BRUT Y TYWYSOGYON

BRUT Y TYWYSOGYON

OR

The Chronicle of the Princes

PENIARTH MS. 20 VERSION

TRANSLATED WITH INTRODUCTION AND NOTES

by

THOMAS JONES

UNIVERSITY COLLEGE OF WALES, ABERYSTWYTH

BOARD OF CELTIC STUDIES, UNIVERSITY OF WALES
HISTORY AND LAW SERIES, No. XI.

CARDIFF
UNIVERSITY OF WALES PRESS
1952

First Edition 1952
Reprinted 1985

© University of Wales, 1952

ISBN 0 7083 0103 7

All rights reserved. No part of this book may be reproduced, stored in a retrieval system, or transmitted, in any form or by any means, electronic, mechanical, photocopying, recording or otherwise, without clearance from the University of Wales Press.

J D LEWIS A'I FEIBION CYF. GWASG GOMER LLANDYSUL DYFED

*This work is dedicated to
the memory of*
SIR JOHN EDWARD LLOYD

PREFACE

THIS is the first of three volumes it is hoped to publish to provide texts and translations of the three versions of *Brut y Tywysogion*. The present translation of the Peniarth MS. 20 version, the Welsh text of which was published in full for the first time in 1941, will be followed by critical texts and translations of the Red Book of Hergest version, which has never been critically edited, and of *Brenhinedd y Saesson*, of which there is one unreliable printed edition but no translation available. The delay in publication is due in part to the fact that most of the work on the two volumes to follow had to be completed before the present translation and notes could be written.

It is right that I should acknowledge my debt to many scholars without whose help this volume and the two to follow could not have been produced. Professor J. Goronwy Edwards, Director of the Institute of Historical Research, has checked the chronology and made valuable suggestions which I have incorporated in the translation and notes. My colleagues Professor T. Jones Pierce and Professor Gwyn Jones have respectively given me useful advice on the rendering of Welsh legal and technical terms and saved me from doing too much violence to English idiom in my attempt to be as literal as possible in my translation. To Professor G. J. Williams I am indebted for many references to MSS. Others who have helped in various ways are Professors David Williams and R. F. Treharne, Father Aubrey Gwynn S.J., Dublin, Mr. Garfield Hughes, and last, but not least, my wife who spent many weary hours in assisting me to check my English versions against the three Welsh texts. Any merit this volume may have is largely due to these willing helpers who must not be held responsible, however, for its many imperfections. Nor must I forget the unfailing courtesy of Dr. Elwyn Davies, Secretary to the University of Wales Press Board, and the great care and patience shown by Messrs. William Lewis (Printers) Ltd., Cardiff.

The dedication of the book to the memory of Sir John Edward Lloyd is a small token of my gratitude for the encouragement which he gave me in the task I had undertaken and for the help I received from his *History of Wales* and *The Welsh Chronicles*. Many years ago Sir John had made careful transcripts of the greater part of the annals preserved in BM. Cotton

MS. Domitian A 1 and in the *Breviate of Domesday Book* in the Public Record Office. Through the good services of his daughter, Mrs. Garmon Jones, and of Professor R. T. Jenkins, these transcripts were placed at my disposal to enable me to check the readings in Ab Ithel's *Annales Cambriae*. Moreover, Sir John in his later years had thought of translating the Peniarth MS. 20 text of the *Brut*, but it appears from his papers that he had not started on the work. It is my sincere hope that the present rendering, inferior though it must be to the one which Sir John would have produced, is not altogether unworthy of the memory of the great Welsh historian who made such valuable contributions to the study of *Brut y Tywysogion*.

THOMAS JONES.

UNIVERSITY COLLEGE OF WALES,
    ABERYSTWYTH.

CONTENTS

	Page
PREFACE	vii
INTRODUCTION:	
§1. Explanatory	xi
§2. Survey of Previous Work on *Brut y Tywysogion*	xiv
§3. Contents and Origin of *Brut y Tywysogion*	xxxv
§4. Manuscripts of the Peniarth MS. 20 Version	xliv
§5. The Peniarth MS. 20 Version	lix
§6. Chronology of the Peniarth MS. 20 Version	lxiv
§7. The Translation and Notes	lxxiv
ABBREVIATIONS	lxxvi
BRUT Y TYWYSOGYON: THE CHRONICLE OF THE PRINCES	1
NOTES	129
APPENDIX: LIST OF SAINTS' DAYS	223
INDEX	224

INTRODUCTION

§1. Explanatory

THE text which follows is a close literal translation of the Peniarth MS. 20 version of the Welsh chronicle called *Brut y Tywysogion* or 'Chronicle of the Princes,' which contains the history of Wales from the end of the seventh century to the year 1282, in the first place, and thence, in a later continuation of the original text, to the year 1332.[1] This version of *Brut y Tywysogion* is on the whole the most complete, though not always the most reliable, of several versions now extant, three of them authentic and important as sources for the history of medieval Wales, and others owing much to the manipulations of later antiquaries, in particular Edward Williams (or Iolo Morganwg), a successful Welsh literary forger of the late eighteenth and early nineteenth centuries. As it is intended to supply, in two volumes which are to follow, critical texts and translations of the two other authentic versions of the same Welsh chronicle—the Red Book of Hergest version of *Brut y Tywysogion* and the third version entitled *Brenhinedd y Saesson*[2] or 'The Kings of the Saxons'—it will be convenient at this point to anticipate certain remarks that will be made in the second section of this Introduction by listing and classifying all the Welsh texts that have at various times been regarded as versions of *Brut y Tywysogion*,[3] even though, as will be shown, some of them are independent of the true *Brut y Tywysogion*, and others, partly based on one or more versions of the *Brut*, owe much of their contents to late interpolations.

The principal texts which have been included under the generic title of *Brut y Tywysogion* are the following:

(1) *Brut y Tywysogion:* Peniarth MS. 20 version.
    The extant MSS. which contain texts of this version are listed below, xliv–lix[4].

(2) *Brut y Tywysogion:* Red Book of Hergest version.
    The text as found in the Red Book of Hergest (Jesus College, Oxford, MS. CXI) has been thrice printed in full: (*a*) in MA ii. (London, 1801) 391–467

---

[1] For the original Welsh text *see* Thomas Jones, *Brut y Tywysogyon. Peniarth MS.* 20. Cardiff. University of Wales Press. 1941.
[2] Sometimes this text has been incorrectly called *Brut y Saesson* or 'The Chronicle of the Saxons' through confusion with another text correctly so called.
[3] As, for example, in Egerton Phillimore's article 'The Publication of Welsh Historical Records,' in *Y Cymmrodor* xi. (1890–91) 133–75.
[4] The list of MSS. in Pen. 20, xvi–xxi, is incomplete.

(=602-51 in the Denbigh edition), (*b*) in BT, with a translation into English, and (*c*) in RBB 257-384. Moreover, the text up to the year 1066 was printed in *Monumenta Historica Britannica* 841-55, with an English translation. Unfortunately, the Red Book of Hergest text is defective in very many places, and what is urgently required is a critical text of the Red Book version based on all the early extant copies. I have prepared such a critical text on the basis of Peniarth MS. 18, Mostyn MS. 116, the Red Book of Hergest, Peniarth MS. 19, and Llanstephan MS. 172, and it will be published, with translation and notes, in the near future.

(3) *Brenhinedd y Saesson* or 'The Kings of the Saxons.'

Excluding late transcripts, there are only two copies of this text now extant in MSS: (*a*) BM. Cotton Cleopatra MS. B v., ff. 109-62*b*, and (*b*) NLW MS. 7006, called the 'Black Book of Basingwerk.' In (*a*) the text ends with the year 1197, but in (*b*) it is continued down to 1461. The text of (*a*) was printed, under the incorrect title *Brut y Saesson* in MA ii. (London, 1801) 468-582 (=652-84 in the Denbigh edition), but it teems with errors of transcription. I have prepared a critical edition, based on (*a*) and (*b*), which will be published, with translation and notes, to form a third volume in this series on *Brut y Tywysogion*.

(4) *Brut y Saesson* or 'The Chronicle of the Saxons.'

This consists of a summary chronicle of the history of England, but including notices of some Welsh events, from the coming of the Saxons down to the year 1381.[1] An incomplete list of MSS. containing copies of this text is given in RBB xxiii-iv., and the Red Book of Hergest text has been printed, ib. 385-403.

(5) *Teyrnassedd y Saesson* or 'The Rule of the Saxons.'

This text, described by J. Gwenogvryn Evans as 'a sort of paraphrase of *Brut y Tywysogion*,'[2] is found in Jesus College, Oxford, MS. CXLI and in NLW MS. 5277, 513-715, the latter being a transcript made by John Jones of Gellilyfdy in 1608 from the Jesus College MS.

---

[1] J. Gwenogvryn Evans in RBB xxiii incorrectly describes it as 'a kind of summary of *Brut y Tywysogion*.'
[2] RWM ii. 37.

(6) *Brut Aberpergwm* or 'The Aberpergwm Chronicle.'
On this text see below, xxviii–xxx, xxxiv.

(7) *Brut Ieuan Brechfa* or 'The Chronicle of Ieuan Brechfa.'
On this text see below, xxviii and xxxiv, note 2.

As will be shown in what follows, it is now recognized that (6) and (7) above, though largely based on versions of the authentic *Brut y Tywysogion*, are the forgeries of Iolo Morganwg. *Brut y Saesson*, listed under (4) above, is a bald and meagre compilation mainly concerned with English history. Composed towards the end of the fourteenth century it is of but little historical value, although it contains a few details about events in Wales[1] which are not given in any version of *Brut y Tywysogion*. Text (5) above, *Teyrnassedd y Saesson*,[2] which appears to date from the late fifteenth century, has never been printed so far as I know, but an examination of its contents shows that it is unimportant as a source for Welsh history.

The texts with which we are concerned in this volume and in the two volumes to follow, are those listed (1), (2), and (3) above. They are three independent and authentic Welsh versions of a lost Latin original, possibly called *Cronica* (or *Historia*) *Principum Walliae* (or *Britanniae*), which in turn was closely related to the three sets of annals published in *Annales Cambriae*[3] and to the *Cronica de Wallia*.[4]

However, before proceeding to deal with the Peniarth MS. 20 version of *Brut y Tywysogion*, it will be useful to survey the work that has already been done, both in manuscript and in print, on the variant versions of this chronicle. Such a survey, it is hoped, will show the defects of all previous editions of the text and at the same time justify the production of yet another three volumes containing texts and translations of the different versions of this Medieval Welsh chronicle which has been described as 'the greatest monument of Welsh historiography in the Middle Ages.'[5]

---

[1] A few such additional details are found too in the still more meagre text called, after its opening words, *O Oes Gwrtheyrn Gwrtheneu* ('From the Time of Gwrtheyrn Gwrthenau'). For a printed version of the Red Book of Hergest text see RBB 404–6.

[2] This title is the one found in NLW MS. 5277.

[3] *Annales Cambriae*, edited by the Rev. John Williams ab Ithel. Rolls Series. London, 1860.

[4] *See* Thomas Jones, *Cronica de Wallia and other Documents from Exeter Cathedral Library MS. 3514*. Cardiff, 1946. Reprinted, with indexes, from B xii. 27–44.

[5] J. E. Lloyd, *The Welsh Chronicles*. Sir John Rhŷs Memorial Lecture. British Academy. London, 1928, 21.

§2. Survey of Previous Work on *Brut y Tywysogion*

Scholars outside Wales, and indeed many in Wales, first realized that there existed a chronicle in Welsh tracing the history of Wales under the princes, when there appeared in 1584 a book entitled *The Historie of Cambria, now called Wales*,[1] edited by Dr. David Powel of Ruabon. As the full title of the book shows, the greater part of the text consisted of an English translation by Humphrey Llwyd (or Lloyd) of an old Welsh chronicle, which the editor had corrected, augmented, and continued. In his preface 'To the Reader' Dr. Powel attempts to describe the nature of the contents of the book and the origin of the Welsh text on which it was based. Caradog of Llancarfan, he tells us, 'collected the successions & actes of the Brytish Princes after Cadwalader, to the yeare of Christ 1156,' and copies of his compilation were kept in the abbeys of Conway and Strata Florida and augmented with accounts of what happened year by year down to 1270. Of the resulting complete compilation down to the year 1270 there were in his day, Powel maintains, 'a hundred copies at the least, whereof the most part were written two hundred yeares ago.'[2] This 'Brytish' or Welsh chronicle was translated into English, with certain additions from various English chroniclers, by Humphrey Llwyd, who died before his translation could be published. For some time after Llwyd's death in 1568 the translation remained with Sir Henry Sidney, Lord President of Wales, who, eager to see it published, asked Dr. David Powel to prepare it for the press. After some hesitation Powel agreed to undertake the work, and he corrected Llwyd's version by comparing it with 'two ancient copies' of the original Welsh text.[3] Powel admits, too, that he 'augmented and continued' Llwyd's text. After the greater part of the book had been printed Powel received a 'larger copie of the same translation, being better corrected,' from Robert Glover, Somerset Herald. Had this copy been brought to his notice earlier, the book then in the press, Powel maintains, would have been more correct.

---

[1] The full title is *The historie of Cambria, now called Wales: A part of the most famous Yland of Brytaine, written in the Brytish language above two hundreth yeares past: translated into English by H. Lloyd Gentleman: Corrected, augmented and continued out of Records and best approued Authors*, by David Powel Doctor in diuinitie. London, [1584].

[2] Powel, [ix].

[3] Powel nowhere uses the title *Brut y Tywysogion* or *Brut*. Both he and Llwyd refer to the original Welsh text by expressions such as 'compilations,' 'collections,' 'the Brytishe booke.'

It is obvious, as has long been recognized, that the original Welsh text from which Llwyd made his translation[1] and of which Powel used 'two ancient copies' in editing Llwyd's work, was some copy of one or more version of the texts now known as *Brut y Tywysogion*. Llwyd's text is founded on the *Brut* down to the year 1270. After recording the death of Gruffudd, lord of Bromfield, in that year, he begins the next section with these words:

> 'At this place leaueth the Brytish booke, and writeth no further of the end of this prince [*sc*. Llywelyn ap Gruffudd], but leaueth him at the highest and most honorable staie that anie prince of Wales was in, of manie yeares before: the writer (peraduenture) being abashed or rather ashamed to declare the vtter fall and ruine of his countrie men, wherevnto their own pride and discord did bring them, as it doth euidentlie appeare to him that searcheth out their histories. But I intending to finish the historie during the gouernment of the Brytaines, have sought out in other Chronicles written in the Latine toong, speciallie in the Chronicle of Nicholas Triuet . . . and such other, asmuch as I could find touching this matter.'[2]

These words obviously imply that the Welsh text used by Llwyd did not continue beyond the year 1270, and they were interpreted as such by Powel who, after the entry recording the death of Gruffudd, lord of Bromfield, adds this note:

> 'Here endeth the Brytish copie.
> That which foloweth vnto the death of this Prince [*sc*. Llywelyn ap Gruffudd] was collected by HUMFREY LHOYD, Gentleman.'[3]

It is strange, to say the least, that Llwyd should have continued the history down to the very year—1282—with which the majority of the complete copies of *Brut y Tywysogion* end. And yet a comparison of Llwyd's text, as edited by Powel, shows that after the year 1270, as Llwyd himself states, it is in no way dependent on any version of *Brut y Tywysogion*. Nor does Powel, in editing the section of Llwyd's work covering the period 1271–82, seem to have added any passages based on the *Brut*, a fact which seems to imply that the 'two ancient copies' of the Welsh original which he used, also ended with the year 1270. Not one of the many copies of the *Brut* which have survived in manuscripts ends at this exact point, so that it appears that the family of MSS. to which Llwyd's and Powel's

---

[1] Llwyd claims that he was the first to translate the Welsh chronicle: 'I was the first that tooke the province in hand to put these things into the English tonge for that I wolde not have the inhabitants of this Ile ignorant of the Histories and Cronicles of the same.' (Llanstephan MS. 172, f. 24*a*.)
[2] Powel, 237.
[3] Ib., 236.

copies belonged, has died out.[1] The Thelwall MS. text of the Peniarth MS. 20 version (listed F below, p. li) of the *Brut*, copied in 1577, continues only a few lines beyond the end of Llwyd's original, but Llwyd could not have used this MS. for he had completed his translation by 17 July, 1559, according to a note by Dr. John Dee in BM. Cotton MS. Caligula A vi. Moreover, although we know that the Thelwall MS. text was in its present incomplete form at the end of the seventeenth century, it cannot be proved that it, or any cognate text, was similarly incomplete in Llwyd's time.

It is irrelevant to this Introduction to discuss the relationship between Llwyd's English text, which is extant in MSS., and the variant versions of *Brut y Tywysogion*, and the relationship between Llwyd's work and the printed *Historie of Cambria* as edited by Dr. Powel. This has been investigated in a dissertation[2] by Mr. Ieuan M. Williams, who, after an analysis of Llwyd's English version and a comparison of it with the Welsh versions of the *Brut*, has shown that Llwyd used copies of the three independent versions of the Welsh text, although he does not exclude the possibility that he translated directly from some Welsh version, no longer in existence, which was a composite text based on the three independent versions now extant. It is to be regretted that Llwyd's text, as distinct from Powel's edition of it, has never been printed, although three copies, not one of which is in the translator's own handwriting, are known to exist.[3] Mr. Ieuan M. Williams has clearly shown that Llwyd's text is more than a mere translation of any known version of the *Brut*,[4] although some such version or versions formed the basis of it, and that Powel made many changes and additions in preparing it for the press.[5]

The *Historie of Cambria* was for centuries the only history of Wales available and it was reprinted in various forms right down to the nineteenth century. Moreover, Powel's views on the origin and authorship of the original Welsh chronicle were

---

[1] Llwyd is known to have possessed a MS. described in a catalogue (BM. Add. MS. 36659, 164) as '*Chronicle in Welche*, Vetusti.' Llwyd's notes on BM. Cotton MS. Cleop. B v (which contains the earliest text of *Brenhinedd y Saesson*) and his signature on f. 223 show that this MS. once belonged to him.

[2] *Hanesyddiaeth yng Nghymru yn yr unfed ganrif ar bymtheg, gan gyfeirio'n arbennig at Humphrey Lluyd a David Powel*. University of Wales M.A. dissertation, 1951. See also Williams's article on Humphrey Llwyd and his works in *Llên Cymru* ii, 110 ff.

[3] (1) BM. MS. Cotton Caligula A vi once in the possession of Dr. John Dee; (2) Ashmolean MS. 847, written by Robert Glover, Somerset Herald, and once owned by Dr. John Dee. This is probably a transcript of (1); (3) Llanstephan MS. 177, dated 1573. On these MSS. see Williams, op. cit., 44–50.

[4] For an analysis of Llwyd's text as compared with the *Brut*, see op. cit., 78–87.

[5] For Powel's changes and additions, see ib., 98–106.

accepted, either fully or in a modified form, as late as the early part of this century. A new edition under the title *The History of Wales* was published in 1697 (London), 'newly augmented and improved by W. Wynne, M.A., and Fellow of Jesus Colledg [*sic*], Oxon.'[1] Reprints of Wynne's 'augmented and improved' edition appeared in 1702 (London), 1774 (London), and 1812 (Merthyr Tydfil), and a German translation of it by P. G. Hübner was published in 1725.[2] Later, in 1832, Wynne's edition was again reprinted in a revised and augmented edition by Richard Llwyd, Bard of Snowdon, of Llannerch Brochwel. Of greater practical use, however, than any of these several reprints of Wynne's edition of the text was the reprint, which appeared in 1811 (London), of the original 1584 edition.

What was needed, however, was not successive reprints of the *Historie of Cambria* as revised by various editors, but a reliable edition of the original Welsh chronicle which had been used by Llwyd and Powel. It was not until 1801 that any complete text of the Welsh *Brut* was printed,[3] but long before that date several Welsh antiquaries had shown an interest in the various versions of it which they found; and two or three of them, as we shall see, appear to have been making preparations for a printed edition. The famous Dr. John Dee interested himself not only in Llwyd's English version but also in the Welsh text. In 1575 he received from his cousin 'Olyver Lloyd of the Welshe Pole' a copy of Llwyd's version of the 'Brytishe booke'[4]—now BM. Cotton MS. Caligula A VI; and later, Robert Glover, Somerset Herald, made for him a special

[1] On the identity of the editor W. Wynne *see* R. T. Jenkins, 'William Wynne and the History of Wales' in B vi. 153 ff. For references to Wynne *see* also R. T. Gunther, *Life and Letters of Edward Lhwyd*. Oxford, 1945, 313, 318.

[2] *Die Historie van Walles*, in sich haltend derer Printzen von Walles Leben und Thaten, von Cadwalader ... biss auf Lhewelinum ... vormahls geschrieben in Brittischer Sprache von Caradoco Llancarvanensi; nachtmahls von D. Powel in Englischer publiciret, und von Mr. Wynne vermehret; ietzo aber aus dieser ins Teutsche gebracht. Coburg, 1725. 8°.
A Welsh translation of selections from the *Historie of Cambria* is in NLW MS. Add. 11-D (Williams MS. 213), 159–237, under the title: 'Byr gynwisiadau allan o Gronicl David Powel, Doctor o Ddifiniti o'r twysog cyntaf o'r Brutaniaid hyd y twysog diweddaf o honunt fal i mae i'w weled yn y deudedic Gronicl.' The text was written in 1694. Certain passages from the *Historie of Cambria* were translated into Welsh by George Wm. Griffith in Llanstephan MS. 8: *see* below, lv-vi.

[3] An incomplete text, in modernized orthography, of the Peniarth MS. 20 version was printed in *Trysorfa Gwybodaeth*. Carmarthen. 1770, 1–120. On this text *see* below, lvii.

[4] Cf. the following note in Robert Glover's hand on the fly-leaf in Ashmolean MS. 847: 'This booke was given to Mr. J. D(ee) of Mortlake by his cousyn Mr. Olyver Lloyd of the Welsh Pole 1575 Mense Novembris. die. 12. At Mortlake.' Cf. Williams, op. cit., 46, where it is argued that 'this booke' refers to BM. Cotton MS. Caligula A VI, from which Ashmolean MS. 847 was copied.

B

transcript—now Ashmolean MS. 847—of Llwyd's translation.[1] However, other MSS. known to have been in his possession and notes written by him on certain folios of BM. Cotton MS. Caligula A vi show that Dee was conscious of the necessity of checking Llwyd's version by comparison with the original Welsh chronicle. According to a catalogue of his MSS. drawn up by him in 1593 he possessed not only a copy of the Latin chronicle called 'Annals of St. Davids' as found in BM. Cotton MS. Domitian A 1, but also at least one chronicle in Welsh. The text described as 'Annales Regulorum Cambricorum a Cadowaladro ad Leolini tempora, *lingua Brytannica sive Cambrica*'[2] can hardly be other than a copy of some version of *Brut y Tywysogion*. Moreover, Dee's notes in BM. Cotton MS. Caligula A vi show that he had gone to the trouble to compare Llwyd's rendering with some copy of the *Brut*, possibly the very one listed in his catalogue; and in one place[3] in his notes he gives a quotation from the *Brut*, with a translation of it. He also had in his possession, according to the catalogue, a text described as 'Hystoriae Britanniae et Angliae fragmentum, *Gallice* conscriptum.'[4] However, Dee's interest in Welsh history and the fact that he possessed at least one copy of the Welsh chronicle is no justification for suggesting that he was contemplating an edition of *Brut y Tywysogion*. It is clear, however, that even after 1584, when Powel's edition of *The Historie of Cambria* appeared, Dee realized that the ultimate source of importance was the Welsh text.

Later, the well-known antiquary Robert Vaughan (1592–1667) of Hengwrt in Merioneth had a better grasp of the problem and far better opportunities for doing something more important than merely checking Llwyd's English version. He had the qualifications necessary for producing an edition of the Welsh text; and some of his MSS. now extant and references by later scholars to other MSS. now lost show that he had done considerable work in investigating numerous copies of *Brut y Tywysogion*. His labours, however, did not produce a printed edition.[5] He made transcripts of various versions, collated many copies

---

[1] J. O. Halliwell, *The Diary of Dr. John Dee and the Catalogue of his Library MSS.* Camden Society. London, 1842, 72. Halliwell wrongly refers to Ashmolean MS. 846.
[2] Ib., 78.
[3] BM. Cotton MS. Caligula A vi, f. 205a.
[4] Halliwell, op. cit., 79, No. 123. The words '*Gallice* conscriptum' seem to show that this fragmentary text was in French, and it is vain to speculate whether it bore any relationship to *Brenhinedd y Saesson*, which combines Welsh and English history.
[5] Some of Vaughan's notes were incorporated in William Wynne's edition (1697) of the *Historie of Cambria*.

INTRODUCTION

of them, and translated one version into English. NLW MS. 13074 (formerly Llanover MS. 15 and earlier Hengwrt MS. 88) contains Vaughan's transcript of parts of the version of *Brenhinedd y Saesson* found in the Black Book of Basingwerk (NLW MS. 7006). In the latter part of the eighteenth century the Rev. Evan Evans, better known as Ieuan Fardd and Ieuan Brydydd Hir, tells us that he had seen and copied 'a very fair manuscript which was collated with ten old copies on vellum by Mr. Robert Vaughan of Hengwrt' and that Vaughan had 'proposed to print another edition (*sc.* of Powel's *Historie of Cambria*) about the year 1660, but was prevented by Percy Enderby's printing his *Cambria Triumphans*, to the great loss of the curious, as no body ever had nor could have so good materials as his valuable collection of MSS. afforded'[1] (NLW MS. 2041 (=Panton MS. 75), 9–10). The only work which Robert Vaughan published was *British Antiquities Revived or A Friendly Contest touching the Soveraignty of the Three Princes of Wales in Ancient Times*... (Oxford, 1662).[2] Here Vaughan often refers to and more than once quotes from versions of the *Brut* which he had consulted; and he seems to refer to different versions by different names. Most often he refers to 'Caradoc of Lancarvan' or 'Caradocus Lancarvanensis,'[3] but he also names 'the Book of Conway'[4] in contexts which seem to show that it contained a text of the *Brut*. Other expressions used by him are 'the British history of the Princes,'[5] 'the Chronicle,'[6] and 'the Chronicles.'[7] That he had consulted many copies and that he had noticed certain differences between them is suggested by the words 'Caradocus Lancarvanensis... who wrote in the dayes of Henry the First, *testifies in some copies of his Annals* ...'[8] Once he refers to Humphrey Llwyd and Dr. David Powel as 'the translators of the Chronicle of Wales,'[9] and he generally distinguishes between the parts of the *Historie of Cambria*

---

[1] William Jones, F.R.S., stated that Powel's *Historie of Cambria* was 'reprinted in a quarto volume Oxford 1663 by William Hall, with the valuable notes of Robert Vaughan of Hengwrt, Esqr:' (quoted by the Rev. Evan Evans NLW MS. 1997 (=Panton MS. 28), 94). William Jones's full statement is again quoted, with slight variants, in Panton MS. 17, f. 10 *a–b*. It is probable that Jones has confused a new edition of Sir John Price's *A Description of Wales*, published by Thomas Ellis, with notes by Robert Vaughan (Oxford, 1663) with a new edition of *The Historie of Cambria*. In any case *The Historie of Cambria* (1584) contained as its first part (1–22) 'A description of Cambria now called Wales: Drawne first by Sir Iohn Prise knight, and afterward augmented and made perfect by Humfrey Lhoyd Gentleman.' CB 191 states that nearly all the printed sheets of the 1663 edition of *A Description of Wales* were sold as waste paper.

[2] The references quoted here are to the reprint published at Bala in 1834.

[3] 13, 15, 28, 29, 30, 46, 47, 61, 62, 72.

[4] For Egerton Phillimore's suggestion that 'the Book of Conway' is identical with Peniarth MS. 20, *see* below, lxiii.

[5] 43. [6] 43. [7] 77. [8] 67. [9] 56.

translated by Llwyd and the additions made by Powel. Moreover, he makes a clear distinction bweteen 'the English History of the Princes of Cambria'[1] and the original Welsh texts. One quotation[2] from the *Brut* is almost certainly derived from some copy of the Peniarth MS. 20 version. In addition to collating various copies of *Brut y Tywysogion*, Vaughan made an English translation of one version, but it was never printed. It had long been known from a letter which Vaughan wrote to archbishop James Ussher on 14 April, 1651, that he had translated into English a version of the *Brut* which was in a MS. in his own library at Hengwrt.[3] In this letter Vaughan refers to the translation and to the original text which he had used:

> 'In pursuance of your request, and my promise, I have at last sent you the Annals of Wales, as out of the ancient copy which you saw with me: I did faithfully translate them into the English tongue, as near as I could, word for word, wherein (knowing my weakness) I labored not so much to render a sweet harmony of speech, as the plain and simple phrase of that age wherein it was written. . . . There was a leaf wanting in my book, which defect (viz. from 900, to An. 950) and some passages besides, I was fain to make up out of other ancient copies; whereof, though we have many in Wales, yet, but few that agree verbatim with one another. . . .'[4]

I recently discovered that Vaughan's translation is extant in B.M. Lansdowne MS. 418, ff. 111–196*b*.[5] As I expected, the translation is made from the text of the *Brut* which is in Peniarth MS. 20, which once belonged to Vaughan's library at Hengwrt. I have shown[6] that Vaughan filled the lacuna in the text caused by the loss of a leaf (now pp. 71-2) in the MS. by translating the corresponding passage from some copy of *Brenhinedd y Saesson*. Vaughan's English version is a good straightforward translation of the Peniarth MS. 20 text, but I had completed my own translation of the same text before I discovered it.

In the letter to Ussher quoted above Vaughan shows that he was aware of certain differences between various versions of *Brut y Tywysogion*: 'but few,' he says, 'agree verbatim with one another.' Nevertheless he does not seem to have appreciated the full significance of these textual variations and he did not

---

[1] 14. [2] 29.
[3] Vaughan's letter is printed in *The Cambrian Register* ii. 473-5 (cf. Panton MS. 28, 116).
[4] Loc. cit.
[5] *See* 'Cyfieithiad Robert Vaughan o "Frut y Tywysogion" ' in *The National Library of Wales Journal* v. 291-4. Edward Owen, *Catalogue of the MSS. Relating to Wales in the British Museum* i. 87, incorrectly described the Lansdowne MS. translation of the *Brut* as 'an early seventeenth century translation into *Latin*.'
[6] Loc. cit., 292-4.

attempt a classification of the copies then extant.[1] Like others before and long after him Vaughan seems to accept Powel's opinion that the author of the original Welsh down to 1156 was Caradog of Llancarfan, and he does not conceive the possibility of the Welsh texts being derived from a Latin original.

Towards the end of the seventeenth century one of many Welsh antiquaries who took an interest in *Brut y Tywysogion* was Bishop Humphrey Humphreys of Bangor. He not only collated copies of it but also seems to have begun a translation, as is shown by a letter which he wrote from Bangor on 29 January, 1693/4 to Mr. Lewis Anwyl of Porthdinllaen[2]:

> 'I have taken the pains to compare not only several antient copies of Caradoc of Llann Carfan & the Clera,[3] but several other annals of our affairs. . . .
>
> I take the David Morganius in Vossius to be the same with Meurig ap Dafydd o Forgannwg, and his annals to be nothing but a copy of Caradoc of Llan Carfan, with a continuation to the time of Edward the fourth, under whom Vossius saith his Morganius flourished, with a preface of the situation of our country, which I have seen in pretty old Manuscripts written about the time of the author, and I am in hopes to compass, and have at present an imperfect translation of it, which I compared and corrected by the old MS. The history of the Cumbrian princes is (or at least was) in the library of Hengwrt, for Mr. Vaughan quotes it in MS. notes on an old Welsh Chronicon which he translated, of which I have a copy; but I could not find it there, though Mr. Eubule Thelwal assured me he saw it in Mr. Vaughan's own hand, who could make little of it.'

Passing by mere copyists who transcribed texts of *Brut y Tywysogion*, the next antiquary who gave serious attention to copies in MSS., possibly with the intention of producing an edition, was William Maurice (*fl.* 1640–80) of Cefn-y-braich, Llansilin. He made transcripts himself and had others made by his amanuenses. His own extant MSS., and notes which he wrote in earlier MSS. which he used and which still survive, show that he had seen and examined many texts of *Brut y Tywysogion*, including copies of all three authentic versions.

---

[1] He at least knew of copies outside his own library. In NLW MS. 5262, 66–8, in a catalogue of South Walian MSS. he refers to a copy of *Brut y Tywysogion* in the possession of 'Wil Meuruc of St. Nicholas' in Glamorgan. Cf. G. J. Williams, *Traddodiad Llenyddol Morgannwg*, Cardiff, 1948, 151, note 32.

[2] The quotation is from a transcript of the letter made by the Rev. Evan Evans (Ieuan Fardd) in NLW MS. 1997 (Panton MS. 28), 96–101.

[3] Humphreys, by his use of the term 'Clera,' accepts Powel's view that Caradog's chronicle was continued at the abbeys of Conway and Strata Florida and that the entries made in these two monasteries were 'conferred together ordinarilie euerie third yeare, when the Beirdh which did belong to those two Abbies went from the one to the other in the time of their Clêra.' Powel, p. ix, explains 'Clêra' as being the 'ordinarie visitation' of the bards, 'which they vse euerie third yeare.'

We know from glosses in his hand that the text of Peniarth MS. 266 had been examined by him; and a text of the *Brut* transcribed by the Rev. Evan Evans in 1794 into NLW MS. 2043 (Panton MS. 77-8) from an exemplar copied for Maurice in 1672, shows that he had had access to Robert Vaughan's collection of MSS. The text which Evans copied is described thus:

> Chronica vel Annales Principum Cymmerice [*glossed* vulgo Cambrice] a Cadwaladro Rege usque ad Leolini ultimi exitum, et deinceps usque ad annum 1332 Cymbrice [*glossed* Wallice] scripti: et nunc demum cum variantibus lectionibus, ex collatione decem exemplarium membranaceorum, praecipue Roberti Vachani de Hengwrt Armigeri, et Codicis Plaswardensis aliorumque aliquot notae vetustioris Manuscriptorum transcripti auspiciis Gulielmi Mauricii Lansilinatis, Anno post Christum natum 1672 vulgaris computi.[1]

Some of the MSS. used for the collation can be traced. On f. 135*b* of vol. ii. of Evans's transcript, after the words *ag yn gystal eu harogleu ar dydd i claddesid* (=Peniarth MS. 20, 302*a*, 11=127 in the translation in this volume) we find the note:

> 'Hactenus vet[us] exemplar Hist[orie][2] Cambrice in Bibliotheca Vachaniana.'

The 'vetus exemplar' in Vaughan's library at Hengwrt can have been none other than Peniarth MS. 20. The annals are described as extending from the time of Cadwaladr to the death of Llywelyn in 1282 and thence continued to the year 1332. This suggests that most of the texts which Maurice used for his collation did not go beyond the year 1282, that is, that they were probably copies of the Red Book of Hergest version, but that a continuation to 1332 was found in the 'vetus exemplar.' And there is such a continuation in Peniarth MS. 20. However, in Evans's transcript, and so presumably in the original written for Maurice, the chronicle is continued to the year 1461. The text on vol. ii. 136*a*–139*a* is derived, according to a rubric,[3] from a MS. written by William Salesbury, and that on ff. 139*a*–141*b* from a MS. copied by John Jones of Gellilyfdy in the Fleet prison in 1635 and 1636.[4] This latter MS. may be safely identified with Peniarth MS. 264, which contains, in addition to a Welsh version of *Dares Phrygius* and *Brut y Brenhinedd* (both transcribed in 1635),

---

[1] NLW MS. 2043 (Panton MS. 77-8), f. 1*a*. Cf. the following statement by the Rev. Evan Evans in NLW MS. 1997 (Panton MS. 28), 7: 'BRUT Y TYWYSOGION or THE HISTORY OF THE PRINCES OF WALES from Cadwaladr the last British king till Edward the fourth's time, *I copied from a very fair Manuscript, which was collated with ten old copies on vellum by Robert Vaughan of Hengwrt, and was lent me some years ago, with many other Manuscripts, by Sir Watkin Williams Wynn of Wynstay Bart.*' Evans seems to refer to the same MS. as that which he transcribed in 1794.

[2] Glossed 'Annal.'

[3] 'Sic MS. transcriptum per Gulielmum Salesbury de Llann Sannan', f. 139*a*.

[4] 'Hucusque exemplar magnum Jo. Jo. transcriptum apud Fletam Ann. 1635 and 1636 in folio'.

a text of *Brenhinedd y Saesson*, the transcription of which was completed on 15 June, 1636.[1] Further evidence of Maurice's interest in various chronicles in Welsh is supplied by Wynnstay MS. 10, which contains a copy of *Brut y Saesson* written by an amanuensis of Maurice's and apparently derived from an original copied by John Jones of Gellilyfdy. In 1688 Thomas Sebastian Price of Llanfyllin compiled 'The correct Annales of Brittaine ... gathered out of severall Authors printed and manuscript, but most especially out of *Brut y Tywysogion*, or the Annals of the Princes of Wales herewith inserted.' These Annals are in NLW MS. 1599 (Kinmel MS. 99), and they contain a copy of the Peniarth MS. 20 version of the *Brut* written in two different hands: 51-2, 55, are in William Maurice's own hand, whereas 55-137 are in an unknown seventeenth century hand, probably that of one of Maurice's amanuenses.[2] Again, Maurice transcribed 'the Hengwrt copy'—possibly Peniarth MS. 20—of *Brut y Tywysogion* into Wynnstay MS. 81,[3] which is now lost or destroyed.

The extant MSS. of Moses Williams (1685-1742)[4] seem to show that he had been making preparations for an edition of *Brut y Tywysogion*. Not only did he collect MSS. which contained versions of the chronicle, but he also made transcriptions himself. Llanstephan MS. 62, which once belonged to Dafydd ap Ieuan of Llangrallo (or Coychurch)[5] came into his hands as a gift from D. J. Powell of Talgarth.[6] Llanstephan MS. 63 contains a transcript by Moses Williams of the Red Book of Hergest text of the *Brut*, and in it he quotes variants from other texts, some of which we can identify: 'MS. Cott.', from which variants are quoted (ff. 92*b*, 111*b*, 170*b*), is certainly BM. Cotton MS. Cleopatra B v, which, as we have seen, contains a copy of *Brenhinedd y Saesson*. Other variants derive from Llanstephan

---

[1] Further proof that Maurice used Peniarth MS. 264 is supplied by a note on a fly-leaf to that MS. ('Guil. Mauricius Lansiliens: libro huic operculum impertit orbo 1660'), by the letters WM marked on the outside of the front cover, and by another note on p. 75: 'Gulielmus Mauricius Lansiliens. hunc MS. operculavit orbum. An. Dm̄i. 1660'.

[2] *See* Thomas Jones, 'Copi Richard ap John o Scorlegan a "Chopi Thomas Prys o Llanfyllin" o "Frut y Tywysogion" ' in *The National Library of Wales Journal* v. 199-206. Cf. below, liii-iv.

[3] *See* Angharad Llwyd, 'Catalogue of Welsh MSS., etc., in North Wales,' *Trans. Cym.*, 1828, 55. According to this catalogue there were copies of *Brut y Tywysogion* in Wynnstay MSS. 2, 61, 80, 81, 82.

[4] *See* John Davies, *Bywyd a Gwaith Moses Williams*. Cardiff, 1937.

[5] Cf. 176: 'llyma lyfyr Dafydd ap Jevan o blwyf Llangrallo tyst o Sion ap Rys o Dre Lales ag o Ddafyð Thomas Dafydd ag o Tomas Howel Lle[wely]n ac o Gryffyth Treharn, per me Thomam Johnes.'

[6] Cf. 1: 'M. Wiliams A.M. R.S. Soc. Ex dono D. J. Powell.'

MS. 62. At the end of f. 249a of Llanstephan MS. 63 (*see* above) Williams has this note:

> 'NB. Here endeth the Copy H[umphrey] Ll[wyd] & D[avid] P[owel] perused. Ergo they did not see Ll[yfr] Coch Hergest.'

And on f. 256b this note occurs:

> 'Hic deficit Cod. MS. quo me donavit D. Joannes Powel de Talgarth.'[1]

This 'Cod. MS.' is Llanstephan MS. 62. In Llanstephan MS. 64, a companion volume to Llanstephan MS. 63, Moses Williams has drawn up an index to the Llanstephan MS. 63 transcript of the Red Book of Hergest *Brut*; and Llanstephan MS. 132, also written by Moses Williams, contains a similar index to some version of the text. Still another indication of Williams's interest in the various versions of the *Brut* is found in the number of texts which he collected and which he has briefly described in Llanstephan MS. 57, Part II (f. 5a):

> '[1]—[Brud] y Seison a'r Tywysogion .Bib. Cott. Cleopatra B. v. p. 109. M. W. Chart.
> [2]—[Brud] y Tywysogion. L. K. H. M. W. Chart.
> [3]   Ał ex dono J. Powell.
> [4]   Ał ex dono ejusdem J.P. imperfect[us].
> [5]   Ał cum Notis Anglicanis ex dono W. Lewis.
> [6]   Ał Bib. Cott. Cleopatra B. v. M.W. Chart. ? an potius Brud y Seison.'[2]

The MS. referred to in [2] must be Moses Williams's own transcript, in Llanstephan MS. 63, of the Red Book of Hergest text. The MS. denoted [1] appears to be Llanstephan MS. 128, and [3] and [4] refer to Llanstephan MSS. 62 and 61 respectively. The text with notes in English, which had been received from W. Lewis[3] [5], is probably Llanstephan MS. 8.[4] The reference in [6] to a transcript of a text entitled [*Brud*] *y Tywysogion* from Cleopatra MS. B v in the Cotton library is probably an error, for that MS. contains *Brenhinedd y Saesson*, and so [6] may be a duplicated notice of the transcript described under [1]. Despite his labours on the *Brut*, however, Moses Williams did not live to produce an edition of the Welsh text and his MSS. were

---

[1] At the end of Llanstephan MS. 27 (Red Book of Talgarth) there is a note by J. D. Powell of Talgarth to Moses Williams (19 September, 1719): 'I hereby quit claim in ye first place, to ye old parchm[en]t MSS. I lent you; tis for you & yrs. *Cradocks Chron. is also ready at your service as I promised.*'

[2] Moses Williams has drawn a line through the words *? an potius Brud y Seison.*

[3] This W. Lewis may be W. Lewis of Margam who is known to have been in correspondence with Edward Lhuyd in 1696 and who was known to Thomas Wilkins: see G. J. Williams, *Traddodiad Llenyddol Morgannwg*, 101, 165.

[4] Llanstephan MS. 8 contains a text of *Brut y Tywysogion*, with notes in English, transcribed by George William Griffith of Penybenglog in Pembrokeshire. See below, lv–vi.

bought from his widow by William Jones, F.R.S., from whom they eventually passed into the Shirburn library, where they remained until they were bought in 1899 by Sir John Williams who later bequeathed them, as part of the Llanstephan collection, to the National Library of Wales.[1]

Towards the end of the eighteenth century a group of Welsh scholars and antiquaries connected with the first Cymmrodorion Society and the later Gwyneddigion Society[2] in London laid an ambitious scheme, with the financial backing of Owain Jones (Myvyr), to publish a corpus of ancient Welsh texts, both prose and poetry. Foremost among them were the Rev. Evan Evans, Lewis Morris, Edward Jones, and the Rev. Richard Davies of Holywell. Each one of these men was engaged in searching for MSS. containing Welsh texts, and more than one of them devoted his attention to various copies of *Brut y Tywysogion*. The greatest scholar of them and the one best equipped to edit an ancient text was undoubtedly the Rev. Evan Evans. Certain transcripts which he made of the *Brut* are still extant: reference has already been made (xxii above) to his transcript, in NLW MS. 2043 (Panton MS. 77–8), of a text of the *Brut* copied for William Maurice in 1672; and NLW MS. 1976 (Panton MS. 6–7) contains a copy of the Red Book of Hergest text which he made in 1784 from an earlier transcript made directly from the Red Book by the Rev. Richard Davies of Holywell in 1781.[3] Of greater immediate interest, however, is Evans's own statement,[4] written on 8 June, 1785, of his plan for an edition of *Brut y Tywysogion* with translation and notes:

'I have taken great pains to collect everything that Mr. Vaughan left in Manuscript [*sc.* on *Brut y Tywysogion*] and likewise have transcribed from the old Monkish historians which I borrowed from Llan Fordaf library abundance of materials to publish another edition of this Welsh Chronicle. *I propose to preserve Dr. Powel's notes & Mr. Vaughan of Hengwrt's by themselves, in the history distinct from the Text, & I propose likewise to publish the British original with an English translation.* And all the passages from the English Monkish historians that treat of our affairs shall be set down in order of time in the appendix both to

---

[1] *See* RWM ii. v–vi.
[2] *See* R. T. Jenkins and Helen M. Ramage, *A History of the Honourable Society of Cymmrodorion*. *Y Cymmrodor* l. London, 1951.
[3] The Rev. Richard Davies's transcript was later printed in *The Myvyrian Archaiology of Wales* ii. (London, 1801), 391–467. Davies sent his transcript to Owain Jones (Myvyr) on 11 September, 1799, along with a letter (BM. Add. MS. 15030, 199–200) in which he states: 'Gyda'r llythyr hwn y derbyniwch Frut y Tywysogion, yr hwnn a scrifennais allan o'r Llyfr Coch o Hergest.... Y rhai hyn a farnodd Iolo Morganwg sydd gyda mi y pryd hwn, yn angenrheidiol.'
[4] NLW MS. 2041 (Panton MS. 75), 1–11. For another passage from the same statement *see* above, xix.

confirm and illustrate the history. This hath cost me more pain & trouble than all the rest. A good history of Wales being yet among the Desiderata. It is requisite in order that it may be brought to perfection, that I should have access to the British Museum, where there are still many British Manuscripts, the copies of which are lost with us in Wales.'

Unfortunately, nothing came of Evans's ambitious plans, and the texts of the *Brut* which he had transcribed did not find a place in the corpus of ancient Welsh texts which was later published in *The Myvyrian Archaiology of Wales*. Another antiquary who was equally interested in texts of the *Brut* was Edward Williams (or Iolo Morganwg), but his motives, as will be seen, were not above suspicion. When he was in Dolgellau in 1799[1] he made a transcript of *Brenhinedd y Saesson* (BM. Add. MS. 15003) from Robert Vaughan's copy in Llanover MS. B 15 (formerly Hengwrt MS. 88), which then belonged to Robert Davies of Gwisaney. Another incomplete transcript of the same text in Iolo's hand is found in Llanover MS. C 65, written in 1800. Bearing directly on some of the texts of *Brut y Tywysogion* which appeared in *The Myvyrian Archaiology of Wales* ii. (London, 1801) is Iolo's own list, in Llanover MS. C 70, 127, of MSS. which were in his possession in 1800, in which he refers to several versions of *Brut y Tywysogion:*

Ysgriflyfrau gan Iolo Morganwg 1800
1. Caradoc Llancarvan   Tre bryn.
2. Un Aberpergwm.—Un Trëos.—
   —Un Ieuan Brechfa—Glan y Lai.[2]
3. Brut y Saeson   Blaenau Gwent.—
   —Un Antoni Powel.
4. Un Gwisanae neu Llannerch.[3]
   un Watkin Powel o Ben y Fai.'

The above list appears to be an attempt at some kind of classification of the texts of the *Brut* which Iolo possessed, some of them no doubt in his own handwriting. It may be that by *Brut y Saeson* (3) Iolo really means *Brenhinedd y Saesson*.[4] Whatever

---

[1] According to Iolo's letter to Owain Myvyr, written on 12 November, 1799: BM. Add. MS. 15024, ff. 297-8.

[2] Cf. Iolo's words in BM. Add. MS. 15003, 56: '. . . in numerous S[outh] W[alia]n MSS. the words meibion, meini, creigydd, ceirw & are written Myibion, Myini, cryigydd, & this is writing from the ear rather than according to grammatical propriety. *The copy of Caradoc Llancarfan in the possession of the Rev[d]. Mr. Basset of Llanelai near Llantrisant in Glam.* has throughout this kind of Orthography in such diphthong words.' On the Rev. Thomas Basset *see* G. J. Williams, op. cit., 25, 96, 318.

[3] It may be assumed that this refers to the copy of Llanover MS. B 15 in BM. Add. MS. 15003 or to the incomplete copy of the same text in Llanover C 65, both mentioned above.

[4] In MA *Brenhinedd y Saesson* is given the incorrect title *Brut y Saeson*. Cf. Iolo's words in Llanover MS. 11, 72: '*Brut y Saeson* is in the Gwentian dialect, and is in several of its copies attributed to Caradoc of Lancarvan.'

the nature and origin of some of his texts may be, it is to Iolo's credit that his classification in the above list does show an awareness of certain differences that existed between the various texts which were collectively known as *Brut y Tywysogion*. This awareness is likewise reflected in his remarks[1] on the text of *Brenhinedd y Saesson* in BM. Cotton MS. Cleopatra B v:

> 'There is a MS. in the British Museum Bibl. Cotton. Cleopatra B. v. P. 136 Plut. XIX A. that seems to have been that (or the same as it word for word) whence Guttyn Owain wrote his extracts, omitting some, not all, of the fabulous stories of Geoffrey. *The continuation from Cadwalader down to the last Princes, and later, is also there, as in the foregoing copy,*[2] *this is, I find by some MSS. in N[orth] W[ales] attributed to Caradoc of Llancarvan, tho' it differs greatly, I should say entirely, from the S[outh] Walian copies that I have seen of Caradoc, and with the last agrees the copy that was translated by Dr. Powel.*'

Iolo's claim in the above quotation that the South Walian copies of 'Caradoc' were in agreement with the copy which Llwyd (not Powel, as Iolo says) translated, must be borne in mind when we discuss some of the texts of *Brut y Tywysogion* which were later printed in the long projected corpus of ancient Welsh texts. In 1801 the first two volumes of *The Myvyrian Archaiology of Wales* appeared, edited by Owen Jones (Myvyr), Edward Williams (Iolo Morganwg), and Dr. William Owen Pughe. The second volume contains 'a collection of historical documents,' including four versions of *Brut y Tywysogion*. These chronicles, the editors inform us in 'The Preface' to vol. ii. of MA, were 'known under the common appellation of *Brut y Tywysogion,* or the Chronicle of the Princes' and 'were written by Caradog of Llangarvan, who flourished in the middle of the twelfth century.' The four versions are then described in these words:

> 'Two copies of them [*sc.* 'the chronicles'] are printed entirely, because they have not the least identity with respect to composition or course of narration. The second copy is printed on the lower half of the page,[3] with the text of another valuable chronicle entitled *Brut y Saeson*, or Chronicle of the Saxons; a name which it bears, not because that it is peculiarly a history of the Saxons, but from its connecting with the affairs of Wales a general review of the transactions of all Britain. To accompany the two last mentioned Chronicles, at the bottom of the page[3] is also given another, which appears to be a short summary of the history of Wales, and which was thought might possibly be of use towards illustrating some of the transactions recorded in the others.'[4]

---

[1] BM. Add. MS. 15003, 57.

[2] Iolo's copy was made not directly from the Cotton MS., but from a transcript in the hand of Robert Vaughan. *See* above, xxvi.

[3] In the second edition of MA (Denbigh, 1870) the texts are not so arranged, but are printed consecutively.

[4] MA 385.

The four texts described in the above quotation are the following:

(1) *Brut y Tywysogion* as found in the Red Book of Hergest, printed from the transcript made in 1781 by the Rev. Richard Davies:[1] MA ii. (1801) 391–467 (=MA (1870) 602–31).

(2) *Brut y Saesson* from BM. Cotton MS. Cleopatra B v: MA ii. (1801) 468–582, upper half of the pages (=MA (1870) 652–84). The text is incorrectly called *Brut y Saesson*: in the MS. the title is *Brenhinedd y Saesson*. The transcript upon which the text is based must have been carelessly done, for the printed version teems with errors, often of the most elementary kind. There is no indication who the transcriber was.[2]

(3) *Brut y Tywysogion*: MA ii. (1801) 468–582, on the lower half of the pages up to the place (470) where text (4) begins, and thence on the middle part of the pages (=MA (1870) 685–715). It is stated, both at the beginning and at the end of this text, that it was copied by Iolo Morganwg for Owain Myvyr in 1800 from another copy which he had made in 1790 from the book of the Rev. Thomas Richards, curate of Coychurch, who had copied it in 1764 from Mr. George Williams of Aberpergwm's book.[3] The events recorded in this version extend from the year 660 to 1196.

(4) *Brut Ieuan Brechfa*: MA (1801) 470–565 on the lowest part of the pages (=MA (1870) 716–20). This text, which covers the period 686–1150, purports to derive from a copy made by Mr. Rhys Thomas, printer, of Cowbridge, from 'the Book of Ieuan Brechfa' which contained excerpts 'from the books of Caradog of Llancarfan and other ancient books of history.'[4]

---

[1] *See* xxv above.

[2] It is known that Iolo Morganwg had transcribed parts at least of the text from the Cotton MS. Writing to Owain Myvyr on 9 July, 1800, Iolo says (BM. Add. MS. 15030, 14–5): 'You will find also what I copied some years ago from the British Museum of *Brut y Saeson*, which is I find by many MSS. in North Wales attributed to *Caradoc Llangarfan*. This will spare Mr. Owen some trouble at the Museum.' These words, however, seem to imply that Iolo had not made a complete transcript of the text.

[3] 'Yr Hanes uchod a gopïwyd o Lyfr George Williams o Aber Pergwm Ysgweier, genyf i Thomas Richards Curad Llan Grallo, yn y flwyddyn 1764. A minnau Iorwerth ab Iorwerth Gwilym ai copiais o Lyfyr y Parchedig Mr. Richards yn [y] flwyddyn 1790. Ac ai dadgopiais ef i Owain Myfyr, yn Mesyryd y flwyddyn 1800.' (MA 685.) 'Yr hanes uchod a ysgrifenwyd o Lyvyr George Williams, Esq. o Aberpergwm, genyf fi Thomas Richards Curad Llangrallo, yn y flwyddyn 1764. A minnau Iorwerth ab Iorwerth ai hysgrifenais o Lyvyr y Parchedig Mr. Richards yn y flwyddyn 1790.' (Ib. 715.)

[4] MA 716, 720.

In MA, therefore, we have four versions of *Brut y Tywysogion,* and it appears that they were all accepted as authentic variant versions.¹ In the light of later revelations about texts (3) and (4) it is interesting to read that part of the editors' preface which calls attention to the differences between the various versions:

> '... the different copies of the Chronicle—but more particularly that by Caradoc—are not alike, with respect to their phraseology—a circumstance which may induce persons to suspect the authenticity of one copy, and to give to another the preference. But such variations, however, in ancient manuscripts, may be accounted for, on the idea of the very great possibility, and even probability, that each of the very various copies attributed to the same author may be equally authentic. Many, perhaps most, of the copies of *Caradoc of Llangarvan* differ from each other in mode of expression, and in length, or brevity of narration.'²

The preface goes on to explain why these differences should be, to defend the action of the editors in 'publishing the obviously authentic copies that are known' and to maintain that 'where each of such copies agree sufficiently in facts and dates, it would be rather difficult to show good reasons why the authenticity of one should be supposed greater than that of another.'³

For many years after the appearance of MA, the four texts were accepted as authentic by scholars, although the editors of MA had themselves stated that 'perhaps a critic of sagacity might detect some interpolations'⁴ in the text purporting to derive from George Williams of Aberpergwm's book. Aneirin Owen, editor of the *Ancient Laws and Institutes of Wales,* was a good critical scholar but he does not seem to have doubted the authenticity of the Aberpergwm *Brut;* and although this text was not included in the *Monumenta Historica Britannica* (1848), in the preparation of which Owen collaborated, he made a translation of it, which was published, along with the original Welsh, in 1863 after Owen's death.⁵ Before this, however, Thomas Stephens of Merthyr, in an article entitled 'The Book of Aberpergwm, improperly called The Chronicle of Caradoc,'⁶

---

¹ Dr. W. Owain [-Pughe], writing to George Chalmers on 20 February, 1801, quotes passages referring to the Welsh kingdom of Strathclyde from both the Red Book of Hergest version and that derived from the book of Mr. George Williams ((3) above), obviously regarding the two texts as equally authentic : *see* NLW Add. MS. 146, 275.
² MA 385.   ³ MA 386.   ⁴ Ib., 387.
⁵ *Brut y Tywysogion.* The Gwentian Chronicle of Caradoc of Llancarvan. With a translation by the late Aneirin Owen, Esq. Printed for the Cambrian Archaeological Association. London, 1863.
For letters on the subject of *Brut y Tywysogion* between Aneirin Owen and the Rev. W. J. Rees of Cascob, *see Archaeologia Cambrensis,* III. iv. (1858) 208-12.
⁶ *Archaeologia Cambrensis,* III. iv. (1858) 77-96.

had critically examined this text and had come to the conclusion that it could not be dated earlier than the sixteenth century, calling attention to manifest errors in the text. It is certain that Aneirin Owen had prepared the text (based on MA) of the Aberpergwm *Brut* or 'the Gwentian Chronicle,' as he calls it, and the translation for inclusion in the *Monumenta Historica Britannica*,[1] the editors of which he helped with the Welsh material. The *Monumenta* includes a text of the *Brut,* with an English translation, down to the year 1066 (841–55), and in a note[2] to the text Owen explains what MSS. he had used: the main text is that of the Red Book of Hergest, with variants from two MSS. at Hengwrt, B [=Peniarth MS. 19] and C [=Peniarth MS. 20], BM. Cotton MS. Cleopatra B v and the Black Book of Basingwerk [=NLW MS. 7006]. The dates embodied in the text, Owen further explains, are taken from MS. C, and the marginal chronology is from BM. Cotton MS. Cleopatra B v. It is to be noticed that Aneirin Owen made use of the Peniarth MS. 20 text, which appears to have been unknown to the editors of MA. Owen's attempt to form a composite text was, to say the least, not very satisfactory in view of the extent to which the texts used, on his own admission, varied both in content and phraseology.[3] We know, however, that at least one other Welsh antiquary had been in touch with the Record Commissioners and that he had sent them a translation of a part of *Brenhinedd y Saesson* for inclusion in the *Monumenta Historica Britannica,* but it was not used by the editors. This translation was prepared by the Rev. Henry Parry of Llanasa who sent it on 30 May, 1829, to Henry Petrie. It is a translation of *Brenhinedd y Saesson* for the years 681–977, but it is not clear what copy of the Welsh text Parry had used.[4] Later Thomas Duffus

---

[1] *Monumenta Historica Britannica or Materials for the History of Britain from the earliest period to the end of the reign of King Henry VII.* Published by command of Her Majesty. London, 1848. Only the first volume (extending to the Norman conquest) appeared, edited by Henry Petrie and, after the former's death, by [Sir] Thomas Duffus Hardy.

[2] 841, footnote *a*. The *Monumenta* also includes the *Annales Cambriae* down to the year 1066: 830–40. In the preface (95) it is suggested, for the first time, that the *Brut* is a translation from Latin.

[3] Owen's difficulties are suggested by the following note, op. cit., 841: 'Such of their respective variations as require translation have been separated from those which are merely verbal. . . . this MS. [BM. Cotton MS. Cleopatra B v] consists of the usual Welsh text, mixed with a Welsh version of considerable portions of the Winchester Annals of Ricardus Divisiensis and of a few excerpts taken from other English writers, which it has not been thought necessary to notice as various readings.'

[4] Parry's Welsh original does not appear to have been either that of BM. Cotton MS. Cleopatra B v or that of the Black Book of Basingwerk. It is clear from Parry's letter that he only translated part of his original: 'With your curious copy of the *Chronicon Walliae,* etc., I send a close English version of the *Welsh Annals,* as far as they go together,' *Archaeologia Cambrensis* III. ix. (1863) 59. The *Chronicon Walliae* must have been some copy of the Annals in BM. Harleian MS. 3859.

Hardy placed this translation at the disposal of the editors of *Archaeologia Cambrensis*, in which journal[1] it was printed along with the original letter which Parry had sent, with the translation, to Henry Petrie.

In 1860 appeared the well-known Rolls edition of *Brut y Tywysogion*,[2] edited and translated by the Rev. John Williams ab Ithel (1811–62).[3] Since this edition of the *Brut* was the only one which offered an English translation of any of the authentic versions, much use has been made of it down to our own days, although it has long been recognized that Ab Ithel's method of editing the Welsh text was unscholarly and that his translation is often at fault. Slavishly following the example of Aneirin Owen, much of whose MS. materials he used without acknowledgement,[4] Ab Ithel attempted to form a composite text from MS. texts which, as we now know, represented three independent versions of the *Brut*. The MSS. used were the Red Book of Hergest (Ab Ithel's A), Peniarth MS. 18 (B), Peniarth MS. 20 (C), BM. Cotton MS. Cleopatra B v (D), and the Black Book of Basingwerk (E)—the same MSS., with the exception of B, as those which Aneirin Owen had used. The main text is that of the Red Book of Hergest, but variants are given from the other MSS. and some additional passages incorporated from Peniarth MS. 20. This last named MS. is described by Ab Ithel in his introduction[5] as 'a Venedotian MS. on vellum, agreeing in matter with the preceding [*sc*. the Red Book of Hergest and Peniarth MS. 18], but totally differing in phraseology.' He might also have added that the texts of MSS. D and E, i.e. BM. Cotton MS. Cleopatra B v and the Black Book of Basingwerk, differed partly in matter and completely in phraseology down to the year 1197, from that of the Red Book of Hergest and Peniarth MS. 18. In view of these differences between the texts which he used the proper thing for Ab Ithel to do would have been to publish three parallel texts based respectively on (1) the Red Book of Hergest and Peniarth MS. 18, (2) Peniarth MS. 20, and (3) BM. Cotton MS. Cleopatra B v and the Black Book of Basingwerk. This was

---

[1] III. ix. (1863) 60–67.
[2] *Brut y Tywysogion* or, *The Chronicle of the Princes*, edited by the Rev. John Williams ab Ithel, M.A. London, 1860.
[3] *See* James Kenward, *Ab Ithel: An Account of the Life and Writings of the Rev. John Williams ab Ithel*. Tenby and London, 1871. This *Life* first appeared in the *Cambrian Journal*, 1862–4. G. J. Williams, 'Ab Ithel,' *Llenor* xii. 216–30; xiii. 88–100.
[4] *See* the review [by H. Longueville Jones] in *Archaeologia Cambrensis*, III. vii. (1861) 93–103; Ab Ithel's reply, ib. 169–71; and Jones's further remarks, ib. 263–7.
[5] Op. cit. xlv.

later realized by Mr. Egerton Phillimore in his survey of Welsh historical material in manuscript,[1] in which he has a long 'note' (170–175) on the shortcomings of Ab Ithel's text and translation. Phillimore's survey was of great service in that the need for a thorough examination of all MS. versions of the *Brut* was emphasized in it, and a plea made for a new critical edition of the texts.

In 1890 the Red Book of Hergest text of *Brut y Tywysogion* was published in RBB 257–384,[2] as also was the Red Book *Brut y Saesson* (385–403) and the summary of events which begins *O Oes Gwrtheyrn Gwrtheneu* (404–6). This can at least be relied upon as a faithful reproduction of the Red Book text, but it represents only one copy of one version of the *Brut*, and that copy, as we now know, one that is defective in several places. In recent years it has become increasingly clear that the Red Book copyist was rather negligent, and a comparison of his text of the *Brut* with earlier ones representing the same version, such as those of Peniarth MS. 18 and Mostyn MS. 116, shows that his readings are incorrect and that there are many important omissions. Since 1890, partly because of the excellent way in which the text was reproduced, too much authority has been given to the Red Book text. That there were defects in it was first seen in 1898 when the first part of the first volume of RWM was published: a collation of the Red Book text with that of Mostyn MS. 116, which J. Gwenogvryn Evans examined and described for the Historical Manuscripts Commission, showed that the latter MS. contained a text far more correct than that of the Red Book.[3] In RWM i. 57–62 the variant readings of Mostyn MS. 116 as compared with the Red Book text printed in RBB were listed, but only so far as the variants affected the sense. Evans does not claim to have noted all the variant readings.

The next substantial contribution to the study of the chronicle was made by the late Sir John Edward Lloyd, who in the preparation of his *History of Wales*, first published in 1910, had used the variant versions of the *Brut*, along with the *Annales*

---

[1] 'The Publication of Welsh Historical Records, *Y Cymmrodor* xi. (1890–91) 133–75. This article was read as a paper before the Cymmrodorion section of the National Eisteddfod at Brecon in August, 1899.

[2] A popular edition, in modernized orthography, of the first part of the RBB text, ending with the appointment of the Lord Rhys as justiciar of South Wales (cf. below 68, 39–40), was produced by [Sir] O. M. Edwards, in *Brut y Tywysogion*, Caernarvon, n.d. So far as I know, the second volume, announced in the Preface to the first, never appeared.

[3] Aneirin Owen had seen and catalogued the Mostyn MSS., then at Gloddaeth (see 'Catalogue of Welsh MSS. in North Wales. No. II.' in *Trans. Cym.*, 1843, 400 ff.), but he did not use the Mostyn MS. 116 text of the *Brut*. Nor did Ab Ithel.

Cambriae, among his main original sources. In his preface he states that he had intended to include in this work a critical account of the 'chronicles included in *Annales Cambriae* and *Brut y Tywysogion*,' but that he had not done so because he had come to the conclusion that the task would have to be separately undertaken. However, he explains briefly that he regarded '*Brut y Tywysogion* and *Brut* (or *Brenhinedd*) *y Saesson* as two independent translations of a Latin original partially (but by no means fully) represented in MSS. B and C of *Annales Cambriae*.' It is clear that in 1910 Sir John Edward Lloyd had not realized the importance of the Peniarth MS. 20 text of *Brut y Tywysogion* and its complete independence of the Red Book of Hergest version. It is probable that he had been misled by the description of this text by J. Gwenogvryn Evans in RWM ii. 342, a description which had appeared in 1899. It is unfortunate that Evans cannot have examined the text very closely for he describes it as 'apparently based on that of Mostyn MS. 116,'[1] but adds that 'the wording is changed more or less throughout' and that in some places its contents differ from those of RBB and Mostyn MS. 116. However, he did draw attention to the fact that the chronicle in Peniarth MS. 20 did not end with the year 1282, as does that of RBB, but continued in three different hands to the year 1332. This continuation for the years 1283–1332 was printed in full in RWM ii. 343–6.

Many years were to elapse before Sir John Edward Lloyd produced the 'full and systematic discussion' of the Welsh chronicles which he had promised in the preface to his *History of Wales*. When the discussion came, in 1928, in his British Academy lecture on 'The Welsh Chronicles,'[2] Sir John had long recognized the importance of the Peniarth MS. 20 text, which he now rightly regarded as representing a third version of the chronicle. In this short but masterly treatment of the texts, based on a lifetime's use and consultation of them,[3] many things seen but dimly by others were clearly and convincingly demonstrated for the first time. It was shown, in the first place, that Caradog of Llancarfan, who since the days of David Powel had been regarded as the author of the *Brut* down to the year 1156,[4]

---

[1] On the text in Mostyn MS. 116, *see* above, xxxii. It contains an earlier and more correct text of the Red Book of Hergest version. The Peniarth MS. 20 text, which represents an independent version, is in no way based upon it.

[2] *The Welsh Chronicles*. The Sir John Rhŷs Memorial Lecture. British Academy. London, 1928.

[3] For an appreciation of this lecture *see* R. T. Jenkins, *Llenor* xxxvi. 83–4.

[4] As late as 1889 even so sound a scholar as Egerton Phillimore regarded Caradog as 'the author of the oldest form of the *Brut* as far as 1120.' *Trans. Cym.*, 1890–91, 150.

could have no claim to the authorship either in part or in full, but that the chronicle had been attributed to him by someone who had taken too seriously the words of Geoffrey of Monmouth in his colophon to the *Historia Regum Britanniae*,[1] where he states (no doubt with his tongue in his cheek) that he 'remits as subject matter to Caradog of Llancarfan,' his contemporary, 'the kings of the Britons who since the time of Cadwaladr have succeeded in Wales.' In the second place, it was proved that there were three Welsh versions of *Brut y Tywysogion* represented by the texts of (1) the Red Book of Hergest (and the earlier and more correct Mostyn MS. 116 and Peniarth MS. 18), (2) Peniarth MS. 20, and (3) *Brenhinedd y Saesson*, as found in BM Cotton MS. Cleopatra B v and the Black Book of Basingwerk. Thirdly, the Abergwm *Brut* printed in MA was dismissed as one of the literary forgeries of Iolo Morganwg,[2] a fact which had been suspected since Professor G. J. Williams had published his *Iolo Morganwg a Chywyddau'r Ychwanegiad*[3] (National Eisteddfod Association, London, 1926). In the fourth place, the view expressed in the preface to the *Monumenta Historica Britannica*[4] that the variant texts of the *Brut* were translated from a chronicle written originally in Latin, was amply confirmed, and it was argued that the three versions represented three independent translations of an original, now lost, which bore a close relationship to the three sets of annals published under the title *Annales Cambriae* in the Rolls series. Lastly, Sir John Edward Lloyd briefly analysed the contents of the *Brut* and showed that there were reasons to believe that the texts used by the final redactor of the complete Latin chronicle probably derived from three monastic centres in Wales, St. Davids (down to about the year 1100), Llanbadarn-fawr (from about 1100 to about 1175), and Strata Florida (from about 1175 to 1282), with additions from records kept in other Cistercian houses in Wales.[5]

A further contribution to the study of the *Brut* was made by Dr. Robin Flower who, sometime before the outbreak of World War II, discovered a set of annals for the years 1190–1266

---

[1] HRB, 556: 'Reges autem eorum (sc. Britonum) qui ab illo tempore (sc. Adelstani) in Gualiis successerunt, Karadoco Lancarbanensi contemporaneo meo in materia scribendi permitto.'

[2] *Brut Ieuan Brechfa* shows signs of being a similar forgery by Iolo Morganwg.

[3] Cf. op. cit., 198, 214.

[4] *See* above, xxx, footnote 2.

[5] In *A History of Carmarthenshire* i. (Cardiff, 1935) 195 the same scholar suggests that certain non-Cistercian houses may have made some contributions. He tends to regard some sections in MS. B of AC as having originated in Talley Abbey, the only Premonstratensian house in Wales.

(called *Cronica de Wallia*) in Exeter Cathedral Library MS. 3514,[1] which was written in the third quarter of the thirteenth century. These annals are closely related to the corresponding sections of the annals in BM. Cotton MS. Domitian A I (MS. B of Ab Ithel's *Annales Cambriae*) and to the various versions of the *Brut*, in particular that of Peniarth MS. 20.[2]

When Sir John Edward Lloyd delivered his lecture on 'The Welsh Chronicles,' not one of the three versions of *Brut y Tywysogion* had been satisfactorily edited nor was there available a sound translation of any one of them. The text of the Red Book of Hergest had been published once in part (down to 1066 in the *Monumenta Historica Britannica*) and thrice in full (in MA, BT, and RBB), and translated once in part (in the *Monumenta*) and once in full, if not very correctly (in BT). However, there was no critical edition, based on all the early MSS., available of the Red Book version. *Brenhinedd y Saesson* had been printed once (in MA), but in a very unsatisfactory way, and there was no complete translation of it.[3] The Peniarth MS. 20 version had never been printed nor translated, though it is now clear that it is the fullest version of the three. In 1941 I published a diplomatic edition of the Peniarth MS. 20 text, with variants from three later copies.[4] In a review of that edition Professor J. Goronwy Edwards regretted that the text was not accompanied by an English translation.[5] In the present volume I offer such a translation and also try to show in the notes where and how the Peniarth MS. 20 version differs in substance from that of the Red Book of Hergest and from *Brenhinedd y Saesson*, of which I have also prepared critical texts with translations for publication in the near future.

§3. CONTENTS AND ORIGIN OF *BRUT Y TYWYSOGION*

Brut y Tywysogion in its three variant forms consists of a chronicle, written in the form of annals, which extends from the year 680 (RB), 681 (Pen. 20), or 683 (BS), to 1282 (RB), 1332 (Pen. 20), 1197 (BS in BM. Cotton MS. Cleopatra B v), or 1461 (BS in the Black Book of Basingwerk). Since the entries in Peniarth MS. 20 for the years 1282–1332 have been added to the main text by two if not three later copyists,[6] it is clear

---

[1] *See* Thomas Jones, *Cronica de Wallia and other Documents from Exeter Cathedra Library MS. 3514*. Reprinted (with indexes) from B xii. 27–44.
[2] *See* Pen. 20, xi–xiii.
[3] For a translation of part of it (the years 681–977) *see* above, xxx.
[4] *Brut y Tywysogyon. Peniarth MS. 20.* Cardiff, 1941.
[5] EHR lvii. (1942), 370–5.
[6] *See* below, xlv.

that the original terminal point for both the RB version and that of Peniarth MS. 20 was the same, i.e. the year 1282. One cannot decide what the original terminal point of BS was, for the text in the Cotton MS. is probably incomplete;[1] and the later portions of the text in the Black Book of Basingwerk seem to be based in part on RB and in part on Peniarth MS. 20. BS down to the year 1088 seeks to combine a summary of Welsh events, as derived from the same source as that of RB and Peniarth MS. 20, with contemporary events in England as recorded in some version of the *Annales de Wintonia*. Thus, of the three variant versions of *Brut y Tywysogion*, the most closely related are RB and Peniarth MS. 20. With the exception of some details and two or three more important passages found in the one and not in the other,[2] and many slight variations of meaning which can be explained as errors of transcription or translation,[3] they are in close agreement in their matter as in their title. Strictly speaking these are the only two versions called *Brut y Tywysogion*;[4] and, as the title implies, they contain a history of Wales under the princes, or from the death of Cadwaladr—regarded as the last supreme king of the Britons—to the death of Llywelyn ap Gruffudd, the last independent prince of Wales, in 1282.

The language and style of the three versions, along with certain names of persons and of places which show Latin declensional forms, make it clear that the original was written in Latin.[5] Down to the year 1282 RB and Peniarth MS. 20 agree so closely in substance and differ so completely in phraseology that it is safe to conclude with Lloyd[6] that they represent two independent translations of the same original, although a close comparison of the two Welsh texts shows that there were minor variations in the contents as well as in the readings of the copies[7] from which the two translations were made. The

---

[1] In the MS. (which is a composite one) f. 162*b* is practically illegible due to its having been an outside page. The text continues to the last line and so must have carried on the entries through 1198. Gutun Owain, in compiling his BS in the Black Book of Basingwerk, must have used as his original a text which ended at the same point, for after 1198 his compilation seems to be a combined summarized version of RB and Pen. 20. And yet there are some indications that his original of BS was not the Cotton MS.

[2] *See* below, lx–xi.

[3] *See* the Notes, *passim*.

[4] On the Welsh word *Brut* (French and English *Brut*, Latin *Brutus*) derived from *Brutus*, the eponymous hero of Britain in Geoffrey of Monmouth's *Historia Regum Britanniae*, used in the sense of 'chronicle' or 'history,' *see* RBB, v–vii.

[5] *See* Lloyd, *The Welsh Chronicles*, 9–13.

[6] Ib., 12–13.

[7] These variations are commented on in the Notes to this volume.

Welsh sections of BS are on the whole briefer than the texts of RB and Peniarth MS. 20 down to 1197, the last legible date in the Cotton MS. text of BS, but it is obvious that they represent a condensed version of the same original Latin chronicle. At present it is difficult to say whether BS is a direct translation of a Latin chronicle which combined a summary of the text from which RB and Peniarth MS. 20 are derived, with sections from the *Annales de Wintonia*, or whether it is a compilation made in Welsh by a chronicler who used both the fuller Latin chronicle underlying RB and Peniarth MS. 20 and the Winchester Annals. So far as I know, there is no Latin chronicle agreeing with BS in its combination of Welsh and English history, now extant. The difference in language and style between the Welsh sections of BS, on the one hand, and both RB and Peniarth MS. 20 on the other, is sufficient evidence that the compiler of BS did not use either of the two full versions of *Brut y Tywysogion* down to the year 1197.

From what has been said above it is obvious that the important text, if ever a copy of it could be found, would be the original Latin chronicle underlying RB, Peniarth MS. 20, and BS. Unfortunately, it does not seem to have survived, and no one has succeeded in tracing any reference to it. And yet minor variations in the contents of the three Welsh versions show that they are not based on one and the same copy of the Latin original, or, in other words, that at least three (probably more) copies of it once existed. It is certain that it was compiled at some monastic house in Wales, and it is equally certain that the Welsh versions were made in similar institutions. After its compilation copies of it would then reach other monastic houses, more especially those which belonged to the same Order. And since it is unlikely that three different Welsh versions of it would be produced in the same house, it may not be too rash to suggest that the three Welsh versions were made at three, or at least two, separate monastic centres. The compiler of the Latin text, like many other compilers of historical texts, must remain anonymous, unless new evidence is discovered. Lloyd has clearly proved[1] that he was not Caradog of Llancarfan, a known contemporary of Geoffrey of Monmouth's,[2] as had been believed since the latter part of the sixteenth century. Nor is there any real evidence to support the theory put forward by

---

[1] Op. cit., 5–8.
[2] On Caradog of Llancarfan and the works written by him *see* J. S. P. Tatlock's article on him in *Speculum* xiii. 139 ff.

Edward Owen,[1] and later supported by Dr. Mary Williams,[2] that the author of part of the compilation was Bleddri ap Cedifor, who is mentioned in the *Brut, s.a.* 1116: *see* 41, 10 below.[3] Whoever the compiler was, it is probable that he wrote the original Latin chronicle towards the end of the thirteenth century, possibly fairly soon after the year 1282 which marks the end of RB and of the Peniarth MS. 20 version in its original form and which appears, therefore, to have been the end of their common original.[4] In any case the year 1282, which saw the fall of Llywelyn ap Gruffudd, the last prince of Wales, would be the natural terminal point for a chronicle of the princes of Wales even if the chronicler lived considerably later. It is obvious that the compiler intended the work to be a continuation of Geoffrey's *Historia Regum Britanniae*, which closes with Cadwaladr, and that the suggestion for its compilation came from Geoffrey's colophon, which has been quoted above. In the MSS., texts of the Welsh versions are often found following that of the Welsh translations of Geoffrey's *Historia*.[5] This is true of RB, Peniarth MS. 20, and BS. In fact, the very first sentence of BS contains a reference to the last sections of the *Historia*:

> '*After the profound, tempestuous plague and the dire famine, which were mentioned above, had come to pass in the time of Cadwaladr the Blessed*, the Saxons came and conquered England from the one sea to the other and held it under five kings, as it had been before in the time of Hors and Hengist, when they expelled Gwrtheyrn Gwrthenau from the bounds of England.'[6]

The italicized words in the above quotation refer to HRB 530–35 and the words 'which were mentioned above' show that the text was originally intended to follow Geoffrey's *Historia*. This seems to suggest that there was once a Latin text from which BS was directly translated and in which passages from the Latin

---

[1] 'A Note on the Identification of the "Bleheris" of Wauchier de Denain,' RC xxxii. (1911) 5–16, especially 13–5.
[2] 'More about Bleddri,' *Études Celtiques* ii. (1937) 219–45. For a bibliography on Bleddri (Breri, etc.) *see Romanic Review* xxxii. (1941) 16, note 77. It should be pointed out that the identification of Bleddri (Breri, etc.) with Bleddri ap Cedifor has not been proved.
[3] The *Bleddyn* of Pen. 20 is an error for *Bleddri*: *see* note *ad loc*.
[4] It must be more than a coincidence that the annals in Cotton MS. Domitian A 1, which continue to 1288, originally ended in 1282: the years 1283–8 were written up from time to time, as appears from the MS.
[5] Cf. J. S. P. Tatlock, *The Legendary History of Britain*. Berkeley and Los Angeles, 1950, 432. In some MSS. the whole series *Y Bibyl Ynghymraec, Ystorya Daret, Brut y Brenhined,* and *Brut y Tywysogion* are linked together to supply a history from the Creation to 1282.
[6] '*Gwedy daruot yr anodun vall dymhestylus a'r newyn girat, a dywetpwyt vchot, yn oes Catwaladyr Vendigeit*, y doeth y Saesson a goresgyn Lloegyr o'r mor pwy gilid a'y chynal a dan pymp brenhin, val y buassei gynt yn oes Hors a Hengist, pan deholassant Gortheyrn Gortheneu o deruynev Lloegyr. . . .' (BM. Cotton MS. Cleopatra B v, f. 109*a*).

chronicle underlying RB and Peniarth MS. 20 and from the *Annales de Wintonia* had already been combined and that the 'contamination' was not first effected in the Welsh BS. In any case, both in BM. Cotton MS. Cleopatra B v and in the Black Book of Basingwerk, the text of BS follows immediately after a Welsh version of the *Historia*,[1] and the above quotation from the beginning of BS shows that the two texts were meant to be linked together. RB and Peniarth MS. 20 are not formally linked with the Welsh versions of Geoffrey's work by any such sentence, but they too are regarded as a natural sequel to the *Historia* and often follow it in the MSS. The opening section on Cadwaladr and the references to the prophecies of Merlin (Myrddin)[2] as set forth in the *Historia* afford a link between *Brut y Tywysogion* (RB and Peniarth MS. 20) and Geoffrey's work.

The compiler, then, probably lived towards the end of the thirteenth century[3] and intended his 'Chronicle of the Princes' to be a sequel to Geoffrey's 'History of the Kings of Britain.' There is considerable indirect evidence to suggest where the compiler worked and what sources he used. The *Brut* bears all the marks of being the work of a historiographer working in a monastery, and most of the monastic foundations in Wales were Cistercian, and the many references in the text to the establishment of houses of that Order in Wales seem to show that the original Latin chronicle was composed in one of these Cistercian houses. And the fact that events at Strata Florida[4] are given greater prominence that those at any other monastic foundation favours the conclusion that it was there that the original text was compiled[5]. The reference in the *Brut* (both RB and Peniarth MS. 20) to the *Annals* of Strata Florida[6] shows that the compiler had been able to consult them as one of his

---

[1] *See* J. J. Parry, *Brut y Brenhinedd*. Cotton Cleopatra Version. Cambridge, Mass., 1937.

[2] *See* below, 1, 119.

[3] The original chronicle was certainly composed after 1286, for both in Pen. 20 and RB reference is made *s.a.* 1280 (120 below) to the fire at Strata Florida when Einion Sais was abbot. We know from the annals in the Breviate of Domesday Book that this fire took place in 1286: *see* AC, 109. S.a. 1200 (below 80) it is said that the virtues of Gruffudd ap Cynan ab Owain, whose death is recorded, shall be remembered 'so long as the men that *now are* shall live.'

[4] *See* Index *s.n.* 'Strata Florida.'

[5] Note that on 64 below, *s.a.* 1164(=1165), as in RB, *s.a.* 1163 (=1165), the founding of Strata Florida is recorded and that in both versions it is said that 'a community of monks *came* to ... Strata Florida.' In BS, however, *s.a.* 1164(=1165) it is said that 'a community *went* to Strata Florida.'

[6] *See* below, 108. The fact that the reference to these *Annals* is found in the RB version (cf. RBB 371, 24–5) as well as in that of Pen. 20 shows that it derives from the lost Latin original. Cf. EHR lvii. 371–2.

sources. And what can be gathered about the probable place of origin of two out of four Latin sets of annals closely related to the *Brut* favours the same conclusion.

The four sets of annals are the following:

(1) The annals from 444 to 954 in Harleian MS. 3859, ff. 189a–193a, col. 2.[1] Lloyd has argued that this document was composed at St. Davids although in its earlier parts other material of an annalistic nature, but not particularly Welsh in origin, had been used in its compilation.[2]

(2) The annals in BM. Cotton MS. Domitian A 1, which, partly based on some form of (1), commence with the Creation and continue to the year 1288. Lloyd has argued on the internal evidence of its latest sections that this text too was compiled at St. Davids.[3]

(3) The annals preserved on the fly-leaves of the *Breviate of Domesday Book* in the Public Record Office and copied about the year 1300. The final entry is given *s.a.* 1286, and for the last fifty years of the period which it covers the text appears to be a chronicle of Strata Florida. It is probable that it was compiled there.[4]

(4) The *Cronica de Wallia*, a set of annals for the period 1190–1266, but with no entries for the years 1217–27, 1229, 1232, 1249–53, 1263. The text in Exeter Cathedral Library MS. 3514—the only copy that seems to have survived—was copied about 1280. Again internal evidence suggests that it originated in Strata Florida. Long passages are in complete verbal agreement with (3) above and may be regarded, so far as they go, as the original of the corresponding passages of the RB and Peniarth MS. 20 *Brut*. It is probable that (4) is derived from (3) above or that both are derived from a common original.

Lloyd came to the conclusion 'either that the compiler of the Latin original of the *Brut* had many other sources before him

---

[1] For a diplomatic reproduction of the text *see* Egerton Phillimore, 'The *Annales Cambriae* and Old-Welsh Genealogies from Harleian MS. 3859,' *Y Cymmrodor* ix. (1888), 141–83.
[2] Op. cit., 14.
[3] Ib., 14–5.
[4] Ib., 15–6. Lloyd has shown that (2) and (3) have a common origin, for in both there is a lacuna from the middle of 1151 to that of 1153. This lacuna is not found in any text of *Brut y Tywysogion*. Ab Ithel formed a composite text of (1), (2), and (3) in his *Annales Cambriae*. Rolls Series. London, 1860. Lloyd has printed the texts of (2) and (3) for the years 1035–93 in parallel columns in *Trans. Cym.* viii. 166–79.

beyond the three[1] which have survived' or—and this is the view which he favoured—'that the two principal texts[2] in *Annales Cambriae* began as mere skeletons or outlines of the chronicle which was then being built up as the foundation of the *Brut*.'[3] The annals of Strata Florida to which reference is made in the *Brut* (below, 108) cannot be (2), (3), or (4) above, for they contain no entry about the matter there recorded. On the basis of an analysis of the contents of the *Brut* Lloyd further argues that the main source down to about 1100 was a St. Davids document, from about 1100 to 1175 a Llanbadarn document, and from 1175 to 1282 a Strata Florida document. This does not mean that all the entries in any one of these periods come exclusively from one of the three monastic centres named. On the contrary, some of the entries reflect other documents which derived from other Cistercian houses in Wales, such as Llantarnam (or Nant Teyrnon), Aberconwy, Basingwerk (not originally Cistercian, but transferred from Savigny to Cîteaux in 1147), Strata Marcella, Cwm-hir and Whitland.[4] Although the complete Latin compilation has not survived many of the original Latin entries, which were embodied in it and subsequently translated thrice into Welsh, may still be traced in one or more of the four sets of Latin annals listed above.[5] And so, in a way, we still have the Latin original of many passages of the *Brut*. The notes to this volume will make it clear that the compiler of the complete original chronicle committed errors in using some of his sources and that the Welsh translators often went astray in their translation. However, the RB and Peniarth MS. 20 versions of the *Brut* are in such close substantial agreement that with the help of the *Annales Cambriae* and the *Cronica de Wallia* large portions of the original Latin text can be reconstructed. Down to 951(=953) the entries in the *Brut* are really translations of those in Harleian MS. 3859, which the compiler had incorporated in his Latin chronicle, with a few additions from other sources or from a fuller version of the text than that preserved in the Harleian MS. The only entries in the *Brut* which have no parallel in the latter are the following:

[1] The *Cronica de Wallia*, (4) above, had not been discovered when Lloyd published *The Welsh Chronicles*.
[2] I.e. (2) and (3) above.
[3] Op. cit., 16.
[4] Ib., 16–20. One passage in the *Brut* (both RB and Pen. 20) shows that the compiler had read Gildas, *De Excidio Britanniae*: see note on 25, 26–7, p. 162 below.
[5] The texts of the *Brut* contain evidence that the compiler of the original Latin chronicle in some places combined the texts of the Latin annals listed (2) and (3) above: see below, notes on 16, 17–9; 20, 5–6.

(1) *s.a.* 842 'Two years after that died Idwallon.'
(2) *s.a.* 873 '. . . and the battle of Ynegydd in Anglesey took place. And Einion Fonheddig, bishop of Menevia, died.'
(3) *s.a.* 890 'Eight hundred and ninety was the year of Christ when the Black Norsemen came to Gwynedd.'
(4) *s.a.* 907 '. . . in which Maelog Cam, son of Peredur, was slain.'
(5) *s.a.* 908 '. . . and bishop of all Ireland and a man of great piety and charity, son of Culunnán, who by his own wish was slain in battle.'
(6) *s.a.* 909 'And Cerbhall, son of Muirecan, king of Leinster, died, making a sure end.'
(7) *s.a.* 918 'And Ireland and Anglesey were ravaged by the folk of Dublin.'
(8) *s.a.* 920 '. . . by Meurig, his brother.'
(9) *s.a.* 921 'And bishop Nercu died.'
(10) *s.a.* 935 'by the men of Ceredigion.'
(11) *s.a.* 944 'And Ussa ap Llawr and . . .'
(12) *s.a.* 950 'And the Gentiles slew Dwnwallon.'

Nor are any of the above entries, which are in the *Brut* but which are not in Harleian MS. 3859, to be found in the annals in BM. Cotton MS. Domitian A 1 and the *Breviate of Domesday Book*. It follows from this that the compiler of the Latin original of the *Brut* either used a fuller version of the annals preserved in Harleian MS. 3859 or that he added the entries listed above from other sources. The only entry in Harleian MS. 3859 which has no parallel in the *Brut* is AC *s.a.* 947 'Eadmund rex Saxonum jugulatus est.' For the period 951(=953) to 1282 the compiler must have used many sources in addition to the chronicles preserved in Cotton MS. Domitian A 1 and in the *Breviate of Domesday Book*. Most of the material in which Welsh events are recorded appear to be based on earlier records made fairly soon after the events described.

The *Brut*, like many other medieval chronicles, is uneven in its treatment of various periods of history. Thus, whereas the early period of over four hundred years (680–1087) occupies about seventeen pages of the translation, the events of the year 1217 alone occupy about three pages. Sometimes the narrative is very meagre, at other times it is full and detailed. The final compiler is hardly to be blamed for this, for the meagreness and fullness of his text reflects the original sources which he used, and they in their turn are a measure of the interest or lack of interest which the various annalists took in the events which they recorded. Some passages, the account of the attack on Aberystwyth castle in 1116, for example, seem to be eye-witness accounts, whereas others consist of a series of statements that are almost cryptic in their bare sentences. It is difficult to know how far the compiler has occasionally expanded his sources after the manner of a literary historian, but it is safe, it appears to me, to assume that he has done so here and there. Take the entries *s.a.* 1020 (=1022) on 12 below. The studied contrast between Rhain's confident attack and his ignominious retreat and the Welsh proverb quoted reflect the literary artist at work. This impression is confirmed by a comparison of this passage in the *Brut* with the corresponding entries in the Cotton MS. Domitian A 1 and in the *Breviate of Domesday Book,* which I quote in parallel columns:

Breviate of Domesday Book	*Domitian A. I*
Reyn Scotus mentitus est se esse filium Mareduc qui obtinuit dextrales Britones; quem Seisil rex Venedocie in hostio Guili expugnauit, et occisus est Reyn. Eilaf uastauit Demetiam. Meneuia fracta est.	Lewelin filius Seissill, rex Uenedotie, pugnauit contra Reyn, qui dicebat se esse filium Maredut; et deuictus est Reyn in ostio Guili. Eilaph uenit in Britanniam et uastauit Dyuet et Meneuiam.[1]

It appears that the compiler of the *Brut* has combined the two passages quoted above and, whilst adhering closely to them in their last two entries, has allowed himself considerable freedom in the retelling of the entry about Rhain the Pretender. His best told tale, that of the abduction of Nest by Owain ap Cadwgan,[2] has no entry corresponding to it in AC, and it may owe much of its detail not only to the compiler's imagination but also to tradition. Evidence of the same literary inclination are the many short speeches which are attributed to some of the persons whose actions are described,[3] the Welsh proverbs quoted,[4] the many set rhetorical panegyrics of princes and clerics,[5] and the obvious attempts to attain dramatic effect.[6] It is clear that the compiler was a Welshman, but the sentiments and sympathies expressed are not consistently Welsh throughout the chronicle, probably because they reflect the sources which were partly Welsh and partly Norman in origin. Like Gildas, Geoffrey of Monmouth and Gerald of Wales before him he regards as punishment inflicted by God for past sins, the troubles

[1] AC, 23, and footnote 2.
[2] 28.
[3] *See*, for example, the words attributed to Iorwerth ap Bleddyn on 32–3.
[4] 12, 44.
[5] Cf. 'Le chroniqueur féodal ne se contente pas de raconter les faits glorieux et d'évoquer les grands hommes, il en fait le panégyrique, et souvent sans mesure et sans sens critique': Paul Rousset, 'La Conception de l'Histoire à l'époque féodale' in *Mélanges d'Histoire du Moyen Âge*, 623–33. Presses Universitaires de France. Paris, 1951.
[6] E.g. 34, 39–40, 48.

that have befallen the Welsh, but he glories in the leaders who strove to keep the Welsh nation alive and to resist the enemies who had resolved 'that the Britannic race should be annhilated.' Like other medieval chroniclers, he records many marvels including blood-rain, comets, eclipses, plagues, and various omens, in all of which he sees the hand of God. But, despite many defects common to his period, he has compiled a sober chronicle which has long been recognized as a source of first importance for the history of medieval Wales and as one that cannot be neglected for some aspects of the history of England,[1] France, and Germany.[2] Even though the suggestion for compiling the chronicle in its full form seems to have come from Geoffrey of Monmouth's colophon, it is fortunate that the unknown compiler did not try too often to emulate Geoffrey's flights of fancy but took his historian's role seriously, giving us for the most part real history rather than romantic pseudo-history like that which his more famous predecessor fabricated.

§4. Manuscripts of the Peniarth MS. 20 Version

When I edited the Peniarth MS. 20 text of *Brut y Tywysogion* in 1941, four copies only of this version were known to me, viz. Peniarth MS. 20, 65–302; Mostyn MS. 143, 35–178; Mostyn MS. 159, 144–231; and Peniarth MS. 213, 11–496—from this point on the Peniarth MS. 213 follows the RB version. These, too, were the only copies known to the late Sir John Edward Lloyd.[3] In the meantime, however, a more thorough examination of all known MSS. containing versions of *Brut y Tywysogion* has shown that Lloyd's list of MSS. is incomplete and that it must be revised. At present ten MSS. are known to contain texts, complete or incomplete, of the Peniarth MS. 20 version, although some of them show a combination of this version with that of RB. It is known also that another copy was contained in a MS., now lost, which formed part of the Wynnstay library; and yet another copy is known to exist in a MS. which was offered for sale to the National Library of Wales about ten years ago and cannot now be traced. Because of these recent additions to the list of MSS. containing texts of the Peniarth MS. 20 version and because the information

---

[1] Cf. Lloyd, op. cit., 20.

[2] Passages from the *Brut*, as edited by Ab Ithel, were printed with a Latin translation in *Monumenta Germaniae Historica:* Scriptorum Tomvs xxvii, 446–8. Hanover, 1885. The prefatory remarks (444–6) by Felix Liebermann are based on the introduction to BT.

[3] *The Welsh Chronicles*, 22–3.

given about the texts then known to me in the Introduction to the 1941 edition is in Welsh, it will be necessary to give fairly full details about all the texts now known.

Before the MSS. are listed, however, there is one point that must be stressed: not one of the texts that have come to light since 1941 affects the printed text, and the one MS. of importance for the Peniarth MS. 20 version of the *Brut* is still Peniarth MS. 20 itself. The newly discovered MSS. are, with one exception, of late date, and they are derived from an archetype closely related to one of the three MSS.—B, C, and D below —of which the variant readings were recorded in the 1941 edition. However, the new copies of the Peniarth MS. 20 version show that it was better known, in comparison with the RB version, than had hitherto been thought. And since much work still remains to be done on Welsh MSS. from the point of view of their origin and lineal descent, it is important to try to define the inter-relationship of the copies of the Peniarth MS. 20 version of the *Brut;* for conclusions reached about the affiliation of copies of this text may be of some assistance to other researchers concerned with other texts which are found in the same MSS.

A. Peniarth MS. 20 (formerly Hengwrt MS. 51), 65–302.

This MS., which has been described in RWM ii. 342, contains, in addition to the *Brut*, *Y Bibyl Ynghymraec*[1]—a Welsh version of the *Promptuarium Bibliae* attributed to Petrus Pictaviensis, and a Welsh 'Grammar.'[2] The main text of the *Brut* (681–1282) is written two columns to a page, except for 204–5, which contain the Latin verses printed below,[3] with twenty-eight lines to each column. In the continuation for the years 1282–1332, written by later hands, the number of lines to a page varies, although the bi-columnar arrangement is kept: 292–3 have thirty-one lines to a page, 294–5 have thirty, and 296–301 have twenty-five. The text ends in the eighteenth line of the first column on 302. The main text is slightly ornamented: there are coloured capitals on 65, 172, 193, 196, 254, 261, 269, and 283; and on 163, 245, 275, 290, 293, 294, 295, 296, and 300 spaces have been left for ornamental capitals which were never executed. In many places in the text small capitals have been touched with red. A peculiarity of the script is the use of the symbol *q̃* (rather like the usual contraction

---

[1] *See* Thomas Jones, *Y Bibyl Ynghymraec*. Cardiff, 1940.
[2] *See* G. J. Williams ac E. J. Jones, *Gramadegau'r Penceirddiaid*. Cardiff, 1934, 39–58.
[3] 77–8.

for the Latin -*que*) for the soft spirant sound denoted by 'dd' in modern Welsh, but it is not used in the other texts in the same MS. And it is only in the first sections of the *Brut* that it is used: from the beginning of the text (65*a*, 1)[1] to 89*a*, 8, *q3* is used consistently, and the first example of -*d* (='dd') occurs in 89*a*, 9, 'yn y diwe*d*.' From this point to 101*a*, 7, both *q3* and *d* are used, but the use of the former symbol is gradually discarded: the last example is 101*a*, 7, 'ar q3adleuoed.' So far as I know, Peniarth MS. 20 is the only MS. where *q3* is used for 'dd,' and it seems to be an orthographical experiment by the copyist[2] who appears to have been more familiar with transcribing Latin or French texts.[3] Errors of transcription show that the text of the *Brut* has been copied from an earlier MS. In several places the original lettering has been retraced in a very black ink by a later and rather unskilful hand, and in the 1941 edition the letters so retraced were printed in italics. The dates added outside the columns in the MS. are all in a comparatively late hand, but there are many marginal corrections, additions, and rubrics in a hand contemporary with that of the main text. One folio (pp. 101–2) of the vellum has been torn and parts of the text have been thereby lost: in the 1941 edition these missing sections were restored by comparison with later copies of the text and printed within square brackets. One complete folio (pp. 71–2) is lost and so there is a lacuna in the text for the years 900–949. This lacuna occurs in all other copies of the text— excepting those in which the missing section has been supplied from the RB version—which seems to prove that all the other texts of this version of the *Brut* are derived from Peniarth MS. 20, either directly or indirectly. In the 1941 edition and in the translation below (the italicized entries on 6–7) the passage corresponding to the lacuna in Peniarth MS. 20 is supplied from Mostyn MS. 116, *which represents the independent RB version.* We know from a letter which Robert Vaughan of Hengwrt wrote to James Ussher, archbishop of Armagh,[4] on 14 April, 1651, that the lacuna in Peniarth MS. 20 existed at that date.

The problem of the date and provenance of Peniarth MS. 20 is difficult to resolve. Various opinions have been given on

---

[1] In the references to Peniarth MS. 20 *a* and *b* denote the first and second column respectively.
[2] The Rev. John Davies of Mallwyd had noticed the use of the symbol *q3*, but he does not say in what MS. *See* his *Antiquae Linguae Britannicae* . . . *Rudimenta* (Editio Altera, 1809), 29–30. Cf. Pen. 20, xvii.
[3] Note the occasional use of *s* for Welsh hard *c*: Pen. 20, 166*b*, 5 a oru\3c [*sic*], 170*a*, 9 a orus.
[4] *See* the quotation from the letter on xx above.

the date of the MS.: Aneirin Owen's 'sixteenth century'[1] is certainly too late, although this opinion was blindly accepted by the uncritical Ab Ithel,[2] who did not have enough palaeographical experience to give an opinion of his own. Mr. W. W. E. Wynne of Peniarth thought it dated from the early fourteenth century.[3] One would expect the most authoritative printed opinion to be that of J. Gwenogvryn Evans, but on two different occasions he has assigned the handwriting of the Peniarth MS. 20 scribe to both the fourteenth and the fifteenth century. In RWM i. 342 he describes the MS. as one written in the fifteenth century, and in RBB xxii he ascribes a similar date to the *Dares Phrygius* of BM. Cotton MS. Cleopatra B v, ff. 223 ff., which he says was written by the scribe of Peniarth MS. 20. There can be no doubt that the same scribe wrote Peniarth MS. 20 and the *Dares Phrygius* of the Cotton MS.: a comparison of a photostat facsimile of the *Dares Phrygius* with the main text of Peniarth MS. 20 proves that this is so. This is further confirmed by the occurrence of *yw y* (for the preposition *y* with the infixed pronoun, 3 sing. and pl.) in the three texts of Peniarth MS. 20 and in the *Dares Phrygius* of BM. Cotton MS. Cleopatra B v.[4] Later, however, when Gwenogvryn Evans came to catalogue and describe the Welsh MSS. in the British Museum, he assigned the *Dares Phrygius* of the composite Cotton MS. to the middle of the fourteenth century:

> 'The *Laws* (fol. 165–222) have 20 lines to the page and are in a hand of about 1350.... The *Dares Phrygius* (fols. 223–50, bi-columnar, 28 lines to the column) belongs to the same school of writing as the *Laws*, if it is not actually from the same hand, but a little later.'[5]

The difficulty of dating Peniarth MS. 20 and the *Dares Phrygius* of the Cotton MS. has been discussed by me in the Introduction to the edition of *Y Bibyl Ynghymraec,* where the date suggested for the *Dares Phrygius* (and so for Peniarth MS. 20) by Dr. Robin Flower was accepted. Dr. Flower was of the opinion that the handwriting was of the second half of the fourteenth century, and it is wise to accept this considered opinion of an expert palaeographer.[6]

The question of the provenance of the MS. is even more difficult. We have seen that in 1651 it formed part of Robert

---

[1] *Brut y Tywysogion.* Cambrian Archaeological Society. London, 1863, pp. xvii–xviii.
[2] BT xlv–xlvi.
[3] *Archaeologia Cambrensis* III. xv. 222.
[4] For a list of passages where *yw y* occurs in Pen. MS. 20 and in the *Dares Phrygius* in the Cotton MS. see B viii. 19 ff; *Y Bibyl Ynghymraec* xc.
[5] RWM ii. 952–3.
[6] See *Y Bibyl Ynghymraec* lxxxix.

Vaughan's library at Hengwrt, but there is no information whence and how it reached Hengwrt. More than once this MS. has been described as 'Venedotian,'[1] but on what evidence it is difficult to say. There is reason to believe that Gutun Owain, when he compiled his *Brenhinedd y Saesson* in the Black Book of Basingwerk, used Peniarth MS. 20,[2] along with a copy of the RB version, for the period 1198–1332, and so it appears that in the second half of the fifteenth century the MS. was either at Valle Crucis—where Gutun Owain, according to his own testimony, spent nearly forty years of his life[3]—or possibly in the monastery of Basingwerk, where Gutun is also known to have spent some of his time.[4] Moreover, as will be shown below, Professor J. Goronwy Edwards has argued that the continuation of the *Brut* for the years 1282–1332 was compiled at Valle Crucis.[5]

Yet in spite of the above evidence, which seems to show that Peniarth MS. 20 was somewhere in North Wales, probably at Valle Crucis, in the second half of the fifteenth century, the form *yw y* (with intrusive *w*) which is consistently used in the three main texts of Peniarth MS. 20 and in the *Dares Phrygius* of the Cotton MS. for the preposition *y* with the infixed pronoun 3 sing. and plur., seems to suggest that the scribe was a South Walian. The use of *iw ei* (*eu*) has been noted in the works of Rhys Morgan[6] of Pencraig Nedd, near Neath, William Rosser[7] of Cadoxton, near Neath, the Rev. William Williams of Pantycelyn,[8] near Llandovery in Carmarthenshire, and Elizabeth Davies[9] of Neath—the four writers lived in the late eighteenth and the nineteenth century. I know of no example of *yw y* used at any time by a writer from North Wales. This is scanty evidence, it must be admitted, for our knowledge of Welsh dialects in modern, let alone medieval times, is very slight. For what it is worth, however, in the light of our present knowledge, the use of *yw y* in Peniarth MS. 20 suggests

---

[1] Aneirin Owen, op. cit., xvii–xviii; BT xlv. J. Gwenogvryn Evans, RBB xxii, states that Pen. MS. 20 'is in Venedotian orthography,' but it is difficult to know what he means by this.

[2] This will be demonstrated in my edition of *Brenhinedd y Saesson*.

[3] E. Bachellery, *L'Œuvre Poétique de Gutun Owain*, 139, 147. Paris, 1950–1.

[4] Ib. 183.

[5] EHR lvii. 370–5.

[6] John Jones, *Almanac*, 1739: 'englynion . . . *iw eu* canu.'

[7] *Y Ddwy Hatling* 4, Cowbridge [1790?]: 'ni roddodd etto lythyr-ysgar *i'w ei* Eglwys yng Nghymru.'

[8] *See* B viii. 17.

[9] In a ballad, *c*. 1850–60: 'A'r viewers *i'w ei* viewio'; 'I'r creigiau *i'w ei* guddio.' I am indebted to Professor G. J. Williams for the examples quoted from the works of William Rosser and Elizabeth Davies.

some kind of a connection with South Wales. It may be that the MS. was originally copied somewhere in South Wales and in some way reached Valle Crucis or some other North Walian monastery by the second half of the fifteenth century, or that the MS. was originally copied somewhere in North Wales by a scribe who hailed from South Wales. The evidence does not warrant our going beyond these vague suggestions, but it is well to make them for any light that can be thrown on the provenance of this MS. may help to decide where the Peniarth MS. 20 version of the *Brut* was originally translated from the lost Latin chronicle. It is to be noted that the form *yw y* is not found in the continuation of the *Brut* on pp. 292–302 of Peniarth MS. 20 (cf. 296*b*, 2 *yw* diua, 297*a*, 19 *ew* gastell). Moreover, the main texts of Peniarth MS. 20 and the *Dares Phrygius* of BM. Cotton MS. Cleopatra B v, copied by the same scribe, and the continuation of the Peniarth MS. 20 *Brut*, along with the *Brut y Brenhinedd* and the *Brenhinedd y Saesson* of the Cotton MS., all copied by another scribe, seem to be the products of the same scriptorium.[1] It may be pointed out, for what the evidence is worth, that some errors of transcription made by the Peniarth MS. 20 scribe, but immediately corrected by him in most cases,[2] suggest that the MS. was copied by someone who was more preoccupied with place-names in Powys or central Wales than with those either of North or South Wales. This again adds a little more weight to the suggestion that the scriptorium was that of Valle Crucis, whereas the consistent use of *yw y* favours the view that the scribe himself was a South Walian.[3]

B. Mostyn MS. 143, 35–178.

This is a MS. of the sixteenth century,[4] and the text of the *Brut* which it contains is incomplete at the beginning and at the end. It begins with the words *tiwssog abergelav* ('leader of Abergelau,' cf. below 4, 23) and ends with *y rufel a oedd* ('the war which had been,' cf. below 105, 27). Besides the lacuna for the years 900–949—which corresponds to the lost folio in A —several other passages have been lost:

---

[1] Cf. RBB xxii; *Y Bibyl Ynghymraec* lxxxviii–lix; Pen. MS. 20, xviii–xix.

[2] Cf. Peniarth MS. 20, 278*b*, 'karrec *houa*' corrected to 'karrec *faylan*'; 283*a*, 'kedewein' corrected (by a hand contemporary with that of the original scribe) to 'hyrvryn.' Egerton Phillimore, loc. cit. 155, suggested that Pen. MS. 20 was the 'Book of Conway' quoted by Robert Vaughan, but the suggestion, possible though it be, cannot be substantiated. Cf. Lloyd, op. cit. 23.

[3] It may be that the use of *yw y* in Pen. MS. 20 derives from an earlier MS. on which the former is based.

[4] *See* RWM i. 124–6.

(1) Peniarth MS. 20, 105*a*, 1 -*aw*—109*a*, 21 *yr awr hon* (=28, 8—30, 11 below);
(2) Peniarth MS. 20, 147*b*, 13 *ac ef*—150*a*, 3 *y lladawd* (=50, 1—30, 11 below);
(3) Peniarth MS. 20, 176*b*, 12 *y llosges*—178*b*, 20 *mwrchath wedy* (=64, 9—65, 12 below);
(4) Peniarth MS. 20, 192*b*, 17 *ar llys oll*—195*a*, 13 *a thec* (=72, 6—73, 21 below);
(5) Peniarth MS. 20, 203*b*, 17 *or ay keissyei*—207*b*, 2 *kastell dinefwr* (=77, 31—79, 32 below);
(6) Peniarth MS. 20, 209*a*, 27 *gruffud a gafas*—224*b*, 5 *rys yeuanc* (=80, 26—87, 37 below).

C. Mostyn MS. 159,[1] 144-231.

This text of the *Brut* was transcribed early in 1587 by David ap Jenkin Amhredydd of Machynlleth for Huw Lewis of Dyffryn yr Hafod Wen in Llangurig, as the colophon shows:

> 'And so ends this book of the Chronicle of the Princes which David ap Jenkin wrote for Huw Lewis of Dyffryn yr Hafod Wen when the year of Christ was one thousand five hundred and eighty-seven, and he finished it on the second day of the month of May.'[2]

The text of the *Brut* is incomplete and ends with the words *gan Rosser mortimer kastell mylienydd* (cf. 106, 15 below). There is a lacuna for the years 900-949 (as in ABD). Also the passage corresponding to Peniarth MS. 20, 105*a*, 1—109*a*, 21 (=28, 8—30, 11 below) has been lost (as in BD), as also the passage corresponding to Peniarth MS. 20, 203*b*, 25 *a llyma*—205, 22 *ruitura dolore* (=77, 34—78, 45 below).

D. Peniarth MS. 213 (formerly Hengwrt MS. 332), 11–532.

This MS. is in the handwriting of the well-known scribe John Jones of Gellilyfdy. The text, of which the first ten pages are lost, begins *dolic: ac y llosges Myniw. Ac y bv varvolaeth ar yr ysgrybyl yn holl ynys Brydain* (=3, 16-8 below). Up to a point corresponding to Peniarth MS. 20, 269*a*, 26-7 *abit kreuyd amdanaw* (=109, 4 below) this text agrees with the Peniarth MS. 20 version, but then it follows the RB version. The text of 496–520 corresponds to RBB 372, 20—378, 9, but this is followed by a lacuna (due to the loss of 521-6) corresponding to RBB

---
[1] This is the MS. called 'Gloddaith MS. 15' in Aneirin Owen's catalogue in *Trans. Cym.*, 1843, 405.
[2] The original Welsh has been quoted in Pen. MS. 20, xx. One of the three MS. copies of Humphrey Llwyd's English version of the *Brut* (*see* above, xvi), Llanstephan MS. 177, was copied by a certain Ieuan ap Dafydd ap Jenkin, who may have been a son of the Ieuan ap Dafydd ap Jenkin who copied Mostyn MS. 159.

378, 9 *or rei ereill*—380, 4 *gregorij bap*. On 527–32 the text corresponds to RBB 380, 4 *Y vlwydyn*—381, 19 *porthmyn*, but much has been lost because the corners of the leaves are torn. Many pages are missing from the MS.: 1–10, 147–50, 327–30, 521–6.[1]

Since John Jones follows the RB version from 496 on, it appears that the original MS. from which he transcribed, was incomplete, unless, of course, he found the Pen. 20 and the RB versions already combined in the MS. he was copying.

E. NLW MS. 7006 D, Black Book of Basingwerk.

As was shown above, this MS. contains a version of *Brenhinedd y Saesson*, probably written by Gutun Owain in the second half of the fifteenth century. Down to the year 1197 the text is in close agreement, though containing many minor variants, with the text of BS in BM. Cotton MS. Cleopatra B v. For the years 1197–1282 Gutun Owain seems to have combined the Peniarth MS. 20 and RB versions, probably using Peniarth MS. 20 itself for the text of the former version. Since the RB version ends with the year 1282, the text of BS in this MS. follows Peniarth MS. 20, 292*a*, 1—302*a*, 18 for the years 1282–1332. E, therefore, contains only a part of the Peniarth MS. 20 version, and this is found on 299*a*, 1—305*a*, 20.[2]

F. Thelwall MS.

About ten years ago Mr. Bernard Halliday of Leicester offered this MS. for sale to the National Library of Wales, Aberystwyth. The Library did not buy it, and its present location is unknown.[3] The MS. contained the following items:[4]

(1) *The History of Gruffudd ap Cynan*, in Welsh.

(2) *Interdictio Papae adversus Lewelinum*.

(3) *Literae Lewelini Principis Walliae ad clerum Angliae*.

(4) The arms of John Trevor.

(5) *Ystoria Dared*.

(6) *Brut y Brenhinedd*, with the following colophon:

---

[1] Variant readings from MSS. B, C, D above are given as footnotes to the 1941 edition of the Pen. MS. 20 *Brut*.
[2] Transcripts of E are found in Pen. MS. 264 (by John Jones of Gellilyfdy), Mostyn MS. 211, and NLW MS. 1591 (by Angharad Llwyd).
[3] On 7 November, 1950, Mr. Bernard Halliday informed Mr. B. G. Owens, M.A., that the MS. was not in his possession.
[4] I am indebted for the list of contents to Mr. E. D. Jones, B.A., of the National Library of Wales.

'Gwallter archiagon Rrydychen a droes y darn hwnn o'r kronigl o Lading i Gymraeg. *A minnav Edward Kyffin a'i ail essgrivennodd fo i Sion Trevor Trevalyn yssgwier pann oedd Oed Krist 1577.*'[1]

(7) *Brut y Tywysogion. Inc.* Pann oedd oed yn Arglwydd ni Iessu Grist yn 681 yr aeth Kydwaladr Vendigaid i Lydaw at Alan nai Selyf a gwedi i fod yn ymddiddan a'r angel ef aeth i Rvfain o'i arch ef. *Desin.* . . . deng mlynedd a thrvgaint a devkant a mil oedd Oed Krist pan fv farw Mredydd ap Grvffydd, arglwydd Hirfryn, yn i gastell ehvn yn Llanymddyfri trannoeth gwedi Gwyl Sain Lvwck Efengylwr (=115, 30-33 below).

The *Brut y Tywysogion* in this MS. was a text of the Peniarth MS. 20 version. It contained the Latin verses (below 77-8), but, like MSS. B, C, D, it omitted the passage corresponding to Peniarth MS. 20, 105*a*, 1—109*a*, 21 (=28, 8—30, 11 below). The beginning and end of the text prove that it was closely related to that of Mostyn MS. 159, but the fact that the Latin verses are in the former but not in the latter show that the one is not directly transcribed from the other.

This MS. was once in the possession of Richard Davies of Llannerch and is the one described as 'Vol II Fol: Chart' in Edward Lhuyd's *Parochialia* i. 98-9.[2] It was still at Llannerch early in the second half of the eighteenth century, as is known from the words of Lewis Morris:[3]

'There is a Copy of Brut y Brenhinoedd in Llannerch library A.D. 1760. It is a Folio wrote upon Paper. In which there is this note of the writer of it. [Then follows the colophon by Edward Kyffin in 1577 as quoted above.] . . . This was copied by Dewi Fardd 1760.'[4]

Further evidence that Dewi Fardd, i.e. Dafydd Jones of Trefriw, had this MS. in 1760 is found in a letter which Lewis Morris wrote on 4 July, 1760, to the Rev. Evan Evans[5]:

'D. Jones tells me of a Llannerch copy of Brut y Brenh. in folio on Paper at his house, wrote by Edward Kyffin for John Trevor of Trefalun.'

[1] '. . . And I Edward Kyffin rewrote (copied) it (*sc. Brut y Brenhinedd*) for John Trevor, Trefalun, Esq., when the year of Christ was 1577.'
[2] *Parochialia*, being a Summary of Answers to 'Parochial Queries' . . . issued by Edward Lhwyd. Parts I, II, and III. Edited by Rupert H. Morris. Published by the Cambrian Archaeological Assoc. as supplements (April, 1909, 1910, July, 1911) to the *Archaeologia Cambrensis*. London.
'Vol. iv' of the Llannerch MSS., described ib. 99, contained a copy of the RB version of *Brut y Tywysogion*. This MS. seems to have disappeared.
[3] BM. Add. MS. 14935, 536.
[4] *See* on Cardiff MS. 2. 388 below, which contains Dewi Fardd's transcript.
[5] Hugh Owen, *Additional Letters of the Morrises of Anglesey. Y Cymmrodor* xlix, Part II, 468.

INTRODUCTION   liii

Thomas Duffus Hardy[1] lists a Welsh version of Geoffrey's *Historia* in 'MS. Downing. XVI cent.', which had the following note:

'Walter, Archdeacon of Oxford, translated this part of the Chronicle from Latin into Welsh, and Edward Kyffin copied it for John Trevor of Trevalun, Esq. A.D. 1577.'

This note is in close agreement with the colophon to *Brut y Brenhinedd* in the Thelwall MS. The latter, however, had 'And *I, Edward Kyffin* . . .' where the Downing MS.—if the original Welsh, which is not quoted, has been faithfully rendered —had 'And *Edward Kyffin.*' If the Thelwall MS. and the Downing MS. are not one and the same, as I think them to be, the latter must be a transcript of the former.[2]

G. NLW MS. 1599 E (Kinmel MS. 99).

This MS. contains 'The Correct Annales of Brittaine from the Incarnation of our Saviour Jesus Christ to this present yeare . . . gathered out of severall Authors printed and manuscript, but most especially out of *Brut y Tywysogion*, or the Annales of the Princes of Wales herewith inserted. By Thomas Sebastian Price of Llanvylling Esqr. 1688.'[3] This title and all the writing to the end of p. 50 are written in the hand of Thomas Sebastian Price[4] and the text is in English, but on ff. 51-2, 55-137, there is a Welsh text of *Brut y Tywysogion* (Peniarth MS. 20 version), written in two different hands: ff. 51-2, 55, are in the hand of William Maurice of Llansilin, and the rest, ff. 56-137, in an unknown seventeenth century hand, probably that of one of Maurice's amanuenses. The last entry in Maurice's hand is at the end of f. 55:

'Blwydyn gwedy hynny y bu farw Elbodu Arçesgob Gwyned'[5]

(=Peniarth MS. 20, 67*b*, 14=3, 13-4 below), and the first entry on f. 56 is:

'Tair blynedd ar hvgain a 800 oedd oed Krist pan losged Deganwy gan y Saesson ac y distrywiwyd Powys'

(=Peniarth MS. 20, 68*a–b*=4, 1-3 below and footnote).

It would appear on first sight that the passage corresponding to Peniarth MS. 20, 67*b*, 14—68*a*, 25 (=3, 15—3, 34 below),

[1] *Descriptive Catalogue of MSS. relating to the Early History of Great Britain* i, Part 1 (London, 1862), 351 (No. 830).
[2] The MS. is again referred to by W. F. Skene in his *Four Ancient Books of Wales* i, 24-6. Edinburgh, 1868.
[3] *See* above, xxiii. This MS. is the one described by Angharad Llwyd, *Trans. Cym.*, 1828, 38, as Caerwys MS. 16.
[4] On Price *see* Richard Williams, *Montgomeryshire Worthies*, Second Edition, 252, Newtown, n.d.; G. J. Williams, *Llythyrau at Ddafydd Jones o Drefriw*, 27, Aberystwyth, 1943.
[5] After this there is a note by William Maurice: 'Hucusque rescriptum per W.M.'

has been lost, but this is not the case, for f. 57 has been misplaced in binding the MS. The text of the *Brut* has the following characteristics:

(1) it shows the usual lacuna for the years 900–949;
(2) it has a lacuna corresponding to Peniarth MS. 20, 105*a*, 1—109*a*, 11, cf. MSS. B, C, and D;
(3) unlike MS. C, it does not omit the Latin verses (=77, 34 —78, 45 below).

It follows from (3) that the text of G, like that of F, is not derived from C.

(4) The text is incomplete and ends (f. 137*b*) with the words:

'Blwyddyn wedi hynny y bv farw Richard o Clar, Jarll Kaer Loiw'

(=Peniarth MS. 20, 276*b*, 21=112, 26–7 below).

Following this, there is a note by William Maurice:

'Hij Annales continuantur in pag[ina] 89ᵇ nostrae Brut y Tywys[ogion] ad obit[um] Jarλ Clâr. Anno 1210.'

Wynnstay MS. 81, as described by Angharad Llwyd in her catalogue,[1] contained a copy of *Brut y Tywysogion* transcribed by William Maurice. The reference in the above note by Maurice may be to that MS. See below on MS. L.

H. Cardiff MS. 2. 388, ff. 110*a*–149*a*.

This is a transcript made in 1761 by Dafydd Jones (Dewi Fardd) of Trefriw.[2] The text of *Brut y Tywysogion* is preceded by that of *Brut y Brenhinedd*, which ends on f. 109*b* with this colophon:

'Gwallter Archiagon Rhyd-ychain a droes y darn hwn o'r Cronigl o Lading i Gymraeg. Ac Edward Kyffin a'i ail ysgrifennodd fo i Sion Trefor, Trefalyn ysgwier, pan oedd Oed Crist 1577. A minnav Dewi Sion o Dref y rhyw yw'r Trydydd ysgrifennydd yn oed Ein Iachawdwr. 1761 Maihefin 9.'

The first paragraph of this colophon agrees with those in the Thelwall and Downing MSS.—if they are not one and the same MS.—and David Jones states in the second paragraph that his copy, completed on 9 June, 1761, is a direct transcript from the text written by Edward Kyffin. Since it is a transcript, David Jones's text exhibits the same peculiarities as does F above.

[1] *Trans. Cym.*, 1828, 55 '[Wynnstay] 81. *Brut y Tywysogion*, from 680 to 1332, written by William Morys, from the Hengwrt Copy.' This copy, apparently a transcript of Pen. MS. 20, cannot now be traced.
[2] *See* on Cardiff MS. 1.1 (K below).

I. Llanstephan MS. 58 (Shirburn MS. E. 6), 1–32.

This MS., like Llanstephan MS. 8 (*see* J below), was copied by George William Griffith of Penybenglog in Pembrokeshire.[1] The text of the *Brut* has been described by J. Gwenogvryn Evans in RWM ii. 554:

> 'An abridged copy of *Brut y Tywyssogion* to the year 1101, with marginal commentary in English. A brief account of Howel's Laws is interpolated in the text after the year 913 . . .'

This description is correct so far as it goes, but Evans did not realize that the text of the *Brut* represents the Peniarth MS. 20 version. The MS. must have been in the hands of Iaco ab Dewi, for at the top of p. 1 he has written 'Pryd Tywysogion Cymru.'[2]

The text begins (p. 1):

'Pan oedd oed Krist chwechant ag vn a phedwar igain,'

and ends (p. 32):

'. . . y geisiassant ymysgysodi canys ny allent ymgredy i'r brenin' (=p. 23, 3–5 below).

The text is closely related to that of MS. C above. There is no lacuna for the period 900–949, *but this section has been supplied from some copy of the RB version.*

J. Llanstephan MS. 8 (Shirburn MS. C. 2).

J. Gwenogvryn Evans, RWM ii. 441, assigns this MS. to the 'early 17th century,' but he did not notice that a clue to the name of the scribe lies in the initials 'G.W.G.' on f. 131*b*. They stand for George William Griffith, the Pembrokeshire antiquary, who, as we have seen, copied Llanstephan MS. 58. J contains a Welsh text of the Peniarth MS. 20 version of the *Brut* interspersed with passages taken from Powel's notes in his 1584 edition of the *Historie of Cambria*. The text follows the Peniarth MS. 20 version to f. 113*b* (=Peniarth MS. 20, 263*b*, 6), the very point at which C ends. There is no lacuna for the years 900–949 but, as in I, this section has been supplied from some copy of the RB version. The readings are in close agreement with the text of C; and, as in C, the Latin verses are wanting. The lacuna common to B, C, and D corresponding

---

[1] On this scribe and other MSS. written by him *see* Francis Jones, 'Griffith of Penybenglog. A Study in Pembrokeshire Genealogy,' in *Trans. Cym.*, 1938, 125 ff.

[2] Llanstephan MS. 58 must be the MS. to which Egerton Phillimore refers in *Y Cymmrodor* xi. 163: 'There is also a bit of the *Brut* in a 17th-century hand at Shirburn Castle, which, though not itself written by Iago ab Dewi, has a page-heading in his hand.'

to Peniarth MS. 20, 105–9 is not found in J, but it must have existed in an earlier MS. from which it derives, *because the passage in J follows the RB version.*

On f. 113*b* after 'a chastell Melienydh gan Rosser Mortimer' (106, 14–5 below) the scribe has this note:

> 'The end of the first copy. After writing the first copy I came across another copy which contained more of the history of the Britons, and following that I finished the task I had begun, as I desired.'[1]

This 'second copy' contained a text of the RB version, and the transcription of it ends (f. 128*b*) with the colophon:

> 'The end of the second copy which I found. That which follows I translated from D. Powel's book.'[2]

The passages translated from Powel's *Historie of Cambria* continue to f. 131.

K. Cardiff MS. 1. 1, 1–9.

This text, entitled 'Cronigl Cymru yn fyrr' (The Chronicle of Wales in brief), was transcribed by Dafydd Jones of Trefriw, as was H above. The *Brut* ends on p. 9 with the words:

> 'Ac yn niwedd y flwyddyn honno y llas Cariadog ap Gruffydd ap Rhys ap Howel ei frawd.'

(Cf. Peniarth MS. 20, 86*b*, 25–87*a*, 1=p. 17, 15–6 below.)

The text has been much abbreviated throughout, but a comparison of selected passages in H and K makes it very doubtful whether these two texts, though both copied by the same scribe, are derived from the same original. In any case, they are closely related.

L. NLW MS. 2043 (Panton MS. 77–8).

This text was copied in 1774 by the Rev. Evan Evans from an original made for William Maurice, Llansilin, in 1672: see above, xxii, xxv. As far as f. 123*b*—*Mefenydd*, the text is that of the RB version, but f. 123*b* A Duw Sul y Blodeu—f. 135*b* contain the text of Peniarth MS. 20, 292*a*, 1—302*a*, 11.

M. Wynnstay MS. 81.

This MS., now lost, existed in the early part of the nineteenth century, for it was catalogued by Angharad Llwyd.[3] The fact that the chronicle in this MS. continued down to 1332,

---

[1] 'Terfyn y coppi kyntaf. Wedy ysgrifenny y copi kyntaf y kyfwrddais a choppi arall rhwn oedd yn cynnwys yndo ychwaneg o stori'r Britanniaid, ag wrth hwnnw y gorphenais vynorchwyl [*sic*] dechreuedig, val y dymynais.'

[2] 'Terfyn, r, ail gopi y gefais. Hynny sydh yn kanlyn y gyfieithies i o lyfr D: Powel.'

[3] See her description quoted above, liv, note 1.

INTRODUCTION lvii

together with the reference by Angharad Llwyd to the 'Hengwrt copy' as its original,[1] suggests that it was a transcript of the Peniarth MS. 20 text. It is possible, therefore, that this is the copy of the *Brut* to which William Maurice refers in his note on f. 137*b* of NLW MS. 1599: see liv above.

N. Cardiff MS. 2. 135 (Tonn MS. 18),[2] 93–236.

This text was transcribed in 1766 by William Bona[3] of Llanpumsaint (Carmarthenshire), who states in a colophon (236) that his original was in the handwriting of Iaco ab Dewi, who, in his turn, had copied (in 1717) from a MS. written by George William Griffith.[4] It was shown above[5] that Llanstephan MS. 58, which contains an abridged copy of the Peniarth MS. 20 version of the *Brut*, had been in the hands of Iaco ab Dewi. However, Iaco's original for his copy of the *Brut*, which was transcribed by William Bona, was not Llanstephan MS. 58, but Llanstephan MS. 8. So far as I know, Iaco ab Dewi's transcript is no longer in existence.[6] The passages in English quoted in Llanstephan MS. 8 from Powel's notes to the *Historie of Cambria* have been rendered into Welsh in Cardiff MS. 2. 135, but it is impossible to say whether the rendering is to be attributed to Iaco ab Dewi or to William Bona.

The text in Cardiff MS. 2. 135 is closely related to the text of the *Brut* published in a Welsh periodical called *Trysorfa Gwybodaeth, neu, Eurgrawn Cymraeg* (Carmarthen, 1770), edited by Peter Williams. Fifteen issues only of it appeared, and in each issue there are eight pages of a partly modernized version of the *Brut*, making 120 pages in all. The text bears the title (1) 'Brut y Tywysogion, O amser Cadwaladr, brenhin diweddaf Brydain hyd at Lewelyn y diweddaf o dywysogion Brydain &.' It begins 'Cadwaladr. / Pan oedd oed ein Harglwydd Crist 681,' and it ends (120) 'Ond o'r diwedd y cyhuddwyd ef wrth y brenhin, ac y dywedpwyd fod || (=Peniarth MS. 20, 126*b*, 24–7: cf. 39, 15–6 below). This printed text of the *Brut* has the same additions (from the *Historie of Cambria*) as are found in Cardiff

---

[1] Ib.
[2] This is Cardiff MS. 58 in RWM ii. 264.
[3] On this scribe *see* Garfield H. Hughes, *The National Library of Wales Journal* iii. 52–3, in an article on Iaco ab Dewi.
[4] 'Terfyn pryd Tywysogion y Bryttanieid ynGhymry wedi ei scrifennu allan o hen Lyfr-scrifen o law un Siors William Gr. gynt o Benybenglog gan Iaco ab Dewi Ebrill 24. 1717. A'r waith hon drachefn o scrifen law Iaco ab Dewi gan Wiliam Bona o Lanpumsaint Mai 22. 1766.'
[5] *See* lv.
[6] Mr. Garfield H. Hughes, who has made a special study of Iaco ab Dewi's work, has failed to trace it.

MS. 2. 135 and its original Llanstephan MS. 8. It certainly seems to derive either from the lost transcript of Llanstephan MS. 8 made by Iaco ab Dewi or from Cardiff MS. 2. 135. The latter was transcribed, as we have seen, by William Bona of Llanpumsaint, near Carmarthen, in 1766, and *Trysorfa Gwybodaeth* was published at Carmarthen in 1770.

The following diagram represents the inter-relationship of the various MS. copies of the Peniarth MS. 20 version of *Brut y Tywysogion* reviewed above. An unbroken line shows direct transcripts, and a broken line shows those texts that are indirectly derived from others. There are some readings in B, C, and D which appear more correct than those of Peniarth MS. 20, but the fact that the lacuna for 900–949 occurs in all MSS. later than Peniarth MS. 20, with the exception of those in which the corresponding section has been supplied from the RB version, shows that no text earlier than that of Peniarth MS. 20 is represented by any of the later copies. In any case, many of the variant readings of B, C, and D (the last in particular) and allied texts are the result of a collation of the Peniarth MS. 20 version with that of RB and *Brenhinedd y Saesson*.

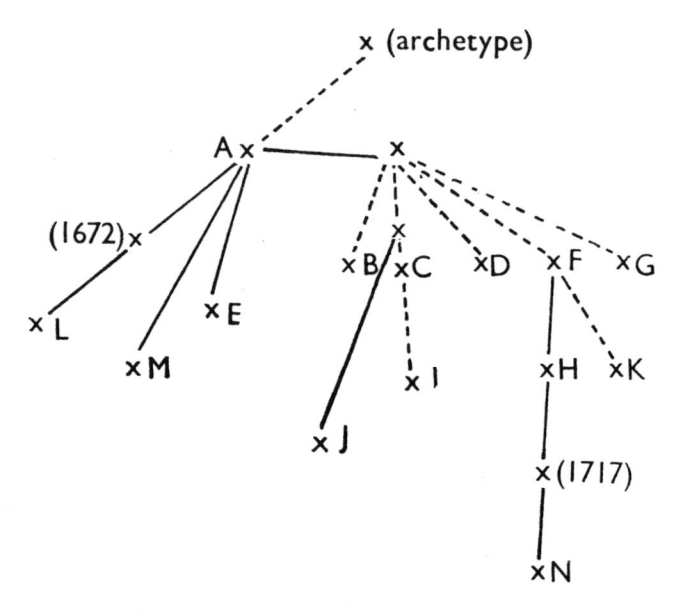

The only MS., therefore, which is of importance for the establishment of the text is Peniarth MS. 20. What errors had occurred in copies which connected it with the archetype, one cannot now say, but the Notes will show that the text is certainly faulty in some places. Whether the errors which involve names of persons and places are those of transcription or of translation cannot be decided in the absence of a text earlier than that of Peniarth MS. 20. However, errors which are common to this version and that of RB and, in some cases, BS as well, probably derive from the Latin original.

§5. The Peniarth MS. 20 Version

This version is in general substantial agreement with the RB version down to the year 1282, where the latter ends and where the former originally ended. And both Peniarth MS. 20 and RB are in similar agreement with those sections of BS—down to the year 1197—which represent a more summary version of the common Latin original. But it must be stressed that the evidence of one must not be accepted without comparison with that of the other two. The three Welsh texts are complementary to each other, and a careful examination of them enables us to decide, to a considerable extent, what the evidence of the original chronicle was at any particular point. On the whole, the least dependable version is that of BS, but in several places it contains details which are not found either in Peniarth MS. 20 or in RB. Sometimes its readings help us to decide whether Peniarth MS. 20 or RB is more likely to be correct, according to whether they agree with the former or the latter. Often BS agrees with neither, and the translation contained in it has misinterpreted the original Latin. In all three versions, as is clear from a comparison of them with one another and with the four Latin texts described above (lx) as containing considerable sections of the original Latin chronicle, there are manifest mistranslations and many errors in the names of places and persons. The fact that some mistakes are common to the three versions show that they already existed in the common original,[1] whereas other differences between the Welsh texts[2] can only be explained as the result of variations in the copies of the original text used by the three translators.

It is useful to compare the merits and demerits of the two main versions, that of Peniarth MS. 20 and that of RB, down to the year 1282, their original terminal point. Both texts show marks of translation in their language and style and are not to be compared, as examples of medieval Welsh prose, with texts

---

[1] *See* notes on 22, 28; 25, 25; 58, 6; 58, 35; 62, 12; 70, 18; 102, 11; 108, 11; 110, 11; 117, 35.
[2] *See* notes on 19, 7; 20, 15–6; 23, 14; 43, 5–6; 53, 23; 59, 15; 92, 39–40.

written originally in Welsh. Both contain obvious mistranslations of the original Latin, and both appear to have suffered at the hands of successive scribes. Some errors in the Peniarth MS. 20 text have been corrected by another scribe contemporary with the one who transcribed the main text. On general linguistic grounds the Peniarth MS. 20 version appears to have been produced earlier than that of RB,[1] but the style of the latter is on the whole better than that of the former, probably because the translator attempted a less literal translation. None the less, there are scores of Latinisms in both versions, and in many cases it is only with the help of AC and CW or by trying to retranslate the Welsh back into Latin that we can decide the exact meaning in certain contexts.

The notes to this volume show the differences in content between the Peniarth MS. 20 and RB versions. The fuller and more complete version is undoubtedly the former: it contains many small phrases and sentences here and there and even whole passages of varying length which are not found in the latter version.[2] The glowing rhetorical panegyrics of Welsh princes, generally accompanying the notice of their death, are considerably longer and more fullsome in Peniarth MS. 20 than in RB. On the other hand, there are places in the text where RB is slightly fuller than the corresponding passages in Peniarth MS. 20.[3] These additional passages, whether short or long, both in Peniarth MS. 20 and in RB, sometimes have a parallel in BS. However, despite its being undoubtedly the fuller version of the two, Peniarth MS. 20 presents a version (at least in the form in which it has survived) which is in many places less correct than that of RB, and in other places less precise.[4] But there are places (less in number) where Peniarth MS. 20 is more

---

[1] This is a general impression: the linguistic forms of neither version have been systematically analysed.

[2] See notes on 1, 21–2; 2, 29; 4, 22–3; 4, 24–5; 4, 27; 5, 24; 7, 29; 9, 25; 14, 7; 17, 30–1; 18, 1–2; 24, 9–10; 25, 18; 25, 26; 27, 13; 27, 20; 49, 1; 54, 19–22; 58, 24–5; 62, 7–9; 74, 1–3; 75, 14–5; 75, 18; 75, 22–3; 76, 34; 77, 31–78, 45; 79, 35–6 ; 80, 5; 80, 34–8; 81, 5; 81, 11–15; 81, 17–19; 81, 20–2; 82, 13; 82, 40; 86, 20–1; 89, 9; 93, 4; 93, 28; 93, 35–6; 97, 11–12; 97, 28; 99, 3–4; 99, 12–22; 103, 36–8; 104, 6–9; 105, 20–1; 106, 29; 106, 39–40; 107, 8; 107, 17; 109, 2; 109, 21; 110, 19–20; 111, 15–7; 118, 3.

[3] See notes on 1, 2; 8,16; 20, 15–6; 32, 8–9; 39, 25–6; 41, 13; 41, 33–5; 53, 29; 54, 14; 59, 25–6; 61, 27; 69, 11; 72, 32; 75, 2; 76, 15–6; 81, 36; 87, 11–2; 88, 8; 104, 20; 111, 10; 113, 16–7; 116, 13; 118, 41–2; 119, 2; 119, 7–8; 119, 9–10; 119, 24.

[4] See notes on 2, 33–4; 3, 4–5; 3, 11; 3, 24; 8, 18; 9, 3–5; 10, 21–2; 10, 29; 13, 14; 13, 16; 14, 2; 14, 35; 16, 23–4; 17, 19; 17, 23–5; 17, 25–6; 18, 22–3; 19, 5–6; 20, 6–7; 21, 9; 21, 15–6; 27, 26; 32, 15; 34, 5; 36, 32–3; 39, 25–6; 43, 24; 43, 34–7; 49, 23–4; 49, 24–5; 50, 12–3; 50, 35–6; 53, 32–3; 61, 2; 62, 12; 63, 40–64, 1; 65, 4–5; 65, 38–9; 67, 10–11; 70, 30; 72, 3–4; 75, 14; 76, 1–2; 76, 3; 87, 9–11; 87, 11–12; 89, 39–90, 2; 90, 22; 95, 29–30; 97, 32; 103, 18; 105, 32–3; 106, 10–11; 107, 20–3; 109, 16; 110, 29–34; 114, 1; 115, 15–7.

correct and detailed than RB.[1] The number of points in which RB appears to be more correct than Peniarth MS. 20 is greater than that in which the Peniarth MS. 20 version appears to be more correct than that of RB. The comparative fullness and correctness of the two versions shows that they must be studied together and that it is only by weighing the evidence of the one against the other and the combined evidence of both, whether it agrees or not, against the evidence of the three texts of AC and that of CW, as is done in the notes, that the original text of the lost Latin chronicle can be recovered.

The principal passage in the main text of the Peniarth MS. 20 version which has no parallel in RB (or BS) is that containing the Latin poem of eighteen elegiac couplets, 'composed,' as the text says, 'when the Lord Rhys died' (77, 78)[2] and the eleven verses, consisting of five elegiac couplets and a concluding hexameter, which formed the epitaph on his sepulchre (78). The Lord Rhys was buried at St. Davids, but he had been a benefactor of the monastic houses of Strata Florida, Whitland, and Talley. The two sets of verses were probably composed at one or other of these four houses, but there is no evidence to decide at which of them. Neither of them is found in AC or CW, but in the latter the rhetorical passage which bewails the death of Rhys[3] and which is in close agreement with Peniarth MS. 20, ends with the words 'Heu! heu! iam Wallia uiduata dolet ruitura dolore' which bear a marked resemblance to and an obvious connection with the concluding hexameter of the epitaph in Peniarth MS. 20:

'Wallia iam viduata dolet ruitura dolore.'

This seems to suggest that the text from which CW is derived contained a copy of the epitaph. The fact that neither the verse panegyric nor the epitaph occur in RB and BS appears to prove that they were not found in the original Latin chronicle but that they were added either to some copy of it used by the translator of Peniarth MS. 20 or included in this Welsh version. This seems to be an argument in favour of regarding the Peniarth MS. 20 version as one produced in South Wales, probably at one of the four monastic houses mentioned above.

---

[1] *See* notes on 2, 8–9; 11, 26; 12, 7; 27, 12; 37, 35; 37, 36–7; 38, 11; 40, 37–41, 1; 46, 26–7; 50, 30; 50, 32; 54, 19–22; 59, 25–6; 61, 24; 62, 7–9; 65, 7–8; 66, 37; 68, 19; 80, 7–8; 80, 9; 82, 27; 90, 34–5; 94, 24; 101, 7; 104, 20 (second note); 109, 2; 110, 6–7; 115, 10–1; 116, 23–5.
[2] For another set of Latin elegiac couplets in praise of Rhys (from the chronicle in the Breviate of Domesday Book) *see* AC 61. No Welsh elegy on Rhys is extant.
[3] 5.

The one lacuna of importance in the Peniarth MS. 20 version as compared with that of RB, is of an accidental nature. The entries for the period 900–949 are missing through the loss of a leaf (=71–2) in Peniarth MS. 20. In the present translation the lacuna has been filled by supplying the corresponding passage from the RB version.[1]

Another important difference between the Peniarth MS. 20 and RB versions is that fuller chronological data are given in the former, as too in BS. Down to the year 1091=1095 RB gives definite dates only at the beginning of each decade, but Peniarth MS. 20 and BS give dates—in many cases incorrect—for each successive entry by reference to the number of years that had elapsed between each event recorded. Hence much of the chronology of RB before the year 1091=1095 has to be decided with the aid of the fuller data given in Peniarth MS. 20 and BS. Not once does RB supply the Golden Number by reference to the *primus decemnouenalis* as do Peniarth MS. 20 and BS in a few places.[2]

Beyond the year 1282 no comparison between Peniarth MS. 20 and RB is possible, for the continuation for the years 1282–1332, which occurs in the former,[3] is not found in the latter. This continuation of the text in Peniarth MS. 20 is an obvious addition and it is not written by the scribe who wrote the main text. Like the chronicle for 681–1282 it is clearly a translation, as the occurrence of Latin declensional forms in the Welsh text shows,[4] apart from considerations of language and style. Unlike the main text, the continuation has retained the annalistic arrangement of its original, and many annals have been left blank—1299, 1303, 1304, 1305, 1309, 1310, 1315, 1316. The linguistic evidence shows that the main text and the continuation were rendered from Latin into Welsh by two different translators: it has already been shown that the form *yw y* which is consistently used by the translator of the main text is not used by the translator of the continuation.[5] Professor J. Goronwy Edwards has cogently argued that the continuation was compiled at Valle Crucis,[6] but like the main text of the *Brut* it seems to be a conflation of more than one set of annals derived

---

[1] *See* the translation, 6–7 below. The passage from RB has been printed in italics to stress the fact that it is from another version independent of that of Pen. MS. 20.
[2] *See* below, 11, 12, 15, 17.
[3] *See* below, 120, 20–127, 9.
[4] 'y seithuet dyd o *Julius*' (Pen. MS. 20, 295*a*, 7); 'dyw gwyl Mathev Apostol vi. kalann y *Martii*' (ib., ll. 10–11); 'dyw gwil seynt *Geruasii et Prothasii*' (ib., 295*a*, 27–295*b*, 1); 'dyw gwyl seyn *Kenelmi* vrenhyn' (ib., 300*b*, 13–4).
[5] *See* above, xlviii–xlix.
[6] EHR lvii (1942), 372–5.

from several places. The chronological confusion of the continuation is probably the result of such a conflation. While many of the entries are concerned with events in north-east Wales and with the diocese of St. Asaph in particular,[1] others refer to events on the South Wales border and probably derive from some monastic house in that area.[2] The script of the continuation bears a marked resemblance to that of *Brut y Brenhinedd* and *Brenhinedd y Saesson* in BM Cotton MS. Cleopatra B v and these three texts may be by the same hand. And the linguistic evidence suggests that *Brut y Brenhinedd* and *Brenhinedd y Saesson*, as found in the Cotton MS., are the work of one and the same translator.

All the evidence, however, is insufficient to decide the provenance of the Peniarth MS. 20 version of the *Brut*. J. Gwenogvryn Evans and others refer to the RB version as the 'Strata Florida version'[3] but I have failed to find any real evidence in support of this. It is probable that the source of this appellation and that of the title 'Book of Conway' which Robert Vaughan gave to some version of the *Brut* merely reflect Powel's statement in the *Historie of Cambria* that 'severall copies' of Caradog of Llancarfan's original compilation 'were afterward (*sc.* after 1156) kept *in either of the Abbeis of Conwey and Stratflur*, which were yearelie augmented as things fell out, and conferred together ordinarlie euerie third yeare.'[4] The many examples of *yw y* seem to show that the scribe who copied Peniarth MS. 20 was a South Walian, but the copy of the *Brut* in this MS. is a transcript from an earlier MS., which may not have contained the form *yw y*. The inclusion of the Latin eulogy and epitaph on the Lord Rhys is at least some evidence in favour of regarding the Peniarth MS. 20 version, like the Latin copy of the chronicle on which it was based, as deriving from some monastic house in South Wales which had benefited from the benefactions of Rhys. But there is no evidence to decide whether the place was Strata Florida, Whitland, or Talley. One can only hope that further progress in Welsh linguistic and historical studies will help to solve the problem.

[1] Ib.

[2] Mr. E. St. John Brooks has called attention to the agreement between the annalistic memoranda at the end of Trinity College, Dublin, MS. D. 4. 1 and some of the entries in the continuation of the Pen. MS. 20 version. He suggests that the former were written at Abergavenny. See his article 'The *Piers Plowman* Manuscripts in Trinity College, Dublin,' in *The Library* vi, Nos. 3/4 (December, 1951), 141–53.

[3] RBB xxii. Ab Ithel, AC xliv and Egerton Phillimore, *Y Cymmrodor* xi. 164, note 4, seem to regard the Pen. MS. 20 and RB versions as deriving from Strata Florida.

[4] Powel, p. [ix].

§6. CHRONOLOGY OF THE PENIARTH MS. 20 VERSION[1]

In the translation which follows the chronicler's dates are given first in ordinary type and what appear to be the true dates are given in bold face. The textual chronology, like that of many other medieval chronicles, is often incorrect: some events are pre-dated and others post-dated by a varying number of years. From about the year one thousand on it is fairly easy to determine the true dates by examining references in the text to events which can be accurately dated from other independent evidence. A comparison of Peniarth MS. 20, RB, and BS, reveals that their chronology is often at variance in any particular place. The problems involved in attempting to determine the true dates are further complicated by the confusion in the chronology of the three texts in AC and of CW, upon which the original Latin chronicle underlying Peniarth MS. 20, RB, and BS was partly based. Errors in the chronology of AC, in particular the text in BM. Harleian MS. 3859, must in many cases have been carried over into the original of the *Brut* in its variant versions. Moreover, it should be remembered that the dates in Arabic numerals given in AC by the editor assume that *annus I* of the text is to be equated with the year A.D. 444. This is no more than a conjecture based on the assumption, probable though it be, that the earliest entries in the Harleian set of annals began as notes on a copy of the Paschal Cycle of Victorius of Aquitaine.[2]

The chronological data given in Pen. 20, as also in BS, are fuller and generally more correct than those in RB. In several places an early corrector of the text of Peniarth MS. 20 has altered the dates of certain annals as copied by the original scribe.[3] As in RB and BS, the dates given in Peniarth MS. 20 are those according to the Christian era, but there are signs here and there of inconsistency in the date with which the year is begun. In most places, both in the main text and in the continuation for the period 1282–1332, the date of the commencement of the year is 25 March, but in others it is 25 December.[4] This inconsistency probably reflects the varying dates for the commencement of

---

[1] Many comments on the chronology of RB, BS, and AC are found in the valuable footnotes to HW. The evidence of the Pen. MS. 20 version invalidates a few of them, as is shown in the Notes.

[2] E. Anscombe has argued that *annus I* of AC=445: see his articles 'The Exordium of the "Annales Cambriae",' in *Ériu* III, 117 ff.; 'The Date of the first settlement of the Saxons in Britain' in ZCP III, 492 ff.; vi. 339 ff. H. M. and N. K. Chadwick, *The Growth of Literature* i. (Cambridge University Press, 1932), 147, note 1, favour the equation *annus I*=446.

[3] *See* notes on 49, 1; 62, 7–9; 72, 20–1.

[4] *See* the note on 51, 7, where the scribe, if not the chronicler, has hesitated in which annal to place the accession of Stephen, which took place on 25 December.

the year in the different annals of varying date and provenance used in the compilation of the original Latin chronicle. Peniarth MS. 20 gives specific dates every ten or twenty years, and the intermediate events are said to have occurred so many years after the last decennial date or after the preceding event. There are four references[1] to the decemnovenial year or the first year of the nineteen year Cycle of Dionysius Exiguus. Only once is the Dominical letter given: see 107 below, *s.a.* 1247.

What follows in this section is an attempt to show how the dates given in bold face in the translation as the true dates were determined. It will be seen that absolute certainty is impossible in a number of places, more especially in the early part of the chronicle, and it must be emphasised that in such cases the date given as true is only approximate. It will be convenient to divide the period covered by the *Brut*, that is 681–1332, into shorter sections, for the problems involved differ in number and complexity in the various sections.

(1) *Chronicler's* 681–899

The first item is given *s.a.* 681 in Peniarth MS. 20, 682 in AC, 680 in RB, and 683 in BS. AC appears to be correct, for the 'mortality in Ireland' recorded two years later seems to be identical with the 'Mortalitas paruulorum' recorded in AU *s.a.* 683 (=684) and in CS *s.a.* 680 (=684). The first item in Peniarth MS. 20 of which the date is independently verifiable is the death of Aldfrid *s.a.* 704, which is correct. At this point, then, the chronology of Peniarth MS. 20 is correct, and, working back from it, it appears that its 681=682.

S.a. 705 Peniarth MS. 20 records the death of Pippin the Great: in RB the date is 710 and in BS 713. Pippin died in 714; and so Peniarth MS. 20 is here nine years in arrear. The explanation of this discrepancy in Peniarth MS. 20 between the chronicler's date and the true one is that AC has nine blank years between this annal and that in which the death of Aldfrid is recorded. It must be either that the blank *anni* of AC were ignored by the compiler of the original Latin chronicle, or that the translator of Peniarth MS. 20 (or his particular copy of the original) went astray. The fact that RB dates this annal 710 and that BS dates it 713—each being four years and one year respectively in arrear—seems to show that the error is due to the Peniarth MS. 20 translator or to the copy of the original which he used. Osred, king of Northumberland, died in 716; and so

---

[1] *See* 11, 12, 15, 17.

Peniarth MS. 20 becomes ten years in arrear, and is so presumably for the following annal as well. The question whether the chronicler's dates 720 and 721 are the true ones cannot be solved through lack of conclusive evidence. There is, however, an argument in favour of their being correct. *S.a.* 723 Peniarth MS. 20 records the battle of Mynydd Carno, but this date is manifestly in arrear: contrast AC 728, AU 728 (=729). Accepting AU 728 (=729) as being more likely to be correct[1] than that of AC, we have Peniarth MS. 20 723=729; and so it appears that the chronicler's 720 and 721 are correct. The death of Bede *s.a.* 735 is correct. For reasons fully explained in the note on 2, 12 (p. 132) it appears that Peniarth MS. 20 736=749: it is probable that thirteen blank *anni* in AC have been ignored. In AC the battle of Mygedog is dated 750, and 749 (=750) in AU, whereas in Peniarth MS. 20 it is placed one year after the death of Owain, king of the Picts, *s.a.* 736=749, i.e. in 750. For the years 750–68 the chronology of Peniarth MS. 20 seems to be correct.

The death of Cynioedd is given *s.a.* 774 in Peniarth MS. 20, *s.a.* 776 in AC, whereas the true date is 775: *see* AU *s.a.* 774=775. This suggests by inference that Peniarth MS. 20 773=774 and 774=775, and that the dates given in AC are at this point one year in advance. Assuming a similar error in AC for the next three annals, we have Peniarth MS. 20 775=776, 776=777, and 779=783. After 784=783 AC has ten blank *anni*, which have been omitted in the chronology of Peniarth MS. 20, before the annal recording the coming of the Pagans to Ireland and the harrying of Rechra. Hence Peniarth MS. 20 is here ten years in arrear and its 785=795, whereas BS gives the correct date.[2] It continues to be a decade in arrear for the two following annals, where the chronology of BS is again correct.

For the years 807–11 the dates in Peniarth MS. 20 seem to agree with those of AC; and as there are no independent verifiable data one can only assume that they are correct. *S.a.* 811 the death of Owain ap Maredudd and the burning of Degannwy are recorded in the same annal, as also in BS; RB does not show the division into annals. In AC, however, the two events are placed in two separate annals, those for 811 and 812 respectively. Since the authority of MS. A of AC is greater than that of any version of the *Brut*, it appears that the Latin original (as reflected

---

[1] AU gives much fuller chronological data than AC, so that it is easier to reckon the true date. The same is true of CS.

[2] *See* note on 3, 1–3, p. 133.

INTRODUCTION lxvii

in Peniarth MS. 20 and BS) has here dropped an annal. Allowing for this and another probable error in AC *s.a.* 815 (MS. A)[1] the Peniarth MS. 20 dates are one year behind for the period [812]–819. Again the absence of entries the dates of which would be independently verifiable, makes absolute certainty impossible.

For the years 823–49 the chronology seems to be correct. Of the entries for the years 850–6, the only date that can be checked is that for the death of Cynioedd, *s.a.* 856, which is given in AU *s.a.* 857 (=858). Here Peniarth MS. 20 seems to be two years in arrear; and it has been assumed that it is so for the three preceding entries. Peniarth MS. 20 records the death of Maelsechlainn *s.a.* 860, but in AU it is given *s.a.* 861 (=862) and in AC *s.a.* 860 (=861). The chronology of Peniarth MS. 20 reflects the apparent error in AC. From 860 to 887 it is one year in arrear, as can be checked at several points: *s.a.* 866 is recorded the ravaging of York, which AU places *s.a.* 866 (=867); *s.a.* 870 comes the destruction of Dumbarton, placed in AU *s.a.* 869 (=871), and *s.a.* 878 the death of Rhodri, placed in AU *s.a.* 877 (=878). Again, the death of Aedh macNeill is recorded in AU *s.a.* 878 (=879), and the death of Cerbhall *s.a.* 887 (=888).

From 889 to 897 Peniarth MS. 20 is two years in arrear, but only one year in 898 and 899. The probable reason for the change from two years to one year in arrear is that AC has a blank *annus* between the death of Elstan (=Peniarth MS. 20 Ethelstan) and the death of Alfred, whereas there is no such blank *annus* allowed for in the *Brut*.

(2) *Chronicler's* 900–[949]

There are difficulties in determining the true chronology of the events recorded during this period: the text of this section of the *Brut* is missing in Peniarth MS. 20, and in the translation the lacuna is filled by the corresponding section in the RB version, which gives only the decennial dates in its early part. Hence the chronology of the years 900–49 must be determined by reference to that of AC and BS and to certain entries which are independently verifiable. AU *s.a.* 907 (=908) and 908 (=909) supplies the dates of the death of Cormac and Cerbhall respectively. Hence—and allowing for a blank *annus* in AC between the death of Rhodri (=RB Rhydderch) ap Hywel and the battle of Dinmeir (=RB Dinneir)—we have the dates 903,

---

[1] *See* note on 3.23.

lxviii BRUT Y TYWYSOGYON

904, 905, 907, 908, 909. And so the death of Asser falls in 910. Between the death of Asser *s.a.* 909 (=910) and the coming of Otir to Britain *s.a.* 913 (=914) AC has three blank *anni*, and so RB 910=914. Between the coming of Otir and the death of Anarawd ap Rhodri AC has another blank *annus*, and so the death of Anarawd seems to fall in 916. After this entry AC has a blank *annus* again, hence the date 918 for the ravaging of Ireland[1] and the death of Æthelflæd. Following this, AC has yet another blank *annus*, and so Clydog ap Cadell's death is placed in the year 920. The death of bishop Nercu, recorded in RB and BS, is not recorded in AC, but since there is a blank *annus* in AC between the death of Clydog and the battle of Dinasnewydd, it is probable that the date is 921. The date 922 for the battle of Dinasnewydd is confirmed by AC, which is hereabouts consistently one year in arrear.

The RB date of 920 for Hywel's journey to Rome is at variance with AC 928 (=929). That RB is here nine years in arrear in its dating is accounted for by its being already four years in arrear at 910 (=914) and by its having omitted another five blank *anni* shown in AC between the battle of Dinasnewydd and Hywel's pilgrimage to Rome. Athelstan died in 939, but the preceding dates 935, 937, 938 are only tentative. CS records Amlaibh's death *s.a.* 940 (=941) and so at 940 RB appears to be one year in arrear, and AC one year in advance, of the true reckoning. In determining the dates of the four annals that follow it has been assumed that AC is correct in showing no blank *anni*. The date 949 for the death of Hywel the Good is accounted for by the fact that after the annal for 946 (=945) and before that for 950 (=949) AC records the death of king Edmund *s.a.* 947 (=946) and has two blank *anni* 948-9 (=947-8) after the year 945. In AC and BS the death of Hywel, the murder of Cadwgan ab Owain, and the battle of Carno are all placed *s.a.* 950 (=949), and it has been assumed that they were so placed in the Latin original of the *Brut*, on the evidence of AC and BS.

(3) *Chronicler's* 950-1062

For the period 950-72 the chronicler's dates seem to be consistently two years in arrear: thus the death of Congalach is placed *s.a.* 954 whereas AU and CS place it *s.a.* 955 (=956). From 974 to 1003 the dates are only one year in arrear: thus the death of Edgar is placed *s.a.* 974 (=975), the mortality *s.a.*

[1] This is confirmed by AU: *see* note on 6, 26-7.

986 (=987) is recorded in AU *s.a.* 986 (=987), the death of Gluniairn *s.a.* 988 (=989) is recorded in AU *s.a.* 988 (=989), and the burning of Armagh *s.a.* 995 (=996) is found recorded in AU *s.a.* 995 (=996) and in CS *s.a.* 994 (=996). It appears that the ravaging of Dublin *s.a.* 999 (=1000) and the death of Imhar of Waterford *s.a.* 1001 (=1002) have been misplaced, as is pointed out in the notes on 11, 1 and 11, 5-6 (pp. 147-8). In Peniarth MS. 20, too, the death of Cynan ap Hywel is placed *s.a.* 1002 (=1003), but this is at variance with AC, where Cynan's death is placed in the third year after the ravaging of Dyfed, and with BS, which records his death two years after the death of Imhar. It may be that Peniarth MS. 20 has omitted a blank *annus*.

However, the reference *s.a.* 1004 to the *annus decemnouenalis* shows that here the chronicler's reckoning is three years in arrear, the true date being 1007. *S.a.* 1012 (=1013) we have the first indication of the date of the commencement of the year for the chronicler: Sweyn's death is placed in the same year as that in which he drove Ethelred from his kingdom. Sweyn died in February, 1014, according to modern reckoning, i.e. in 1013 if we reckon the beginning of the year from 25 March. It is to be noticed that MSS. B, C, D of Peniarth MS. 20 state that Sweyn died in the year following that in which he expelled Ethelred, i.e. in 1014. The chronology of B, C, D at this point reflects a 'correction' made in a common original which, as we have seen, derived from Peniarth MS. 20; and the correction must have been made by a scribe who did not reckon the commencement of the year from 25 March. Cnut's accession *s.a.* 1015 (=1016) is post-dated by one year. MS. B of AC has a blank *annus* between the events recorded *s.a.* 1015 and 1016 respectively in Peniarth MS. 20: this blank *annus* has been ignored in Peniarth MS. 20 and so its dates from 1016 to 1062 are two years in arrear. And this can be checked at certain points: *s.a.* 1024 the *annus decemnouenalis* is obviously 1026, and *s.a.* 1062 the *annus decemnouenalis* is 1064.

(4) *Chronicler's* 1064-1129

There is some confusion in the date of the entry *s.a.* 1064: Donnchadh's death is recorded in AU *s.a.* 1064 and in CS *s.a.* 1061 (=1064). BS, however, like Peniarth MS. 20, places it two years after the *primus decemnouenalis* in 1064. But AC omits the reference to the *annus decemnouenalis* and has two blank *anni* between the death of Joseph and the defeat of Harold. It appears, therefore, that 'two years' *s.a.* 1064 is an error in Peniarth MS. 20 and BS for 'one year.' This probable error has been taken into account in arriving at the equation 1064=1065. AU, however, places the death of Donnchadh in 1064.[1]

It is difficult to determine the true date of the battle of Mechain recorded *s.a.* 1068 in Peniarth MS. 20 as in BS. Whereas Peniarth MS. 20 dates it *'three* years' after the encounter between the two Harolds (*s.a.* 1065=1066), i.e. in 1068, MSS. B, C, D of Peniarth MS. 20 date it *'two* years' after the same event. This, however, represents no discrepancy for the same MSS. B, C, D date the encounter between the two Harolds *'two* years' after the death of Donnchadh, i.e. in 1066, whereas Peniarth MS. 20 dates it in the following year, i.e. in 1065. MSS. B and C of AC have two blank *anni* between the two entries which are given *s.a.* 1066 and 1069 respectively. BS, however, records the battle between the two Harolds *s.a.* 1066 and the battle of Mechain *s.a.* 1068. The latter date seems to be an error in BS, and the equation 1068=1069 in the translation follows Peniarth MS. 20 and AC.

From 1070 to 1101 the dates are two years in arrear, as can be checked at several points: the death of Diarmaid, son of Mael-na-mbo, recorded *s.a.* 1070, is placed *s.a.* 1072 in AU; *s.a.* 1081 the *annus decemnouenalis* is really 1083; Toirrdelbhach's death is recorded *s.a.* 1084, but AU records it *s.a.* 1086; William I's death, recorded *s.a.* 1085, is post-dated by two years; the death of Maelcoluim, recorded *s.a.* 1091, was in 1093; William Rufus went to Normandy in March, 1094, but the chronicler's date is 1092, and he died in August 1100, not in 1098 as in the chronicle; Hugh the Fat died on 27 July, 1101, and so the chronicler's 1099=1101; king Magnus was slain in 1103, and so the equation 1101=1103 is correct.

The annal for 1104 (true date) which is found blank in MS. C of AC, has been omitted in Peniarth MS. 20, RB, and BS, and so, therefore, in the common Latin original which must have followed some copy of text B in AC. Because of this omission the chronicler's dates become *three* years in arrear and continue to be so down to 1130 (=1133). This can be checked at several points: Alexander, son of Maelcoluim, *s.a.* 1104 died in January, 1107;[2] Henry I's return from Normandy, *s.a.* 1112, was in 1115; Gilbert fitz Richard *s.a.* 1114 died in 1117; the death of Muircertach *s.a.* 1116 was on 13 March, 1119,[2] according to AU; the

---

[1] *See* note on 15, 12.
[2] The dates imply that the commencement of the year in this section was 25 December.

loss of the White Ship *s.a.* 1117 took place in 1120; Henry I's marriage to Adela was solemnized on 29 January, 1121, but the chronicler's date is 1118.[1] It appears from the dates given to the death of Alexander, son of Maelcoluim, to that of Muircertach, and to Henry's marriage, that the beginning of the year is reckoned from 25 December.

It is to be noted that the annal for 1119 (=1122) is not in RB and AC, but that it is in BS. It has been accepted as correct: see note on 49. 1 on p. 170. That it is correct and that the chronicler's dates are still three years behind is shown by the chronicler's date (1123) for Henry's return from Normandy, which was in September, 1126.

(5) *Chronicler's* 1130–1249

Originally the years 1130–33 (=1133–6) were blank, as is shown by the text of the first paragraph on 51. Later entries must have been added, for the next annal, the chronicler's 1134, records the death of Henry I, which took place on 1 December, 1135. Therefore at this point the dating is one year in arrear and it continues to be so down to 1169 (=1170). The death of Miles, earl of Hereford, that of Robert, son of king Henry, that of Robert, bishop of Hereford, and that of David, king of the Scots, are all post-dated by one year. So, too, the death of king Stephen, that of Roger, earl of Hereford, and that of Toirrdelbhach.[2]

The chronicler's 1070 seems to be the correct date. By modern reckoning Thomas Becket was murdered on 29 December, 1170, but it is placed in 1171 by the chronicler because, in this section, the beginning of the year is reckoned from 25 December. The chronicler's dating continues to be correct down to 1206: Henry's return to England from Ireland *s.a.* 1172, the death of pope Alexander *s.a.* 1181 and that of Henry the Younger *s.a.* 1183, are all correctly dated. The death of Richard, archbishop of Canterbury, which occurred on 16 February, 1184, by modern reckoning, is placed *s.a.* 1183; and this is correct if we reckon the beginning of the year from 25 March. Again, the death of Henry *s.a.* 1189 and that of king Richard *s.a.* 1199 are correctly dated. So, too, *s.a.* 1205, the death of Hubert, archbishop of Canterbury. Some entries appear to have been misplaced: *see* notes on 73, 6 and 74, 17–8.

---

[1] The dates imply that the commencement of the year in this section was 25 December.
[2] *See* note on 62, 7–9.

The chronicler's 1207 is one year in arrear, for the events recorded under that year took place in 1208. It appears that the annal for the true date 1207 has been omitted in Peniarth MS. 20, as in RB, BS, and CW. MS. D of Peniarth MS. 20 is correct with its *Two* years after that.' As a result of the error in Peniarth MS. 20 the years 1207-11 are all one year in arrear. Thus John's visit to Ireland, *s.a.* 1209, took place in 1210. With the chronicler's 1212 the chronology rights itself for the events of 1212 (true date) have been recorded under two separate annals, i.e. the chronicler's 1211 and 1212; *see* note on 86, 38. The chronology continues to be correct down to 1249. King John's visit to Poitou is placed in 1214: but since he sailed in February, 1214, by modern reckoning, the dating of the commencement of the year is at this point 25 December. The death of pope Innocent III, that of king John, that of the earl of Chester, and that of Richard, earl of Pembroke, are all correctly dated. Henry III's marriage, which took place on 20 January, 1236, by modern reckoning, is placed in 1235, thus showing that at this point also the year is reckoned from 25 December.

(6) *Chronicler's* 1250–82

The chronicler's 1250 is one year ahead of the true date for Alexander III, king of Scotland, died on 8 July, 1249. This error is common to Peniarth MS. 20, RB, and BS, and so it probably goes back to the original Latin chronicle: *see* the note on 108, 36–8, where it is pointed out that the footnote (1) in HW ii. 694 needs to be emended. From 1251 to 1256 the chronology is correct: thus Henry III's visit to Burgundy and his return therefrom are correctly placed in 1253 and 1254 respectively, and Louis's return from Jerusalem in 1254. However, the events of 1257 have been recorded under two separate annals so that the chronicler's 1258 is really the second half of 1257, and his 1259 is 1258. Henry III went to France in November, 1259, but this event is recorded *s.a.* 1258. The chronicler's reckoning at 1259 is correct once again and it continues to be so down to 1282, although some events, which are probably additions, seem to have been misplaced. The election of pope Clement IV in 1265,[1] the death of Henry III in 1272, the election of pope Gregory X in the same year, Edward's return from Jerusalem in 1274, are all correctly dated. Dafydd took the castle of Hawarden on 21 March, 1282,

---

[1] Clement IV was elected Pope on 15 February. Hence the date 1265 is correct in the chronicle only if we reckon the year from 25 December.

according to modern reckoning, but this meant 1281 (120) for the chronicler for whom the year at this point began on 25 March.

Chronicler's 1282–1332

This section is a later addition to the chronicle in Peniarth MS. 20 and is not in RB. The chronology is in many places incorrect, some of the events recorded being misplaced by one, two, three, and even four years. These errors probably reflect a conflation of more than one set of annals. From 1282 to 1285 the chronology is correct, but in 1289 the chronicler is two years ahead in his dating of the siege of Dryslwyn castle. The dates 1290–2 are correct, but the death of Bevys de Clare seems to have been placed too early. Einion, bishop of St. Asaph, died on 5 February, 1293,[1] by modern reckoning, and so the chronicler's 1292 is correct according to the reckoning whereby the year began on 25 March. If the latter was the case, however, the election of Llywelyn ap Llywelyn ab Ynyr as bishop, which took place on 6 April, 1293,[2] should have been placed in a separate annal. That an error was made at this point is proved by the chronicler's dates for the years 1293 to 1295 being one year in arrear. Gilbert earl of Clare's death on 7 December, 1295, is placed two years too late. The date of the battle of Falkirk is correct, but the death of John, earl of Warrene, is four years behind the true date (27 September, 1304). Benedict XI's death on 7 July, 1304, is placed in 1301, and the chronicler's 1302 is likewise three years in arrear. There are no entries for the years 1302–5, but the dates 1306–8 are correct. The years 1309 and 1310 are blank. The birth of Edward III (13 November, 1312) is placed one year too early, as also are Gaveston's death, the election of Llywelyn as bishop of St. Asaph and the 'battle in the Pools.' Dafydd ap Bleddyn was consecrated bishop on 12 January, 1315,[3] according to modern reckoning, so that the chronicler's date—1314—is correct if he reckoned the year as commencing on 25 March: but he has placed Dafydd's consecration in the year following that in which bishop Llywelyn died and in which Dafydd was elected 'on the eve of the feast of John at Midsummer.' There is obvious confusion here between the dates (25 December and 25 March) from which the commencement of the year was variously reckoned. The equation 1314=1315 is correct according to the reckoning from 25 December.

[1] Le Neve i. 67.
[2] Ib.
[3] Ib. 68.

There are no entries for the chronicler's 1315 and 1316. Llywelyn Bren's revolt, his seizure, and 'the discord between the king and the barons,' are dated two years too early if we reckon the beginning of the year from 25 March. From 1320 to 1332 the chronicler's dates are correct; but the execution of the earl of Lancaster and the coronation of Edward III, which took place respectively on 22 March, 1337, and 29 January, 1327, according to modern reckoning, are correctly dated only if the commencement of the year is reckoned from 25 December. On the other hand Warenne's return from Gascony is correct only if the year is reckoned from 25 March.

§7. THE TRANSLATION AND NOTES

A few words of explanation are needed on the translation and the notes which follow. The translation is that of the Peniarth MS. 20 text of the Peniarth MS. 20 version of the *Brut:* it does not claim to be a translation of a completely critical text of that version. A few obvious emendations have been incorporated in the English rendering, but they are confined to emendations of this one text; and any emendations which involve the Peniarth MS. 20 version as such, and, beyond it, the Latin original on which it is based, are reserved for the notes. The translation is designed to be as literal and as close to the Welsh original as is possible without doing too much violence to English idiom. The Welsh text, being a translation from Latin, is not conspicuous for any graces of style and is often ambiguous in its references to persons whose actions are recorded. Words given within square brackets have been added by me either for the sake of clarity or to help to render into fairly natural English, certain Welsh words and expressions which could not be translated literally. For Welsh names of places and persons I have adopted the forms used in HW, and with such English names I have generally followed the forms given in *The Handbook of British Chronology* (R.H.S., London, 1939). The dates of the many saints' days mentioned in the text have not been incorporated in the translation but have been listed in the Appendix on 223. The dates in ordinary type are the chronicler's and those that follow in bold face are the editor's, as representing the true dates: but, as was explained in the above section on chronology, in some places in the first sections they can only be approximate.

The notes are not intended as a commentary on the historical content of the *Brut*. Their main purpose is to facilitate the task of trying to recover the evidence of the original Latin text which underlies Peniarth MS. 20, RB, and BS. These three versions have been carefully compared with each other and with the texts of AC and CW, and the notes are primarily designed to draw attention to the many discrepancies between them and wherever possible, to show which version is most likely to be correct. In the early sections of the chronicle comparison with AU and CS proved useful. Hence the many quotations from RB, BS, AC, CW, AU, and CS. Attention is called to mistranslations from the original Latin wherever they can be traced with the help of the cognate texts. The translation should not be used without consulting the notes wherever the sign † is found in the text: in most cases the note shows that the text is corrupt or is at variance with those of RB and BS. It is hoped that until the texts and translations of RB and BS appear, this translation of Peniarth MS. 20 together with the notes will supply students with the combined substantial evidence of the three versions of the *Brut*.

ABBREVIATIONS

AC	. .	*Annales Cambriae.* Ed. John Williams ab Ithel. Rolls Series. London, 1860.
ASE	. .	*Anglo-Saxon England.* F. M. Stenton. Oxford, 1943.
AU	. .	*Annals of Ulster.* Vol. i. Ed. W. M. Hennessy. Vol. ii. Ed. B. Mac Carthy. Rolls Series. London, 1887 and 1893.
B .	. .	*Bulletin of the Board of Celtic Studies.* Cardiff, 1921–.
BB	. .	*Black Book of Basingwerk* (NLW MS. 7006).
BD	. .	*Brut Dingestow.* Ed. Henry Lewis. Cardiff, 1942.
BS	. .	*Brenhinedd y Saesson* in BM. Cotton MS. Cleopatra B.v. and NLW MS. 7006.
BT	. .	*Brut y Tywysogion.* Ed. John Williams ab Ithel. Rolls Series. London, 1860.
BTl	. .	*The Book of Taliesin.* Ed. J. Gwenogvryn Evans. Llanbedrog, 1910.
CA	. .	*Canu Aneirin.* Ed. Ifor Williams. Cardiff, 1938.
CACW	. .	*Calendar of Ancient Correspondence concerning Wales.* Ed. J. G. Edwards. Cardiff, 1935.
CB	. .	*Cambrian Bibliography.* William Rowlands. Llanidloes, 1869.
CLlH	. .	*Canu Llywarch Hen.* Ed. Ifor Williams. Cardiff, 1935.
CPS	. .	*Chronicles of the Picts and Scots.* Ed. W. F. Skene. Edinburgh, 1867.
CS	. .	*Chronicum Scotorum.* Ed. W. M. Hennessy. Rolls Series. London, 1866.
CW	. .	*Cronica de Wallia and Other Documents from Exeter Cathedral Library MS.* 3514. Ed. Thomas Jones. Reprinted, with indexes, from B xii. (November, 1946) 27–44.
EHR	. .	*English Historical Review.* 1886–.
G .	. .	*Geirfa Barddoniaeth Gynnar Gymraeg.* J. Lloyd-Jones. Cardiff, 1931–.
HB	. .	*Historia Brittonum* in *Nennius et L'Historia Brittonum.* Ferdinand Lot. Paris, 1934.
Hemingburgh	.	*Chronicon Domini Walteri de Hemingburgh.* Ed. Hans Claude Hamilton. 2 vols. London, 1848–9.
HRB	. .	The *Historia Regum Britanniae* of Geoffrey of Monmouth. Ed. Acton Griscom. London, New York, Toronto, 1929.
HW	. .	*A History of Wales.* John Edward Lloyd. Second edition. London, 1912.
LL	. .	*The Text of the Book of Llan Dâv.* Ed. J. Gwenogvryn Evans. Oxford, 1893.

ABBREVIATIONS

Le Neve	*Fasti Ecclesiae Anglicanae.* John Le Neve. Corrected and continued by T. Duffus Hardy. 3 vols. Oxford, 1854.
LW	*Littere Wallie.* Ed. J. Goronwy Edwards. Cardiff, 1940.
MA	*The Myvyrian Archaiology of Wales.* Ed. Owen Jones (Myfyr), Edward Williams (Iolo Morganwg), and W. O. Pughe. Second edition. Denbigh, 1870. References to the first edition (3 vols., London, 1801–1807) are specifically noted where necessary.
ONR	*Old Norse Relations with Wales.* B. G. Charles. Cardiff, 1934.
OP	*The Description of Penbrokshire by George Owen.* Ed. Henry Owen (with notes by Egerton Phillimore). Four parts. London, 1892, 1897, 1906, 1936.
Pen. 20	*Brut y Tywysogyon. Peniarth MS. 20.* Ed. Thomas Jones, Cardiff, 1941.
PKM	*Pedeir Keinc y Mabinogi.* Ed. Ifor Williams. Cardiff, 1930.
Powel	*The Historie of Cambria now called Wales.* Ed. David Powel. Reproduction of original 1584 edition. London, 1811.
RB	*Critical text* (prepared for publication) *of the 'Red Book of Hergest Version' of 'Brut y Tywysogion.'* The symbols for the various MSS. used are: L = Llanstephan MS. 172 M = Mostyn MS. 116 R = Red Book of Hergest (Jesus College, Oxford; MS. CXI) P = Peniarth MS. 18 T = Peniarth MS. 19
RBB	*The Text of the Bruts from the Red Book of Hergest.* Ed. John Rhŷs and J. Gwenogvryn Evans. Oxford, 1890.
RC	*Revue Celtique.* Paris, 1870–.
RP	*The Poetry in the Red Book of Hergest.* Ed. J. Gwenogvryn Evans. Llanbedrog, 1911.
RWM	*Reports on Manuscripts in the Welsh Language.* J. Gwenogvryn Evans. Historical Manuscripts Commission. London, 1898–1910.
Trans. Cym.	*Transactions of the Honourable Society of Cymmrodorion.* London, 1822–.
VSB	*Vitae Sanctorum Britanniae et Genealogiae.* Ed. A. W. Wade-Evans. Cardiff, 1944.
ZCP	*Zeitschrift für celtische Philologie.* Halle, 1897–.

Brut y Tywysogyon
THE CHRONICLE OF THE PRINCES

PENIARTH MS. 20. 65*a*. 1

[681–682]. Six hundred and eighty-one† was the year of Christ when there was a great mortality† in the island of Britain.† In that year Cadwaladr ap Cadwallon, the last king that was over the Britons, went to Rome; and there he died on the twelfth day from the Calends of May.[1]† And thenceforth the Britons lost the crown of kingship, and the Saxons obtained it, as Myrddin had prophesied to Gwrtheyrn Wrthenau.†

And after Cadwaladr there succeeded Ifor son of Alan,[2]† king of Brittany, not as king but as leader; and he held dominion over the Britons for forty-eight years; and then he died. And after him succeeded Rhodri Molwynog.

[683–684]. Two years after that, there was a mortality in Ireland.†

[684–685]. And in the year next to that the earth quaked.†

[688–689]. Four years after that, was the rain of blood† in the island of Britain and Ireland, and the milk and the butter turned into blood.

[690–691]. Two years after that, the moon reddened as it were to the colour of blood.†

[704–704]. Seven hundred and four was the year of Christ when Aldfrid, king of the Saxons, died. And he was buried at Damnani.†

[705–714]. A year after that,† the night became as bright as day.† And Pippin the Great, king of the Franks, died.

[706–716]. A year after that, died Osred, king of the Saxons.

[707–717]. A year after that, the church of Michael† was consecrated.

---

[1] Six hundred . . . May]. When the year of Christ was six hundred and eighty-one, Cadwaladr the Blessed went to Brittany, to Alan, nephew of Selyf. And after he had conversed with the angel he went to Rome at his behest. And then the Saxons ruled the island of Britain. And five years after his going to Rome he died, when the year of Christ was six hundred and eighty-eight, on the twelfth day from the Calends of May; and in Rome was he buried. C.
[2] Assan *retraced in MS.*, Alan C.

[720–720]. Seven hundred and twenty was the year of Christ when the hot summer befell.

[721–721]. A year after that, died Beli, son of Elffin.† And the battle of Heilyn† in Cornwall took place, and the battle of Garthmaelog† and the battle of Pen-cŵn[1]† in the South. And in those three battles the Britons prevailed and obtained the victory.

[723–729]. Two years after that was the battle of Mynydd Carno.†

[735–735]. Seven hundred and thirty-five was the year of Christ when Bede the Wise died.

[736–749]. A year after that, died Owain, king of the Picts.†

[750–750]. Seven hundred and fifty was the year of Christ when the battle which was called Gwaith[2] My[g]edog[3]† took place between the Picts and the Britons. And then Talargan,[4]† king of the Picts, was slain. And Tewdwr ap Beli died.

[754–754]. Four years after that, died Rhodri, king of the Britons.

[757–757]. Three years after that, died Ethelbald, king of the Saxons.

[760–760]. Seven hundred and sixty was the year of Christ when the battle between the Britons and the Saxons, which was called Gwaith[2] Henffordd,† took place. And Dyfnwal ap Tewdwr died.

[768–768]. Eight years after that, Easter was changed for the Britons, Elfoddw, a servant of God,† changing it.

[773–774]. Seven hundred and seventy-three was the year of Christ when Ffyrnfael ab Idwal† died.

[774–775]. A year after that, died Cynioedd, king of the Picts.†

[775–776]. The year next after that, died Cuthbert the abbot.†

[776–777]. The year next to that, Offa harried the men of the South.†

[779–783]. Three years after that, in the summer, the Britons were harried along with Offa.†

---

[1] Penkwn *with* coed *written above* kwn MS.
[2] *Gwaith* 'battle.'
[3] Mietouc MS., Megedawc C.
[4] Talargarn MS.

[785–795]. Seven hundred and eighty-five was the year of Christ when the Pagans came to Ireland, and Rechra was harried.†

[786–796]. A year after that died Offa, king of Mercia, and Maredudd, king of Dyfed, in the battle at Rhuddlan.†

[788–798]. Two years after that, Saxons slew[1] Caradog, king of Gwynedd.

[807–807]. Eight hundred and seven was the year of Christ when Arthen, king of Ceredigion, died. And then there was an eclipse of the sun.

[808–808]. A year after that died R[hun],[2]† king of Dyfed, and Cadell[3] of Powys.

[809–809]. A year after that, died Elfoddw, archbishop of Gwynedd.

[810–810]. Eight hundred and ten was the year of Christ when the moon darkened on Christmas day. And Menevia was burnt. And there was a mortality upon the animals in all the island of Britain.

[811–811]. A year after that, died Owain ap Maredudd.

[–812]. And Degannwy was burnt by fire of lightning.†

[812–813]. A year after that there was war between Hywel and Cynan, and Hywel prevailed.†

[815–814]. Three years after that† there were great thunders and many things were burnt. And Gruffudd ap Rhun† died. And then Griffri† ap Cyngen was slain through the treachery of Elise, his brother. And then Hywel of the island of Anglesey obtained the victory, and Cynan was driven[4] into flight, and many of his host were slain.

[817–816]. Two years after that, Hywel was driven a second time from Anglesey. And king Cynan died. And the Saxons ravaged the mountains of Eryri and took Rhufoniog by force.

[818–817]. A year after that the battle of Llan-faes† took place.

[819–818]. A year after that, Coenwulf ravaged the land of Dyfed.

---

[1] Saxons slew] Offa had a dyke made as a defence between him and the Welsh so that it might be easier for him to resist the attack of his enemies. And that is called Offa's Dyke from that day to this. And there Saxons slew C.
[2] Beli C.
[3] + king C.
[4] and he drove Cynan D.

[823–823]. Eight hundred and twenty-three was the year of Christ when the Saxons destroyed the arch† of Degannwy and took the kingdom of Powys for their own.[1]†

[825–825]. Two years† after that,[2] died Hywel.

[831–831]. Eight hundred and thirty-one was the year of Christ when there was an eclipse of the moon.† And Sadyrnfyw,† bishop of Menevia, died.

[840–840]. Eight hundred and forty was the year of Christ when Bonheddig,[3] bishop of Menevia,† ruled.

[842–842]. Two years after that, died Idwallon.

[844–844]. Two years after that, the battle of Cedyll took place. And Merfyn[4] died.

[848–848]. Four years after that, the battle of Ffinnant† took place. And the men of Brycheiniog slew Ithel, king of Gwent.

[849–849]. A year after that, Saxons slew Meurig.[5]

[850–852]. Eight hundred and fifty was the year of Christ when the Pagans slew Cyngen.†

[853–855]. Three years after that, Anglesey was ravaged by the Black Host.

[854–856]. A year after that, Cyngen,† king of Powys, died in Rome.

[856–858]. Two years after that, died Cynioedd, king of the Picts.† And Ionathal, leader† of Abergelau, died.

[860–861]. Eight hundred and sixty was the year of Christ when Maelsechlainn[6] died.†

[862–863]. Two years after that, Cadweithen was expelled.†

[864–865]. Two years after that, she ravaged Glywysing.†

[865–866]. A year after that, died Cynan of Nanhyfer.†

[866–867]. A year after that, York was ravaged by a host of Black Gentiles.†

---

[1] the Saxons . . . own] Degannwy was burnt by the Saxons and Powys was destroyed CD.
[2] + the said CD.
[3] Einion the gentle-born CD.
[4] + Frych CD.
[5] + king of Gwent CD.
[6] + of Ireland BCD.

[869–870]. Three years after that, the battle of Bryn Onnen took place.

[870–871]. Eight hundred and seventy was the year of Christ when the fortress of Dumbarton was destroyed by the Pagans.[1]†

[871–872]. A year after that, Gwgan ap Meurig, king of Ceredigion, was drowned.

[873–874]. Two years after that, the battle of Banolau† and the battle of Ynegydd in Anglesey took place. And Einion Fonheddig, bishop of Menevia†, died.

[874–875]. A year after that, Himbert[2]† assumed the bishopric of Menevia.

[875–876]. A year after that, Dwngarth,† king of Cornwall, was drowned.

[876–877]. A year after that, the Sunday battle took place in Anglesey.†

[877–878]. A year after that, Rhodri and Gwriad, his brother,† were slain by the Saxons.

[878–879]. A year after that, died Aedd, son of Mell.†

[880–881]. Eight hundred and eighty was the year of Christ when the battle of the Conway, which was called 'the avenging of Rhodri,'† took place.

[882–883]. Two years after that, died Cadweithen.†

[885–886]. Three years after that, Hywel died in Rome.

[887–888]. Two years after that, died Cerbhall.[3]†

[889–891]. Two years after that, died Suibhne,† the most learned of the Irish.

[890–892]. Eight hundred and ninety was the year of Christ when the Black Norsemen came to Gwynedd.†

[891–893]. A year after that, died Hyfaidd† ap Bleddri.

[893–895]. Two years after that, Anarawd came, along with the Saxons, to harry Ceredigion and Ystrad Tywi.

[894–896]. A year after that, the Norsemen ravaged England and Brycheiniog and Gwent and Gwynllŵg.[4]†

---

[1] when the Pagans destroyed the fortress of Dumbarton BCD.
[2] Hunbert BD., Hunberth C.
[3] Cerbhall] Cadell ap Rhodri, his brother BCD.
[4] and Gwynllwg]—BCD.

[895–897]. A year after that, bread failed in Ireland because of vermin which fell from heaven having two teeth after the fashion of moles; and those devoured all the food, and they were destroyed through fasting and prayer.

[897–898]. Two years after that, died king Ethelstan.†

[898–899]. A year after that, died Alfred, king of Wessex.†

[900–903]. Nine hundred was the year† [*Mostyn MS.* 116.144] *of Christ when Igmund came to the island of Anglesey and he held Maes Rhosmeilon.†*

[–904]. And then the son of Merfyn† was slain by his own folk.† And Llywarch ap Hyfaidd died.

[–905]. And Rhydderch† ap Hyfaidd's head was struck off on the feast-day of Paul.†

[–907]. And the battle of Dinneir† took place, in which Maelog Cam,[1] son of Peredur, was slain. And then Menevia was destroyed.

[–908]. And bishop Gorchwyl† died. And Cormac died, king and bishop of all Ireland and a man of great piety and charity, son of Culennán, who by his own wish was slain in battle.†

[–909]. And Cerbhall, son of Muirecan, king of Leinster,† died, making a sure end.†

[–910]. And Asser, archbishop of the island of Britain,† died; and Cadell ap Rhodri.†

[910–914]. *Nine hundred and ten was the year of Christ when Otir came to the island of Britain.*

[–916]. And Anarawd ap Rhodri, king of the Britons, died.†

[–918]. And Ireland and Anglesey were ravaged by the folk of Dublin. And queen Æthelflæd died†.

[–920]. And Clydog ap Cadell was slain by Meurig, his brother.

[–921]. And bishop Nercu died.

[–922]. And the battle of Dinasnewydd took place.

[920–929]. *Nine hundred and twenty was the year of Christ when king Hywel the Good, son of Cadell, went to Rome. And Elen died.*

[930–935]. *Nine hundred and thirty was the year of Christ when Gruffudd ab Owain was slain by the men of Ceredigion.†*

[–937]. And the battle of Brun† took place.

[–938]. And Hyfaidd† ap Clydog and Meurig, his brother,† died.

---

[1] *cam* 'crooked'; i.e. 'Crook-back.'

[-939]. *And Athelstan, king of the Saxons, died.*

[940-941]. *Nine hundred and forty was the year of Christ when king Amlaibh† died.*

[-942]. *And Cadell ab Arthfael was poisoned. And Idwal ap Rhodri and Elisedd, his brother,† were slain by the Saxons.*

[-943]. *And Lwmberth,† bishop of Menevia, died.*

[-944]. *And Ussa ap Llawr and Morlais, bishop of Bangor, died.*

[-945]. *And Cyngen ab Elisedd was poisoned. And Eneurys, bishop of Menevia, died. Strathclyde was ravaged by the Saxons.*

[-949]. *And king Hywel the Good, son of Cadell, the head and glory of all the Britons, died.†*

And Cadwgan ab Owain† was slain by the Saxons. And then the battle of Carno† took place between the sons of Hywel [Peniarth MS. 20. 73] and the sons of Idwal.[1]

[950-952]. *Nine hundred and fifty was the year of Christ when Dyfed was laid waste*[2] *twice by the sons of Idwal, Iago and Ieuaf.*[3] *And the Gentiles slew Dwnwallon.†*

[951-953]. *A year after that, died Rhodri ap Hywel.*[4]†

[952-954]. *A year after that, there was a great slaughter between the sons of Idwal and the sons of Hywel at the place which is called Gwrgystu:† the battle of Conwy Hirfawr. And Anarawd ap Gwri*[5] *was slain.† And after that, Ceredigion was ravaged by the sons of Idwal.*[6] *And Edwin ap Hywel† died.*

[953-955]. *A year after that, Iarddur ap Merfyn† was drowned.*

[954-956]. *A year after that, died Edwin ap Hywel.† And*[7] *Congalach, king of Ireland, was slain.†*

[955-957]. *A year after that, Gwgan ap Gwriad*[8] *was slain. And the hot summer befell.*

[958-960]. *Three years after that, Owain*[9] *ravaged Y Gorwydd.†*

---

[1] Nine hundred ... Idwal]. When the year of Christ was nine hundred, was the battle of the sons of Idwal BC,—D.
[2] burnt BCD.
[3] and Ieuaf] and Ieuan, sons of Idwal Foel ab Anarawd ap Rhodri Mawr BCD.
[4] + the Good BCD.
[5] Gwri] Gwiriad ap BCD.
[6] And ... Idwal]. And the sons of Idwal ravaged Ceredigion BCD.
[7] died Edwin ... and]—BCD.
[8] + ap Rhodri BCD.
[9] + ap Hywel Dda BCD.

[959–961]. A year after that, there was a mighty plague in the month of March, the sons of Idwal[1] ruling.† And Holyhead and Llŷn were ravaged by the sons of Amlaibh.[2]

[960–962]. Nine hundred and sixty was the year of Christ when Idwal ap Rhodri[3] was slain.

[961–963]. A year after that, the sons of Gwyn[4] were slain. And Tywyn was ravaged by the Gentiles. And Meurig ap Cadfan died.

[962–964]. A year after that, died bishop Rhydderch.

[964–966]. Two years after that, died Cadwallon ab Owain.

[965–967]. A year after that, the Saxons ravaged the kingdoms[5] of the sons of Idwal, with Aelfhere as their leader.†

[966–968]. A year after that, Rhodri ab Idwal was slain. And then Aberffraw was ravaged.

[967–969]. A year after that, Ieuaf ab Idwal was seized by Iago, his brother, and was imprisoned.†

[968–970]. A year after that, Einion ab Owain ravaged[6] Gower.

[969–971]. A year after that, Madog,† son of Harold, ravaged Penmon.

[970–972]. Nine hundred and seventy was the year of Christ when Godfrey, son of Harold, ravaged the island of Anglesey; and with great treasure[7]† he subdued the island.

[971–973]. A year after that, there was a great fleet along with Edgar, king of the Saxons, at Chester.†

[972–974]. A year after that, Iago was expelled from his kingdom through the victory of Hywel. And Meurig ab Idwal was blinded[8]† and Morgan died.

[974–975]. Two years after that, died Edgar, king of the Saxons. And Dwnwallon, king of Strathclyde, went to Rome. And Idwallon ab Owain† died.

---

[1] Owain ap Hywel Dda BCD.
[2] the sons of Amlaibh the Irishman ravaged Holyhead and Llŷn BCD.
[3] + the Great BC.
[4] + ap Gollwyn CD.
[5] kingdom BCD.
[6] + the land of BCD.
[7] fame BCD.
[8] seized C.

[976-977]. Two years after that, Einion ravaged¹ Gower for the second time.

[977-978]. A year after that, Gwrmid ravaged Llŷn for the second time. And Hywel ap Ieuaf² and the Saxons† ravaged Clynnog Fawr.³†

[978-979]. A year after that, Iago was captured by the Gentiles, after Hywel ap Ieuaf had prevailed⁴ and had obtained possession of his kingdom.†

[979-980]. A year after that, Idwal⁵ was slain. And thereupon Custennin ap Iago and Godfrey, son of Harold, ravaged Llŷn and Anglesey. And thereupon Custennin was slain by Hywel ap Ieuaf⁶ in the battle which was called Gwaith Hirbarwch.†

[981-982]. Nine hundred and eighty-one was the year of Christ when Dyfed was ravaged by the men of Godfrey, son of Harold, and Menevia and Llanweithefawr.†

[982-983]. A year after that, Brycheiniog and all the lands of Einion ab Owain were ravaged by the Saxons, with Aelfhere as their leader, and Hywel ap Ieuaf⁷ and Einion slew many of their hosts.†

[983-984]. The year next to that, Einion ab Owain was slain by the great men of Gwent. And their noble bishop† died.

[984-985]. A year after that, Hywel ap Ieuaf⁸† was slain through the treachery of the Saxons. And Cadwallon ap Ieuaf slew Ionafal ap Meurig.†

[985-986]. A year after that, Maig ap Ieuaf⁹† was slain. And Maredudd ab Owain slew Cadwallon ap Ieuaf† in victorious battle and gained possession of his territory, that is,¹⁰ Gwynedd and Anglesey, which he subdued with great treasure.¹¹†

[986-987]. A year after that, Llywarch ab Owain was deprived of his eyes. And Godfrey, son of Harold, and with him the Black Host, ravaged all the island of Anglesey† and captured two

---

¹ + the land of BCD.
² Ieuan BCD.
³ Fawr]—CD.
⁴ by the Gentiles . . . prevailed] by the men of Hywel ap Ieuan (Ieuan *altered to* Ieuaf D) BCD.
⁵ + Fychan ab Idwal Foel BCD.
⁶ Custennin . . . Ieuaf] Hywel ap Ieuan ab Idwal slew Custennin (. . . Ieuaf . . . Cwstennin D) BCD.
⁷ Ieuan BC.
⁸ Ieuan BCD.
⁹ Meurig ap Ieuan BC, Meurig (or Maig) ap Ieuaf D.
¹⁰ that is]—BCD.
¹¹ through great treachery BCD.

thousand men; and Maredudd ab Owain¹ took the remainder†
to Ceredigion and Dyfed. And then, too, there was a mortality
upon the cattle in all the island of Britain.†

[987–988]. A year after that, died Ieuaf² ab Idwal and Owain
ap Hywel. And Llanbadarn and Menevia and Llanilltud and
Llancarfan and Llandudoch were ravaged.

[988–989]. A year after that, Gluniairn,† son of Amlaibh, was
slain, and Maredudd ab Owain gave a penny from every person†
as a tribute to the Black Host. And then there was a great
mortality upon men because of famine.

[989–990]. A year after that, Owain ap Dyfnwal was slain.

[990–991]. Nine hundred and ninety was the year of Christ
when Maredudd ab Owain ravaged Maeshyfaidd.†

[991–992]. A year after that, Edwin† ab Einion and Edylfi† the
Saxon and with him³ a great host, ravaged all the territory of
Maredudd in Deheubarth, that is, Ceredigion and Dyfed and
Gower and Cydweli. And he took hostages† from the whole
territory. And for the third time he ravaged Menevia. And
Maredudd ravaged Glamorgan by hiring Gentiles and ransoming
the captives.⁴† And Cadwallon, his son, died.

[992–993]. A year after that, hostages from amongst the sons of
Meurig were in Gwynedd,† and the island of Anglesey was
ravaged on Ascension Thursday.

[993–994]. A year after that, there was a pestilence of famine in
the territory of Maredudd ab Owain. And there was a battle
between Maredudd and the sons of Meurig near Llangwm,⁵ and
the sons of Meurig prevailed; and there† Tewdwr ab Einion was
slain.

[994–995]. A year after that, Sweyn,† son of Harold, ravaged
Man.

[995–996]. A year after that†† Idwal ap Meurig was slain. And
Armagh† was ravaged and burnt.

[998–999]. Three years after that, Menevia was harried, and
bishop Morgenau was slain.† And Maredudd ab Owain, the
most praiseworthy king of the Britons, died.

---

¹ ab Owain]—BCD.
² Ieuan BCD.
³ them BCD.
⁴ nobles BCD.
⁵ near Llangwm] And that was near Llangwm D.

[999–1000]. A year after that, the Irish ravaged Dublin.† And Cynan ap Hywel held Gwynedd.

[1000–1001]. One thousand was the year of Christ when the Gentiles ravaged Dyfed.

[1001–1002]. A year after that, died Mor ap Gwyn. And Imhar of Waterford died.†

[1002–1003]. A year after that,† Cynan ap Hywel was slain.

[1003–1004]. A year after that, Gwlfach and Ubiad† were blinded.[1]

[1004–1007]. A year after that, was the first year that was called *Decemnouenalis*.[2]

[1011–1012]. One thousand and eleven was the year of Christ when Eadric and Ubis,† the Saxons, ravaged Menevia. And Iarddur,† the monk, from Bardsey, died.

[1012–1013]. A year after that, Sweyn, son of Harold, father of Cnut, son of Sweyn, invaded the territory of Ethelred, son of Edgar,† king of the Saxons, and drove him in flight from his kingdom, and he gained possession of his kingdom and brought it under his sway.[3] And that year[4] he died.

[–1014]. And Brian, king of Ireland, and Murchadh, his son, and many other kings led hosts against Sitriuc, king of Dublin, son of Amlaibh, and against Maelmordha, king of Leinster. For those had allied themselves together against Brian. And Sitriuc hired long ships and[5] pirate ships full of armed men to assist him; and the leader of those was called Brotor.† And after there had been a hard battle between them and a great slaughter on either side, Brian and Murchadh, his son, were there slain, and Brotor, leader of the ships, and king Maelmordha were slain.†

[1014–1015]. Two years after that, Owain ap Dyfnwal was slain.[6]

[1015–1016]. A year after that, Cnut, son of Sweyn, gained possession of the kingdom of England and Denmark and Great Germany.

[1] seized BC.
[2] A year ... Decemnouenalis]—BCD.
[3] gained possession of it BCD.
[4] that year] the year next to that BCD.
[5] ships and]—BCD.
[6] deceased CD.

[1016–1018]. A year after that,† Llywelyn ap Seisyll† slew Aeddan ap Blegywryd and his four sons.

[1019–1021]. Three years after that, Meurig ab Arthfael was slain.

[1020–1022]. One thousand and twenty was the year of Christ when a certain Irishman lied in saying that he was son to king Maredudd. And he would have himself called Rhain.† And he was accepted by the men of the South and he held territory. And against him rose up Llywelyn ap Seisyll, king of Gwynedd and the supreme and most praiseworthy king of all Britain.† And in his time, as the old men were wont to say, the whole land from the one sea to the other was fruitful in men and in every kind of[1] wealth, so that there was no one in want nor anyone in need within his territory; and there was not one township empty or desolate.

And Rhain[2] weakly and feebly gathered a host, and, as is the custom with the Irish, he boastfully incited his men and he promised them that he would prevail. And he confidently[3] went against his enemies. But they, calmly steady, awaited that presumptuous inciter. And he made for the battle bravely fearless.† And after there had been great slaughter on either side equally, with the men of Gwynedd fighting steadily, Rhain, the Irishman, and his host were defeated. For, as is said in the Welsh proverb, 'Urge on thy dog, but go not with him,' so was he brave† in attack but of a foxy manner in turning to flight. And the men of Gwynedd, pursuing them cruelly vengeful, slaughtered them and ravaged the whole land, and carried off all the chattels.† And he himself was never seen again. That battle was at the mouth of the river Gwili, at Abergwili.[4] And thereupon[5] Eilaf came to the island of Britain.† And he ravaged Dyfed. And Menevia was destroyed.

[1021–1023]. A year after that, died king Llywelyn. And Rhydderch ap Iestyn held the kingdom of the South.

[1023–1025]. Two years after that, died bishop Morgynnydd.[6]†

[1024–1026]. A year after that, was the first year that was called *Decemnouenalis*.[7]

---

[1] every kind of]—BCD.
[2] + the Irishman BCD.
[3] proudly confident C, proudly fearless D.
[4] And he . . . Abergwili]—BCD.
[5] then BCD.
[6] Morgynnydd *with* eneu *written above* MS.
[7] A year . . . Decemnouenalis]—CD.

[1025-1027]. A year after that, Cynan ap Seisyll was slain.

[1031-1033]. One thousand and thirty-one was the year of Christ when the Irish slew Rhydderch ap Iestyn. And Iago ab Idwal held the kingdom of[1] Gwynedd after Llywelyn.† And the sons of Edwin, Hywel and Maredudd, held the kingdom of the South.

[1032-1034]. A year after that was the battle of Irathwy[2]† between the sons of Edwin and the sons of Rhydderch.

[1033-1035]. A year after that, Maredudd ab Edwin was slain by the sons of Cynan,[3] and the Saxons slew Caradog ap Rhydderch. And Cnut, son of Sweyn, king of England and Denmark and Germany, died. And after his death Eilaf fled to Germany.

[1037-1039]. Four years after that, the gentles[4]† captured[5] Meurig ap Hywel. And Iago, king of Gwynedd, was slain.† And in his place[6] Llywelyn, his son,[7] ruled;† and he, from the end of his reign to its beginning[8], hounded the Pagans and the Saxons in many battles, and he prevailed against them and slaughtered them and ravaged them. He had his first battle at Rhyd-y-grog† on the Severn, and there he prevailed. And in that year he pillaged Llanbadarn and held all Deheubarth, and he drove Hywel ab Edwin in flight from his kingdom.

[1038-1040]. A year after that, died Erfyn,[9]† bishop of Menevia.

[1039-1041]. A year after that, the battle of Pencadair took place; and there Gruffudd defeated Hywel, and he seized his wife and took her for his own.

[1040-1042]. One thousand and forty was the year of Christ when the battle of Pwlldyfacht† took place. And there Hywel defeated the Gentiles who were ravaging Dyfed. And in that year Gruffudd was captured by the Gentiles of Dublin.[10]

[1041-1043]. A year after that, Hywel ab Owain, king of Glamorgan, died in his old age.

[1] the kingdom of]—BCD.
[2] Irathwy *with* Hiraethwy *written above* MS., Hiraythwy CD.
[3] the sons of Cynan slew Maredudd ab Edwin BCD.
[4] y bonhedigyon *with* cenedloed *written above by later hand* MS.,—C.
[5] avenged B, escaped C.
[6] in his place]—BCD.
[7] Ll., his son] Gruffudd ap Llywelyn BC, Gruffydd ap Llywelyn of The Golden Torque son of Seisyllt D.
[8] from the beginning of his life to its end BCD.
[9] Henry BCD.
[10] the men of Dublin captured Gruffudd ap Llywelyn BCD.

[1042–1044]. A year after that, Hywel ab Edwin gathered a fleet of the gentles† of Ireland with the intention of ravaging[1] the whole kingdom. And Gruffudd ap Llywelyn encountered him; and there was a mighty battle and many of the host of the foreigners and of his own host were slain at the mouth of the river Tywi. And there Hywel was slain and Gruffudd prevailed. And then Enilfre and Maccus† the monk died.

[1043–1045]. A year after that, Joseph, Teilo's bishop,† died in Rome. And there was great deceit and treachery between Gruffudd and Rhys,† sons of Rhydderch, and Gruffudd ap Llywelyn.

[1045–1047]. Two years after that,† about seven score men of Gruffudd ap Llywelyn's war-band were slain through the treachery of the leading men of Ystrad Tywi. And to avenge those men, king Gruffudd ravaged Dyfed and Ystrad Tywi. And in that year there was great snow, lasting from the Calends of January to the feast of Patrick.

[1047–1049]. Two years after that, all Deheubarth was ravaged.†

[1050–1052]. One thousand and fifty was the year of Christ[2] when a fleet from Ireland foundered in the South.

[1054–1056]. Four years after that, Gruffudd ap Llywelyn slew Gruffudd ap Rhydderch. And after that, Gruffudd ap Llywelyn moved a host against the Saxons, and he arrayed his army at Hereford. And against him rose up the Saxons, and with them a mighty host and with Ranulf† as their leader; and they drew up their army and prepared for battle. And Gruffudd, fearless and with a well-ordered army, fell upon them; and after bitter-fierce fighting the Saxons, unable to withstand the onslaught of the Britons, turned to flight after a great slaughter of them. And Gruffudd pursued them to within the walls of Hereford, and there† he massacred them and destroyed the walls and burned the town. And with vast spoil he returned home eminently worthy.

[1056–1058]. Two years after that, Magnus,† son of Harold, king of Germany, ravaged the kingdom of England with the help and chieftainship of Gruffudd ap Llywelyn,[3] king of the Britons.

[1] a fleet ... ravaging] to BCD.
[2] And three years after that BC.
[3] + of the Golden Torque D.

[1057–1059]. A year after that, died Owain ap Gruffudd.

[1061–1063]. One thousand and sixty-one was the year of Christ when Gruffudd ap Llywelyn was slain,[1] after innumerable victories and taking of spoils and treasures of[2] gold and silver and precious purple raiment, through the treachery of his own men,[3]† after his fame and glory had increased and after he had aforetimes been unconquered, but was now left in the waste valleys,[4] and after he had been head and shield and defender to the Britons.

And then died Joseph, bishop of Menevia.

[1062–1064]. A year after that, [was]† the first *Decemnouenalis*.[5]

[1064–1065]. Two years after that, Donnchadh, son of Brian, died on his way to Rome.†

[1065–1066]. A year[6] after that, Harold, king of Denmark, thought to subdue the Saxons. And against him in a sudden battle there rose up the other Harold, king of the Saxons, son of earl Godwin: and he had first been an earl,[7] but thereupon, after the death of Edward, king of the Saxons, he raised himself through oppression to the very height of kingship. And through innate treachery† he invited the other unarmed from the ships[8] to the land, and there he slew him. And as he was enjoying the glory of victory, a certain man called William the Bastard, leader of the Normans, and with him a mighty host, came against him; and after a mighty battle and a slaughter of the Saxons, he despoiled him of his kingdom and of his life, and he defended[9] for himself the kingdom of the Saxons with victorious hand and a mighty noble host.

[1068–1069]. Three[10] years after that,† the battle of Mechain took place between Bleddyn and Rhiwallon, sons of Cynfyn, and Maredudd and Ithel,† sons of Gruffudd. And there the sons of Gruffudd fell, Ithel[11]† in the battle and Maredudd of cold

---

[1] One thousand ... slain] And (—D) when the year of Christ was one thousand and sixty-one, Gruffudd ap Llywelyn (+ap Seisyllt D) died, slain by his own men through treachery BCD.
[2] treasures of]—BCD.
[3] through ... men]—BCD.
[4] places BCD.
[5] A year ... Decemnouenalis]—BCD.
[6] Two years BCD.
[7] and he ... earl]—BCD.
[8] and his ships BCD.
[9] won BCD.
[10] Two BCD.
[11] the sons of Gruffudd fell, Ithel] Ithel ap Gruffudd fell BCD.

in flight. And there Rhiwallon ap Cynfyn was slain. And Bleddyn ap Cynfyn ruled after his victory. And Maredudd ab Owain ab Edwin held the kingdom of the South.

[1070–1072]. One thousand and seventy was the year of Christ when Maredudd ab Owain was slain by the French and Caradog ap Gruffudd ap Rhydderch on the banks of the Rhymni. And Diarmaid, son of Mael-na-mbo, the most praiseworthy and bravest king of the Irish—terrible towards his foes and kind towards the poor† and gentle towards pilgrims—was slain in an unforeseen and unexpected battle.

[1071–1073]. A year after that, the French ravaged Ceredigion and Dyfed. And Menevia and Bangor were ravaged by the Gentiles. And Bleuddydd, bishop of Menevia, died; and Sulien assumed the bishopric.

[1072–1074]. A year after that, the French ravaged Ceredigion by itself.[1]†

[1073–1075]. A year after that, Bleddyn ap Cynfyn was slain through the evil-spirited treachery of the princes and leading men of Ystrad Tywi,† he who eminently held the kingdom of all[2] the Britons after Gruffudd,[3] his brother.[4] And it was Rhys ab Owain who slew him. And after him Trahaearn ap Caradog, his first-cousin, ruled over the kingdom of Gwynedd; and Rhys ab Owain and Rhydderch ap Caradog held[5] the South. And Gruffudd, grandson of Iago, gained possession of Anglesey,† and Cynwrig ap Rhiwallon was slain by the men of Gwynedd.

That year the battle of Camddwr took place between Goronwy and Llywelyn, sons of Cadwgan, and Caradog ap Gruffudd, and Rhys ab Owain and Rhydderch ap Caradog, who fell there together.†

In that year was the battle of Bron-yr-erw between Gruffudd and Trahaearn.

[1074–1076]. A year after that, Rhydderch ap Caradog was slain by Meirchion ap Rhys ap Rhydderch, his first-cousin, through treachery.

[1075–1077]. A year after that, was the battle of 'Gweunytwl'† between Goronwy and Llywelyn, sons of Cadwgan, and Rhys ab Owain; who were defeated a second time.†

[1] a second time BCD.
[2] all]—BCD.
[3] + ap Llywelyn ap Seisyllt BCD.
[4] + by the same mother D.
[5] gained possession of BCD.

[1076–1078]. A year after that, was the battle of Pwllgwdig,† in which Trahaearn, king of Gwynedd, obtained the victory;¹† and by the grace of God he avenged the blood of Bleddyn ap Cynfyn, his first-cousin, who was the most beloved and the most merciful of all kings and who wrought good to all and who did harm to no one. He was gentle towards his kinsmen and generous towards the poor and merciful towards pilgrims and orphans and widows. And he was a defence for the weak and the strength of the learned and the honour of the churches and the foundation and comfort of the lands† and generous towards all; terrible in war, beloved and meek in peace and a defence for all. And thereupon the whole war-band of Rhys fell, and he himself fled like a wounded frightened stag through the thorns and the briars before the hounds.

And at the close of that year Caradog ap Gruffudd† slew Rhys and Hywel, his brother. And Sulien resigned his bishopric, and Abraham assumed it.²

[1077–1079]. A year after that, Rhys ap Tewdwr began to rule.

[1078–1080]. A year after that, Menevia was pillaged.† And Abraham, bishop of Menevia, died.† And Sulien was induced against his will to assume the bishopric a second time.

[1079–1081]. A year after that was the battle of Mynydd Carn.³† And there Trahaearn ap Caradog† and Caradog⁴ and Gruffudd and Meilyr, sons of Rhiwallon, and Rhys ap Tewdwr were slain.† And after him came Gruffudd, grandson of Iago, together with Irish, to help him.† And Gwrgenau ap Seisyll was slain through treachery by the sons of Rhys Sais. And in that year William, king of England and Wales and much of France,⁵† came on the Menevia pilgrimage.⁶

[1081–1083]. One thousand and eighty-one was the year of Christ when the first *Decemnouenalis* was.†

[1083–1085]. Two years after that, Sulien a second time† resigned his bishopric, and Ewilfre† assumed it.

---
¹ + over Rhys ab Owain BCD.
² + Here the Lord Rhys ap Tewdwr the Great ab Einion ab Owain ap Hywel Dda ap Cadell began to rule Deheubarth D.
³ Carno BCD.
⁴ + and Gruffudd ap Cynan (+ ap Iago D) prevailed BCD.
⁵ and many Frenchmen BCD.
⁶ + The year of Christ was 1080 when the building of Cardiff, a town in Glamorganshire, was commenced D.

[1084–1086]. A year after that, died Toirrdelbhach, king of the Scots or the Irish.†

[1085–1087]. A year[1] after that, William the Bastard, prince of the Normans and king of the Saxons and the Britons[2] and the Scots, died after exceeding great glory in this changeable world and after being favoured with fame and innumerable victories and riches.[3] And after him succeeded[4] William,[5] his son.

[1086–1088]. A year after that,[6] Rhys ap Tewdwr was expelled from his kingdom by Madog and Cadwgan and Rhiryd, sons of Bleddyn. And he fled to Ireland. And after he had gathered a fleet there, he returned and gave battle at Llech-y-crau.[7]† And there the two[8] sons of Bleddyn,[9] Madog and Rhiryd, were slain. And then[10] Rhys ap Tewdwr gave treasure to the pirates—Scots and Irish—who had come to his aid.

[1087–1089]. A year after that, the shrine of David was taken by stealth from the church; and close to the city it was completely despoiled. And in that year there was a great earthquake throughout the whole island.†

[1089–1091]. Two years[11] after that,† Sulien, bishop of Menevia, the most learned and most pious of the bishops of the Britons, and the most praiseworthy for the instruction of his disciples and his parishes, died in the eightieth year of his age and the nineteenth year of his episcopate† on the eve of the Calends of January.

And then Menevia was destroyed by the men of the Isles.[12] And Cedifor ap Gollwyn died. And his sons, Llywelyn and his brothers, called in Gruffudd ap Maredudd, whom Rhys ap Tewdwr encountered in the battle near Llandudoch;† and he drove him to flight and pursued him and captured him, and at last he slew him.[13]

---

[1] Three years BCD.
[2] Welsh C.
[3] and riches]—BCD.
[4] came BCD.
[5] + the Red CD.
[6] And in that year D.
[7] Llechryd y Crau BC, Llechyd D.
[8] two]—BC.
[9] + ap Cynfyn D.
[10] there BCD.
[11] A year BCD.
[12] the men of the Isles destroyed Menevia BCD.
[13] + A year after that (+ that is 1090 D) William the Red, king of England, destroyed fifty-two mother-churches to make the new forest near Southampton BCD. *In D there is a marginal entry*: aditio.

[1091–1093]. One thousand and ninety-one was the year of Christ, when Rhys ap Tewdwr, king of the South, was slain by Frenchmen who were inhabiting Brycheiniog—with whom fell the kingdom of the Britons. And after his death Cadwgan ap Bleddyn plundered Dyfed on the Calends of May.† And within two months of that,† the French overran Dyfed and Ceredigion— what was not in their power before that†—and made castles in them and fortified them. And then the French seized all the lands of the Britons. And Maelcoluim, son of Donnchadh, king of the Picts and the Scots, and Edward, his son, were slain by the French.[1] Queen Margaret, wife of Maelcoluim,[2] when she heard that her husband and her son had been slain, placing her trust in God, prayed that she might not live longer than that in this world. And God listened to her prayer and then[3] by the seventh day she died.†

[1092–1094]. A year after that, king William,[4] son of William the Elder, who first[5] defeated the Saxons in glorious war,† went to Normandy to defend the kingdom of Robert, his brother, who had gone to Jerusalem to fight against Saracens and to defend Christendom. And while he stayed there, the Britons, being unable to bear the tyranny and injustice[6] of the French, threw off the rule of[7] the French, and they destroyed their castles in Gwynedd† and inflicted slaughters upon them. And the French brought a host to Gwynedd; and against them came Cadwgan ap Bleddyn, and he defeated them and drove them[8] to flight, inflicting great slaughter upon them. And that battle was in Coedysbys.† And at the close of that year the castles of Ceredigion and Dyfed were all taken except two castles, Pembroke and Rhyd-y-gors;† and they were all razed to the ground and the spoils carried off by them, and Ceredigion and Dyfed were ravaged.

[1093–1095]. A year after that, the French ravaged[9] Gower and Cydweli and Ystrad Tywi, and they remained waste. And in the middle of autumn William, king of England, moved a host against the Britons, but they sought a defence[10] in their woods

---

[1] the French slew BCD.
[2] Margaret, queen of the Picts BC, Margaret, queen of the Picts and the Scots D.
[3] then]—BCD.
[4] king William] William the Red BCD.
[5] —BCD.
[6] battle engagements BD.
[7] the rule of]—BCD.
[8] *Emend* gyrrawnt MS. *to* gyrraw[d wy]nt.
[9] + the land of BCD.
[10] + together BC.

and their¹ wilderness, and he returned home empty-handed and having gained naught.

[1094–1096]. A year after that, died William fitz Baldwin, who had established the castle of Rhyd-y-gors by command of the king of England. And after his death the garrison left the castle² empty.† And then Brycheiniog and Gwent and Gwynllŵg did homage to³† the French, and the French moved a host to Gwent and after they had gained naught they returned home empty-handed. And the Britons slew them in the place called Celli Tarfawg.† And thereupon the French led frequent raids into Brycheiniog and thought to destroy⁴ the land completely. And when they had failed to have their will in aught, they returned home; and then they were slain by the sons of Idnerth ap Cadwgan, Gruffudd and Ifor,⁵ in the place called Aber-llech. The castles, however,⁶ still remained intact, with their garrisons in them.†

In that year Uchdryd ab Edwin and Hywel ap Goronwy and many other leaders and the war-band of Cadwgan ap Bleddyn went to the castle of Pembroke and despoiled it completely, and ravaged the land; and they returned home with vast spoil.

[1095–1097]. A year after that, Gerald the officer, to whom had been given the keepership of the castle⁷ of Pembroke, ravaged all the bounds of Menevia. And William, king of England, a second time moved a great host and folk without number against the Britons. And the Britons, placing their trust, not in themselves, but in the Lord of Heaven, Creator of created things, with fastings and prayers and alms and severe penances, avoided the assault of the French: for the French, not daring to invade the woods or the wilderness against the Britons, but foraging about⁸ and encompassing the open fields, returned home dejected and empty-handed. And so the Britons defended their land fearlessly.

[1096–1098]. A year after that, the French a third time moved hosts against the men of Gwynedd, with two earls as their leaders, namely, Hugh, earl of Shrewsbury, and another⁹ [*sc.* Hugh]† along with him. And they made for the island of

---

¹ the BCD.
² after ... castle] the castles were left BCD.
³ opposed D.
⁴ with the intention of destroying BCD.
⁵ they were slain ... Ifor] the sons of Idnerth ap Cadwgan, Gruffudd and (ap BC) Ifor, slew them BCD.
⁶ —BCD.
⁷ castles D.
⁸ watching BCD.
⁹ Hugh the Fat, earl of Chester D.

Anglesey. And the men of Gwynedd, as was their custom, retreated to the strongest and wildest places[1] they had. And after counsel they occupied Anglesey. And they called in pirate ships from Ireland to defend them. But the latter for rewards brought the French into the island.† Cadwgan ap Bleddyn and Gruffudd ap Cynan, for fear of treachery by their own men, left the island and fled to Ireland. And after the French had come into the island, they slew many of the island. And as they stayed there,[2] Magnus,† king of Germany, approached the island of Anglesey, and a fleet with him, thinking to conquer[3] all the island of Britain. And after king Magnus had heard that the French were minded to ravage the whole land and to destroy it utterly, he hastened to attack them. And as they were shooting at one another, the one side from the sea and the other from the land, then† earl Hugh wounded king Magnus in his face.† And then by a sudden resolve Magnus withdrew from the bounds of the land; and the French took all who were in the island, both great and small, to the Saxons.† And after that, since the men of Gwynedd could not suffer the laws and injustice of the French, they rose up a second time in opposition to them, with Owain ab Edwin, who had before that brought the French to Anglesey, as their leader.

[1097–1099]. A year after that, Cadwgan ap Bleddyn and Gruffudd ap Cynan returned from Ireland. And, after making peace with the French, they received a portion of the land and the kingdom. Cadwgan ap Bleddyn received a portion of[4]† Powys and Ceredigion, and Gruffudd ap Cynan received Anglesey.† Llywelyn ap Cadwgan was slain by the men of Brycheiniog.[5] Hywel ab Ithel went to Ireland.

In that year died Rhygyfarch the Wise, son of bishop Sulien, greatly lamented by all, for he was[6] the most learned of all the race of the Britons and there had not been before him his equal nor after him his like nor in his lifetime his peer,[7] without his having received instruction from anyone save from his own father. And he died in the forty-third year of his age.

[1098–1100]. A year after that, died William, king of England, who was king after the other William,[8] his father. And this is

[1] corners BCD.
[2] in Ireland, and then BCD.
[3] subdue BCD.
[4] a portion of] *marginal addition* MS.,—BCD.
[5] the men of Brycheiniog slew BCD.
[6] for he was]—BCD.
[7] there had not been . . . peer] there was not his like before or after BCD.
[8] after William the Bastard BCD.

how he died: as he was going a-hunting with knights of his, he[1] and Henry, his youngest brother,[2] and a knight of his (Walter Tyrrell was his name)† was aiming with an arrow at[3] a stag, he unintentionally hit the king with the arrow, so that he died. And Henry entrusted his brother to those[4] who were there[5] and commanded that a royal funeral service be done for him. And he himself went to Winchester, where the king's treasure was kept; and he seized it for himself and summoned to him all his brother's household. And thereupon he gained possession of London, the city that is head of the whole kingdom of England. And then all the French and the Saxons gathered[6] to him; and after he had been crowned king in England, he took[7] the daughter of Maelcoluim, king of the Picts, by queen Margaret, for his wedded wife, and her name was Matilda. For William, his brother, had died without an heir, because he had always used concubines.

And then Robert, his eldest brother, returned from Jerusalem after obtaining the victory. And Thomas, the archbishop, died at York. And after him came Gerard, bishop of Hereford; for king Henry raised him to a rank higher than that which had been his. And then Anselm was a second time made archbishop in Canterbury by king Henry. And that Anselm had before that left his archbishopric because of king William's oppression, for he (*sc.* the king) would do nothing just nor anything that appertained to the commandments of God.

[1099–1101]. A year after that, died Hugh the Fat, earl of Chester. And there succeeded[8] after him a son of his, young in age:[9] his name was Roger.† And the king because of remembrance and love of his father set him in his father's place. In that year died Goronwy ap Cadwgan and Gwyn† ap Gruffudd.

[1100–1102]. One thousand and one hundred was the year of Christ when there was treachery between Henry, king of England, and Robert, earl of Shrewsbury, who was called de Bellême, and Arnulf, his brother, who had come to Dyfed

---

[1] of his, he]—BCD.
[2] + along with him BCD.
[3] and a knight . . . at] and one of his knights was trying to shoot BCD, + and the name of the knight who slew him was Sir Walter Tyrrell D.
[4] the men BCD.
[5] + along with him BCD.
[6] turned BCD.
[7] took . . . for his wedded wife] married BCD.
[8] came BCD.
[9] a young son whom he had BCD.

and had established the castle¹ of Pembroke. And when the king heard that they were working treachery against him, he summoned them to find out the truth concerning that. But they sought pretexts² to make an excuse, for they could not trust themselves to the king.³ And the king rejected their excuses after learning of their treachery. And when they knew that the king had learned of their treachery, and they dared not show themselves to him,⁴ they occupied their castles and fortified them, and summoned help to them from all sides and summoned to them the Britons who were under them, together with their leaders, namely, the sons of Bleddyn ap Cynfyn, Cadwgan, Iorwerth and Maredudd. And they received them with honour, and gave them gifts and promised them many things and gladdened the land with liberty. And a second time† they fortified their castles and encompassed them with ditches and strong walls and prepared provision and gathered together knights and gave them gifts. Robert occupied four castles, namely, Arundel and Blyth† and Bridgenorth—and it was against Bridgenorth that the whole treachery had been aimed, for he had built that without the king's permission—and Shrewsbury. Arnulf occupied Pembroke alone. And immediately after that they assembled hosts and summoned the Britons along with them and carried off spoils and returned home happy.

And whilst they were doing that, Arnulf thought to make peace with the Irish and to seek aid from them. And he sent messengers, that is, Gerald his officer, and many others, to Ireland and he asked for the daughter of king Muircertach† for his wife. And that he obtained easily. The messengers came back⁵ joyful. King Muircertach sent his daughter and many armed ships along with her to the aid of his son-in-law.⁶ And for that reason the earls⁷ waxed proud against the king, without wishing for peace or agreement from him.

And king Henry gradually gathered a host. And first he took the castle of Arundel. And thereupon through agreement and promises he gained possession of⁸ Blyth.† And at last he came towards the castle of Bridgenorth, and with him a great host. And after surveying the castle from a distance he took

---

¹ castles BCD.
² —BCD.
³ to the king]—BCD.
⁴ And after . . . him] and not daring (able D) to trust the king BCD.
⁵ + home D.
⁶ to his aid BCD.
⁷ earl BCD.
⁸ + the castle of BCD.

counsel as to how he might capture the earl or subdue him or drive him out of the whole[1] kingdom. And he resolved in council to send messengers to the Britons; and he summoned to him in particular Iorwerth ap Bleddyn, and he promised him more than he would obtain from the earl. And he gave to Iorwerth freely, without rent or payment, that portion of Wales which was in the hands of those earls,[2] for his lifetime so long as the king lived; that was Powys and Ceredigion and half of Dyfed—the other portion was in the hands of fitz Baldwin—and Ystrad Tywi† and Cydweli and Gower.

And when Iorwerth ap Bleddyn was going towards the king's castle, he sent his war-band to plunder the territory of earl Robert. And the war-band, cruelly and hostilely executing their lord's behest, gathered vast plunder and ravaged the land and pillaged it: for the earl had before that ordered his men to take their flocks and herds and all their chattels into the land of the Britons, for he placed trust in them, not supposing that he would meet with opposition from them, not remembering the wrongs that the Britons had formerly suffered at the hands of Roger, his father, and Hugh,[3] his brother, and at the hands of their men, which were held in remembrance by the Britons.

Cadwgan, however,[4] and Maredudd, sons of Bleddyn, were with the earl, knowing naught of that. And when the earl heard that, he despaired; and not trusting the help that was with him, because Iorwerth and his men had deserted him—for Iorwerth was foremost of the Britons and the most powerful— he sought a truce of the king to make peace with him or to leave the kingdom altogether.

Whilst they were about those things, Arnulf and his men had gone to meet his wedded wife and the fleet that had come to his aid. In the meantime, Magnus, king of Germany, and with him a fleet, came a second time to Anglesey; and after felling for himself some trees for timber† he returned to Man. And there he built three castles and a second time filled Man, which he had previously left desolate, with his men. And he asked for the daughter of Muircertach,† king of Ireland, as wife for his son. And he obtained her easily and gladly. And he set him up as king over that island. And there he stayed that winter. And when earl Robert heard that, he sent messengers to him to

---

[1] —BCD.
[2] the earl, and that BCD.
[3] —BCD.
[4] —BCD.

beg help for himself; but he obtained none from him.¹ And when the earl saw that he was besieged on all sides, he asked permission of the king to leave the kingdom; and the king granted it to him. And then he left all that was his and sailed to Normandy. And then the king² sent to Arnulf and commanded him to go after his brother and to leave the kingdom or else to come at the king's will with his head in his lap. And when Arnulf heard that, he preferred to go after his brother than to submit to [the king's]³ will, and he surrendered his castle to the king; and the king sent a garrison to keep it.

And after that, Iorwerth ap Bleddyn made peace with his brothers and he shared the territory with them. And after a short while he seized Maredudd, his brother, and imprisoned him in the king's prison.⁴ And he made peace with Cadwgan, his brother, and gave him Ceredigion and a portion of Powys. And thereupon Iorwerth went to the king, thinking that he would have his promises from the king. But the king did not keep faith with him, but took from him Dyfed and the castle⁵† and gave them to a certain⁶ knight called Saer. And Ystrad Tywi and Cydweli and Gower he gave to Hywel ap Goronwy. In that year Goronwy ap Rhys was seized and he⁷ died in his prison.

[1101–1103]. A year after that, Magnus, king of Germany, came from Man, and a few ships with him, and he hoisted sails against the men of Scotland† and ravaged their bounds. And the Scots,† as is the custom of the Scots or the French,† like ants rising from their caves when there is a shower of warm⁸ rain,† came in bands after their spoils. And when they saw the king with but a small force with him, they fell upon him. And as the custom of the men of Denmark is, through proud desire to obtain victory, without regard for the great numbers of his⁹ enemies and the smallness of his own force, he arrayed his army. And after valiant fighting on both sides and after many of both parties had been slain, then¹⁰ at last because of pressure from the great numbers of the other host on all sides,¹¹ king Magnus was slain.

¹ from him]—BCD.
² he BC.
³ BCD,—MS.
⁴ in the king's prison] *marginal entry* MS.,—BCD.
⁵ and the castle]—BCD.
⁶ —BCD.
⁷ was seized and he]—BCD.
⁸ —BCD.
⁹ their BCD.
¹⁰ —BCD.
¹¹ from all lands BCD.

And then king Henry summoned Iorwerth ap Bleddyn by deceitful means to Shrewsbury to be judged before the king's council. And when he came thither, the whole proceeding turned against him. And after arguing[1] with him for the whole of that day they adjudged him, according to their judgment, guilty. And in the end, not by law but through might and power and violation of the law, they placed him in the king's prison. And then there was great lamentation amongst all the Britons for their hope and strength and safety and splendour and comfort.

[1102–1105]. A year after that,† Owain ab Edwin died after a long illness. And Richard fitz Baldwin repaired the castle of Rhyd-y-gors. And Hywel ap Goronwy, to whom king Henry had entrusted the keeping of Ystrad Tywi and Rhyd-y-gors and their bounds, after being expelled gathered spoils; and he burned the houses and the crops and ravaged the greater part of the whole land; and he slew many of the French as they were returning home, and he encompassed the land on all sides and occupied it except for the castles and their garrisons.

In the meantime king Henry ejected Saer from Pembroke, and he entrusted the castle and its bounds to Gerald: he had been officer to Arnulf.

[1103–1106]. A year after that,† Hywel ap Goronwy was slain through the treachery of the French who were keeping Rhyd-y-gors. And it was Gwgan ap Meurig, the man who had nurtured a son of Hywel's, and the man in whom Hywel placed greater trust than in anyone, who deceived him. For he invited[2] him to his house and thereupon sent to the French in the castle and informed them of the night and what place.† And they came by night about cock-crow and surrounded the hamlet and the house and raised a shout around the house. At that shout Hywel vigorously arose from his slumber[3] and sought his arms and called upon his comrades and sought his sword, which he had placed[4] above his head, and his spear, which he had placed below his feet. But Gwgan had removed them while he was asleep. And when Hywel sought his comrades and thought that they were ready to fight along with him, they had fled at the first shout. And then he too fled. And Gwgan pursued him and did not give him up until he caught him, as he had promised

---
[1] contending BCD.
[2] had invited BCD.
[3] from his slumber] himself BCD.
[4] which ... placed]—BCD.

the French.† And after Gwgan's comrades had come to him, they strangled him. And after he had been strangled[1] until he was well-nigh dead, they brought him to the French. And the French cut off his head and took it to the castle.

In that year there appeared a[2] star wonderful to behold, having a thick beam of light turned back behind like a pillar, and the beam long and having great lustre and signifying what came to pass thereafter: for Henry, emperor of Rome, after many[3] victories and a pious life, then died. And his son obtained the Empire and became emperor.

And then Henry, king of England, sent knights to subdue Normandy. And earl Robert, his[4] brother,† and Robert de Bellême and William de Bretagne, his uncle,† met them and drove them to flight. And then they sent to the king to seek aid from him. And then the king himself, and with him a mighty host of knights and great numbers of foot-soldiers,[5] went across the sea. And the earl and his host vigorously encountered him, but because of the great numbers of the king's host he was forced to flee. And the king pursued him and captured him together with William, his uncle,† and sent them to prison in England. And then he gained possession of all Normandy.

And at the close of that year Meurig and Griffri, sons of Trahaearn ap Caradog, were slain by† Owain ap Cadwgan.

[1104–1107]. A year after that, Maredudd ap Bleddyn escaped from prison and regained possession of his land. And Edgar,† son of Maelcoluim, died. And Alexander, his brother, ruled in his place.

[1105–1108]. A year after that, a folk of strange origin and customs, with nothing known of where they had been concealed in the island for many years before that, were sent by king Henry to Dyfed. And they occupied the whole cantref called Rhos, near the estuary of the river called Cleddyf, and drove away all the inhabitants[6] from the land. And that folk had come from Flanders, the land that lies near the Sea of Britain, because the sea had overwhelmed the land and its bounds and had thrown sand all over the ground, so that the whole land was unfruitful. And at last, since there was no place for them[7] to live either on

[1] And . . . strangled]—BCD.
[2] + great BCD.
[3] countless D.
[4] and his BCD.
[5] men BCD.
[6] garrisons BCD.
[7] for them]—BCD.

the coast, because of the sea, or in the hinterland, because of the great numbers of people living in it,[1] and because they could not remain all together—therefore that folk came to beg of king Henry a place wherein to live and to dwell. And he sent them to Rhos. And there they still remain, the inhabitants having lost their land.

In the meantime Gerald, the officer of Pembroke castle, built the castle in the place called Cenarth Bychan.† And he fortified it with ditches and walls and thought to place there for safe keeping his wife and sons and his wealth and all his valuables.

[1106–1109]. A year after that, Cadwgan ap Bleddyn prepared a royal feast for the leading men of his land. And he invited Owain, his son, from Powys to the feast. And he held that feast at Christmas in honour of Jesus Christ. And when the feast was ended, Owain heard that Nest, daughter of the lord Rhys ap Tewdwr, wife of Gerald the officer, was in the said castle. And when he heard, he went, and with him a small force, to visit her as though she were a kinswoman—and so she was, for Cadwgan ap Bleddyn and Gwladus, daughter of Rhiwallon, who was mother to Nest, were first cousins: for Bleddyn and Rhiwallon were brothers, sons of Cynfyn by Angharad, daughter of king Maredudd. And after that, at the instigation of the Devil, he was moved by passion and love for the woman, and with a small company with him—about fourteen men—he made for the castle by night. And unknown to the watchers, he came into the castle over the wall and the ditch,† and surrounded the building where Gerald and Nest, his wife, were sleeping. And he raised a shout around the building and set fire to the buildings and kindled them. And Gerald awoke from his slumber and was afraid when he heard the shout, and knew not what he should do. And his wife said to him, 'Go not to the door, for there are thine enemies around it, but come with me.' And thus he did. And she led him to the privies which adjoined the building. And through the pit of the privies he escaped. And when Nest knew for certain that he had escaped, she shouted from within and said, 'Why do you shout in vain? He whom you were seeking has escaped.' And then they came inside and searched for him everywhere. And when they did not find him, they seized Nest and her two sons and the third son, whom Gerald had by a concubine, and a daughter. And they utterly pillaged the castle and burned it. And he violated Nest and lay with her and then returned home.

[1] living in it]—BCD.

Cadwgan, his father, was not in the place, for he had gone to Powys to pacify some men who were opposed to Owain, his son, and had deserted him.

And when Cadwgan heard that story, he was grieved and was frightened for two reasons: because of the violation of the lady, and because of fear of king Henry on account of the injury to his officer. And when he returned, he sought in every way to restore the woman and the spoil, but he was not allowed. And Owain, because the woman was for ever saying unto him, 'If thou wilt have me true and keep me for thyself, release my sons to their father,'—and in his infatuation for the woman, he released the two sons and the daughter.

And when Richard, bishop of London, who was then officer to the king at Shrewsbury, heard that, he thought to avenge upon Owain the injury done to Gerald. And he summoned to him the two sons of Rhiryd ap Bleddyn, namely, Madog and Ithel, and spoke to them thus, 'Do you wish to please king Henry and to win friendship from him for ever? And he will honour and exalt you over and above any of your fellow landholders and he will make all your kinsmen envious of you.' 'We do,' said they. 'Go then,' said he, 'and seek Owain ap Cadwgan and seize him, if you can. But if you can not, expel him and his father from the territory, for he has done wrong against the king, and he has done injury and shame to the lord king and great loss to Gerald his officer in respect of his wife and his sons and his castle and his spoils. And I will give you the truest and most faithful companions, namely, Llywarch ap Trahaearn, whose brothers Owain slew,† and Uchdryd ab Edwin.' And they believed that and gathered hosts and came together and made for his land. And Uchdryd sent a force into the land and he ordered that everyone who fled to him should receive protection. And many went to him. And some went to Arwystli, others to Maelienydd, others to Ystrad Tywi. And the greater part of them went to Dyfed, where Gerald was supreme. And as he was minded to put them to death, it happened that on that day Walter, chief justice of Gloucester, the man to whom the king had entrusted the government of the kingdom of England, had come to Carmarthen. And he defended them from being put to death. Those of them who went to Arwystli, the men of Maelienydd met them, and they were destroyed. Those of them who went to Uchdryd escaped unharmed. Those of them who went to Ystrad Tywi, Maredudd ap Rhydderch received them kindly. Cadwgan and

Owain made for a ship that was at Aberdyfi, which had come before that from Ireland with merchandise in it.

Madog and Ithel, his brother, and Llywarch came to meet Uchdryd, and they encamped at the ford called the ford of 'Corruonet.'† And at last Uchdryd came. And as he was coming thither, they desired to travel by night until day arose, to ravage the land. And he answered, 'If it please you, there is no need for that,' said he. 'But Cadwgan and Owain, his son, ought not to be scorned, for they are praiseworthy men of note; and it may be that they shall have much help that they have not at this moment. And therefore it is not proper for us to go so unawares as that, but rather to array our host and go in broad daylight.' And by those words they were pacified a little, and thereby the inhabitants[1] were able to escape. On the following day they came into the land. And after seeing it deserted, they reproached themselves and accused Uchdryd and said that those were the wiles of Uchdryd and[2] that it was not proper for anyone to associate with him. And they foraged about[3] and obtained nothing save Cadwgan's stud. And after obtaining it, they burned the houses and the barns and the crops and returned again to the castles.[4]† And they destroyed some of those who had fled for sanctuary to Llanbadarn, others they did not kill.

And then they heard[5] that some had stayed in the place where there is a privilege and[6] a sanctuary of David the bishop and which is called Llanddewifrefi, along with the priests of the church. And they sent their accursed, evil-spirited company[7] thither to violate the sanctuary of the church and to kill the inhabitants.[8] And after that they returned after ravaging and plundering the whole land except the precincts of the saints themselves—David and Padarn.† And after that, Owain, and a few comrades who had been burning the castle along with him, sailed to Ireland. And king Muircertach, the chief of the Irish, received him honourably, for it was with him that he had been before that, when the war in Anglesey had been waged by the two earls, having been sent by his brother with gifts for the king.

Cadwgan hid himself in the land of Powys. And he sent messengers to Richard, the king's officer, and he obtained from him a truce until he should make peace with the king on whatever

---

[1] garrison BCD.
[2] + then they said CD.
[3] kept watch BC.
[4] castle BCD.
[5] found BCD.
[6] a privilege and]—BCD.
[7] those accursed men BCD.
[8] and . . . inhabitants]—BCD.

terms he could. And the king thereupon received him and left him in a township which he had had from his wife, who was a Frenchwoman, daughter of Picot of Sai.

In the meantime, Madog and Ithel, sons of Rhiryd, seized Cadwgan's and his son Owain's portion of Powys and they governed it infamously and unsuccessfully: for there was no peace between themselves.

And when all that was over, Cadwgan redeemed his territory in Ceredigion from the king, through great entreaties, for a hundred pounds. And all who had been scattered everywhere gathered together there again; for before that it was the king's command that no one was to dwell in Ceredigion, neither natives[1] nor strangers, and that no one was to maintain them. And it was on this condition that the king gave his land to Cadwgan: that there was to be no comradeship at all between him and Owain, his son, and that he was not to allow him to come to land, and that he was not to help him with any kind of counsel or support. And after that, some of those who had gone to Ireland along with Owain returned, and they lurked concealed with kinsmen of theirs without doing anything openly.[2] And after that, Owain returned, but he made his way, not to Ceredigion, but to Powys. And he sought to send messengers to the king. But there was no one who would dare to go on the errand.

And at that time there was discord between Madog and the French[3] because of certain[4] Saxons who had committed robberies[5] in their lands. And after committing wrongs there, they had fled to Madog. And Richard the officer had sent to demand them from Madog for their having done wrong to the king. But he refused him and did not give them to him; and thereby[6] he too did wrong. And when he knew not what to do, he sought[7] friendship of Owain and he obtained it. And then they, who before that were enemies, were reconciled. And each of them swore to the other with a great oath that neither of them would make peace with the king without the other, and that neither of them would commit treachery or betrayal against the other. And then they journeyed together wheresoever fate led them, whether upwards or downwards. And they burned the homestead of a certain leading man. And

[1] garrisons BCD.
[2] anything openly] any harm BCD.
[3] Saxons BCD.
[4] of certain] some of the CD.
[5] robbery BCD.
[6] then BD, there C.
[7] compelled BCD.

whatever they could plunder, that they did, whether horses or raiment or aught else.

[1107–1110]. A year after that, king Henry[1] remembered that Iorwerth ap Bleddyn was in prison. And he sent messengers to him to ask him what he would give for being released from prison. And because of the great weariness and length of imprisonment he promised more than he could come by, and said, 'Whatsoever he wishes I shall give him.' And he demanded as hostages Iorwerth and Ithel, sons of Rhiryd, his brother,† and[2] three hundred pounds of silver, which he was to pay in whatsoever form he could,[3] in horses, in oxen, in other things. And then Henry, son of Cadwgan by the Frenchwoman, his mother, was given as hostage, and a hundred marks were paid for him. And his territory was given to Iorwerth, and he paid much, and Cadwgan then released him.†

And in the meantime Owain and Madog were committing much mischief on the lands[4] of the French and the Saxons.[5] And whatever they carried off, either by violence or by stealth, they carried it into Iorwerth's territory. And there they were staying. And then Iorwerth sent messengers to them, at first kindly, and he said thus: 'God has placed us in the midst and in the hands of our enemies and has brought us so low that we cannot do aught according to our will. And frequently it happens to us Britons that no one will associate with us in food or drink or counsel or help, but that we are sought and hunted from place to place and are at last placed in the hands of the king to be imprisoned or put to death or to do whatever is willed with us. And, above all, we have been commanded[6] not to enter into agreement with anyone,[7] because of distrust in us: for none could believe that the father and uncle would not desire benefit and good for their sons and nephews. And, therefore, if we were to enter into agreement with you in a small matter we would be accused of violating the king's command, and our territory would be taken from us, and we ourselves would be imprisoned or put to death.[8] Therefore, as friend I beseech you, and as lord I command you, and as kinsman I pray you, that you come not henceforth into my territory nor into

---

[1] king Henry] the king BCD.

[2] as hostages . . . and] hostages of Iorwerth, and then the sons of Rhiryd (+ ap Bleddyn D), his brother, went for BCD.

[3] which . . . could] or their value, whatever it was BCD.

[4] to the land BCD.

[5] and the Saxons]—CD.

[6] he has commanded us BCD.

[7] you BCD.

[8] be at last imprisoned BCD.

Cadwgan's territory, any more than into other land that lies around it. For there is greater enmity towards us than towards others, and it is easier to find a charge[1] against us.' But they scorned that command, and thenceforth they frequented the territory even more than before, and they scarcely shunned their own presence.†

And then Iorwerth sought to pursue them and he assembled many men and hunted them from place to place. And they stole away a few at a time and got together and made for Uchdryd's territory as far as Meirionnydd. And when the sons of Uchdryd and their war-band, whom Uchdryd had left defending their land, heard that, they sent to Meirionnydd to bid everyone assemble together to drive them out of their[2] land. For they had come first of all to Cyfeiliog, where the sons of Uchdryd were, but they failed to drive them out. And the men of Meirionnydd gathered to the sons of Uchdryd. And as Owain and Madog were quartered in Cyfeiliog, they thought to go on the following day to be quartered in[3] Meirionnydd, without desiring to do mischief there, but only to be quartered. And when they were on their way, lo, the men of Meirionnydd in a well-ordered troop[4] meeting them in the roughest place and raising a shout and attacking them. They, not suspecting that, at first fled[5]—until Owain came. And when the men of Meirionnydd saw Owain ready to fight and coming on bravely, they took to flight. And the others pursued them and ravaged the land, burning the houses and the crops and killing the stock—as much as they found, but carrying nothing off thence.

And thereupon Madog returned to Powys and Owain made his way to Ceredigion, where his father was ruling. And he stayed there, he and his comrades. And his comrades went on forays to Dyfed and they plundered the land and seized the people and carried them off with them bound to the ships which Owain had brought with him from Ireland. And still they stayed in the land. On another occasion they summoned hotheads from Ceredigion to add to the numbers along with them, and by night they came to a township of Dyfed and slew all that they found, and despoiled others and carried others off with them as prisoners to the ships, and thence sold them to their folk. And after burning the houses and killing the animals and carrying others off with them, they returned to

[1] calumny BCD.
[2] the BCD.
[3] to be quartered in] to BCD.
[4] in . . . troop]—BCD.
[5] at first fled] fled into the valley BCD.

Ceredigion, and they quartered and stayed there, coming and going without regard for Cadwgan's good or the king's interdiction.

Again, some of them kept watch on a road along which a certain bishop from Flanders† was coming; and his name was William Brabant.[1] And after encountering him they slew him. And at that time Iorwerth and Cadwgan had gone[2] to king Henry's court to seek a parley of the king. And whilst they were conversing peacefully with the king, lo, a brother of the slain man coming and informing the king that Owain ap Cadwgan's comrades had slain his brother. And when the king heard that, he said to Cadwgan, 'What sayest thou to this?' Cadwgan said,[3] 'I know not.'[4] And the king said to him, 'Since thou, Cadwgan, canst not keep thy land from thy son's[5] comrades, lest they do harm any more to my men, I shall give the land to such as will keep it. And I shall keep thee with me on this condition: that thou art not to set thy feet on thine own land any more. And I will provide for thee from my own until I shall have taken counsel what I should do concerning thee.' And the king gave him two shillings of silver daily for his expenses. And he placed neither shackle nor fetter upon him,[6] but allowed him to go freely wheresoever he desired, save to his own land.

And when Owain heard that his father had been dispossessed of[7] his territory, he went to Ireland, he and Madog ap Rhiryd. After that, king Henry sent a messenger to Gilbert fitz Richard, who was a mighty, powerful man and a friend of the king, and eminent in all his deeds. And he came forthwith to the king. And the king said to him: 'Thou wert always asking of me a portion of Wales. Now I will give thee the land of Cadwgan ap Bleddyn. Go and take possession of it.' And he accepted it gladly from the king. And he gathered a host and came to Ceredigion and took possession of it and made two castles in it, one opposite Llanbadarn-fawr, near the estuary of[8] the river called Ystwyth,[9] and another near the estuary of[10] the river called Teifi, in the place called Dingeraint, where earl Roger had before that made a castle.

[1] Brabant]—BCD.
[2] went BC.
[3] —BCD.
[4] + said he BCD.
[5] thy son Owain's BCD.
[6] And he allowed him not to be imprisoned BCD.
[7] forced from BCD.
[8] the estuary of]—BD.
[9] on the banks of the Ystwyth C.
[10] the estuary of]—BCD.

A short while after that, Madog ap Rhiryd returned from Ireland, unable to suffer the evil ways and evil customs of the Irish. And Owain stayed a short while after him. And Madog made for Powys, but Iorwerth, his uncle, with dread of the king and his law still upon him, did not receive him kindly, lest the king should hold him guilty if he agreed with him in aught, while he was in hiding from place to place without showing himself to Iorwerth. For [Iorwerth][1] had made a decree that no one should mention to him anything about him.

In the meantime Madog thought to work the betrayal of Iorwerth in whatsoever way he could. And he secretly joined in friendship with Llywarch ap Trahaearn. And so ended that year.

[1108–1111]. A year after that, after Madog had considered[2] the betrayal of Iorwerth, he sought a time and place.[3] And as Iorwerth was one day coming to Caereinion, Madog fell upon him by night under cover of darkness, and the comrades of Llywarch ap Trahaearn along with him to help him. And they raised a shout around the house where Iorwerth and his comrades were. And with the shout Iorwerth and his comrades awoke; and from within they defended the house. And Madog burned the house. And Iorwerth's comrades, when they perceived that, fled through the fire and left Iorwerth by himself in the house. And when Iorwerth perceived that,[4]—that the house was falling upon him—he sought to sally forth. And the men outside received him with spears. And thus slain and burnt he fell. And when king Henry heard that Iorwerth had been slain, he gave Powys to Cadwgan ap Bleddyn and he promised peace to Owain, his son, and he bade messengers be sent after him to Ireland.

And Madog, he and his comrades, after Iorwerth had been slain and they realised that they had done wrong against the king, they lurked in woods and thought to work the betrayal of Cadwgan as well. And Cadwgan, as his custom was, not wishing to hurt anyone, he and some of the elders of the land with him came to Welshpool[5] and there he thought to stay and to make a castle. And there, however, was an easy and nearest way for Madog. And Madog sent spies to ascertain where Cadwgan was staying. And those returned and said, 'He

[1] —MS., BCD.
[2] cunningly devised BCD.
[3] and place]—BCD.
[4] —BCD.
[5] Trallwng Llywelyn MS., Trallwng-ym-Mhowys (= 'the Pool in Powys') BCD.

whom we were seeking afar is close at hand.' And then Madog
and his comrades rushed thither forthwith. And Cadwgan, not
suspecting any harm, neither fleeing nor fighting, after all his
comrades had fled, was then slain.

And then Madog, after Cadwgan had been slain, sent
messengers to Richard, bishop of London, who at that time held
the king's place,† to beseech him to give him the land on account
of which that deed had been committed. And when the bishop
had considered the matter, he granted him a truce, not out of
love for him, but out of love for the land, for he knew that they
were all killing one another. And he gave him the portion that
had once belonged to him and to Ithel, his brother. And when
Maredudd ap Bleddyn heard that, he went to the king's court to
seek the land of Iorwerth ap Bleddyn. And the king gave it
him to keep until Owain ap Cadwgan should come. In the
meantime Owain came, and he went to the king and obtained his
land from the king by giving hostages and promising much
money. And Madog, too, promised hostages and much money.
And still he kept to his truce until the[1] year ended.

[1109–1112]. A year after that, earl Robert, who was called
Robert[2] fitz Roger de Bellême, was seized and king Henry
imprisoned him; and his son committed[3] an act disagreeable to
the king.

[1110–1113]. One thousand one hundred and ten was the year
of Christ when it chanced that, after Maredudd ap Bleddyn had
sent his war-band to make a raid upon the land of Llywarch ap
Trahaearn, a man met with them as they were journeying through
the land of Madog ap Rhiryd. And they seized him and asked
him where Madog was that night. And he began to deny that
he knew where he was, but at last under pressure he admitted
that he was close at hand. And they bound the man and sent
spies to search where he was,—whilst he was lurking close at
hand till it should be day.† And when it was[4] morning, they
suddenly fell upon him and after slaying many of his men they
seized him and took him to Maredudd. And Maredudd joyfully
received him and placed him in durance in shackles till Owain ap
Cadwgan should come. But Owain was not at home then.
And when Owain heard that, he came in haste and Maredudd
placed him in Owain's hands. And Owain took him joyfully

[1] that BCD.
[2] who . . . Robert]—BCD.
[3] king . . . committed] and he was imprisoned. King Henry imprisoned him for committing BCD.
[4] when it was] in the BCD.

and gouged his eyes out of his head and let him go thus. And the portion of Powys that was his, namely, Caereinion and a third of Deuddwr and Aberriw, they divided between them.

[1111–1114]. A year after that, Henry, king of England, moved a host against the men of Gwynedd and above all to Powys. For it was judged by him that Owain had done wrong; for Gilbert fitz Richard had accused him of thefts which Owain's men and comrades, so he stated, were committing in his land. And whatever others committed, it was alleged against them and it was them he accused before the king. And the king believed everything as though it were true against him. And in the meantime also the son of Hugh, earl of Chester, had accused Gruffudd ap Cynan and Goronwy ab Owain. And out of hate for them they set their minds upon exterminating all the Britons, so that the name of the Britons[1] should never more be called to mind from that time forth. And king Henry gathered a host over all the island of Britain, from the promontory of Penwith in Cornwall to the promontory of Blathaon in Scotland, and all those combined together against the men of Gwynedd and Powys. And when Maredudd ap Bleddyn heard that, he repaired to the king and entered into friendship with the king. And after Owain had learnt that, he gathered his men and all their chattels along with them and moved into the mountains of Eryri; for that was the wildest and safest place to which to retreat.

In the meantime, the king got together three hosts: one from Cornwall and Deheubarth and French and Saxons from Dyfed,[2] with Gilbert fitz Richard as their leader, and another host from the North and Scotland with two leaders over them, namely, Alexander, son of Maelcoluim, and the son of Hugh, earl of Chester, and the third host along with himself. And then the king, and two hosts with him, came to the place called Murcastell. And Alexander came, he and the earl, to the place called Pennant Bachwy.† And whilst that was being done, Owain sent messengers to Gruffudd and to Goronwy ab Owain to ask them to make a firm peace with their enemies† who were, so they said,[3] bent upon exterminating them out of the world or casting them into the sea, so that the name of the Britons should not be remembered. And they made a common agreement

---

[1] the name . . . Britons] their name BCD.
[2] got together . . . Dyfed] placed a host of French and English, and Cornwall and Deheubarth and Dyfed BCD.
[3] so they said]—BCD.

that not one of them should come to terms or make peace without his fellow.

And after that, the son of Maelcoluim and the other earl sent messengers to Gruffudd ap Cynan to ask him to come to the king's peace; and by promising much to him he was deceived into agreeing with them. And the king sent to Owain to ask him to come to his peace and to leave those from whom he would not receive any constant support at all.[1] But Owain did not agree† to that.[2] And thereupon, lo, a certain one coming to Owain and saying to him, 'Be careful and see that thou[3] act wisely. Gruffudd ap Cynan and Goronwy ab Owain† have made their peace with the son of Maelcoluim and with the other earl, and they have promised them peace from the king and their land free, without tribute and without castles,[4] so long as the king might live.' But still Owain did not agree. And after that, the king sent other messengers to Owain; and along with those he sent to him Maredudd ap Bleddyn, his uncle, to promise him much good. And when Maredudd saw Owain, he said to him, 'See that thou art not late in coming to the king's peace, for fear lest others should forestall thee in obtaining the king's friendship before thee.' And he believed, and went to the king. And the king joyfully received him, and a large host along with him, and did him honour and praised him. And the king said to him, 'Since thou hast come to me of thy free will and since thou didst believe the words of my messengers, I will exalt thee and raise thee up higher than anyone of thy kin, and I will reward thee for it with worthy gifts. And I will give thee thy land free, so that all thy kin shall feel envy towards thee.' And when Gruffudd heard that Owain had made peace with the king, he too sent to the king to seek peace of him. And the king took him into his peace upon his paying him a large tribute. And after the king had returned to England, he said[5] to Owain, 'Come with me and I will reward thee as may be fitting. And this I will tell thee: I am going to Normandy, and if thou wilt come with me, I will fulfil to thee everything that I have promised thee. And I will make thee a knight.' And he went with him and went across the sea with him. And the king fulfilled to him everything that he had promised him.

[1112-1115]. A year after that, king Henry returned from Normandy, and Owain ap Cadwgan along with him. And

---

[1] and to leave . . . all] promising that he would not render help to the others BCD.
[2] with the king but sent to ask for peace unconditionally BCD.
[3] see that thou]—BCD.
[4] tax BCD.
[5] *Emend* dyweduc MS. *to* dywedut.

Geoffrey,[1]† bishop of Menevia, died. And after him there succeeded one from Normandy,[2]—his name was Bernard†—whom king Henry made bishop in Menevia in contempt of the clerics of the Britons.

In the meantime there came a certain[3] young man, who was a son of the king of the South, to wit, the son of Rhys ap Tewdwr, whom some of his kinsmen had taken when a boy to Ireland; and there he stayed until he was a grown man. And at last, tired of exile, he came to his own land, to Dyfed; and his name was Gruffudd ap Rhys. And he stayed for about two years with his kinsmen,[4] a part thereof with Gerald, the officer of Pembroke castle, as was said before this above,—for the latter's wife was Nest, daughter of Rhys, a sister to the said young man called[5] Gruffudd—at other times with friends of his, sometimes in hiding, sometimes openly proclaimed. And at last he was accused before the king, and it was said that everyone's mind was upon him, to raise him to be a lord and to leave the overlordship of the king.

And when he[6] heard that for certain, he thought to go to Gruffudd ap Cynan to seek to defend his life[7] along with him. And after messengers had been sent to him, Gruffudd promised him that he would receive him gladly if he would come to him. And when Gruffudd ap Rhys and Hywel, his brother, heard that, they went—and many others along with them—to Gruffudd ap Cynan. And at last[8]† Gruffudd received them kindly and gladly.†

And the king, as it was the custom of the French to deceive men with promises, promised much good to Gruffudd ap Cynan for obtaining Gruffudd ap Rhys for him alive to be imprisoned; and if he could not get him alive to send him his head. And that he promised him, and he came to his land.† And forthwith he asked where Gruffudd ap Rhys was staying. And Gruffudd ap Rhys was informed that Gruffudd ap Cynan had come[9] from the king's court and that he was enquiring for Gruffudd ap Rhys[10] everywhere. And some of those who loved Gruffudd ap Rhys said to him, 'Shun the presence of Gruffudd ap Cynan until thou

[1] Griffri BCD.
[2] of the Normans BCD.
[3] —BCD.
[4] gyuathrachwr MS., gyfathrachwyr CD. *Translation based on* CD.
[5] to the said ... called] to the above C, of BD.
[6] Gruffudd BC, Gruffudd ap Rhys D.
[7] seek defence BCD.
[8] at last] then BD, there C.
[9] + home BCD.
[10] him BCD.

know how the world may turn.' And even as they were saying that, lo, one with a shout, saying, 'Behold, horsemen coming.' And scarcely had he gone through the doorway, when lo, horsemen in haste and panting, seeking him. And he could do nothing but flee to the church of Aberdaron. And after Gruffudd ap Cynan had heard that he had fled to the church, he sent servants to drag him from the church; but the prelates of the land did not allow the sanctuary of the church to be violated. And after he had been left in the church† he fled thence to Deheubarth till he came¹ to Ystrad Tywi. And when news of that had been heard and² many had gathered to him, he made violent attacks upon the Flemings and the French. And thus ended that year.

[1113–1116]. In the year after that, Gruffudd ap Rhys took the castle that was near Arberth and burned it in the first attack that he made. Thereupon he attacked the other³ castle, which was at Llandovery, belonging to the leader Richard fitz Pons, the man to whom king Henry had given Cantref Bychan, with the intention of burning it, but he failed to do so because of the garrison who were custodians along with Maredudd ap Rhydderch ap Caradog, the man who held the chieftainship of the said Cantref Bychan under Richard fitz Pons. However, he burned the outer castle. And after many of his men had been wounded, and others slain, he turned back again. And after that he sent his comrades to make an attack upon a castle which earl Henry, who was called de Beaumont,⁴ had at Swansea, but again they achieved nothing, because of the garrison, but the burning of the outer castle; and they turned back again after some of them had been slain. And after hearing that, many young hotheads gravitated to him from everywhere and they carried off many spoils.

And the French took counsel and summoned to them the chieftains of the lands,⁵ to wit, Owain ap Caradog ap Rhydderch, to whom a portion of Cantref Mawr in Ystrad Tywi had been given by king Henry; and Maredudd ap Rhydderch, who was mentioned above; and Rhydderch ap Tewdwr and his sons, Maredudd and Owain—and their mother† was Hunydd, daughter of Bleddyn; and Gruffudd ap Llywelyn and the latter† were brothers by the same mother,⁶ Angharad, daughter of

¹ to Deheubarth . . . came]—BCD.
² news . . . and]—BCD.
³ other] *marginal addition*.
⁴ who . . . Beaumont]—BCD.
⁵ of the lands]—BCD.
⁶ and Gruffudd . . . mother] brother of Gruffudd ap Llywelyn ap Seisyllt BCD.

Maredudd, king of the Britons; and Owain, son of Caradog by Gwenllïan, daughter of the same king Bleddyn[1]; and many others. And the French asked each of those if they were true to king Henry. And they all answered that they were. And the French said, 'If it is so, as you say,[2] in order that what you profess in your words may be shewn[3] by your deed, each one of you, as it falls to his lot, must keep the king's castle at Carmarthen, that is, Owain ap Caradog for two weeks, and Rhydderch and his sons for another two weeks, and Maredudd ap Rhydderch ap Caradog for another two weeks.' And to Bleddyn ap Cedifor† was entrusted the castle of Robert Courtemain,[4]† which was at Abercorram.†

And after that matter had been settled and arranged, Gruffudd ap Rhys sent spies to Carmarthen to see whether he could either breach the castle or burn it. And when it chanced that he found a time when it would be easy for him to besiege the castle, it chanced that then Owain ap Caradog was keeping his turn on the castle. And Gruffudd ap Rhys gathered his men and his comrades together and he assaulted the castle by night. And when Owain heard the shout and the tumult around the castle by the men attacking, he quickly arose from where he was with his comrades. And he made for the place where the troop's shout was greatest,[5] thinking that his comrades were with him; but they were not, for they had fled and had left him alone in the stress;[6] and he was slain there. And after the outer castle had been burnt and the towers had escaped, they returned to the woods, and much spoil with them.

And thereupon young hotheads of the land gathered[7] to him, thinking because of those attacks that he had overcome everything. A castle that was in Gower he burned outright and he slew many within it.[8] William of London, through fear of him, left the castle that was in his charge and his cattle and his men. And after all those things had been done,† he thought to make his way to Ceredigion after he had been invited by certain men,† namely, Cedifor ap Goronwy and Hywel ab Idnerth and Trahaearn ab Ithel: those, over and above anyone from Ceredigion, were adhering to him, because of kinship and relationship. And when they had decided upon that in council,

---
[1] daughter of Bleddyn, his mother BCD.
[2] as you say]—BCD.
[3] what you say in your words will be shewn BCD.
[4] Tort MS., Cortmayn BCD.
[5] the shout and tumult were greatest BCD.
[6] in the stress]—BCD.
[7] turned BCD.
[8] within it]—BCD.

they left† Dyfed full of diverse peoples—Flemings and French and Saxons—and of their own folk;[1]—and those, even though they were of the same race as the men of Ceredigion, nevertheless had a hostile heart towards the men of Ceredigion because of the uneasiness which the men of Ceredigion frequently used to cause them; and, what was more, they scorned the fear of[2] Henry, king of England, the man who had subdued under his authority all the island of Britain and its mighty ones; and many men besides beyond the sea he had subdued under his authority, some by his might and main, others by innumerable gifts of gold and silver, and the man against whom no one could be of avail save God himself, who had bestowed that authority upon him.

And then, when Gruffudd ap Rhys came to Ceredigion, he came first to the place called Is-Coed and the spot which belonged to Gilbert fitz Richard,[3] with Flemings dwelling in it, and which was called Blaen-porth.† And that he attacked first. And on a certain day he besieged the tower throughout the day; and many from the tower were slain, and one of his men too was slain, and he burned the greater part of the town, without gaining anything but that. And then he turned back. Thereupon the men of the land as it were suddenly gathered to him, and they harried the Saxons whom Gilbert had brought in to fill the land, which was before that as it were empty because of a scarcity of people and well-nigh deserted;[4] and they plundered and despoiled them and burned their houses, and directed their course to the place called Penweddig. And they surrounded the castle of Ralf,† officer to Gilbert, which was at the place called Ystrad Peithyll. And they laid siege to it and overcame it; and they slew many[5] within it and burned it by night, and they encamped at the place called Glasgrug, about a mile from Llanbadarn, and did wrong to the church: for they carried off cattle from the sanctuary for their dinner.

And they thought to lay siege the following day to the castle of Aberystwyth, and it was their desire to win possession of it. And then Ralf,† the officer, who was constable over that castle, the man whose castle had been burned before that and whose men had been slain, in wrath at his loss sent messengers that night under cover of night to the castle which Gilbert his lord had made at Ystrad Meurig, to ask that help be sent to him.

[1] garrisons BCD.
[2] and, to cause them disturbance, they went to BCD.
[3] and the . . . Richard] a place which belonged to Richard the Fleming C.
[4] well-nigh deserted] they ravaged them BCD.
[5] + men BCD.

And the men who were keeping that castle sent the greatest number they could. And they came to him by night. On the following day Gruffudd ap Rhys and Rhydderch, his uncle, along with him and his sons,[1] Maredudd and Owain, arose and did not draw up or arrange their force aright save for placing the standards in the van;† and like a furious rabble without a ruler over them they made their way towards the castle of Aberystwyth, where Ralf the officer and—without their knowing—his supporters were, till they came to Ystrad Antarron opposite the castle. The castle was situated on the top of a small hill with the river Ystwyth flowing between them and the place whither they were coming. And there was a bridge across the river. And as they were there, thinking to make engines to shoot at the castle and deliberating in what way they could breach the castle, the day almost slipped away from them till it was time of Nones. And then the garrison, as it is the way with the French to do everything with diligence and circumspection, sent archers to the bridge to shoot at them and to annoy them so that, should any of them come rashly against them unarmed, mailed knights could suddenly rush upon them and seize them. And when the Britons saw the archers so boldly approaching the bridge, they sallied imprudently against them, and as it were marvelled why they dared to make for the bridge so boldly. And as they were thus shooting at one another from either side of the bridge,† lo, a mailed knight making for the bridge. And some of the men encountered him on the bridge. And as he bore down upon them with great force, his horse was wounded. And after the horse had been wounded and whilst it was fretting with pain, the knight fell; and as all the spearsmen were intent upon doing him hurt, with his corselet[2] and his armour protecting him,[3] lo, someone making a rush and getting him out from amongst the troop. And he arose and fled. And when his comrades[4] saw him fleeing, they too all fled. And the Britons pursued them to the end†† of the mountain, but the rear troop did not follow their comrades, but they kept the ford and the bridge behind them should they perchance be pursued, and to be a support for their comrades.† And when the French from the brow of the hill saw those fleeing, they swooped down upon them and slew them without mercy. And then all the inhabitants of the land were dispersed throughout the lands nearest them, some with their animals with them, others having

[1] his sons]—BCD.
[2] and when . . . corselet] and as he was unable to take off his corselet BCD.
[3] protecting him] a hindrance BD, preventing them C.
[4] friends BCD.

left all their chattels without care for aught save they should find protection for their lives, so that the whole land was waste.†

And during those events Henry, king of England, sent to Owain ap Cadwgan to ask him to come to him. And Owain forthwith went. And the king said to him, 'My most beloved Owain, dost thou know that[1] accursed petty[2] thief Gruffudd ap Rhys, who is molesting my magnates? And since I believe that thou art true to me, I would have you be in the van of my son and his host in order to drive him away. And I will make Llywarch ap Trahaearn a comrade to thee. For it is in you two that my hope lies. And when thou comest back, I will worthily repay thee for it.' And then Owain felt glory in himself on account of the promise. And he gathered his men, and Llywarch along with him. And they proceeded against Gruffudd ap Rhys as far as Ystrad Tywi, where they supposed Gruffudd ap Rhys was hiding; for it was a land wild with woods and difficult to approach, and easy for those acquainted with it to encounter their enemies. And when the host of Owain and the king's son and their supporters came to the limit of the land, they sent their hosts in bands into the woods, each one in his sector. And they pledged one another that not one of them would spare one person, neither man nor woman, neither boy nor girl, but that whomsoever they caught they would not let any one go, but kill or hang him or cut off his members.† And when the inhabitants[3] of the land heard that, each one, as best he could, sought to defend himself. And they dispersed, some into the woods to lurk, others to flee to the other lands around them, others to the castles nearest to them to seek protection from the place whence they had come;—as is said in the Welsh proverb, 'The dog licketh the spear with which he is wounded.' And after the host had dispersed into the woods, it chanced that Owain, and a few men—about ninety—along with him, made for the woods in his sector. And as they were searching the woods, lo, they could see the tracks of the people making for the woods, and from the woods fleeing with their cattle towards the castle of Carmarthen, with which they had made peace. And Owain pursued them and he came upon them wellnigh close to the castle. And after seizing them, he returned to his comrades.

And meanwhile a host of the Flemings from Rhos chanced to come to Carmarthen to meet the king's son; and along with

[1] the D.
[2] —BC.
[3] garrisons BCD.

them Gerald, officer of Pembroke, was coming. And as those were coming, lo, some in flight making it known with cries that Owain ap Cadwgan had carried off by force all that was theirs. And when the Flemings heard that, they were fired with the old hate that formerly existed between them and Owain; for many a time had Owain done them hurt. Instigated also by Gerald, the man from whom Owain had carried off his wife, and whose castle he had burned, and whose spoil he had carried off, they thought to pursue Owain. But Owain, not thinking that there was any opposition at all to him, went slowly on his way. And they pursued him, and forthwith they came to the place where Owain was, and the spoil with him. And when Owain's comrades saw the multitude coming after them, they said to Owain, 'There is a multitude pursuing us, whom we have no power to encounter.' And he replied to them and said, 'Let there be no fear upon you without cause.[1] Nothing can be done,' said he, 'with the Flemings.' And then he attacked them boldly,† and they too stood manfully; and with shooting on either side Owain was wounded till he was slain. And after he[2] had been slain, his comrades fled. And when Llywarch ap Trahaearn heard that, he and his comrades returned home.

And after he† had been slain, his brothers held his portion of Powys, save that which Owain had taken from Maredudd, namely, Caereinion, which had belonged to Madog ap Rhiryd ap Bleddyn. And his brothers' names were these: Madog, son of Cadwgan by Gwenllïan,† daughter of Gruffudd ap Cynan; Einion, son of Cadwgan by Sannan, daughter of Dyfnwal; Morgan, son of Cadwgan by Ellylw,[3]† daughter of Cedifor ap Gollwyn, the man who had been lord over all Dyfed; Henry, son of Cadwgan by the Frenchwoman his wife, daughter to Picot, a leader of the French;[4] and by her there was another son, his name was Gruffudd; the sixth son was Maredudd by Euron, daughter of Hoeddlyw ap Cadwgan ab Elystan.

After that, Einion ap Cadwgan and Gruffudd ap Maredudd ap Bleddyn made a solemn pact with the king,† and they made an attack upon the castle which Uchdryd ab Edwin, who was first-cousin to Maredudd ap Bleddyn, had made: for Bleddyn and Iwerydd, mother of Owain and Uchdryd, were brother and sister, not by the same mother, but by the same father;[5] for

[1] without cause]—BCD.
[2] Owain BC, Sir Owain ap Cadwgan ap Bleddyn ap Cynfyn D.
[3] Elliw BCD.
[4] from France BCD.
[5] were brother . . . father] brother and sister by the same mother and the same father BCD.

Angharad, daughter of Maredudd, was the mother of Bleddyn; Cynfyn ap Gwerystan was their father. And the castle which has been mentioned was situated in the place that is called Cymer in Meirionnydd. For Cadwgan ap Bleddyn had given Meirionnydd and Cyfeiliog to Uchdryd on this condition: that he should be a true, inseparable friend to him and his sons and a helper against all opposition that might come upon them. He, however,[1] was opposed to Cadwgan and his sons. And above all, after the death of[2] Owain he thought nothing of Cadwgan's other sons; and therefore he had made the castle that was mentioned above. And then those who were mentioned above took that in anger; and they made an attack upon the castle and burned it, some of the garrison fleeing and others coming over to them. And then they seized for themselves all Meirionnydd and Cyfeiliog and Penllyn, and they apportioned them amongst them, to each one his portion. And to Gruffudd ap Maredudd there came as portion Mawddwy and Cyfeiliog and half of Penllyn; and to Cadwgan's son[3]† came the other half of Penllyn and Meirionnydd. And thus ended that year, irksome to everyone.

[1114-1117]. A year after that, Gilbert fitz Richard died of a long infirmity. And king Henry stayed in Normandy, with war still between him and the king of France.

[1115-1118]. The year next after that, treachery was bred between Hywel ab Ithel, who held Rhos and Rhufoniog, and Rhiryd and Llywarch and their other[4] brothers,† sons of Owain ab Edwin ap Goronwy.† And Hywel sent messengers to Maredudd ap Bleddyn and to Madog and Einion, sons of Cadwgan ap Bleddyn, to beseech them to come to his aid. For it was through their support and help that he held and maintained what land had fallen to his lot. And when they heard that he was hard-pressed, they gathered about four hundred kinsmen and comrades and a war-band of theirs, which they had ready, and went to meet him to Dyffryn Clwyd, which was a land of theirs. The sons of Owain,[5] too, and Uchdryd, their uncle, gathered their men and brought the French from Chester to their aid. And they came up against Hywel and Maredudd and the sons of Cadwgan[6] and their supporters. And after there had

---
[1] —BCD.
[2] after the death of]—BCD.
[3] sons BCD.
[4] —BCD.
[5] + ab Edwin BCD.
[6] and their sons BCD.

been a hard battle† and many had been slain on either side, the sons of Owain and their men fled, after Llywarch ab Owain and Iorwerth ap Nudd—he was a praiseworthy, eminent man—had been slain in the battle, and after many others had been slain and many[1] had been wounded, and they willingly returned empty-handed. And Hywel was wounded in the battle, and on the fortieth day after coming home he died. Maredudd and the sons of Cadwgan, although they had won the victory, did not dare to take possession of the land because of the French, but they returned home.

[1116–1119]. A year after that, died Muircertach, the man of greatest power and authority and victory of the men of Ireland.

[1117–1120]. A year after that, king Henry thought to return to England from Normandy, after peace had been arranged between him and the king of France. And he bade† his mariners equip ships and make them ready. And when they were ready, he had his two sons—one by his wedded wife, whom he desired to be his heir to his kingdom, and another by his concubine—sent towards England in the ship that was considered the best,[2]† and with them many leading men and ladies, about two hundred, of those known to be most worthy of the love of those sons. And after they had boarded the ship about the fall of night, a storm overtook them and the sea became very rough. And the ship bore down upon rocks unknown to the sailors. And those wrecked the ship;[3] and all the company that was in it together with the king's sons were drowned, so that not one person escaped. And the king was in another ship; and although the storm hit him hard, he escaped and came to land. And when he heard that his sons had been drowned, he was grieved. And thus ended that year.

[1118–1121]. A year after that, king Henry married a daughter of a certain[4] prince from Germany; for before that, since the death of the daughter of Maelcoluim, he was wont to use concubines.

And after that, as soon as summer came and the roads were dry and it was easy to find and to follow paths, the king moved a mighty host against the men of Powys, where Maredudd ap Bleddyn and the sons of Cadwgan ap Bleddyn, Einion and

---

[1] + others BCD.
[2] the best ship that could be found BCD.
[3] And the ship was wrecked BCD.
[4] —BCD.

Madog and Morgan, were lords. And when they heard that, they sent messengers to Gruffudd ap Cynan, who held the island of[1] Anglesey, to ask him whether he would unite with them against the king; and they told him that together they could hold the wild parts of their lands against the king.[2] But he had made peace with the king, and he informed them that, if they fled near his bounds, he would come[3] against them and would despoil them. And when Maredudd and the sons of Cadwgan learned that, they decided in council to keep themselves within their own bounds and to guard and defend them.

And the king approached the bounds of Powys. And Maredudd sent young men to way-lay the king, to a certain[4] counter-slope the way along which he was coming, in order to engage him with bows and arrows and to cause confusion among his host with missiles. And it chanced that the king came that way at the time when those young men had gone to[5] the counter-slope. And those young men met the king and his men; and with a great tumult and shouting they sent missiles and keen arrows amongst the host. And after some had been slain and others had been wounded, one of the young men drew his bow and discharged an arrow amongst the host; and without his knowing how it was going, it went right through the host until it reached the king; but because of the corselet and the armour that were about him it did him no harm, but the arrow recoiled. And the king had a great fright, exactly as though the arrow had gone through him. And there and then he ordered tent to be pitched. And he asked who were they who were so bold as to attack him as daringly as that. And he was told that certain[6] young men, whom Maredudd ap Bleddyn had sent, were they who had done that. And he sent them a truce for them to come to him. And they came. And he asked them who had sent them; and they answered that it was Maredudd ap Bleddyn. He then asked them, 'Can you get hold of Maredudd?' said he. 'We can,' said they. And then he asked them to bring Maredudd to his peace. And Maredudd and the sons of Cadwgan came to his peace. And after they had made peace with the king, the king returned to England after imposing a heavy tribute of animals upon Maredudd and the sons of Cadwgan—about ten thousand head. And so ended that year.

[1] the island of]—BCD.
[2] and they told . . . king]—BCD.
[3] be BCD.
[4] a certain] where there was a CD.
[5] were on BCD.
[6] —BCD.

[1119–1122]. A year in which there was [peace].¹†

[1120–1123]. The year of Christ was one thousand one hundred and twenty when Gruffudd ap Rhys slew Gruffudd ap Sulhaearn.

[1121–1124]. A year after that, died Einion ap Cadwgan, to whom belonged a portion of Powys, and who had taken Meirionnydd from Uchdryd, and who bequeathed it, when he died, to Maredudd, his brother. And when that Maredudd came to take possession of it, he was driven back by Maredudd ap Bleddyn, his uncle. And then Ithel ap Rhiryd ap Bleddyn was released from his prison by king Henry. And when he came to seek a portion of Powys, he obtained none.

And when Gruffudd ap Cynan heard that Maredudd ap Cadwgan had been driven back by his uncle,² Maredudd ap Bleddyn, he sent his two sons,³ Cadwallon and Owain, and with them a mighty host, to Meirionnydd; and they carried off with them to Llŷn all the men of Meirionnydd and all their chattels. And after that they moved a host, thinking to drive all Powys into exile. But, as the Welsh cannot fully accomplish their thoughts, they came back again empty. And Maredudd ap Bleddyn and the sons of Cadwgan ravaged much of the territory of Llywarch ap Trahaearn,⁴ because he had helped the cause of the sons of Gruffudd ap Cynan and had made a pact with them.

[1122–1125]. A year after that, [Gruffudd ap]⁵ Maredudd ap Bleddyn† slew Ithel ap Rhiryd ap Bleddyn in the presence of Ithel's father,† who was brother to Maredudd. And a little after that, Cadwallon ap Gruffudd ap Cynan, the man who was mentioned above, slew his three uncles, namely, Goronwy and Rhiryd and Meilyr, sons of Owain ab Edwin: for Angharad, daughter of Owain, was wife to Gruffudd ap Cynan⁶ and mother of Cadwallon and Owain and Cadwaladr and many daughters.

In that year treachery was begotten between Morgan and Maredudd, sons of Cadwgan ap Bleddyn; and Morgan with his own hand slew Maredudd, his brother.

[1123–1126]. A year after that, king Henry returned from Normandy after pacifying those who had had disagreement with him.†

---

¹ And the year next after that there was peace (was peaceful D) CD.
² his uncle]—BC.
³ his two sons]—BCD.
⁴ + ap Gwyn BCD.
⁵ —MS., BCD.
⁶ Cynam MS., Cynan BCD.

[1124–1127]. A year after that, Gruffudd ap Rhys was expelled by king Henry from the portion of land which the king had given to him, because he had been accused without cause by the French who were dwelling along with him.

At the close of that year died Daniel, son of Sulien, bishop of Menevia, the man who was mediator between Gwynedd and Powys concerning any between whom there was trouble in those lands; and none of them found any fault in him, but rather that he was peaceful and beloved by all. And he held the position of archdeacon in Powys when he died.

[1125–1128]. A year after that, died Gruffudd [ap Maredudd][1]† ap Bleddyn. And[2] Llywelyn ab Owain was seized by Maredudd, his uncle, his father's brother,† and placed in the hands of Payn fitz John; and the latter sent him to the castle of Bridgenorth to be interned.

Towards the end of that year Morgan ap Cadwgan went to Jerusalem because of the murder of his brother, and as he was returning he died in the island of Cyprus in the Tyrrhene Sea.†

[1126–1129]. A year after that, Llywelyn ab Owain slew Maredudd ap Llywarch after he had been expelled from his land, the man who had slain [the son of] Meurig, his first-cousin, and had gouged out the eyes of Maredudd and Griffri, his two first-cousins, and who had blinded his two brothers.†

[1127–1130]. A year after that, Llywelyn ab Owain slew in Powys Iorwerth ap Llywarch. And soon after that, Maredudd ap Bleddyn† caused Llywelyn ab Owain to be castrated and to have his eyes gouged out. In that year Ieuaf ab Owain was slain by his first-cousins, that is, the sons of Llywarch.

At the close of that year Madog ap Llywarch was slain by Meurig,† his first-cousin.

[1128–1131]. And before the end of the year next after that, Meurig's eyes were gouged out of his head and he was castrated.†

[1129–1132]. A year after that, Iorwerth ab Owain was slain. In that year Cadwallon ap Gruffudd ap Cynan was slain in Nanheudwy by Cadwgan ap Goronwy and Einion ab Owain, his first-cousins.† And soon after that, Maredudd ap Bleddyn, the splendour and defence of the men of Powys, died after having done penance on his soul and[3] body and worthily receiving the Body of Christ.

[1] D,—MS.
[2] And ... Tyrrhene sea]—CD.
[3] soul and]—CD.

[1130-1133—1133-1136†]. In the four years after that, that is, in the year of Christ one thousand one hundred and thirty and the three years next after that, there was nothing that might be placed on record.†

[1134-1135]. The first year after that, that is, the fourth year,† king Henry, son of William the Bastard, king of England and Wales, died in the first month of winter† in Normandy. And† Stephen, his nephew, who was called Stephen of Blois, took the sceptre by force, and he manfully subdued the south of all England.

[1135-1136]. A year after that, Morgan ab Owain slew Richard fitz Gilbert.[1]

And thereupon Owain and Cadwaladr, sons of Gruffudd ap Cynan, the splendour of all Britain and her defence and her strength and her freedom, like two kings, like two generous ones, two fearless ones, two brave ones, two fortunate ones, two pleasant ones, defenders of the churches, guardians of the poor, slayers of their enemies and tamers of warriors, surest help for all those who fled to them, while they surpassed all in strength of body and soul, held supremacy over all Wales and moved a mighty, fierce host to Ceredigion; and in the first attack they burned Walter's Castle. And thereupon, stirring their wings, they laid siege to the castle of Aberystwyth and burned it, having along with them Hywel ap Maredudd and Madog ab Idnerth and the two sons of Hywel, Maredudd and Rhys. And after they had burned the castle of Richard de la Mare and the castle of Dineirth and Caerwedros, they returned home.

Towards the close of that year they came a second time to Ceredigion, and along with them a numerous host, about six thousand footsoldiers and two thousand mailed horsemen ready for battle. And along with them, as support for them, there came Gruffudd ap Rhys and Hywel ap Maredudd from Brycheiniog and Madog ab Idnerth and the two sons of Hywel. All those directed their forces towards Cardigan.† And against them came Stephen the constable† and Robert fitz Martin and the sons of Gerald and William fitz Odo,† and all the Flemings and all the knights† from the estuary of the Neath to the estuary of the Dyfi.† And after fierce fighting, then the Flemings and the Normans, according to their usual custom, took to flight as their place of refuge. And with some slain and others burnt, and others trampled under horses' feet,† and others carried off

---
[1] fitz Gilbert] and Gilbert his son BD, fitz Gilbert his son C.

into captivity and others drowned in rivers like fools, and having lost of their own men about three thousand, they returned home weak and despondent. But Owain and Cadwaladr, having honourably won the victory, returned to their land, and along with them a great abundance of captives[1] and spoils and costly raiment and fair armour.

[1136–1137]. A year after that, died Gruffudd ap Rhys, the light and excellence and strength of all South Wales.

In that year Gruffudd ap Cynan, prince of Gwynedd and head and king and defender and pacifier of all Wales, ended his temporal life in Christ, and died after many perils by sea and land and after innumerable victories in wars and the winning of spoils, after great wealth of gold and silver, after gathering [the men of][2] Gwynedd together from the several lands whither the Normans had dispersed them, after building many churches and consecrating them to God and the saints—after receiving extreme unction and communion and confession and repentance for his sins, and becoming a monk and making a good end in his perfect old age.

In that year died Ieuan, high-priest of Llanbadarn, the most learned of the learned, having led a pious life without mortal sin till his death, which he found in the Lord Christ on the third day from the Calends of April.†

In that year, for the third time, the sons of Gruffudd ap Cynan came into Ceredigion, and they burned the castle of Ystrad Meurig and Stephen's Castle† and Humfrey's Castle and Carmarthen.

[1137–1138]. A year after that, the empress came to England to subdue England for her son,† who was called Henry; for she was a daughter of Henry the First, son of William the Bastard. In that year there was an eclipse of the sun on the twelfth day from the Calends of April.

[1138–1139]. A year after that, Cynwrig ab Owain was slain by the friends and followers of Madog ap Maredudd.[3]†

[1139–1140]. A year after that, died Madog ab Idnerth. And the sons of Bleddyn ap Gwyn slew Maredudd ap Hywel.

[1140–1141]. The year of Christ was one thousand one hundred and forty when Rhys ap Hywel slew Hywel ap Maredudd ap Rhydderch of Cantref Bychan.

[1] wealth BCD.
[2] —MS., BCD.
[3] + ap Bleddyn ap Cynfyn BCD.

[1141-1142]. A year after that, Hywel ap Maredudd ap Bleddyn was slain by his own men without its being known, however, who slew him. And Hywel and Cadwgan, sons of Madog ab Idnerth, were slain.

[1142-1143]. A year after that, Anarawd ap[1] Gruffudd, the hope and glory of the men of Deheubarth, was slain by the followers of Cadwaladr ap Gruffudd, of whom he[2] had no fear. And when Owain, his [*sc*. Cadwaladr] brother, heard of that, he took it grievously; for he had promised his daughter to[3] Anarawd.[4]† And he thought to despoil Cadwaladr of his territory. And then Hywel ab Owain[5] sought Cadwaladr's portion of Ceredigion; and he burned Cadwaladr's castle at Aberystwyth. Then Miles, earl of Hereford, was slain by the arrow-shot of one of his knights[6] in shooting a stag.

[1143-1144]. A year after that, when Cadwaladr saw that he was expelled by Owain, his brother, from the whole kingdom, he gathered a fleet from Ireland along with him and came to land at Abermenai, and as leaders over it along with him Otir, son of the other Otir, and the son of Turcaill and the son of Ischerwlf.† But then, however, Owain and Cadwaladr made peace through the counsel of their leading men, as befitted brothers. And when the Irish† heard that, they seized Cadwaladr; and he contracted to pay them two thousand head of cattle† for his release. And thus he freed himself from them. And when Owain heard that his brother was free, he fell upon them and made an assault against them. And they, with some of them killed and others captured, fled ignominiously in the direction of Dublin.

In that year Welsh pilgrims† were drowned† on their way to Jerusalem.

In that year Hugh fitz Ranulf repaired the castle of Cymaron,[7] and a second time subjugated Maelienydd. And the castle of Colunwy† was built a second time, and Elfael was a second time subjugated to the French.

[1144-1145]. A year after that, Hugh de Mortimer seized Rhys ap Hywel and imprisoned him, after some of his men had been slain and others captured. And Hywel ab Owain and Cynan,

---
[1] Angharat verch MS., *with* Anarawd vab *in margin by later hand*; Yngharad vz *with* Anarawd vab *written above* B, Anarawd ap CD.
[2] ... arnei MS., arnaw BCD.
[3] for he had been promised a daughter of CD.
[4] y Gadwaladyr MS., *with* Anarawd *in margin by later hand*.
[5] Hywel and Owain, sons of Gruffudd ap Cynan BCD.
[6] men BCD.
[7] CD, Cymerau MS.

his brother, ravaged Cardigan. And after a fierce battle had taken place there, they returned to their land with victory and having won great spoil. In that year earl Gilbert, son of the other[1] Gilbert, came to Dyfed and overran it; and he built the castle of Carmarthen and another castle in Mabudryd.

[1145–1146]. A year after that, Sulien ap Rhygyfarch ended his temporal life, the man who had been a foster-son and thereafter a teacher in the church of Llanbadarn—he was a man of age and mature in accomplishments, a speaker and pleader[2] for his people and a mediator for various kingdoms, peaceful towards[3] men of the church and an ornament of secular judgments—after receiving extreme unction and communion and confession on the twelfth day from the Calends of November.[4]†

In that year Meurig ap Madog ap Rhiryd† was slain through the treachery of his own men. And Maredudd ap Madog ab Idnerth was slain by Hugh de Mortimer.

In that year Cadell ap Gruffudd overcame by force the castle of Dinefwr,[5]† which earl Gilbert had built. Soon after that, he and Hywel ab Owain overcame the castle of Carmarthen, and they granted† their lives to the prisoners who were there. Soon after that, Cadell and his brothers, Maredudd and Rhys, overcame the castle of Llanstephan by a severe struggle, after many of their enemies had been slain and others wounded. Soon after that, a multitude of French and Flemings, with the sons of Gerald and William fitz Hai† as leaders over them, came without warning to lay siege to that castle. And when Maredudd ap Gruffudd, the man to whom the castle had been entrusted, saw his enemies come without warning, he urged his men to fight manfully. And he himself rose superior to his age: for a boy though he was in age, he showed nonetheless the action of a man, battling in person with his enemies and urging his men to fight. And when the enemies saw how very few were the defenders, they raised ladders against the walls. And he bore with his enemies until they were on the ladders; and then he came, he and his men, and overturned the ladders so that his enemies were in[6] the ditch, many of them being slain and the others put to flight. And thus did he a boy[7] defeat many men proven in arms and battles.

[1] the other]—BCD.
[2] counsellor BCD.
[3] pacifier of BCD.
[4] October *with* November *written above* B, October CD.
[5] Dinehwr MS., Dinefwr BCD.
[6] and . . . in] and threw his enemies into BCD.
[7] a boy]—BCD.

At the close of that year died Rhun ab Owain, a praiseworthy young man, whom the ancestry of his forebears had formed strong: for he was comely in appearance and kind of word and pleasant towards all, and generous and gentle in his home, and harsh towards his enemies, and pleasant towards his comrades; he was tall, and his flesh white, with curly flaxen hair, a long face,[1] large, merry, blue eyes, a long stout neck, a broad chest, a long waist, stout thighs, long legs, long slender feet, long straight toes. And when the news of his death reached Owain,[2] he fell into so great a sorrow that neither the splendour of sovereignty nor the entertainment of bards nor the solace of courtiers nor the sight of costly objects could raise him from his conceived sorrow and grief. God, however, of his accustomed goodness saw good to show mercy to the race of the Britons, so that it should not be wrecked completely like a ship when it has lost its steersman, and be despoiled of its chief, and He preserved Owain for them as leader. And as unbearable sorrow had disturbed the prince's mind and brought it low, even so did divine providence raise it up. For there was a castle called Mold,—and that many had besieged in vain, without gaining success. And when the eminent prince and his courtiers and war-band along with him came round it, neither the nature of the place nor its strength nor its forces could defend it from being burnt and completely destroyed; and many of the garrison were slain and others captured and imprisoned. And when the lord knew of that, he laid aside all his sorrow and all his grief, and he vigorously returned to his natural state of mind and gladness.†

[1146-1147]. A year after that, the king of France, who was called Louis, and the emperor of Germany, and a vast multitude of earls and barons along with them, went to Jerusalem.

In that year Cadell ap Gruffudd and his brothers, Maredudd and Rhys, and William fitz Gerald and his brothers moved a host to Wizo's Castle. And having despaired of their own forces, they summoned Hywel ab Owain to their aid. For through the numbers and doughtiness of his host and their readiness in war, and through the wisdom of his counsel, they hoped to gain the victory. And forthwith Hywel, as he was eager to win fame and glory, had a host assembled. And after assembling the bravest and readiest host, and the one most eager for the fame and honour of their lord, he made his way towards the said Wizo's

---

[1] a long face ... straight fingers] and every place on his body, in addition to that, God had fashioned worthily BCD.
[2] + his father BC.

Castle. And the said barons received him gladly. And there and then he encamped before the castle. And the entire course of the battle was shaped by his counsel and ruling. And thus at last all his friends attained to the highest glory and fame. And after Wizo's Castle had been taken through him, with great toil and conflict, Hywel joyfully returned home victorious.

And soon after that, strife was begotten between the sons of Owain, Hywel and Cynan, and Cadwaladr, their uncle. And then Hywel, from the one direction, and Cynan, from the other, came together to Meirionnydd; and there they called[1] to them[2] the men of the land† who had fled for sanctuary to the churches, maintaining towards them the sanctuary and honour of the churches. And thence they turned their army towards the castle of Cynfael, which Cadwaladr had built. And keeping the castle was Morfran, abbot of Whitland.† And a fervent demand for the castle was made to him, now with harsh threats, now again with many gifts; but he refused them, for he preferred to die honourably than to lead a life of shame through treachery to his lord. And when Hywel and Cynan saw that, they launched an attack against the castle and took the castle by force. And it was with difficulty that the keeper of the castle escaped through friends, after some of his men had been slain and others had been wounded.

In that year died earl Henry,[3]† son of king Henry, after he had waged war against king Stephen for twelve years.

In that year died earl Gilbert, son of the other Gilbert.

[1147–1148]. A year after that, Uchdryd, bishop of Llandaff, a man of exceeding great praise, defender of the Church, and repeller of its enemies, died in his perfect old age. And after him Nicholas ap Gwrgant became bishop.

In that year Bernard, bishop of Menevia, a man of great art and praise, after innumerable toils on sea and land for the freedom of the church of Menevia, died in the thirty-third year of his episcopate. And after him David fitz Gerald, archdeacon of Ceredigion, became bishop.

In that year died Robert, bishop of Hereford, full of perfect life and works of mercy; he was a pious man and a provider for the poor and an eminent ornament of the Church. And after him Gilbert, abbot of Gloucester, became bishop.

---

[1] they called to them the men] *emend* law (*Pen. MS.* 20. 96 *b*. 3) *to* [y] law.
[2] to them]—CD.
[3] Henry *with* Rhobert *written above* B, Bossed C, Rhobert prince of Gloucester D.

In that year there was a great mortality in the island of Britain.†

[1148–1149]. A year after that, Owain ap Gruffudd ap Cynan built a castle in Iâl. And Cadwaladr ap Gruffudd ap Cynan built a castle at Llanrhystud; and he gave his portion of Ceredigion to Cadwgan, his son.†

Towards the end of the[1] year Madog ap Maredudd built the castle of Oswestry, and he gave Cyfeiliog† to Owain and Meurig, sons of Gruffudd ap Maredudd.

[1149–1150]. A year after that, Cadell ap Gruffudd repaired the castle of Carmarthen, for the strength and splendour of his kingdom; and he harried Cydweli.

In that year Owain, prince of Gwynedd, imprisoned Cynan, his son.

In that year Hywel ab Owain seized Cadfan, son of Cadwaladr, his uncle,† and gained possession of his territory and his castle.

Soon after that, Cadell and Maredudd and Rhys, sons of Gruffudd, came to Ceredigion and they gained possession of Is-Aeron.

In that year Madog ap Maredudd, king of Powys, thought with the help of Ranulf, earl of Chester, to rise up against Owain. And after the host of his supporters[2] had been slain at Coleshill, they fled.

[1150–1151]. It was the year of Christ one thousand one hundred and fifty when Cadell and Maredudd and Rhys, sons of Gruffudd, took Ceredigion from Hywel ab Owain, save for one castle which was at Pen-gwern in Llanfihangel.† The castle of Llanrhystud they took after a long siege of it. And after that, Hywel ab Owain took that castle by force, and burned it after killing all the garrison of the castle. Soon after that, Cadell and Maredudd and Rhys, sons of Gruffudd, repaired the castle of Ystrad Meurig. And after that, some men from Tenby came upon Cadell ap Gruffudd, as he was hunting, and they did him injury and left him half-alive for dead. And immediately after that, Maredudd and Rhys fell upon Gower and took the castle of Aberllwchwr† and burned it. In that year the two of them built the castle of Dinefwr.[3]† In that year Hywel ab Owain built the castle of Humfrey's son† in the valley of the Cletwr.

[1] that BCD.
[2] chiefs BCD.
[3] Dinehwr MS., Dinevwr BD.

[1151-1152]. A year after that, Owain ap Gruffudd caused Cunedda ap Cadwallon, his nephew, his brother's son, to be castrated and his eyes to be gouged out of his head. In that year Llywelyn ap Madog ap Maredudd slew Stephen fitz Baldwin. In that year Cadwaladr was expelled from Anglesey by Owain, his brother; and Simon, archdeacon of Cyfeiliog,[1]† a man of great authority and dignity, died.

[1152-1153]. A year after that, Maredudd and Rhys, sons of Gruffudd, directed their armies to Penweddig; and they laid siege to the castle of Hywel ab Owain[2] and subdued it. Soon after that, the sons of Gruffudd breached the castle of Tenby by treachery at night, and they gave it for custody to William fitz Gerald. And after that, Rhys ap Gruffudd, and a large host with him, ravaged the castle of Ystrad Cyngen.† After that, in the month of May, Maredudd and Rhys made for the castle of Aberafan; and after killing many and burning houses they carried off with them thence vast booty. And thereupon Rhys ap Gruffudd, having gained a victory, ravaged Cyfeiliog.

In that year died David, king of the Scots, a man of great piety.

In that year† prince Henry came to England and subdued it all.

Towards the end of that year died Ranulf, earl of Chester. In that year Cadell ap Gruffudd went on a pilgrimage, about the Calends of Winter;† and he entrusted all his authority to Maredudd and Rhys, his brothers, until he should come back.

[1153-1154]. A year after that, died king Stephen, the man who held the kingdom of England by force after king Henry, after prince Henry had come a second time to England and gained possession of the whole kingdom. That year died Gruffudd† ap Gwyn.

[1154-1155]. A year after that, Maredudd ap Gruffudd ap Rhys, lord of Ceredigion and Ystrad Tywi and Dyfed, a man of great prowess and justice and mercy, died in the twenty-fifth year of his age. In that year died Geoffrey, bishop of Llandaff.† In that year died Roger, earl of Hereford.

[1155-1156]. A year after that, when Rhys ap Gruffudd heard that Owain, prince of Gwynedd, his uncle, was coming with a great host to Ceredigion, he vigorously gathered a host. And

---

[1] Clynnog BCD.
[2] ab Owain] *marginal addition* MS.,—BCD.

he came as far as Aberdyfi, and there he raised a ditch† to give battle. And soon after that he had a castle built there.

In that year Madog ap Maredudd had a castle made in Caereinion, near Cymer. That year Meurig, nephew of the said Madog, escaped from his prison. Soon after that, the church of Mary was built† at Meifod. In that year died Toirrdelbhach,† king of Connaught.

[1156-1157]. A year after that, Henry, king of England, led a mighty host to Chester,† in order to subdue Gwynedd. And there he pitched camp: he was grandson to Henry the Great, son of William the Bastard. And Owain, prince of Gwynedd, after summoning to him his sons and his leading men, and gathering together a mighty host, encamped at Basingwerk. And he raised a ditch† there to give battle to the king. And when the king heard that, he sent his host† and many earls and barons beyond number, and with them a strong force fully equipped, along the shore† towards the place which Owain was holding. And the king and an innumerable armed host, fearless and ready for battle, came through the wood which was between them,[1] which was called the wood of Hawarden. And there Cynan and Dafydd, sons of Owain, encountered him, and there they gave him a hard battle. And after many of his men had been slain he escaped to the open country.[2] And when Owain heard that the king was coming from the one side, and he saw the earls and a mighty host on the other side, he left that position.[3]† And the king gathered his host together and came as far as Rhuddlan.[4] And Owain encamped at Tâl Llwyn Pynna.[5]† And he harassed the king both by day and by night. And Madog ap Maredudd, lord of Powys, chose for himself his place between the king and Owain, where he might have the first encounter.

While those things were happening, the king's fleet approached Anglesey. And after leaving the grooms and the exposed, unarmed men in the ships,† the commander of the ships and the head seamen and the armed men[6] all came to land and plundered the church of Mary and the church of Peter and other churches.† But the saints did not let them get away scot-free, for God took vengeance for it upon them.[7] For on the

[1] which ... them]—BCD.
[2] to ... country] from the field + and he was pursued to the marsh of Chester BCD.
[3] + a second time BCD.
[4] as far as Rhuddlan] after him BCD.
[5] Tal Llwyn Pennant BCD.
[6] and the armed men]—BCD.
[7] But the saints ... them] But God did not let it go scot-free for them, without avenging it upon them BC.

following day there was a battle between them and the men of Anglesey; and the French, according to their usual custom, fled and some of them were captured, others were slain, others were drowned, and it was only with difficulty that a few of them escaped back to the ships, after Henry, son of king Henry, and all the chief seamen, for the greater part, had been slain. And then the king made peace with Owain; and Cadwaladr received back his land. And the king returned to England. And Iorwerth Goch ap Maredudd took the castle of Iâl and burned it.

[1157-1158]. A year after that, Morgan ab Owain† was slain through treachery by the men of Ifor ap Meurig, and along with him the best poet that was: Gwrgant ap Rhys.[1] Iorwerth, his brother, gained possession of Caerleon and Owain's land.

And after all the princes of Wales save Rhys ap Gruffudd alone had made peace with the king, Rhys on his own carried on war against the king; and he moved all[2] Deheubarth and their wives and children and all their animals to the forest-land of the Tywi. And when the king heard that, he sent messengers to Rhys to tell him that it was to his advantage to come to the king's court before the king brought French and Saxons and Welsh against him. And after taking counsel of his leading men he repaired to the king's court. And against his will he made peace with the king upon his being allowed Cantref Mawr and another cantref, which the king chose to give him, and that whole and not divided. But the king did not hold to that for him, but gave him various portions within the lands of various barons. And though Rhys understood that deceit, nevertheless he patiently took those portions and held them in peace.

In the meantime Roger, earl of Clare, though he was in haste to come to Ceredigion, nevertheless did not dare to come until Rhys had made peace with the king. And on the second day from the Calends of June he came to Ystrad Meurig. And on the following day† he provisioned the castle and took Humfrey's Castle and the castle of the Dyfi† and the castle of Dineirth and the castle of Llanrhystud.

And while those things were being done, Walter Clifford, the man who then owned the castle of Llandovery, gathered spoil from Rhys's territory, which was next to him, and slew his men. And Rhys sent messengers to make that known to the king. But the king did not will that reparation should be made

[1] + was he BCD.
[2] + the men of BCD.

to him. And then Rhys's war-band went against Llandovery, and Rhys took the castle.†

Einion ab Anarawd ap Gruffudd, nephew to Rhys,— a young lad in age but manly in strength—because he saw Rhys, his uncle, freed from his oath, and also because he was eager to abolish his people's bondage, made for Humfrey's Castle, and he slew the knights and the other keepers who were there, and won huge spoil and steeds and armour.

And when Rhys ap Gruffudd saw that he would get nothing willingly save what he won with his arms, he made for the castles which the earls and the barons had built all over Ceredigion, and he burned them all. And when the king of England heard that, he came a second time, and a mighty host with him, to Deheubarth. And after Rhys had given him hostages,† he returned to England, and immediately after that went across the sea.

[1158–1159]. A year after that, Rhys ap Gruffudd conquered the castles which the French had set up all over Dyfed and he burned them all. And thereupon he led his host against Carmarthen and besieged the castle. And then came Reginald, son of king Henry, and a vast multitude of French and Saxons and Flemings and Welsh with him. And then Rhys left the castle and gathered all his men and their possessions to the mountain that is called Cefn Rhestr Main.† And then earl Reginald and the earl of Bristol and the earl of Clare and two other earls and Cadwaladr ap Gruffudd and Hywel and Cynan, sons of Owain ap Gruffudd,† encamped at Dinwileir.[1]† And without daring to attack Rhys where he was, they returned home after a bootless journey. And they offered Rhys a truce. And he accepted it, and gave his men leave to go[2] to their own land.

[1159–1160]. A year after that, Madog ap Maredudd, prince of Powys, died at Winchester† after receiving communion and confession and penance upon his body. He was a man of great praise, whom God had formed with physical beauty and fashioned with wisdom untold, and filled with doughtiness and adorned with generosity. He was generous and kind and meek towards the poor and the meek,† and harsh and unkind towards the warlike mighty. And he was brought to be buried to Meifod, where his burial-place was, and he was honourably buried in the church of Tysilio.

[1] + and measured out a castle there BCD.
[2] to go] BCD,—MS.

Soon after that, Llywelyn, his son, in whom lay the hope of all Powys, was slain. And then Cadwallon ap Madog ab Idnerth seized Einion Clud, his brother, and sent him as a prisoner to Owain ap Gruffudd. And Owain in turn gave him to the French. And through comrades of his† he escaped from Winchester† by night.

[1160–1161]. In the year of Christ one thousand one hundred and sixty naught happened.[1]

[1161–1162]. A year after that,† died Angharad, wife of Gruffudd. In that year died Maredudd,† bishop of Bangor. In that year Hywel ap Ieuaf took by treachery the castle of Tafolwern† in Cyfeiliog. And because of that† Owain ap Gruffudd fell into such great sorrow that neither the splendour of sovereignty nor the solace of aught else in the world could win him from his conceived grief. And although unbearable grief afflicted the mind of prince Owain, nonetheless through the providence of God, sudden joy raised him up. For the said Owain moved a host to Arwystli and came to Llandinam; and thence he carried away vast spoil. And the men of Arwystli gathered together from all sides, about three hundred men, along with Hywel ap Ieuaf, their lord. And they went after the spoil as far as Llanidloes.[2]† And when Owain saw his foes coming suddenly, he urged his men to fight manfully; and the foes were turned to flight and slain, so that scarcely a third escaped back. And when the prince saw that, he laid aside his conceived sorrow and returned to his original state of mind and gladness. And he repaired his castle a second time.

[1162–1163]. A year after that, Carreg Hofa fell before Owain ap Gruffudd and Owain ap Madog and Maredudd ap Hywel. In that year, Henry, king of England, came to Deheubarth, and a mighty host with him, as far as Pencadair. And after Rhys ap Gruffudd had given him hostages, he returned again to England. And then Einion ab Anarawd was slain in his sleep by a man of his own; and his name was Gwallter ap Llywarch. And Cadwgan ap Maredudd was slain by Walter fitz Richard.

In that year Rhys ap Gruffudd took Cantref Mawr, which was a large district, along with land that was at Dinefwr. In that year died Cedifor ap Daniel, archdeacon of Ceredigion. In that year died Henri ab Arthen, an eminent teacher excelling all clerics.

[1] In ... happened] When the year of Christ was 1161 (1160 D) there was nothing to be recorded that year save the consecration of Thomas as archbishop (bishop C) in Canterbury by the counsel of Henry, king of England BCD.
[2] Gorddwr Hafren BCD.

[1163–1164]. A year after that, when Rhys ap Gruffudd saw that the king would not keep aught of his promise to him, and that he could not live worthily, he manfully made for the land of Roger, earl of Clare; for it was at his instigation that Einion, his nephew and leader of his host, had been slain. And he breached the castle of Aber-rheidol and the castle of Mabwynion and burned them. And he gained possession of all Ceredigion and inflicted repeated slaughters and conflagration and despoilings upon the Flemings. And thereupon all the Welsh united together to throw off the rule of the French.

[1164–1165]. A year after that, Dafydd ab Owain ravaged Tegeingl, and he took all its people and all their chattels with him into Dyffryn Clwyd. And when the king of England thought that there was fighting against his castles which were[1] there, he moved a host with great haste and came to Rhuddlan, and he encamped there three nights. And he returned again to England and gathered a host beyond number of the picked warriors of England and Normandy and Flanders and Gascony and Anjou and all the North and Scotland. And he came to Oswestry, thinking to annihilate all Welshmen. And against him came Owain and Cadwaladr, sons of Gruffudd ap Cynan, and all the host of Gwynedd with them, and Rhys ap Gruffudd and with him the host of Deheubarth, and Owain Cyfeiliog and Iorwerth Goch ap Maredudd and the sons of Madog ap Maredudd and the host of all[2] Powys with them, and the two sons of Madog ab Idnerth and their host. And they gathered together fearlessly and boldly into Edeirnion, and pitched tents there at Corwen. And as they were thus on both sides staying in their tents, without the one daring to attack the other, at last the king of England was enraged; and he moved his host into the wood of Dyffryn Ceiriog,† and he had that wood cut down, and felled to the ground. And there a few picked Welshmen, in the absence of their leaders, manfully and valorously resisted them. And many of the bravest on either side were slain. And the king and his armies advanced, and he pitched his tents on the Berwyn mountain. And he stayed there a few days. And then there came upon them a mighty tempest of wind and bad weather and rains, and lack of food; and then he moved his tents into England. And in rage he had the eyes of the hostages, who had been long kept with him, gouged out; namely, two sons of Owain's, Rhys and Cadwallon, and Cynwrig and Maredudd, sons

[1] which were]—BC.
[2] all the host of BC.

of Rhys,† and several others. And for the second time, after he had changed his counsel, he moved a host to Chester. And there he encamped many days, until ships from Dublin and from the other towns of Ireland came to him. But since that number of ships was not sufficient for him, he rewarded the ships of Dublin with much wealth and sent them back to their land. And he himself and his host returned a second time to England.

In that year Rhys ap Gruffudd attacked the stronghold of Cardigan and the castle, and he destroyed and burned them; and he carried off vast spoil. And he occupied the castle of Cilgerran and captured Robert fitz Stephen and imprisoned him.

In that year, through the will of God and at the instigation of the Holy Spirit, a community of monks came to the place called Strata Florida. In that year† died Llywelyn ab Owain Gwynedd, the flower and splendour of the whole land, for he surpassed everyone in measure of praise, and his praise [was surpassed] by his intelligence, and his intelligence by his speech, and his speech by his manners.

[1165–1166]. A year after that, the French from Pembroke and the Flemings came to the castle of Cilgerran, and they strongly laid siege to it. And after many of them had been slain, they returned again empty-handed. They came to Cilgerran a second time and laid siege to the castle in vain, without gaining aught of it.

In that year Basingwerk† was destroyed by Owain ap Gruffudd. In that year Diarmaid MacMurchadha was driven from his territory.† And he came to Normandy to the king of England to complain to him and to beg that his territory be restored to him. In that year Iorwerth Goch was driven from his territory in Mochnant by the two Owains. And they shared Mochnant between them: Uwch-Rhaeadr to Owain Cyfeiliog, and Is-Rhaeadr to Owain Fychan.

[1166–1167]. A year after that, Owain and Cadwaladr, sons of Gruffudd, from Gwynedd, and Rhys ap Gruffudd from Deheubarth united to drive Owain Cyfeiliog in flight from his territory; and they took Caereinion from him and entrusted it to Owain ap Madog. And thereupon they attacked Tafolwern and gave it to Rhys ap Gruffudd, for it was said to be within his bounds. Soon after that, Owain Cyfeiliog and a host of the French with him came to the castle of Caereinion, which the Welsh had built; and he took and destroyed it, and burned it, and slew all the castle garrison.

Towards the end of that year Owain and Cadwaladr, princes of Gwynedd, and Rhys from Deheubarth, gathered together with their hosts to attack the castle of Rhuddlan. And they besieged it for three months; and after taking the castle and destroying it, and burning it, and after they had won the victory,† they returned again joyfully to their lands.

[1167–1168]. A year after that, Gwrgenau, abbot of Llwythlawr,† and Llawdden, his nephew, were slain by Cynan ab Owain.

[1168–1169]. A year after that, Robert fitz Stephen went to Ireland with a host of vast numbers along with Diarmaid MacMurchadha after he had been released from the prison of Rhys, his kinsman.† And they came to land at Wexford, and they laid siege to it and took it.

[1169–1170]. A year after that, Meurig ab Addaf[1]† was slain by his own first-cousin,† Maredudd Bengoch, through treachery in his sleep. At the end of that year, Owain ap Gruffudd ap Cynan, prince of Gwynedd, the man who was of great goodness and very great nobility and wisdom, the bulwark of all Wales, after innumerable victories, and unconquered from his youth, without ever having refused anyone that for which he asked, died in the month of December,† after taking penance and communion and confession and [making] a good end.

[1170–1170]. One thousand one hundred and seventy was the year of Christ when Dafydd ab Owain slew Hywel ab Owain, his eldest brother.

[1171–1171]. A year after that,† Thomas, archbishop of Canterbury, a man of great piety and saintliness and righteousness, was slain† by the counsel and at the instigation of Henry, king of England, on the fifth day from Christmas, before the altar of the Trinity in his own church at Canterbury, attired in his ecclesiastical vestments, and with the image of the Cross in his hand.

In that year, earl Richard, son of Gilbert Strongbow,[2]† went across the Irish Sea, and along with him a strong force of knights. And on the first attack he took Waterford. And he made an alliance with king Diarmaid and took his daughter for his wedded wife. And with his help he took Dublin, bringing into it a large fleet.†

---

[1] + of Builth BCD.
[2] + earl of Shropshire BCD.

In that year died Rhobert ap Llywarch. In that year died Diarmaid, king of Leinster, and he was buried in the city called Ferns.

In that year there was very great dissension between the king of England and the king of France because of the murder of archbishop Thomas. For the king of England had given to the king of France many sureties, namely, Henry, prince of Burgundy, and Theobald, his brother, a young lad, sons of Theobald, the good prince of that land and chief ruler of Flanders, that he would never do injury to the archbishop, when he gave him friendship.[1] And when Pope Alexander heard of the archbishop's death, he sent letters to the king of France and to the other sureties to bid them, upon pain of excommunication, to compel the king of England to come to the court of Rome to make amends for the death of the archbishop. And they harassed him on that account. But he sent messengers to the Pope's court to make known the reasons why he could not go to Rome. And then a great part of the year had gone by.

And while those events were taking place beyond the sea, Rhys ap Gruffudd gathered a mighty host to subdue Owain Cyfeiliog, his son-in-law;[2]† for on as many occasions as he could, he opposed Rhys. And Rhys forced him to submit to him, and took seven hostages from him.

In the meantime the king feared the sentence of the Pope of Rome; and he left the regions of Scotland† and came to England, and said that he desired to go to subdue Ireland. And he gathered to him all the leaders of England and Wales. And Rhys came to him where he was in the Forest of Dean about the last feast of Mary in the autumn. And he made friends with the king and made peace with him; and he promised him three hundred horses and four thousand oxen and fourteen† hostages. And thereupon the king approached Deheubarth. And on that journey, on the river Usk, he took Caerleon-on-Usk from Iorwerth ab Owain ap Caradog ap Gruffudd. And for that reason Iorwerth and his two sons, Owain and Hywel, whom he had had by Angharad, daughter of Uchdryd, bishop of Llandaff, and Morgan, son of Seisyll ap Dyfnwal by Dyddgu,† daughter of Owain, sister to Iorwerth, and many others destroyed all Caerleon to the tower and ravaged nearly all the land. And the king and a mighty host,† as was said, came to Pembroke on the eleventh day from the Calends of October. And then he gave

---
[1] support BD.
[2] his son-in-law]—BCD.

to Rhys all Ceredigion and all Ystrad Tywi and Ystlwyf and Efelffre. And that summer Rhys built Cardigan and its castle, which he had before that destroyed, when he took it from the earl of Clare; and in its taking he had captured Robert, son of Stephen by Nest, daughter of Rhys ap Tewdwr—and that Nest was aunt to Rhys, and that Robert was first-cousin to him. And brothers of that Robert were David, bishop of Menevia, and William fitz Gerald, and many others.

And so Rhys went from the castle of Cardigan to Pembroke to parley with the king. And he parleyed with him on the seventh† day from the Calends of October. And it was a Saturday. And on that day and the following Rhys bade all the horses which he had promised the king to be gathered to Cardigan by his coming, so that they might be ready to be sent to the king. And Rhys returned on Sunday and chose eighty-six horses.† And on the following day he set out towards Pembroke. And when he arrived there, he heard that the king had gone to Menevia on a pilgrimage. And at Menevia the king made an offering of material for two capes of brocaded silk for the use of the cantors, to serve God and David in that church. He also made an offering of a handful of silver, about ten shillings. And David fitz Gerald, the man who was then bishop of Menevia, begged the king to take meat at his court. But the king would not stay, to avoid excessive expense for the bishop; but he himself, and the bishop and three canons along with him, went into the hall to dine. And the king sat down; and earl Richard, who had come from Ireland to be reconciled with the king—for he had gone to Ireland against the king's will—and many others took their meat standing. And forthwith after their dinner, the king and his company mounted their horses in heavy rain—it was the feast of Michael—and came to Pembroke. And when Rhys heard that, he sent the horses to the king so that he might come to parley with the king after he had received the horses. And after the horses had been brought, the king took thirty-six of the choicest, and said that it was not because of any need in the world that he took them, but in order to requite Rhys a second time.† And having thus pleased the king, Rhys came to Whitland, and he found grace and favour before the king. And the king gave him Hywel, his son, who had been a hostage with the king for a long time before that. And he gave him a deferment concerning the other hostages whom he was due to give anew; and concerning the tribute, too, he granted a respite till the king should return from Ireland.

Thereupon a fleet was got ready, but the wind was not fair: for it was cloudy weather, and in that season the corn hardly ripened at all in Wales. And when the feast of Pope Calixtus came, the king sent to fetch ships to the harbour to have them put out to sea. And that day he went on board the ships. And when they reached the sea, the wind was still not favourable. And so the king, and a small company along with him, returned to land. And on the following day—it was Sunday evening—the king went on board the ships, with all weeping and he himself weeping. And on the following day, the sixteenth day from the Calends of Winter, with a prosperous wind he came to land in[1] Ireland. And there he stayed that winter without doing any harm to the Irish.

[1172–1172]. The year next after that, mortality befell those who had gone with the king to Ireland[2] because of the novelty of the unaccustomed foods, and also because the ships had not been able to sail with merchandise in winter, on account of the fury of the Irish Sea.

In that year, in the month of February,† died[3] Cadwaladr ap Gruffudd ap Cynan. And the king returned to England, messengers having been sent to him by the Pope and by Louis, king of France, and he left many earls and barons in Ireland—and that on the Friday after the Sunday of the Passion. And he stayed at Pembroke on Easter eve and Easter day; and on Easter Monday, after he had had parley with Rhys, he set out towards England. And the parley between them took place at Laugharne on the way.

And whilst he was going from Cardiff through the new town on the Usk,† he sent to Iorwerth ab Owain to bid him come to discuss peace with him. And he granted him and his sons a truce whilst they should be engaged therein. And when Owain ap Iorwerth—he was an excellent young man—at the request and instigation of his father, was making ready to go to the king's court along with his father, the earl of Bristol's men coming from Cardiff slew him. And after he had been slain, Iorwerth, his father, and Hywel, his brother, and many others, placing no trust in the king, ravaged the lands around Gloucester and Hereford, pillaging and burning and slaying without mercy. And the king left Rhys ap Gruffudd as justice on his behalf in all Deheubarth and went to France.

[1] land in]—BCD.
[2] were . . . in Ireland BCD.
[3] ir varw MS. *emend to* bu varw; by varw BCD.

In the meantime, in the month of August, Seisyll ap Dyfnwal and Ieuan ap Seisyll ap Rhiryd were seized by the king's men through treachery at Abergavenny.[1]†

[1173–1173]. A year after that, the temperature of the air was at its best during winter and spring and the month of May, till Ascension Thursday. And that day there were great thunders and great showers and a furious whirlwind, so that all the leaves of the trees fell to the ground. And insects that year devoured the leaves of the trees,[2] so that nearly all the trees of the woods were rent.

In that year† many men and animals died, nor was it surprising: for that year[3] there was born to Rhys a son† by the daughter of Maredudd, his brother.

In the meantime, whilst the king of England, Henry the Elder, was staying beyond the sea, Henry the Younger, his son, came to him to ask him what he might do or what he ought to do after his being ordained new king. For although he was king with many knights under him, yet he had no means whereby he could reward them, unless he obtained it from his father. And that was in Lent. And his father replied to him that he would give him for expenses twenty pounds daily of the money of that land. And the son, when he heard that, said that he had never heard of a king being a paid servant, and that he would not be such. And therefore the son,[4] after he had taken counsel, journeyed to the city of Tours to seek money on loan from the burgesses. And the father, when he heard that, sent secretly to the burgesses to forbid them to make any loan to his son. And forthwith he sent leading men from his court to keep friendly watch lest his son should go anywhere thence. And when the son had learned that, he feigned being merry and had his watchers made drunk with choice wine. And after they had been made drunk and were sleeping heavily, he arose by night, and a few men along with him, and went to the king of France, his father-in-law.

In the meantime Rhys ap Gruffudd sent Hywel, his son, to king Henry the Elder beyond the sea, to serve him at his court, so that he might the more thereby have kindness from the king, and so that the king might place greater trust in him.[5] And the king received him with honour and love, and thanked Rhys much for his fidelity.

---

[1] † and they were imprisoned in the castle of Abergavenny D.
[2] to the ground. And insects ... devoured the leaves of the trees]—BCD.
[3] that year]—BCD.
[4] the son]—BCD.
[5] the king ... in him]—BCD.

And then, however, the young king caused great disturbance to his father's territory with the support and help of his father-in-law and the sons of Theobald, prince of Burgundy and ruler of Flanders. And whilst the kings were thus contending beyond the sea, Iorwerth ab Owain of Caerleon† began to lay seige to Caerleon on Wednesday, the fifteenth day from the Calends of August. And he took it by force on a Saturday, having captured, on the Friday before that, all who were defending the bailey. And for those the castle was surrendered on the following day. And after that Hywel ap Iorwerth by night drew towards Gwent Is-Coed on the seventeenth day from the Calends of September; and on the following day, Friday, he won it all except the castles; and hostages were given to him by the leading men of the land.

That year Dafydd ab Owain of Gwynedd gained possession of all Anglesey, after driving Maelgwn, his brother, to Ireland.

[1174–1174]. A year after that, Dafydd ab Owain gained possession of all Gwynedd, after expelling all his brothers and uncles.† In that year Maelgwn was seized by Dafydd, his brother, and imprisoned. In that year died Cynan ab Owain, prince of Gwynedd.

[1175–1175]. A year after that, Hywel ap Iorwerth of Caerleon, unknown to his father, seized Owain Pen-carn,† his uncle; and he gouged his eyes out of his head and castrated him, lest he should beget issue who might hold authority over Caerleon. And on the following Saturday the French gained possession of Caerleon, having driven Iorwerth and Hywel, his son, out of it.

In that year king Henry the Elder made peace with Henry the Younger, his son, after a vast destruction of Normandy and of the lands next to it. Then Dafydd ab Owain seized through treachery Rhodri, his uterine† brother. And he harshly imprisoned him in shackles for seeking a portion of his patrimony from him. That same Dafydd then married the king's sister— Emma was her name—because he thought that he could hold his territory in peace thereby. But before the end of the year Rhodri escaped from his brother's prison, and he drove Dafydd, his brother, from Anglesey and across the Conway.

At that time, when he went to the king's council to Gloucester on the feast of James the Apostle, Rhys ap Gruffudd took with him all the princes of Wales who had incurred the king's displeasure, namely: Cadwallon ap Madog, his first-cousin, of Maelienydd, Einion Clud,† his son-in-law, of Elfael, Einion ap Rhys, his other son-in-law, of Gwerthrynion, Morgan ap Caradog ap Iestyn of Glamorgan, his nephew by Gwladus, his sister, Gruffudd ab Ifor ap Meurig of Senghenydd, his nephew by Nest, his sister, Iorwerth ab Owain of Caerleon, Seisyll ap Dyfnwal of Higher Gwent,† the man to whom Gwladus, Rhys's sister, was then married. All those returned along with Rhys, having obtained peace, to their own lands, yielding Caerleon to Iorwerth ab Owain.

And immediately after that, Seisyll ap Dyfnwal was slain through treachery in the castle of Abergavenny by the lord of Brycheiniog. And along with him Geoffrey, his son, and the best men of Gwent were slain. And the French made for Seisyll's court; and after seizing Gwladus, his wife, they slew Cadwaladr, his son. And on that day there befell a pitiful massacre in Gwent. And from that time forth, after that treachery, none of the Welsh dared place trust in the French. In that year Cadell ap Gruffudd died of a long infirmity and after assuming the habit of the Order in Strata Florida. And there he was buried. In that year a certain imperfect monk slew with a knife Richard, abbot of Clairvaux,† in a certain monastery near the city of Rheims.

[1176–1176]. A year after that, died Cynan, abbot of Whitland. And David, bishop of Menevia, died. And after him Peter became bishop.

At Christmas in that year the Lord Rhys ap Gruffudd held court in splendour at Cardigan, in the castle. And he set two kinds of contests there: one between bards and poets, another between harpists and crowders and pipers and various classes of music-craft. And he had two chairs set for the victors. And he honoured those with ample gifts. And of the harpists, a young man from Rhys's court won the victory. As between the bards, those of Gwynedd prevailed. Each of the suitors† obtained from Rhys that which he sought, so that no one was refused. And that feast, before it was held, was announced for a year through all Wales and England and Scotland and Ireland and the other islands.[1]

In that year the king assembled a council in the middle of Lent to London, to confirm there the laws of the churches[2] in the presence of a cardinal from Rome, who had come thither for

---

[1] † That castle and the castle of Cilgerran he had won a little before that, not through strength but by means of contrivances devised by the man and his own war-band, who was called Cedifor ap Dinawol, namely, hooked ladders which grasped the walls where they were placed. And to that man Rhys gave many gifts and freedom on his lands within his principality. And to that Cedifor he gave one of his daughters for wife C.
[2] Church BCD.

that. And because of strife that arose between the archbishop of Canterbury and the archbishop of York, the council was wrecked. For the archbishop of Canterbury had first occupied a seat.† And as the two bishops on the following day were disputing about their rights in the presence of the cardinal and all the court, certain men came behind the archbishop of York, as he sat on the cardinal's right, and drew the chair from under him and overturned him and his chair together, so that his back went heavily on to the floor; and he only just escaped with his life after he had been trampled upon and struck with feet and with hands.

[1177–1177]. A year after that, Einion Clud was slain. And Morgan ap Maredudd was slain. And Rhys ap Gruffudd built the castle of Rhaeadr-gwy.

[1178–1178]. A year after that, the sons of Cynan waged war against Rhys ap Gruffudd.

[1179–1179]. A year after that, Cadwallon† was slain. And a community was set up at Nant-teyrnon† near Caerleon,[1] which is called Dewma.[2]

[1180–1180]. In the year one thousand one hundred and eighty there was nothing that might be placed on record.†

[1181–1181]. A year after that,† died Pope Alexander. And after him Lucius succeeded as Pope. In that year Adam, bishop of St. Asaph, died at Oxford, and he was buried in the monastery of Osney.

[1182–1182]. A year after that, Ranulf de Poer was slain by young men from Gwent,† and many knights along with him.

[1183–1183]. A year after that, died king Henry the Younger. And Richard, archbishop of Canterbury, died.†

[1184–1184]. A year after that, died Rhydderch, abbot of Whitland. And Meurig, abbot of Cwm-hir, died.

[1185–1185]. A year after that,† the Patriarch came from Jerusalem to England to seek help from the king of England, lest the Saracens and the Jews should harry all the land of Jerusalem. And he went back with a multitude of knights and foot-soldiers along with him.

---

[1] + others call it the monastery of Dewma (Vegma C), others the monastery of Caerleon-on-Usk CD.
[2] which ... Dewma] *addition in* MS.

In that year the sun changed its colour on the day of the Calends of May; and, as some say, it was under an eclipse. In that year died Dafydd, abbot of Strata Florida. And Hywel ap Ieuaf, lord of Arwystli, died; and he was honourably buried at Strata Florida. And Einion ap Cynan died at Strata Florida.

[1186-1186]. A year after that, died Pope Lucius;† and after him Urban the Third succeeded as Pope.

In that year† a community went from Strata Florida to Rhedynog Felen in Gwynedd. And Peter, abbot of Clairvaux,† died. And Cadwaladr ap Rhys was slain in Dyfed, and he was buried at Whitland.

[1187-1187]. A year after that,† died Ithel, abbot of Strata Marcella.† And then Owain ap Madog, a man of great praise, beloved, strong and comely and generous, an ornament of good manners, was slain by the two sons of Owain Cyfeiliog, Gwenwynwyn and Cadwallon,[1] through treachery by night at Carreg Hofa.† And then Llywelyn ap Cadwallon[2] was unjustly seized by his brothers, and his eyes were gouged out of his head. And then Maelgwn ap Rhys, the shield and bulwark of all Wales, ravaged the town of Tenby and burned it. He was of brightest fame and beloved by all, and comely of face, though he was of a moderately sized body; harsh towards his enemies, and genial and kind towards his comrades, ready with gifts; in his home meek, in war a victor; all his neighbours dreaded him; like to a lion was he in his actions, and like a lion's whelp roaring in chase; the man who frequently slew the Flemings and who drove them to flight many a time.

[1188-1188]. A year after that, the Pagans and the Saracens came to Jerusalem, and they took the whole city on the first assault on Ash Wednesday, and carried off the Holy Cross with them. And the Christians whom they found in the city, some of them they killed and others they carried off with them into bondage.† And for that reason Philip, king of France, and Henry, king of England, and Baldwin, archbishop of Canterbury, and a multitude beyond number of Christians took the Cross.

[1189-1189]. A year after that, died Henry, king of England. And after him Richard, his son, the best and doughtiest knight, became king.

In that year Rhys ap Gruffudd took the castle of St. Clears and Abercorram and Llanstephan. In that year Maelgwn ap

---

[1] a Chaswallawn MS.
[2] D, Kaswallawn MS.

Rhys—the light and splendour and excellence and the shield and bulwark of all Deheubarth and its liberty, the dread of the Saxons, the best knight, a second Gawain†—was seized and imprisoned by his father and his brother.

[1190–1190]. One thousand one hundred and ninety was the year of Christ when Philip, king of France, and Richard, king of England, and Baldwin, archbishop of Canterbury, and earls and barons beyond number and a multitude of others, went as Crusaders to Jerusalem.†

In that year Rhys ap Gruffudd built the castle of Cydweli, and Gwenllïan, daughter of Rhys, the flower and beauty[1] of all Wales, died.

[1191–1191]. The year after that, died Gruffudd Maelor, lord of Powys, the most generous of all the princes of the Britons. In that year died Gwion, bishop of Bangor, a man of great piety and honour and dignity. And there was an eclipse of the sun.

In that year died† the most saintly man, Baldwin, archbishop of Canterbury. And Einion of Porth† was slain by his brother. And Rhys ap Gruffudd[2] took the castle of Nevern.[3]† And Owain ap Rhys died at Strata Florida.

[1192–1192]. The year after that, Maelgwn ap Rhys escaped from the prison of the lord of Brycheiniog. In that year Rhys ap Gruffudd took the castle of Lawhaden. And Gruffudd ap Cadwgan died.

[1193–1193]. A year after that, a certain earl seized Richard, king of England, as he was coming from Jerusalem; and he placed him in the emperor's prison. And for his release therefrom an immense tax and collection of money were imposed throughout all England, so much so that neither monks nor churchmen had either gold or silver to their name, not even the furnishings of the church and its chalices and its relics,[4] which they were not forced to give up entirely to the queen and the servants of the king.†

In this year Rhodri ab Owain subdued all the island of Anglesey through the help of the son[5] of Godred;† and before the end of the year after that he was expelled by the sons of Cynan ab Owain.

---

[1] + of all the women BC.
[2] Gruffudd ap Rhys CD.
[3] *Emend* Nyner MS. *to* Nyuer; Dinefwr B, Vyner *with* Din[e]vwr *in margin* D.
[4] furnishings and chalices BCD.
[5] sons BCD.

In that year the war-band of Maelgwn ap Rhys manfully breached the castle of Ystrad Meurig with slings and catapults.† In that year Hywel Sais ap Rhys took Wizo's Castle by treachery, and captured its owner, Philip fitz Wizo, and his wife and two sons. And that same Hywel, after he had seen that all his castles could not be held unless one of them were demolished, gave leave to Maelgwn, his brother, and his host to destroy the castle of Lawhaden. And after the Flemings had learned that, they gathered to the said castle on an appointed day; [and][1] without warning they rushed to attack those brothers, and after making a slaughter of their men they drove them to flight. And soon after that the Welsh gathered together, and they razed the said castle to the ground at their pleasure.

In that year Anarawd ap Rhys[2]† in his greed for worldly power† seized his two brothers, Madog and Hywel, and had their eyes gouged out of their heads.

[1194-1194]. A year after that, Maelgwn ap Rhys gave the castle of Ystrad Meurig to his brother for his hostages.† And Rhys ap Gruffudd for the second time built the castle of Rhaeadr-gwy. In that year Rhys ap Gruffudd was seized by his sons and was imprisoned†; but Hywel Sais deceived Maelgwn, his brother, and released his father from prison; and he took the castle of Nevern,[3] which belonged to Maelgwn.† And the sons of Cadwallon burned the castle of Rhaeadr-gwy. And Richard, king of England, returned from Jerusalem.

[4]In that year Llywelyn ap Iorwerth and the two sons of Cynan ab Owain and Rhodri ab Owain united together against Dafydd ab Owain,† and they drove him to flight and took from him all his territory except three castles.

[1195-1195]. A year after that, Roger Mortimer came with a host to Maelienydd. And he built a castle in the place called Cymaron and drove away the two sons of Cadwallon. The two sons of Rhys ap Gruffudd, namely, Rhys and Maredudd, took the castle of Dinefwr by treachery, and the castle of Cantref Bychan with the consent of the men of the land. And in that year they were a second time seized through treachery by their father at Ystrad Meurig, and they were imprisoned.†

[1196-1196]. A year after that, died the bishop of Bangor. And Rhys ap Gruffudd gathered a mighty host, and he fell upon

---

[1] —MS., BCD.
[2] + ap Gruffudd BCD.
[3] *Emend* Nyner MS. *to* Nyuer; Dinevwr BC, Vyner *with* Denewr *above* D.
[4] + *Marginal gloss*: 'The beginning of Llywelyn ap Iorwerth's conquest.' MS.

Carmarthen and destroyed and burned it to the ground, after the constable† of the castle alone had escaped. In that year he overcame the castle of Colunwy,† having with him a mighty host and many supporters of his, and he burned it to the ground. And thereafter that same Rhys and his host marched manfully against the castle of Radnor and took it and burned it. And after it had been burnt, on that day Roger de Mortimer and Hugh de Sai arrayed a mighty host in the valley near that town, and they placed their forces armed with corselets and shields and helmets against the Welsh. And when Rhys perceived that, as he was a great-hearted man, he armed himself like a lion with a strong hand and daring heart, and attacked his enemies and drove them to flight; and after driving them he manfully pursued them and slew them. And then the Marchers, oppressed with excessive terror, lamented that slaughter. And forthwith the same Rhys took Painscastle in Elfael.† And after taking it and making a pact with William de Breos, he left it in his peace.

In that year Hubert,[1]† archbishop of Canterbury, justice of all England and of all the kingdom, having gathered innumerable princes and earls and barons and knights, and the princes[2] of Gwynedd along with him, went against the castle of Gwenwynwyn at Welshpool.[3] And after laboriously laying siege to it with various kinds of catapults and slings, at last, when through a marvellous device sappers had been sent into the earth and had tunnelled under the castle, they forced the garrison to surrender the castle; and all the garrison escaped with their arms free and in peace, except for one who was slain. And thereupon, about the end of the year, Gwenwynwyn gathered his men, and he manfully laid siege to that castle and forced it to surrender to him, upon his pledging the garrison their lives and freedom to depart with their arms.

In that year died Gruffudd, abbot of Strata Marcella.†

[1197–1197]. A year after that,† there was an exceeding great mortality in all the island of Britain and France upon every kind of person. And that pestilence killed an untold number of people and a multitude of gentlefolk and many princes. And it spared no one. In that year, on the fourth day from the Calends of May, died Rhys ap Gruffudd, prince of Deheubarth and the unconquered head of all Wales. And his dire fate brought him low that year,—which should be narrated with

---

[1] Hu MS., *probably due to wrong extension of contraction* H. (= Hubertus).
[2] and earls . . . princes]—BCD.
[3] + and many earls, barons and knights (+ of England D) along with him BCD.

tears and recorded with grief worthy of[1] an elegy, for it was fraught with loss for everyone. That said Rhys, since he was sprung from the most gentle stock, and since he himself was the renowned head of his kindred, made his worthiness match his lineage; and thus he increased twofold the nobleness of his mind, a counsellor as he was of his kinsmen and a conqueror of the mighty, and a defender of the vanquished, powerful stormer of fortresses, inciter of armies, and assaulter of hostile troops. Like to the bravery of a forest boar growling, or to the lion lashing the ground with its tail in anger, even so would he rage amongst his enemies. Alas for the glory of battles and the shield of knights, the defender of his land, the splendour of arms, the arm of prowess, the hand of generosity, the eye and lustre of worthiness, the summit of majesty, the light of reason,[2] the magnanimity of Hercules! A second Achilles in the sturdiness of his breast, the gentleness of Nestor, the doughtiness of Tydeus, the strength of Samson, the valour of Hector, the fleetness of Eurialius,[3] the comeliness and face of Paris, the eloquence of Ulysses, the wisdom of Solomon, the majesty of Ajax!

Nor is it strange that we should lament the death that should cause so great a loss as that. And cruellest, tempestuous Fate, sister to Atropos, without knowing how or desiring to spare anyone, ventured[4] to approach with envious hand the personage of such a man as that;—he whom before that Fate, mother of human nature, had aided from the beloved commencement of his youth; and thereupon she suffered to be forgotten the height of her Wheel,[5] when she cast this man to the ground. Alas for the sure defence of the poor and their protection, raiment for the naked, food for the needy, drink for the thirsty! Alas for the ready abundance of gifts for all who sought them! Pleasant of speech, his deed[6] an adornment; the worthiness of manners, kind of speech, comely of face, meek and just towards all.

And these are the Latin metrical verses that were composed when the Lord Rhys died:

> Nobile Cambrensis cecidit dyadema decoris,†
> Hoc est, Resus obit, Cambria tota gemit.
> Resus obit; non fama perit, sed gloria transit;
> Cambrensis transit gloria, Resus obit.
> Resus obit, decus orbis abit, laus quoque tepescit;

---

[1] worthy sorrow and BCD.
[2] of majesty . . . reason]—BCD.
[3] Curialius MS.
[4] begged BCD.
[5] her Wheel] her gift BCD.
[6] deeds CD.

In gemitum[1] viuit Cambria, Resus obit.
Semper Resus obit populo quem viuus amauit;
Lugent corda, tacent corpora, Resus obit.
Resus obit, vexilla cadunt regalia signa.
Hic iam nulla leuat dextera, Resus obit.
Resus obit, ferrugo tegit galeam, tegit ensem;
Arma rubigo tegit, Cambria, Resus obit.
Resus abest, inimicus adest, Resus quia non est.
Iam tibi nil prodest, Cambria, Resus abest.
Resus obit, populi plorant, gaudent inimici;
Anglia stat, cecidit Cambria, Resus obit.
Ora rigant elegi cunctis mea fletibus isti,
Cor ferit omne ducis dira sagitta necis.
Omnis lingua canit Reso preconia, nescit
Laudes insignis lingua tacere ducis.
Ploratu plene vite laxantur habene.
Meta datur meri laus sine fine duci.
Non moritur, sed subtraitur quia semper habetur
Ipsius egregium nomen in orbe nouum.
Camber, Locrinus Reso rex Albaque nactus
Nominis et laudis inferioris erant.
Cesar et Arthurus, leo fortis vterque[2] sub armis,
Vel par vel similis Resus vtrique fuit.
Resus Alexander in velle pari fuit alter,
Mundum substerni gliscit vterque sibi.
Occasus solis tritus Resi fuit armis,
Sensit Alexandri solis in orbe manum.
Laus canitur cineri sancto; cantetur ab omni
Celi laus regi debita spiritui.
Penna madet lacrimis quod scribit thema doloris,
Ne careat forma littera cesset ea.

After those, these are metrical verses of Latin which are an eulogy on his sepulchre and which were composed after he had been buried:

Grande decus tenet iste locus, si cernitur ortus;
Si quis sit finis queritur, ecce cinis:
Laudis amator, honoris odor, dulcedinis auctor,
Resus in hoc tumulo conditur exiguo;
Cesaries quasi congeries solis radiorum
Principis et facies vertitur in cineres.
Hic tegitur, sed detegitur quia fama perhennis,
Non sinit illustrem voce latere ducem.
Colligitur tumba cinis hac, sed transuolat vltra
Nobilitas claudi nescia fune breui.
Wallia iam viduata dolet ruitura dolore.†

And after the death of the Lord Rhys, Gruffudd, his son, ruled his kingdom after him,—he who was thereafter exiled by

[1] gemitu D.
[2] Vtherque D.

Maelgwn ap Rhys, his brother, the man who was then without a portion of his patrimony. And his war-band with him, and the war-band of Gwenwynwyn as well, they came to Aberystwyth; and there they captured Gruffudd ap Rhys and slew some of his men and imprisoned others. And they gained possession of the whole land of Ceredigion and its castles, and sent Gruffudd to Gwenwynwyn's prison; whom Gwenwynwyn after that gave willingly to the Saxons. And Gwenwynwyn subdued Arwystli. And then Llywelyn ap Iorwerth seized Dafydd ab Owain.

In that year died Owain Cyfeiliog, after he had assumed the habit of the Order at Strata Marcella. In that year died Owain ap Gruffudd Maelor and Owain of Brithdir, son of Hywel ap Ieuaf, and Maelgwn ap Cadwallon of Maelienydd. In that year Trahaearn Fychan of Brycheiniog, a brave eminent man and of gentle lineage, with the niece of the Lord Rhys—his sister's daughter—as his wife, came incautiously to Llan-gors, to the court of his lord, William de Breos, and there he was seized and imprisoned. And as a pitiful example and with unusual cruelty he was bound by his feet to the tail of a strong horse, and was thus drawn along the streets of Brecon as far as the gallows; and there his head was struck off and he was hanged by his feet; and he was for three days on the gallows,† after his brother and his son and his wife, niece of the Lord Rhys, had fled from such peril as that.

[1198–1198]. A year after that, Maelgwn ap Rhys, after handing over Gruffudd, his brother, to the Saxons, took the castle of Cardigan and the castle of Ystrad Meurig, and gained possession of them. In that year a community from Cwm-hir went to reside at Cymer in Nannau in Meirionnydd.

In that year the youngest sons of the Lord Rhys took the castle of Dinefwr from the French.†

In that year Gwenwynwyn gathered a mighty host to seek to win for the Welsh their original rights and to restore their bounds to their rightful owners, which they had lost through the multitude of their sins,† and that about the feast of Mary Magdalene, with the help and support of all the princes of Wales. And after they had assembled together, they laid siege to Painscastle in Elfael†; and for three weeks they were laying siege to it without any recourse to catapults or slings. And when the Saxons learned that, they were amazed; but nevertheless they then set free Gruffudd ap Rhys, the man who was in their prison.† And they gathered all the might of England, and they sent to seek to make peace with the Welsh. And the Welsh said that they would burn their cities for the Saxons once they had taken the castle, and that they would carry off their spoils and destroy them too. And the Saxons, being unable to suffer that, as God showed thereafter,† fell upon the Welsh and immediately drove them to flight and slew untold numbers of them like sheep. And in that wretched slaughter Anarawd ab Einion and Owain ap Cadwallon† and Rhiryd ap Iestyn and Rhobert† ap Hywel were slain; and Maredudd ap Cynan was captured and imprisoned. And so the Saxons returned joyfully to their land, enriched with the spoils of the Welsh.

In that year Gruffudd ap Rhys manfully sought[1] a portion of his patrimony from Maelgwn, his brother, and he obtained it save for two castles, namely, Cardigan and Ystrad Meurig. And one of them, namely, Cardigan, soon after that Maelgwn swore upon many relics in the presence of monks and ecclesiastics to give on an appointed day to Gruffudd, his brother, in return for his receiving from him hostages, for keeping peace with him. And he scorned the oath and did not restore the castle in spite of receiving the hostages. And those hostages, soon after that, divine power snatched from Gwenwynwyn's prison.

In that year died Peter, bishop of Menevia.

[1199–1199]. A year after that, Maelgwn ap Rhys gathered a host and fell upon the castle of Dineirth, which Gruffudd had built; and of as many men as he found there some he slew and others he imprisoned. And Gruffudd took the castle of Cilgerran by treachery† and held it.

In that year, as king Richard was laying siege to the castle of a baron of his who was against him, one from the castle wounded him with a bolt-shot, so that his life came to an end. And then John, his brother, was raised to be king after him.

[1200–1200]. One thousand and two hundred was the year of Christ when Gruffudd ap Cynan ab Owain died, making a good end, after assuming the habit of the Order at Aberconwy, the man† who was known by all in the island of Britain because of the abundance of his gifts and his gentleness and his goodness. Nor is it strange, for so long as the men that now are shall live, they will remember his fame and his praise and his deeds.

In that year, about the feast of Mary Magdalene, Maelgwn ap Rhys, for fear and also in hatred of Gruffudd, his brother, sold to the Saxons the lock and stay of all Wales, the castle of

---

[1] gathered BCD.

Cardigan, for a small worthless price. In that year there was built a monastery in Iâl, which is called Llynegwestl.†

[1201–1201]. A year after that, Llywelyn ap Iorwerth, being a young man graced with generosity and worthiness, gained possession of the cantref of Llŷn and Eifionydd,† after driving out Maredudd ap Cynan because of his treachery.

In that year the community of Strata Florida went to the new church on the eve of Whit Sunday, after it had been nobly and handsomely built.

About the feast of Peter and Paul after that, Maredudd ap Rhys was slain in Carnwyllion,† an eminent young man, a terror† to his enemies, the love of his friends, like a flash of lightning-fire between armed hosts, the hope of the men of the South, the dread of England, the honour of cities and the splendour of the world. And Gruffudd, his brother, gained possession of his castle at Llandovery, and along with it the cantref in which it was. He was† a wise, prudent man, and, as was hoped, he would in a short while have restored the March† of all Wales, if only his envious fate had not snatched him away on the feast of James the Apostle after that. And to tell† of him in a few words and to give praise to the eminent father—not in age, but in manners and strength—in that year died the Gruffudd of whom we are speaking, son to the Lord Rhys and a prince of Wales by right and inheritance, after assuming the habit of the Order at Strata Florida; and there he was honourably buried.

In that year the earth quaked greatly and marvellously in Jerusalem.

[1202–1202]. A year after that, Maredudd ap Cynan was expelled from Meirionnydd, because of his treachery, by Hywel ap Gruffudd, his nephew, his brother's son, and he was despoiled of all his possessions except his horse. In that year the Welsh took the castle of Gwerthrynion on the eighth day from the feast of Peter and Paul. And its owner at that time was Roger de Mortimer. And they forced the garrison to submit to them, and they burned the castle to the ground.

In that year† Llywelyn ap Iorwerth moved a mighty host to Powys,[1] to subdue Gwenwynwyn and to gain possession of his territory: for though he was a kinsman to him by blood and a near relation, yet he was a man most hostile to him in deeds. And Llywelyn summoned to him all his kinsmen and all his leaders, and those swore to him unanimously to war against

---

[1] to Powys]—CD.

Gwenwynwyn. And after questioning them earnestly, each one revealed his conscience. And after Llywelyn had realised that Elise ap Madog would not willingly agree in that matter, Llywelyn with all his heart devised to make peace with Gwenwynwyn; and he sent to him, and drove Elise from all his land and completely deprived him of his patrimony. And after that, through the intercession of men of the Church and laymen arranging[1] peace between Llywelyn and Gwenwynwyn, Llywelyn of his mercy allowed Elise the castle of Crogen† and seven small townships along with it. And so Llywelyn returned again after he had taken the castle of Bala.

In that year Rhys Ieuanc ap Gruffudd, son of Lord Rhys the Great, by diligence† and invention, took the castle of Llandovery on the feast-day of Michael.

[1203–1203]. A year after that, Rhys ap Gruffudd took the castle of Llanegwad. In that year Llywelyn ap Iorwerth expelled Dafydd ab Owain from Gwynedd; and he died in England. In that year the castle of Llandovery and the castle of Llangadog were taken by catapults and slings by Gwenwynwyn and Maelgwn, and the garrisons that were in them were driven away. In that year Maelgwn ap Rhys completed the castle of Dineirth.

[1204–1204]. A year after that, Hywel, son of Lord Rhys the Great, was slain in Cemaes through betrayal[2]† by the men of Maelgwn, his brother†; and he died after he had assumed the habit of the Order at Strata Florida, and he was honourably buried in the same grave as[3]† Gruffudd, his brother.

In that year Maelgwn ap Rhys lost as it were the bolts and stays of all his territory and all else he had to his name, to wit, Dinefwr and Llandovery. And those castles the sons of Gruffudd, his brother, manfully took.

In that year William Marshal, and a great host with him, came against the castle of Cilgerran, and he took the castle.

[1205–1205]. A year after that, died Hubert, archbishop of Canterbury and legate to the Pope of Rome and chief counsellor† of all England.

In that year Maelgwn ap Rhys caused a certain Irishman to slay with a battle-axe,† on the Monday before Ascension Thursday, Cedifor ap Gruffudd, a praiseworthy man, gracious, strong and generous, by treachery and unjustly,† him and his

---

[1] y furyfhaut MS. *with* –t *added above line. Read* y furyfhau.
[2] *Emend* o vrath MS. *to* o vrat. *Cf.* drwy dwyll (RB version); CW p. 6, dolo.
[3] in . . . as] like CD.

four sons, after they had been seized. And those sons were sprung from the most gentle stock, for their mother was Susanna, daughter of Hywel by the daughter of Madog ap Maredudd.

[1206–1206]. A year after that, cardinal John came from Rome to England, and he gathered together bishops and abbots and monks beyond number, and held a stately synod wherein to confirm the laws of the Church.

In that year Maelgwn ap Rhys built the castle of Abereinion. In that year there came to the estuary of the Ystwyth such an abundance of fish that their like was never heard of.

[1207–1208†]. A year[1] after that, Christianity was interdicted throughout all England and Wales because John, king of England, opposed the election of the archbishop of Canterbury.

In that year William de Breos, a man of gentle lineage and discreet, was banished by the king of England from all his land to Ireland because of enmity and envy towards William the Younger. His son and his wife and his grandsons were banished along with him, in disgrace and with the loss of their possessions.

In that year Gwenwynwyn was seized at Shrewsbury by the king. And Llywelyn ap Iorwerth made for his territory and gained possession of it all and his castles and his townships. And when Maelgwn ap Rhys learned that, for fear of Llywelyn he razed the castle of Ystrad Meurig to the ground. And he burned Dineirth and Aberystwyth. Llywelyn, however, in spite of that did not abandon his purpose, but he came to Aberystwyth and there he built the castle again and gained for himself the cantref of Penweddig and held it; and the other portion, between the Dyfi and the Aeron, he gave to the sons of Gruffudd, his [*sc*. Maelgwn's] nephews.

In that year Rhys Fychan took the castle of Llangadog, unmindful of the pact which he had made with his nephews, and unheedful of the service which they had rendered to him when he took the castle of Dinefwr on the feast-day of Michael.

[1208–1209]. A year after that, Rhys and Owain, sons of Gruffudd, manfully attacked the castle of Llangadog, and after killing some and capturing others of the garrison, they burned the castle.

[1209–1210]. A year after that,† John, king of England, and a mighty host with him, about Whit Sunday went to Ireland. And he took the land and the castle[2] of the sons of Hugh de Lacy

---
[1] Three years C, Two years D.
[2] castles D.

from them. And after he had subdued all the people of Ireland, and had seized the wife of William de Breos and William the Younger, her son, and his wife and his son and his daughter, about the Calends of August he returned to England. And William the Younger and Matilda of St. Valéry, his mother, he had put to a horrible death in the castle of Windsor.

In that year the earl of Chester again built the castle of Degannwy, which Llywelyn ap Iorwerth had destroyed for fear of the king. And the same earl built the castle of Holywell. And Llywelyn ravaged the land of that said earl. And then Rhys Fychan made peace with the king, and he subdued the castle of Llandovery with the king's help. And the garrison surrendered the castle, after they had despaired of any kind of support, upon their being given their lives and their safety and what was theirs and all their chattels free and sixteen steeds. And that was on the last feast-day of Mary in the autumn.[1]

In that year, about the feast of Andrew the Apostle, Gwenwynwyn recovered his land with the support of the king of England. And then Maelgwn ap Rhys was joyful because of that, and he made a mutual pledge with the king. And forthwith, unmindful of the oath and pledge he had given to Rhys and Owain, his nephews, sons of Gruffudd, he gathered a mighty host of French and Welsh; and he attacked the cantref of Penweddig, and encamped at Cilcennin. And Rhys and Owain, sons of Gruffudd, and their war-band of picked men, about three hundred men, fell upon the host by night, and killed some and captured others, and drove the others to flight. And in that battle Cynan ap Hywel, nephew of Maelgwn, and Gruffudd ap Cadwgan, Maelgwn's chief counsellor, were captured, and Einion ap Caradog and many others were slain. And Maelgwn, after many of his men had been slain and others had been captured, shamefully fled on foot by night and escaped.

That year Ingelard,[2] sheriff of Gloucester, fortified the castle of Builth, after the Welsh, however, had slain many of his men there before that.†

That year, on the feast-day of Thomas the Martyr, died Matilda de Breos, mother of the sons of Gruffudd ap Rhys, after taking penance and receiving communion and confession at Llanbadarn-fawr, and after assuming the habit of the Order; and she was buried at Strata Florida by the side of Gruffudd, her wedded husband.

[1] in the autumn]—CD.
[2] engelart MS. *with* b *added after* –l– *above line.*

[1210–1211]. In the year of Christ one thousand two hundred and ten Llywelyn ap Iorwerth led frequent attacks against the Saxons, harassing them cruelly. And because of that, John, king of England, gathered a mighty host and made for Gwynedd, planning to dispossess Llywelyn and to destroy him utterly. And he summoned to him along with him all the princes of Wales, namely, Gwenwynwyn of Powys and Hywel ap Gruffudd ap Cynan and Madog ap Gruffudd Maelor and Maredudd ap Rhobert of Cydewain and Maelgwn and Rhys Fychan, sons of the Lord Rhys. And the king came as far as Chester. And then Llywelyn ap Iorwerth had Perfeddwlad and Anglesey and all their chattels moved to the wilderness of Eryri. And the king came, according to his plan, to the castle of Degannwy. And there the host suffered lack of food to such an extent that an egg was sold for a penny-halfpenny; and they found the flesh of their horses as good as the best dishes. And because of that the king, having lost many of his men, about Whit Sunday returned in shame to England without having fulfilled aught of his mission. And after that, about the Calends of August, he returned again to Gwynedd, and with him a host that was greater and fiercer; and he built castles therein, and went across the river Conway towards the mountains of Eryri; and he sent some of his men to the city of Bangor to burn it. And Rhobert, bishop of Bangor, was seized in his church, but he was ransomed for two hundred falcons.

And then Llywelyn, being unable to suffer the king's rage, sent his wife, the king's daughter, to him by the counsel of his leading men to seek to make peace with the king on whatever terms he could. And after Llywelyn had accepted safe conduct to go to the king and to come away from him free, he went to the king and was reconciled to him on condition of his giving the king hostages from amongst the leading men of the land, and of his binding himself to give the king twenty thousand cattle and forty steeds. And he granted, too, to the king all Perfeddwlad and what appertained to it, for ever. And then all the princes of Wales made peace with the king, except the two sons of Gruffudd, son of Lord Rhys the Great, namely, Rhys and Owain. And the king with great joy and victory returned to England.

And he commanded Falkes, sheriff of Cardiff, to take all the host of Glamorgan and Dyfed with him, and Maelgwn and Rhys Fychan, sons[1] of the Lord Rhys, and their hosts along with him, to force the sons of Gruffudd ap Rhys to yield or else to

---

[1] *Emend* vab MS. *to* veibion.

drive them from all the kingdom. And the said Falkes and Maelgwn and Rhys Fychan, having gathered together all their might, made for the cantref of Penweddig. And the said Rhys and Owain, sons of Gruffudd, being unable to encounter such great might as that, sent messengers to Falkes to draw up peace for them; for there was no place for them to flee to in all Wales. And they granted to the king all their land between the Aeron and the Dyfi. And forthwith Falkes built a castle for the king at Aberystwyth. And Rhys and Owain went to the king under the safe conduct of Falkes; and the king received them into reconciliation and into peace. And while they were on their way to the king's court, Maelgwn and Rhys Fychan repented of their reconciliation with the king, and they fell upon the new castle at Aberystwyth and razed it to the ground. And when Rhys and Owain returned from the king's court reconciled to the king, they made a disturbance in Maelgwn's land, Is-Aeron, and carried off from it vast spoil, after killing many of Maelgwn's men, amongst whom was slain Bachglas: he was a strong young man.

In that year died Gruffudd ab Ifor[1] and Maredudd ap Caradog.†

[1211–1212]. A year after that, Llywelyn ap Iorwerth, prince of Gwynedd, being unable to suffer the injuries which the men from the new castles† were inflicting upon him, made a solemn pact with the princes of Wales, namely, Gwenwynwyn, Maelgwn ap Rhys, Madog ap Gruffudd Maelor, Maredudd ap Rhobert. And he rose up against the king, and by the end of two months he laid siege to all the castles which the king had built in Gwynedd, and took them all except two, Degannwy and Rhuddlan. And they laid siege to the castle of Mathrafal in Powys, which Robert Vieuxpont had built. And the king came with a mighty host and beat them off from that castle. And he himself set fire to the castle and burned it.

In that year Robert Vieuxpont hanged at Shrewsbury Rhys ap Maelgwn, an excellent boy not yet seven years old, who was a hostage with the king. In that year died Rhobert, bishop of Bangor.

[1212–1212 *continued*]. A year after that,† there was a battle in Spain between the Christians and the Saracens. And there were slain of the Saracens and the Pagans seventy thousand† men and three thousand women.

[1] Iorwerth CD.

In that year three leaders of gentle birth from Wales were hanged in England, namely, Hywel ap Cadwallon, Madog ap Maelgwn, Meurig Barach.†

In that year Pope Innocent the Third absolved three princes, namely, Llywelyn ap Iorwerth and Gwenwynwyn and Maelgwn ap Rhys, from the oath and allegiance they owed to the king of England. And he enjoined upon them, for the remission of their sins, to direct friendly endeavour and action against the iniquity of that king. And he interdicted the churches for five years in all England and Wales, except for the territory of those three princes and those who were leagued with them.† And they by unanimous counsel gained possession of† Perfeddwlad, which was before that in the hands of the king, and that with spirited manliness.

[1213–1213]. A year after that, when Rhys[1] ap Gruffudd, grandson of the Lord Rhys, saw that he alone had no portion of his patrimony, he sent messengers to the king to seek by his help a portion of his patrimony. And the king commanded Falkes,† sheriff of Hereford, and Falkes, sheriff of Cardiff, to support him manfully. And they were commanded to drive Rhys Fychan from all Ystrad Tywi, unless he gave the castle of Llandovery and its appurtenances to the sons of Gruffudd ap Rhys. And after they had been summoned for this purpose, Rhys Fychan gave answer and said that he would not share with them a single acre of land. And then Rhys ap Gruffudd, full of rage and indignation, moved a mighty host from Brycheiniog and came by force to the land of Ystrad Tywi; and in the place called Trallwng Elgan† he encamped. And on the following day, the Thursday next after the feast of St. Hilary, there came to him Falkes, sheriff of Cardiff, and Owain, his [*sc*. Rhys's] brother, and a host along with them. And on the following day they marched thence,† with Rhys as leader in the van of the first troop, and Falkes in the van of the second troop, and Owain in the van of the rear troop. And Rhys Fychan encountered the first troop. And after they had fought hard, Rhys Fychan was there and then driven to flight, after many of his men had been slain and others had been captured. And whilst Rhys Ieuanc was fighting, Rhys Fychan went and fortified the castle of Dinefwr with men and arms, and he completely burned the town of Llandeilo-fawr and made off. But Rhys Ieuanc came before the castle. And on the following day he had ladders placed against the walls, and armed men to scale the walls. And on

---
[1] + Ieuanc D.

the first assault the whole castle was taken, except for the tower. And in that all the garrison gathered together and they defended strongly with missiles and stones and other engines. And from without archers and crossbow-men were shooting missiles, and sappers digging, and armed knights making unbearable assaults, till they were forced before the afternoon to surrender the tower. And they gave three picked hostages that they would surrender[1] the castle unless help came to them by the following day,† upon their being allowed in safety their lives and their limbs and their arms. And so it happened. And after the castle had been taken and the land of[2] Cantref Mawr had been overrun, Rhys Fychan, he and his wife and his sons, and all his chattels, went to Maelgwn, his brother, the castle of Llandovery having been fortified with men and arms and other things for the defence of the castle.

And Rhys Ieuanc went to Brycheiniog. And along with a mighty host of French and Welsh he came a second time before[3] Llandovery. And before they encamped, the garrison surrendered the castle on condition that they should be granted their lives and their members.

In that year John, king of England, went to the archbishop of Canterbury to do penance. And he recalled the archbishop and the bishops[4] and the clerics who had gone into exile because of the interdict upon the churches. And for the oppressive wrong he had done to the Church of England he bound himself and all his heirs and all his kingdom in England and Wales and Ireland to God and Peter and Paul and Pope Innocent and to all his successors in the Faith for ever. And he did homage thereupon, paying to the Church of Rome every year a thousand marks of silver for every service and custom which he was bound to observe to that end. And he swore, too, that he would restore everything that he had taken from the Church.

In that year Rhys Fychan was seized† at Carmarthen, after he had deserted the Welsh, and he desired to make a pact with them a second time. And he was placed in the king's prison.

In that year Llywelyn ap Iorwerth took the castle of Degannwy and the castle of Rhuddlan,† and he gained possession of them.

[1214-1214]. The year after that, John, king of England, and along with him a vast multitude of fighting men, sailed to Poitou. And after the count of Flanders and the count of

---

[1] y rodynt D, ony rodynt MS.
[2] the land of]—CD.
[3] a second time before] to CD.
[4] bishop BCD.

Boulogne and the count of Hainaut and Otto, emperor of Rome, his nephew, and Salisbury, his brother, and many others from amongst knights and leaders had made a solemn pact with him, he rose up with great turmoil and war against Philip, king of France. And the emperor Otto, and the said counts along with him, molested the king of France from the direction of Flanders, and king John from the direction of Poitou, and they sought to harass the kingdom of France on every side of it. And the eminent king Philip sent Louis, his son, into Poitou to oppose the king of England as best he could. And he himself, and with him his counts, and the French came into Flanders against the Emperor and the counts. And the emperor and the counts, marvelling in a way that the king of France was so boldly coming against them, came to fight with him. And after fighting long, through God's providence[1] the victory fell to the king of France, the emperor ignominiously fleeing, and the count of Flanders and the count of Boulogne and the earl of Salisbury being captured at Vernon.† And the king of England for that reason feared to continue war against the king of France. And after making a seven-years' truce with him, he returned to England. And he restored[2] to the clerics almost all that had been taken from them.

In that year died Geoffrey, bishop of Menevia.

[1215–1215]. A year after that, strife arose between John, king of England, and the Northerners of England and many other leading men of the realm, because they were not getting from him the laws and the good customs that had been in the age of king Edward and king Henry, the first king[3] of the kings of England†; for he had sworn, when he was absolved, to give them to the kingdom. And that strife spread so much that all the leading men of England and the princes of Wales made a pact together against the king that no one of them, without the consent of all the others, would make peace or agreement or truce with the king until he gave to the Church its liberty and its rights, whereof he and his ancestors before him had long deprived the Church, and until there should be restored to each one of them their laws[4] and their power and their castles, which he had taken from them without law or truth or justice. And after the archbishop of Canterbury and his bishops and earls and barons had asked and instructed him† whether he would restore

---
[1] vision BCD.
[2] to England ... restored]—BCD.
[3] Edward and king ... king] Edward the first king BCD.
[4] until ... laws] until their laws should come to each one of them BCD.

to them their laws, he answered that he would not restore, that he would not give to the Church or to the barons or to the kingdom, laws or anything through fear of them. And he took the Cross.

And then the men of the North from the one side rose up against him, and the Welsh from the other side. And in the first expedition the men of the North subdued the city of London. And Llywelyn ap Iorwerth, prince of Gwynedd, and the Welsh made for Shrewsbury; and the town and the castle were surrendered to them without resistance. And then Giles de Breos, the man who was bishop at Hereford, son to William de Breos, since he had been the first and foremost of the confederates against the king, sent Reginald de Breos, his brother, to Brycheiniog; and the Welsh of that land received him honourably. And about the Calends of May he took the castle of Pencelli and Abergavenny and White Castle and Grosmont† and Skenfrith† before the end of three days. And thereupon, when bishop Giles came, the castle of Radnor and Hay and Brecon and Builth and Blaenllyfni were surrendered to him without any resistance. And he left Painscastle and the castle of Colunwy† and the cantref of Elfael to Gwallter Fychan ab Einion Clud.

And whilst that was taking place in Brycheiniog, Rhys Ieuanc ap Gruffudd, son of the Lord Rhys, and Maelgwn ap Rhys, his uncle, were reconciled. And together they fell upon Dyfed, and they subdued all the Welsh of Dyfed, except for Cemaes. The castle of Arberth and the castle of Maenclochog they burned, and Cemaes they plundered. And then Maelgwn and Owain, son[1] of Gruffudd, went to Llywelyn, to Gwynedd. Rhys Ieuanc ap Gruffudd moved his host to Cydweli, and he subdued it and the commot of Carnwyllion, and he burned the castle. And thence he went to Gower, and set fire to the castle of Loughor and burned it. And he made for the castle of Hugh de Meules at Tal-y-bont,[2]† and the garrison sought to hold it against him. But he took it by force and burned some[3] of the garrison and slew others. And on the following day he made his way towards Seinhenydd, and for fear of him the garrison burned their town. But he, not desisting from his plan, made for the castle of Oystermouth, and on the first day he took the castle, and there he encamped that night. And on the following day he burned the castle and the town. And he took all the

---

[1] ap D, veibion MS.
[2] Talybonet MS., Talybonedd BD.
[3] many BCD.

castles of Morgannwg† before the end of three days. And he returned joyful with victory. And thereupon Rhys Fychan was released from the king's prison, after his son had been given as a hostage for him, and two other hostages along with him.

That year Iorwerth, abbot of Talley,[1] was made bishop at Menevia, and Cadwgan, abbot of Llandyfâi,[2]† bishop at Bangor. And then Giles, bishop of Hereford, son of William de Breos, made peace with the king of England and joined in a pact with him for fear of the Pope. But as he was returning from the king's court, he died of a severe illness at Gloucester about the feast of Martin. And as his heir to his patrimony came Reginald de Breos, his brother. And he took for his wedded wife the daughter of Llywelyn ap Iorwerth, prince of Gwynedd.

In that year Pope Innocent the Third assembled a council from all Christendom to the Lateran church in Rome on the feast of Simon and Jude. And in that council the laws of the Church were renewed, and the aiding of the land of Jerusalem, which had been oppressed by Saracens for many years before that, was discussed.

In that year Llywelyn ap Iorwerth, by counsel of† all the princes of Wales along with him, led a host, by their common counsel, against Carmarthen. And by the fifth day the castle was surrendered to them, and they razed it to the ground. And thereupon they overthrew to the ground[3] Llanstephan and St. Clears and Laugharne. And thereupon on the eve of the feast of Thomas the Apostle, they came into Ceredigion, and they took the new castle in Emlyn.† And they subjugated the men of Cemaes, and the castle of Trefdraeth was surrendered to them; and by the common counsel of the princes it was razed to the ground. And when the garrison of Cardigan saw that they could not hold out in their castle, they surrendered the castle on the feast-day of Stephen the Martyr. And on the feast-day of John the Evangelist the castle of Cilgerran was surrendered to them. And thereupon Llywelyn, prince of Gwynedd, and all the other princes who had come with him returned again joyful with victory to their lands. And these are the names of the princes who were with Llywelyn ap Iorwerth: from Gwynedd there were Hywel ap Gruffudd ap Cynan and Llywelyn ap Maredudd; from Powys there were Gwenwynwyn ab Owain Cyfeiliog and Maredudd ap Rhobert and the war-band of Madog ap Gruffudd Maelor; from Deheubarth there were the two sons

---

[1] of Talley] o Ta*ll*. MS. *with* Tal-y-llychau *written above*;—BCD.
[2] Llanndefit MS., Llandevic BCD.
[3] And thereupon . . . ground]—BC. And thereupon they destroyed the castle of D.

of Maelgwn ap Cadwallon and Maelgwn, son of the Lord Rhys, and Rhys Ieuanc and Owain, sons of Gruffudd ap Rhys, and Rhys Fychan, son of the Lord Rhys. And these are the names of the castles which they took then: Seinhenydd, Cydweli, Carmarthen, Llanstephan, St. Clears, Laugharne, Trefdraeth, Cardigan, Cilgerran. And while that war lasted, so great was the mildness of the air and the fine weather that a winter as mild as it was never seen nor heard of before that.

[1216–1216]. A year after that, there was an apportioning of land between the sons of the Lord Rhys, Maelgwn and Rhys Gryg,[1] and Rhys and Owain, sons of Gruffudd, son of the Lord Rhys, at Aberdyfi,† after almost all the leading men of Wales had been assembled there before the Lord Llywelyn and all the learned men of Gwynedd. And to Maelgwn, the eldest son of the Lord Rhys, came three cantrefs of Dyfed, namely, Cantref Gwarthaf and the cantref of Cemaes and the cantref of Emlyn, and Peuliniog and the castle of Cilgerran; and of Ystrad Tywi there came to him the castle of Llandovery and two commots, Hirfryn and Mallaen, and the manor of Myddfai†; of Ceredigion there came to him two commots, Gwynionydd and Mabwynion. To Rhys Ieuanc and Owain, his brother, came the castle of Cardigan and the castle of Nantyrarian and three cantrefs of Ceredigion along with them. To Rhys Gryg came the castle of Dinefwr and Cantref Mawr, except the commot of Mallaen, and Cantref Bychan, except Hirfryn and Myddfai, and the commot of Cydweli and the commot of Carnwyllion.

That year Gwenwynwyn, lord of Powys, made a solemn pact with John, king of England, and he renounced and scorned[2] the oaths and pledges and charters which he had given to Llywelyn ap Iorwerth and to the princes and the leading men of Wales and England, and he renounced the homage he had done to Llywelyn and the hostages whom he had given to him. And when Llywelyn learned that, it vexed him. And he sent bishops and abbots and other men of great authority to him, and with them the tenor of the cyrographs and the charters and the pact and the homage which he had done to him, to beseech him to return. And when he had gained nothing thereby, he gathered a host and summoned to him almost all the princes of Wales, and went to Powys and drove Gwenwynwyn in flight to the earl of Chester†; and he subdued for himself all his land and gained possession of it.

[1] † This Rhys Gryg has been called Rhys Fychan in every place previously. Both names are the same D.
[2] violated BCD.

In that year Louis, the eldest son of the king of France, at the call and request of the confederates from England, and with him a great host of French, came to England, about the feast of the Trinity, after receiving hostages from the confederates.† And king John feared his coming to England, and had the harbours held by a mighty force of armed men. And when he saw Louis approaching towards the land, he left the coastland and fled towards Winchester and the valley of the Severn. And Louis marched towards London, and there the earls and the barons who had invited him received him with honour. And he received their homage and gave to each one his rights. Soon after that he went to Winchester. And when king John heard that, he burned the town and fortified the castle and withdrew. And Louis laid siege to the castle; and at the end of a few days the castle was surrendered to him. And king John, and with him a multitude of armed men, went towards the March and came to Hereford. And he sent envoys to Reginald de Breos† and to the princes of Wales, and begged of them to be reconciled to him in every way; but they would not have it. And he made for Radnor and Hay and he laid siege to them and overthrew the castles to the ground, and he burned Oswestry† and destroyed it all.

In that year, about the feast of St. Benedict, died Pope Innocent the Third. And after him succeeded Honorius the Third.

And about the feast of St. Luke the Evangelist, John, king of England, died at Newark; and he was taken to Worcester and was buried honourably in the church of Mary† near the grave of St. Wulfstan. And forthwith Henry, his son, a boy nine years old, was elected king. And through some of the leading men and bishops of England, on the feast-day of Simon and Jude, by the authority of Gualo,[1]† a cardinal from Rome and legate in England, he was consecrated king in England.† And he was crowned at Gloucester. And he then took the Cross.

In that year died Hywel ap Gruffudd ap Cynan, an eminent young man beloved by everyone,† and he was buried at Aberconwy.

[1217–1217]. A year after that, a council was held at Oxford by those who were supporters on the side of[2] king Henry. And a peace and a truce between them and Louis, son of the king[3] of France, and the Northerners were there discussed. And since there could be no success, at Lent Louis sailed to France to take

---
[1] Gwallter *underlined* MS., Gualo *in margin*.
[2] on the side of] of BCD.
[3] son of Philip, king B, eldest son of Philip, king D.

counsel of Philip, his father, concerning the things he should do in England. And upon that the king's men rose up against his men and made fierce attacks upon them. And they came to Winchester and subdued the castle,[1] and took the castles which had been surrendered to Louis before that. And they drew to them many of the confederates.

And then Louis came a second time to England and a small force with him. And then the Northerners and the French were bolder because of his coming. And they made for the city of Lincoln and subdued it and laid siege to the castle. And the garrison manfully and faithfully made a defence and sent messengers to William Marshal, earl of Pembroke and governor of the kingdom at that time, and others of the leading men of the kingdom, to seek aid of them. And those by common counsel agreed to aid the garrison, and that they preferred to end their lives worthily together for the freedom of the kingdom than to suffer any longer the unjust and insufferable taxes and laws of the French. And so with an armed troop of knights they made for Lincoln. And after arraying their forces outside the gates, they fell upon the city. And the Northerners and the French arrayed their forces, too, and mounted the walls and manfully made a defence. And after protracted fighting on either side, at last, through God's providence, the troop at the head of which were the earl of Chester and Falkes de Breauté† came into the castle through an unfamiliar door. And they made for the town, and without warning they inflicted great slaughter on the Northerners and the French. And when the Northerners and the French saw that, they were thrown into confusion, and like madmen they yielded to flight with all of them seeking a place to hide even as their fate gave to them. And then the king's men attacked the city gates and destroyed them and came inside, while the others fled. And there they commenced to slay them and to overthrow them and to seize and imprison them. And in that battle the earl of Winchester and the earl[2] of Hereford and Robert fitz Walter were captured. The count of Perche, well-nigh the gentlest born of the French, was slain. And Simon de Pessi and Hugh de Roch and Gilbert de Clare and Robert de Ropell and Reginald† de Crescy, constable of Chester, and Gerald de Furnevaus and many of the others—almost more than could be counted of the foremost—were drowned in the river. And so the king's men returned joyful with victory and giving praise and glory to God.

[1] And they came ... castle]—BCD.
[2] Henry de Bohun earl D.

And then Louis, son of the king of France, was greatly afraid, and he desisted from besieging the castle of Kent,[1]† and he hastened to London. And he sent messengers to France to seek help. And the king's men kept the sea-ports, and boldly awaited the coming of the French, and besieged Louis in London. And the French, and with them a vast multitude, put to sea. And they sailed across the seas; and in the estuary of the Thames there was a naval battle between them and the king's men. And at last, through lack of wind, the victory fell to the English. And after killing the French and capturing them, they joyfully went in victory to the port.

During those events Reginald de Breos made peace with the king. And when Rhys and Owain, sons of Gruffudd, saw that their uncle had renounced his pact with the leading men of the kingdom, they rose up against him and took from him the cantref of Builth, and gained possession of it all except the castle.

And Llywelyn ap Iorwerth also was enraged on account of that reconciliation. And he moved a host against Reginald, and made for Brycheiniog and arrayed forces, and went against Brecon and planned to destroy the town completely. And the burgesses, unable to resist him, came to him; and with the help of Rhys Ieuanc ap Gruffudd they made peace with him, and gave him five hostages from amongst the most gentle folk of the town against their paying him a hundred marks for peace for the town.

And thence he turned his course towards Gower over the Black Mountain; and there many of his sumpters were lost. And he encamped at Llan-giwg.[2] And when Reginald† saw what destruction he was causing, he came, and six knights along with him, and surrendered to Llywelyn. And on the following day Llywelyn gave him the castle of Seinhenydd.† And he entrusted it to the keeping of Rhys Gryg. And there Llywelyn stayed for a few days.

And thence he turned his course towards Dyfed[3] and he came as far as Cefn Cynfarchan. And messengers came to him from the Flemings to sue to him for peace.[4] And Llywelyn kept to his plan. And he made for Haverford and arrayed his troops to lay siege to the town. And Rhys ap Gruffudd, and with him a host of the men of the South, went through the river Cleddyf to be the first to lay siege to the town. And behold Iorwerth, bishop of Menevia, and with him monks and clerics, coming to

---

[1] Canterbury C.
[2] BC. *Emend* Llanngync MS. *to* Llanngyuc.
[3] + against the Flemings *above line* D.
[4] to accept peace from him BC.

the Lord Llywelyn, prince of Gwynedd, and planning terms of peace with him on behalf of the Flemings. And these were the terms, to wit, that they should give twenty picked hostages from Rhos and Pembroke, against their giving him by the feast of Michael a thousand marks of silver, or else that they should surrender themselves to him to hold their land and territory under him.† And after that was ended, all returned joyfully to their lands.

And in the meantime peace was discussed between the king of England and Louis, son of the king of France. And peace was made between them in this wise: the king of England gave to all the barons of England and the kingdom all their laws[1] and all their customs for which they had stirred up war against king John; and on either side the prisoners, who had been captured because of the war, were released; and a large sum of money was promised to Louis, and he forswore the land of England for ever. And after he had been absolved from the sentence of excommunication, he sailed towards France. And then the churches in all England were absolved.

In the meantime William Marshal laid siege to Caerleon and he took it; for the Welsh had no desire to agree to the peace which the barons had made, because they were still bound to their oath or else had been scorned and ignored in that peace. And then Rhys Gryg overthrew Seinhenydd and all its castles to the ground.† And he drove all the English away from that land and took from them of their chattels as much as he pleased; and he drove with them their wives and children without a hope of their ever returning. And he divided their lands for Welshmen to occupy.

[1218–1218]. A year after that, Christianity was restored to the Southerners. And the castle of Carmarthen and Cardigan were given to the Lord Llywelyn, prince of Gwynedd, to keep. And Rhys ap Gruffudd alone of all the men of the South, by counsel of the Lord Llywelyn, made for the king's court and did him homage.

In that year many Crusaders went to Jerusalem, along with whom went the earl of Chester and earl Ferrars† and Brian de L'Ile† and many others of the leading men of England. In that year, about the Calends of June, a host of the Christians went to the city that is called Damietta,[2] with the king of Jerusalem and the Patriarch of Jerusalem and the master of the Templars and

---
[1] rights BC.
[2] *Emend* Dannecham MS. *to* Damietham.

the master of the Hospital and the duke of Austria as leaders at their head. And they went across the sea and they took the city. And the pilgrims in ships laid siege to the tower which had been built in the middle of the river, and they took it and slew many of the Saracens and captured others.

[1219–1219]. A year after that, Rhys Gryg took the daughter of the earl of Clare for his wedded wife, and John de Breos took Margaret, daughter of the Lord Llywelyn, for his wedded wife.

In that year Almighty God delivered to the host of the Christians, after afflicting them for long, the city of Damietta, in the land of Egypt, built upon the river Nile. And it was not by the strength of men, but by the powers of God that it was taken:† for by the providence of God there was in the city such mortality upon the people that the living could hardly bury the dead. For on the day the city was taken there were in it three thousand people dead along the streets[1] like dogs. And there forthwith an archbishop was created to the praise and honour of the Trinity from Heaven.

[1220–1220]. One thousand two hundred and twenty was the year of Christ when the body of St. Thomas, archbishop of Canterbury, was raised by Stephen Langton, archbishop of that same place and the chiefest in all England and a cardinal in Rome, and it was placed with honour in a fair noble shrine skilfully fashioned of gold and silver and adorned with various kinds of precious stones and gems; and it was placed in the church of the Trinity with pomp of service and the devotion of all the clerics of the realm and many of the people.†

In that year, about the feast of Ieuan y Coed,[2]† Llywelyn, prince of Gwynedd, gathering to him the princes and leading men of all Wales, moved a mighty host against the Flemings of Rhos and Pembroke because of the frequent attacks they made upon the Welsh against the Welsh† and for violating the terms of the peace and the truce which the king and the leading men of England had made between the English and the Welsh. And on his first expedition he took by force the castle of Cardigan,† which first the Welsh had destroyed and then the Flemings had repaired. And after the castle had been taken by force, some of the garrison were slain, and others burnt and others bound in prison; and the castle was all thrown to the ground. And thereupon† he destroyed Wizo's Castle[3] and he burned the town.

---

[1] along the streets] and the stench BCD.
[2] + the Baptist, the last of the two BD.
[3] kastell y wys MS. *emend to* kastell gwys.

And on the third day he burned the town of Haverford all to the gates of the castle. And so throughout that week he traversed Rhos and Daugleddau, inflicting immense slaughter on the people every day. And at last, having made a truce till the Calends of May, he returned joyfully.

[1221-1221]. A year after that, strife arose between Llywelyn ap Iorwerth and Gruffudd, his son, because of the cantref of Meirionnydd, which the said Gruffudd had subjugated because of the multitude of injuries which the men of that cantref had done to him and to his men. And Llywelyn took that subjugation angrily; and he gathered a host and went against Gruffudd and threatened to avenge that attack heavily upon him and upon his men. And Gruffudd, having arrayed his troops ready to fight, boldly awaited the coming of his father. And when wise men on either side saw that there was excessive danger on either side, they urged Gruffudd to surrender himself and all his possessions to his father's will. And also they urged Llywelyn to receive him peacefully and mercifully, and to remit to him all his anger from a good heart. And so it came to pass. However, Llywelyn took from Gruffudd, his son, the cantref of Meirionnydd, of which he had gained possession, and the adjoining commot of Ardudwy. And he began to build a castle in it.

At that time Rhys Ieuanc quitted the fellowship of the Lord Llywelyn, for he was angered because Llywelyn had given the castle of Carmarthen to Maelgwn ap Rhys and had not given to himself the castle of Cardigan, which had before that come to him from the apportioning of the lands of Deheubarth. And he went to Rhos to William Marshal, earl of Pembroke. And Llywelyn came to Aberystwyth and subdued for himself the castle and all the land attached to it and returned again. And Rhys Ieuanc went to the king's court, and he complained to the king of the injury which the Lord Llywelyn had done to him. And the king summoned to him Llywelyn and all the earls and the barons of the March, to Shrewsbury. And there Rhys was reconciled to Llywelyn, his uncle, and Llywelyn received him into conciliation. And Llywelyn swore to him that he would do to him concerning the castle of Cardigan the very same as he had done to Maelgwn concerning Carmarthen.

In that year the host of the Christians who were in the city of Damietta in the land of Egypt went towards the tower of Babylon† to lay siege to it. But divine vengeance came upon them inasmuch as the river Nile flooded against them, so that they were just penned between two rivers, so that countless numbers of them were drowned, and the Saracens imprisoned the majority of the others on the eighth day from the last feast of Mary in the autumn,† so that they were forced for their lives[1] and their prisoners to surrender the city of Damietta back to the Saracens. And after making an eight years' truce the Saracens escorted them to Acre. And at that time naught was known about the Cross, but by the mercy of God it was restored to them.

In that year, about the feast of Nicholas, John de Breos by leave and counsel of the Lord Llywelyn, repaired the castle of Swansea.†

[1222–1222]. A year after that, died Rhys Ieuanc ap Gruffudd,† son of the Lord Rhys, a young man eminent for his praise and his eloquence and his sense and his prudence and his wisdom; a light to the aged[2]; bounty and renown and a jewel to the young; the honour and glory and splendour and unconquered bulwark of knights; pillar and tower and shield of his country; father and shepherd and foster-father of clerics; the steadfastness and nobleness and peace and commendation of peoples; the ship and haven and defender of the weak; the trampler and terror and fear of his enemies; the one hope for all Deheubarth. Moreover, he died after long infirmity of illness and pain, after taking communion and confession and making a good end, in the month of August, and after assuming the habit of the Order of the White Monks at Strata Florida. And after him Owain, his only brother, succeeded to his patrimony, but he received only a portion[3] of his brother's patrimony; and the other portion Llywelyn gave to Maelgwn ap Rhys.

In that year William Marshal, earl of Pembroke,[4] went across the Irish Sea.

[1223–1223]. A year after that, William Marshal[5] brought a large fleet and a multitude of knights and foot-soldiers from Ireland to Deheubarth; and he came to land at Menevia about Palm Sunday. And thereupon, on Easter Monday, he moved his mighty host to Cardigan; and forthwith the castle was surrendered to him. On the Wednesday following he went to Carmarthen; and there too the castle was surrendered to him forthwith. And when the Lord Llywelyn heard that, he sent

---

[1] for their lives]—BC.
[2] light . . . aged]—BCD.
[3] ac ny chauas kyfrann MS., . . . onid kufran BCD. *Emend* MS. *to* ac ny chauas [onyt] kyfrann *or* ac *y kauas* kyfrann.
[4] earl of Pembroke] *marginal addition* MS.,—BCD.
[5] + earl of Pembroke BCD.

Gruffudd, his son, and with him a large number of men to oppose that said earl; for it was to the keeping of the said Llywelyn that the king had entrusted those castles. And when the said Gruffudd heard that the earl was coming towards Cydweli, he and the leading men of Wales with him went thither. And Rhys Gryg feared treachery by the burgesses of Cydweli, and sought to take them along with him into the safety of the woods. And when they would not go, he burned all the town and its churches.[1]† And when the earl Marshal heard that, he went across the Tywi to Carmarthen bridge. And Gruffudd received him and gave him a hard battle. And after fighting for the most part of the day on either side, each of the two hosts withdrew from the other to their tents, many having been slain and wounded on either side. And then Gruffudd returned to Gwynedd because of lack of food.

And the earl repaired the castle of Carmarthen; and after repairing it he made for Cilgerran and there he began to build an ornate castle of mortar and stones. And soon after commencing the work, lo, letters coming to him from the king and from the archbishop of Canterbury, to bid him come in his own person before the king to make reparation for what wrongs he had done, and to receive reparation from the prince for what wrongs had been done to him too. And the earl obeyed the letters, and he sailed in a ship to England, and with him a small company, after leaving all his host at Cilgerran to hold the work he had begun, and bidding them give support where they should see peril. And both of them, that is, the prince and the earl, came before the king and the archbishop and the council at Ludlow, but they failed to be reconciled. And the earl planned, with the help of the earl of Salisbury, de Piggott of Ewyas,† to return through his territory to his own land, but he failed to do so; for the Lord Llywelyn had sent Gruffudd, his son, and Rhys Gryg along with him, and with them a mighty host, against them. And those seized the road against them in Carnwyllion. And Llywelyn himself and all his forces along with him came to Mabudryd. And there he awaited tidings concerning his men and concerning the earl's coming.

[1224–1224]. A year after that, a community was sent from Whitland to the 'White Strand,'† in Ireland.

[1225–1225]. A year after that, died Cedifor, abbot of Strata Florida.

---

[1] church C.

[1226-1226]. A year after that, died Louis, the eminent king of France.

[1227-1227]. A year after that, Rhys Gryg was seized by Rhys Fychan, his son, at Llanarthnau; but he was released in return for the castle of Llandovery.

In that year Maredudd, son of the Lord Rhys, archdeacon of Ceredigion, died in the church of Mary at Lampeter†; and his body was borne to Menevia, and Iorwerth, bishop of Menevia, buried him honourably near the grave of the Lord Rhys, his father, in the church of David.

[1228-1228]. A year after that, Henry, king of England, and with him a vast host of the might of all England, came to Wales, planning to subdue the Lord Llywelyn and all the Welsh. And he encamped in the place that is called Ceri. And there† all the Welsh gathered together in unity with their prince. And then by fierce attacks upon their enemies,[1] they caused great confusion amongst them. And there William the Younger, son of Reginald de Breos, a man eminent in arms, young though he was, was captured; and he was imprisoned wounded. And for his freedom he was forced to give the castle of Builth and all the land, and therewith a large sum of money to the Lord Llywelyn. And the king, after peace had been arranged between him and Llywelyn, and after the leading men of Wales who were there had done him homage[2] without kingly honour, he returned to England.

[1229-1229]. A year after that, died Iorwerth, bishop of Menevia.

[1230-1230]. One thousand two hundred and thirty was the year of Christ when king Henry sailed across the sea, and with him a huge hosting of armed men and ships, to seek to win back his territory in Normandy and Anjou and Poitou. And because of an unfortunate tempest and ill-fated mortality he was foiled of his purpose. And soon after that he returned empty-handed to England.

In that year died William Canton of Cemaes. And Llywelyn ap Maelgwn Ieuanc died in Gwynedd, and he was honourably buried at Aberconwy.

In that year William de Breos the Younger, lord of Brycheiniog, was hanged by the Lord Llywelyn in Gwynedd,

---

[1] And then ... enemies] with fierce hearts and BCD.
[2] and the leading men of Wales had then done homage to him BCD.

after he had been caught in Llywelyn's chamber with the king of England's daughter, Llywelyn's wife.

[1231–1231]. A year after that, Maelgwn, son of the Lord Rhys, died at Llannerch Aeron; and he was buried at Strata Florida in the chapter-house.†

In that year king Henry built Painscastle in Elfael.

In that year strife grew afresh between the Lord Llywelyn and the king, and Llywelyn destroyed Baldwin's Castle and Brecon and Hay† and Radnor, and burned them all. And thence he went towards Gwent; and he came to Caerleon and burned all the town to ashes, losing, however, gentlefolk in the fighting.† And thereupon he took the castle of Neath and the castle of Cydweli, and he threw them[1] to the ground.

In that year Maelgwn Ieuanc ap Maelgwn, son of the Lord Rhys, manfully made for the town of Cardigan, and he ravaged it all and burned it completely up to the castle gate; and he slew all the burgesses whom he found in it, and returned again in victory with vast spoil and booty. And forthwith after that he came back and broke the bridge over the Teifi, which was close by the town. The same Maelgwn and Owain ap Gruffudd and their men, and with them the Lord Llywelyn's men, went a second time to the town of Cardigan; and they laid siege to the castle. And after a few days they breached it with catapults, till the garrison was forced to surrender the castle and to leave it.

[1232–1232]. A year after that, John de Breos was drawn at his own horse's tail; and so he died a cruel death. And then died the earl of Chester. And Abraham, bishop of St. Asaph, died.

[1233–1233]. A year after that, Richard, brother of Henry, king of England, repaired the castle of Radnor, he being an earl in Cornwall.[2] And that castle the Lord Llywelyn had destroyed two years before that.

In that year Llywelyn, and a mighty host along with him, went to Brycheiniog, and he burned all the towns and castles that were in that land, and he carried many spoils away with him. And he manfully laid siege to the castle of Brecon every day for a whole month with catapults, and he threw the walls to the ground. And yet he left the castle for fear, and burned the whole town. And as he was returning he burned the town of Clun† and gained possession of the land that was attached to it, that is, the valley of the Teme.† And thereupon he marched to

---

[1] they were thrown BCD.
[2] Yngkerhyw *retraced* MS., Yngherniw BCD.

Castell Coch† and razed it to the ground; and he burned the town of Oswestry.

In that year strife arose between Henry, king of England, and Richard Marshal, earl of Pembroke. And the earl made a solemn pact and agreement with the Lord Llywelyn and with the Welsh. And forthwith he and Owain ap Gruffudd gathered an exceeding[1] numerous host along with them; and they burned the town of Monmouth, after making a great slaughter therein of the king's men who were dwelling therein to strengthen it. And thereupon they took these castles: Cardiff, Abergavenny, Pencelli, Blaenllyfni, Bwlchydinas, and they destroyed them all except Cardiff.

In that year Maelgwn Ieuanc ap Maelgwn ap Rhys and Rhys Gryg and Owain ap Gruffudd and their followers and all the leaders of Deheubarth, and with them the Lord Llywelyn's host and the host of Richard, earl of Pembroke, all combined together, laid siege to the town and castle of Carmarthen for three months at a stretch, and they destroyed† the bridge on the Tywi, but it profited them but little. For the sailors came armed, with the tide, and again mended the bridge. And when the Welsh saw that, they returned home.

In that year Rhys Gryg, son of the Lord Rhys, died at Llandeilo-fawr, and he was buried at Menevia, near the grave of the Lord Rhys, his father.

In that year Maelgwn Fychan ap Maelgwn ap Rhys repaired the castle of Trefilan, which his father had built before that.†

[1234–1234]. A year after that, Richard, earl of Pembroke, a young knight eminent in arms, of great wisdom and renown and praise, went to Ireland. And there in the battle his barons and his knights treacherously deserted him, and he was mortally wounded. And at the end of a fortnight he died.

In that[2] year Gruffudd, son of the Lord Llywelyn, was released from prison after he had been six years in prison.

In that year Cadwallon ap Maelgwn of Maelienydd died at Cwm-hir.

[1235–1235]. A year after that, Owain ap Gruffudd, a man† of gentle lineage and of graceful manners—he was wise and generous and of great fame—died at Strata Florida on the Wednesday next after the eighth day from Epiphany. And he was buried in the chapter-house of the monks, close by the grave of Rhys Ieuanc, his brother.

[1] exceeding]—BC.
[2] the same BCD.

In that year† king Henry married the daughter of the count of Provence; and the wedding-feast was held at Christmas in London, all the bishops and all the earls and most of the barons of England having been invited.

[1236–1236]. A year after that, died Madog ap Gruffudd Maelor, the man† who surpassed all for the renown of his manners and for generosity and piety: for he was an outstanding founder of monasteries, he was a supporter of the needy and the poor and the indigent. And he was honourably buried in the monastery of Llynegwestl, which he himself had built. In that year died Owain ap Maredudd ap Rhobert of Cydewain. In that year died the bishop of London and the bishop of Lincoln and the bishop of Worcester.† In that year there was a mighty tempest of wind one night before Christmas eve, so great that it destroyed countless[1] houses and churches; and it killed many people and animals, and many woods were rent by it.

In that year Pope Gregory the Ninth relieved Cadwgan, bishop of Bangor, a man of great accomplishments and learning, of his episcopal care; and he habited himself as a monk at the monastery of Dore.† In that year Gilbert, earl of Pembroke,† took by treachery the castle of Morgan ap Hywel, which is called Machein.† And after making a great fortification around it[2] he gave back the castle for fear of the Lord Llywelyn.

[1237–1237]. A year after that, the Lady of Wales, wife of Llywelyn ap Iorwerth and daughter to the king of England,— her name was Joan—died in Llywelyn's court at Aber in the month of February; and her body was buried in a consecrated enclosure which was on the shore-bank.† And there after that bishop Hywel† consecrated a monastery for the Barefooted Friars† to the honour of the Blessed Mary. And the prince built it all at his cost for the soul of his Lady. In that year died John, earl of Chester, and Cynwrig, son of Lord Rhys the Great.

In that year Otto, a cardinal from Rome and legate of the Pope, came to England, sent by Pope Gregory the Ninth.[3]

[1238–1238]. A year after that, on the day after the feast of St. Luke the Evangelist, all the princes of Wales swore allegiance and fealty to Dafydd, son of the Lord Llywelyn, at Strata Florida. And forthwith Dafydd took from Gruffudd, his brother, Arwystli and Ceri and Cyfeiliog and Mawddwy and Mochnant and Caereinion, and allowed him to hold Llŷn alone. In that

[1] a number of BC.
[2] around the castle dyke BCD.
[3] the Ninth]—BC.

year Maredudd ap Madog ap Gruffudd Maelor slew Gruffudd, his brother. And forthwith the Lord Llewelyn took from him all his territory.[1]

[1239–1239]. A year after that, died Maredudd Goeg,[2]† son of the Lord Rhys, prince of Deheubarth; and he was buried at Whitland. In that year died the bishop of Winchester.† In that year a son was born to Henry, king of England, and his name was Edward. In that year Dafydd ap Llywelyn seized Gruffudd, his brother, breaking his oath with him; and he imprisoned him and his son in the castle of Cricieth.

[1240–1240]. One thousand two hundred and forty was the year of Christ when the Lord Llywelyn ap Iorwerth ab Owain Gwynedd, prince of Wales, a second Achilles,[3]† died after he had assumed the habit of the Order at Aberconwy; and he was buried honourably there. And after him ruled Dafydd, his son by Joan,[4] daughter of John, king of England.

And that Dafydd, in the month of May following, did homage to Henry, king of England, his uncle, at Gloucester.[5] And the barons of Wales in the summer after that did homage to the king.† And then[6] the English remembered their old custom and† sent Walter Marshal, and with him great might, to fortify the castle of Cardigan.

[1241–1241]. A year after that, Otto, cardinal[7] and legate of the Pope, departed from England. And the emperor Frederick thereafter seized him, and with him a great number of archbishops and bishops and abbots and many other ecclesiastics because of the war which had long been between the emperor and Pope Gregory; and the Pope had excommunicated the emperor.

And after the cardinal had departed from the kingdom, the king gathered a mighty host to subdue all the Welsh† and to receive their homage. And he fortified a castle at Diserth† in Tegeingl, and took hostages from Gwynedd† from Dafydd, his nephew, summoning Dafydd to London to the council that had

---

[1] In that year . . . territory]—BCD.
[2] + (in other books save this alone he is called Maredudd Ddall) D. *Coeg* = 'one-eyed'; *dall* = 'blind.'
[3] a second Achilles]—BCD.
[4] Jonet BD.
[5] his uncle at Gloucester]—C, + others said that Llywelyn was seized in Brycheiniog, through the treachery of the men of the land, by Lord Mortimer and taken to the king and there beheaded: but that Llywelyn was Llywelyn ap Gruffudd ap Llywelyn ap Iorwerth D.
[6] there BCD.
[7] Otto, cardinal] the cardinal BCD.

been appointed there. And he gave to Gruffudd ap Gwenwynwyn his rights† in Powys, and to the sons of Maredudd ap Cynan their territory† in Meirionnydd; and he took Gruffudd, son of the Lord Llywelyn, and all the prisoners who were with him, and brought them to London to his prison.

That year died Pope Gregory the Ninth.

[1242–1242]. A year after that, king Henry sailed to Poitou soon after Easter. And he planned to win from the king of France the lands which the king of France had taken from him before that. And in that year he failed to do so; but after losing† earls and barons, he stayed with the queen at Bordeaux.

In that year these castles were fortified in Wales: by Maelgwn, the castle of Garth Grugyn; by John de Monmouth, the castle of Builth; by Roger de Mortimer, the castle of Maelienydd. In that year died Gruffudd ap Maredudd, son of Lord Rhys the Great, who was then archdeacon in Ceredigion.

[1243–1243]. A year after that, Henry, king of England, returned from Bordeaux, safe and in good cheer, he and his men. And after that he unrighteously oppressed Welshmen and many others.

[1244–1244]. A year after that, died Rhys Mechyll ap Rhys Gryg. In that year, as Gruffudd ap Llywelyn and some of his men along with him were in the king of England's prison in London, he planned to escape, and threw a rope through the tower window and sought to escape along it; but through ill-fate the rope broke and he fell, so that his neck was broken. And when Dafydd, his brother, heard that, he was moved by great anger, and he summoned to him all his leading men and swooped like a lion† amongst his enemies and drove them all away from his bounds, save for those who were in the castles. And he sent letters and messengers to all the princes of Wales and united them all with him, save Gruffudd ap Madog and Gruffudd ap Gwenwynwyn and Morgan ap Hywel. And he inflicted many losses upon those that year. And thus he forced them to submit to him.

In that year, Maredudd ap Rhobert, eminent counsellor[1] of Wales, died after having assumed the habit of the Order at Strata Florida.

[1245–1245]. A year after that, the heirs of William Marshal received their patrimony in peace.†

---

[1] supporter D.

In that year Henry, king of England, gathered a mighty host from all his kingdom and from Ireland. And he came to Degannwy, planning to subdue all the Welsh. And there he fortified for himself a castle against the will of Dafydd ap Llywelyn, and left knights of his there, and returned to England. And to commemorate his act, he left many corpses of his men dead in Gwynedd unburied, some in the sea, others on land.

[1246–1246]. A year after that, it was a rainy year.† In the month of March,[1] the shield of Wales, Dafydd ap Llywelyn, died in his court at Aber; and his body was buried at Aberconwy with the body of his father. And since he had no heir of his body, there ruled after him two nephews of his, namely, two sons of Gruffudd ap Llywelyn, Owain Goch and Llywelyn. And those, by counsel of the wise men of the land, divided the territory into two halves between them.

In that year the king of England sent Nicholas de Meules, his justice, from Carmarthen,† and some of the princes of Deheubarth who were in the place along with him, namely, Maredudd ap Rhys Gryg and Maredudd ab Owain, to dispossess Maelgwn Ieuanc. And when Maelgwn heard that, he fled to Owain and Llywelyn, sons of Gruffudd ap Llywelyn, and their followers; and they left their territory, since they had to, to men foreign to them.† And when the king learned that, he summoned to him each one of the leaders, who were under him, against Owain and Llywelyn and Maelgwn and Hywel ap Maredudd of Glamorgan, who also had fled to[2] Gwynedd after the earl of Clare had despoiled him completely of his territory. And when they learned that, they and their followers fled to the mountains and the wilderness.

In that year died Ralf de Mortimer. And after him Roger, his son, ruled in his patrimony.

[1247–1247]. A year after that, Hywel ab Ednyfed, bishop of St. Asaph, died at Oxford; and there he was buried. In that year Anselm the Fat, the honourable bishop of Menevia, died in the month of March.

In that year, on the twentieth day of the month of February, the twelfth day from the moon's prime, with this letter—F— marking Sunday, about vesper-time the earth greatly and dreadfully quaked throughout the whole kingdom.†

[1] A year ... March] One thousand two hundred and forty-six was the year of Christ when D.
[2] + the land of D.

[1248-1248]. A year after that, Louis, the eminent king of France, he and his three brothers with him, and a mighty host of Christians, set out for Jerusalem after Easter. And at the end of that year he sailed across the Great Sea.†

In that year, in the month of July, Gruffudd, abbot of Strata Florida, made a settlement with king Henry concerning a debt which the king had demanded of the monastery a long time before that, remitting to the abbot and the community half the debt, that is, three hundred and fifty marks, and taking it at fixed intervals,† as is recorded in the *Annals* of the monastery.†

In that year Owain ap Rhobert† obtained his rights, namely[1] Cydewain, and Rhys Fychan ap Rhys Mechyll obtained his castle, namely, Carreg Cennen, which his mother had treacherously[2] placed in the hands of the French, out of enmity towards her son.

In that year the king granted to the abbot of Strata Florida and the abbot of Aberconwy the body of Gruffudd ap Llywelyn, when they came to seek it; and they took it with them to Aberconwy, where it lies.†

[1249-1249]. A year after that, Louis, the most eminent king of France, and with him his three brothers and the queen, went to the city of Damietta, which Almighty God delivered to him after the Saracens had left it. And after that, in the summer following, the Saracens captured that said king, after Robert, his brother, and about thirty thousand of the Christians had been slain. And for his release and safe conduct[3] and that of his men to Acre, he delivered Damietta to the Saracens and an immense sum of money therewith. And he returned safely thence. And within a few days after that† God gave him victory over his enemies and over the enemies of Christ, and vengeance for his own men by the capture of many of the Saracens and the killing of countless numbers of them. For he stayed, he and the queen and his host, at Acre, and he sent his two brothers to France to gather aid for him in men and horses and arms[4] and money.

[1250-1249]. One thousand two hundred and fifty was the year of Christ when the king of Scotland died, and he left an only son as his heir.†

---

[1] in D.
[2] drwy dwyn MS. *Emend to* drwy dwyll, *as in* D.
[3] and safe conduct]—D.
[4] gold D.

[1251–1251]. A year after that, Gwladus, daughter of Llywelyn ap Iorwerth, died at Windsor.[1]† And about the end of that year Morgan,† son of the Lord Rhys, died at Strata Florida after assuming the habit of the Order.

[1252–1252]. A year after that, in the summer, the earth withered with the over excessive heat of the sun, so much that it gave hardly any of its wonted fruit, and the sea and the rivers gave not their fish as they were wont, and the trees gave not their wonted fruits. And towards the end of the autumn of that year there came so much rain that it covered the face of all the earth, after it had hardened, so that it could not absorb so much water, because of its great dryness. And on account of that so great were the floods that they submerged many houses and rent the trees and the orchards and broke the mills and caused many other losses.

That summer died Gwilym ap Gwrwared,† steward to the king over the land which had belonged to Maelgwn Ieuanc. That man carried off spoil from Elfael at the king's command, because the men of Elfael sought to make use of the pastures of Elfed† as though by right.

[1253–1253]. A year after that, about August,† king Henry sailed to Burgundy,† and with him a mighty host, after entrusting the kingdom of England to Edward, his son, and to Richard, earl of Cornwall, his brother, and to the queen.

In that year, in Lent, Thomas, bishop of Menevia, returned from the court of Rome.

[1254–1254]. A year after that, Louis, the eminent king of France, returned from Jerusalem, after he had been six years in the Holy Land, and with him his queen and his host.

In that year king Henry returned from Gascony to England, having left Edward, his son, there holding those lands. In that year Gwenllïan, daughter of Maelgwn Ieuanc, died at Llanfihangel Gelynrhod on the feast-day of St. Catherine; and her body was buried honourably at Strata Florida in the chapter-house of the monks.

[1255–1255]. A year after that, died Maredudd ap Llywelyn of Meirionnydd, and he left as heir his only son by Gwenllïan, daughter of Maelgwn. And immediately after the feast of John the Baptist, Rhys, Maelgwn's only son, died after assuming the habit of St. Benedict at Strata Florida; and his body was buried in the chapter-house beside his sister.

---

[1] + (she was wife to Ralf de Mortimer of Wigmore, mother of Sir Roger Mortimer) D.

In those days strife arose between the sons of Gruffudd ap Llywelyn, Owain Goch and Dafydd, his brother, on the one side, and Llywelyn on the other side. And Llywelyn, trusting in God, fearlessly awaited the coming of his brothers against him,† and with them a mighty host. And unperturbed in the fighting, in the space of an hour he captured his brothers and imprisoned them,† after many of their men had been slain and others put to flight. And he gained possession of all their lands without any opposition to him.

In that year died Margaret, daughter of Maelgwn, wife of Owain ap Rhobert.† In that year the great bell of Strata Florida was bought for twenty-seven marks and five shillings and two cows.† And it was raised on the feast-day of Bartholomew the Apostle, and it was consecrated by the bishop of Bangor. In that year, towards the end of summer,† died Thomas Wallis, bishop of Menevia.

[1256–1256]. A year after that, Edward, son of king Henry, he then being earl of Chester, came to survey his lands and his castles in Gwynedd round about August. And after his return to England† the gentlefolk of Wales, despoiled of their liberty and their rights, came to Llywelyn ap Gruffudd and revealed to him with tears their grievous bondage to the English; and they made known to him that they preferred to be slain in war for their liberty than to suffer themselves to be unrighteously trampled upon by foreigners. And the said Llywelyn, at their instigation and by their counsel and at their request, made for Perfeddwlad, and with him Maredudd ap Rhys Gryg; and by the end of the week he gained possession of it all.† And after that he took the cantref of Meirionnydd into his hands. And the land that belonged to Edward in Ceredigion, he gave to Maredudd ab Owain, and Builth he gave to Maredudd ap Rhys, despoiling Rhys, his nephew, and expelling him from his territory and giving it to Maredudd, and keeping naught for himself, but only fame and honour.† And after that he took Gwerthrynion from Roger de Mortimer and held it in his own hand.

In that year Master Richard de Carew was consecrated bishop in Menevia by the Pope.

[1257–1257, *first half*]. A year after that, Llywelyn ap Gruffudd, and Maredudd ap Rhys and Maredudd ab Owain along with him, went against the land of Gruffudd ap Gwenwynwyn, and he gained possession of it all except the castle of Welshpool and a portion of the valley of the Severn and a little of Caereinion. And the castle of Bodyddon† he destroyed.

And after that, Rhys Fychan ap Rhys Mechyll gathered a host past telling of barons and knights from England; for it was in England that he was then. And he set out thence for Carmarthen in Whitsun week. And thence they came to the castle of Dinefwr. And after he had come to the castle, the garrison seized him. And thereupon they manfully fell upon the host, and they captured the best barons and knights of them, and they slew of the others about two thousand and more.† And after that the princes went to Dyfed. And they burned the castle of Abercorram and Llanstephan and Arberth and Maenclochog and all the towns that adjoined them.

[1258–1257, *second half*]. A year after that,† Llywelyn ap Gruffudd took the land of Cemaes. And after that, Llywelyn ap Gruffudd came to Deheubarth about the feast of John the Baptist.† And after making peace between Maredudd ap Rhys and Rhys, his nephew, he took those and others along with him, and they subdued the castle of Trefdraeth. And thence they went together and burned all Rhos except Haverford. And thereupon they made their way to Glamorgan; and there, after many had been captured and many had been slain, they took the castle of Llangynwyd.† And thence they turned back. In that year died Maelgwn Ieuanc, and his body was buried in the chapter-house at Strata Florida.

And thereupon, about the first feast of Mary in the autumn, Henry, king of England, and with him a mighty host, came to Degannwy. And he stayed there till the last feast of Mary in the autumn. And then he returned to England.

During that time the church of Padarn was burnt. And soon after that, Llywelyn ap Gruffudd made peace with Gruffudd ap Madog, and he dispossessed Gruffudd ap Gwenwynwyn of his land.

[1259–1258]. A year after that, all the Welsh made a pact together, and they gave an oath to maintain loyalty and agreement together, under pain of excommunication upon whomsoever of them broke it. And Maredudd ap Rhys went against that oath, without keeping his oath.

In that year strife arose in England between the foreigners, about the feast of John the Baptist.

In that year, at the beginning of autumn, Dafydd ap Gruffudd and Maredudd ab Owain and Rhys ap Rhys, and many leading men along with them, went to parley with Maredudd ap Rhys and Patrick de Chaworth, to Emlyn. And that Patrick was seneschal to the king at Carmarthen. And then Patrick and Maredudd swooped down upon Llywelyn's men, and they broke the truce. And then Patrick was slain, and with him many knights and foot-soldiers.

[1259–1259]. About the end of that year king Henry sailed to France to parley with the king of France.†

[1260–1260]. One thousand two hundred and sixty was the year of Christ when Llywelyn ap Gruffudd, immediately after Epiphany, went to the land of Builth; and he took that land from Roger de Mortimer, who ruled it at that time, except for the castle and the town of Llanfair. And so, after he had traversed all Deheubarth without doing injury to anyone, he returned again. And after that, as men from the castle were opening the gates for the others who were without, behold Llywelyn's men leaping in by night and taking the castle. And so it was taken without so much as an arrow-shot, and such men and horses and arms and equipment as were in it; and it was destroyed to the ground. And then Owain ap Maredudd of Elfael came to Llywelyn's peace.

[1261–1261]. A year after that, died Gwladus, daughter of Gruffudd, who was wife to Rhys Ieuanc ap Rhys Mechyll. In that year, a little after the Calends of Winter, died Owain ap Maredudd, lord of Cydewain.

[1262–1262]. A year after that, died Richard de Clare, earl of Gloucester.

That year, about the feast of Andrew the Apostle, certain people by their own counsel came from Maelienydd by treachery† to the new castle,† which then belonged to Roger de Mortimer. And they took the castle and seized Hywel ap Meurig, who was constable of the castle, and his wife and his sons and his daughters, after killing the gate-keepers. And they made that known to the Lord Llywelyn's seneschal and constable. And those came in haste and burned it to the ground. And when Roger heard that, he came with many leading men as his supporters in arms. And he stayed within the castle walls† for a few days. And the Lord Llywelyn's officers made that known to him. And he gathered a host and came to Maelienydd, and he received the homage of the men of the land, and took two other castles; and he gave Roger and his men leave to return. And he himself went, he and his host, to Brycheiniog, at the request of the leading men of Brycheiniog, to receive their homage. And after receiving their homage he returned again.

[1263–1263]. A year after that, a little before Easter, John Lestrange the Younger, he being constable and bailiff over Baldwin's Castle, gathered a mighty host. And he came by night through Ceri upwards to Cydewain. And after he had gathered vast spoil he returned along the way downwards from Cydewain.† And when the Welsh heard that, they gathered in pursuit of them and slew two hundred of the English, some in the field, others in the barn of Aber-miwl. And a little after that, John Lestrange had that barn burnt because of that slaughter. And a little after that, the Welsh were slain near the valley of the Clun.† At that time Edward was moving in the March, and burning townships in Gwynedd.† And after that, he returned to England. And after he had gone to England, Dafydd ap Gruffudd forsook the fellowship of Llywelyn, his brother.†

At that time the barons of England and some of the earls and the Welsh rose up against Edward and the foreigners, both clerics and laymen, and desired to cast them forth from all the kingdom of England. And they took the strong towns and the cities and the castles on every side, and they burned the foreigners' towns and destroyed their courts. And then Llywelyn ap Gruffudd and his host drew near to the castles that were on his land, namely, Carreg Faelan and Degannwy, and after taking them he destroyed them. And Gruffudd ap Gwenwynwyn took the castle of Yr Wyddgrug† and destroyed it.

[1264–1264]. A year after that—the strife that had been since the preceding year between Henry and Edward, his son, and their supporters, on the one side, and the earls and the barons, on the other side, not forgotten†—the king of Germany and the king of England and their sons and their confederates gathered on a Wednesday to the field of Lewes, to fight against the earls and the barons, who were seeking the laws and the rights of the kingdom, and with the intention of capturing them. And after a mighty battle on that field, the purpose was reversed; and the earls and the barons captured the kings and king Henry's two sons, namely, Edward and Edmund, and twenty-five other barons along with them, after many knights and other leading men, round about ten thousand of the kings' men, had been slain. And after that the earls and the barons, after they had taken counsel, released the king of Germany† and left all the other men in their prison.

In that year Wales had peace from the English, and Llywelyn ap Gruffudd was prince over all Wales. Then died Llywelyn ap Rhys ap Maelgwn, on the eighth day from Epiphany.†

[1265–1265]. A year after that, Edward, son of Henry, king of England, escaped from Hereford, from the prison of Simon de Montford, on the Thursday before the feast of the Trinity, by the counsel and through the stratagem of Roger de Mortimer. And after his escape, he gathered a mighty host of earls and barons who joined with him; and on the Tuesday next after August† he came to the field of Evesham. And against him came earl Simon and his host to fight with him. And in that fighting fell Simon and his sons† and most of the nobles who supported him.

That year, in the month of March, Maredudd ab Owain, defender of all Deheubarth and counsellor of all Wales, died at Llanbadarn-fawr; and he was buried at Strata Florida in the chapter-house of the monks. In that year Pope Clement the Fourth was elected.

[1266–1266]. A year after that, the two sons of Simon de Montford escaped from the prison of the king of England. And they sailed to France to seek aid and counsel of their kinsmen and their friends, and they fortified their castle of Kenilworth† with strong men and arms and victuals. And when king Henry and Edward, his son, heard of that, they gathered a mighty host from all England after the feast of John the Baptist, and went to lay siege to that said castle. And the garrison of young men that was in the castle manfully held the castle against the whole host of England till the eve of the feast of Thomas the Apostle. And then from lack of victuals they surrendered the castle to the king, upon their being allowed the safety of their lives and their members and their raiment and their weapons.

[1267–1267]. A year after that, Llywelyn ap Gruffudd made a pact with the earl of Clare. And after that, the earl gathered a mighty host and made for the city of London; and forthwith through the deceit and treachery of the burgesses of the town he took the city. And when king Henry and Edward, his eldest son, heard of that, they gathered a host and laid siege to the city, and forced the earl and his men to submit to them upon certain conditions. After that, on the feast-day of Pope Calixtus,† peace and concord were arranged between Henry, king of England, and the Lord Llywelyn, prince of Wales, with Ottobon, the Pope's legate, as mediator between them, at Baldwin's Castle.† And for that peace and agreement he promised to the king thirty thousand marks of the king's sterling.† And the king granted that the prince should receive the homage of the barons of Wales, and that the barons should maintain themselves and their followers wholly under the prince, and that there should be princes of Wales from that time forth, and that they should be so named.† And to testify to that for ever, the king, with the consent of his heirs, granted his charter thereto under his seal and also the legate's seal to the prince. And that was also ratified by the authority of the Pope.

In that year Charles, king of Sicily, killed Conrad, nephew to the emperor Frederick, and Manfred, the emperor's son, in a battle on a field in Apulia.†

In that year the Sultan of Babylon† took the city of Antioch and ravaged it completely, killing all the men and women, after having before that ravaged all the land of Armenia.

[1268–1268]. A year after that, Goronwy ab Ednyfed, steward to the prince, a man eminent in arms and generous with gifts, and wise of counsel and true of deed and pleasant of words, died on the eve of the feast of St. Luke the Evangelist. That year died Joab, abbot of Strata Florida.†

[1269–1269]. A year after that, Gruffudd ap Madog ap Gruffudd Maelor and Madog Fychan, his brother, died on the same day† in the month of December; and they were buried in the monastery of Llynegwestl.

[1270–1270]. One thousand two hundred and seventy[1] was the year of Christ when Maredudd ap Gruffudd, lord of Hirfryn,† died in his castle at Llandovery on the day following the feast of St. Luke the Evangelist;† and he was buried at Strata Florida in the chapter-house of the monks.

In that year, in the month of October, Llywelyn ap Gruffudd took the castle of Caerffili.

In that year Louis, king of France, died while his son and the Pope's legate were on their way going to Jerusalem. And Edward, son of king Henry, went to Jerusalem.[2]†

[1] *Emend* ar hugeint MS. *to* a thrugeint.
[2] And Edward . . . Jerusalem] *marginal entry* MS.

[1271–1271]. A year after that, [Maredudd ap]¹ Rhys Gryg,† a brave, powerful man, died in his own castle at Dryslwyn on the sixth day from August;† and his body was taken to Whitland and was honourably buried in the great church on the steps in front of the altar. Three weeks after that, on the eighth day from the feast-day of St. Lawrence, Rhys Ieuanc ap Rhys Mechyll died in his own castle at Dinefwr; and he was buried in the monastery of Talley.

[1272–1272]. A year after that, Henry, king of England, son of John, died on the feast-day of St. Cecilia the Virgin after his having reigned fifty-six years, one month and one week; and he was buried in London in a new monastery. And after him Edward, his eldest son, reigned.†

In that year, on the feast-day of St. Denis, Pope Gregory the Tenth was elected.

[1273–1273]. A year after that, about the feast of Mary [after that of] St. Brigit, Owain and Gruffudd, sons of Maredudd ab Owain, gave Cwmwd Perfedd to Cynan, their brother.

[1274–1274]. A year after that, about Low Easter, Llywelyn ap Gruffudd went to survey his castle of Dolforwyn.† And he summoned Gruffudd ap Gwenwynwyn to him. And after reproaching him for his infidelity and his deceit, he took from him the cantref of Arwystli and thirteen townships between the Rhyw and the Luggy, and a portion of Cyfeiliog beyond the Dyfi.† And he seized Owain, his eldest son, and took him with him to Gwynedd.

In that year Edward came from the land of Jerusalem, and† Pope Gregory the Tenth held a general synod at Lyons on the day of the Calends of May.

In that year, on the Sunday after the first feast-day of Mary in the autumn, Edward, son of Henry, was consecrated and crowned king.

In that year, about the feast of Andrew the Apostle, Llywelyn ap Gruffudd sent messengers to Gruffudd ap Gwenwynwyn, to the castle of Welshpool. And he welcomed them, so it appeared, and invited them to their meat to the castle. And that night he had them served unstintingly with food and drink. And forthwith he went from the castle to Shrewsbury, and he bade the garrison imprison the prince's messengers. And when Llywelyn heard of that, he gathered the host of all Wales to lay siege to the castle. And he took the castle and released

¹ —MS.

his messengers from the prison, and he burned the castle and subdued all the territory of Gruffudd ap Gwenwynwyn without opposition to him, and placed officers of his own in every place in the territory.

In that year there was an exchange of two commots, namely, Cwmwd Perfedd and the commot of Pennardd, between Cynan and Rhys Fychan; and to Cynan came Pennardd, and to Rhys Cwmwd Perfedd.

[1275–1275]. A year after that, a little before Ascension Thursday, king Edward held a council of all the realm in London. And there he laid down new statutes and laws for the welfare of his realm.

In that year, on the fifteenth day from the Calends of August,† died Owain ap Maredudd ab Owain; and he was buried at Strata Florida, in the chapter-house of the monks, beside his father's grave.

In that year, about the last feast of Mary in the autumn, king Edward came from London to Chester; and he summoned to him the Lord Llywelyn to render him his homage. And the prince summoned to him the barons and the leading men of all Wales. And after taking counsel of them, he did not go to the king's court because his fugitives were with the king, and the king commending and maintaining them, namely, Dafydd ap Gruffudd and Gruffudd ap Gwenwynwyn. And the king in rage returned to England. And the prince came back.

That year the earth quaked in Wales, about the last feast of Mary, at the time of the third hour of the day.†

In that year merchants from Haverford† seized Amaury, son of Simon de Montford, sailing with Eleanor, his sister, for Gwynedd; and both of them were placed in the king's prison. And that Eleanor the prince had married through words uttered by proxy; and after that she was released through the intercession of Pope Innocent and the leading men of England. And a marriage was solemnized between Llywelyn and Eleanor, on the feast-day of St. Edward the king, at Winchester,† with king Edward there and then going to a liberal expense for the wedding banquet. And by her the prince had a daughter, who was called Gwenllïan. And Eleanor died giving birth to her; and she was buried in the monastery of the Barefooted Friars at Llan-faes in Anglesey. And that Gwenllïan, after the prince's death, was taken into captivity to England; and before her coming of age she was made a nun against her will. And after

Amaury had been released from the king's prison, he forthwith set out for the court of Rome.

In that year died Cadwgan Fychan of Ystrad.†

[1276–1276]. A year after that, Llywelyn frequently sent messengers to the king's court to seek to arrange peace between them, but he did not succeed at all. At last, about the feast of Mary [after that of] St. Brigit, the king held a council at Worcester. And there he set up three hosts to war against the Welsh: one he sent to Chester, with himself at its head; the second to Baldwin's Castle, and at its head the earl of Lincoln and Roger de Mortimer. And those gained possession of Powys for Gruffudd ap Gwenwynwyn, and Cydewain and Ceri and Gwerthrynion and Builth for Roger de Mortimer; and the earl of Hereford gained possession of Brycheiniog. And the third he sent to Carmarthen, and at its head Pain de Chaworth.

[1277–1277]. A year after that, a little after Easter, the earl of Lincoln and Roger de Mortimer came to lay siege to the prince's castle of Dolforwyn. And they took it by the end of a fortnight† for lack of water. And then Rhys ap Maredudd ap Rhys and Rhys Wyndod, nephew of the prince, made a pact with Pain de Chaworth. And Llywelyn, brother of Rhys Wyndod, and Hywel ap Rhys Gryg left their land and went to Llywelyn. And Rhys [Fychan ap Rhys] ap Maelgwn went to Roger de Mortimer, his kinsman, and promised in his hand submission to the king. And last of all Deheubarth, there submitted to the English the two sons of Maredudd ab Owain, Gruffudd and Cynan, and Llywelyn ab Owain, their nephew. And then Pain, and with him a mighty host, came to subjugate three commots above the Aeron,—Nanhuniog and Mefenydd and Cwmwd Perfedd. And the above four barons—Rhys ap Maredudd and Rhys Wyndod from Ystrad Tywi and the two sons of Maredudd ab Owain from Ceredigion—made for the king's court to tender him their homage. And the king deferred accepting their homage till the first† council; and two of them, Gruffudd and Rhys ap Maredudd, he released home, and the other two, Rhys Wyndod and Cynan, he detained in the court with him. And Llywelyn ab Owain because of his not being of age was placed in his ward. And after that, about the feast of John the Baptist,† the above four rendered their homage to the king at Worcester, and Rhys Fychan ap Rhys[1] ap Maelgwn along with them.

That year Edmund, the king's brother, built a castle at Aberystwyth.† And Edward came to Perfeddwlad and he

---

[1] Fychan ap Rhys *added in margin*.

fortified Flint with a huge ditch. And he came to Rhuddlan and fortified it, too, with a ditch.†

That year, about August,† Rhys Fychan ap Rhys[1] ap Maelgwn, for fear of his being seized by the English from Llanbadarn, and the men of Genau'r Glyn and all their chattels with them, fled to Gwynedd to Llywelyn and left their land empty. And the English occupied all their territory. And after that,† Edmund and Pain returned to England from Aberystwyth and left Roger de Meules to keep the castle. And after that,† Rhys Wyndod and Cynan ap Maredudd came by permission from the king's court.

And about the beginning of autumn the king sent many of his host in ships to burn Anglesey and to carry off much of its corn. After that the prince came, about the Calends of Winter, to Rhuddlan to the king and made peace with him. And the king invited him to London at Christmas; and he went at the invitation. And in London he tendered his homage to the king on Christmas day. And after staying there a fortnight he returned again. Thereupon, about the feast of Andrew, the king had Owain Goch, the prince's brother, and Owain ap Gruffudd ap Gwenwynwyn released from the prince's prison. And then Owain Goch received the cantref of Llŷn from the prince.

[1278-1278]. A year after that,† king Edward and Edmund, his brother, gave Eleanor, daughter of Simon de Montfort, their kinswoman, as wedded wife to the prince. And they were married on the feast-day of Edward the king in the cathedral church of Worcester. And that night their† wedding-banquet was held. And on the following day the prince, and his wife with him, returned to Wales.

[1279-1279]. A year after that, king Edward had his money changed, and the halfpenny and the farthing were made round. And then was verified the soothsaying of Myrddin when he said, 'The form of exchange shall be split, and its half shall be round.'†

[1280-1280]. One thousand two hundred and eighty was the year of Christ[2]† when Master Richard de Carew, bishop of Menevia, died on the Monday next before the feast of St. Ambrose, the Calends of April. And after him came Thomas de Bec.

[1] Fychan ap Rhys *added in margin*.
[2] *The following entry has been added by another hand in the margin, to be taken after* Christ: when Dafydd broke with the king of England on the thirteenth day before the Calends of April.

That year died Phylip Goch, abbot† of Strata Florida. And after him came Einion Sais, under whom the monastery was after that burnt. After that, on the eve of the feast of Mary [after that of] St. Brigit, Thomas, bishop of Menevia, sang the first Mass that he sang in his diocese at the high altar in the church of Strata Florida. Thereupon, on the feast-day of David, he was consecrated bishop on his throne at Menevia.

[1281–1281]. A year after that,† Dafydd ap Gruffudd took the castle of Hawarden on the feast-day of St. Benedict, after slaying all the garrison except Roger de Clifford, lord of the castle, and Pain de Gamage. Those he imprisoned.

[1282–1282]. A year after that, Gruffudd ap Maredudd and Rhys Fychan ap Rhys[1] ap Maelgwn, on the feast-day of Mary at the Equinox, took the castle and the town of Aberystwyth; and they burned them and destroyed the walls, but granted their lives to the garrison because of the imminence of the days of the Passion. That day Rhys [ap Rhys]† ap Maelgwn[2] gained possession of the cantref of Penweddig and Gruffudd of the commot of Mefenydd.†

On Palm Sunday took place the breach between Llywelyn ap Gruffudd and Edward, king of England. And the autumn after that, the king and his host came to Rhuddlan. And he sent a fleet of ships to Anglesey, with Hywel ap Gruffudd ab Ednyfed as leader at their head; and they gained possession of Anglesey. And they desired to gain possession of Arfon. And then was made the bridge over the Menai†; but the bridge broke under an excessive load,† and countless numbers of the English were drowned, and others were slain. And then was effected the betrayal of Llywelyn in the belfry at Bangor by his own men.

And then Llywelyn ap Gruffudd left Dafydd, his brother, guarding Gwynedd; and he himself and his host went to gain possession of Powys and Builth. And he gained possession as far as Llanganten. And thereupon he sent his men and his steward to receive the homage of the men of Brycheiniog, and the prince was left with but a few men with him.† And then Roger Mortimer and Gruffudd ap Gwenwynwyn, and with them the king's host, came upon them without warning; and then Llywelyn and his foremost men were slain on the day of

[1] Fychan ap Rhys *added in margin* MS.
[2] ap Maelgwn *in margin* MS.

Damasus the Pope, a fortnight to a day from Christmas day; and that day was a Friday.†

[1283-1283]. The year next to that was commenced the castle of Aberconwy, and Beaumaris and Caernarvon and Harlech. And on the fifth day from the end of the month of April, Edward of Caernarvon was born.† And that summer the king gained possession of all Gwynedd, and Dafydd ap Gruffudd went into outlawry, and the king took hostages from Gwynedd. And the autumn after that, Dafydd ap Gruffudd and Owain, his son, were seized, and they were taken† to Rhuddlan as prisoners; and thereupon they were taken to Shrewsbury. And then† Dafydd ap Gruffudd was executed, and Owain was taken to prison to Bristol.

[1284-1284]. A year after that,[1] the king held a fair at Moel-yr-Wyddfa. And he had a tournament held at Nefyn in Llŷn. And thereupon the king went towards England exultantly happy with victory.

[1285-88-1285-88]. After that there were four years of continued peace at a stretch, without anything to be recorded for that length of time.†

[1289-1287]. A year after that, the breach came between the king of England and Rhys ap Maredudd, lord of Dryslwyn. And then the king's host from Wales and from England came against Dryslwyn. And then John Pennardd,[2] leader of the men of Gwynedd, was drowned. And at last by a long seige they took the castle, and drove Rhys ap Maredudd into outlawry.

[1290-1290]. One thousand two hundred and ninety was the year of Christ when the Jews were expelled from the realm of England. In that year Rhys ap Maredudd was seized in the woods of Mallaen through the treachery of his own men.

[1291-1291]. Anno. j°. died Bevys de Clare, brother of Gilbert, earl of Clare; he was the foremost person in England, and the most powerful.

[1292-1292]. Anno. ij°. died Einion, bishop of St. Asaph. He was called 'The Black Friar of Nannau.' And he was the best man and the strongest in maintaining his diocese that anyone saw.

---
[1] *In the MS. there is a marginal entry to be read after* that: Edward of Caernarvon was born.
[2] Penlard MS.

[–1293]. In that year Llywelyn ap Llywelyn ab Ynyr† was elected bishop at St. Asaph.

[1293–1294]. Anno. iij. Geoffrey Clement,† justice of Deheubarth, was slain at 'Y Gwmfriw' in Builth.† And there was a breach between Welsh and English on that feast of Michael. And Cynan ap Maredudd and Maelgwn ap Rhys were chief over Deheubarth, and Madog ap Llywelyn ap Maredudd† over Gwynedd, and Morgan ap Maredudd over Morgannwg.

[1294–1295]. Anno. iiij. Edward, king of England, came with a great host into Wales, and he overran Wales. And Madog ap Llywelyn and his son were seized. And Cynan was seized at Hereford and was executed.†

And at that[1] time the men of Scotland and the men of Flanders were warring against England.

[1295–1296]. Anno. v. The king and his host went to subdue Scotland; and Sir John Balliol, king of Scotland, and his son were seized; and he was expelled from this island.†

[1296–1297]. Anno. vj. The king and his host went to subdue Flanders, and peace was made between them.

[1297–1295]. Anno. vij. died Gilbert, earl of Clare, the man of gentlest blood and the most powerful of the English.†

[1298–1298]. Anno. viij. There was a great massacre of the Scots at Falkirk in Scotland. And the sun reddened on that day in the beginning of autumn.†

[1299–]. Anno. ix.

[1300–1304]. Anno dm̄. m̊. ccc°. John, earl of Warenne, died.†

[1301–1304]. Anno. j°. The Pope of Rome† died. And the cardinals were confined for long at Perugia because they would not elect a Pope.

[1302–1305]. Anno. ij. William Wallace was drawn.

[1303–]. Anno. iij.

[1304–]. Anno. iiij.

[1305–]. Anno. v.

---

[1] *Emend* en MS. *to* en [er].

[1306-1306]. Anno. vj. There was a breach between the men of Scotland and the king of England.

[1307-1307]. Anno. vij. Edward, king of England, went to subdue Scotland. And coming thence, at the town called Burgh-on-Sands the eminent king died on the seventh day of July.
In the same year, on the feast-day of Matthew the Apostle, the sixth day from the Calends of March, Edward Caernarvon, his son, was crowned.

[1308-1308]. Anno. viij. Piers Gaveston began to govern the realm at his pleasure. And the other leaders took that ill.

[1309-]. Anno. ix.†

[1310-]. Anno dm. m. cccx.

[1311-1312]. Anno. j. Edward the Third was born.†

[1312-1312]. Anno. ij. Piers Gaveston was slain on the feast-day of Stt. Gervasius and Protasius,† near Warwick, after he had been lured out of the castle.

[1313-1314]. Anno. iij. Llywelyn, bishop of St. Asaph, died, and Dafydd ap Bleddyn was elected in his place on the eve of the feast of John at Midsummer. And on that day occurred the encounter in the Pools,† and Gilbert the Younger, earl of Clare, and many of the men of England besides, were slain by the Scots. And the king of England ignominiously fled from that encounter.

[1314-1315]. Anno. iiij. Dafydd,† bishop of St. Asaph, was consecrated.

[1315-]. Anno. v.

[1316-]. Anno. vi.

[1317-1315]. Anno. vij. The war of Llywelyn Bren took place.

[1318-1316]. Anno. viij. Llywelyn Bren was seized.†

[1319-1317]. Anno. ix. There was discord between the king and the barons.

[1320-1320]. Anno dm. m. ccc°. xix°. The barons came fully armed to the council at London, and they wanted to seize the king and Sir Hugh the Younger, unless he placed his seal to the letters of the barons. And he wept and did their will.

[1321–1321]. Anno. j. The queen came to the castle of Leeds; and there she was prevented from entering. And she complained to the king. And because of that the war between the barons and the king commenced. And then the king sent a host against the castle to destroy it, and bade that Sir Bartholomew of Badlesmere[1] be captured; for that castle belonged to him. And there the barons went against Sir Hugh's territory, and they overran all Morgannwg. And after that had been made known to the king, he came to Shrewsbury that Christmas. And there the Rogers came to the king's will. And they were taken as prisoners to the White Tower in London. And the king, and the host of Gwynedd with him, came to Hereford. And there he was for the feast of Mary [after that of] St. Brigit, and the barons and their host at Gloucester. And soon after that† the barons burned Bridgenorth. And thence they went to Burton-on-Trent, and there they were dispersed. And thence they came to Boroughbridge. And there Sir Andrew of Harclay came and cut them off from the bridge. And there the earl of Hereford was slain, and the earl of Lancaster was seized and taken to Pontefract, to his own castle as prisoner by the king. And there his head was struck off on the Monday following the feast of Benedict the abbot in the same year.†

[1322–1322]. Anno. ij. The barons were everywhere pursued, and the Clifford, Mowbray, Tyeis, Badlesmere[2] and many others were seized, and they were slain, drawn and hanged; and others were imprisoned. The Audley and the Berkleys and many others were imprisoned.†

[1323–1323]. Anno. iij. Sir Hugh caused the queen to be hated and to be placed on livery. And there was war in Gascony against the king in that year.

[1324–1324]. Anno. iiij. The earl of Warenne was chosen to go as leader of a host to Gascony. And he went with his host to Bordeaux after the feast of St. Brigit.†

[1325–1325]. Anno. v. The queen and Edward, her son, and the countess of Warenne went to Paris as messengers from the king of England to the king of France.† And that Christmas the earl of Warenne came from Bordeaux.†

[1326–1326]. Anno. vi. On the Thursday next after the feast-day of Michael, the queen and her son and the earl of Kent

---

[1] Baddesmere MS.
[2] Baddesmere MS.

and Roger Mortimer and the brother of the count of Hainaut landed in England at St. Edmondsbury. And thereupon they made for London. And the king came towards Morgannwg. And on the feast-day of Luke the Evangelist the earl of Arundel was seized by the burgesses of Shrewsbury in the monastery.†

On the Sunday next before the feast of Stt. Simon and Jude the king and Sir Hugh the Younger fled across the Severn to Morgannwg from Bristol. And there Sir Hugh the Elder was seized and drawn. And on the day following the feast-day of St. Edmund the archbishop, the earl of Arundel was slain at Hereford. And on the day following the feast-day of St. Clement the Pope, Sir Hugh the Younger and Simon Reding were drawn at Hereford. And the king was taken prisoner by them.

And on the next feast-day of Mary [after that of] St. Brigit, his son was crowned king.† He was the third Edward. And there the betrothal between him and the daughter of the count of Hainaut† was made.

[1327–1327]. Anno. vij. The leaders of England went to York, after the feast of Gregory the Pope, against the Scots; but it was hardly of avail.

[1328–1328]. Anno. viij. About the feast of Peter, at the beginning of autumn, peace was made between England and Scotland. And the daughter of the king of England was given to the son of the king of Scotland.

In that year Roger Mortimer had a council held at Salisbury about the Calends of Winter, and they wanted to kill the earl of Lancaster, and they argued strongly on either side. And they came to Worcester that Christmas. And about the feast of Paul the Apostle they were pacified at Leicester. And after the feast of Mary [after that of] St. Brigit, the burgesses of London were compelled, some to ransom their necks, others to be hanged, for having helped the earl of Lancaster.

[1329–1329]. Anno. ix. The king of England was compelled to go to France to do homage to the king of France. And the earl of Warenne stayed at Dover to await him, and Roger Mortimer and the queen in Kent.

In that year the tournament was held at Dunstable.† In that year, after the feast of Gregory the Pope, a council was held at London. And Sir Edmund de Woodstock came to the council. And Roger Mortimer had him seized and had his head struck off on the Monday following the feast-day of St. Edward the king and martyr, without justice, without judgement in the world. And on the following day his ordained knight, Sir Ralf de Hermer, was slain. And many others fled from the land, when they saw that a man of such high rank as the earl of Kent, and an uncle to the king, his father's brother, and near kinsman to the old queen, was not respected.[1]

[1330–1330]. Anno dm. m. ccc. xxx. A son was born to Edward the Third at Woodstock about the Calends of May.

In that year Llywelyn ap Hofa, archdeacon of St. Asaph, died after the feast of John at Midsummer.

In that year a third part of the sun was darkened on Tuesday, the feast-day of St. Kenelm the king.

In that year Roger Mortimer was seized at Nottingham on the feast-day of Luke, in the night. And he was taken to London; and there he was executed on the eve of the feast of Andrew.† And on the feast-day of St. Catherine before that, occurred the great wind wherewith the belfry of Wrexham fell. And one night before Christmas eve there was a great wind, and on the third day after Christmas day.

[That][2] year came the harmful tempest which did not allow the corn to ripen till winter came, and there was much that was never reaped.†

In that year, after Christmas, the earl of Arundel's son was given his rights.

[1331–1331]. Anno. j. About the Calends of May the market at Wrexham, which was formerly on Sunday, was changed: it was changed to Thursday from that time forth.

In that year, in autumn, a site for a fortification was first measured at Bryneglwys in Iâl.† In that year a jousting tourney was held on the feast of Michael at Cheap in London.†

In that year died many of the leading men of Wales: Goronwy ap Tudur of Anglesey and Tudur ab Adda, archdeacon of Meirionnydd, and Madog ap Llywelyn, the best man that ever was in Bromfield, on the eve of the feast of Matthias the Apostle at the end of the month of February; and he was buried in his own church at Gresford.†

---

[1] *In the MS., opposite the last statement in this paragraph there is a marginal entry by another hand*: In that year died Master Philip at Hereford on the feast of Hilary and then he was buried in the cloister in the burial place on the south side of the church.

[2] *Insert* honno *in Welsh text.*

[1332-1332]. Anno. ij. After the Calends of May the body of Harold, king of England, was found in the church of John at Chester, after it had been buried more than two hundred years before that. And his body and his crown and his raiment and his leathern hose and his golden spurs were found as whole and smelling as good as on the day that they were buried.†

In the same year, about the feast of Michael, Edward de Balliol, and with him a small host, went to seek to gain possession of Scotland.†

NOTES

page line

1   1   **Six hundred and eighty-one ... and then he died** (l. 10): The first two paragraphs of the text are based partly on AC and partly on the concluding sections of Geoffrey of Monmouth's *Historia Regum Britanniae*, XII, XV–XIX: see HRB 530–35. For the date 681 in the text, ctr. 682 in AC, 680 in RB, and 683 in BS. MS. C shows an attempt to bring the chronology into line with that of Geoffrey's *Historia*. Cf. HRB 534 Tunc Cadualadrus abiectis mundialibus propter dominum regnumque perpetuum uenit Romam & a Sergio papa confirmatus inopinato etiam morbo correptus *duodecima autem die Kalendarum Maiarum anno ab Incarnatione Domini d.cl.xxxix* a contagione carnis solutus celestis regni aulum ingressus est. Not one of the three MSS. of AC refer to Cadwaladr's going to Rome: MS. A only records his death, but MSS. B and C say that he went to Brittany.

1   2   **a great mortality ... Britain**: cf. AC *s.a.* 682 Mortalitas magna fuit in Britannia. This bald statement has been developed by Geoffrey of Monmouth, HRB 530: Accessit etiam aliud infortunium quia fames dira ac famossissima insipienti populo adhesit, ita ut tocius cibi sustentaculo uacaretur provincia, excepto uenatorie artis solatio. Quam etiam famem pestifera mortis lues consecuta est que in brevi tantam populi multitudinem strauit quantam non poterant uiui humare.

1   2   **Britain**: After this there is an additional entry in RB: Ac o dechreu byt hyt yna yd oed blwydyn eisseu o petwarugein mlyned ac wyth cant a phumil, 'And from the beginning of the world till then there was one year short of five thousand eight hundred and eighty years.' This RB entry is not in BS.

1   4–5   **and there he died ... May**: See HRB 534 quoted above on 1.1. Lloyd has shown in HW i. 230 and footnote 9 that Cadwaladr died in the pestilence of 664 and that Geoffrey has identified him with Caedwalla of Wessex, thus placing his death on 20 April, 689. The *Saxon Genealogies* in the *Historia Brittonum*, *c.* 64 record Cadwaladr's death in the plague which occurred during the reign of Oswy of Northumbria: HB 204 Osguid, filius Eadlfrid, regnavit viginti octo annis et sex mensibus. *Dum ipse regnabat, venit mortalitas hominum, Catgualatr regnante apud Brittones post patrem suum et in ea periit.*

1   6–7   **as Myrddin ... Gwrtheyrn Wrthenau**: The reference is to Merlin's prophecy to Vortigern in HRB 387: Arripiet mortalitas populum cunctasque nationes euacuabit. Residui natale solum deserent & exteras culturas seminabunt. *Rex benedictus* parabit navigium & in aula duodecim inter beatos annumerabitur. Erit miseranda regni desolatio.

For a Welsh commentary from Peniarth MS. 16. 29*b* on Merlin's prophecies see BD 246 on 105. 3. In it *E brenin bendigedic* (rex benedictus) is explained as denoting Cadwaladr.

For *Gwrtheyrn Wrtheneu* (Pen. 20) RB and BS give the older form with the initial consonant of the adjective unmutated: RB [G]wrtheyrn

page line

Gortheneu, BS Gortheyrn *Gortheneu*. Gwrtheneu (*Gortheneu*) < *gor* (intensive prefix) + *tenau*, 'thin' = 'very thin.' See CA lxxix, footnote 2.

1 8 **Ifor son of Alan**: see HRB 534–35. The entry in BS is much fuller than the corresponding one in Pen. 20 and RB: Ac val yd oedynt velly yn gwledychu yn hedwch dagnauedus a gwedy peidiaw o'r dymhestyl, ef a doeth Juor vab Alan ac Ynyr y nei ... y dir Lloegyr ac ev llu git ac wynt; sef oed hynny teir blyned a phedwar vgeint a chwechant gwedy geni Duw. Ac yn ev herbyn wyntheu y doeth y Saesson, ac ymlad ac wynt yn wychyr creulon calet. Ac yn yr ymlad hwnnw y llas lluossog-rwyd o bop tu. Ac o'r diwed y goruu Ivor ac y goresgynnws Kerniw a Dyfneint a Gwlat yr Haf. Ac yna yd aeth y Saesson y gynullau ev nerthoed attadunt y dyuot am benn Ivor. Ac yna yd aeth gwyrda ryngthunt ac y tagnavedwit wynt. Ac yna y kymyrth ef Ethelburga yn wreicka idaw. Ac ef a beris gwneithur freitur y meneich yn Glastingburie ar y gost ehun, a hynny drwy llywodraeth Aldelmus, manach sant o'r ty hwnnw.

'And as they were thus ruling in peaceful quiet and after the tempest had ceased, Ifor son of Alan and Ynyr, his nephew, ... came to the land of England and their host with them; that was three and four-score and six hundred years after the birth of God. And against them came the Saxons and fought with them savagely, fiercely and stubbornly. And in that fighting a multitude was slain on either side. But in the end Ifor prevailed and conquered Cornwall and Devon and Somerset. And then the Saxons went to gather to them their forces to come against Ifor. And then leading men went between them and peace was made between them. And then he took Aethelburh to be his wife. And he had the refectory of the monks at Glastonbury made at his own cost, and that under the direction of Aldelm, a saintly monk from that house.'

BS has identified Ifor son of Alan with Ini of Wessex who married Aethelburh and who is said to have gone to Rome. Cf. *Annales de Wintonia* in *Annales Monastici* (Rolls Series), ii. 6.

1 12–3 **a mortality in Ireland**: AU *s.a.* 683 (= 684) and CS *s.a.* 680 (= 684) have 'Mortalitas *paruulorum*.'

1 14 **the earth quaked**: RB Ac yna y crynawd y daer *yn Llydaw*, 'And then the earth quaked *in Brittany*'; BS ... y crynws y daear *yn Manaw*, 'the earth quaked *in Man*'; AC *s.a.* 684 Terrae motus *in Eubonia* (MS. A., *Eumonia* MS. B, *Brittania* MS. C); AU *s.a.* 684 (= 685) Terre motus *in insola*, i.e. in the island of Ireland; CS *s.a.* 681 (= 685) terrae motus *in Hibernia insola*. The difference here and elsewhere between Pen. 20, RB and BS shows that there were minor variations in the underlying Latin versions used by the Welsh translators and that those variations reflected differences in the various MSS. of the *Annales Cambriae* which were used in the compilation of the Latin chronicle.

1 15 **the rain of blood**: on 'blood-rain' see *Classical Philology* ix. 442.

1 18–9 **the moon ... blood**: cf. AC *s.a.* 690; also AU *s.a.* 691 Luna in sanguineum colorem *in natali sancti Martini* uersa est; CS *s.a.* 688 Luna in sanguineum colorem *in natale Sancti Martini*.

1 21–2 **And he was buried at Damnani**: This second part of the entry for 704 is not in RB and BS, which merely state that Aldfrid, king of the

NOTES

page line

Saxons, died. AC *s.a.* 704 Alchfrid (MS. A, Aelfrid MS. B, Adelstan MS. C) rex Saxonum obiit (moritur MS. C). Dormitatio Adomnan,— the last two words being in MS. A only. Cf. AU *s.a.* 703 (= 704) *Adomnanus* lxx. vii aetatis suae, abbas Iae, *pausat*; CS *s.a.* 700 (= 704) *Adomnanus* lxxviii anno aetatis suae in nono Kalendarum Octobris, Abb Iae, *quieuit*. The reference is to the death of Adamnán. Pen. 20 has mis-translated *dormitatio*; and *Adomnani* has been taken as a place-name.

1 23 **A year after that**: i.e. in the year 705. Ctr. RB *Deg mlyned a seithcant* oed oet Crist . . . , 'Seven hundred and ten was the year of Christ . . .'; BS *Anno Domini d.cc.xiii* . . . Between this entry and the preceding, AC has nine blank *anni*. This explains why the date in Pen. 20 is here nine years in arrear.

1 23-4 **the night . . . day**: AC *s.a.* 714 Nox lucida fuit sicut dies; AU *s.a.* 713 (= 714) and CS *s.a.* 710 (= 714) Nox lucida *in autumno*. In AC and BS the two entries for 714 (true date) are in the same order as that of Pen. 20, but in RB the order is reversed.

1 26 **the church of Michael**: the reference is to Mont St. Michel. MS. A of AC has Consecratio Michaelis archangeli ecclesie, whereas MS. B has Consecratio S. Michaelis *in monte Gargano*, and MS. C Consecratio S. Michael ecclesie. *Garganus* is the name of a mountain in Apulia: see G s.v.

2 3 **Beli, son of Elffin**: AC *s.a.* 722 Beli filius Elfin (MS. A, *Elphin* MS. B, *Elphini* MS. C) moritur (obiit MS. B) cf. AU *s.a.* 721 (= 722) Maelcorgis o Druim ing, *Bile mac Eilpin rex Alocluathe*, moriuntur. AU shows that Beli was king of Dumbarton or Alcluathe. See OP iii. 259, note 1.

2 3-4 **the battle of Heilyn**: The original reading in Pen. 20 was *y vrwydyr ynGhernyw a elwir Gweith Garthmaelawc*, but a later hand has deleted *a elwir* and written *heilyn* in the margin for insertion after *vrwydyr*. RB vrwydyr *Heilin*, BS ryvel *Heil*, AC bellum *Hehil* (MS. A, *Heil* MS. B, *Heyl* MS. C). Here, as elsewhere, the marginal entry in Pen. 20 seems to reflect a collation of the text with that of RB.

2 5 **Garthmaelog**: for possible identifications of this place-name see HW i. 197 and note 15. Cf. G s.v. 'garth.'

2 5 **Pen-cŵn**: Pen. 20 *Penkwn*, with *kwn* underlined and *coed* written above it by a later hand, showing the influence of RB or BS. RB *Pen Coet*, BS *Pencoet*, AC *s.a.* 722 cat *Pencon* (bellum *Pentun* MS. C). Cf. BT1 61. 19 gweith *pencoet*. On the evidence *Pencoet* appears to be the more correct form. *Pencon* is probably an error for *Pencoit* (an older orthographical form of *Pencoet*) with *-it* wrongly transcribed as *-n*. Assuming that Pen-coed is correct, see OP iii. 226, note 1 for possible identifications—(1) Pen-coed near Coychurch in the Vale of Glamorgan; (2) Pen-coed between Caer-went and Caerleon; (3) Pen-coed west of Ross in Herefordshire.

2 8-9 **the battle of Mynydd Carno**: RB vrwydyr y *Mynyd Carn*, BS ryuel *Mynyd Carno*, AC *s.a.* 728 Bellum mortis (*montis* MSS. B, C) *Carno*. The form *Carno* is more correct than *Carn*. AU *s.a.* 728 (= 729) has a fuller entry: *Bellum Monithcarno iuxta stagnum Loogdae*, inter hostem Nectain et exercitum Oengusa, et exactatores Nectain ceciderunt, hoc

o

page line

est, Biceot mac Moneit et filius eius, Finguine mac Drostain, Feroth mac Finguinne, et quidam multi; et familia Oengussa triumphavit. It is obvious that this battle was fought in Central Scotland, not in Wales. It is probable that the fact that a well-known battle was fought in 1081 at Mynydd Carn in Wales has influenced the RB text here.

2 12 **A year after that, died Owain, king of the Picts**: Pen. 20, RB, BS and AC agree in placing this entry in the annal following that which records the death of Bede, and so the date appears to be 736. But it appears that 'Owain, king of the Picts' (AC *Ougen*, rex Pictorum) is to be identified with *Oengus*, son of Fergus: cf. AU *s.a.* 735 (= 736) *Oengus* mac Fergusso *rex Pictorum* . . . But we know from AU that Oengus survived till 750: cf. *s.a.* 749 (= 750) Aithbe flatho Oengussa, 'End of the reign of Oengus.' It is to be noted that AC has thirteen blank *anni* between the annal recording the death of Owain and that recording the battle of 'Mocetauc.' It may be that these blank *anni* should have preceded the annal giving the death of Owain. This would mean that Owain's death would be dated 749, thus agreeing with the actual date in AU for the end of his reign. AU does not state that he died in that year. AU *s.a.* 760 (= 761) has: *Mors Oengusa* mic Fherghussa, *regis Pictorum*—but this cannot be proved to be the same person.

There is another possible explanation of the entry in AC, Pen. 20, RB and BS. AU *s.a.* 735 (= 736) records the death of Brude, son of Oengus, son of Fergus. It may be that *Brudeus filius* was dropped before *Ougen* in the entry in AC. This explanation, however, does not account for the *rex Pictorum* in AC. Hence the first explanation given above is to be preferred and has been adopted in deciding the chronology.

2 14 **Gwaith My[g]edog**: Pen. 20 Gweith *Mietouc* (Mictaut Megedawc MS. C); RB Gweith *Maes Edawc* (*al. Maes y Dawc, Maes Ydawc*); BS Gweith *Mecgetawc* (*al. Megedawc*); AC *s.a.* 750 Bellum inter Pictos et Brittones, id est, Gueiht *Mocetauc*; AU *s.a.* 749 (= 750) *Bellum Cato hic* inter Pictones et Brittones, in quo cecidit Talorggan mac Ferggussa, frater Oengussa. The readings of AC and BS are to be preferred, as representing Mod. Welsh *Mygedog*. Pen. 20 *Mietauc* is probably a corruption of *Mi[c]etauc*, an orthographical variant of AC *Mocetauc*. The form may be a place-name, a proper noun or an adj. See B viii. 232–34 on *mygedorth*. RB *Maes Edawc* appears to be a corruption of *Mocetauc* with *–c–* (before *–e–*) pronounced as 's', and the first element rationalized as *maes* 'field.'

2 15 **Talargan**: i.e. Talorgan, son of Fergus. Cf. AU in the passage quoted in the preceding note.

2 23 **Gwaith Henffordd**: so too RB and BS, but AC *s.a.* 760 gueith *Hirford*. *Henffordd*, if correct here, is the Welsh form for Hereford. *Hirford* represents an older form, before the change of *r* to *n*.

2 26 **Elfoddw, a servant of God**: For his death see below *s.a.* 809, where he is called 'archbishop of Gwynedd.' Nennius in his preface to the *Historia Brittonum* describes himself as 'Elvodugi discipulus.' See HB 16, 115–118, 145, 147.

2 28 **Ffyrnfael ab Idwal**: RB Fernuail vab *Idwal*, BS Ffermael vab *Jdwal*, but AC *s.a.* 775 Fernmail filius Iudhail (MS. A, *Idwal* MS. B, *Ydwal*

page line

MS. C). *Iudhail* represents Mod. Welsh 'Ithel,' and is the correct name here: cf. the Pedigrees in HB . . . Fernmail *map Iudhail*. See G *s.v.* 'Ffyrnuael.'

2 29 **A year . . . Picts**: so too BS, but the entry is not in RB. Cf. AC *s.a.* 776 *Cenioyd* rex Pictorum obiit; AU *s.a.* 774 (= 775) Mors *Cinadhon* regis Pictorum. MS. *Kymoyd* (BS *Cemoyd*) has been emended to *Kynioyd*.

2 30 **Cuthbert the abbot**: so too RB and AC *s.a.* 777, but BS *seint Cubertus abbat*, '*Saint* Cuthbert the abbot.' The reference is not to St. Cuthbert, who died in 758, but to Cuthbert, abbot of Wearmouth and a pupil of Bede's.

2 31–2 **The year . . . men of the South**: RB Ac yna y bu distryw y Deheubarthwyr gan Offa vrenhin, 'And then was the harrying of the men of Deheubarth by king Offa'; BS gwyr Deheubarth Kymre a diffeitheassant yr ynys hyt ar Offa, brenhin Mers, 'the men of South Wales harried the island as far as Offa, king of Mercia'; AC *s.a.* 778 Vastatio Brittonum dextralium apud (ab MS. C), rege Saxonum (last two words in MS. C only). AC *apud* Offa is probably a mistake in copying *ap = ab*. Pen. 20 and RB give the correct meaning, but BS has mistranslated probably in an attempt to give a meaning to *apud Offa*. But see RC xlix. 163 where Loth shows that *apud* is used in the *Historia Brittonum* in the sense of *contra*; also HB 55, note 3.

2 33–4 **Three years . . . Offa**: RB Petwarugein mlyned a seithcant oed oet Crist pan diffeithawd Offa vrenhin y Brytanyeit yn amser haf, 'Seven hundred and eighty was the year of Christ when king Offa ravaged the Britons in the season of summer'; BS D.CC.lxxxiiij yr haf y diffeithws y Kymre kyuoeth Offa, 'In the year seven hundred and eighty-four, in the summer, the Welsh harried the kingdom of Offa'; AC *s.a.* 784 Vastati[o] Brittonum cum (ab MS. C) Offa in aestate. Pen. 20 has obviously translated '*cum* Offa,' but Phillimore suggests that *cum* of MS. A of AC is a mistake in translating Old Welsh *cant* (Mod. Welsh *gan*), which could mean 'by' as well as 'with': see *Y Cymmrodor* ix. 162, note 5. RB gives the correct sense, but BS has again mistranslated. See also OP iii. 261, note 1; RC xlix. 158.

3 1–3 **Seven hundred and eighty-five . . . harried**: RB Deg mlyned a phetwarugein a seith cant oed oet Crist pan doeth y Paganyeit yn gyntaf y Jwerdon, '*Seven hundred and ninety* was the year of Christ when the Pagans came first to Ireland'; BS DCC.lxxxxv yd aeth Paganyeit gyntaf y Iwerdon ac y diffeithwyt Rechreyn, 'In the year *seven hundred and ninety five* the Pagans first went to Ireland and Rechra was harried'; AC Vastatio *Rienuch* ab Offa (MS. C only). Primus adventus gentilium apud dexterales ad Hiberniam (MS. A, Gentiles venerunt ad Hiberniam MS. C). Pen. 20 *Rechrenn* and BS *Rechreyn* represent the Irish genitive of *Rechra* (i.e. Lambey Island, Co. Dublin). Cf. AU *s.a.* 794 (= 795) Loscadh *Rechrainne* o geinntibh, 'The burning of Rechra by Gentiles.' BS alone of the Welsh versions gives the correct date. Pen. 20 is a decade in arrear, probably because AC has a blank decade after the preceding entry.

AC Vastatio *Rienuch* ab Offa, since it is found in MS. C only, is open to suspicion. If it is correct, *Rienuch* can well represent *Rheinwg*, the name of a district in South Wales so-called after Rhain: see HW i.

page line

281-282. It is possible, however, that MS. C of AC has here gone astray and that *Rienuch* is an error for some form of Rechra, in which case 'ab Offa' would be incorrect. On the entry of MS. C of AC see *Y Cymmrodor* xi. 140, note 3. See also CLlH 97 for the form *Rieinwc*.

3   4-5   **A year after that ... Rhuddlan**: RB Ac y bu varw Offa vrenhin a Maredud, brenhin Dyfet. Ac y bu vrwydyr yn Ruḋlan, 'And king Offa and Maredudd, king of Dyfed, died. *And there was a battle at Rhuddlan*'; BS DCC.lxxxxvi y bu varw Offa, brenhin Mers, ac y bu varw Moredud, brenhin Dyvet. Ac y bu ymlad Rudelan, 'In the year seven hundred and ninety-six died Offa, king of Mercia, and Maredudd, king of Dyfed, died. *And the battle of Rhuddlan took place*; AC *s.a.* 796 Offa rex Merciorum et Morgetiud rex Demetorum morte moriuntur, *et bellum Rudglann* (Offa rex obiit. Bellum Rudlan. Maredud rex Demetorum obiit MS. C). Pen. 20 has mistranslated in saying that Maredudd died 'in the battle of Rhuddlan.' RB and BS are here more correct.

3   11   **R[hun]**: The emendation of Pen. 20 *r*[. . .] is confirmed by Pen. 20 *s.a.* 814 Gruffud vab *run*. That RB and BS *Rein* is the correct form here and *s.a.* 814 is proved by AC *s.a.* 808 *Regin* (*Reyn* MS. C) rex Demetorum. AC *Regin* is the old Welsh form corresponding to Medieval Welsh *Rein* and Mod. Welsh *Rhain*.

3   20   **A year ... lightning**: In Pen. 20 and BS the death of Owain and the burning of Degannwy are given in the same annal. RB does not show division into annals in this section. AC *s.a.* 811 and 812 divides them into two separate annals.

3   22   **... and Hywel prevailed**: RB, BS and MSS. A and B of AC agree, but ctr. MS. C of AC ... sed victor fuit *Kenan*.

3   23   **Three years after that**: in MS. A of AC there is *one* blank *annus* between the notice of the 'war between Hywel and Cynan' and that of the 'great thunders,' etc. RB does not show the analistic divisions, but BS places the 'war between Hywel and Cynan' *s.a.* 812 and the 'great thunders,' etc. *s.a.* 815, thus agreeing with Pen. 20 in having *two* blank *anni* between the two notices. However, it is to be noticed (*Y Cymmrodor* ix. 163, note 9) that *an*[*nus*] is repeated once too often in this decade in MS. A of AC. In MSS. B and C of AC there are no blank *anni* between the two notices. Hence the chronology in the text.

3   24   **Gruffudd ap Rhun**: RB *Tryffin* vab *Rein*, BS *Grufud* vab *Rein*, AC *s.a.* 814 *Trifun* (MS. A, Trifin MS. B) filius *Regin*. RB *Tryffin* is more correct than Pen. 20 and BS *Grufud*, and RB and BS *Rein* more correct than Pen. 20 *Run*. See above on 3.11. Cf. *Y Cymmrodor* ix. 175 [T]*riphun* map *regin*.

3   25   **Griffri**: so too RB and BS, but AC *Griphiud* (Grifri MS. B).

3   32   **Llan-faes**: so too RB and AC, but BS is more precise: Gweith Llanvaes y Mon, 'the battle of Llan-faes *in Anglesey*.'

4   2   **the arch of Degannwy**: RB *castell* Deganwy, 'the castle of D.'; BS –Degannwy; AC *s.a.* 822 Arcem Decantorum (Arx Deganhui MS. B) a Saxonibus destruitur (Saxones *arcem Degannoe* destruxerunt MS. C). The Pen. 20 translator seems to have read *arcum* for *arcem*.

NOTES   135

page line

4 2–3 **and took ... own**: RB Ac yna y duc y Saeson brenhiniaeth Powys yn eu medyant, 'And then the Saxons took the kingdom of Powys under their rule.' BS ac y distrywywt Powys, 'and Powys was harried.' AC et regionem Poyuis in sua potestate traxerunt (MS. A, Powis in suam potestatem traxerunt MS. B, et regionem Poweis vastaverunt MS. C). Pen. 20 and RB seem to reflect MSS. A and B of AC, but BS is closer to MS. C.

4 4 **Two years after that**: so too BS, but in AC the death of Hywel is placed in the *third* annal after that recording the destruction of Degannwy.

4 6 **eclipse of the moon**: RB Deg mlyned ar hugein ac wyth gant oed oet Crist pan vu diffyc ar y lleuat *yr wythuet dyd o vis Racuyr*, 'Eight hundred and thirty was the year of Christ when there was an eclipse of the moon *on the eighth day from the month of December*'; BS DCCC.xxxi y bu diffic ar y ll[e]uat *viii Kalendas Nouembres*, 'In the year eight hundred and thirty-one there was an eclipse of the moon *on viij Kal. Nou.*' AC (MS. B only) *s.a.* 831 Eclipsis lunae.

4 6 **Sadyrnfyw**: MS. *Saturbin*, which is to be emended to *Satur[n]biu*. RB *Saturbiu*, BS *Saturbin*, AC *Satur biu* hail (MS. A), Satur wiu (MS. B,) Sadurnven (MS. C). The form *Saturnbiu* occurs in Old Welsh. See *An Inventory of the Ancient Monuments in Anglesey* cxi; LL xlvi, xlvii (from the 'Book of St. Chad').

4 9 **when Bonheddig, bishop of Menevia, ruled**: RB pan wledychawd Meuryc escob y Mynyw, 'when *bishop Meurig* ruled in Menevia'; BS y kyssegrwit escob Mynyw, '*the bishop of* Menevia was consecrated'; AC *Nobis* episcopus in Miniu regnavit (MS. A), Novus episcopatum suscepit (MS. B), Novis est episcopus Menevensis (MS. C). The Pen. 20 translator has read *nobilis* for *Nobis* (the proper name) and rendered it by *bonhedic*. The Welsh of Pen. 20 could be translated as 'when the gentle-born (*bonhedic*) bishop of Menevia ruled.' With RB 'bishop Meurig' cf. below on 9.21. BS appears to have translated *Novus est episcopus Menevensis*. For the proper name *Nobis* (*Novis*) see LL 216, 217, 262, 270, 303, 312. MSS. C D of the Pen. 20 version give *Einion vonheddic* with which cf. Pen. 20 below *s.a.* **874** where this bishop's death is recorded.

4 13 **the battle of Ffinnant**: MS. *fumant*, but the emendation is confirmed by RB [g]weith *Finant*, BS Gueith *Fynnant*, AC *s.a.* 848 Gueit *Finnant*. Since the next sentence mentions 'the men of Brycheiniog,' it is probable that the place here meant is Ffinnant near Aberysgir in Brycheiniog, although there are two places so named in Montgomeryshire: (1) in the parish of Llansanffraid in Mechain, (2) in the parish of Trefeglwys. Also there is a farm bearing the name near Brechfa in Carmarthenshire.

4 16–7 **when the Pagans slew Cyngen**: RB Ac y tagwyt Kyngen *y gan y Kenedloed*, 'and Cyngen was strangled *by the Gentiles*'; BS y llas Kyngen *y gan y wyr ehun*, 'Cyngen was slain *by his own men*'; AC Cinnen *a gentilibus* jugulatur (MS. A), Cengen *a gentibus* occisus est (MS. B). BS has misinterpreted *a gentilibus* or *a gentibus*, possibly reading *a gente*.

4 20 **Cyngen**: RB and BS agree, but AC gives *Cinnen* (MS. A), *Cengen* (MS. B), *Fygen* (MS. C).

page line

4 22–3 **Two years ... Picts**: not in RB, but in BS and AC. The latter *s.a.* 856 gives the proper name as *Cemoyth* (altered from *Cemoith*). Read *Cenioyth* as in AC (MS. A) *s.a.* 776. Cf. AU *s.a.* 857 (= 858) *Cinaedh mac Ailpin, rex Pictorum*, ⁊ *Adulf, rex Saxan, mortui sunt.*

4 23 **Ionathal, leader of Abergelau**: RB *Jonathal, tywysawc* Abergeleu, 'Ionathal, leader of Abergelau'; BS *Jonathan, pennaeth* Abergeleu, 'Jonathan, chief of Abergelau'; AC *Ionathan princeps* Opergelei (Abergeleu MS. B). Pen. 20 and RB have translated *princeps* as *tywysawc*, 'leader,' but BS *pennaeth*, 'chief' is more apposite since the reference is to Ionathal as head of the *clas* at Abergelau.

4 24–5 **Eight hundred ... died**: Cf. AU *s.a.* 861 (= 862) *Maelsechnaill mac Maelruanaigh ... ri hErend uile ii Kalendas Decembris, iii. Feria, anno regni sui xui°, defunctus est*, 'Maelsechnaill son of Maelruanaigh, king of all Ireland, died on the 2nd of the Kalends of December, on a Tuesday, in the sixteenth year of his reign.' So too CS *s.a.* 862. This entry is not in RB, but is in BS and in MSS. B and C of AC. It appears to have been misplaced by a year in AC.

4 26 **Two years ... expelled**: so too RB, but BS *Ac yn y vlwydyn honno y bu Cat Gweithen*, 'And in that year was *the battle of Gweithen*'; AC *s.a.* 862 *Catgueithen* (MS. A, *Cadweithen* MS. B) *expulsus est*. This entry is not in MS. C of AC. BS has mistranslated by taking the personal name *Catgueithen* as *cat* (battle) and *Gueithen*. [*Gweithen*, in its Old Welsh form, *Gueithgen*, is found in LL 144.26]. For *Catgueithen* (= Cadweithen) as a personal name see LL 183.21, 204.6 and cf. G s.v. 'geni.' Cf. below on 5.22.

4 27 **Two years ... Glywysing**: not in RB, but BS *y diffeithwyt Glyuissig ac yd alltudwyt wynt*, 'the Glywysing were ravaged and exiled'; AC *s.a.* 864 *Duta* (*Dutta* MS. B) *vastavit Gliuisigng*. The entry is not in MS. C of AC. The Pen. 20 translator seems to have read *Dicta* or *ista* for *Duta*, taking it to refer to Cadweithen in the preceding entry. However, AC *Duta* is correct: for examples of the Saxon personal name Duta or Tuta see LL 218.17, 218.19, 221.9, 222.9, 223.14, and W. G. Searle, *Onomasticon Anglo-Saxonicum* s.n. 'Tuta,' etc.

4 28 **Cynan of Nanhyfer**: MS. *Kynan nawd niuer* which could be taken to mean 'Cynan host-protector,' but RB *Nant Niuer* and BS *Nant Niver* prove that Pen. 20 *nawd niuer* is to be emended to *Nant Niuer*, the Old Welsh form of Nanhyfer. Cf. AC *s.a.* 865 *Ciannant in mer* (*Chian Nant Newer* MS. C), which is for *Cian Nantnimer*. Note that where Pen. 20, RB and BS have *Kynan*, AC has *Cian*: this last may be an error for *Cian* = *Cinan*. However, *Cian* is an authentic form (see G s.v.), though not necessarily correct here; but since it occurs in MS. A of AC it should not be lightly set aside. Phillimore OP ii. 440-41 accepts *Cian* as the correct form and points out that this name may be commemorated in *Rhiw Gian* (later > *Rhigian*) in the parish of Trefdraeth or Newport, Pem. Cf. also ib. ii. 87.

4 29–30 **York ... Black Gentiles**: RB *ac y diffeithwyt kaer Efrawc yg kat Dubkynt*, 'and York was ravaged in the battle of the Black Gentiles'; BS *y diffeithwyt Caer Effrauc, ac y bu Cat Dubgynt*, 'and York was ravaged, and the battle of the Black Gentiles took place'; AC *s.a.* 866.

page line

Urbs Ebrauc vastata est, *id est cat Dub gint*. The Pen. 20 translator seems to have read *i cant* for 'id est cat,' the RB translator seems to have read *in cat*, and the BS translator *et cat* by confusing the contractions for *et* and *id est*.

Dubgynt is a compound < Old Welsh *dub* (= *duf* > modern *du*, 'black') + *gynt* < Lat. *gentes*, meaning 'Black Gentiles.'

With this entry cf. AU *s.a.* 866 (= 867) Bellum for Saxanu tuaiscerta i Cair Ebhroc, re nDub Ghallaib, in quo cecidit Alli rex Saxan aquilonalium, 'A battle [was gained] over the Northern Saxons, in York, by the Black Foreigners, in which Alli, king of the Northern Saxons fell.'

The *Alli* of AU is Aelle, king of Northumbria.

5   4   **when the fortress of Dumbarton . . . Pagans**: so too RB, but BS y torret *twr* Alclut, 'the *tower* of Dumbarton was destroyed'; AC *s.a.* 870 *Arx* Alt Clut a gentilibus fracta est. With this entry cf. AU *s.a.* 869 (= 871) Obsesio *Ailech cluathe* a Norddmannis. i. Amlaibh et Imhar, duo reges Norddmannorum obsederunt arcem illum et destruxerunt in fine .iiii. mensium arcem et predauerunt; CS *s.a.* 871 Amlaib ocus Imar do tricchecht arisi do *Ath Cliath* a Alban díbh cédoibh long, ocus creach mor daine .i. do Saxanaib ocus do Brentnachaibh do tabairt leo docum hErinn, 'Amlaibh and Imhar came again to *Ath-cliath* from Alba with two hundred ships, and a great band of men, that is, of Saxons and Britons, was brought by them to Ireland.' CS has *Ath-cliath*, 'Dublin,' where AU has *Ail-cluathe*, 'Dumbarton.' AU seems to be correct. Cf. ONR p. 11.

5   7   **Banolau**: MS. *Y Bann Goleu*; RB *Bangoleu*; BS *Banngoleu*; AC *Bannguolou* (MS. A), *Bannoleu* (MS. B). See G s.v. 'goleu.'

5   8–9   **Einion Fonheddig, bishop of Menevia**: RB *Meuryc*, escob bonhedic, 'Meurig, a gentle-born bishop'; BS escob Mynyw, 'the bishop of Menevia'; AC *s.a.* 873 *Nobis et Mouric* moriuntur (MS. A), *Novus episcopus et Meuruc* moriuntur (MS. B), *Novis* episcopus moritur (MS. C). RB has translated *nobilis episcopus Mouric* (cf. above on 4.9), BS does not give the bishop's name, but it is difficult to see how the Pen. 20 translator arrived at Eyn̄ (= Einion).

5   10   **Himbert**: RB Lwmbert, BS Lunberth, AC *s.a.* 874 Llanwerth (MS. B only). BS *Lunberth* is confirmed by the same form in LL 238–239.

5   12   **Dwngarth**: RB Dungarth, BS Dungarth, AC Dungarth (MS. A), Dumnarth (MS. B). The first three of these forms represent *Dunarth* but the fourth is for *Dyfnarth*. Whether the former or the latter be more correct here, Pen. 20 *Dwngarth* seems to represent an earlier *Dungarth*. For other examples of *Dunarth* and *Dyfnarth* as variants see G s.v. 'Dunart (—th).' This *Dunarth*, it has been suggested, is the same person as the *Doniert* commemorated on a stone at St. Cleer near Liskeard: see *Archaeologia Cambrensis* V. xii. 52, 57.

5   14–5   **the Sunday battle . . . in Anglesey**: Pen. 20, RB and BS have Gweith Duw Sul y Mon. Cf. AC Gueith Diu Sul in (en MS. B) Mon (Bellum die Dominica apud Mon MS. C). ONR 6 comments on this battle: 'Probably this was a sudden encounter with the Norsemen, who, being the only heathen antagonists of the period, forced the Christian

page line

Welsh to take up arms in spite of religious principles.' It is probable that after being worsted in this battle Rhodri ap Merfyn fled to Ireland, as recorded in AU *s.a.* 876 (= 877): Ruaidhri mac Muirminn, rex Brittonum, du tuidheacht docum nErend for teiched re Dubghallaibh, 'Rhodri son of Merfyn, king of the Britons, came to Ireland, fleeing before the Black Foreigners.' Cf. CS *s.a.* 877 Ruaidri mac Muirminn, Rex Britannorum, do toighecht cum Erenn, for teithedh re Duph Gallaib, 'Rhodri son of Merfyn, king of the Britons, came to Ireland, fleeing from the Black Foreigners.'

5 16 **Rhodri and Gwriad, his brother**: so too RB and BS; AC *s.a.* 877 Rotri et *filius* ejus Guriat (MS. A), but MS. B reads *frater* for *filius*. AU *s.a.* 877 (= 878) records the death of Rhodri but does not mention Gwriad: Ruaidhri mac Muirminn, rex Brittonum, a Saxonibus interemptus.

5 18 **Aedd, son of Mell**: RB Aed vab *Mellt*, BS Aed vab *Mell*, AC *s.a.* 878 Aed map *Neill* moritur. Cf. CPS 8 Aed filius *Niel*; ib. 10 Aed filius *Neil* moritur; ib. 109 Mors Aeda meic *Neill*; AU *s.a.* 878 (= 879) *Aedh* finn liath mac *Neill* caille, rex Temoriae, in xii. Kl. Decimbrium i nDruim in ascland i crich Conaille dormiuit. The entry in CS *s.a.* 879 agrees with AU but it adds that Aedh died on the sixth day of the week.

To give the form *Mell* (Pen. 20 and BS) and *Mellt*, with intrusive –*t*, (RB) in Welsh it is probable that the *ni*— of a form *niel(l)* was read as *m*—.

5 20–1 **the battle of the Conway ... the avenging of Rhodri**: so too BS, but RB pan vu weith Conwy *y dial Rodri o Duw*, 'when the battle of the Conway took place *for God to avenge Rhodri*'; AC Gueit Conguoy digal *Rotri a Deo* (MS. A), Bellum Congui *Dial Rotri* (MS. B), Bellum Conui, id est *Dial Rotri* (MS. C). The words 'avenging of Rhodri' imply that the Britons were in this battle victorious against the Saxons and so avenged the death of Rhodri in 878 at the hands of the Saxons.

5 22 **Cadweithen**: see above on 4.26.

5 24 **Two years ... Cerbhall**: not in RB, but cf. BS y bu varw Cerball, 'Cerbhall died'; AC *s.a.* 887 Cerball defunctus est; AU *s.a.* 887 (=888) Cerbhall mac Dungaile, rex Osraighi, subita morte periit; CS *s.a.* 888 Cerball mac Dunlainge, Rí Osruidhe, subita morte [periit].

5 25–6 **Suibhne, the most learned of the Irish**: Cf. AU *s.a.* 890 (= 891) Suibne mac Mailehumai, ancorita et scriba optimus Cluana macc U *Nois*, dormiuit; CS *s.a.* 891 Suibne mac Maoiluma, ancorita Cluana muc *Nois*, quieuit.

5 28 **when the Black Norsemen came to Gwynedd**: For Pen. 20 *y Wyned*, 'to Gwynedd,' RB has eilweith y Gastell Baldwin, 'a second time to Baldwin's Castle,' and BS has drachevin hyt ar Gwinn, 'again as far as Gwinn.' There is no corresponding entry in any of the MSS. of AC. Egerton Phillimore, in his notes to OP iv. 693–4, suggests that the Latin original of the Welsh texts meant *Mons Blandinus* or *Mont Blandin*, the name of the site at St. Peter's Abbey at Ghent. 'The Norsemen's host went from Fulham to Ghent, "and sat there one year," in 880, about 12 years before they went to *Bononia* or *Boulogne*, in 892. ... It looks as though the events of the year 880 and those of 892, and the names of

NOTES

page line

some *Baldwin* of Flanders, Mont *Blandin*, and some form of Boulogne (and perhaps also *Baldwin* de Bollers' castle at Montgomery) had been confused by a Welsh annalist writing in a remote situation with few works of reference, say at St. David's or Llancarvan in the early 12th century.' This, however, is not very convincing. It should be noted that Pen. 20 has nothing corresponding to RB *eilweith*, 'a second time,' and BS *drachevin*, 'again,' a point which weakens Phillimore's suggestion. ONR 14–15, written before the publication of the Pen. 20 text, accepts the RB version but calls attention to that of BS. Baldwin's Castle, however, was not built until 1093 so that the RB reading here is suspect—although ONR 15 shows that the Norsemen were active in the region of the eastern border of Powys about this time. Since the RB version bungles so often, the readings of Pen. 20 and BS (its *Gwinn* may reflect a contraction in the original Latin) are to be preferred here.

5 29 **Hyfaidd**: MS. *Henweith*, RB *Heinuth*, BS *Henneth* are all corruptions of an Old Welsh form of *Hyfaidd*. Cf. AC *s.a.* 892 *Himeyd* (MS. A), *Hiveid* (MS. C). Cf. on 6.36.

5 32–3 **England and Brycheiniog and Gwent and Gwynllw̃g**: so too BS, confirmed by AC *s.a.* 895 Nordmani (Hordmani MS.) uenerunt et uastauerunt Loycr et Bricheniauc et Guent et Guinnliguiauc. Ctr. RB y diffeithawd y Normanyeit Loegyr a Brecheinoc *a Morganwc* a Gwent *a Buellt* [a] Gwnllwc, 'the Normans ravaged England and Brycheiniog *and Morgannwg* and Gwent *and Buellt* [and] Gwynllwg.'

6 5 **king Ethelstan**: the scribe of Pen. 20 wrote *Edelstan vrenhin y Saesson*, 'Ethelstan, king of the Saxons,' but a later hand has drawn a line through *y Saesson*. RB *Elstan* vrenhin y Saeson, BS *Elstan* brenhin y Saesson, AC *Elstan* rex Saxonum (MS. B only). This reference to the death of *Edelstan* or *Elstan* may be an error: cf. AU *s.a.* 897 (= 898) *Aided mac Laigni, rex Ulath*, a sociis suis per dolum occisus est; CS *s.a.* 898 *Aided mac Laighne, Rí Uladh*, a sociis per dolum [occisus est]. AC, RB and BS *Elstan* suggest that Pen. 20 *Edelstan* is wrong. *Elstan* may be for the later form *Elystan*: see G *s.n.*

6 6 **Wessex**: MS. *Euwas*, RB *Iwys*, BS *Gynoys* (read *Gyuoys*), AC *s.a.* 900 rex *Giuoys*, i.e. the *Gewisse*, the original name of the West Saxons. See Stenton, ASE 21, n. 1.

6 7 **Nine hundred was the year**: The text of Pen. 20 is here defective: a leaf (= pp. 71–72) is missing, leaving a lacuna for the years 900–950. This lacuna occurs in all the extant versions of the Pen. 20 text. It is known that the leaf was missing in Pen. 20 as early as the seventeenth century: see *Cambrian Register* ii. 473–475 and *The National Library of Wales Journal*, V. 291. In the present translation the missing section has been supplied (as in Pen. 20) from Mostyn MS. 116. 144a–144b, *which represents the independent RB version.*

6 8–9 **and he held Maes Rhosmeilon**: BS ac a gynhelijs *Mays Meleriaun*, 'and he held Maes Meleriawn'; AC *s.a.* 902 et tenuit *maes Osmeliaun*. This last form is the more correct, representing the Old Welsh form of *Osfeilion* or *Ysweilion* (near Llan-faes in Anglesey), < *Osfael* + *ion*, 'the land of Osfael.' The Genealogies in BM Harleian MS. 3859 give *Osmail* as the name of one of Cunedda's sons: see *Y Cymmrodor* ix. 183. On *Osmeliaun* see Phillimore, OP ii. 296; ONR 17.

page line

6 10 **the son of Merfyn**: BS *y llas Meruyn vab Rodri*, 'and *Merfyn ap Rhodri* was slain'; AC *Merwyn filius Rodri* (MS. B), *Mervin rex filius* Rodri (MS. C). RB is here corrupt, and BS correct.

6 10 **by his own folk**: MS. *y gan y genedyl*; BS *y gan y wyr ehvn*, 'by his own men'; AC *a gentilibus* (MS. C only). It appears that both RB and BS have mistranslated *gentiles*, the Gentiles, i.e. probably the Norsemen. See ONR 18–19. Cf. notes on 4.16–7; 7.17.

6 12 **Rhydderch ap Hyfaidd**: BS *Rodri vab Himeith*; AC *s.a.* 904 *Rostri* (MS. A), *Rodri* filius Heweid (MS. B). RB *Ryderch* is an error due to a wrong extension of a contraction. On AC *Rostri* (MS. A) see Phillimore, *Y Cymmrodor* ix. 167, note 6; OP iii. 210–11.

6 12–3 **on the feast-day of Paul**: BS *yn Arwystli*, 'in Arwystli'; AC *in Arguistli*. Here again RB is corrupt.

6 14 **Dinneir**: MS. *Dinneir* with *th* added above line by later hand to give *Dinneirth* (Dinneirt MSS. R, T); BS *Diuuieir*; AC *s.a.* 906 *Dinmeir* (MS. A), *Dynerth* (MS. C). The *nn* of MS. *Dinneir* and of *Dinneirt* (MSS. R, T) make it improbable that the correct form is *Dineirth*. Phillimore, OP iv. 493 thinks that the forms *Dinmeir* and *Dinneirth*, taken together, point to a place called *Din Meirch* and refers to a township called *Llandinier* near Garthmyl.

6 16 **Gorchwyl**: BS *Gorchywyl*, which agrees with AC *s.a.* 907 *Guorchiguil* (MS. A), *Gorchewil* (MS. B).

6 16–8 **And Cormac ... in battle**: BS *A Cormoc, vrenhin ac escob holl Iwerdon a gwr mawr y grefyd a'y gardawt, mab Culennan, a las yn yr ymlad hwnnw*, 'And Cormac, king and bishop of all Ireland and a man of great piety and charity, son of Culennán, was slain in that battle'; AC *s.a.* 907 ... *obiit, et Cormuc rex* (MS. B), *Cormuch rex Hyberniae obiit* (MS. C),—entry not in MS. A. Cf. AU *s.a.* 907 (= 908) *Bellum etir firu Muman* ⁊ *leith Cuinn* ⁊ *Laighniu, in quo occisus est Cormac mac Cuileannain rí Caisil, cum aliis regibus praeclaris*, 'A battle between the men of Munster and the Leth-Chuinn [i.e. the northern half of Ireland] and Leinstermen, in which *Cormac mac Cuileannain, king of Caisel*, was slain, together with other famous kings'; CS 907 (= 908) *Bellum Bealaigh Mugnai re Laignibh ocus re Leith Cuinn for feraib Muman, in quo Cormac mac Cuilennain, Rí Caisil, scriba optimus atque episcopus et ancorita et sapientissimus Gaoidiol occisus est*, i. *Fiach H. Ugfadan o Dennlis isse ro mharb Cormac* (i.e. Fiach Ua Ugfadan, from Dennlis it was that slew Cormac).

The phrase 'by his own wish' (MS. *o'e uod*) of RB does not occur in BS or in AC. In the translation *o'e uod* has been rendered 'by his own wish,' taking it as '*o'e uodd*' since –*d* regularly = –δ in Mostyn MS. 116. If, however, as is possible, we have here a sporadic example of –*d* = –*d*, the last part of the sentence must be rendered 'who was slain as a result of his being in a battle.' This would appear to mean that Cormac, who is described in CS as '*episcopus et ancorita*,' was slain as a result of his being—contrary to what was expected of a bishop—in the battle of Bealach Mughna, in which the men of Leinster and Northern Ireland defeated the men of Munster.

6 19 **Leinster**: MS. *Langesy*, BS *Laginensium*. That BS is here correct is proved by AU *s.a.* 908 (= 909) *Cerball mac Muirecan, rex optimus*

page line

Laginensium, dolore mortuus est; CS *s.a.* 908 (= 909) Cearball mac Muirigen, Rí *Laigen*, (= king of Leinster) dolore mortuus est.

6   20 **making a sure end**: MS. *o keugant diwed*, BS *yn diwed yr ymlad*, 'at the end of the battle.' This entry is not in AC, but AU and CS (see preceding note) say that Cerbhall died of *anguish* (*dolore*). The variant versions of RB and BS point to a confusion between some form of *certus* and *certamen*.

6   21 **archbishop of the island of Britain**: BS archescop y Brutannyeit, 'archbishop of the Britons'; AC *s.a.* 908 Asser (MS. A), *episcopus* (MS. B), *episcopus Britannie* (MS. C).

6   22 **and Cadell ap Rodri**: in BS and AC the death of Cadell is placed in the annal following that containing the notice of the death of Asser. Cf. CS *s.a.* 908 (= 909) Caittell mac Ruadhrach, Rí Bretan, moritur, 'Cadell son of Rhodri, king of Britain, dies'.

6   25 **And Anarawd ... died**: Cf. CS *s.a.* 915 (= 916) Anoroit mac Ruarach, Rí Bretan, moritur, 'Anarawd son of Rhodri, king of Britain, dies.'

6   26-7 **And Ireland ... Æthelflæd died**: BS *s.a.* 914 y diffeithwyt Iwerdon y gan wyr Dulyn. Ac y bu varw Eldfled vrenhines, 'Ireland was ravaged by the men of Dublin. And queen Æthelflæd died.' AC *s.a.* 917 has only 'Aelfled regina obiit.' BS, it will have been noticed, does not mention 'Anglesey' under this annal, but *s.a.* 915 it has: y diffeithwyt Mon y gan [wyr] Dulyn, 'Anglesey was ravaged by [the men of] Dublin. AU *s.a.* 917 (= 918) records, immediately before the death of Æthelflæd, a battle between the Foreigners of Ireland and the men of Alba on the banks of the Tyne, whereas CS *s.a.* 918 (= 919) records the battle of Dublin in which the Irish were defeated by the Foreigners.

6   34 **by the men of Ceredigion**: so too BS, but these words are not in AC.

6   35 **the battle of Brun**: BS ymlad y Brune, 'the battle of the Brune'; AC *s.a.* 838 (MS. A only) Bellum *Brune*. It appears that the reference is to the battle of Brunanburgh. For early forms of the name see Alistair Campbell, *The Battle of Brunanburgh*. London, 1938. pp. 157-58.

6   36 **Hyfaidd**: MS. Hennyrth, BS Hymeith, AC Himeid (MS. A), Hewed (MS. B), Hiveid (MS. C). Emend MS. to *Hemeyth* or some such form. The BS and AC forms are correct, representing variant orthographical forms of modern *Hyfaidd*. Cf. on 5.29.

6   36 **his brother**: not in BS and AC.

7   2-3 **king Amlaibh**: BS ... y bu varw Abloyc, brenhin Iwerdon, '... *Amlaibh, king of Ireland*, died.' Cf. CS *s.a.* 940 (= 941) Amlaibh mac Gotfrit, Rí Finngall ocus Dupgall, mortuus est, 'Amlaibh son of Godhfrith, king of the White Foreigners and of the Black Foreigners, died.'

7   5 **his brother**: BS y *vab*, 'his son,' AC et *filius* ejus (MS. A), cum *filio* Elissed (MS. B).

7   6 **Lwmberth**: MS. Lwmbert, BS Lunberth, AC Lumberth (MS. A), Lunweth (MS. B), Luvert (MS. C). Cf. above on 5.10

page line

7 10–1 **And king Hywel ... died**: BS places Hywel's death in 948 (= 949) but AU records it *s.a.* 949 (= 950).

7 12–4 **And Cadwgan ... sons of Idwal**: BS records the death of Hywel, the slaying of Cadwgan, and the battle of Carno *s.a.* 947 (= 949), but in MS. A of AC the death of Hywel is placed *s.a.* 950 (= 949) and the slaying of Cadwgan and the battle of Carno *s.a.* 951 (= 950). Since RB does not here show the divisions into annals, the chronology of the text is based on MS. A of AC.

7 13 **the battle of Carno**: BS ymlad *Caerno*, 'the battle of Caerno' (ymladd Karno, 'the battle of *Carno*, MS. B); AC *s.a.* 950 bellum *Carno* (MS. A), juxta *Nant Carno* (MS. C). HW i. 344 follows MS. C of AC.

7 17 **And the Gentiles slew Dwnwallon**: so too BS: ac y llas Dungwallaun y gan ev gwyr wynt. Anno. ix^c.lj y bu varw Rodri vab Howel, 'And Dwnwallon was slain *by their men*. Anno ix^c.lj died Rhodri ap Hywel.' The italicized words seem to be a mistranslation of *a gentilibus* or *a gentibus*, correctly rendered by Pen. 20. AC does not record the death of Dwnwallon. RB seems to have combined two separate entries: Ac yna y bu varw Dyfynwal a Rodri, meibon Hywel, 'And then died *Dyfnwal* and Rhodri, sons of Hywel.' AC *s.a.* 954 has *Rotri* (*Rodri* MSS. B and C) *filius Higuel* (*Hoeli* MS. B, *Howel* MS. C), moritur (obiit MS. B).

7 18 **Rhodri ap Hywel**: see the preceding note.

7 20–1 **at the place ... Conwy Hirfawr**: RB yg *gweith Conwy yn Llan Wrst* (sic), 'at the battle of the Conway at Llan-rwst; BS yn lle gelwir *Gurgustu nev Gweith Conwy Hirmaur*, 'in the place called "Gurgustu" or the Battle of Conwy Hirfawr'; AC *s.a.* 954 in loco qui dicitur *Gurguist* (MS. B only). Pen. 20 *Gwrgystu*, BS *Gurgustu* seem to be errors for Old Welsh *Gurgust* (> Gwrwst), the second element in Llan-rwst.

7 21–2 **And Anarawd ap Gwri was slain**: RB Ac y llas Hir Mawr ac Anarawt y gan y pobloed. Meibon oed y rei hyny y Wryat, 'And Hirfawr and Anarawd were slain by the Gentiles. Those were sons of Gwriad'; BS agrees with Pen. 20: ac y llas Anaraut vab Gwry, 'and Anarawd ap Gwri was slain'; AC *s.a.* 954 Anaraut filius *Guiriat* occisus est (MS. B), ... *Guriat* (MS. C).

7 23 **Edwin ap Hywel**: so too RB, BS and MS. C of AC (Edywyn), but MS. B of AC has *Guin* filius Hoeli. It is pointed out in HW i. 337, note 61, that the form *Guin* is due to a misunderstanding of *Etguin* (Old Welsh form of *Edwin*) as *et Guin*. In Pen. 20 the death of Edwin ap Hywel is again recorded *s.a.* 954 (= 956), but this second entry is not in RB, BS and AC.

7 24 **Iarddur ap Merfyn**: RB *Hayardur* vab *Meruyn*, BS *Hayardur* vab *Mervyn*, AC *Haardus* filius *Meuruc* (MS. B only).

7 25 **A year ... Hywel**: See above on 7.23. Pen. 20 is incorrect here.

7 25–6 **And Congalach ... slain**: Not in AC. Cf. AU *s.a.* 955 (= 956) Conghalach mac Maelmithidh, ... ri Erend, do marbad do Gallaib (Atha cliath) ⁊ Laignib oc Taig Guirann il Laignib, 'Congalach son of Maelmithidh, ... king of Ireland, was slain by Foreigners (of Dublin) and Leinstermen at Tech Guirann in Leinster; CS *s.a.* 955

page line

(= 956) Congaluch mac Maoilmithidh, Rí Eirenn, do marbadh cona riograidh do Galloibh Atha cliath ocus la Laignibh, 'Congalach son of Maelmithidh, king of Ireland, was slain, together with his chieftains, by the Foreigners of Dublin and by Leinstermen.'

7 29 **Three years ... Y Gorwydd**: not in RB, but cf. BS Anno ix^c.lviij y diffeithws Oweyn *Goryuyd*, 'Anno ix^c.lviij Owain ravaged *Goryfydd*'; AC *s.a.* 959 Oweyn vastavit *Goher* (MS. C only). In HW i. 345, note 85, it is suggested that the correct reading is *Goruynyd*, 'Gorfynydd,' which is actually found in the MS. B of BS. But see G s.v. 'goruynyd.'

8 1–2 **A year ... ruling**: RB Ac y bu diruawr *eira* vis Mawrth, a meibon Idwal yn gwledychu, 'And there was great *snow* in the month of March, the sons of Idwal ruling'; BS Ac y gwledychaud meibion Jdwal drwy *nerth* diruawr mis Maurth, 'And the sons of Idwal ruled with great *strength* in the month of March.' Since there is no corresponding entry in AC, it is difficult to see how these variant translations of the same Latin original were arrived at. However, Pen. 20 and RB are probably more correct than BS, for the first part of the entry seems to correspond to CS *s.a.* 959 (= 960) *Plaig* mor for innilibh la *sneachta* ocus galra, 'A great *plague* upon cattle by *snow* and distempers.'

8 12 **with Aelfhere as their leader**: so too RB, but the phrase is not in BS. It is suggested in HW i. 350, note 108, that it may be that in Pen. 20 and RB the notice of 983 has been doubled.

8 16 **and was imprisoned**: RB alone adds: a gwedy hyny y croget, 'and after that he was hanged.'

8 18 **Madog, son of Harold ... Penmon**: RB Ac y diffeithawd *Marc* vab Herald *Benmon*, 'And *Mark* son of Harold ravaged Penmon'; BS y diffeithwyt Penn Mon y gan *y Paganyeit a Mactus* vab Harald, 'Penmon was ravaged *by the Pagans and Mactus* son of Harold'; AC (MS. B only) *Mon* vastata est *a filio* Haraldi. Stenton ASE 364 gives the name as *Maccus*, which would be correctly reflected by BS *Mactus*. Cf. ONR 24, 31. For the form *Maccus* cf. below 14.7, and W. G. Searle, *Onomasticon Anglo-Saxonicum* 344. Pen. 20 *Madog* is an error, possibly due to a wrong extension of a contraction, or to misreading *Mact.* as *Mad*[*og*].

8 21–2 **when Godfrey ... the island**: RB pan diffeithawd Gotbric vab Herald Von; ac *o vawr ystryw* y darystygawd yr holl ynys, 'when Godfrey son of Harold ravaged Anglesey; and *through great cunning* he subdued the whole island'; BS y diffeithwyt Mon y gan Gotfrit vab Harald ac a'y goresgynnawt *yn drethawl ydaw*, 'Anglesey was ravaged by Godfrey son of Harold and he overran it [and made it] *tributary to him*.' In Pen. 20 I printed 'a thrwy δiruawr *so*[*r*]*r*.' In the MS (74, col. a, l. 28) there is a smudge over the last two letters. Recently Mr. Hanson of the National Library of Wales treated this spot in the MS., and it is now clear that what the scribe originally wrote was ... *fofz*. Then he changed the –*fz* into –*lz* (hence the smudge), thus giving *solt*, which must be for *swllt*, 'treasure.' Cf. Pen. 20, 11, col. b, l. 23, drwy *swllt* mawr, 'with great treasure.' There is no corresponding entry in AC: Pen. 20 and BS are tolerably in agreement, and it may be that RB has translated some form of *sensus* for *census*.

page line

8 24 **at Chester**: MS. ȳGhaer llion; RB yg *Kaer Llion ar Wysc*, 'at Caerleon-on-Usk'; BS hyt *ynGhaer Llion ar Wysc*, 'to Caerleon-on-Usk'; AC *s.a.* 973 in urbe Legionum. Pen. 20, RB and BS have wrongly identified the *Urbs Legionum* of AC with Caerleon-on-Usk instead of Caerleon-on-Dee, i.e. Chester. See HW i. 349, note 105, ASE 365, ONR 31. In Medieval Welsh *Kaerllion* is the regular form for Caerleon (-on-Usk) and *Kaerlleon* the form for Chester. The translation is based on the emendation of *ȳGhaer llion* to *ȳGhaer lleon*.

8 27 **was blinded**: RB *hedychwyt* (*clefychwyt* MSS. R, T), 'was pacified' ('sickened' R, T); BS a *dallwyt*, 'was blinded'; AC *s.a.* 974 Meuric filius Idwal *caecatus est* (MS. B, *occiditur* MS. C). Pen. 20, BS and AC (MS. B) agree. RB *hedychwyt* must be a scribal error or a mistranslation.

8 29-30 **And Dwnwallon . . . died**: RB Ac yd aeth *Dwnwallawn*, vrenhin Ystrat Clut, y Rufein. Ac y bu varw *Idwallawn* vab *Einawn*, 'And Dwnwallon, king of Strathclyde, went to Rome. And Idwallon ab Einon died'; BS ac y kyrchawd *Dungwallaun*, brenhin Strat Clut, Ruvein. Ac y bu varw *Jdwallawn* vab *Oweyn*, 'and Dwnwallon, king of Strathclyde, made for Rome. And Idwallon ab *Owain* died' ; AC *s.a.* 975 *Idwalan* filius *Owein* obiit (MS. B only) It appears as if two separate entries, from different sources but referring to the same person, have been combined, with corruption of proper names. Cf. AU *s.a.* 974 (= 975) *Domnall mac Eogain, ri Bretan, in ailithri*, Foghartach abb Daire, mortui sunt, '*Domnall son of Eogan, king of the Britons, in pilgrimage*, [and] Foghartach, abbot of Daire, *died*'; CS *s.a.* 973 (= 975) Domnall mac Eogain, Rí Bretan, in clericatu quieuit. The Old Welsh form corresponding to Irish *Domnall* would be *Dumngual* or *Dumnagual*: for both forms see *Y Cymmrodor* ix. 172, 174. It is probable that *Dwnwallon* and *Idwallon ab Owain* (*Einon* RB) are errors for *Dyfnwal* and *Dyfnwal ab Owain* respectively.

9 3-5 **A year after that . . . Clynnog Fawr**: the Pen. 20 scribe wrote *Gyueilyawc Vawr*, but a later hand has drawn a line under these two words and written *Gelynnoc Vawr* at the foot of the column. MSS. C and D of the Pen. 20 version read *Gylynnawc*. RB Ac y diffeithwyt *Llwyn Kelynawc Vawr* . . . is to be emended to . . . Llyyn [a] Kelynawc Vawr. Cf. BS y diffeithwyt *Lleyn a Chelynnauc Vaur* yr eilweith y gan Hywel vab Ieuaf a'r Saesson y gyt ac ef, '*Llŷn and Clynnog Fawr* were ravaged for the second time by Hywel ap Ieuaf and the Saxons along with him.' See HW i. 351, note 116, where it is suggested that *Saesson* of Pen. 20, RB and BS (and so of the common Latin original) is a mistake for 'Gentiles.'

9 6-8 **Iago was captured . . . kingdom**: RB Ac yna y delit Jago, ac y goruu Hwel ap *Jeuaf*, ac y gweresgynwys kyuoeth Jago, 'And then Iago was captured and Hywel ap Ieuaf prevailed and he took possession of Iago's territory'; BS y dalpwyt Jago *y gan wyr* Howel vab *Jeuaf*, ac ef a wledychws kyuoeth Iago, 'Iago was captured by the men of Hywel ap *Ieuaf*, and he ruled Iago's territory'; AC *s.a.* 979 Iago captus est Hoelo filio *Idwal* triumphante et regnum eius possidente (MS. B), Iago captus est *a gentilibus* Ieuaf tenente regnum ejus (MS. C). It appears that the original Latin combined the *a gentilibus* of MS. C of AC with MS. B. BS seems to have translated *a gente*. Cf. notes on 4.16; 6.10; 7.17.

page line

9   12   **Gwaith Hirbarwch**: RB *Hirbarth*, BS *Hirbaruch*, AC ——.

9   14–5   **when Dyfed ... Llanweithefawr**: RB *pan diffeithawd Gotbric vab Herald Dyuet a Mynyw. Ac y bu weith Llan Wenawc* (*Wanawc* MSS. RT), 'when Godfrey son of Harold ravaged Dyfed and Menevia. *And the battle of Llanwenog took place*'; BS is nearer to Pen. 20: *y diffeithwyt Dyvet a Myniw a Llangweithenauc y gan wyr Gotfrit vab Harald*, 'Dyfed and Menevia *and Llanweithenawg* were ravaged by the men of Godfrey son of Harold'; AC *s.a.* 982 *Gothrit et Haraldus vastaverunt Devet et Meneviam* (MS. B), *Vastatio Dyvet et Meneviae a Godisric filio Haraldi* (MS. C). BS *Llangweithenauc* appears to be a better reading than Pen. 20 *Llannweitheuawr*: cf. LL 278 where *Gueithenauc* occurs as a proper name.

9   16–9   **Brycheiniog ... of their hosts**: so too RB and BS; AC *s.a.* 983 *Hoelus filius Idwal et Alfre dux Anglorum vastaverunt Brecheinauc et totam regionem Einaun filii Owini, sed Einaun ex eis multos occidit* (MS. B), *Einiaun filius Owein pugnavit contra Saxones, Alfre existente eorum duce, et contra Howel filium Ieuaf, et multos interfecit ex eis* (MS. C). See note on 8.12.

9   21   **And their noble bishop died**: RB *Ac y bu varw Bonhedic escob*, 'And bishop Bonheddig died'; BS ——, AC ——. It is probable that the translators of Pen. 20 and RB read *nobilis episcopus* for *Nobis episcopus*; and since there is no corresponding entry in BS and AC, this sentence in Pen. 20 and RB may have been misplaced. See on 4.9.

9   22   **Hywel ap Ieuaf**: so too RB and BS, but AC *s.a.* 985 *Howelus filius Idwal* (MS. B, *Ieuaf* MS. C).

9   24   **Cadwallon ap Ieuaf ... Meurig**: so too RB and BS. AC has no entry corresponding to 'And Cadwallon ... Meurig.'

9   25   **Maig ap Ieuaf**: RB has no entry corresponding to 'Maig ap Ieuaf was slain,' but cf. BS *y llas Meyc* (*Mevric* MS. B) *vab Jeuaf*; AC *s.a.* 986 *Meuric filius Idwal occisus est* (MS. B only). *Meyc* (= Maig) of Pen. 20 and BS is an authentic proper name (cf. LL 209, 231, VSB 315, 319) but is incorrect here.

9   26   **Cadwallon ap Ieuaf**: so too RB and BS, but AC *s.a.* 986 *Catwalaun filium Idwal* (MS. B only). *Ieuaf* is correct. Cf. 9.23.

9   28   **with great treasure**: MS. *drwy swllt mawr*; RB *o diruawr ystryw a challder*, 'by great stratagem and cunning'; BS *yn drethawl ydaw*, 'tributary to him.' With these variant versions cf. note on 8.21–2 above.

9   31   **the island of Anglesey**: so too RB, BS and MS. B of AC, but MS. C of AC reads *Meneviam*. AU *s.a.* 986 (= 987) has: *Cath Manand ria mac Aralt ⁊ rias na Danaraib ubi mille occisi sunt*, 'The battle of *Man* by the son of Harold and by the Danes, where one thousand were slain.' In spite of the early confusion (cf. on 16.23–4) between the Latin forms for Man (*Eubonia, Eumonia*) and for Anglesey (*Monia, Mona*) there are no grounds for doubting the readings of Pen. 20, RB, BS and MS. B of AC here. *Meneviam* (MS. C of AC) must be an error.

10   1–2   **and Maredudd ab Owain ... Dyfed**: RB *a'r dryll arall onadunt a duc Meredud ap Ywein gyt ac ef y Geredigyawn a Dyvet*, 'and *the remainder of them* Maredudd ab Owain took with him to

page line

Ceredigion and Dyfed'; BS *a'r gwedilyon* a duc Moredut vab Oweyn ganthaw hyt yng Keredigiaun a Dyvet, 'and *what remained*, Maredudd ab Owain took with him to Ceredigion and Dyfed'; AC *s.a.* 987 *reliquias vero Maredut secum asportavit ad Keredigean et ad Demetiam*. Pen. 20 and RB *y dryll arall* and BS *gwedilyon* are independent variant translations of *reliquos* which appears to have been an error in the common Latin original for the *reliquias*, 'relics,' of AC. The verb *asportavit* suggests that *reliquias* is the original correct reading in AC.

10 3 **in all the island of Britain**: so too RB, but BS *yn holl Kymre*, 'in all Wales.' Cf. AU *s.a.* 986 (= 987) *Beidgdibudh mor co ro la ár doeine ┐ indeli i Saxanaibh ┐ Bretnaibh ┐ Goidhelaibh*, 'A sudden great mortality which caused a slaughter of people and cattle *in Saxonland and Britain and Ireland*.' Variant interpretations of *Britannia* account for the difference between Pen. 20 and RB, on the one hand, and BS, on the other. Cf. on 12.30 and 57.1-2.

10 7 **Gluniairn**: MS. Glwmayn, RB ——, BS *Glumayn*. Emend Pen. 20 and BS to *Gluniairn*, 'Iron-knee.' Cf. AU *s.a.* 988 (= 989) *Glun iairn ri Gall do marbad dia moghaidh fein i meisce*, 'Gluniairn, king of the Foreigners, was slain by his own servant, in drunkenness'; CS *s.a.* 987 (= 989) *Glun iarainn, mac Amlaibh, Righ Gall, do marbadh da moghadhaigh feisin .i. Colbáin*, 'Gluniairn son of *Amlaibh*, king of the Foreigners, was slain by his own servant, i.e. Colbain.'

10 8-9 **and Maredudd . . . Black Host**: Pen. 20 and RB *o bob dyn*, 'from every person'; BS *am bop gwr*, 'for every man'; AC *s.a.* 989 *Maredut redemit captivos a gentilibus nigris, nummo pro unoquoque dato* (MS. B), *Maredut censum reddit nigris gentibus, scilicet nummum pro unoquoque homine* (MS. C). BS gives the better sense. The Latin original seems to have been in agreement with MS. C of AC.

10 13 **Maeshyfaidd**: lit. 'Hyfaidd's Plain (or Field).' The reference here is to the vill, not to the district later so called. See *Trans. Cym.* 1899-1900. 125; HW i. 346, note 87.

10 14 **Edwin ab Einion**: so too RB and BS, but AC *s.a.* 993 *Guyn filius Eynaun* (MS. B), *Owein filius Eyniaun* (MS. C). *Edwin* is correct. With *Guyn* here in MS. B of AC cf. 7.23 above.

10 14 **Edylfi**: RB *Eclis*, BS ——, AC *s.a.* 993 *duce Edelisi Anglico*.

10 17 **hostages**: RB adds *eilweith*, 'a second time.' This whole sentence is not in BS and AC.

10 18-20 **And Maredudd . . . the captives**: RB *A Maredud a huryawd y Kenedloed a dothoedynt yn y ewyllys gyt ac ef, ac a diffeithawd Gwlat Vorgan*, 'And Maredudd hired along with him the Gentiles, who had come into his power, and he ravaged Glamorgan'; BS *Ac yn dyuot o diffeithiaw Gwlat Vorgant y doeth Moredud yn ev hewyllys*, 'And coming from ravaging Glamorgan, Maredudd came into their power.'

10 21-2 **hostages . . . in Gwynedd**: RB *Ac yna y duc meibon Meuryc gyrch hyt yg Gwyned*, 'And then the sons of Meurig *led a raid* into Gwynedd'; BS *. . . a gwarchadw o veibion Meuric Gwyned*, 'and the sons of Meurig besieged Gwynedd.' Since there is no corresponding entry

page line

in AC, one cannot be sure what phrase in the original Latin has yielded the above variant versions, but it appears as if there has been confusion between *obsides* and *obsederunt*. RB and BS seem to give better sense than Pen. 20 here.

10   27   **and there**: so too RB and BS, but AC *s.a.* 994, after referring to the battle of Llangwm, adds the apparently separate entry: Teudur filius Einaun occisus est.

10   29   **Sweyn**: MS. *Ywein* is to be emended to *Y[s]wein*. Cf. RB *Yswein*, BS *Suein*, AC *s.a.* 995 *Sweyn*. For another example of a foreign name changed into a familiar native one, see above on 8.8.

10   31   **A year after that**: so too BS, but AC (which does not record the ravaging of Armagh) places the death of Idwal ap Meurig *two* years after the ravaging of Man by Sweyn.

10   31-2   **And Armagh was ravaged and burnt**: Pen. 20 *Arthinatha*, RB *Arthmarcha* and BS *Arthmatha* are to be emended to *Arthmacha*, 'Armagh.' Cf. AU *s.a.* 995 (= 996) Tene diait do ghabail Aird Macha, co na farcaibh dertach na damliac na h-erdaimh na fidnemedh ann cen loscadh, 'Lightening seized Ard-Macha, so that it left neither oratory nor stone-church nor porch nor church-grove without burning'; CS *s.a.* 994 (= 996) Airgialla dargain Ard Macha, go rugsat fiche ced bó este. Ard Macha do losccadh, taigibh, templaibh ocus a chloigthec, 'The Airghialla plundered Ard-Macha, and took 2,000 cows out of it. Ard-Macha was burned—houses, churches, and its belfry.'

10   33-4   **Three years ... slain**: RB Ac y dipoblet Mynyw *y gan y Kenedloed*, ac y llas Morgeneu esgob y gantunt, 'And Menevia was pillaged *by the Gentiles*, and bishop Morgenau was slain by them'; BS y dibobylat Mynyw *o genedyl anffydlawn*; ac y lladassant Morgeneu, escop Mynyw, 'Menevia was pillaged by heathen folk; and they slew Morgenau, bishop of Menevia'; AC *s.a.* 999 Menevia vastata est (vastatur MS. C) *a gentilibus*, et Morganeu episcopus ab eis occisus est (occiditur MS. C). Pen. 20 has dropped *a gentilibus* in translating. Cf. Giraldus Cambrensis, *Itinerarium Kambriae* ii. Cap. I (Rolls vi. 104) *Morgeneu*, qui primus inter episcopos Meneviæ carnes comedit, *et ibidem a piratis interfectus est*.

11   1   **the Irish ... Dublin**: This entry (also in RB and BS) is not in AC. Cf. AU *s.a.* 998 (= 999) Slogad la Brian, ri Caisil, co Gleann mamma, co tangadar Gaill Atha Cliath dia fhuabairt, co Laignibh imaille friu, co remaidh forro, ┐ co roladh a n-ár, im Aralt mac Amlaimh ┐ im chulen mac nEtigen, ┐ im maithibh Gall olchena. *Do luidh Brian iarsin i nAth Cliath, co ro ort Ath Cliath leis*, 'A hosting by Brian, king of Caisel, to Glen-Mama, where the Foreigners of Ath-cliath [i.e. Dublin], together with the Leinstermen, came to attack him; but they were routed and put to slaughter, including Aralt son of Amlaimh, and Culen son of Etigen, and other chiefs of the Foreigners. Brian went afterwards to Ath-cliath; *and Ath-cliath was pillaged by him*'; CS *s.a.* 997 (= 999) Sluiaiccedh mor la Maolsechlainn mac Domnaill, ocus le Brian mac Cinnedigh go Glen mama, go ttancuttar Gaill Atha Clíath da ffobairt, gur raoinedh for Galloibh ocus gur lad anár, im Aralt mac Amlaibh, ocus um Culen mac Etigen, ocus um maithibh Atha cliath, et go ndechadh

P

page line

Maolseclainn ocus Brían iarsin a nAth clíath, go rappatur seachtmainn ann, go rugsat a or ocus a airged ocus a brait, ocus gur innarbsat an Righ .i. Sitriug mac Amlaibh, 'A great hosting by Maelsechlainn, son of Domhnall and by Brian, son of Cennedigh, to Glen-mama; and the Foreigners of Ath-cliath came to attack them; but the Foreigners were defeated and slaughtered, together with Aralt son of Amlaibh, and Culen son of Etigen, and the nobles of Ath-cliath, and Maelsechlainn and Brian afterwards went to Ath-cliath and expelled the king, i.e. Sitriuc son of Amlaibh.'

11 5–6 **And Imhar of Waterford died**: Pen. 20 and BS *Porthalarchi* (RB *Porth Talarchi*) corresponds to *Port Lairge*, the Irish name for Waterford. The date of Imhar's death is supplied by AU *s.a.* 999 (= 1000) Imhar ri Puirt Lairgi do ec, 'Imhar, king of Waterford, died'; and CS *s.a.* 998 (= 1000) Imar Puirt Lairge moritur. The entry in Pen. 20, RB and BS (and so in the common Latin original) seems to have been misplaced. It is not in AC.

11 7 **A year after that**: BS places the death of Cynan ap Hywel *two* years after the death of Mor ap Gwyn and Imhar of Waterford, and AC places it in the *third* year after the ravaging of Dyfed, thus agreeing, it seems, with BS. In RB the annals are not shown in this section. Since BS and AC here agree, it may be that Pen. 20 has omitted a blank *annus*.

11 8 **Gwlfach and Ubiad**: RB Gwlfac ac *Vryat*, BS Gulfach ac *Vbiat*, AC ——.

11 13 **Eadric and Ubis**: MS. Eutris ac Vbis, RB Entris ac Vbis, AC Edris et Ubis.

11 14 **Iarddur**: MS. Yardur, RB Hayarndrut, BS Haeardur (Haiarnddur MS. B). With the BS form cf. LL 226. 2 *Heardur*.

11 16–7 **Ethelred, son of Edgar**: MS. Eldryd vab *Elgar*, but RB Eldryt vab *Etgar*, BS Edelret ——, AC *s.a.* 1014 Edelrit filius *Etgar*.

11 26 **Brotor**: MS. *Brodr*, with *Derotyr* written above by later hand (result of collation with RB), RB Derotyr, BS Brodr. AU *s.a.* 1014 Brotor shows that Pen. 20 and BS have preserved the correct form.

11 29 **. . . were slain**: for a fuller account of this attack on Dublin see AU *s.a.* 1014 and CS *s.a.* 1012 (= 1014).

12 1 **A year after that**: BS places the slaying of Aeddan and his sons in the annal (1016) immediately following that (1015) in which the slaying of Owain ap Dyfnwal is recorded. The entry about Cnut in Pen. 20 *s.a.* 1015 is found in RB between the slaying of Owain ap Dyfnwal and the slaying of Aeddan and his sons, but the division into annals is not shown. MS. B of AC has a blank *annus* between the reference to Cnut and that to the slaying of Aeddan and his sons, but there is no such blank *annus* in MS. C. In the chronology MS. B of AC has been followed.

12 1 **Llywelyn ap Seisyll**: so too RB and BS, the latter adding *brenhin Gwyned*, 'king of Gwynedd,' but AC *s.a.* 1018 a *Grifino filio Lewelin* rege Britonum (MS. B), a *Lewelino* (MS. C).

NOTES

page line

12 7 **And he would ... Rhain**: RB *ac y mynawd y alw ehun yn vrenhin*, 'and he had himself called king'; BS *a Rein oed y henw*, 'and Rhain was his name'; AC *s.a.* 1022 *Reyn Scotus mentitus est se esse filium Maredut* (MS. B), ... *contra Reyn, qui se dicebat esse filium Maredut* (MS. C). It appears that the translator of RB read *regem* for *Regin*, the Old Welsh form of *Rhain*.

12 9–10 **Llywelyn ap Seisyll ... Britain**: RB *Llywelyn ap Seisyll, goruchaf vrenhin Gwyned a phenaf a chlotuorussaf vrenhin o'r hol Vrytanyeit*, 'Llywelyn ap Seisyll, supreme king of Gwynedd and foremost and most praiseworthy king of all the Britons'; BS *Llywelyn vab Seissyll, y brenhin clotuorussaf a wydit o'r mor pwy gilid*, 'Llywelyn ap Seisyll, the most praiseworthy king of whom was known from the one sea to the other'; AC *Seisil rex Venedotiae* (MS. B), *Lewelin filius Seisill, rex Venedotiae* (MS. C).

12 20–1 **bravely fearless**: MS. *yn lew δiargysswr*. RB *yn hy diofyn* proves that *lew δiargysswr* of Pen. 20 is not a scribal error for *yn [l]lew diargysswr*. Cf. below on 12.24–5.

12 24–5 **so was he brave in attack**: MS. *ynteu yn lew yn kyrchu*. Since this is in contrast with 'the foxy manner' of Rhain's retreat, the words of the text could conceivably mean 'so was he *a lion* in attack,' taking *lew* < *llew*, not < *glew*. So too RB *ef a gyrchawd yn lew ehofyn*, 'he attacked *bravely fearless*,' or 'he attacked *as a fearless lion*.' However, since in the preceding case *lew* is definitely a form of *glew*, it is more than likely that it is to be taken as such here too. Hence the translation. In both these cases there is no phrase corresponding in BS and AC.

12 28 **all the chattels**: After *chattels* (MS. *da*) a later hand has added in the margin *hyt y Mars*, 'as far as the March.' This addition comes from RB. It is not in BS.

12 30 **to the island of Britain**: RB *Ynys Prydein*, 'the island of Britain'; BS *y dir Kymmre*, 'to the land of *Wales*'; AC *Eilaf vastavit Demetiam. Menevia fracta est* (MS. B), *Eilaph venit in Britanniam et vastavit Dyvet et Meneviam*. BS is correct: in Pen. 20 and RB *Britannia* has been taken to mean 'Britain,' whereas the context shows that here it means 'Wales.' See HW i. 350, note 112. Cf. on 10.3 above and on 18.17–8; 57.1–2 below.

12 34 **Morgynnydd**: MS. *Morgynnyd* altered to *Morgeneu* by a later hand; RB *Morgeneu*, BS *Morgynnyd*, AC *s.a.* 1025 *Morgannuc* (MS. B only). Cf. Giraldus Cambrensis, *Itinerarium Kambriae* i. Cap 2 (Rolls vi. 104) *Morgennith* (= Morgynnydd).

13 4 **after Llywelyn**: MS. *yn ol Lliwelyn* added by another (early) hand in the margin. Cf. RB *wedy Llywelyn ap Seissyll*, BS *gwedy Llywelyn*.

13 7 **the battle of Irathwy**: so too RB, but BS [g]*weith Hiraethwy*, AC *s.a.* 1034 *Gueith Hiradus* (MS. B), *Bellum Iratur* (MS. C). See OP iv. 569. The AC forms may be for *Hiraduc*, 'Hiraddug.'

13 14 **the gentiles**: MS. *y bonheδigyon* with *cenedloed* ('Gentiles') written above by a later hand; RB *Kenedloed*, 'Gentiles'; BS *yr anfydloneon*, 'the heathen'; AC *s.a.* 1039 *Gentiles* (MS. C only). RB and BS are correct, but in Pen. 20 *Gentiles* has been mistranslated. Cf. on 14.2 below.

page line

13   15   **Iago ... was slain**: BS alone says that he was slain by Gruffudd ap Llywelyn: see the next note. The Irish chroniclers say that he was slain 'by his own men': AU *s.a.* 1039 Iaco ri Bretan *a suis* [occisus est]; CS *s.a.* 1037 (= 1039) Iaco Rí Bretan *a suis* occisus est. Cf. HW i. 358, note 2, *Trans. Cym.*, 1899–1900. 126 and note 3.

13   16   **Llywelyn, his son, ruled**: Pen. 20 has here gone astray, for Llywelyn was not the son of Iago, and it was Gruffudd ap Llywelyn who became king of Gwynedd after Iago ab Idwal. RB is here correct: Ac y llas Jago, vrenhin Gwyned. Ac yn y le ynteu y gwledychawd Gruffud ap Llywelyn ap Seissyll, 'And Iago, king of Gwynedd, was slain. And in his place ruled Gruffudd ap Llywelyn ap Seisyll.' BS makes Gruffudd responsible for Iago's death: Ac y llas Jago vab Jdwal, brenhin Gwyned, *y gan Grufyd vab Llywelyn*, ac a oresgynnws y gyfoeth ac a'y gwledychws, 'And Iago ab Idwal, king of Gwynedd, was slain *by Gruffudd ap Llywelyn*, and he gained possession of his territory and ruled it.' MS. B of AC does not record Iago's death, but MS. C records it along with the beginning of Gruffudd's reign, in a way which could possibly mislead a translator: Iacob rex Uenedocie occiditur pro quo Grifut ab Leuuelin regnauit. See the preceding note.

13   20   **Rhyd-y-grog**: MS. *Ryd y Groc* ar Hafren; RB *Ryt*[*y*] *Groes* ar Hafren; BS *Ryt y Groes* ar Hafren; AC *s.a.* 1039 Bellum *in vado Crucis super Sabrinam* (MS. B only). The form in Welsh texts which are not translations is *Ryt y Groes*, e.g. *Breudwyt Ronabwy* (ed. Melville Richards) 3. 28, note 37–8. This was translated as *Vadum Crucis*, which the Pen. 20 translator has rendered as *Ryd y Groc*. It appears from this that the Pen. 20 translator did not know of the place called Rhyd-y-groes. The exact locality of the ford has been much debated, but the weight of evidence favours some spot near Buttington. See *Trans. Cym.*, 1899–1900, 129–130, OP iv. 618–19, 649–50.

13   23   **Erfyn**: MS. *Heruini*, RB *Hennin* (*Henrim* MSS. RT), BS *Hermini*, AC *s.a.* 1040 *Erwyn* (MS. B), *Hervin* (MS. C). Giraldus Cambrensis loc. cit. gives the bishop's name as *Eruin*. The personal name *Ermin* (= Mod. Welsh *Erfyn*) is attested: cf. *Book of St. Chad* LL xlv. 3, 5; ib. 4, 5. See G s.v. 'ermin' and R. J. Thomas, *Enwau Afonydd a Nentydd Cymru*. Cardiff. 1938. p. 205.

13   28   **the battle of Pwlldyfach**: MS. *Pwlldyuech*, but RB *Pwll Dyfach* and BS *Pwll Dyuach* give the correct form: cf. AC *s.a.* 1042 Bellum *Pullduwath* (MS. B only). Pwlldyfach (pronounced locally 'Pwlldyfarch') is some five miles NW. of the town of Carmarthen. See *Trans. Cym.*, 1899–1900. 132, note 2, HW ii. 360, and ONR 42.

14   2   **a fleet of the gentles of Ireland**: RB a llyges o *genedyl* Iwerdon, 'a fleet of the *folk of Ireland*'; BS llynghesseu o'r *Gwydil*, 'fleets *of the Irish*'; AC *s.a.* 1044 accepta classe *gentilium*. Again Pen. 20 has mistranslated some form of *gentiles*, 'Gentiles': cf. 13.14 above. RB seems to have translated *gentis*.

14   7   **Enilfre and Maccus**: the entry 'And then ... died' is not in RB and AC, but cf. BS Ac y bu varw *Gvilfre* a *Mactus* manach, 'And Gwilfre and Mactus the monk died.' *Enilfre* may be an error for *Euilfre* = 'Ewilfre': cf. 17.33.

NOTES

page line

14 8 **Teilo's bishop**: so too RB and BS, but AC *episcopus Landavensis* (MS. B only).

14 9–11 **great deceit ... Gruffudd ap Llywelyn**: RB Ac y bu diruawr dwyll a brat gan Ruffud *a Rys*, meibon Ryderch, yn erbyn Gruffud ap Llywelyn, 'And there was great deceit and treachery by Gruffudd and Rhys, sons of Rhydderch, against Gruffudd ap Llywelyn'; BS Ac y bu *lladua* vawr y rwng meibion Ryderch, Grufud *a Rys*, a Grufud vab Llywelyn, 'And there was a great massacre between the sons of Rhydderch, Gruffudd and Rhys, and Gruffudd ap Llywelyn'; AC *Seditio* magna orta fuit inter Grifud filium Lewelin et Grifud filium Riderch. BS seems to have translated *caedes*. AC does not mention Rhys.

14 12 **Two years after that**: so too BS *s.a.* 1045, after the death of Joseph and the treachery between the sons of Rhydderch and Gruffudd ap Llywelyn recorded *s.a.* 1043. MS. C of AC has a blank *annus* between the two entries, i.e. between 1145 and 1147 of the text, and so agrees with Pen. 20 and BS. MS. B of AC, however, has no such blank *annus* here and seems to assign the slaughter of Gruffudd ap Llywelyn's war-band to the year 1146.

14 18–9 **was ravaged**: RB ac y *bu diffeith* holl Deheubarth, 'and all Deheubarth *was waste*'; BS y *diffeithwyt* y Dehev oll, 'all the South was laid waste'; AC *s.a.* 1048 tota dextralis patria *deserta est* (MS. B), *destructa est, metu gentilium* (MS. C).

14 26 **Ranulf**: MS. Rāndwlf, RB Reinwlf, BS Randwlf. The correct form is Ralf (*Rawlf* in Welsh): see HW ii. 365, *Trans. Cym.*, 1899–1900. 133.

14 32 **and there**: RB is in substantial agreement with Pen. 20, but BS adds one detail: a thra uuant ar ev bwyt y kyrchyssant y gaer, 'and while they (*sc.* the Saxons) were at their meat, they (*sc.* the Welsh) fell upon the fortress.'

14 35 **Magnus**: MS. Rodri Mawr, RB Magnus, BS Magus, AC Magnus. In the MS. *Rodri* is to be deleted as an unfortunate addition and *Mawr* regarded as a translation of the personal name *Magnus*. Cf. below 21.9 on *Mawrus*.

15 3–6 **was slain ... through the treachery of his own men**: RB ... pan dygwydawd Gruffud ap Llywelyn ... *drwy dwyll y wyr ehun*, '... when Gruffudd ap Llywelyn fell ... *through the treachery of his own men*'; BS *y bu varw* Grufud vab Llywelyn, 'Gruffudd ap Llywelyn *died*'; AC *s.a.* 1063 Grifinus filius Lewelini ... *dolo suorum occisus est* (MS. B), Grifud filius Lewelin ... *cecidit* (MS. C). BS seems nearer to MS. C of AC.

15 11 **[was]**: supply *y bu* in MS. after *hynny*.

15 12 **Two years ... Rome**: AU records the death of Donnchadh, son of Brian, *s.a.* 1064: Donnchadh, mac Briain, aírdrí Muman (do athrigadh ⁊) *do ec i Roim* i n-a ailithri, 'Donnchadh, son of Brian, high-king of Munster (was deposed and) *died in Rome* in his pilgrimage.' Cf. CS *s.a.* 1061 (= 1064) Donnchadh mac Briain daíthrighadh ocus *a dol do Roim* da ailtri conderbailt i naítrighe .i. i Mainister Ztepain, 'Donnchadh, son of Brian, was dethroned and going to Rome on his pilgrimage he died in penitence, i.e. in the monastery of Stephen.' AC has no entry

page line

referring to Donnchadh, but BS (like Pen. 20) records his death *two* years after the *primus decemnouenalis*, i.e. in 1064. It is to be noted, however, that AC has only *two* blank *anni* between the death of Joseph, bishop of Menevia, and the defeat of Harold by William. It appears, therefore, that 'Two years' *s.a.* 1064 is an error in Pen. 20 and BS (and so, probably, in the original Latin) for 'One year.' The notice of Donnchadh's death is in RB too, but that text does not show the division into annals. The probable error in Pen. 20 and BS has been taken into account in determining the chronology.

15 19-20 **And through innate treachery**: MS. a thrwy *dadawl* dwyll. RB drwy *wladawl* dwyll, BS ——, AC ——. Literally rendered Pen. 20 means 'and through *ancestral (fatherly)* treachery,' and RB means 'through treachery *(characteristic) of the land*.' To account for these variants one assumes that there was in the common Latin original some word *patrius* or *patritus*. *Tadawl* (Pen. 20) would be a good literal translation of *patrius* in the sense of 'innate,' 'inborn,' and *gwladawl* (RB) would be a mistranslation suggested by the word *patria*. Harold Godwinesson was not popular in Wales and it would be natural for a Welsh chronicler to think that English treachery was innate, inborn or inherited from their fathers. So, too, *gwladawl* (RB) might have the sense of the treachery characteristic of the land of England i.e., 'native,' 'inherent.'

15 28 **Three years after that**: MSS. B, C, D of the Pen. 20 version give '*Two* years after that': so too BS, which records the battle between the two Harolds *s.a.* 1066 and the battle of Mechain *s.a.* 1068. AC, however, has *two* blank *anni* between these two events (in MSS. B and C) and so is in agreement with Pen. 20.

15 30 **Ithel**: so too RB and BS, but AC *s.a.* 1068 *Idwal* (MSS. B and C). *Ithel* is wrong here and in the next sentence, where AC again gives *Idwal*.

15 31 **Ithel**: see the preceding note.

16 8-9 **kind towards the poor**: RB hynaws wrth *y ki[w]dawtwyr*, 'kind towards his own people'; BS ——; AC ——. It is obvious that Pen. 20 has translated *indigentes* whereas RB has translated *indigenas*. Cf. on 20.15-6. In reading *indigentes* the translator of Pen. 20 was linking this phrase with the one that follows, but RB in reading *indigenas* was obviously contrasting it with the preceding one and thinking of the cliché (in passages like this) which praises a man for his prowess against his foes and for his kindness towards his own folk. The death of Diarmaid, son of Mael-na-mbo, is recorded in AU *s.a.* 1072 and in CS *s.a.* 1069 (= 1072). There the battle is called the 'battle of Odhbha,' waged by Diarmaid against Conchobhar Ua Maelsechlainn.

16 16 **by itself**: RB yr eilweith, 'a second time'; so too BS yr eil weith; AC *iterum* (MS. C), which agrees with RB and BS. Pen. 20 *ehun* (by itself) seems to be in contrast to *Ceredigyawn a Dyved*, 'Ceredigion and Dyfed' of the preceding annal. But on this entry and the first entry *s.a.* 1071 see OP iv. 629-30.

16 17-9 **A year after that ... Ystrad Tywi**: This is a good example of how the original Latin chronicle combines the texts of MSS. B and C of AC: Bledint filius Kenwin *dolo ducum* Stratewy a Reso filio Owini occiditur (MS. B); Bledin filius Kenuin *dolo malignorum hominum* de Estratewy a Res filius Owein occiditur.

NOTES

page line

16 23-4 **And Gruffudd ... Anglesey**: RB Ac yna yr ymladawd Gruffud ap Kynan, wyr Iago, a *Mon*, 'And then Gruffudd ap Cynan, grandson of Iago, *besieged Anglesey*'; BS Grufud hagen, nei James, a oed yn gwarchadw *Manaw*, 'Gruffudd, however, nephew of James, was defending *Man*'; AC Grifud autem *nepos Iacob non* obsedit (MS. C only). AC *non* is to be emended to *Mon*, 'Anglesey.' RB is here more correct than Pen. 20 and BS. Pen. 20 seems to have translated *obtinuit* or *occupavit*. BS has rendered *nepos* as *nei* instead of *wyr*, *Iacob* as *James* instead of *Iago*, and has confused *Mon* with *Manaw*. Confusion between the Latin names of Anglesey and Man is old: see HW i. 184. In AC, Pen. 20 and BS Gruffudd ap Cynan is called *nepos Iacob* or the Welsh equivalent, upon which Lloyd, *Trans. Cym.*, 1899-1900, 154, note 2, thus comments: 'MS. C of *Annales Cambriae* speaks of Gruffydd on his first appearance as 'Grifud nepos iacob,' and thus, I think, clearly shows its character as derived from a contemporary record. A few years later, no one would have dreamt of calling him anything but Gruffydd ap Cynan; in 1075, however, nothing was known in Wales of Cynan, and it was as Iago's grandson this young man of twenty claimed the Venedotian crown.'

16 26-9 **That year ... together**: RB Ac yna y bu y vrwydyr yg Kamdwr rwg Goronw a Llywelyn, meibion Kadwgawn, a Charadawc vab Gruffud gyt ac wynt, a Rys vab Ywein a Ryderch vab Caradawc. [A Goronw a Llywelyn a oruuwyt, a Charadawc] y gyt a rei hyny, 'And then was the battle at Camddwr between Goronwy and Llywelyn, sons of Cadwgan, and Caradog ap Gruffudd along with them, and Rhys ab Owain and Rhydderch ap Caradog. [And Goronwy and Llywelyn were defeated, and Caradog] along with them.' The words in square brackets are not in the MSS. of RB. I have supplied them, assuming an error of haplography. BS is ambiguous: y bu ymlad Camdwr y rwng meibion Cadwgavn, nyt amgen, Goronw a Llywelyn, gyt a Caradauc vab Grufud, o'r neill parth, a Rhys vab Oweyn a Ryderch vab Caradauc, o'r parth arall, y rei a oruuwyt arnadunt, 'the battle of Camddwr took place between the sons of Cadwgan, viz. Goronwy and Llywelyn, along with Caradog ap Gruffudd, on the one side, and Rhys ab Owain and Rhydderch ap Caradog, on the other side,—who were defeated.' AC *s.a.* 1073 bellum Camdubr inter filios Kadugaun et inter Res et Rederch, qui uictores fuerunt (MS. C only). AC makes it clear that Rhys and Rhydderch were victorious. Pen. 20, however, seems to have mistranslated, for Goronwy and Llywelyn were not slain: *s.a.* **1077** they fought in the battle of 'Gweunytwl' and 'were defeated a second time.' The second *inter* of AC is intrusive and explains the unnecessary second *yrŵg* 'between' (which I have not included in the translation) of Pen. 20, 21*b*, 26. For the site of the battle of Camddwr see *Trans. Cym.*, 1899-1900, 174, note 1, OP iv. 443.

16 35 **the battle of 'Gweunytwl'**: RB Gweunottyl, BS Gweun y Nygyl, AC *s.a.* 1075 Guinnitul. The place has not been identified, but see OP iv. 443.

16 36-7 **between Goronwy ... second time**: RB rwg [Goronw] a Llywelyn, meibon Kadwgawn, a Rys vab Ywein *a Ryderch vab Caradawc*, y rei a oruuant eilweith, 'between [Goronwy] and Llywelyn, sons of

page line

Cadwgan, and Rhys ab Owain *and Rhydderch ap Caradog*, who prevailed a second time'; BS *rwng meibion Cadwgawn yr eilweith a Rys vab Oweyn, ac y goruuwyt ar Rys yr eil weith*, 'between the sons of Cadwgan the second time, and Rhys ab Owain, and Rhys was defeated the second time'; AC *s.a.* 1075 inter filios Cadugon, Goronui et Lewelin, et Resum filium Owini; *et ab eo victi sunt* (MS. B), inter filios Kadugaun, id est Lewelin et Gronoui, et inter Res filium Owein, *qui iterum victi sunt* (MS. C). The translator of BS has blundered, probably misled by *qui iterum . . . sunt* of AC MS. C: the *qui* is plural, as *victi sunt* shows, and so refers to Llywelyn and Goronwy, but because it follows immediately after *Res filium Owein* it was regarded as singular by the translator, who must have been nodding here. It appears from this that BS understood 'who were defeated' as referring to Rhys and Rhydderch in his account of the battle of Camddwr. See on 16.26-9. Note that RB alone says that Rhys ab Owain *and Rhydderch ap Caradog* fought in the battle of 'Gweunytwl': but the entry for **1076** (found in Pen. 20, RB, BS and AC), referring to the death of Rhydderch ap Caradog, proves that his name is intrusive here in RB, due to a doubling of the entry for **1075**.

17 1 **battle of Pwllgwdig**: In RWM i. 57 *Llan wnda* is given as the reading of the RB version in Mostyn MS. 116, and Lloyd, HW i. 393, note 114, has relied on this supposed variant to support Fenton's identification of Pwllgwdig with Goodwick in Pembrokeshire. But this variant reading is not in Mostyn MS. 116, which agrees with The Red Book of Hergest and Peniarth MS. 19 in reading *Pwll Gwdyc*. Strangely enough, this supposed variant is not given in the original MS. of RWM (NLW Gwenogvryn Evans MS. 59), so that it must have been added in the proofs. Its provenance is a mystery. Unfortunately, this non-existent variant has been used in OP iv. 606-7, and *The National Library of Wales Journal*, V. 3. 216, note 7.

17 2 **in which Trahaearn . . . victory**: RB *Ac yna y goruu Trahaern brenhin Gwyned*, 'And then Trahaearn, king of Gwynedd, prevailed'; BS *y bu ymlad Pullgudic y rwng Trahaearn, brenhin y Gweyndit, a Rys vab Oweyn, ac y goruu Trahaearn*, 'the battle of Pwllgwdig took place between Trahaearn, king of the Venedotians, *and Rhys ab Owain*, and Trahaearn prevailed.' BS alone here names Rhys ab Owain as Trahaearn's adversary, but it is supplied in MSS. B, C, D of Pen. 20, probably under the influence of BS. Pen. 20 and RB in omitting Rhys's name at this point agree with AC *s.a.* 1076 Bellum Pullgudic *in quo Trahern, rex Norwallie, victor fuit* (MS. B), Bellum Pullgudic *in quo Traharn, rex Venedocie, uictor fuit* (MS. C). In both Pen. 20 and RB the reference to 'avenging the blood of Bleddyn ap Cynfyn' implies that Trahaearn's adversary was Rhys, for MS. C of AC, RB and BS state that he was responsible for the death of Bleddyn ap Cynfyn in 1075. Pen. 20, too, mentions Rhys at the end of this entry.

17 10 **the lands**: MS. *gwladoed*, so too RB. Here, as elsewhere, *gwlad* is a technical term, like *cantref* and *cwmwt*, denoting a territorial division.

17 15 **Caradog ap Gruffudd**: so too Pen. 20 and BS, but AC *s.a.* 1076 Resus et Hoelus frater eius a *Trahairn filio Caraduc* occisus est (MS. B), In fine uero huius anni Res et Howel eius frater a *Cradauc filius Grifud* occiduntur (MS. C). MS. B of AC is here at fault.

NOTES

page line

17 19 **Menevia was pillaged**: RB, BS, and AC are more precise: RB y diffeithwyt Mynyw yn druan *y gan y Kenedloed*, 'Menevia was woefully ravaged *by the Gentiles*'; BS y diboblet Mynyw yn druan *y gan wyr anfydlon*, 'Menevia was woefully pillaged *by heathen folk*'; AC *s.a.* 1078 Menevia *a Gentilibus* vastata est (MSS. B and C).

17 20 **Abraham . . . died**: so too RB and BS. MS. B of AC does not record Abraham's death, but MS. C does: Et Abraham *a Gentilibus* occiditur.

17 22 **the battle of Mynydd Carn**: see *Trans. Cym.*, 1899-1900, 154, *Y Cymmrodor*, xi. 167, HW ii. 384 and note 88, OP iv. 415.

17 23-5 **And there Trahaearn ap Caradog . . . were slain**: RB Ac yna y llas Trahaern ab Caradawc a Chradawc vab Gruffud [a Meilyr ap Ruallawn *y gan Rys ap Tewdwr*], 'And then Trahaearn ap Caradog and Caradog ap Gruffudd [and Meilyr ap Rhiwallon] were slain [*by Rhys ap Tewdwr*]; BS Ac yno y llas Trahaearn vab Caradauc a meibion Riwallawn, Caradauc a Grufyd a Meilir, *y gan Rys vab Teudwr*, 'And there Trahaearn ap Caradog and the sons of Rhiwallon, Caradog and Gruffudd and Meilyr, were slain by Rhys ap Tewdwr'; AC Bellum montis Carn in quo Traharn filius Carad[auc] et Caradauc filius G[rifin]i et Meiler filius Ruallan a Reso filio [Teu]dur et a Grifino filio Conani occisi sunt (MS. B), Bellum montis Carn in quo Traharn filius Cradauc et Cradauc filius Grifud et Meilir filius Ruallaun *et Res filius Teudur et Grifud filius Eynaun* [emend to *Cynan*] *filius Iacob* occiduntur (MS. C).

Pen. 20 and MS. C of AC are wrong in saying that Rhys ap Tewdwr was slain in this battle. And MS. C of AC is wrong in saying that Gruffudd ap Cynan was slain there. BS has bungled in calling 'Caradog *and* Gruffudd and Meilyr' 'sons of Rhiwallon'. They were Rhys ap Tewdwr's adversaries, i.e. Caradog *ap* Gruffudd and Meilyr ap Rhiwallon, together with Trahaearn ap Caradog. These names are correct in Pen. 20, RB (as emended) and AC: see A. Jones, *The History of Gruffydd ap Cynan*. Manchester. 1910. 124-30.

17 25-6 **And after him . . . help him**: It appears from this that the Pen. 20 translator regarded Gruffudd ap Cynan as successor to Rhys ap Tewdwr after the (supposed) death of the latter in the battle of Mynydd Carn. Ctr. RB [Ac y doeth Gruffud], wyr Iago, ac Yscotteit gyt ac ef yn ganhorthwy idaw, '[And Gruffudd], grandson of Iago [came], and Irish along with him to help him' (*sc.* Rhys ap Tewdwr); BS canys Grufud, nei Jago, ac Yscottieit llidiauc a doeth yn borth idaw, 'for Gruffud, grandson of Iago, and fierce Irish came to his aid,'—i.e. to the aid of Rhys ap Tewdwr. As the text of Pen. 20 stands 'to help him' can only refer to Gruffudd ap Cynan, but RB, BS, and *The History of Gruffudd ap Cynan*, loc. cit. show that in its original Latin context it must have meant 'to help Rhys ap Tewdwr.' Therefore, either Pen. 20 is a mistranslation or, less probably, this sentence was misplaced in the original Latin.

17 28-9 **William . . . France**: The words of Pen. 20 could also mean 'William, king of England and Wales, *together with many Frenchmen* came on the Menevia pilgrimage,' but RB and BS support the version given in the text: RB Gwilim Bastard, brenhin y Saesson *a'r Freinc* a'r Brytanyeit, 'William the Bastard, king of the Saxons and *the French* and

page line

the Britons'; BS William, *Duc Normandi* a brenhin Lloegyr a Chymre, 'William, *duke of Normandy* and king of England and Wales.'

17 30-1 **One thousand ... was**: Before this entry, BS *s.a.* 1080 (= 1082) has an additional entry: y dechrewt edeiliat Caer Dyf, 'the building of Cardiff was begun.' This is not in RB and AC, but cf. the variant reading of D (Pen. 20 version), which probably shows the influence of BS.

17 32 **a second time**: RB y *dryded* weith, 'the *third* time,' BS ——, AC ——. Pen. 20 is correct. Sulien had become bishop for the second time in 1080, after the death of Abraham.

17 33 **And Ewilfre assumed it**: RB ac y kymerth *Wilfre*, 'and *Wilfre* assumed it'; BS ac y kymyrth *Gwilfret* hay [*sic*], 'And *Gwilfred* assumed it'; AC (MS. B only) Sulgenius episcopatum reliquit, cui *frater* successit.

18 1-2 **A year ... Irish**: This entry, which is in BS too, is wanting in RB and AC. Cf. AU *s.a.* 1086 Tairrdelbach hUa Briain, ri Erenn, do ec i Ciun-choradh, 'Toirrdelbach Ua Brian, king of Ireland, died in Cenn-coradh.' AU further states that he died on Tuesday, 14 July, in his seventy-seventh year.

18 11 **Llech-y-crau**: MS. Llech y Kreu, RB Llychcrei, BS y Llechryt, AC Pen Llecheru (MS. B), Penlethereu (MS. C). This place-name has not been identified. See HW ii. 398, note 136. It is unlikely that BS y Llechryt is correct.

18 17-8 **And in that year ... island**: RB yn holl *Ynys Prydein*, 'in all *the island of Britain*'; BS dros wyneb *Kymre*, 'all over *Wales*'; AC Terremotus ingens per totam *Britanniam* fuit (MS. C only). For *Britannia* variantly translated as 'Britain' and 'Wales' see 10.3; 12.30; 57.1-2.

18 19 **Two years after that**: MSS. B, C, D of Pen. 20 read '*A year* after that,' which may reflect a collation of Pen. 20 with BS. In the latter the despoiling of the shrine of David is recorded under 1088 = 1090, and the death of Sulien in the following year, i.e. 1089 = 1091. RB does not show the division into annals in this section. AC places the despoiling of the shrine of David in 1088 = 1089 and then shows a blank *annus* (1089 = 1090) before recording the death of Sulien 'LXXV aetatis suae anno' in 1089 = 1091 (MS. C only). Whereas Pen. 20 has counted the blank *annus* in AC between the despoiling of St. David's and the death of Sulien, BS seems to have omitted it. Since Pen. 20, RB, and BS agree in saying that Sulien died in his eightieth year, AC 'LXXV' is probably an error for 'LXXX.'

18 22-3 **the nineteenth year of his episcopate**: RB unuet [ulwydyn] eisseu o vgein *o'e gyssegredigaeth*, 'the twentieth year but one *from his consecration*'; BS Ac vn vlwydyn eissiev o vgeint y buassei yn escob, 'And he had been bishop one year short of twenty.' Now Sulien was bishop of Menevia from 1073 to 1078 and again from 1080 to 1085, making a total of *twelve* years. This is confirmed by the following lines in a poem composed by Ieuan, one of Sulien's four sons, and preserved in Corpus Christi Coll., Cambridge MS. 191 (cf. Haddan and Stubbs, *Councils and Ecclesiastical Documents*, i. 663):

> Qui (*sc.* Sulgenus) quoque post tantam populorum famine famam,
> Cunctorum precibus superatus, summus ut esset,
> *Uallis* iam *Rosinae presul deducitur*, ecce,
> Uitam quo puram David perfecit ouanter.

NOTES

page line

> En igitur Sulgenus adest, mihi iam pater almus,
> Pontificis David cathedram qui rexit amoenam:
> *Bis reuocatus* ibi *duodenos* egerat *annos.*
> Soli nam Christo secretam ducere uitam
> Deuouens totam pompossam liquerat illam.

The statement in Pen. 20 that Sulien died 'in the nineteenth year of his episcopate' is not correct, and 'of his episcopate' (MS. o'y esgobod) is probably a mistranslation of 'de episcopatu,' i.e. from his being made bishop. RB 'from *his consecration*' gives the correct and required meaning. Sulien first became bishop in 1073, but we do not know on what day and in what month. If he was consecrated before 25 December, and if the commencement of the year be reckoned from that date, 31 December in the nineteenth year falls in 1092: but if the commencement of the year be reckoned from 25 March, it falls in 1091. Since Pen. 20 and BS agree in placing Sulien's death in 1091, it appears that in the original Latin chronicle the commencement of the year was reckoned here from 25 March, and that the entry about Sulien's death was taken from a source which reckoned the commencement of the year from 25 December. BS appears to have dropped a blank *annus* between 1088 (= 1089) and 1089 (= 1091).

18 28 **Llandudoch**: i.e. St. Dogmaels. BS *Llandydoch* and AC *s.a.* 1089 *Llandedoc* (MS. B only) confirm the Pen. 20 reading as against RB *Llann Wdach*.

19 5 **on the Calends of May**: MS. duw Kalan Mei; RB *yr eil dyd o Uei*, 'the second day from May'; BS *ychydic kyn* Kalan Mei, '*a little before* the Calends of May'; AC pridie Kalendarum May (MS. B only). The day before the Calends was regularly expressed either by *pridie Kal* . . . or by *ij Kal* . . ., the latter usage being due to the fact that the Middle Ages usually adhered to the Roman inclusive method of reckoning. It is possible that in Pen. 20 *kyn*, 'before' has been dropped before *Kalan*; and if this is so, Pen. 20 and RB are consistent in so far as they refer to the day before the Calends of May.

19 5–6 **And within two months after that**: RB and BS are more precise: RB Ac yna, deu uis wedy hynny, *amgylch Kalan Gorffennaf*, 'And then, two months after that, *about the Calends of July*'; BS A deu vis gwedy hynny, *ynchylch Kalan Gorffennaf*, 'And two months after that, about the Calends of July.' Cf. AC *Circiter Kalendas Iulii* (MS. B), Postea *circa Kalendas Iulij* (MS. C).

19 7 **what was not in their power before that**: MS. ar (ac B, C, D) nyd ytoeð yn y medyant kȳn no hȳny. RB and BS give versions different from that of Pen. 20: RB y rei a'e kynhalassant gantunt etwa, 'which they have held to this day'; BS ac y gwledychassant yr hynny hyt hediw, 'and they have ruled them from that to this day.' It is obvious that the translator of Pen. 20 has read *quae non etiam tenuerunt* in the original Latin, whereas the translators of RB and BS have read *quae etiam tenuerunt*.

19 9–15 **And Maelcoluim . . . she died**: cf. CS *s.a.* 1089 (= 1093) Maolcoluim mac Donnchadha, Rí Alban, do marbadh do Frangcoibh, ocus Edbard a mac, et Margarita, ben Maolcoluim, dhéc da chumadh,

page line

'Maelcoluim, son of Donchadh, king of Scotland, and Edward his son were slain by the French, and Margaret, wife of Maelcoluim, died of grief for him.'

19   17   **who first defeated the Saxons in glorious war**: The Pen. 20 text, like the translation, is ambiguous, as the relative clause may refer to 'William the Elder' (i.e. William the Conqueror) or to 'king William' (i.e. William Rufus). Cf. RB *Ac yna yd aeth Gwillym Goch uap Gwillym Hynaf, yr hwn kyntaf a oruu ar y Saesson o glotuorussaf ryfel, hyt yn Normandi,* 'And then William Rufus, son of William the Elder, who first defeated the Saxons in most glorious war, went to Normandy'; BS *Willim Goch vab William Bastart a aeth hyt yn Normandi,* 'William Rufus, son of William the Bastard, went to Normandy.' If the relative clause in Pen. 20 and RB—not in BS—refers to William Rufus, the 'glorious war' must refer to Rufus's campaigns in the north of England and Scotland in 1091–92. If not, the reference is to the battle of Hastings.

19   22–3   **and they destroyed their castles in Gwynedd**: RB is in substantial agreement with Pen. 20, and refers to the destruction of the castles in Gwynedd, but BS is somewhat different: *Ac yn y vlwydyn honno y bv mynych ymgyrchu y rwng y Kymre a'r Freinc a oed yn gwledychu yna Keredigion a Dyvet,* a *dwyn anreithiev a mynych lladuaev o bop parth,* 'And in that year there were frequent attacks between the Welsh and *the French who were then ruling Ceredigion and Dyfed,* and they carried off spoils and [inflicted] frequent slaughters on both sides.' Cf. AC *s.a.* 1092 (= 1093) Britanni jugum Francorum respuerunt, *Wenedociam, Cereticam* et *Demetiam* ab iis et eorum castellis emundaverunt (MS. B), Britanni Francorum jugum respuunt et castella *in Norwallia* diruunt (MS. C). Pen. 20, RB, and MS. C of AC probably give the more correct version here, for it is shown in HW ii. 403 that the rising began in Gwynedd.

19   27   **in Coedysbys**: MS. *yn y Koed Yspys;* RB *yg Koet Ysbwys;* BS *yng Koet Yspes.* The place has not been located.

19   29   **Rhyd-y-gors**: 'a ford on the Tywi, a mile south of the old Roman fort of Carmarthen and the church of Llandeulyddog,' HW ii. 401. Cf. Lloyd B viii. 44–5, *A History of Carmarthenshire,* i. 129.

20   5–6   **And after ... empty**: so too RB *A gwedy y uarw ef yd edewis y keitweit y castell ynn wac,* 'And after his death the keepers left the castle empty'; BS *yd edewyt y castell yn wac o wercheitweit,* 'the castle was left empty of a garrison'; AC quo (*sc.* Willielmus filius Baldewini) mortuo castellum *vacuum* reliquitur (MS. B), eo mortuo castellum *a custodibus deseritur* (MS. C). Here again the original Latin of the *Brut* seems to have combined MSS. B and C of AC.

20   6–7   **And then ... did homage to the French**: MS. *Ac yna y gwrhaawd* Brycheinyawc *a Gwent a Gwenllywc y'r Freig,* but MS. D of the Pen. 20 version gives *gwrthnebodd,* 'resisted' for *gwrhaawd.* RB and BS show that Pen. 20 is here corrupt, due to mistranslation or to miscopying; RB *Ac yna y gwrthladawd Bryttanyeit Brechenniawc a Gwent a Gwenllwc arglwydiaeth y Freinc,* 'And then the Britons of Brycheiniog and Gwent and Gwynllŵg *threw off the rule of the French*'; BS *Gwyr Brecheynavc*

page line

a gwyr Gwent a gwyr Gwenllyvc a *wrthnebassant gorthrymder* y Freinc, 'The men of Brycheiniog and the men of Gwent and the men of Gwynllŵg *resisted the oppression of* the French.' Cf. AC Brecheinauc et Guent et Guenliunc [*sic*] *iugum Francorum respuunt* (MS. C). In Pen. 20, 26*a*, 8–10, *Francorum iugum respuunt* is rendered by *y gwrthladassant arglwydiaeth y Freing*; hence it is almost certain that here the Pen. 20 text should be emended to: Ac yna y *gwr[t]h[l]a[d]awd* Brychēinyawc a Gwent a Gwenllywc *arglwydiaeth y Frēig*, 'And then [the men of] Brycheiniog and Gwent and Gwynllŵg threw off the rule of the French,' thus bringing it into agreement with RB, BS, and MS. C of AC. Since this emendation is rather involved, at least in its confirmation, and since the error in Pen. 20 may be due to mistranslation rather than to miscopying, it has not been incorporated in the text of the translation but reserved for this note. If there is no copying error in Pen. 20, it must be that the translator read *iugum recipiunt* for *iugum respuunt*.

20 10 **Celli Tarfawg**: MS. *Kelli Taruawc* with *Carnant* written above by a later hand; RB Celli *Carnant*; BS Kelli *Carnawc*; AC Celli *Darnaut* (MS. B), Kelli *Caruanc* (MS. C). On linguistic grounds the RB form appears to be the more correct; but since the place has not been identified absolute certainty is impossible. See HW ii. 406, note 30.

20 15–6 **The castles ... in them**: RB *A'r kiwdawdwyr* a trigassant yn eu tei *ynn diofyn* yr bot y kestyll etwa ynn gyuan a'r castellwyr yndunt, 'And *the inhabitants* stayed in their houses *unafraid* although the castles were still intact and the garrisons in them'; BS Ac ev kestyll a edewit yn gyfan ac *ev tlodeon* a drigassant yn ev tei *yn ergrynedic*, 'And their castles were left intact and their *poor folk* stayed in their houses *trembling* [*with fear*].' Pen. 20 has nothing corresponding to RB 'And *the inhabitants* stayed in their houses *unafraid*' and BS 'and their *poor folk* stayed in their houses *trembling* [*with fear*].' It is obvious that RB has translated *indigenae* whereas BS has translated *indigentes*: cf. on 16.8–9 above. RB is here to be preferred to BS.

20 34–6 **with two earls ... with him**: RB a deu tywyssawc yn y blaen, a Hu, iarll Amwythic, yn bennaf arnunt, 'with two leaders in the van, and with Hugh, earl of Shrewsbury, as chief over them'; BS a deu dywyssauc arnadunt, nyt amgen, Hugone Goch, Jarll Amhwythic, a Hugone Vras, Jarll Caerlleon, 'with two leaders over them, to wit, Hugh the Red, earl of Shrewsbury, *and Hugh the Fat, earl of Chester*.' BS makes the meaning of Pen. 20 clear. AC has *Hugo comes urbis Legionum*, et *alter Hugo* (MS. B), ... contra *duos Hugones consules Francorum* (MS. C).

20 36–21 5 **And they made for the island of Anglesey ... into the island**: RB agrees in substance with Pen. 20, but BS supplies additional details: A gwedy ev dyuot hyt yn Gwyned y kiliws y Gweyndit y'r annealwch mal y gnottahassant gynt. Ac y doethant wyntev hyt yn agos ar y mor kyverbyn a Mon, *y lle y gelwyt Aber Lliennauc, ac y gwnaethant gastell yno*. A gwedy gwelet o'r Gweyndyt na ellynt ymerbynnieit ac wynt, achubeit Mon a orugant y geisiaw amdiffyn y gan wyr Jwerdon neu herwlonghev y ar vor. *A gwedy gwybot o'r Freinc hynny, kymryt a orugant Oweyn vab Edwyn yn ev blaen y vynet y Von*, 'And after they (*sc.* the French) had come to Gwynedd, the men of Gwynedd fled to the wilderness as they had been accustomed to do in the past. And they (*sc.* the

page line

French) came up near to the sea opposite Anglesey, *to the place called Aberlliennog, and they made a castle there.* And after the men of Gwynedd had seen that they could not encounter them, they occupied Anglesey to seek protection from the men of Ireland or pirate ships at sea. *And after the French had learnt that, they took Owain ab Edwin in their van to go to Anglesey.*'

BS does not mention the treachery of the 'pirates,' but AC *s.a.* 1098 agrees with Pen. 20 and RB. For Aberlliennog see *The History of Gruffydd ap Cynan,* 29, 50, 139, 174.

21   9   **Magnus**: MS. 28*b*, 26 *Mawrus*: cf. MS. 29*a*, 4, 16 ; 36*a*, 24; 36*b*, 27; RB *Magnus*, BS *Magnus*. Pen. 20 *Mawrus* seems to be *Mawr*, 'big' (a literal translation of *magnus*) + *us*!

21   15   **then**: MS. *ac yna* emended to *yna*.

21   15–6   **earl Hugh . . . face**: Pen. 20 has mistranslated. RB and BS correctly state that Magnus slew earl Hugh of Shrewsbury: RB *y brathwyt Hu Jarll yn y wyneb; ac o law y brenhin ehun yn y vrwydyr y dygwydawd,* 'earl Hugh was wounded in his face; and by the hand of the king himself he fell in the battle'; BS *y brathwit iarll Amwithic yn y wyneb o law brenhin Norwei yn y golles y eneit,* 'the earl of Shrewsbury was wounded in his face by the hand of the king of Norway so that he lost his life.' Cf. AC *s.a.* 1098 *alter comes sagitta in facie percussus occubuit* (MS. B), *alter consulum vulneratus in facie cecidit* (MS. C). This is confirmed by Giraldus Cambrensis, *Itinerarium Kambriae,* ii. cap. vii, although Gerald has confused Hugh, earl of Shrewsbury, with Hugh, earl of Chester. See also HW ii. 409–410, ONR 117–122.

21   17–8   **and the French . . . to the Saxons**: RB *A dwyn a oruc y Freinc oll, a mawr a bychan, hyt ar y Saesson,* 'And he took all the French, both great and small, to the Saxons'; BS *Ac yr edewys yr holl Freinc Ynys Von ac y doethant y Loegyr at Saesson,* 'And all the French left the island of Anglesey and came to England, to Saxons'; AC *Magnus abivit, Franci vero majores et minores secum ad Angliam perduxerunt* (MS. B only). Pen. 20 gives the correct version. RB has translated '*Magnus abivit, Francos* vero majores et minores secum ad *Anglos perduxit.*' BS has completely blundered.

21   26–7   **a portion of Powys**: MS. *Powys* with *rann o,* 'a portion of' added in the margin. This correction is confirmed by RB *a chyfran o* Powys, 'and a portion of Powys,' and BS *a ran o* Bowys, 'and a portion of Powys.' Cf. AC *s.a.* 1099 *partem* terrae suae capiens (MS. B), *partem* regni sui accepit (MS. C).

21   27–8   **Gruffudd ap Cynan received Anglesey**: MS. *Gruffud ap Kynan a gauas* Mon. So too RB *a Gruffud a gauas* Mon, 'and Gruffudd *received* Anglesey.' Ctr. BS *Grufud a werchetwys* (*gedwis* MS. B) Mon, 'Gruffudd *besieged* (*held* MS. B) Anglesey'; AC *s.a.* 1099 *Grifinus filius Conani Mon obsedit* (MS. B), *Grufud filius Kenan Moniam obsedit* (MS. C).

22   3   **Walter Tyrrell was his name**: MS. *Wat' Tirel oed y henw* added in the margin by an early corrector of Pen. 20. This is not in RB, but cf. BS: *ef a rodes y uuha yn law Sir Water Tirell,* 'he (*sc.* the king) placed his bow in the hand of Sir Walter Tyrrell'. AC (MSS. B and C) merely state that the king was slain *a quodam milite*.

page line

22 28 **Roger**: a mistake for *Richard*. This mistake, due to a wrong extension of the contraction R., is found in Pen. 20 (Roger), RB (Roger), BS (Roger), and AC (MS. C) *Rogerus*, and so derives from the Latin original. See HW ii. 463, note 3.

22 30 **Gwyn ap Gruffudd**: RB *Ywein* vab Gruffud, but BS agrees with Pen. 20: *Gwynn* vab Gruffud. AC *s.a.* 1101 refers to the death of Goronwy ap Cadwgan, but does not mention Gwyn (or Owain) ap Gruffudd.

23 14 **a second time**: RB Yg kyfrwg hynny, 'In the meantime'; BS Ac yna, 'And then.' It is obvious that Pen. 20 has translated *iterum* where RB has translated *interea*, which would appear to be the better reading here.

23 18 **Blyth**: MS. castell *Blidense*; RB *Blif*; BS castell *Blydense*. Probably, the original Latin had *castellum Blidense*. No remains of a castle have been found at Blyth, but Tickhill, since it belonged to the honour of Blyth, was sometimes called 'castellum *Blidense*.' The castle meant here is that of Tickhill. Cf. below 23.25.

23 27 **the daughter of king Muircertach**: MS. merch Murcard vrenhin; so too RB merch Murtart vrenhin, BS merch Murcard, brenhin Iwerdon, 'the daughter of Muircertach, king of Ireland.' In the three versions the phrase implies that Arnulf's wife was Muircertach's only daughter: but we know that another daughter of his married Sigurd Magnusson. See below 24.36 and cf. HW ii. 413, note 44. A more correct translation of the original Latin (? filiam Murcardi) would have been *merch y Vurcard vrenhin*, 'a daughter of king Muircertach's.'

23 35 **Blyth**: see on 23.18.

24 9-10 **and Ystrad Tywi**: not in RB, but cf. BS git ac Ystrat Tywi 'along with Ystrad Tywi.'

24 32-3 **and after ... timber**: RB a gwedy torri llawer o wyd defnyd, 'and after felling many trees for timber,' but BS ac a vriwaud *adeiliadev prenn*, 'and he destroyed *wooden buildings*.' Pen. 20 and RB seem to give the correct sense: BS has probably mistranslated some form of *materies*. See HW ii. 414, note 45.

24 36 **the daughter of Muircertach**: MS. merch Murcard, RB merch Mwrchath, BS merch *Murcardi* (which has retained the genitive of the original Latin). See above on 23.27. Here again the original Latin has not been rendered correctly in any of the three versions.

25 18 **and the castle**: not in MSS. B, C, D of Pen. 20, nor in RB, but cf. BS Dyvet *a'r castell*, 'Dyfed *and the castle*.'

25 25 **against the men of Scotland**: MS. yn erbyn gwyr *yr Alban*; RB ... a diffeithaw a oruc teruyneu *Prydein*, '... and he ravaged the bounds of Scotland'; BS ... y diffeithiaw tervynev *Llychlyn*, '... to ravage the bounds of *Scandinavia*.' All three texts have blundered here: this attack by Magnus (in which he fell, as correctly stated by Pen. 20, RB, and BS) was not upon Scotland, still less upon Scandinavia: rather it was against Ulster. Cf. CS *s.a.* 1099 (= 1103) Magnus Rí Loclainne ocus na ninnsibh,

162   BRUT Y TYWYSOGYON

page line

fer ro triall forbaisi for Erinn uile, do marbadh *ar crech dUlltoibh*, 'Magnus, king of Lochlann and of the Isles, a man who attempted an attack against all Ireland, was slain *on a foray by the Ultonians*'; AU *s.a.* 1103 Maghnus, ri Lochlainni, do marbadh *for creich i n-Ultaibh*, 'Magnus, king of Lochlann, was slain *on a foray by the Ultonians.*' The Pen. 20 and RB versions can be explained as mistranslations of *adversus Scottos*, the latter word having been misunderstood as 'the men of *Scotland*' instead of 'the men of Ireland,' but it is difficult to see how the translator of BS arrived at his version.

MS. C of AC *s.a.* 1103 incorrectly states that Magnus was slain at Dublin: Magnus rex *apud Dulin* occiditur.

25   25-6   **And the Scots**: MS. a'r *Albaenwyr*, RB y *Prydeinwyr*, BS y *Llychlynwyr*. See the preceding note on 25.25.

25   26   **or the French**: not in RB and BS. It may be that the original Latin was *Scottorum vel Pictorum*, and that *Pictorum* was taken for *Pictauiensium* and rendered as *y Freing*, 'the French' in Pen. 20. Cf. '*Scottorum Pictorumque*' in the quotation from Gildas on 25.26-7.

25   26-7   **like ants . . . warm rain**: this simile, in its original Latin, seems to have been an echo of Gildas, *De Excidio Britanniae*, cap. xix: quasi in alto Titane incalescenteque caumate *de artissimis foraminum caverniculis* fusci vermiculorum cunei, tetri Scottorum Pictorumque greges . . . Where Pen. 20 has *gogofeu*, 'caves,' RB has *o gnyghaf tylleu y gogofeu*, 'from the very narrow holes of their caves,' which agrees still closer with the words of Gildas.

26   11   **A year after that**: the annal for 1104 (true date) is wanting in Pen. 20, as also in RB and BS. And so Pen. 20 becomes three years in arrear. The annal for 1104 (true date) is wanting in MS. B of AC, but in MS. C a blank *annus* is shown.

26   23   **A year after that**: ctr. RB Y ulwydyn *honno*, 'That year.' BS agrees with Pen. 20 in placing the death of Hywel ap Goronwy in the year following that in which the death of Owain ab Edwin is recorded, i.e. *s.a.* 1103 = 1106. So too AC.

26   28-9   **and informed them . . . place**: RB a menegi vdunt teruynedic le ar aros amser yn y nos, 'and informed them of an appointed place wherein to wait for a time during the night'; BS y venegi hynny, 'to inform [them] of that.'

27   1   **the French**: a marginal addition in MS. Not in RB and BS.

27   12   **And earl Robert, his brother**: if Pen. 20 is correct, 'Robert, his brother' (*sc*. king Henry) can refer only to Robert, duke of Normandy: but MSS. B, C, D of Pen. 20 read *a'i vrawd*, '*and* his brother,' i.e. 'earl Robert [de Bellême] and his brother,' although Robert de Bellême is specifically mentioned. RB (which seems to have omitted words here by haplography) has: A chyhwrd ac wynt a wnaeth Robert iarll o Vethlem, 'And earl Robert of Bellême encountered them.' BS Ac yn ev herbyn y doeth Robert iarll *ac Ernwlf y vraut* a Robert de Beleem a William o Moretania, 'And against them came earl Robert and *Arnulf his brother* and Robert de Bellême and William of Moretania.' But Arnulf was the brother of Robert de Bellême, not of Robert, duke of Normandy.

page line

27 13 **William de Bretagne, his uncle**: RB ——, BS William o *Moretania, y gevynderw*, 'William of *Moretania*, his *first-cousin*.' William of Mortaigne is meant, and he was *first-cousin* (not 'uncle' as Pen. 20 says) to king Henry II.

27 20 **his uncle**: RB ——, BS *y gevynderw*, 'his *first-cousin*,' which is correct: see on 27.13.

27 24 **by**: MS. 39*b*, 27, *ap* emended to *y gan*. It may be that the scribe of Pen. 20 (who seems to have been more accustomed to copying Latin texts) absentmindedly wrote the Latin *ap* (= *ab*) instead of the Welsh *y gan*, 'by.'

27 26 **Edgar**: RB *Edwart* is incorrect, probably due to a wrong extension of the contraction *E.* or *Ed.* Maelcoluim had a son called Edward, but he died in 1093: see *s.a.* The entry 'And Edgar ... in his place' is not in BS which, however, has the following entry (not in Pen. 20 and RB): Ac y bu varw Herwaldus, escop Llandaf; ac y doeth yn y le yntev Worgen. Ancell archescob a'y kyssegrws yng Keint, 'And Herewald, bishop of Llandaff, died; and in his place came Urban. Archbishop Anselm consecrated him in Canterbury.'

28 8 **Cenarth Bychan**: MS. 40*b*, 28–41*a*, 1 *Keugarth Vachaw* emended to *Kengarth Vachan*; cf. RB [K]enarth Bychann, BS Kengarth Vachan; AC *s.a.* 1107 castellum *Chenarth Bechan* (MS. B), castellum de Kilgarran (MS. C). On the situation of Cenarth Bychan see HW ii. 418, note 59.

28 26 **he came ... the ditch**: RB y doeth ef ... y'r castell ... *wedy* [g]*wneuthur clawd dan y trotheu ynn dirgel*, 'he came into the castle *after having secretly made a hole under the threshold*.' No details are given in BS.

29 28 **whose brothers Owain slew**: so too RB Llywarch ap Trayhayarnn, *y gwr y lladawd Owein y urodyr*, 'Llywarch ap Trahaearn, the man whose *brothers* Owain slew.' Ctr. BS canys Oweyn a ladassei y vraut ef, 'for Owain had slain his *brother*.' BS has read *fratrem* where Pen. 20 and RB have read *fratres*. The correct reading must have been *fratres*, for in 1106 (see above *s.a.*) Owain had slain Meurig and Griffri, sons of Trahaearn, as recorded in Pen. 20, RB and BS.

30 4–5 **the ford of 'Corruonet'**: RB *Ryt Cornuec* (MS. P), *Coruuec* (MSS. M, T), *Corunec* (MS. R); BS Ryt *Coruonec*. The situation of this ford has not been determined and so the correct form of the place-name cannot be decided. Phillimore, OP iv. 434–35, suggests that it is the same ford as that later called *Rhyd Meirionnydd*, 'in the Cyfoeth y Brenin division of Llanfihangel Genau'r Glyn parish ... being half a mile up the northern fork of the brook which joins the sea at Wallog, between Aberystwyth and Borth.' Near it, as Phillimore points out, there is a place called *Moel Cerneu*. 'This "ford" is on the direct straight road from Borth to the church and village of Llanbadarn Fawr, crossing the Clarach at Llangorwen; which road furnished a route by which the position then blocked by the castles of Castell Gwallter (Llanfihangel) and Ystrad Peithyll ... lying along the modern main road, could be turned.'

30 21 **to the castles**: RB y *pebylleu*, 'to their *tents*'; BS y ev *kestyll*, 'to their castles.'

Q

page line

30 28–30 **And after that they returned ... Padarn**: RB A gwedy hynny yn orwac hayach yd ymhoelassant *eithyr cael anuolyanus anreith o gyulyeoed y seint, Dewi a Phadarnn*, 'And after that they returned wellnigh empty-handed *save for having taken infamous spoil from the precincts of the saints, David and Padarn*'; BS ... *ac anreithiaw yr eglwissev yn llwyr* lle buessint, '*and they utterly pillaged the churches* where they had been.'

32 8–9 **And he demanded ... his brother**: RB is fuller: Ac ynn gynntaf yd erchis gwystlon y [Uadawc] uap Ridit o ueibon goreugwyr y wlat. *Yr eil weith* yd erchis *Ithel y urawt*, 'And in the first place he demanded hostages of [Madog] ap Rhyddid from amongst the sons of the best men of the land. *The second time* he demanded Ithel, his brother.' Pen. 20 is incorrect in calling the sons of Rhiryd 'Iorwerth and Ithel': they were Ithel and *Madog*. Note the variant reading of MSS. B, C, D of Pen. 20.

32 15 **and Cadwgan then released him**: ctr. RB Ac yna y gollygawd ef mab Cadwgawn, 'And then he released Cadwgan's son'; BS ac y talawd yntev yn lle y vab Cadogon, 'and then he (*sc*. Iorwerth) forthwith requited Cadwgan's son.' RB is here the correct version.

33 5–6 **and they scarcely shunned their own presence**: so too RB Ac abreid y gochelynt gynndrycholder *y gwyr ehunein*, 'And they but scarcely shunned the presence of *the men themselves*.' There is no phrase corresponding to this in BS. Pen. 20 is ambiguous, and RB only slightly less so. The meaning seems to be that in frequenting the territory of Iorwerth and Cadwgan, Owain and Madog only just kept out of the way of Iorwerth and Cadwgan. At least, this is the meaning apparent in RB, and such therefore appears to be the meaning of Pen. 20. It is just possible that both Pen. 20 and RB have mistranslated some such phrase as *vix suam presentiam celabant*, 'they scarcely *concealed* their own (*sc*. Owain and Madog) presence,' using *gochel* for *celu*: but this supposition is unnecessary.

34 5 **a certain bishop from Flanders**: ctr. RB *hennafgwr o'r Flemisseit*, 'an *elder* of the *Flemings*'; BS *primas o Flandrys*, 'a *chief man* from Flanders.' BS has obviously retained the original Latin word (which was eventually borrowed into Welsh: see *Cywyddau Dafydd ap Gwilym a'i Gyfoeswyr* (1935) XXXV. 30, LXIII, 22) which Pen. 20 has rendered as *esgob*, 'bishop,' and RB as *hennafgwr*, 'elder.' RB is correct here, for William of Brabant was 'a distinguished member of the Flemish colony' in Rhos. See HW ii. 420, and note 60. On the variant meanings of *primas* see J. S. P. Tatlock, *The Legendary History of Britain* (Berkeley and Los Angeles. 1950), 264, note 32. Cf. on 82.35 below.

36 6–7 **who at that time ... place**: RB y gwr a oed ynn kynnal lle y brenhin ac yn y lywaw *ynn Amwythic*, 'the man who was holding the king's place and directing it *at Shrewsbury*'; BS yr hwn a oed yn medu yna Swyd Amhwythic, 'he who was then governing *the county of Shrewsbury*.'

36 32–3 **whilst he ... day**: RB and BS seem to give a better meaning, especially in conjunction with the sentence which follows. RB A llechu a *orugant wynteu* yny oed oleu y dyd trannoeth, 'And *they* (*sc*. the war-band) lay in hiding until it was light on the following day'; BS Ac yna dodi

page line

    gwyliadurieit arnaw y nos honno, 'And then they placed men to watch him that night.' Pen. 20 has probably mistranslated here.

37 35 **Pennant Bachwy**: RB *Penaeth Bachwy*, BS *Pennant Bachwy*. RB *Penaeth* is to be emended to *Pennant*. *Bachwy* (now *Bacho*) is the name of a small stream which joins the Clywedog near Staylittle, and there are references to a place there called *Pennant Bacho*: see OP iv. 646. But Lloyd, HW ii. 463, note 6, has pointed out that this *Pennant Bachwy* (*Bacho*) would be 'very far from any line which we can suppose the Earl of Chester to have taken in his march against Gruffydd. Either the original chronicle substituted for an unfamiliar name one with which he was acquainted or the meeting-place of the southern contingent has been accidently assigned to the northern.' In his account of the campaign Lloyd, HW ii. 463, assumes that king Alexander and the earl of Chester 'set out from Chester by the coast road leading to the mouth of the Conway.' Phillimore, OP iv. 647-48, suggests that *Pennant Bachwy* is a mistake for *Pennant Machnwy*, 'which was perhaps . . . the older name of Pennant *Machno*, now called Penmachno.' There is some confirmation of Phillimore's suggestion in the fact that MS. C of Pen. 20 reads Pennant *Machno*.

37 36-7 **to Gruffudd . . . with their enemies**: RB Yghyfrwg hynny yd anuones Ywein kennadeu at Gruffud *ac Ywein, y vab*, y erchi vdunt gwneuthur yn gadarn hedwch *yrygtunt yn erbyn* y gelynnyon, 'In the meantime Owain sent messengers to Gruffudd and *Owain, his son*, to ask them to make peace firmly *amongst themselves against* their enemies.' Pen. 20 'Goronwy ab Owain' is correct as against RB 'Owain, his (*sc.* Gruffudd ap Cynan) son' (cf. below 38.11), but the latter part of the sentence is more correct in RB than in Pen. 20. There is probably a scribal error in Pen. 20 due to haplography, which can be thus emended: *y erchi vdunt wneuthur kadarn hedwch a'y [gilyd yn erbyn y] gelynyon*, 'to ask them to make a firm peace with [each other against their] enemies.' This would bring it into line with RB.

    The Goronwy ab Owain mentioned in Pen. 20 is Goronwy ab Owain ab Edwin, whose sister Angharad was wife of Gruffudd ap Cynan. One can account for RB *ac Ywein, y vab* if the original Latin was nuntios misit ad G. (= Gruffudd) *et* G. (= Goronwy) *f. E.* (= Ewein for Owain): the translator probably understood the second G. as a contraction for *Gruffudd* and so understood *G. f. E.* as *Griffini filium Ewein* (Owain son of Gruffudd) and not as Goronwy son of Owain. This would be a natural mistake for a translator to whom the name of Owain Gwynedd, son of Gruffudd ap Cynan, was better known than that of Goronwy ab Owain.

38 9 **agree**: Pen. 20, 124, col. *b*, 8, *chydfynawd* is an error of print for *chydfynawd*.

38 11 **Gruffudd ap Cynan and Goronwy ab Owain**: RB Llyma Ruffudd *ac Ywein, y vab*, wedy kymryt hedwch gan vab Moelcolwm a'r Jarll, 'Behold, Gruffudd *and Owain, his son*, have accepted peace from the son of Maelcoluim and the earl'; BS . . . a menegi yr hedychu Grufud a mab Moelculum a'r Jarll, 'and he made known that *Gruffudd* had made peace with the son of Maelcoluim and the earl.' Here again RB *ac Ywein, y vab*, is a blunder, as above, 37.36-7

page line

39 1 **Geoffrey**: MS. *Geffrei*; RB *Jeffre*; BS *Geffrei*; AC *s.a.* 1115 *Wilfre* (MS. B), *Wilfridus* (MS. C). The Latin original of the three Welsh versions must have read *Galfridus*, but Florence of Worcester and Symon of Durham confirm the form *Wilfred*, as in AC. See EHR, xxxiv, 376, No. 346.

39 2 **Bernard**: for the grant of the bishopric of Menevia to Bernard on 19 September, 1115, see EHR xxxiv. 376, No. 347.

39 25-6 **And at last Gruffudd received them kindly and gladly**: The corresponding words in RB and BS suggest that Pen. 20 is here corrupt: RB Yr Howel hwnnw a uuassei ygharchar Ernwlf vab Rosser, Jarll castell Baltwin, yr hwnn y rodassei Wylym vrenhin idaw kyfran o gyuoeth Rys ap Teudwr. *Ac yn y diwed* y diaghassei yr Howel hwnnw yn anafus gwedy trychu y aelodeu o'r carchar. Ac yna yd aruollet wyntwy, ac eraill gyt ac wynt, yn hegar y gan Gruffud vab Kynnan, 'That Hywel had been in the prison of Arnulf fitz Roger, earl of Baldwin's Castle, to whom king William had given a portion of the territory of Rhys ap Tewdwr. And *at last* that Hywel had escaped from prison in a maimed state after his members had been cut. And then they, and others along with them, were kindly received by Gruffudd ap Cynan'; BS Hywel . . . yr hwn a uuassei yng karchar Ernulf vab Rosser, Jarl Montgomeri, ac y rodassei Gwilliam vrenhim gynt ydaw ran o gyvoeth Rys; a gwedy torri y a[e]lodev, y ellwg ymeith a oruc. Ac y doeth yntev ar Grufud vab Kynan, ac y bu lawen wrthaw, 'Hywel . . ., who had been in the prison of Arnulf fitz Roger, earl of Montgomery, and to whom king William had formerly given a part of Rhys's territory; and after his members had been cut, he let him go. And he came to Gruffudd ap Cynan, and he (*sc.* Gruffudd) welcomed him.' As the passage stands in Pen. 20, the *at last* is not much to the point, but in RB, applied to Hywel, it has a meaning. It must be that either the Pen. 20 text is here corrupt or that the translator of Pen. 20 has blundered.

39 25-6 **. . . kindly and gladly**: After this RB and BS have an additional passage which makes the meaning of what follows much clearer and which has probably been dropped by the Pen. 20 scribe: RB Ac yghyfrwg hynny, gwedy clybot o'r brenhin mynet Gruffud ap Rys at Gruffud vab Kynan, annon kenhadeu a wnaeth at Gruffud vab Kynan y erchi idaw dyuot attaw. Ac vuyd vu Ruffud y uynet attaw, 'And in the meantime, after the king had heard that Gruffudd ap Rhys had gone to Gruffudd ap Cynan, he sent messengers to Gruffudd ap Cynan to bid him come to him. And Gruffudd was obedient in going to him'; BS A gwedy dyuot Grufud vab Kynan y lys y brenhin llawen uuwyt vrthaw ac adaw llawer o da idaw yr peri Grufud vab Rys ydaw ay yn vew ay yn varw. Ac yr ymedewys yntev ac wynt, 'And after Gruffudd ap Cynan had come to the king's court, he was welcomed and promised much wealth for obtaining for him (*sc.* the king) Gruffudd ap Rhys either alive or dead. And he left them.' The fact that Pen. 20 later implies (see on 39.31) that Gruffudd had been away from his own land suggests that a short passage corresponding to the additional words in RB and BS has been dropped in Pen. 20.

39 31 **and he came to his land**: This implies that Gruffudd ap Cynan had been outside his own land, probably with the king, as RB and BS state. See above on 39.25-6.

NOTES

page line

40 9 **And after he had been left in the church**: RB *a gwedy y ellwg o'r eglwys*, 'and after he had been *let out of* the church'; BS *a gwedy y adaw onadunt ef yno*, 'and after they had *left* him there.' Pen. 20 and BS seem to have translated the same verbal participle (? *relictus*), but RB seems to have adopted a different reading or to have mistranslated.

40 37–41 1 **and their mother ... king of the Britons**: RB *mam y rei hynny oed Hunud verch Vledyn ap Kynnuyn, y penhaf o'r Bryttannyeit wedy Gruffud ap Llywelyn, y rei a oed ynn urodyr vn vam, kanys Agharat verch Varedud, vrenhin y Bryttannyeit, oed y mam yll deu*, 'the mother of those (*sc.* Maredudd and Owain, sons of Rhydderch ap Tewdwr) was Hunydd, daughter of Bleddyn ap Cynfyn, *the foremost of the Britons after Gruffudd ap Llywelyn*, who were brothers by the same mother, for Angharad, daughter of Maredudd, king of the Britons, was the mother of both of them'; BS *ev mam wynt oed Hvnyd verch Vledynt, y mwiaf o'r Kymry gwedy Grufud vab Llywelyn*, canys wynt oedynt vrodyr vn vam o Agharat verch Voredud, brenhyn Kymre, 'their (*sc.* Maredudd and Owain, sons of Rhydderch ap Tewdwr) mother was Hunydd, daughter of Bleddyn, *the greatest of the Welsh after Gruffudd ap Llywelyn*, for they were brothers by the same mother, by Angharad, daughter of Maredudd, king of Wales.' RB *the foremost of the Britons after Gruffudd ap Llywelyn*, and BS *the greatest of the Welsh after Gruffudd ap Llywelyn* correspond to Pen. 20 *and Gruffudd ap Llywelyn*. RB *who were brothers by the same mother*, and BS *for they were brothers by the same mother* must refer to Bleddyn ap Cynfyn and Gruffudd ap Llywelyn, for their mother, Angharad, daughter of Maredudd ab Owain, was wife consecutively to Llywelyn ap Seisyll (*d.* 1063) and Cynfyn ap Gwerstan. There was probably a slight corruption here in the Latin text underlying RB and BS. With one emendation (see on 40.38) Pen. 20 supplies a better text.

40 38 **the latter**: MS. 129*b*, 22, *wynteu* emended to *ynteu*. See note on 40.37–41.1.

41 10 **Bleddyn ap Cedifor**: MS. *y Vledy^{nt} vab Kediuor*; RB *y Bledri vab Kediuor*; BS *y Vledyn vab Kediuor*. RB *Bledri* (= Bleddri) is the correct form: see OP iii. 213, HW ii. 428, and Edward Owen, 'A Note on the Identification of the "Bleheris" of Wauchier de Denain,' RC xxxii. 5ff. The identification cannot be proved, but the article quotes references to Bleddri in the charters. See also M. Williams, 'More about Bleddri' in *Études Celtiques* ii. 219ff.

41 11 **Robert Courtemain**: MS. Robert *Tort* (*Cort* with *mayn* added MS. B, *Kordmaen* MS. C, *Kortmayn* MS. D); RB Rotpert *Lawgam*, 'Robert Crooked-hand'; BS Robert *Courtemayn*. The Pen. 20 reading together with the RB version (*Lawgam*) show that the translator of RB read *Tort* or *Tortemain*. BS has retained the correct reading, and Pen. 20 has been emended accordingly in the translation.

41 12 **Abercorram**: RB *Aber Cofwy*; BS *Aber Comuyn*. RB and BS are errors in transcribing an earlier form *Aber Couuy*, 'Abercowyn.' *Abercorram* is the spot where the castle of the commot of Laugharne (Talacharn) was situated: cf. *s.a.* 1189 and *s.a.* 1257. *S.a.* 1215 it is called the castle of *Talacharn*. The reference in RB and BS is to another castle,

page line

Abercowyn, from the river Cowyn which flows into the Carmarthenshire Taf at Llandeilo Abercowyn. See G s.v. 'Cowyn'; B xiv. 218; *History of Carmarthenshire* i. 134. On *Abercorram/Talacharn* see OP iii. 240.

41   33   **... had been done**: after this RB has a slight addition : megys y dyweit Selyf, 'Dyrchafael a wna yspryt yn erbyn kwymp dyn' 'as Solomon says, "The spirit becomes haughty against the fall of man".' Cf. BS Ac yno y kyflewnyt a dywat Selif: 'Kyn y kwymp y dyrcheif yr ysbryt,' 'And there was fulfilled what Solomon said, "Before a fall, the spirit becomes haughty".' The reference is to *Proverbs* xvi. 18, 'Pride goeth before destruction, and an haughty spirit before a fall.'

41   33–5   **he thought ... certain men**: RB is fuller: Yna yd aruaethawd ef, yn hwydedic o valchder ac o draha yr anosparthus pobyl a'r ynuyt giwtawt, kyweiraw hyntoed ynuydyon o Dyvet y Geredigyawn a chymryt gwrthwyneb hynt y'r gyfyawnder wedy y alw o ..., 'Then, swollen with pride and presumption of the disorderly folk and the hot-headed inhabitants, he planned to lead hot-headed expeditions from Dyfed into Ceredigion and to follow a path contrary to righteousness after he had been called by ...' The corresponding passage in BS is: A gwedy gwelet o'r anosparthus bobyl o Dyvet hynny, ymgveirav y Geredigion a orugant dwrwy ganhorthwy ..., 'And after the disorderly folk from Dyfed had seen that, they made for Ceredigion through the help of ...'

42   1   **they left**: MS. 131*b*, 24, *ac adaw* emended to *adaw*.

42   16   **Blaen-porth**: RB Blaen Porth *Hodnant*, BS Blaen Porth *Gwydni*. See HW ii, 434, note 116, and OP iv. 433, 441.

42   27   **Ralf**: MS. *Rawlf*; RB *Razon*; BS *Rys*. HW ii. 435 adopts the form *Razo*. The three forms are variant extensions of a contraction R. BS is obviously wrong. For the site of the castle at Ystrad Peithyll, see OP iv. 489.

42   35   **Ralf**: see on 42.27.

43   5–6   **save for placing the standards in the van**: ctr. RB a *heb* ossot arwydon oc eu blaen, 'and *without* placing ensigns in their van.' BS has simply yn dirool, 'disorderly.' It appears that Pen. 20 has translated *nisi* where RB has translated *nec*.

43   24–5   **And as they were thus ... of the bridge**: RB Ac val yd oed y neill rei *yn kyrchu* a'r rei ereill yn saethu, 'And as the one side was *attacking* and the other shooting'; BS Ac yn yr ymseithu hynny, 'And during that shooting at one another.' From the account which follows it appears that the Welsh were armed with *spears*, so that RB seems the more correct version here.

43   34   **to the end of the mountain**: MS. hyd yn *dibēn* y mynyd; RB hyt *ygwrthallt* y mynyd, 'to the *counter-slope* of the mountain'; BS y *ben* y *bryn*, 'to the top of the hill.' It may be that Pen. 20 *dibēn* is a mistake or an alternative form for *dibynn*, 'a steep,' which would give a meaning in agreement with RB.

page line

43 34–7 **but the rear troop ... for their comrades**: RB gives a different version: Y toryf ol eissoes nys ymlidyawd, namyn heb geissaw na phont na ryt kymryt eu ffo a wnaethant, 'The rear troop, however, did not pursue them, but, seeking neither bridge nor ford, they took to flight.' That this is the correct version is proved by the sentence which follows in Pen. 20. The same general meaning is conveyed by BS: A gwedy gwelet o'r gwyr ereill hynny, *fo a orugant*, 'And after the other men had seen that, *they fled*.'

44 2 **... was waste**: after this BS adds Ac y foas Grufud ap Rys hyt yn Ystrat Tywi, canys lle anneal oed hwnnw, 'And Gruffudd ap Rhys fled to Ystrad Tywi, for that was a wild place.'

44 24 **cut off his members**: MS torri y aelodeu, RB trychu y aelodeu, both being euphemisms for castrating.

45 17–8 **he attacked them boldly**: the site of this encounter is not named in any of the Welsh versions, but cf. AC *s.a.* 1116 Owein a Flandrensibus *in Estrat Brunus* occiditur (MS. C only). *Estrat Brunus* is for Ystrad Frwnws, later Ystrad Rwnws, now Ystrad, near the confluence of the Tywi and the Cothi. See HW ii. 422, note 67.

45 22 **he**: i.e. Owain ap Cadwgan.

45 26 **Gwenllïan**: this Gwenllïan cannot be Gruffudd ap Cynan's daughter Gwenllïan (who married Gruffudd ap Rhys) by Angharad. Lloyd, HW ii. 417, note 57, points out that Angharad cannot have had a marriageable daughter at this time, and he suggests that this Gwenllïan was an illegitimate daughter of Gruffudd ap Cynan.

45 28 **by Ellylw**: MS. *oellyl o* emended to *o Ellylo*. Cf. RB *o Ellyllw*, BS *o Elilo*. *Ellylo* and *Ellilo* are variant forms of *Ellylw*: on the latter see G s.v.

45 35 **with the king**: MS. kydaruoll ... a'r brenhin, but *a'r* has been retraced by a later hand, possibly incorrectly. Ctr. RB A gwedy hynny yd ymaruolles Einawn ap Cadwgawn ap Bledyn a Gruffud [ap] Maredud ap Bledyn *y gyt* y dwyn kyrch am benn castell Vchdryt vab Etwin, a oed gefynderw y V[aredud ap B]ledyn *vrenhin*, 'And after that Einion ap Cadwgan ap Bleddyn and Gruffudd ap Maredudd ap Bleddyn made a solemn pact *together* to lead an attack against the castle of Uchdryd ab Edwin, who was first-cousin to Maredudd, son of king Bleddyn'; BS Ac yn hynny kytdyhvnaw a oruc Eynon ap Cadwgon a Grufud ap Moredud ap Bledyn y vynet am ben castell Vchdryt ap Edwyn ...', 'And thereupon Einion ap Cadwgan and Gruffudd ap Maredudd ap Bleddyn united together to go against the castle of Uchdryd ab Edwin ...' As it stands the Pen. 20 text is incorrect, but if *a'r brenhin* is emended to *y brenhin*, the meaning will be in agreement with RB and BS: 'Einion ap Cadwgan and Gruffudd ap Maredudd *son of king Bleddyn* made a solemn pact ...'

46 18 **to Cadwgan's son**: MS *y vab* Kadwgawn, but *veibion* in MSS. B, C, D; RB *y veibon* Cadwgawn, BS *y veibion* Cadwgon, 'to the *sons* of Cadwgan.'

46 26 **their other brothers**: they were Goronwy and Meilyr.

page line

46 26–7 **...sons of Owain ab Edwin ap Goronwy**: ctr. RB...a meibon Ywein ab Etwin, *nyt amgen* (— — MSS. M, R, T) Gronw a Ridit a Llywarch a'e brodyr y rei ereill, '... and the sons of Owain ab Edwin, *namely* (— MSS. M, R, T) Goronwy and Rhiddyd and Llywarch and their other brothers; BS...a meibion Oweyn ap Edwyn, Ririt a Llywarch ac ev brodyr, '... and the sons of Owain ab Edwin, Rhiryd and Llywarch and their brothers.' The RB text is corrupt: *nyt amgen* is not in MSS. M, R, T, and so may be an unnecessary addition in MS. P. However, Owain ab Edwin had a son Goronwy (*d.* 1124) so that RB does make sense, only one would then expect *a'e brawd y llall*, 'and their other brother,' i.e. Meilyr, instead of *a'e brodyr y rei ereill*. It may be that the translator of RB read the contraction for *scilicet* instead of *f.* (= *filius*). If *nyt amgen* of MS. P be omitted, since it is not in MSS. M, R, T, and *ap* be inserted after *Etwin*, RB will be brought into agreement with the correct meaning given in Pen. 20 and BS.

47 1 **a hard battle**: the name of this battle is not given in any of the three Welsh versions, but cf. AC *s.a.* 1118 Bellum *Maismain Cemro*, in quo Lewarch filius Owini cecidit (MS. B), Bellum *Mays Mayn Kembro* in quo Lyuuarch filius Ouuein cecidit (MS. C). Maes Maen Cymro is a township in the parish of Llanynys, near Rhewl, between Dyffryn Clwyd and Cinmeirch. See HW ii. 465, note 14.

47 16 **And he bade**: MS. ac ef a oruc erchi. In a few cases the scribe of Pen. 20 writes a –c– for Welsh *s*, and so *ac ef* may be for *a sef*. If this be not the case here, the text is to be emended to *ac ef a erchis*, which is the reading of MS. C, or to *ac erchi a oruc ef*.

47 20 **the ship that was considered the best**: RB yn y llog oreu a diogelaf, 'in the best and safest ship'; BS ac a dewisswit y gorev onadunt (*sc.* y llonghev), 'and the best of them (*sc.* the ships) was chosen.' The ship was 'La Blanche Nef' or 'The White Ship.' See EHR xxxiv. 513, No. 406.

49 1 **A year in which there was [peace]**: MS Bloidyn y bu hed[uch] added in the margin by the early corrector of the original text. This annal (1119 = 1122) is not in RB and AC, but it is in BS: Pan oyd oed Crist M.C.xix. hedwch uu y vlwydyn honno. 'When the year of Christ was MCxix, there was peace that year.' Since this annal is given in Pen. 20 and BS, in which more attention is paid to chronology than in RB, it is probably correct. The implications of its acceptance are quite important for chronological purposes. It follows that beginning with 1122 the dates of AC (MS. B) fall one year behind, from 1122 (= 1123) to 1125 (= 1126), with the result, for example, that the death of Einion ap Cadwgan can no longer be put in 1123 (as Lloyd, HW ii. 769 puts it), but must be moved to 1124. The dating of AC (MS. B) seems to get right again with the annal for 1127.

49 23–4 **[Gruffudd ap] Maredudd ap Bleddyn**: MS. *Mared.*' ap Bled.'; RB *Gruffud ap* Meredud ap Bledyn; BS *Moredud* ap Bledyn. Pen. 20 and BS are here incorrect. The RB reading is confirmed by AC *Grifinus* filius Meredut (MS. B), *Grifut* filius Maredut (MS. C). Hence the emendation. Moreover, RB, BS, and AC state that Ithel was first-cousin to the man who slew him, and Ithel was first-cousin to Gruffudd

NOTES

ap Mareddudd ap Bleddyn, not to Maredudd ap Bleddyn, who was Ithel's uncle. Cf. the note on 50.11.

49 24-5 **in the presence of Ithel's father**: RB *ygwyd Meredud y tat*, 'in the presence of Maredudd, his father'; BS ——. Pen. 20 has blundered: Ithel's father, Rhiryd ap Bleddyn, could not have witnessed the slaying of his son, for he had died in 1088 (see *s.a.*). RB is correct: Ithel was slain by Gruffudd ap Maredudd in the presence of the latter's father.

49 34-6 **A year ... with him**: Henry returned to England in September, 1126. See EHR xxxiv. 538, No. 523.

50 11 **Gruffudd [ap Maredudd] ap Bleddyn**: MS. *Mared.' ap Bled.'* with line drawn through *Mared.'* and *Gruffud vab* written opposite in the margin; RB *Gruffud ap Bledyn*; BS *Grufud ap Moredud ap Bledin*; AC *s.a.* 1128 Grifinus filius Meredut (MS. B), Grifut filius Maredut (MS. C). BS and AC are correct. The line of deletion through *Mared.'* in Pen. 20 may be a slip by the corrector.

50 12-3 **by Maredudd, his uncle, his father's brother**: RB *y gan Varedud ap Bledyn, y ewythyr, vrawt y hendat*, 'by *Maredudd ap Bleddyn*, his uncle, brother to *his grandfather*'; BS *Ac y delhis Llywelyn ap Owein Moredud ...*, 'And Llywelyn ab Owain seized *Maredudd*'; AC *s.a.* 1128 Lewelin filius Owini captus est a *Maredut* (MS. B), Lewelin filius Owein *ab auunculo suo Maredut* capitur (MS. C). Llywelyn ab Owain could not have been seized by Maredudd [ap Cadwgan], his father's brother, in this year, for Maredudd ap Cadwgan had been slain in 1125 (see *s.a.* above). RB is correct: Llywelyn was seized by Maredudd ap Bleddyn, Cadwgan's brother and 'great-uncle' of Llywelyn. BS has mistranslated possibly through reading *Lewelin filius Owein Maredut capit*. Further proof that Pen. 20 has blundered here is found below *s.a.* 1130, where we have the entry: 'And ... *Maredudd ap Bleddyn* caused Llywelyn ab Owain to be castrated.'

50 17-8 **and as he was returning ... Tyrrhene Sea**: If Pen. 20 means exactly what it says, i.e. that Morgan 'went to Jerusalem' 'towards the end' of 1128, his death at Cyprus on the homeward journey cannot well have been earlier than 1129, and the date of his death given by Lloyd, HW ii. 729 would have to be emended accordingly. BS agrees with Pen. 20: *Yn diwed y vlwydyn yd aeth* Morgant ap Cadogon y Gaerussalem am lad ohonaw y vrawt. A gwedy y dyvot drachevyn hyt yn Cyprys, y bu varw, '*At the end of the year* Morgan ap Cadwgan *went* to Jerusalem because he had slain his brother. And after he had returned as far as Cyprus, he died.' RB, however, says that he died at the end of this year, implying that he had gone to Jerusalem earlier: *Yn diwed y ulwydyn honno y bu varw* Morgan ap Cadwgawn yn Cipris yn ymhoelut o Garussalem, wedy mynet ohonaw a chroes y Garussalem o achaws ry lad ohonaw kyn no hynny Varedud y vrawt, '*At the close of that year* Morgan ap Cadwgan *died* in Cyprus on his way back from Jerusalem, after having gone as a crusader to Jerusalem because he had before that slain Maredudd, his brother.' Cf. AC *s.a.* 1128 Morganus filius Cadugaun propter fratricidium Ierosolimam petiit et inde rediens in insula Cipro obiit (MS. B), Morgan filius Cad.' qui ob fratricidium Ierosolimam

172 BRUT Y TYWYSOGYON

page line

perrexit in reditu in insula Cypres moritur (MS. C)—MS. B implying that he went to Jerusalem in 1128 and MS. C implying that he died in that year. The brother whom Morgan had slain was Maredudd ap Cadwgan: see above *s.a.* 1125.

50   19–23 **A year after that . . . two brothers**: MS. *Lliwelyn* has been added by the early corrector of the text. RB and BS do not mention Llywelyn ab Owain here: RB Y ulwydyn wedy hynny y *gwrthladwyt* Meredud vab Llywarch o'e wlat, y gwr a ladawd *mab Meuryc*, y gefenderw, ac a dallawd *meibon Griffri*, y deu gefendyryw ereill. Ac *Jeuaf ap Ywein* a'e gwrthladawd ac yn y diwed a'e *lladawd*, 'The year after that, Maredudd ap Llywarch was expelled from his land, the man who slew *the son of Meurig*, his first-cousin, and who blinded the sons of Griffri, his other two first-cousins. And it was *Ieuaf ab Owain* who expelled him and who at last slew him'; BS Pan oyd oet Crist M.C.xxvi y lladawt Moredud ap Llywarch y gevynderw gan *vab Meuric* a deu gevynderw gan *meibon Grifri* a dynnawt ev llygeit. A Jeuaf ap Oweyn a dallawt y dev vroder ac a'y deholes o'r wlat ac y llas wynt, 'When the year of Christ was 1126 Maredudd ap Llywarch slew his first-cousin, the son of Meurig, and gouged out the eyes of two first-cousins, the sons of Griffri. And *Ieuaf ab Owain* seized (*or* blinded) his two brothers and expelled them from the land, and they were slain'; AC *s.a.* 1129 Maredut filius Lywarch consobrinum suum *filium Meuruc occidit*; alios duos consobrinos suos filios Griffini, oculis privavit, duos quoque fratres suos Baldewino caecandos tradidit. Ipse vero a *Iowan filio Owini* de patria expulsus occisus est. Madauc filius Lywarch a Meuric consobrino suo occisus est (MS. B), Maredut filius Lyuuarch qui consobrinum suum *filium Meuric* occidit et duos consobrinos suos filios Grifut oculis priuauit duosque fratres suos excecare Bledwino iussit, a *Jeuuab filio Owein* occiditur (MS. C). Pen. 20 *Llywelyn ab Owain* is a mistake for *Ieuaf ab Owain* (d. 1130; see *s.a.*) which is given correctly by RB, BS, and AC (MS. C). Pen. 20 *Meurig* has been emended to [*the son of*] *Meurig* as in RB, BS, and AC (MSS. B and C): Meurig ap Trahaearn, who had been slain by Owain ap Cadwgan in 1106 (see above *s.a.*) was Maredudd ap Llywarch's uncle. Where Pen. 20 gives '*Maredudd and Griffri*, his two first-cousins,' RB, BS, and AC give 'his two first-cousins, the sons of Griffri (or Gruffudd).' The names, as given by Pen. 20, may be correct: in any case they must have been sons of Griffri ap Trahaearn, who was slain in 1106 along with his brother Meurig. For the family connections implicit in this entry, see HW ii. 770, 'Arwystli and Cydewain.' BS has mistranslated.

50   25–6 **Maredudd ap Bleddyn**: MS. *Mared.' a Bled.'* emended to *Mared.' a[p] Bled.'* although the mistake may be a mistranslation (by taking the contraction for *filius* (*f.*) as that for *et*) rather than a scribal error. Cf. RB y gan *Varedud ap Bledyn*, BS *Moredud* ap Bledyn, AC a *Meredut filio Bledint* (MS. B), a *Maredut filio Bledin* (MS. C).

50   30 **Meurig**: RB y gan *Veuryc*, y gefynderw *vab Ridit*, 'by Meurig, his first-cousin, *son of Rhiddyd*'; BS y gan *Meuric*, y gevynderw, 'by Meurig, his first-cousin'; AC *s.a.* 1130 a *Meuruc* consobrino suo (MS. B), a *Meuric filio Meuric* consobrino sno. RB 'son of Rhyddid' is obviously a blunder. Cf. note on 50.32.

NOTES 173

page   line

50   32   **Meurig's eyes ... castrated**: RB *yd yspeilwyt Meuryc ap Ridit o'e deu lygat a'e dwy geill*, 'Meurig ap Rhiddyd was despoiled of his two eyes and his two testicles'; BS *y tynnwyt llygeit Meuric a'y geillev*, 'Meurig's eyes and his testicles were gouged out'; AC *s.a.* 1131 *Meuric filius Meuric* oculis et testibus privatus est (MS. B), *Meuric filius Meuric* oculis privatus est. Again RB *ap Rhyddid* is a blunder. Cf. on 50.30.

50   35–6   **by Cadwgan ap Goronwy and Einion ab Owain, his first-cousins**: ctr. RB *y gan Gadwgawn ap Gronw ap Etwin* [Ywein MSS.], *y gefynderw, ac Einawn ap Ywein*, 'by Cadwgan ap Goronwy ab Edwin, his *first-cousin*, and Einion ab Owain'; BS *y gan y gevynderw* Cadwgon ap Gronw ac Eynion ap Oweyn, 'by his *first-cousin*, Cadwgan ap Goronwy, and Einion ab Owain'; AC *s.a.* 1132 a *consobrino* suo Cadugaun filio Goronou et Eynaun filio Owini (MS. B), a *consobrino* suo Cadugaun filio Gronoe (MS. C). Pen. 20 has mistranslated, reading *a consobrinis suis*.

51   1–4   **In the four years ... on record**: cf. RB [D]*eg mlyned ar hugein a chant a mil oed oet Crist pan vu bedeir blyned ar vntu* heb gael neb ystorya o'r a ellit y gwarchadw y dan gof, 'One thousand one hundred and thirty was the year of Christ when there were four years in succession without there being any history that might be preserved in memory.' This agrees with Pen. 20 in saying that the years 1130–1133 (chronicler's dates) were blank. BS is different: *Pan oyd oet Crist Mil.c.xxx nyt oed dym a dyckit ar gof na'r dwy vlyned nessaf gwedy hynny*, 'When the year of Christ was 1130 there was naught which might be placed on record, nor in *the two years next after that*,' This implies blank *anni* for 1130–1132. BS has an entry for 1133: ... y bu varw Robert, Courtehevse oyd y lyshenw, yn Gaerloiw, mab William Bastart ac yn Jarll y Normannieit; ac y clathpwit yn Gaerdyf, '... died Robert—Courthose was his nickname—at Gloucester, son of William the Bastard and earl of the Normans; and he was buried at Cardiff.' Robert, duke of Normandy, died on 10 February, 1134, and so BS 1133 = 1134. This entry in BS occurs in MS. B of AC. MS. B of AC has the year 1133 blank, and MS. C has *three* blank years between the death of Maredudd ap Bleddyn and the death of Henry I.

51   5   **The first year after that, that is, the fourth year**: according to the text, this would be 1134, i.e. one year behind the true reckoning, since Henry I died on 1 December, 1135. RB and BS likewise are one year behind in their dating here.

51   7   **in the first month of winter**: RB *y trydyd dyd o vis Racuyr*, 'the third day of (or from) the month of *December*; BS iij Idus Novembres. The true date is 1 December.

51   7   **And**: MS. *Blwydyn wedy ac*, with a line drawn through *Blwydyn wedy* by the original scribe. Obviously he had started writing *Blwydyn wedy* [*hyny*], 'A year after that,' and was going to place Stephen's accession in the year following that recording the death of Henry I, i.e. in 1135 (= 1136), which would have been correct counting the beginning of the year from 25 December, for Stephen's accession was on 25 December. RB and BS agree in their dates with the corrected text of Pen. 20, i.e. as it is in the translation.

51   34   **towards Cardigan**: MS. *tu ac Aberteuii*, RB *y Aber Teiui*, BS *hyt yn Aberteiui*, AC *s.a.* 1136 ad *Abertewy* (MS. B), ad *Aberteyui* (MS. C).

174 BRUT Y TYWYSOGYON

page line

51 35 **Stephen the constable**: opposite this, in the margin of the MS., there is a gloss: y Sadwrn Du, 'Black Saturday.' Lloyd has shown that this marginal entry, combined with the statement by the continuator of Florence of Worcester that the battle was fought in the second week of October, seems to show that the date was Saturday, 10 October. The Welsh gloss corresponds to the foot-note 'Blake Saterndey' in MS. C of AC. See Lloyd, *The Story of Ceredigion*. Cardiff, 1937. 54 and note 1.

51 36 **William fitz Odo**: MS. Gwilym vab *Orc*; RB Gwilym ap *Oitt*; BS William vab *Oit*. AC *s.a.* 1136 mentions only 'Stephanus constabularius et filii Geraldi' (MS. B only). Pen. 20 *Orc* may be an error for *Oit* (cf. RB and BS). Lloyd, HW ii. 473, note 46, suggests that the reference is to William fitz Odo, i.e. William de Barri of Manorbier.

51 37 **and all the knights**: RB a'r holl varchogyon *a'r holl Freinc*, 'and all the knights *and all the French*'; BS *a Normannieit* ac ev marchogeon, '*and Normans* and their knights'; AC *s.a.* 1136 et *omnes Franci* (MS. B only).

51 37–8 **from the estuary of the Neath to the estuary of the Dyfi**: so too RB o *Aber Ned* hyt yn *Aber Dyvi*, 'from the estuary of the *Neath* to the estuary of the *Dyfi*'; ctr. BS (y doeth) . . . hyt yn Aber *Dyvi* (*Teivi* MS. B), '(came) . . . to the estuary of the *Dyfi*' (Teifi MS. B); AC *s.a.* 1136 ab hoste *Sabrinae* usque ad *Meneviam* (MS. B only).

51 41 **and others trampled . . . into captivity**: ctr. RB a *thrychu tra[et] meirch ereill*, a dwyn rei ereill yghethiwet, '*and the horses of others had been hamstrung*, and others carried off into captivity'; BS ereill *a las traet ev meirch* ac a dalywyt, 'others *had the feet of their horses cut* and were captured.' Here RB and BS are in general agreement against Pen. 20, but this last is the nearest to AC *s.a.* 1136 et equorum *pedibus conculcati* (MS. B only).

52 22–3 **on the third day from the Calends of April**: i.e. 30 March. This notice of the death of Ieuan is not in BS, nor is it in AC.

52 26 **and Stephen's Castle**: MS. a chastell *Ystyffant*; RB a chastell Llan *Ystyffan*, 'and the castle of *Llansteffan*'; BS a chastell *Ystevyn*, 'and Stephen's Castle'; AC *s.a.* 1137 et castello *Stephani* (MS. B only). Pen. 20, BS, and AC suggest that RB *Llan Ystyffan* is an error for *Ystyffan*, but cf. RB *s.a.* 1227 Pont *Lann Ystyphann* with reference to *Lampeter* bridge, where Pen. 20 has *Llannbedyr Tal Pont Ystyuyn*. In any case, Lampeter and not Llanstephan is meant here. See HW ii. 476, and cf. ib. 427 and note 88.

52 28–9 **A year after that . . . for her son**: On the annalistic reckoning this year is 1137, which (since 1134 = 1135) needs to be 'corrected' by adding one and so equals 1138. But the empress Matilda came to England actually in 1139, which is the year correctly given by AC. At first sight, therefore, the chronicler's 1137 = 1139 here. But MS. B of AC puts the death of Cynwrig ab Owain under 1138, in the annal before that recording the arrival of the empress, whereas Pen. 20, RB, BS, and MS. C of AC put Cynwrig ab Owain's death in the year after the arrival of the empress. It is possible that these two annals have been reversed in Pen. 20, RB, BS, and MS. C of AC and so, it is almost certain, in the common Latin original. If this is correct, Cynwrig ab Owain's death must be put in 1138.

NOTES

page line

52   33–4   **A year after that . . . Madog ap Maredudd**: On the dating of this annal see the preceding note. RB *teulu* and BS [*g*]*wyr* agree with Pen. 20 *kyueillyon a thylwyth*, 'friends and followers.' So too AC a *familia* (MS. B)—but MS. C has *ab Howel filio* Maredut. After recording Cynwrig ab Owain's death, BS has an additional entry: Ac y bu varw Wallter vab Richart, y gwr a seilawd gyntaf manachloc Tyndyrn, 'And Walter fitz Richard died, the man who first founded the monastery of Tintern.'

53   5–10   **A year after that . . . to Anarawd**: In the MS. the original text is: Blwydyn wedy hynny y llas *Angharat verch* Ruffud, gobeith a gogonyant y Deheubarthwyr, y gan dylwyth Katwaladyr ap Gruffud, yr hwn nyt oed *arnei* dim o'y ouyn. A phan gigleu Ewein y *brawt* hynny, gorthrwm y kymyrth arnaw; kanys ef a adawssei y verch y *Gadwaladyr.* A later hand, however, has underlined *Angharat verch* and *Gadwaladyr* and written *Anarawd vab* and *Anarawd* opposite them respectively in the margin. But his corrections are not complete: *arnei* must be changed to *arnaw* and *brawt* to *vrawt*. This brings Pen. 20 into substantial agreement with RB and BS. The translation is based on the fully emended text. Cf. the variants of MSS. B, C, D as given in the footnotes to the translation.

53   19   **Ischerwlf**: RB Cherwlf, BS Cherulf. On the Norsemen mentioned here see ONR 87.

53   22   **the Irish**: MS. y *Gwydyl*; RB y *Germanwyr*; BS y *Gwydil*; AC *s.a.* 1144 *Germanici* (MS. B), *Hybernienses* (MS. C).

53   23   **two thousand head of cattle**: MS. dwyuil o *warthec*; ctr. RB dwy vil o *geith*, 'two thousand *bondmen*'; BS dwy vil o *vorkeu*, 'two thousand *marks*'; AC *s.a.* 1144 duo millia *captivorum* (MSS. B and C). ONR 87 follows RB and AC, which agree with neither Pen. 20 nor BS. Pen. 20 seems to have translated *cattellorum.*

53   29   **Welsh pilgrims**: MS. pererinyon Kymry; RB pererinyon *o Gymry*, 'pilgrims from Wales' or 'Welsh pilgrims'; BS pererinion o *Gymre*, 'pilgrims from Wales' or 'Welsh pilgrims'; AC *s.a.* 1144 Peregrini *de Dyvet et Keredigaun* (MS. C only).

53   29   **were drowned**: RB adds *ar Vor Groec*, 'on the Sea of Greece,' and BS *yn y mor*, 'in the sea.' AC (MS. C only) has merely *submersi sunt*.

53   32–3   **the castle of Colunwy**: MS. kastell *Kolunwy*; so too BS a chastell *Colunwy*; ctr. RB castell *Colwyn*. *Colunwy*, the old Welsh form of *Clun*, and *Colwyn*, the castle in Elfael, are frequently confused in the Welsh texts. Here RB is obviously correct. On *Colunwy* > *Clun* see OP iii. 196, note 2. Cf. below 76.3; 113.12–3.

54   12–3   **on the twelfth day from the Calends of November**: ctr. RB y *decuet* dyd o Galan Hydref, 'on the *tenth* day from the Calends of October'; BS *x* Kalendas *Octobres.*

54   14   **Meurig ap Madog ap Rhiryd**: RB adds: yr hwn a elwit Meuryc Tybodyat, 'who was called *Meurig Tybodiad.*' *Tybodyat* may be a form of *Tyfe(i)diad*, i.e. the Teme.

page line

54 18 **Dinefwr**: MS. *Dinehwr* (*Dinevwr* MSS. B, C, D); RB *Dinweileir*; BS *Dinwileyr*; AC *s.a.* 1147 *Dinweilleir* (MS. B only). Lloyd, HW ii. 511 places 'Dinweiler' in Cantref Mawr, and ib. 501, note 63, it is assumed that the castle of Mabudryd and the castle of Dinwileir were one and the same castle. See also B viii. 39-40 and OP iv. 362, where it is suggested that Dinwileir castle was at Pencader or Gwyddgrug. RB, BS, and AC have the better reading here, for the castle which Cadell destroyed is the same as 'the castle in Mabudryd' mentioned *s.a.* 1145.

54 19-22 **and they granted ... castle of Llanstephan**: The corresponding passage has been lost in RB. Because of this gap in RB, Lloyd, HW ii. 502 erroneously ascribed the defence of Carmarthen rather than that of Llanstephan to Maredudd ap Gruffudd. This mistake has been rectified in *A History of Carmarthenshire*, i. 142 and note †. BS and AC agree with Pen. 20: BS y cavas Cadell vab Gruffud castell Dinwileyr ... a chastell Caer Vyrdyn drwy Howel ap Oweyn ... Ac odyna y doeth Cadell a'y vrodyr, Moredud a Rys, y gastell *Llan Ystiphan* ac ymlad yn gadarn ac wynt a llad llawer oc ev gelynneon a brathu ereill, 'Cadell ap Gruffudd took the castle of Dinwileir ... and the castle of Carmarthen through Hywel ab Owain ... And thereupon Cadell and his brothers, Maredudd and Rhys, came to the castle of Llanstephan and they fought stoutly and many of their enemies were slain and others wounded'; AC *s.a.* 1147 ... castellum Kermerdin adquisierunt *necnon Lanstephan ceperunt* (MS. B), Cayrmerdin inuaserunt et ceperunt *necnon et castellum de Landestephan* (MS. C).

54 25 **William fitz Hai**: MS. Gwilyam vab *Hay*, RB Gwilim ap *Haet* (MS. P, *Aed* MSS. M, R, T), BS William o'r *Hay*, 'William of Hay.' BS has certainly blundered. Above *s.a.* 1136 (see note on 51.36) Pen. 20 mentions a *Gwilym vab Orc* (RB Gwilym ap *Oitt*, BS William vab *Oit*) acting, as here, in combination with 'the sons of Gerald,' i.e. William and Maurice fitz Gerald. In this present instance Lloyd, HW ii. 502, note 64, identifies *Gwilyam vab Hay* with *Willelmus filius Hay*, a son of Nest's, who was lord of St. Clears. Cf. *A History of Carmarthenshire*, i. 142. It is possible, however, that the same person is meant in both instances.

55 27-8 **... and gladness**: It is to be noted that AC puts the capture of Dinwileir, the death of Rhun, and the capture of Mold in the annal for 1147. Lloyd, however, accepts 1146 as the date of these three events: see HW 501, 492, 491 respectively.

56 10-11 **and there they called to them the men of the land**: MS. *ac yno galw a orugant law gwyr y wlat*. The italicized words have been retraced by a later hand, who occasionally makes mistakes. At present no *y* (which one would expect) can be seen between *orugant* and *law*: cf. RB a galu a wnaethant *y law* gwyr y wlat. Pen. 20 [*l*]*law gwyr* might possibly be interpreted as 'dejected men' (on *llaw*, 'small,' 'sad,' 'dejected' see CA 87, 186, 258, *Y Beirniad* vi. 213, vii. 187, viii. 259, PKM 271), but RB is against this. It is possible that the preposition *y* has been covered over by the retraced *orugant*, or that *galw law* is an older form (without preposition) of *galw y law*.

56 15 **Morfran, abbot of Whitland**: MS. Morvran abat *y Tygwȳn* (all the letters retraced by a later hand); RB Moruran abbat *y Ty Gwyn*;

page line

BS Morvran abbat *y Ty Gwyn*. Lloyd rightly finds it difficult to accept this reading, which is found in the three versions, HW ii. 490, note 14: '... it is a wildly improbable assumption that a Cistercian abbot, in the early days of that order's austerity, should have held a castle for a Welsh prince sixty miles from the monastery he ruled. The difficulty is solved if we suppose the true form to be "Y Tywyn" and Morfran to be the head of the "clas" at that place.' See also ib. i. 206 and note 57. It is to be noticed, however, that Pen. 20 has *y Tygwȳn* with the *Ty* and the *gwȳn* not separated, so that it may represent Old Welsh *Tiguinn* = Tywyn, but since the same scribe in the same MS. (73*b*, 23) has *y Tywȳn* for *Tywyn* it is almost certain that his *y Tygwȳn* is for *Y Ty Gwynn*. In any case it would be easy to confuse *Tiguinn* (= Tywyn) with *Ty Gwynn*. But that Lloyd is absolutely correct in his assumption here is proved by a reference in a poem by Llywelyn Fardd (*Hen Gerddi Crefyddol*, ed. Henry Lewis, xxxv. l. 60, p. 86) to Morfran as abbot of the 'clas' of Cadfan in Merioneth, i.e. of Tywyn. That Morfran should be a warrior as well as abbot does not surprise us when we remember Giraldus's story (*Itinerarium Kambriae* ii. cap. 4: Rolls 121) about the lay abbot of Llanbadarn 'cum lancea longa praecedentem,' accompanied by a veritable war-band.

56 24 **Henry, son of king Henry**: ctr. RB *Robert* Jarll vab Henri vrenhin, 'earl *Robert*, son of king Henry'; BS *Robert* iarll, 'earl *Robert*'; AC *s.a.* 1149 *Robertus* comes Henrici regis filius (MS. B), *Robertus* comes *frater* Henrici regis (MS. C). The reference is to Robert of Gloucester, son of Henry I, and Pen. 20 *Henri* is wrong. Note the variants in MSS. B and D.

57 1–2 **in the island of Britain**: so too RB, but ctr. BS yn *Gymre*, 'in Wales.' Here again we have variant translations of *Britannia*. Cf. on 10.3 and 12.30.

57 4–6 **And Cadwaladr ... Cadwgan, his son**: so too RB and BS, but ctr. AC *s.a.* 1151 Catwaladrus castellum Llan Ristut edificavit, et *Catwano* filio suo cum parte sua de Keredigean dedit. AC *Catwan[us]* = *Cadfan* is correct: cf. below *s.a.* 1150 *Cadfan*, son of Cadwaladr.

57 8 **Cyfeiliog**: emend Pen. 20, 98*a*, 28—98*b*, 1 *ogyveilyawc* (which is here a reconstructed text) to *gyveilyawc*, for MSS. B, C, D read *gyveilioc*, *Gyveiliawc* and *Gyfeilioc* respectively. Cf. RB ac y rodes *Gyveilawc* and AC *s.a.* 1151 dedit *Keweilauc* (MS. B, *Keveilauc* MS. C), but ctr. BS rodes ... *y ran o Kyveilyawc*, 'he gave ... *his portion of Cyfeiliog*.'

57 15–6 **Cadfan, son of Cadwaladr, his uncle**: MS. Kadvan vab Kadwaladyr y *ewythr*; RB Catuan vab Catwaladyr, y *gefynderw*, 'Cadfan ap Cadwaladr, his *first-cousin*'; BS Catwaladyr, *y kevynderw*, 'Cadwaladr, his *first-cousin*'; AC *s.a.* 1153 Catwanum *patruelem suum* (MS. B), Caduan *consobrinum suum* (MS. C). There is no real inconsistency between the texts here. In Pen. 20 *y ewythyr* is in apposition to Cadwaladr, who was Hywel ab Owain's *uncle*, and in RB *y gefynderw* is in apposition to Cadfan, who was Hywel's first-cousin. The *consobrinum* of MS. C of AC is therefore correct. The *patruelem suum* of MS. B probably derives from an earlier text which read *Catwanum filium Catwaladri patruelis sui* and which therefore agreed with Pen. 20. BS is corrupt and should be emended to [*Catuan vab*] *Catwaladyr, y kevynderw*, with *y kevynderw* in apposition to *Catuan* (as in RB), or to *Catuan, y kevynderw*. Cf. on 57.4–6.

page	line	
57	28	**castle ... at Pen-gwern in Llanfihangel**: This is the same castle as Castell Gwallter: see OP iv. 489.
57	37	**Aberllwchwr**: MS. *Llychwr* with *Aber* written in the margin; RB and BS *Aber Llychwr*; AC *s.a.* 1154 castellum *Lychur* (MS. B only).
57	38	**Dinefwr**: MS. *Dinehwr* (*Dinevwr* MSS. B, D, as above 54.18); RB *Dinwileir*, BS *Dinwyleyr*. Emend Pen. 20 to *Dinweileir*: see note on 54.18.
57	39	**the castle of Humfrey's son**: so too BS, but RB Gastell *Hwmffre*, 'Humfrey's Castle.' After its repairing in this year by Hywel ab Owain, this castle was known as *Castell Hywel*, 'Hywel's Castle.' See OP iv. 493, No. 15.
58	6	**Cyfeiliog**: MS. *Kyveilyawc* (*Klynnawc* MSS. B, C, D); RB *Kyfeilawc*; BS *Kelynnawc*. MSS. B, C, D of Pen. 20 and BS give the correct reading, but since both Pen. 20 and RB give *Kyveilyawc* (*Kyfeilawc*), the error may derive from the original Latin. See HW ii. 469, note 25.
58	14	**Ystrad Cyngen**: See B viii. 45, where Lloyd argues that this place was somewhere in Northern Ceredigion.
58	21-3	**In that year prince Henry ... Ranulf, earl of Chester**: David, son of Maelcoluim, king of the Scots, died on 24 May, 1153, and Ranulf, earl of Chester, died on 16 December, 1153, but it was on 6 January, 1153 (by modern reckoning) that prince Henry reached England, and this would be in 1152 if the beginning of the year were reckoned from 25 March. The inclusion of this entry *s.a.* 1153 in Pen. 20, RB and BS—and so presumably in the common Latin original—is correct only if the beginning of the year is reckoned from 25 December. The reference below, *s.a.* 1154, is to Henry's later arrival in England on 11 December, 1154, as is shown by the words 'a second time' in Pen. 20.
58	24-5	**about the Calends of Winter**: These words are not in RB and BS. AC tells us that Cadell's pilgrimage was to Rome, but it is placed in 1157 = 1156: Catell *Romam* peregrinacionis causa perrexit (MS. B) Cadell filius Grifud *Romam* peregre proficiscitur (MS. C). See HW ii. 503, and note 67.
58	30	**Gruffudd**: so too BS, but RB *Griffri*.
58	35	**Llandaff**: MS. *Llanndaf*, RB *Llann Daf*, BS *Llandaf*. But Geoffrey (of Monmouth)—the bishop whose death is here recorded—was bishop, not of Llandaff, but of St. Asaph (*Llanelwy*). We know that Nicholas ap Gwrgant was bishop of Llandaff from 1148 to 1163. 'Llandaff' of the three Welsh versions is an error which must derive from the Latin original. Cf. Lloyd, 'Geoffrey of Monmouth,' EHR lvii, 466: 'It can only be conjectured that the scribe who at this time entered up the chronicle, probably at Llanbadarn Fawr, near Aberystwyth, had heard of the death of a Welsh bishop in England, but was misinformed about his see.' See also HW ii. 525, note 154.
59	1	**raised a ditch**: MS. dyrchauel *ffos*; BS y gwnaeth yno *fos a chastell*, 'he made there *a ditch and castle*'; AC *s.a.* 1157 *fossam* fecit (MS. B), *fossam Aberdevi* fecit (MS. C). Ctr. RB ac yno *y gorffwyssawd*, 'and there he halted.'

page line

59   6   **was built**: RB *kyssegrwyt*, BS *kyssegrwit*, 'was consecrated.'

59   6   **Toirrdelbhach**: i.e. Toirrdelbhach Ua Conchobuir: see AU *s.a.* 1156.

59   9   **to Chester**: RB hyt *ymaestir* Caerlleon, 'to the *open land* of Chester'; BS hyt ym *Morva* Kaer Lleon, 'to the *sea-marsh* of Chester'; AC *s.a.* 1158 ad *campestria* Cestriae (MS. B only).

59   14   **raised a ditch**: RB a pheri dyrchauel *clodyeu*, 'and he had *ditches* raised'; BS a dyrchavel *klodiev mawr*, 'and he raised *great ditches*'; AC *s.a.* 1158 *vallum* erexerunt (MS. B only).

59   15   **he sent his host**: RB *rannv* y lu a oruc, 'he *divided* his host'; BS anvon tywyssogyon, jeirll a barwnieit, a llu mawr gantunt hyt yno, 'he sent leaders, earls and barons, and a great host with them thither.' Pen. 20 and BS must have translated *dimisit* where RB has translated *diuisit*.

59   17   **along the shore**: MS. *ar hyt y traeth* added in the margin by the early corrector: cf. RB *ar hyt y traeth*; AC *s.a.* 1158 via littorea. These words are not in BS.

59   25-6   **he left that position**: RB adds a chilyaw *hyt y lle a elwit Kil Ywein*, 'and retreated as far as *the place that was called Cil Owain*.' AC *s.a.* 1158 merely says: et in loco tutiori se recepit (MS. B only). It is clear that RB wanted to connect the place called Cil Owain with this battle, no doubt believing that it was so called after this retreat by Owain. Lloyd, however, has shown, HW ii. 498, note 52, that this place-name is found in *Domesday* and so cannot have had any connection with Owain Gwynedd. Hence the RB addition probably incorporates an unfounded explanation of Cil Owain. Pen. 20 and BS (which do not have this detail) are more reliable.

59   27-8   **Tâl Llwyn Pynna**: MS. *Tallwynpynna*; RB [yn] *Hal* (MS. P, *Thal* MS. M, *Tal* MSS. R, T) *Llwyn Pina*; BS *Tal Llwyn Pennant*. AC *s.a.* 1158 ad Ruthlan progreditur, *ibi*que castra metatus est. See HW ii. 498, note 53, where it is pointed out that Powel identified the place with Bryn-y-pîn above Kinmel. See also OP iv. 554.

59   34   **in the ships**: MS. *ene lloghen* added in the margin by the early corrector. That it is correct is proved by RB yn y llogeu, 'in the ships'; BS ——.

59   36-7   **and other churches**: MS. *ac eglwiss[eu] ereil* added in the margin by the early corrector. Cf. RB a llawer o eglwysseu ereill, 'and many other churches.' BS ——. We know from Giraldus Cambrensis (*Itinerarium Kambriae*, ii. Cap. 7: Rolls 130) that one of 'the other churches' was Llandyfrydog.

60   10   **Owain**: RB calls him 'Owain *Wan*,' i.e. Owain *the Weak*. The epithet appears to be authentic: see J. A. Bradney, *Llyfr Baglan*. London, 1910.   11, note 4.

60   32-4   **And on the second day ... the following day**: RB A gwedy hynny, *dydgweith* kynn Kalan Meheuin, y doeth y Ystrat Meuryc. A *thrannoeth dyw Calan* Meheuin . . ., 'And after that, *a day* before the Calends of June, he came to Ystrad Meurig. And on the following day,

R

page line

the Calends of June ... (or conceivably, "And on the day following the Calends of June").' Pen. 20 'the second day from the Calends' and RB 'one day before the Calends' are alternative ways of expressing 'the day before the Calends,' corresponding respectively to the Latin 'ij Kal.' and 'pridie Kal.' Cf. on 19.5.

60 35 **and the castle of the Dyfi**: RB a chastell *Aber Dyvi*, 'and the castle of Aberdyfi'; BS a *chastell Humfrey ar Dyvi*, 'and Humfrey's Castle on the Dyfi'; AC *s.a.* 1159 castellum *Aberdiwy* (MS. B only). On the site of 'the castle of the Dyfi' see OP iv. 486–87. BS has blundered: 'Humfrey's Castle' (or Castell Gwallter) was distinct from 'the castle of the Dyfi': see above on 57.28.

61 2 **and Rhys took the castle**: RB is more detailed: Ac y doeth Rys attunt ac y goresgynnawd y castell, 'And Rhys came to them and he overcame the castle.' This is in closer agreement with AC *s.a.* 1159 Familia ergo Resi in ultione praedae suae castellum Llanamdewri obsedit, quod Resus *adveniens* primo impetu cepit (MS. B only).

61 14–5 **And after Rhys had given him hostages**: RB A gwedy *mynych wrthwynebu* o Rys a'e wyr *idaw*, 'And after Rhys *had frequently opposed him*'; BS A *chymryt gwystlon* y gan Rys ap Grufud, 'and *he* (*sc.* the king) *took hostages* from Rhys ap Gruffudd.' Pen. 20 and BS give a better sense than RB. See HW ii. 507, note 77. RB seems to have read some form of *obstare* or *obsistere* for some form of *obsides*.

61 24 **Cefn Rhestr Main**: MS. *Keuyn Restyr Mein* (*Yr Escair Main* MSS. B, D, *Egyr Main* MS. C); RB *Keuyn Restyr*; BS *Kyven Rychtir Main*; AC *s.a.* 1160 ad *Resterwein* (MS. B only). It is almost certain that RB has dropped a final element in the place-name and that the Pen. 20 form is correct: at least, it has a meaning, 'the Ridge of the Line of Stones.' Lloyd, B vii. 39, has pointed out that 'an alignment of at least eight stones, pointing east and west, may be traced on Mynydd Llanybydder, not far from Crugiau Edrid,' and concludes that 'we need look no further for the "Cefn Rhestr Main" of the chronicler.' [*Kynen Rychter mein* quoted by Lloyd, loc. cit. as the reading of Pen. MS. 18 (RB version) is incorrect, following the Rolls *Brut y Tywysogion*.]

61 27 **. . . Gruffudd**: After this Pen. 20 seems to have dropped a phrase, either in transcription or in translation, for RB and BS are in substantial agreement in making a slight addition: RB a diruawr luossogrwyd o uarchogyon a phedyt gyt ac wynt, 'and a mighty multitude of horsemen and foot-soldiers along with them'; BS a lluoed mawr ganthunt, 'and great hosts with them.'

61 27 **Dinwileir**: MS. *Dynwylleir*; RB *Dinefwr* (MS. P, *Dinwileir* MSS. M, R, T); BS *Dynwylleir*; AC *s.a.* 1160 *Denweileir* (MS. B only). See notes on 54.18; 57.38.

61 32 **at Winchester**: the place of Madog's death is not given in RB, BS, nor AC. Lloyd, HW ii. 508, note 83, says that he can find 'no authority for the statement of Powel . . . that Madog died at Winchester, except the narrative of Rhys Cain . . .' There can be no doubt that Powel's authority was Pen. 20, but even with this authority it is very

page line

doubtful whether one can accept the statement. *A priori*, one would not expect Madog to die at Winchester, so far from Powys; nor is there any suggestion that that happened, in the elegy to him by Gwalchmei (MA 147-49). Moreover, it is observable that Pen. 20 on more than one occasion has *Caer Wynt*, 'Winchester,' where it is manifestly wrong. See the note on 62.5-6 below, where Pen. 20 gives *Caer Wynt* but RB *Wickwm* (MS. P, *Wiccw* MSS. R, T) and AC *s.a.* 1161 *Wirgonia* (MS. B only). See also notes on 71.4; 72.27; 117.35.

61 36-7 **generous and kind ... the meek**: ctr. RB vfuyd a hegar a hael wrth y tlodyonn, huawdyr wrth yr ufydyon, 'meek and kind and generous towards the poor, *pleasant towards* the meek.' This suggests that Pen. 20 has dropped some words corresponding to RB 'pleasant towards,' and that the text should be emended: hael a hygar ac vvid oed wrth dlodyon ac [huawdyr wrth] vuydyon.

62 5 **through comrades of his**: RB a thrwy y getymeithon a'e deulu, 'and through his comrades and his war-band'; BS o gyghor y wyr a'y vrodyr maeth, 'through the counsel of his men and his foster-brothers'; AC *s.a.* 1161 per collectaneos et familiares suos (MS. B only).

62 5-6 **from Winchester**: o *Gaer Wynt* o hyt nos (*o hyt nos*, 'by night' added by the early corrector of the text, but the corresponding words are in RB, BS, and AC); RB o *Wickwm* (MSS. P, M, o *Wiccw* MSS. R, T); BS ——; AC *s.a.* 1161 de *Wirgonia* (MS. B only). Lloyd, HW ii. 511, note 92, accepts AC *Wirgonia* as an error for *Wigornia*, 'Worcester.' Pen. 20 *Caer Wynt* is suspect here as elsewhere in the text: at least, it is unlikely that Einion Clud's war-band could have ventured as far as Winchester. It may be suggested that the translator of Pen. 20 read *Wītonia* for *Wytynton* (cf. AC *s.a.* 1223) or some such form of Whittington. This supposition, however, would not account for the RB forms *Wickwm* and *Wiccw*. At first sight, *Wickwm* suggests *Wickham* (Berks), *Wycomb* (Leics.) or *Wycombe* (Bucks), but not one of these is likely as the place of Einion Clud's imprisonment. It must have been some place near the Welsh border, and that is why Lloyd followed AC *Wirgonia*. On the principle of the *durior lectio* there is much to be said for the RB forms. RB *Wiccw* (MSS. P, M) suggests some such form as 'de *Wicco*' in the original Latin, and *Wiccus* may have been a Latinized form of *Wich*, on the borders of Cheshire and the Maelor district of Flintshire. On *Wich* see HW ii. 491, note 20.

For *Caer Wynt*, 'Winchester,' in the text as an error for Worcester see on 117.35.

62 7-9 **In the year ... A year after that**: MS. Blwydyn o oet Krist trugeint a chant a mil *ny bu dym*. *Blwydyn wedy hynny y bu varw*, with the words in italics in the hand of the 'early corrector' of the text. It is fairly obvious that the original scribe wrote: Blwydyn o oet Krist trugeint a chant a mil [oed pan vv] varw Angharat, 'The year of Christ [was] one thousand one hundred and sixty [when] Angharad died.' The corrector realised that the original scribe had omitted a blank annal and so he altered the text: he erased [oed pan vv] and wrote *ny bu dym* over the erasure, then added *Blwydyn* outside the column (to the right) and *wedy hynny y bu* in the margin. The above details are given because the

page line

annal for 1160 (= 1161) is not given in RB, which reads (much as Pen. 20 did before the correction): Trugein mlyned a chant a mil oed oet Crist pann uu varw Agkarat, 'One thousand one hundred and sixty was the year of Christ when Angharad died.' Now BS puts Angharad's death in 1161 (= 1162), but under 1160 (= 1161) it has an entry *which does not refer to Welsh events*: gwedy marw Adrianus y barnwit y goruodedigaeth o Freinc a Lloegyr y Alexander, ac y dyrchafwyt yn Bap, 'after the death of Hadrian the supremacy of France and England was adjudged to Alexander and he was raised to be Pope.' AC (MS. B only) has a blank *annus* for 1162 (= 1161).

62 10 **Maredudd**: MS. *Maredud* with *al*[*ias*] *Meuryg* written by a later hand in the margin. RB *Meuryc*, BS *Meuric*. RB and BS give the correct form here, and Pen. 20 *Maredud* is probably due to a wrong extension of a contraction.

62 12 **Tafolwern**: MS. 108*a*, 17–8 kastell *Walwern*; RB castell *Dafalwern*; BS castell *Walwern*. It appears that the translators of Pen. 20 and BS read 'castellum *de Walwern*.' Ctr. MS. 114*a*, 5–6 kyrchu *Dywalwern*. For the error underlying the Pen. 20 and BS versions cf. CW 9, *s.a.* 1212 castellum *de Waluernia* apud Kereynaun . . . obsederunt; AC *s.a.* 1168 castellum *de Walwern* ceperunt. The older forms of *Tafolwern* are *Dywalwern* and *Dafalwern*: see HW ii. 510, note 88, OP iv. 593–94, and G s.v. 'Dywalwern.'

62 12 **And because of that**: so too RB Ac o achos hynny, 'And because of that,' referring presumably to the event recorded in the preceding sentence, i.e. the loss of Tafolwern. Ctr. BS Ac am hynny y kymyrth Owein ap Grufud tristwch yndaw *am varw y vam* hyt na allei dim y digrifhau, 'And therefore Owain ap Gruffudd conceived sorrow *because of the death of his mother* [i.e. Angharad, wife of Gruffudd ap Cynan] so that nothing could give him pleasure.' BS is almost certainly more correct here than Pen. 20 and RB, and has been followed by Lloyd, HW ii. 488 and note 7. Even in Pen. 20 and RB the sentence describing Owain's sorrow suggest a more personal loss than that of a castle, and are in close agreement with the description of his sorrow after the death of his son Rhun, *s.a.* 1146. It is probable that originally the sentence beginning 'And because of that . . .' followed immediately after the sentence referring to the death of Angharad.

62 22 **Llanidloes**: MS. hyt *Licdoef*. (*yn Gorddwr Hafren* MSS. B, C, D); RB ——; BS hyt yn *Gordwr Hafren*. Lloyd, B xi. 49 regards *Licdoef*. as an error for *Licdoef*. = Llanidloes. See his note, loc. cit. on 'Gorddwr Hafren,' also OP iii. 206, note 3, iv. 611–14. For other references see G s.v. 'gordwf(y)r.'

63 30–1 **into the wood of Dyffryn Ceiriog**: so too RB, but BS a dyuot . . . am ben *coet Aber Keiriauc*, 'and came . . . against the wood of *Aberceiriog*.' See HW ii. 516, note 117.

63 40–64 1 **two sons of Owain's . . . sons of Rhys**: RB deu uap Ywein Gwyned, [Katwallawn] a Chynwric, a Maredud ap yr Arglwyd Rys, 'two sons of Owain Gwynedd, Cadwallon and Cynwrig, and Maredudd son of the Lord Rhys'; BS deu vab Owein vrenhin, Catwallawn a Kynwric a Moredud meibion Rys, 'two sons of king Owain, Cadwallon and

page line

Cynwrig, and Maredudd, sons [*sic*] of Rhys.' BS agrees with RB if *meibion* (sons) of the former is emended to *mab* (son), and with this emendation RB and BS seem to be more correct than Pen. 20. Giraldus Cambrensis's description of Cynwrig ap Rhys in 1188 (*Itinerarium Kambriae*, ii. Cap. 4: Rolls vi. 119) shows that he cannot have been amongst the hostages blinded in 1165. Because of this and because we have no reference to a son of Owain called Rhys, it is likely that Pen. 20 'deu vab y Ywein, *Rys a* Chadwallawn, a Chynwric a Mared'. *meibyon Rys*' is a wrong translation for 'deu vab y Ywein, *sef* Cadwallawn a Chynwric a Mared'. *vab* Rys,' 'two sons of Owain, namely Cadwallon and Cynwrig, and Maredudd *son* of Rhys.' MS. C of AC tells us that the hostages who were maimed were twenty-two in number: *obsides eorum numero xxii oculis et testiculis privavit*.

64   14-8   **In that year ... by his manners**: This entry, which is in RB also, is not in BS and AC.

64   25   **Basingwerk**: MS. Dinas Bassin. The reference is to the fortification there, not to the monastery. See OP iv. 562, 574.

64   26-7   **In that year ... territory**: for the expulsion of Diarmaid MacMurchadha, king of Leinster, see AU *s.a.* 1166, where it is shown (ii. 153, note 8) that the date of his expulsion was Monday, 1 August.

65   4-5   **and after taking the castle ... the victory**: RB A gwedy cael y castel[l] a'e torri a'e losci, *a chastell Prystatun* heuyt y gyt ac ef ...', 'And after taking the castle (*sc*. Rhuddlan) and destroying and burning it, *and also the castle of Prestatyn along with it* ...'; BS Ac yno y buant tri mis yn adeiliat castell gvedy torri y castell a gafsant yno a'y llosgi *a chastell Prestattvn* ..., 'And there (*sc*. Rhuddlan) they were three months building a castle, after the castle which they found there had been destroyed and burnt, *and the castle of Prestatyn*'. The reference to the castle of Prestatyn in RB and BS is not in Pen. 20 and AC. See HW ii. 518, note 123.

65   7-8   **Gwrgenau, abbot of Llwythlawr**: RB Gwrgeneu abat, 'abbot Gwrgenau'; BS Ac y llas nei y Wrgenev abat ..., 'And a nephew of abbot Gwrgenau was slain ...' No other reference to a place called *Llwythlawr* is known, although the form of the name could be compared with *Llwythyfnwg*, the name of a small district to the north-east of Elfael. It may be suggested, however, with a fair degree of certainty that *Llwythlawr* is an error for some form of *Llwytlaw*, 'Ludlow.' Except for the omission of the place-name, RB agrees with Pen. 20, but BS seems to have mistranslated, thus omitting the reference to the death of Gwrgenau himself.

65   13   **his kinsman**: Robert fitz Stephen and Rhys were first-cousins, Gruffudd ap Rhys (Rhys's father) and Nest (Robert's mother) being brother and sister. Below *s.a.* 1171 (p. 67) Robert fitz Stephen is explicitly described as Rhys's first-cousin.

65   15   **Meurig ab Addaf**: so too RB, but BS Meurig ap Adam *o Buellt*, 'Meurig ab Addaf *of Buellt*'; AC *s.a.* 1170 Meuruc filius Adam *filius Seisil de Buellt* (MS. B), Meuric filius Adaf (MS. C).

65   15-6   **by his own first-cousin**: so too RB and BS, but AC a *consanguineo* suo.

page	line	
65	22	**in the month of December**: RB mis *Tachwed*, 'in the month of November.' BS does not mention the month. RB is correct: Owain Gwynedd died on 25 November, 1170. See HW ii. 522, note 136.
65	27	**A year after that**: Thomas Becket was murdered on 29 December, 1170. The event is placed in 1171 by the chronicler, reckoning the beginning of the year from 25 December.
65	29	**was slain**: BS alone gives the names of the murderers: Richard Bryton a Hugus Normyrvile [*sic*] a William Traci a Reinallt vab yr Arth 'Richard Breton and Hugh Normerville (*recte* Morville) and William Tracy and Reginald fitz Urse.'
65	34	**earl Richard, son of Gilbert Strongbow**: RB Rickert, *iarll Strifug*, vap Gilbert Bwa Kadarnn, 'Richard, earl *of Chepstow*, son of Gilbert Strongbow'; BS Richard vab Gilbert Stragbow, *jarll Amhwydic*, 'Richard son of Gilbert Strongbow, *earl of Shrewsbury*'; AC *s.a.* 1171 Ricardus *comes de Striguil* (Strugul MS. C).
65	38–9	**bringing into it a large fleet**: MS. 180*a*, 3–5 gan dwyn *llȳges* vawr ydi. Pen. 20 here disagrees with RB and BS, and has almost certainly mistranslated: RB trwy wneuthur *diruawr aerua*, 'committing a *great slaughter*'; BS ac a wnaeth *lladva vaur* yn Dulyn, 'and he made *a great massacre* in Dublin.' RB and BS are confirmed by AC civibus occisis (MS. B) and AU *s.a.* 1170 Tucsat dono ar for Gallaibh Atha-cliath ꝛ Puirt-lairgi ꝛ tuctha tra áir ímda forrusum, 'However, they inflicted *slaughter* upon the Foreigners of Dublin and Waterford, and, on the other hand, many slaughters were inflicted upon themselves.' The translator of Pen. 20 seems to have read some form of *classis* for some form of *clades*.
66	20–1	**to subdue Owain Cyfeiliog, his son-in-law**: MS. 181*a*, 5–7 y darystw̄g Ywein Kyveilyawc *ydaw*, with *gan y verch* added in the margin by the early corrector, for insertion after *ydaw*. The marginal addition shows that the corrector understood *ydaw* as *y daw*. If the addition is ignored the original text could mean either (*a*) to subdue Owain Cyfeiliog *to him* (i.e. under him) or (*b*) to subdue Owain Cyfeiliog, his son-in-law. The word *daw*, without any qualifying phrase, generally means the same as *daw gan uerch*, i.e. son-in-law. RB reads . . . am benn Owein Kyueilawc *y daw* ar ueder y darestwg, '. . . against Owain Cyfeiliog, *his son-in-law* with the intention of subduing him,' and here the syntax does not allow us to regard *y daw* as for *ydaw*, 'to him.' BS is more explicit: i daristwng Owein Kyveiliavc, *y dav gan y verch*, 'to subdue Owain Cyfeiliog, *his son-in-law*.' It is to be noticed that MSS. B, C, D of Pen. 20 omit *ydaw* and *gan y verch*,—rightly so for Owain Cyfeiliog's wife was Gwenllïan, daughter of Owain Gwynedd. Owain, therefore, was not a son-in-law of Rhys ap Gruffudd. However, Rhys ap Gruffudd's wife was Gwenllïan, daughter of Madog ap Maredudd, brother of Gruffudd ap Maredudd, Owain's father, i.e. Gwenllïan was Owain's first-cousin, and so Rhys ap Gruffudd and Owain were relations by marriage. Pen. 20 *ydaw* (read as *y daw*) and RB *y daw* could possibly mean his 'relation,' and so BS alone would be absolutely incorrect. If the marginal addition in Pen. 20 is ignored as a mistake and *ydaw* taken as the 3 sing. masc. of the conjugated preposition *i*, 'to' (which is often found with *darystwng*), there

NOTES

page line

is no reference to Owain as Rhys's son-in-law. It may be that the chronicler has confused Owain's wife Gwenllïan, daughter of Owain Gwynedd, with Rhys's daughter of the same name. In any case, T. F. Tout's statement in DNB that 'the prince of Powys (*sc.* Owain Cyfeiliog) had married Rhys's daughter' is based on the faulty text of the Welsh chronicle.

66   25   **Scotland**: RB *Ffreinc*, 'France'; BS ——. RB is correct: Henry returned from *France* on 3 August, 1171.

66   31   **fourteen hostages**: RB a *phetwar* gwystyl *ar hugeint*, 'and *twenty-four* hostages'; BS a xiiij o wystlon, 'and *fourteen* hostages.'

66   37   **Dyddgu**: RB *Agharat*, 'Angharad'; BS *Dudgu*. RB *Agharat* is a slip due to the occurrence of that name in the previous line. See HW ii. 545, note 47.

66   40   **and a mighty host**: MS. *a dirvaur lv* added in the margin by the early corrector of the text. Cf. RB a dirvawr lu gantaw, 'and a mighty host with him'; BS a llu maur ganthav, 'and a great host with him.'

67   10-1   **on the seventh day**: RB y *deudecuettyd*, 'on the *twelfth* day'; BS ——. RB is correct, for Pen. 20 says above that the king came to Pembroke 'on the *eleventh* day from the Calends of October.' The Pen. 20 translator has read *vii* instead of *xii*.

67   15-6   **eighty-six horses**: so too RB and BS, but it is said above that Rhys had promised three hundred horses.

67   36-7   **but in order to requite Rhys a second time**: RB namyn yr talu diolch y Rys a vei uwy no chynt, 'but in order to give thanks to Rhys that would be greater than before'; BS gan ev diolch y Rhys yn vaur, 'thanking Rhys greatly for them.' Apparently, the meaning is that the king let Rhys off with a tribute of thirty-six horses instead of the three hundred which he had promised and that this decrease in the tribute was the 'requital.'

68   19   **in the month of February**: RB vis *Mawrth*, 'in the month of March'; BS ——. Cadwaladr ap Gruffudd died on 29 February, 1172. RB is here incorrect. See HW ii. 550, note 67.

68   28-9   **the new town on the Usk**: RB y *castell newydd* ar Wysc, 'the *new castle* on the Usk'; BS y *castell newyd* ar Wysg, 'the *new castle* on the Usk.' Pen. 20 y *dref newyd* and RB (and BS) y *castell newyd* are obviously variant renderings of the Latin *Novum Burgum*. The place meant is Newport. See HW ii. 442, note 160.

69   1-3   **In the meantime . . . at Abergavenny**: RB Yg kyfwrwg hynny y delit Seisyll ap Dyfynwal a Ieuan ap Seissyll ap Ridit trwy dwyll y gann wyr y brenhin, *ac y carcharwyt* yg kastell Aber Geuenni, 'In the meantime Seisyll ap Dyfnwal and Ieuan ap Seisyll ap Rhiddid were siezed through treachery by the king's men, *and they were imprisoned in the castle of Abergavenny*'; BS Yn hynny mys Aust y cavas Seissil a[p] Dyvynwal a Jeuan ap Seissill ap Ririt castell Aber Gevenny o dwyll y gan wyr y brenhin, 'Thereupon, in the month of August, Seisyll ap Dyfnwal and Ieuan ap Seisyll ap Rhiryd took the castle of Abergavenny through treachery by the king's men.' BS has mistranslated.

page line

69 11 **In that year**: RB *Yn y ulwydyn honno a'r vlwydynn kyn no hi*, 'In that year *and the year before it.*' BS agrees with Pen. 20.

69 12 **a son**: BS alone gives his name as Meurig.

70 5 **of Caerleon**: RB *o Gwynllwg*, 'of Gwynllŵg'; BS ——. Below *s.a.* 1175 (p. 71, l. 3) Pen. 20 and BS read 'of Caerleon.'

70 18 **uncles**: RB *ewythdred*, 'uncles,' but BS *(a'y) gevynderiw*, '(and his) first-cousins'. Lloyd, HW ii. 551, note 72, has pointed out that in 1174 Dafydd ab Owain had neither 'uncles' nor 'first-cousins' on the male side, and he suggests that *ewythred* (Pen. 20 and RB) and *kevynderiw* (BS) are wrong translations of *nepotes* or some such word.

70 22 **Owain Pen-carn**: Lloyd, HW ii. 771, in his Genealogical Table for Gwynllŵg, gives the name as *Owain Pen Carwn*, following MS. R (with which MS. T agrees) of RB. MS. P of RB is correct: *Ywein Pen Carnn*. *Carwn* of MSS. R, T is derived from *Carun* (MS. M). The epithet *Pen-carn* is topographical and is to be equated with *Rhyd Ben-carn* and *Nant Pen-carn* mentioned by Giraldus Cambrensis, *Itinerarium Kambriae*, i. Cap. 6. For *Pen-carn* cf. CACW 219, 220. The epithet is omitted in BS.

70 30 **his uterine brother**: the adjective in Pen. 20 suggests that Dafydd and Rhodri were brothers by the same mother but not by the same father. RB, however, reads: *y vrawt vn vam vn tat ac ef*, 'his brother *by the same mother [and] by the same father* as he.' BS has *y vraut*, 'his *brother.*' RB is correct for Dafydd and Rhodri were sons of Owain Gwynedd by his second wife Cristin, daughter of Goronwy ab Owain. See HW ii. 549, and note 64.

70 41 **Einion Clud, his son-in-law**: So too RB and BS. But according to Giraldus Cambrensis, *Itinerarium Kambriae*, i. Cap. 1, it was Einion ab Einion Clud who had a daughter of Rhys to wife; and for chronological reasons, Lloyd, HW ii. 545, note 43, regards the latter as the more likely to be meant here. It appears that *filius Einon* was omitted after *Einon* in the Latin original underlying Pen. 20, RB, and BS.

71 4 **of Higher Gwent**: In the MS. 190*b*, 19-20, the scribe first wrote *o Gaer Wynt*, 'from *Winchester*': then he deleted *Gaer*, altered the *-y-* of *Wynt* to *-e-*, giving *Went*, and added *vchaf*. Here again we see the scribe (or the chronicler) revealing his preoccupation with Winchester. Cf. on 61.32; 62.5-6; 72.27.

71 19 **Clairvaux**: Pen. 20 *y Glynn Eglur*; RB *Cleryuawt* (MS. P), *Clerynawt* (MSS. M, R, T); BS *Clerval*. The RB forms are obvious corruptions of some form of Clairvaux. Pen. 20 *y Glynn Eglur*, 'the Clear Valley,' is a literal translation of *Clara Vallis*. Cf. 73.9.

71 31 **Each of the suitors**: RB *A phawb o'r kerdoryon ereill*, 'And all the other *minstrels*'; BS ——. There is no disagreement here between Pen. 20 and RB, for every minstrel would be sueing for gifts! See PKM 137, note on 17.21.

72 3-4 **For the archbishop of Canterbury . . . seat**: RB is more explicit: *Kanys y dyd kynntaf o'r kyghor y[d] achubassei archescob Iorc eistedua y gadeir o'r tu deheu y'r cardinal, yn y lle y dylyei ac y*

page line

gnottaei archescob Keint eisted, 'For on the first day of the council the archbishop of York had occupied the seat of the chair on the right-hand side of the cardinal, where the archbishop of Canterbury had a right and was wont to sit.' There appears to be an omission in Pen. 20. No corresponding details are given in BS.

72 17 **Cadwallon**: i.e. Cadwallon ap Madog. See HW ii. 567 and note 164. RB places the death of Cadwallon and the founding of the monastery at Caerleon in the same year as the war waged by the sons of Cynan against the Lord Rhys, i.e. in 1178. BS agrees in its chronology with Pen. 20.

72 17–9 **And a community ... Dewma**: MS. Ac y gossodet kouent y Nant Thirnon yn emyl Kerllion, with *yr hon a elwir Dewma* added by a later hand. In the margin the rubricator has written *pan doeth kouent gyntaf y vanachloc Devma*, 'when a community first came to the monastery of Dewma.' Cf. RB Ac y dechreuwyt couent y Manachloc *Gaer Llion, yr honn a elwid Deuma*, 'And a community was started in the monastery of *Caerleon, which was called Dewma*'; BS y prypheythwyt couent yn Nant Teyrnon, ereill a'y geilw *manachloc Devma, ereill manachloc Caerllion ar Wysg*, 'a community was established at Nant-teyrnon, *others call it the monastery of Dewma, others the monastery of Caerleon-on-Usk.*' The name Nant-teyrnon was later changed to Llantarnam. For the name 'Dewma' cf. *The Poetical Works of Lewis Glyn Cothi*. Oxford, 1837. i. 96, l. 60:

Llaw Domas ger llaw *Deuma*

and Peniarth MS. 132. 219 (RWM i. 827) Sir Vynyw plwyf *Devma* y penntref bach. See also OP iii. 293–94, note 4, iv. 456, note 1.

72 20–1 **In the year ... placed on record**: MS. 193*a*, 22–26 Pedwarugeīt mlynet a cant amil nybu dym a ellit ydwyn ar gof. Blwydyn gwedy hynny y bu va/rw Alexander Bab. The words *Pedwarugeīt ... va/* have been written by the early corrector over a deletion of the original text. Now RB reads: Petwar vgein mlyned a chant a mil oed oet Crist pann uu uarw Alexander Bap, 'One thousand one hundred and eighty was the year of Christ when Pope Alexander died,' thus omitting the annal for 1180 (true date), for Pope Alexander died in 1181. It is almost certain that the original text of Pen. 20 agreed with RB, but the corrector saw that a blank annal for 1180 had been omitted: hence his correction. Cf. 62.7–9. BS shows the annal for 1180: Anno Domini M.C.LXXX. Ny bu dim o'r a dyckit ar gof yn y vlwydyn honno, 'Anno Domini 1180. There was naught that might be placed on record in that year.' As elsewhere, the chronology of the Latin text used by the translator of BS seems to have been more correct than that of those upon which Pen. 20 and RB were based. It is observable that MS. B of AC has a blank *annus* for 1180.

72 22 **A year after that**: See the preceding note.

72 27 **from Gwent**: MS. o *Went*; RB y gann ieuegtit *Caer Wynt*, 'by the youth of *Winchester*'; BS o *Went*, 'from Gwent.' RB has read some form of *Wintonia* for *Guent* or *Gwencia*. Cf. above on 71.4.

72 29 **And Richard ... died**: according to modern reckoning, Richard died on 16 February, **1184**. In Pen. 20, RB and BS his death is recorded under 1183, which is correct according to the reckoning whereby the year began on 25 March.

page line

72 32 **A year after that**: RB adds *amgylch y Garawys*, 'about Lent'; BS ——.

73 6 **A year after that, died Pope Lucius**: Pope Lucius died on 25 November, 1185. In RB his death is recorded under 1185 (= 1186) and in BS under 1186. It appears, therefore, that this entry was misplaced in the original Latin.

73 8 **In that year**: RB adds *amgylch mis Gorffennaf*, 'about the month of July'; BS ——.

73 9 **Clairvaux**: MS *y Glynn Eglur*, 'the Clear Valley'; RB *y Dyfryn Gloew* (yn *Dyfryn Chwyt* MSS. M, R, T), 'the Bright Valley' [*Chwyt* of MSS. M, R, T being a corruption]; BS *Clervallis*. Pen. 20 *y Glynn Eglur* and RB *y Dyfryn Gloew* are variant literal renderings of *Clara Vallis*. Cf. above on 71.19.

73 12 **A year after that**: ctr. RB Yn y ulwydyn *honno*, 'In *that* year.' BS agrees with Pen. 20. The events recorded *s.a.* 1187 in Pen. 20 and BS, and *s.a.* 1186 in RB, are not recorded in AC.

73 12-3 **Strata Marcella**: MS. *Ystrat Marchell*; RB *Ystrat Marchell*; BS (y) *Trallwng*, 'Welshpool.' There is no disagreement between Pen. 20 and RB on the one hand, and BS on the other, Strata Marcella being close to Welshpool. See HW ii. 599, note 131. Cf. on 76.33.

73 15-7 **slain . . . Carreg Hofa**: RB and BS agree with Pen. 20 in making Gwenwynwyn and Cadwallon responsible for the murder of Owain ap Madog, their cousin, but Giraldus Cambrensis (Rolls vi. 142-3) makes their father Owain Cyfeiliog directly responsible for it. The text *O Oes Gwrtheyrn* (RBB 405) states that Owain was slain at 'Gwern y Vinogyl' (= Gwernyfigyn, near Carreg Hofa). Cf. HW ii. 565.

73 28-33 **A year after that . . . bondage**: Jerusalem was taken by the Saracens in 1187, but the event is placed in the annal for 1188 because it is linked with the following entry.

74 1-3 **the light and splendour . . . Gawain**: this encomium of Maelgwn ap Rhys is not in RB, but BS gives a shorter version: y gwr a oed blodev y marchogeon ac amdiffynnwr Deheubarth Kymre, 'the man who was the flower of knights and the defender of South Wales.'

74 5-9 **One thousand . . . Jerusalem**: The entries in CW start with the annal for 1190, and so from this point onwards we have many long Latin passages which correspond closely to the Welsh chronicles and which in part, like certain passages in AC, may be regarded as their Latin original. CW and AC are of help to determine the exact meaning of the Welsh in certain places.

74 17-8 **In that year . . . Canterbury**: Baldwin died on 19 November, 1190, but in Pen. 20, RB, BS, AC, and CW his death is recorded in the annal for 1191. This misplacement must go back to the original Latin.

74 18 **Einion of Porth**: so too RB and BS. CW *s.a.* 1191 Einion de Porta. Einion of Porth is the same as Einion ab Einion Clud: see HW ii. 567 and note 163. Lloyd, HW ii, 585, note 54, suggests that the brother who murdered Einion was Gwallter ab Einion Clud.

NOTES

page line

74 19 **Nevern**: MS. 197*a*, 18 kastell *Nyner* (emend to *Nyuer*), RB castell *Niuer*; BS castell *Dyneuur*; AC castellum *de Newer* (MS. B, de *Kemmer* MS. C); CW *s.a.* 1192 *Dynneuore*. *Kemmer* of MS. C of AC is an error, so too BS *Dyneuur* and CW *Dynneuore*, which reflect the Latin castellum *de Niuer*: cf. the reading of AC, MS. B. That *Nyuer*, 'Nevern,' is the correct reading here is proved by Giraldus Cambrensis, *Itinerarium Kambriae*, ii. Cap. 2 (Rolls vi. 111–12); there in recording the same event the castle is called castrum ... apud *Nanhever* and castrum ... de *Nanhever*. Nanhyfer is from *Nant Nyuer*. Cf. above on 4.28.

74 32–3 **to the queen and the servants of the king**: RB ymedyant swydogyon y brenhin a'r *teyrnnas*, 'into the hands of the officers of the king and *the realm*'; BS ——; AC ——; CW *s.a.* 1193 reddere ... *regine et regis officialibus*. Pen. 20 agrees with CW, but RB must have read *regis et regni* for CW *regine et regis*.

74 35 **the son of Godred**: RB Gwrthrych, 'Godred'; BS o nerth meibion *Godrich*, 'through the help of the *sons* of Godred.' In considering the RB version it is noticeable that the original scribe of Pen. 20 wrote 'drwy ganhorthwy *Gothrych*' (thus agreeing with RB), but the early corrector of the text added *mab* in the margin for insertion before *Gothrych*. Lloyd, HW ii. 588, note 70, shows that RB (and the original text of Pen. 20) cannot be correct, for Godred had died in 1187. Godred had two sons, Olaf and Reginald, and so there is something to be said for the BS reading. But since Rhodri ab Owain married Reginald's daughter, it appears that the corrected reading of Pen. 20 is the one to be preferred. Note, however, that MSS. B, C, D of Pen. 20 read *meibion*, 'sons,' probably under the influence of BS.

75 2 **with slings and catapults**: Both RB and BS state that the castle was taken *nos Nadolyc*, 'on Christmas eve.'

75 14 **Anarawd ap Rhys**: RB Anarawt ——; BS Anaraut ——, (Anarawd ap yr Arglwydd Rys MS. B); CW *s.a.* 1193 Anaraut filius *Eynaun*. Pen. 20 and MS. B of BS are almost certainly wrong in calling this Anarawd 'son of (the Lord) Rhys': Rhys had no son called by that name. RB and the main MS. of BS are correct in omitting *vab Rys*, but CW is more specific with its *filius Eynaun*. This Anarawd was a son of the Einion ab Anarawd who was slain in 1163 by Gwallter ap Llywarch. See above, *s.a.* 1163 (p. 62, l. 33). Anarawd ab Einion was slain in 1198: see below, p. 80, ll. 7–8.

75 14–5 **in his greed for worldly power**: Not in RB and BS, but cf. CW *s.a.* 1193 *presentis seculi ambicione ductus*.

75 18 **for his hostages**: not in RB, but cf. BS dros y wistlon, 'in return for his hostages.'

75 21 **was imprisoned**: The place of his imprisonment was the castle of Nevern: see *Itinerarium Kambriae*, ii. Cap. 2. CW records the capture of Rhys but does not mention the place of imprisonment.

75 22–3 **and he took ... Maelgwn**: not in RB, but cf. BS Ac y kymyrth meibion *Catwallawn* castell de Nyuer, yr hwn a oed eidiaw Maelgwn, a chastell Rayadyr Gwy ac a'y llosgassant, 'And *the sons of Cadwallon* took

the castle of Nevern, which belonged to Maelgwn, and the castle of Rhaeadr-gwy and they burned them.' AC, like Pen. 20, makes Hywel (not the sons of Cadwallon, as does BS) responsible for the capture of Nevern: Hoelus castellum *Newer* diruit (MS. B only). MSS. B, C, D of Pen. 20 read *Dinevwr* (cf. on 74.19), but in this case it cannot be due to collation with RB or BS.

75 26-8 **and the two sons ... Dafydd ab Owain**: RB *a Rodri ap Ywein a deu vab Kynan ap Ywein yn erbyn Dauid ap Ywein*, 'and Rhodri ab Owain and the two sons of Cynan ab Owain against Dafydd ab Owain'—which agrees with Pen. 20. Ctr. BS *a deu vab Kynan, Rodri ac Owein a dugant kyvoeth Dauid ap Owein*, 'and the two sons of Cynan, Rhodri and Owain, took the territory of Dafydd ab Owain.' BS has mistranslated. For this battle at Aberconwy see HW ii. 588, note 72. The 'two sons of Cynan' are Gruffudd and Maredudd. The account in *Itinerarium Kambriae*, ii. Cap. 8, places Rhodri on the side of Dafydd and not, as here in the chronicle, on the side of Owain and the two sons of Cynan.

75 35-7 **And in that year ... imprisoned**: This implies that Rhys and Maredudd were seized and imprisoned at Ystrad Meurig. Cf. RB *A'r rei hyny yn y vlwydyn hono a delit drwy dwyll y gan y tat yn Ystrat Mèuruc ac a garcharwyt*, 'And those, in that year, were seized through treachery by their father at Ystrad Meurig and were imprisoned.' Ctr. BS which says that they were imprisoned at Ystrad Meurig, implying that they were seized elsewhere: *Ac y delhijs ev tat wynt o dwill ac yn Ystrat Meuric y carcharwit wynt*, 'And their father seized them by treachery and they were imprisoned at Ystrad Meurig.' Lloyd, HW ii. 581 and note 35 has followed BS. However, CW *s.a.* 1195 is in agreement with Pen. 20 and RB: Qui (*sc.* Resus et Mareduch) iterum eodem anno a prefato patre suo *apud Estrathmevrych dolo capti sunt et incarcerati*.

76 1-2 **after the constable of the castle alone had escaped**: MS. 200a, 14-6 *wedy diāg kwnstabyl y castell ehunan*. Ctr. RB ... *ac y llosges hyt y prid eithyr y castell ehun*, ' ... and he burned it to the ground *except for the castle itself*'; BS *ac a'y llosgas ac a'y diffeithawd*, 'and he burned and ravaged it'; AC *s.a.* 1196, Resus filius Griffini Kermerdin *combussit*. RB is correct here and Pen. 20 has mistranslated, as is proved by CW *s.a.* 1196 *eamque* (*sc.* Kaermerdin) incendio solotenus destruxit, tantum *castelli apice euaso*. RB *castell* here seems to mean the keep. The translator of Pen. 20 arrived at his version by taking *apice* (< *apex*) to mean 'head,' 'chief' (as it could in certain contexts), i.e. in the case of a castle, the constable. In its context in CW, however, it means the keep.

76 3 **Colunwy**: MS. 200a, 18-9 *Kolunwy*; RB *Colwyn*; BS *Collvnwy*. The reference, in the sentence that follows, to Radnor suggests that RB *Colwyn* is the correct form here and that Pen. 20 and BS should be emended accordingly. This is confirmed by CW *s.a.* 1196 castellum *Coloin* obsedit. Cf. AC *s.a.* 1196 Resus filius Grifini Kermerdin combussit*, inde exercitum ad Herefordiae partes* ducens Redenor (MS. B). For other examples of confusion between *Colunwy* (= Clun) and *Colwyn*, the castle in Elfael, see 53.32-3; 90.22.

page line

76 15-6 **And forthwith ... Elfael**: RB is fuller: Ac yn y lle yd ymladawd a chastell Paen yn Elvael a blifieu a magneleu ac y kymhellawd y ymrodi, 'And forthwith he laid seige to Painscastle in Elfael with catapults and engines and forced it to surrender.' So too BS: Ac yna eiste wrth y castell a gwneithur ermygyon y ymlad a'r castell. 'And then he blockaded the castle and made engines to besiege the castle.' RB and BS are in closer agreement than Pen. 20 with CW *s.a.* 1196 Nec mora idem uir bellicus castellum Pain apud Eluael obsedit. Quod cum iam *bellicis machinamentis* exsuperans ad dedicionem cogi posset ...

76 19 **Hubert**: MS. *Hu*, 'Hugh'; RB *Henri*; BS *Henri*. These are wrong extensions of the contraction H. (= Hubertus). Cf. HW ii. 583, note 42. *S.a.* 1205, both Pen. 20 and RB give the correct form, *Hubert*.

76 33 **Strata Marcella**: so too RB, but BS y *Trallwng*, 'Welshpool'; CW *s.a.* 1196 *Strathflur*, 'Strata Florida.' There is no real disagreement between Pen. 20 and RB, on the one hand, and BS on the other. See on 73.12-3. CW *Strathflur* is probably incorrect.

76 34 **A year after that**: The long passage (in prose) which follows on the death of the Lord Rhys, should be compared with the corresponding passage in CW *s.a.* 1197. The similar passages in RB and BS are much shorter.

77 22-8 **And cruellest ... to the ground**: the original Latin seems to be represented by CW4, *s.a.* 1197: Hoc enim anno pestifero *Atropos, sororum seuissima* que nemini parcere gnara, cunctis mortalibus inuisa, magni uiri, scilicet Resi, exicium ausa est demoliri, quem instabilitatis mater Fortuna, nature condicionem hoc solo oblita, iugi celsitudine rote passa est permanere suoque ab etatis sue exordio benigno refouerat gremio. Ad tanti ergo obitum uiri accedens ... The translator appears to have read *soror* for *sororum* and *nature condicionis* for *nature condicionem*.

77 36-78 45 **... decoris**: The Latin eulogy and epitaph on the Lord Rhys which follow are not in RB and BS.

78 45 **Wallia ... dolore**: There is an echo of this last line in CW *s.a.* 1197 Heu! heu! iam Wallia uiduata dolet ruitura dolore.

79 23 **on the gallows**: BS adds: ac y [cl]atpwyt yn Y[strat Flur], 'and he was buried at Strata Florida.'

79 32 **from the French**: Except for a few words still legible on f. 162*b* the main text (MS. BM Cleopatra B.V.) of BS ends here. Henceforth all quotations from BS are taken from MS. B, i.e. NLW MS. 7006, 'The Black Book of Basingwerk.' There is reason to believe that Gutun Owain, who is said to have compiled the continuation of BS in NLW MS. 7006, has used versions of both the Pen. 20 and RB texts. Hence any quotation henceforward from BS does not necessarily confirm any particular reading in Pen. 20 or RB as it may be derived from them.

79 35-6 **which they had lost through the multitude of their sins**: Not in RB, but cf. CW *s.a.* 1198 ... restituere fines ac terminos sibi quondam *exigente peccatorum multitudine* subtractos ...

page line

79   39   **in Elfael**: MS *en Eluael* added in the margin by the early corrector of the text. RB ——; CW ——; BS *yn Elvel*.

79   39–43   **and for three weeks . . . their prison**: RB *a gwedy bot yn ymlad ac ef teir wythnos hayach heb wybot y damwein rac llaw*. A phan wybu y Saesson hyny, gollwg a wnaethant Ruffud ap Rys, a oed yg carchar gantunt, '. . . and after having laid siege to it for *nearly three weeks he did not know the future issue*. And when the Saxons learned that, they set free Gruffudd ap Rhys, who was in prison with them'; BS ac ymladd a chastell Paen yn Elvel *heb na bliviav na mangnelav* dair wythnos, 'and they laid siege to Painscastle in Elfael, *without slings or catapults*, for three weeks.' CW *s.a.* 1198 shows Pen. 20 has mistranslated (a mistranslation echoed in BS) and that there may be an omission in RB: castellum Paen obsederunt *per tres fere ebdomadas* cum magna et magna animi exultacione licet minus cauta suis iugiter *bellicis oppugnantes machinamentis*. Jgnorabaut namque quid sibi prepararent miserabiles rei euentus. Anglici enim hoc comperto exterriti Griffinum filium Resi, quem compeditum tunc tenebant, absoluerunt et tocius Anglie robur coadunari fecerunt.

80   5   **as God showed thereafter**: not in RB and BS, but cf. CW *s.a.* 1198 Anglici itaque hoc non ferentes *diuino, ut postea perpatuit, nutu* in eos impetum fecerunt . . . The Welsh translation of the italicized Latin words is not very close, to say the least.

80   7–8   **Anarawd ab Einion and Owain ap Cadwallon**: so too BS, but RB *Anarawt ap Ywein ap Katwallawn* (MSS. M, R, T) is corrupt and should be emended to Anarawt ap [Einon ac] Ywein ap Katwallawn. That Pen. 20 and BS are correct is proved by CW *s.a.* 1198 Arenaut filius Einaun et Owinus Rascop filius Cathwallaun. Emend *Rascop* to *Kascop* (modern Cascob).

80   9   **Rhobert ap Hywel**: MS. *Rotpert* vab Hywel; RB *Rodri* ap Hywel; BS *Rotpert* ap Howel. RB *Rodri* is an error due to a wrong extension of the contraction R. Cf. CW *s.a.* 1198 *Robertus* filius Hewel.

80   27   **by treachery**: MS. *drwy dwyll* added by the early corrector of the text. Not in BS, but cf. RB *drwy dwyll* and CW *s.a.* 1198 . . . *dolo optinuit*.

80   34–8   **the man . . . his deeds**: this encomium of Gruffudd ap Cynan ab Owain is not in RB and BS.

81   1–2   **In that year . . . Llynegwestl**: so too RB, but BS Yr vn vlwyddyn honno yr adeilodd *Madoc ap Gruffydd Maelor* vynachloc Lanegwest *y Nol yr Hen Groes yn Ial*, 'That same year *Madog ap Gruffudd Maelor* built the monastery of Llanegwestl *in the Meadow of the Ancient Cross in Iâl*.' The 'Ancient Cross' may have been the Pillar of Elise, for Edward Lhuyd, *Parochialia*, Pt. i. 123, refers to 'a small mount on *maes y Groes* [the field of the Cross] where Eliseg's pillar was erected.' See OP iv. 531–33. Phillimore, op. cit., 531–32, takes *yn ol* of BS to mean 'in or on the traces of,' but taken in conjunction with the name *Maes y Groes* (see above) it is much more likely to be for *y(n) Nol*, 'in the meadow.' The BS text of NLW MS. 7006 ('The Black Book of Basingwerk') was written by Gutun Owain, a poet of the second half of the fifteenth century. In his poems, he several times mentions the

page line

'ancient Cross': see E. Bachellery, *L'Œuvre Poétique de Gutun Owain*, VIII. 8; XXI. 24; XXII. 25; XXIV. 5; XXXVIII. 22. So also does Guto'r Glyn, another fifteenth century poet: Ifor Williams and J. Llywelyn Williams, *Gwaith Guto'r Glyn*. Cardiff. 1939. CXV. 6, 38; CXVI. 58.

81   5   **and Eifionydd**: not in RB and BS, but cf. CW *s.a.* 1201 cantredum qui uocatur Thlein *cum Euionyd* sibi uiriliter adquisiuit.

81   11   **was slain in Carnwyllion**: Maredudd ap Rhys was slain on 2 July by the followers of William de Londres, lord of Cydweli. Cf. AC *s.a.* 1201 Maredut filius Resi, inclitus adolescens, *a Francis de Kedweli die sancti Swithini occisus est*, cujus corpus ad Kedweli dilatum ibique juxta ecclesiam Sanctae Mariae humatum est (MS. B), Grifut filius Res obiit, et Maredut frater ipsius *ab hominibus de Kedweli occisus est* (MS. C).   CW *s.a.* 1201 states that he was slain *apud Carnewalleun*.

81   11-5   **a terror to his enemies . . . splendour of the world**: this encomium of Maredudd ap Rhys is not in RB and BS, but cf. CW *s.a.* 1201: suis honor, hostibus horror, omnibus amor, inter armatas acies tanquam fulgur egrediens cunctorumque mentibus uel spes unica uel metus existens, omnis honoris honos, decor et decus urbis et orbis.

81   17-9   **He was a wise, prudent man . . . snatched him away**: not in RB and BS, but cf. CW *s.a.* 1201 *uir magnus et prudens nimirum* in formam informia, in normam enormia queque reducens, fortunam ducens et se in anteriora protendens, tempora sibi contemperans et semper successibus instar, *et, ut sperabatur, Kambriae monarchiam in breui reformasset si non tam prepropere, tam premature, tam inopinate eum* sequenti festiuitate Sancti Jacobi apostoli *inuida fatorum series rapuisset*.

81   18   **the March of all Wales**: MS. 211*a*, 6-7 *ardal* holl Gymry. Here, as elsewhere in Pen. 20, *ardal* = the March. But CW *s.a.* 1201 reads 'Kambrie *monarchiam*': for the full quotation see the preceding note. The translator of Pen. 20 must have read *marchiam* for *mārchiam*.

81   20-2   **And to tell . . . strength**: CW *s.a.* 1201 makes it clear that 'the eminent father' is Gruffudd's father, the Lord Rhys: et, ut breui eloquio laudis ad cumulum multa concludam, egregio patri sola fuit etate, non virtute secundus.   The account of Gruffudd's death is much more sober in RB: there is nothing corresponding to 'And to tell . . . right and inheritance' in Pen. 20.

81   36   **In that year**: RB adds *amgylch Gwyl Veir Gyntaf yn y Kynhayaf*, 'about the first feast of Mary in autumn'; BS ——.

82   9   **the castle of Crogen**: RB *gastell*, 'a castle'; BS *gastell Krogen*, 'the castle of Crogen.'   On Crogen Castle and the seven townships here mentioned see Phillimore OP iv. 554, number 8.

82   13   **by diligence**: MS. drwy *astudrwyd*, which may represent *astutia* in the Latin original.   RB ——, AC ——, CW ——.

82   23-5   **Hywel . . . his brother**: AC *s.a.* 1199 gives a different account of Hywel ap Rhys's death: Houelus Seis Resi filius erga Pascha curiam regis Johannis adivit, et in reditu suo apud Strigiul aegritudine correptus obiit, *vel, at alii volunt, a Francis occisus est* (MS. B).   The italicized words

are probably an addition referring to some such account as that given in the *Brut*. See HW ii. 618, note 37, where Lloyd gives his reasons for regarding the account in the *Brut* as the more probably correct. His opinion is confirmed by the agreement of CW with the *Brut*: Howelus filius Resi Magni, iuuenis egregius, spes suorum, horror hostium, *dolo apud Kemmeys ab hominibus Mailgonis uulnere letali est transfixus*.

82 24 **through betrayal by**: MS. 213*b*, 2–3 o *vrath* y gan (*drwy dwyll y gan* MS. D, 'through treachery by'). The emendation of *vrath* to *vrat*, suggested in the footnote to the text, is confirmed by RB *drwy dwyll* (hence the reading of MS. D of Pen. 20) and CW *s.a.* 1204 *dolo*. For the full quotation from CW, however, see the note on 82.23–5: it is just possible that Pen. 20 *o vrath* translates *uulnere letali* and that *dolo* has been left untranslated, whereas RB has translated *dolo* and has not translated *uulnere letali*.

82 27 **in the same grave as**: MS. 213*b*, 9 yn *vn ved* a (yn *unwedd a* MSS. C, D); RB yn *vn wed a*, 'like'; BS *gaer* bedd, '*near* the grave of.' That Pen. 20 is correct is proved by CW *s.a.* 1204 . . . *Griffini fratris sui* conuectus *sepulcro* apud Stratflour honorifice est sepultus. RB *vn wed* (which explains the reading of MSS. C, D of Pen. 20) should be emended to *vn ved*, assuming that *v*– has been read as 6– (= *w*–).

82 35 **chief counsellor**: MS. 214*a*, 4 a phēn *kyghorwr*; RB a phen *prelat*, 'and chief *prelate*'; BS a phenn *kyngor*, 'and chief counsel'; CW *s.a.* 1205 et tocius Anglie *primas*. The variant translations of Pen. 20 and RB reflect the variant meanings of the Latin *primas*. See on 34.5 above.

82 38 **with a battle-axe**: MS. 214*a*, 10–11 a *bwyall enillec*; RB bwell, 'axe'; BS ——. CW *s.a.* 1206 gives the original Latin: Prima die rogacionum Mailgun filius Resi Kediuor filium Griffini, uirum bonum et probum, fortem et largum et inique captum . . . a quodam Hyberniense *securi* interfici fecit. 'Battle-axe' is a tentative translation of *bwyall enillec*. On *en(n)illec* (? or *gen(n)illec*) see B xiii. 76–7; G s.v. 'gen(n)illec.' If *gen(n)ill*– is from Latin *gentilis*, as suggested in G, *bwyall enillec* would mean 'a foreign (? Scandinavian) axe.' It is to be noticed that Giraldus Cambrensis in his *Topographia Hibernica* III. x (Rolls v. 151) states that the Irish had borrowed their big axes from the Norwegians and the Ostmen: (utuntur) *securibus* quoque *amplis*, fabrili diligentia optime chalibatis, *quas a Norwagiensibus et Oustmannis . . . sunt mutuati*.

82 40 **by treachery and unjustly**: RB ——, BS ——, but cf. CW *s.a.* 1206 et *inique captum*: see the full quotation in the note on 82.38.

83 11 **[1207–1208]. A year after that**: This year, which according to the annalistic reckoning of the chroniclers is 1207, is really 1208, i.e. 1207 has been omitted. This is indicated by the '*Dwy* vlynedd wedy hynny' of MS. D. The consequence of this error is that the next five years are *one* year in arrear (i.e. 1207 = 1208, 1208 = 1209, 1209 = 1210, 1210 = 1211, 1211 = 1212) and then the chronology comes right because the chronicler has erroneously put the events of 1212 under two years (i.e. his 1211 on p. 86 and his 1212 on p. 86). So from 1213 onwards the chronicler's chronology is right. The annal for 1207 (true date) has been

NOTES

page line

omitted in RB and BS also. MS. B of AC has the annal for 1207, but it contains no entries relating to Wales. AC correctly records the capture of Llangadog castle (there called *castellum Luchewein*), the interdiction of Christianity (MS. C only) and the banishment of William de Breos under 1208. In CW 1207 = 1208 as in Pen. 20, RB and BS.

83 38 **A year after that**: Allowing for it being one year in arrear, this is correct, for king John went to Ireland in June, 1210. RB, however, says 'Y vlwydyn hono,' 'That year,' so that its 1208 here = 1210. BS agrees with Pen. 20 in its chronology, as also does CW. AC places John's expedition to Ireland in 1210.

84 34–5 **after the Welsh ... before that**: so too RB and BS, but CW is more precise: interfecti sunt *xl uiri ad minus* de exercitu Anglicano.

86 20–1 **In that year ... Maredudd ap Caradog**: not in RB, but CW *s.a.* 1210 records the death of Gruffudd ab Ifor: Eodem anno (*sc.* 1210 = 1211) *Griffinus filius Ivor Gulathmorgan* apud abbatiam de Kaerlyon *obiit*.

86 23–4 **the men from the new castles**: RB [g]wyr y brenhin ... a ed[e]wssit yn y *cestyll* (MSS. P, M, *castell* MSS. R, T) newyd, 'the king's men ... who had been left in the new *castles*' (MSS. P, M, *castle* MSS. R, T). BS [g]wyr y brenin oedd yn *y kastell newydd yn Aber Konwy*, 'the king's men who were in *the new castle at Aberconwy*.'

86 38 **A year after that**: so too RB, but actually this is a continuation of the previous annal, for the 'battle in Spain' is that of Las Navas de Tolosa, fought on 16 July, 1212. See HW ii. 637, note 126. Hence the chronicler's 1212 here = 1212. See above on 83.11.

86 40 **seventy thousand**: RB *deg mil*, '*ten* thousand,' so too BS. CW *s.a.* 1211 agrees with Pen. 20: *lxxM uirorum*.

87 3 **Meurig Barach**: MS. Meuryc *Bartech* (*Barrech* MS. C, *Barr^aech* MS. D); RB Meuruc *Barach*; BS Mevric *Barach*; CW *s.a.* 1211 Meuric *Barrec*. Cf. AC *s.a.* 1277 Adam *Bareth*.

In *Trans. Cym.*, 1894–95, p. 69, S. W. Williams states that the 'three leaders' mentioned in this paragraph 'were executed at Bridgenorth for slaying one William de Moid, in some border feud or petty rebellion of that time.' He identifies Hywel ap Cadwallon with a son of Cadwallon ap Madog, and Madog ap Maelgwn with a son of Maelgwn ap Cadwallon ap Madog and a brother of Cadwallon ap Maelgwn of Maelienydd, who died at Cwm-hir in 1234, as recorded below, p. 103.

87 9–11 **And he interdicted the churches ... with them**: RB and BS represent the original Latin (as found in CW) better. RB A gwahard y Gristonogaeth, *a parassei yr ys pum mlyned gyn no hyny yn Lloegyr a Chymry*, y rydhaawd y Pap y'[r] tri thywyssawc gynneu a'e kyuoetheu a phawb o'r a vei vn ac wynt, 'And the interdiction of Christianity, *which had lasted for five years before that in England and Wales*, the Pope remitted to the three princes fore-mentioned and their territories and all who might be leagued with them'; BS *A gwahard y Gristynogaeth a wnaethoedd yr ys pvmp blwyddyn kyn no hynny yn Lloegr a Chymry.* Ac yna y ryddhaodd

s

page line

y Pab y tri tywyssawc hynny a'i kywethav ac a vai vn ac wynt, 'And *he (sc.* the king) *had interdicted Christianity for five years before that in England and Wales.* And then the Pope absolved those three princes and their territories and those who might be leagued with them.'

That Pen. 20 has mistranslated (as is obvious from the fact that the interdiction was made in 1208) and that RB gives a correct rendering of the original Latin is proved by CW *s.a.* 1211 Sed et interdictum, *quod per quatuor ante annos in tota Anglicana et Wallicana ecclesia durauerat,* in terris illorum tantum et aliorum, qui se illis iungebant, penitus resoluit. BS is here probably based on RB.

87   11–2 **And they by unanimous counsel gained possession of**: MS. 223*a*, 21–3 Ac wynteu o gytduhun gȳgor a orysgȳnassant. RB suggests that there is a lacuna in Pen. 20: Ac wynteu yn gyfun *a gyuodassant yn erbyn y brenhin ac* a oresgynassant yn wrawl y arnaw y Peruedwlat, a dugassei yntev kyn no hynny y ar Lywelyn ap Ioruerth, 'But they, *united together, rose up against the king and* they manfully won from him Perfeddwlad, which he himself had before that taken from Llywelyn ap Iorwerth.' Cf. BS (which may derive here from RB): Ac wyntav yn vvydd gyvvn *a gyvodassant yn erbyn y brenin ac* a orysgynasant yn wrawl y Beruedwlad, a dugassi y brenin i ar Lywelyn kynn no hynny, 'But they obediently united together *rose up against the king* and manfully won Perfeddwlad, which the king had taken from Llywelyn before that.' That the additional phrase (italicized above) in RB and BS is correct is proved by CW *s.a.* 1211 Qui communi consilio *consurgentes* terram de Peruerwalth, quam rex ante inuaserat, uiriliter optinuerunt. Either the scribe of Pen. 20 has dropped some such phrase as *a gyuodassant ac* after *gygor,* or *consurgentes* had been dropped in the copy of the original Latin used by the translator of Pen. 20, or *consurgentes* was left untranslated.

87   19 **Falkes, sheriff of Hereford**: RB synysgal Henford, 'seneschal of Hereford'; so too RB. MS. Fauk*un*, 'Falkes' is not correct: the sheriff of Hereford was Ingelard: cf. above *s.a.* 1209.

87   28 **Trallwng Elgan**: MS. 224*a*, 8–9 *Tallwyn Elgan,* but the emendation to *Trallwng Elgan* is confirmed by RB *Trallwyn* (MS. P, *Trallwng* MSS. M, R, T) *Elgan,* BS *Trallog Elgan.* 'Trallwng Elgan' is the name of a township in the north of the parish of Talley. See HW ii. 641, note 147, and Phillimore, OP iv. 432, 640. Pen. 20 *Tallwyn* and RB *Trallwyn* (MS. P) suggest that the form in the Latin original was *Trallwgn,* with *-gn* = *-ng,* and that RB should be emended to *Trallwgn.* See also *Ymddiddan Myrddin a Thaliesin,* ed. A. O. H. Jarman. Cardiff, 1951. pp. 31–2, and for the sixth century *Elgan* commemorated in the place-name, ibid. 17ff.

87   28–32 **he encamped ... marched thence**: this sequence of events is somewhat different in RB: ... a phebyllyaw yn y lle a elwir Trallwgn (*emended: see note on* 87.28) Elgan *dyw Ieu* wedy yr wythuet tyd o Wyl Seint Hyllar. A *thrannoeth, dyw Gwener,* y deuth ataw Owein y vrawt a Fawcoc (MS. P, Phawcwn MSS. R, T), synyscal Caer Dyf, a'e lluoed. *A thrannoeth* kyrchu a orugant gyuoeth Rys Gryc, 'And he (*sc.* Rhys Ieuanc) encamped in the place called Trallwng Elgan *on the Thursday* after the eighth day from the feast of St. Hilary. And *on the following*

page line

day, *Friday*, there came to him Owain, his brother, and Falkes, seneschal of Cardiff, and their hosts. And *on the following day* they made for the territory of Rhys Gryg.' BS agrees with RB.

88   8   **by the following day**: RB erbyn *echwyd* trannoeth, 'by *noon* the following day.'

88   32   **was seized at Carmarthen**: so too RB y delit ef yg Kaer Vyrdin, 'he was seized at Carmarthen'; BS y daliwyd Rys Gryc yn Ghaervyrddin, 'Rhys Gryg was seized at Carmarthen.' CW *s.a.* 1212 does not state where Rhys Gryg was seized but names Carmarthen as the place of imprisonment: Sequenti aestate Resus filius Resi ab officialibus regis captus est *et apud Kermerdyn diro carceri mancipatus est.* AC (MS. B only) *s.a.* 1213 has a different account, which does not necessarily conflict with the above: Resus Parvus ad Mailgonem se transtulit, et cum eo parum moratus inde ad Francos venit, qui eum post modicum temporis intervallum ceperunt, *et in Angliam duxerunt.*

88   35-6   **the castle of Degannwy ... Rhuddlan**: so too RB and BS, but CW *s.a.* 1212 *tria* castra ... Deganuy scilicet et Rudlan *et Trewphennaun*, optinuerunt. *Trewphennaun* is for *Treffynnon*, 'Holywell.' AC *s.a.* 1213 does not name the castles: *castella* per Norwalliam et Powis a rege firmata, *unum post aliud* valida manu ceperunt.

89   18   **at Vernon**: MS. 227b, 13-4 *yn Vernwn*. Not in RB and BS. The reference is to the battle of Bouvines, but *Vernwn* cannot be other than *Vernon*. The men mentioned were captured in the battle, but they were imprisoned in France: cf. Matthew Paris, *Historia Anglorum* ii. 151 Capti sunt viri praeclari comes Saresbiriensis W[illelmus], comes Flandriae F[errandus], comes quondam Boloniae Reginaldus ... *qui in Franciam trahebantur incarcerandi.* The natural meaning of the Welsh text is that they were captured 'at Vernon,' but this cannot be correct unless *Vernwn* is an error for some form of Bouvines. It could possibly mean that they were held, i.e. imprisoned at Vernon, in which case the site of the battle is not named in the Welsh text.

89   28-9   **king Henry, the first king of the kings of England**: This probably translates some such phrase as 'in tempore ... Henrici primi inter reges Angliae,' i.e. 'Henry the first [of that name] among the kings of England.' RB gann Edwart a Henri, y brenhined kyntaf, 'from Edward and Henry, the first kings ...'; BS gan Edwart ap Alvryd, brenin Lloegr, 'from Edward son of Alfred, king of England.'

89   38-90   1   **And after the archbishop ... their laws**: MS. 228b, 19-25 A gwedy gouyn o archesgob Keint a'e esgyb a yeirll a barwnyeit ydaw *a'y dysgu* a dalei eu kyfreithyeu vdunt ... The words *a'y dysgu* seem to have been misplaced: cf. RB A gwedy *y dyscu* o archescop Keint ac esgyb Lloegyr a'e ieirll a'e barwnyeit velle, a gouyn idaw a rodhei yr hen gyureitheu da y'r teyrnnas ..., 'And after *he had been so instructed* by the archbishop of Canterbury and the bishops of England and her earls and barons, and he had been asked whether he would give to the kingdom the good old laws ...' In RB the meaning is clear.

90   17   **Grosmont**: The original scribe wrote *Mynyd Bras* (MS. 229b, 11-12), which is a literal Welsh rendering of *Grosmont*—but the early

page line

corrector of the text drew a line through it and wrote *Grosmvnt* in the margin. Cf. note on 96.37–8.

90   17   **Skenfrith**: MS. 229*b*, 12–13 *Ynys Kynwric*; RB Ynys *Gynwreid*; BS Ynys *Gynwric*. It is certain that *Ynys Kynwric* here is Skenfrith, for the name occurs along with Pencelli, Abergavenny, White Castle, and Grosmont. RB *Cynwreidd* may be for *Cynwreith*, which is found as a personal name (see G s.v.) and could very well be the second element of the Welsh form underlying Skenfrith. Cf. LL 196 nant cum *Cinreith*. Pen. 20 and BS *Kynwric* is probably incorrect here, being a personal name better known than *Kynwreith*. There was a place called *Aber Kynwric* in Brecknock: see G s.v. 'Kynwric?' On *Ynys Gynwreidd* see OP iii. 182, note 4. See also *Archaeologia Cambrensis*, CI. 27–33 on 'Skenfrith.'

90   21   **Colunwy**: MS. 229*b*, 24–5 *Kolunwy*; RB *Colwyn*; BS *Kolvnwy*. RB is correct, for the reference to Elfael shows that Colwyn castle is here meant. For confusion between *Colunwy* (= Clun) and *Colwyn* cf. on 53.33; 76.3.

90   33–4   **the castle of Hugh de Meules at Tal-y-bont**: RB and BS a chastell Hu, 'and Hugh's castle.' Pen. 20 must have been Powel's source for his reference to 'Talybont' (p. 196). See HW ii. 645, note 168.

91   1   **Morgannwg**: RB *Gwyhyr*, 'Gower'; BS (probably combining Pen. 20 and RB) *Gwyr a Morgannwc*, 'Gower and Morgannwg.' RB is probably correct here.

91   6   **and Cadwgan ... Bangor**: RB ... a Chadwgawn Landifei, *abat y Ty Gwynn*, yn escop *y Mynyw*, '... and Cadwgan [of] Llandyfái, *abbot of Whitland*, [was made] bishop *in Menevia*'; BS ... a Chadogon, *abad y Ty Gwynn*, yn esgob *y Mangor*, '... and Cadwgan, *abbot of Whitland*, [was made] bishop *in Bangor*'; CW s.a. 1214 Caduganus uero abbas de Alba Domo Bangorum (*sc.* sedi) preficitur, uir mire facundie et sapientie. On *Llandyfái* or Lamphey see HW ii. 688, note 201, and OP i. 106, note 7, iv. 460.

91   20   **by counsel of**: MS. *o* (+ *gighor* in margin by the early corrector) holl dywyssogyon Kymry *gyt ac ef*—all retraced by a later hand. Since 'by their common counsel' follows in the same sentence, 'by counsel of' seems unnecessary. The *o* is possibly a slip for *a*—which is what one would expect with *gyt ac ef* following: 'Llywelyn ap Iorwerth, and all the princes of Wales along with him, by their common counsel led a host.' The retracer of the MS. cannot be responsible for the *o*: for if he were, the 'early corrector' would not have added *gighor* in the margin. Cf. RB Llywelyn ap Iorwerth *a chyffredin tywyssogyon Kymry*, 'Llywelyn ap Iorwerth and *the princes of Wales* in general'; BS Llywelyn a thywysogion Kymry, 'Llywelyn and the princes of Wales.'

91   27   **the new castle in Emlyn**: RB y castell, 'the castle'; BS Kastell Emlyn, 'the castle [in] Emlyn.' Cf. AC s.a. 1259 Castelh Nowid (= Castell Newydd), ib. s.a. 1287 castrum ... quod dicitur *Novum Castrum*.

92   12   **at Aberdyfi**: MS. yn Aber*dyvi*; RB yn Aber *Dyui*; BS yn Aber *Dyui*. Ctr. CW s.a. 1215 apud *Aberteiuy* (= Aberteifi or Cardigan). CW is wrong here. On this reference to Aberdyfi see OP iv. 486.

NOTES

page line

92 18-9 **and two commots ... Myddfai**: so too RB and BS. Ctr. CW *s.a.* 1215 ... castellum de Lanamdeuri *cum Kemmut Hirvryn*, but with no mention of the manor of Myddfai. Later in the passage CW says that the sons of Gruffudd received Dinefwr and Cantref Mawr, except *the commot of Mallaen*, Cydweli, Carnwyllion, *Cantref Bychan and Myddfai*.

92 39-40 **to the earl of Chester**: RB (so too BS) hyt ynn *Swyd* Caer Lleon, 'into the *county* of Chester.' CW *s.a.* 1215 eo fugato; AC *s.a.* 1215 sua patria expulsus est (MS. B only). Whereas Pen. 20 has translated 'ad *comitem*,' RB has translated 'ad *comitatum*.'

93 4 **after receiving hostages from the confederates**: Not in RB and BS, but cf. CW *s.a.* 1215 Lodowicus primogenitus regis Francie ad instanciam confederatorum regni Anglie, *susceptis eorum obsidibus* ... Angliam intrauit.

93 17 **And he sent envoys to Reginald de Breos**: RB A *galw ataw a oruc* Reinallt y Brewys, 'And *he summoned to him* Reginald de Breos'; BS Ac yno *galw atto* Reinallt Brewys, 'And there *he summoned to him* Reginald [de] Breos'; CW *s.a.* 1215 *missique nunciis ad* Reginaldum de Breusa.

93 21 **Oswestry**: so too RB and BS, but CW *s.a.* 1215 *Coluin et Croes Oswald* [= Oswestry] combussit et destruxit.

93 28 **in the church of Mary**: not in RB and BS, but cf. CW *s.a.* 1215 in *ecclesia Beate Marie*.

93 32 **Gualo**: MS. *Gwallter*, with *Gualo* in the margin in the 'early corrector's' hand; RB *Valeroe* (MS. P only); BS ———; CW ———.

93 33 **he was consecrated king in England**: RB *y kyssegrawd escob Bad ef yn vrenhin* yg Kaer Loyw, '*the bishop of Bath consecrated him king* at Gloucester'; BS ———; CW ———; AC ———.

93 35-6 **an eminent young man beloved by everyone**: not in RB and BS, but cf. CW *s.a.* 1215 iuuenis egregius et omnibus amabilis.

94 24 **Falkes de Breauté**: MS. 238*b*, 24 *Faukun* with *o Breute* added in the margin by the corrector. RB Ffawckun *Brewys* and BS Ffwc *o Brewys* are obvious errors.

94 38 **Reginald**: MS. 175*b*, 9 *Reinalld*. So too RB and BS. But *Reinalld* is an error for some form of *Roger*, due to a wrong extension of the contraction R.

95 2 **the castle of Kent**: RB *y castell*, 'the castle.' BS agrees with Pen. 20. For *Kastell Keint* (MS.) one would have expected *Kaer Geint* (as in MS. C of the Pen. 20 version), the usual Welsh form for 'Canterbury.'

95 27 **Reginald**: so too BS, but RB Reinallt *ac* ... *Wiliam Brewys* (MS. P), Reinalt Brewys (MS. M), Reinald y Brewys (MSS. R, T). The *ac* ... *Wiliam*, 'and William,' of MS. P of RB is probably a slip.

95 29-30 **And on the following day ... Seinhenydd**: Pen. 20 has mistranslated, for the sense required is that Reginald surrendered Seinhenydd to Llywelyn, as in RB and BS: RB A gwedy gwelet o

page line

Reinallt ac o Wiliam Brewys y diffeithwch yd oed Lywelin yn y wneuthur ar y gyuoeth, ef a gymerth hwe marchawc vrdawl y gyt ac ef ac a doeth *y ymrodi y Lywelin wrth y gyghor, ac a rodes castell Seinhenyd idaw*, 'And after Reginald and William [de] Breos had seen the ravage that Llywelyn was inflicting upon his territory, he took six ordained knights along with him and he came *to surrender himself to Llywelyn at his pleasure, and he surrendered the castle of Seinhenydd to him*' (*sc.* Llywelyn); BS . . . a roddi *i Lywelyn* gastell Seinhenydd . . ., ' . . . and *he* (*sc.* Reginald de Breos) surrendered *to Llywelyn* the castle of Seinhenydd.' Cf. CW *s.a.* 1216 Lewelinus . . . magnum congregauit exercitum ut Reginaldum de Breusa, generum suum, qui confederatus est regi, eo derelicto, dedicioni compelleret. Where Pen. 20, RB and BS mention Seinhenydd, CW loc. cit. has 'Aberthauoe' [i.e. Abertawe, 'Swansea'] and says that the castle there was destroyed and burnt: uillam (*sc.* Brecon) deserens peruenit usque ad *Aberthauoe*, castrum munitissimum, quod in breui sibi redditum solotenus destrui fecit uillamque comburi; cf. AC castellum *Abertaui* primo impetu cepit. See HW ii. 652, note 210.

The error of translation in Pen. 20 is reflected in Powel, p. 200.

96   6–7   **to hold their land and territory under him**: RB . . . ac *a gynhelynt* (MS. P, *y kynhelynt* MSS. M, R, T) *y danaw* yn dragywydawl, ' . . . and that they would *hold themselves under him for ever*'; BS a *chynal* y dano ef vyth, 'and *hold themselves under him always.*' It may be that RB has dropped some such phrase as *y tir a'y dayar* before *y danaw*. Assuming this, the emended text would mean 'and that they would hold [their land and territory] under him.' In any case, the general sense (with or without the emendation in RB) is the same in Pen. 20, RB and BS.

96   24–5   **And then Rhys Gryg . . . ground**: RB Ac yna y distrywawd Rys Gryc *castell Seinhenyd a holl gestyll Gwyr a'e kedernit*, 'And then Rhys Gryg destroyed *the castle of Seinhenydd and all the castles of Gower and their fortifications*'; BS ac y distrywiodd Rys Gryc *gastell Sainhenydd a holl gestyll Gwyr*, 'and Rhys Gryg destroyed *the castle of Seinhenydd and all the castles of Gower.*' On 'Seinhenydd' see *Archaeologia Cambrensis*, CI, 23–4.

96   37   **earl Ferrars**: MS. 244*a*, 5 yarll *Ferwr*; RB Iarll *Marscall*, BS Iarll *Marsial*, 'earl *Marshall.*' R. T. Jenkins has called attention to the apparent discrepancy between RB (and BS) and Pen. 20: see B xi. 101. He suggests that the original Latin was 'comes ferrarius.' One of the meanings of *ferrarius* was a 'shoeing smith'; and *marescallus* had a similar meaning (cf. French *maréchal*). *S.a.* 1223 RB correctly gives 'iarll *Ferwr*,' but here the RB translator seems to have equated *ferrarius* with *marescallus* and to have assumed that the reference was to William Marshall, earl of Pembroke. It may be that *marscal* had been borrowed into Welsh with the meaning 'shoeing smith'—although there is no record of such a borrowing. In any case, it was William Ferrars, earl of Derby, who went on a Crusade in 1218.

96   37–8   **Brian de L'Ile**: MS. 244*a*, 5–6 Brian *o'r Ynys*, with line drawn through *o'r Ynys* (a literal Welsh translation of *de L'Ile*) and *de Lile* written in the margin by the early corrector. Cf. above on 90.18. RB Brian *o Vilis* is corrupt.

97   11–2   **And it was not by the strength of men . . . taken**: not in RB and BS.

NOTES

page line

97 25-7 **and it was placed ... of the people**: RB and BS 'in the Church of the Trinity in Canterbury.'

97 28 **about the feast of Ieuan y Coed**: not in RB. The 'feast of Ieuan y Coed' was on 29 August, i.e. the festival of the Beheading or Decollation of St. John the Baptist. With the name 'Gŵyl Ieuan y Coed' cf. 'Gŵyl Ieuan *y Moch*,' literally 'The festival of John of the Swine.' At the time of this festival it was lawful for the swine to commence pannage in the woods, hence the two names. See *Trans. Cym.*, 1894-5, p. 127.

97 32 **upon the Welsh against the Welsh**: MS. 245*b*, 27-246*a*, 1 am bēn y Kymry yn erbyn/y Kymry. It appears that Pen. 20 is here corrupt. RB *drwy wneuthur mynych gyrcheu ar y Kymry ac aulonydu arnunt*, 'by making frequent attacks upon the Welsh *and harassing them*'; BS *Ac wyntav a wnaethoedd mynech gyrchev ar y Kymry a thorr heddwch*, 'And they had made frequent attacks upon the Welsh *and [committed] a disturbance of the peace.*' RB and BS suggest that something has been dropped in Pen. 20 between *y Kymry* and *yn erbyn*; and the text can be tentatively emended to: am bēn y Kymry [a chyuodi] yn erbyn y Kymry, '(the frequent attacks) which they made upon the Welsh [and rising up] against the Welsh.'

97 35 **the castle of Cardigan**: MS. 246*a*, 10-11 kastell *Aberteiui*; RB castell *Arberth*, 'the castle of Arberth' (= Narberth); BS *Arberth*; AC *s.a.* 1219 castellum *Arberth* (MS. B only). RB, BS, and AC are correct and Pen. 20 *Aberteiui*, 'Cardigan,' is a mistake.

97 39-40 **And thereupon**: RB and BS *A thrannoeth*, 'And *on the following day.*' Cf. AC *s.a.* 1219 *deinde* castellum Wiz *in crastino* adivit. Pen. 20 has either dropped *trannoeth* in transcription or left *in crastino* untranslated. That *in crastino* was in the original Latin is shown not only by AC but also by 'on *the third day*' which follows in the Pen. 20 text.

98 42 **Babylon**: i.e. Cairo, as usual in medieval texts. Cf. 115.18.

99 3-4 **on the eighth day ... autumn**: not in RB and BS.

99 11 **Swansea**: MS. 249*a*, 14-5 *Abertawy*; RB *Seinhenyd*; BS *Abertawy a Sainhenydd*, 'Swansea and Seinhenydd.' Here we have BS combining Pen. 20 and RB. For *Seinhenydd = Abertawe* cf. on 95.29-30; 96.24-5.

99 12-22 **ap Gruffudd ... illness and pain**: this eulogy of Rhys Ieuanc is not in RB. For similar passages omitted in RB see on 80.34-8; 81.11-5; 81.17-9; 103.36-8; 104.6-9.

100 8-9 **And when they would not go ... churches**: ctr. RB *Ac nys gadassant*, namyn kyrchu y dref a *wnaethant* a llosci y tref a'r *eglwys* hyt y prid, 'But *they did not allow him*: rather, *they* attacked the town and burned the town and the *church* to the ground'; BS *A chyrchu Kydweli a'i llosgi, kanis yno y klowsai vod yr Jarll*, 'And [he] attacked Cydweli and burned it, for he had heard that the earl was there.'

100 30 **the earl of Salisbury, de Piggot of Ewyas**: MS. 252*a*, 16-8 yarll *Sarr̄*. o Eyess[e] de Bigote,—all retraced by a later hand. Ctr. RB Iarll *Ferwr* a Henri Pigot (emended from *Rigot* MS. P, *Pigtot* MSS.

page line

M, R, T), arglwyd Euas, 'earl *Ferrars* and *Henry Pigot,* lord of Ewyas'; BS —*Henrri* Pigod, arglwydd Evas, '—*Henry* Pigot, lord of Ewyas.' If Pen. 20 is reliable *yarll Sarr.* must refer to William de Longespée.

100   39   **the 'White Strand' in Ireland**: MS. 252*b*, 15–6 y *Traeth Gwȳn* yn Ywerdon; RB *y Gwyndir* yn Jwerdon, 'the "White Land" in Ireland'; BS y'r *Brynn Wylovus yn Gwyndir* Ewerddon, 'to the *Dolorous Mount in the "White Land"* of Ireland.' The reference is to Tracton, Co. Cork: the official name of the abbey was *Albus Tractus,* of which Pen. 20 y *Traeth Gwȳn* and RB *y Gwyndir* are variant literal translations. The founder of Tracton was Odo de Barri: see Dom D. J. Canivez, *Statuta Capitulorum Generalium Ordinis Cisterciensis.* Louvain, 1933–39. 7 vols. ii. pp. 20, 29. BS is not to be relied upon in this context.

101   7   **Lampeter**: MS. 253*a*, 8–10 Llanbedyr Tal Pont Ystyuyn, i.e. 'Lampeter [at] the end of Stephen's Bridge'; RB *Pont Lann* (MS. P,—MSS. M, R, T) *Ystyphann*, 'the Bridge (of Llan MS. P) Stephen.' RB shows confusion between *Pont Ystyphan*, 'Stephen's Bridge' or Lampeter and *Llann Ystyphann*, 'Llanstephan.' BS agrees with Pen. 20: Llanbedr Tal Pont Ystyfn. See HW ii. 427, and note 88.

101   14   **And there**: RB Ac *o'r tu arall y'r coet*, 'And *from the other side of the wood*'; BS Ac o'r tv arall, 'And *from the other side*.' RB and BS seem to represent the original Latin better: cf. CW *s.a.* 1228 ex opposita nemoris parte.

102   3–5   **A year after that . . . chapter-house**: MS. C of AC places Maelgwn ap Rhys's death in 1230: see HW ii. 674, note 110.

102   9   **Hay**: MS. 255*a*, 21 *ar hay* (retraced by later hand) with *adr* added by later hand to give *a Rhayadr.* This addition is incorrect for *rh* is not found in Medieval Welsh. Moreover RB and BS read *a'r Gelli* and CW *s.a.* 1231 *Haiam.* Welsh *Y Gelli (Gandryll)* = *Hay* (< La Haie (Taillée)).

102   11   **losing, however, gentlefolk in the fighting**: RB kyt kollit bonedigyon yno, 'although gentlefolk had been lost there.' CW *s.a.* 1231 (here in verbal agreement with AC (MS. B) *s.a.* 1231) differs in meaning: Deinde uersus Gwenciam tendens et Carlyon in cinerem redigens castella de Nech et de Kedwelli *et de Kardygan, uilla prius a Mailgone succensa,* prostrauit, *probis parcium illarum hominibus sibi subiugatis* et fidelitate a magnatibus Lewelino prestita universis, preterquam a Morgano filio Howeli Anglicis confederato. It appears that Pen. 20 and RB have translated *probis hominibus ibi sublatis.*

102   38–9   **the town of Clun**: MS. 256*b*, 28–257*a* 1 tref *Golunwy.* So too RB. On Welsh *Colunwy* > *Clun*, see Phillimore, OP iii. 196, note 2.

102   40   **the valley of the Teme**: see Lloyd's note on 'Tempsiter,' B xi. 53–4.

103   1   **Castell Coch**: so too RB and BS. 'Castell Coch' is Powys Castle, but as is pointed out in HW ii. 680, note 140, this castle was in Llywelyn's own territory of Powys Wenwynwyn, and so it is difficult to see why he should burn it. However, CW *s.a.* 1233 has *castrum* quod uocatur *Castelhychoet*, and AC (MS. B) *s.a.* 1233 *castrum* quod uocabatur *Castell*

page line

Hithoet. See Phillimore, OP iii. 233 and (for a criticism of Lloyd, HW ii. 680, note 140) ib. iv. 637-38. *Castelhychoet* of CW, and *Castell Hithoet* of AC, if they do not stand for 'Castell Coch,' have not been identified.

103 18 **and they destroyed . . . the bridge**: ctr. RB Ac ymlad a hi (*sc.* Caer Vyrdin) tri mis, a *gwneuthur* pont ar Tywi a orugant. Ac yna y deuth y llogwyr yn aruawc y gyt a'r llanw y *torri* y pont, 'And they laid siege to it (*sc.* Carmarthen) for three months, and they *made* a bridge on the Tywi. And then the sailors came armed, with the tide, to *break down* the bridge'; BS ac ymladd a hi dri mis a *gwnevthvr* pont ar Dowi. A llongwyr arvoc a *dores* y bont, 'and they laid siege to it for three months and *made* a bridge on the Tywi. And armed sailors *broke down* the bridge.' AC *s.a.* 1233 suggests that RB and BS are correct: Hoc anno Henricus de Trirbelevile succurrit castrum de Cayrmardin obsessum a Ricardo Marscallo et a Walensibus. Qui veniens per alveum fluvii Tewy in quadam nave *fregit* pontem de Cayrmardyn, ubi plures de obstantibus capti sunt, plures submersi. See Lloyd, HW ii. 680, and note 142. Pen. 20 seems to have translated *fregerunt* instead of *fecerunt*; or it may be that his Latin text was faulty.

103 25-6 **repaired the castle of Trefilan . . . before that**: RB y *gorffennawd* Maelgwn Vychan *adeilat* castell Trefilan, yr hwnn a *dechreuassei* Vaelgwn y tat kyn no hynny, 'Maelgwn Fychan *completed the building* of the castle of Trefilan, which Maelgwn, his father, had begun before that'; BS agrees with RB and is probably derived from it. AC *s.a.* 1234 Mailgon filius Mailgon *aedificavit* castellum de Trefilan. (MS. B only.) On Trefilan Castle see OP iv. 491.

103 36-8 **a man . . . great fame**: not in RB and BS.

104 1 **In that year**: Henry's marriage took place on 20 January, 1236, thus falling in 1235 according to the reckoning whereby the year commenced on 25 March. RB and BS and CW agree with Pen. 20, but AC places the marriage in 1236.

104 6-9 **the man . . . the indigent**: not in RB and BS.

104 11-3 **In that year died . . . Worcester**: so too in RB and BS. But no bishop of London is known to have died in 1236, and Hugh of Wells, bishop of Lincoln, died on 12 February, 1235. The reference to the death of a bishop of Worcester is correct: William of Blois died on 18 August, 1236. Owain ap Maredudd died in 1261: see p. 112.

104 20 **. . . Dore**: RB adds Ac yno y bu varw ac y cladwyt, 'And there he died and was buried,'—which is quite correct: he died there on 11 April, 1241. See HW ii. 689, note 203.

104 20 **earl of Pembroke**: MS. 260*a*, 19 yarll *Penvro*, and BS agrees. RB *Pennbrys* (MS. P), *Penbris* (MSS. M, R, T) seem to represent 'Pembridge,' and if so are incorrect, for the 'Gilbert' is Gilbert Marshall, earl of *Pembroke*.

104 22 **Machein**: i.e. modern Machen in Monmouthshire. See HW ii. 701, note 43; OP iv. 593.

204 BRUT Y TYWYSOGYON

page line

104 28 **on the shore-bank**: i.e. on the shore of Anglesey.

104 29 **Hywel**: so too RB and BS. Hywel (ab Ednyfed), who died in 1247 (see *s.a.* below) was not bishop of St. Asaph in 1237. The bishop in 1237 was Hugh. HW ii. 686 is correct in saying that the 'new burying-ground had been consecrated by Bishop Hugh of St. Asaph,' and the *Brut* is equally correct in saying that 'Hywel consecrated a monastery' there.

104 29–30 **a monastery for the Barefooted Friars**: RB vanachloc troetnoeth a elwir Llann Vaes yMon, 'a monastery [for] Barefooted [Friars] which is called Llan-faes in Anglesey'; BS vynachloc Brodyr Troednoeth ac a elwir heddiw Llann Vaes yMon, 'a monastery of Barefooted Friars which is today called Llan-faes in Anglesey.'

105 4 **Maredudd Goeg**: so too BS. *Coeg* = 'one-eyed'. RB Maredudd Dall, 'Maredudd the *Blind.*' Maredudd was blinded by Henry II (see above *s.a.* 1165), after which he became a monk at Whitland, cf. HW ii. 580, note 34.

105 6 **In that year died the bishop of Winchester**: this entry is similarly misplaced in RB and BS: Peter des Roches, bishop of Winchester, died on 9 June, 1238, and so his death should have been placed in the preceding annal.

105 13 **a second Achilles**: RB gwr a oed anawd menegi y weithredoed, 'a man whose deeds it were difficult to narrate'; BS gwr anodd i neb draethv i wroliaeth a'i weithredoedd, 'a man difficult for anyone to set forth his bravery and his deeds'; CW *s.a.* 1240 (= AC MS. B *s.a.* 1240) Obiit magnus ille *secundus Achilles . . . cuius opera sum insufficiens narrare.*

105 17–20 **And that Dafydd . . . the king**: Pen. 20 is here in disagreement with RB, BS, CW, and AC. Cf. RB Mis Mei racwynep yd aeth Dauid ap Llywelin, *a barwneit Kymry gyt ac ef,* hyt yg Kaer Loyw y wrhav y Henri vrenhin, y ewythyr, 'The following month of May Dafydd ap Llywelyn, *and the barons of Wales along with him,* went to Gloucester to do homage to king Henry, his uncle'; BS A mis Mai racwyneb yd aeth Davydd i Gaerloyw, *ef a barwniaid Kymry gyd ac ef,* i wrhav i Henrri, i ewythr, brenin Lloegr, 'And the following month of May Dafydd went to Gloucester, *he and the barons of Wales along with him,* to do homage to Henry, his uncle, king of England'; CW *s.a.* 1240 (= AC MS. B *s.a.* 1240) qui (*sc.* Dauid) mense Maio eiusdem (*sc.* anni) homagium fecit Henrico regi Angliae apud Gloucestriam, *et barones Wallie post ipsum.*

105 20–1 **remembered their old custom and**: not in RB and BS, but cf. CW *s.a.* 1240 (= AC MS. B *s.a.* 1240) Quo mense (*sc.* Maio) Anglici *non inmemores sue consuetudinis* destinauerunt Walterum Marescallum . . .

105 31 **all the Welsh**: RB *tywyssogyon* Kymry, 'the princes of Wales'; —so too BS; CW *s.a.* 1241 omnes *Wallias*; AC *s.a.* 1241 omnes *Walenses* (MS. B. only).

105 32–3 **a castle at Diserth in Tegeingl**: RB *Castell y Careg* yn emyl y Disserth yn Tegeigyl, '*The "Castle of the Rock"* near Diserth in Tegeingl.' BS agrees with RB. With RB and BS cf. CW *s.a.* 1241 (= AC MS. B *s.a.* 1241) *castrum*que firmauit in *forti rupe iuxta Dissarth in Teggeigell.*

NOTES

page line

RB and BS *Castell y Careg* corresponds to *Castellum de Rupe* in *Calendar of the Patent Rolls*, i. 267, 278, 279. The 'rock' was called Dincolin and Carreg Faelan: see HW 699, note 35, and OP iv. 558-60.

105   33   **from Gwynedd**: RB *dros* Wyned, 'for Gwynedd.' BS ——; CW 1241 (= AC MS. B *s.a.* 1241) obsidibus acceptis a Dauid nepote suo *pro* Gwineth sibi relicto.

106   2   **his rights**: MS. 263*a*, *y gyfoeith* with *-fo-* retraced by a later hand. It is almost certain that the original text was *y gyfreith* (cf. i gyfraith MSS. C, D), but that the retracer, finding *kyfoeth* three lines later in the column, altered it to *y gyfoeith*. One would expect to find the same word here and in the next line, and the original scribe of Pen. 20 may have made a mistake, cf. CW *s.a.* 1241 (= AC MS. B *s.a.* 1241) restituendo Griffino filio Gwennainun *ius suum hereditarium* in Powis et filiis Mereduc filij Kenan in Meironyth; RB y holl *dylyet* ym Powys . . . y holl *dylyet* y Meironyd, 'all his *rights* in Powys . . . all his *rights* in Merionnydd'. BS agrees with RB. It is probable that the original Welsh translation read y *gyfreith* . . . eu *kyfreith*.

106   3   **their territory**: see the preceding note.

106   10-1   **after losing earls and barons**: RB wedy *ellwg* (MS. P, *gollwg* MSS. M, R) y (MSS. M, R, —— MS. P) ieirll dracheuen, 'after *sending* the (MSS. M, R, —— MS. P) earls *back*'; BS wedy *gollwng* yr ieirll adref i Loegr, 'after *sending* the earls *home* to England.' RB and BS give the required meaning. Pen. 20 has probably translated *amissis* instead of *remissis*.

106   29   **like a lion**: not in RB and BS, but cf. CW *s.a.* 1244 (= AC MS. B *s.a.* 1244) *tanquam leena* raptis catulis suis.

106   39-40   **A year after that . . . in peace**: this entry is not in RB and BS, but cf. CW *s.a.* 1245 (= AC *s.a.* 1245, MS. B only): Conquieuerunt heredes Willielmi Marescalli in pace. It appears that Pen. 20 has translated *conquisierunt* for *conquieuerunt*.

107   8   **A year . . . rainy year**: not in RB, BS, CW, and AC.

107   17   **his justice, from Carmarthen**: not in RB, but cf. BS vstvs Kaer Vyrdin, 'justice of Carmarthen'; CW *s.a.* 1246 (= AC *s.a.* 1246, MS. B only) Nicholaus de Molins, *senescallus de Kermerdin*, ad terram Mailgonis cum miro exercitu accessit.

107   20-3   **And when Maelgwn heard that . . . foreign to them**: Pen. 20 has mistranslated, for it was not Owain and Llywelyn, sons of Gruffudd, who left their territories, but rather Maelgwn Ieuanc. RB and BS give the correct sense: RB Ac yna y goruu ar Vaelgwn a'e eidaw ffo hyt y Gwyned at Ywein a Llywelin, meibon Gruffud ap Llywelin, gann adaw *y gyuoeth* y estronyon, 'And then Maelgwn and his men were forced to flee to Gwynedd to Owain and Llywelyn, sons of Gruffudd ap Llywelyn, leaving *his territory* to foreigners'; BS Ac yna gorvv ar Vaelgwn ffo i Wynedd at Owain Goch a Llywelyn, meibion Gruffudd ap Llywelyn ap Jerwerth, a gado *i gyuoeth* i estronion, 'And then Maelgwn was forced to flee to Gwynedd to Owain Goch and Llywelyn, sons of Gruffudd ap

page line

Llywelyn ap Iorwerth, and to leave *his territory* to foreigners.' Cf. CW *s.a.* 1246 (= AC *s.a.* 1246, MS. B only) *Mailgone fugato* . . . Dictus tamen Nicholaus ibidem moram non fecit, sed *terris post se in regia potestate relictis.*

107　36-9　**In that year . . . whole kingdom**: RB Y ulwydyn honno, yr vgeinvettyd o vis Hweurawr, y crynawd y dayar yn aruthyr yn gyffredin ar traws yr holl teyrnas, 'That year, on the twentieth day of the month of February, the earth quaked dreadfully throughout the whole kingdom in general'; BS Y vlwyddyn honno y krynodd y ddaiar yr vgeinved dydd o vis Chwefrol, 'That year the earth quaked on the twentieth day of the month of February'; CW *s.a.* 1247 In eodem anno factus est terre motus magnus *per vniversam regionem*; AC *s.a.* 1248 (MS. B only) Terrae motus magnus fuit *in Britannia et Ybernia,* quo terremotu magna pars ecclesiae Menevensis corruit, et plura edificia in patria, et rupes scissae sunt, *xi Kalendas Martii.*

108　4　**the Great Sea**: so too RB, but not in BS. 'The Great Sea' translates *Mare Magnum*, i.e. the Mediterranean.

108　6-10　**made a settlement . . . fixed intervals**: This debt originated in 1212. See EHR LVII, 371, notes 4 and 5: 'It is evident from the Patent Rolls that the abbot was to pay by half-yearly instalments of 25 marks at Easter and Michaelmas; *Cal. Pat R.* 1247-58, pp. 27, 35, 45, 57, 75, 92, 111, 129, 148.'

108　10　**as is recorded in the 'Annals' of the monastery**: RB herwyd val y keffir yn yr *Annyales* y vanachloc, 'as it is found in the *Annals* of the monastery.' Emend RB *Annyales* to *Annales*, but with the form in the text cf. RBB 37, 25 Y*nyaeles* and RP 141*b*, 22 *ynyales*, and on the latter forms see T. H. Parry-Williams, *The English Element in Welsh*. London, 1923. p. 98.

For the significance of this reference to the keeping of 'Annals' at Strata Florida, see EHR LVII. 371-72.

108　11　**Owain ap Rhobert**: so too RB and BS (Ywein vab Rotpert). This is an error for Ywein *vab Maredud* or, more probably, for Ywein [vab Maredud] vab Rotpert. Since the error is common to Pen. 20, RB and BS, it probably derives from the original Latin and so the emendation has not been incorporated in the translation of the text. Cf. below on 110.11.

108　19　**. . . where it lies**: on the evidence of an elegy by Dafydd Benfras, J. Lloyd-Jones, *The Court Poets of the Welsh Princes* (Sir John Rhŷs Memorial Lecture, British Academy, London, 1948) pp. 18-9, suggests that the body was transferred to Aberconwy 'about the month of May.'

108　29　**And within . . . that**: RB Ac *ychydic* wedy hynny, 'And *soon* after that.' RB gives better sense.

108　36-8　**One thousand . . . heir**: Alexander II, king of Scotland, died on 8 July, 1249, and so Pen. 20's '1250' is a year ahead. So too RB and BS. Since the error is common to Pen. 20, RB and BS, it probably derives from the Latin original. It is observable that AC (MS. B) has a blank *annus* for 1250, and this may reflect the error in the original Latin

page line

of the Welsh versions. Lloyd, HW ii. 694, note 1, is not quite right when he says that 'the chronology of B[rut y] T[ywysogion] continues to be correct from 1240 to 1256.' It is wrong in 1250.

109   2   **at Windsor**: not in RB and BS, but cf. AC (MS. B only) *s.a.* 1251 Gladus filia domini Lewelini *apud Windesour* . . . obiit. BS calls Gwladus Ddu 'verch Llywelyn ap Jerwerth Drwyndwn, gwraic briod Syr Randwlff Mortmer,' 'daughter of Llywelyn ap Iorwerth Drwyndwn, the wedded wife of Sir Randulf Mortimer.' Actually, she was wife successively to Reginald de Breos and *Ralf* Mortimer: cf. the reading of MS. D of Pen. 20 in the footnote to the text.

109   3   **Morgan, son of the Lord Rhys**: cf. Exeter Cathedral Library MS. 3514, 522 (= CW p. 15) in a list of the sons of the Lord Rhys: Tercium (*sc.* filium) *Morgan* non habentem partem hereditariam nisi tantum vnam villam Langeby, quam nunc tenent filij sui. Fuit etiam penteulu Griffini fratris, idem secundus ab eo in reverencia et in quibusdam aliis.

109   16   **Gwilym ap Gwrwared**: Pen. 20 is wrong in its statement that Gwilym ap Gwrwared *died* in the summer of 1252, for references to him show that he was alive in 1267: see Lloyd, B viii, 2. Ctr. RB Yn haf y ulwydyn honno y duc Gwilym ap Gwrwaret, gwr a oed synyscal y'r brenhin ar tir Maelgwn Jeuanc, drwy orchymyn y brenhin anreith y ar wyr Eluael am y bot yn keissaw aruer o borueyd Maelenyd megys o vreint, 'In the summer of that year Gwilym ap Gwrwared, the man who was seneschal to the king over Maelgwn Ieuanc's land, by the king's command carried off spoil from the men of Elfael because they were seeking to use the pastures of Maelienydd as though by right'; BS Yn y vlwyddyn honno y duc Gwilym ap Gwrwared, y gwr ydd oedd gadwedigaeth tir Maelgwn Jevangk arno, drwy orchymvn y brenin, anrraith vawr i ar wyr Elvael am i bod yn kleimio porveydd Maelienydd o vraint, 'In that year Gwilym ap Gwrwared, the man with whom lay the keeping of the land of Maelgwn Ieuanc, by the king's command carried off great spoil from the men of Elfael because they were claiming the pastures of Maelienydd by right'; AC *s.a.* 1252 (MS. B only) *Lewelinus* filius Gurwareth tunc balliuus domini Henrici regis in terra que fuerat domini Maelgonis Iunioris, cepit mandato regis predam super uiros de Eluael eo quod quasi hereditario uolebant uti pasturis montium Elenyth. *Lewelinus* is an error for *Gwilim* or some such form. Since RB, BS, and AC are in agreement, the error in Pen. 20 is one of translation or of transcription and does not derive from the Latin original.

109   19-20   **the pastures of Elfed**: RB and BS porueyd *Maelenyd*; AC *s.a.* 1252 pasturis montium *Elenyth*. Phillimore, OP iv. 447, note 1, seems to favour the reading *Maelenyd* because 'Elfael did not approach nearer Elenydd [*sic*] than the lower Ithon,' but this is corrected ib. iv. 502. It is almost certain that AC *Elenyth* is the correct reading. *Elenid* is an old name for the mountains of Pumlumon: see PKM 71, 5, and note p. 259, HW ii. 513, note 100, and G s.v.

109   21   **about August**: not in RB, but cf. BS Awst nessaf, 'The following August'; AC *s.a.* 1253 (MS. B) circa principium Augusti. Actually, Henry III was in France from 6 August, 1253, till 27 December, 1254.

page line

109 22 **to Burgundy**: RB y *Vordews*, BS i *Vwrdias*, 'to Bordeaux'; AC *s.a.* 1253 (MS. B) in *Burgundiam*.

110 3–5 **And Llywelyn . . . against him**: RB Ac yna yd arhoes Llywelin a'e wyr yn diofyn *ym Bryn Derwyn*, trwy ymdiret y Duw, creulawn dyuodyat y vrodyr, 'And then Llywelyn and his men, trusting in God, awaited unafraid *on Bryn Derwin* the fierce coming of his brothers'; BS A gwedy gossod maes o naddvnt *yMrynn Derwin* ac ymladd yn grevlon . . ., 'And after they had joined battle *on Bryn Derwin* and had fought fiercely . . .' Pen. 20 *yn y erbyn* (MS. 271*a*, 28–271*b*, 1), 'against him' may be an error of transcription for *y Mrynn Derwyn*, but since the site of the battle is not mentioned in CW and AC *s.a.* 1255, there is no need to assume this. Cf. AC loc. cit. idem Lewelinus confidens in Domino eorum (*sc.* Owain and Dafydd) indubitanter espectauit horribilem cum magno exercitu *adventum*. On the location of Bryn Derwin see HW ii. 715, and note 127.

110 6–7 **he captured his brothers and imprisoned them**: ctr. RB . . . y *delit Ywein Coch* ac y *foes Dauid*, '. . . Owain Goch was captured and *Dafydd fled*'; BS . . . a daly Owain Goch a'i garcharv. A *Davydd a ffoes*, '. . . and Owain Goch was captured and imprisoned. And *Dafydd fled*'; CW *s.a.* 1255 et predictum *Owinum vna cum fratre suo Dauid*, qui erat dux familie sepe dicti Owini, *tenuit et in carcerem retrusit*; AC *s.a.* 1255 (MS. B) dictum *Owynum et Dauid*, fratres suos . . . *cepit*. Thus AC, followed by Lloyd, HW ii. 715, and note 128, is confirmed by Pen. 20 and CW.

110 11 **Owain ap Rhobert**: so too RB and BS, but AC *s.a.* 1255 (MS. B) Margeria . . . uxor *Owini filii Mareduth* de Kedeueyn. MS. 271*b*, 16–7, *Ywein vab Rotpert* is an error for 'Ywein vab *Maredud*' or more probably, 'Ywein [vab Maredud] vab *Rotpert*.' Since the error is common to Pen. 20, RB and BS it probably derives from the Latin original. Cf. on 108.11 above.

110 12–3 **for twenty-seven marks and five shillings and two cows**: RB yr trugein a dwy vorc ar bymthec ar hugein a dwy uu, which if corrupt might be emended in one of two ways: (1) by inserting *swllt*, 'shilling,' after *trugein*, or (2) by inserting *swllt* after *hugein* and emending *ar hugein* to *ac ugein*. Emendation (1) would give the meaning 'for three-score [shillings] and thirty-seven marks and two cows'; and emendation (2) would give 'for seventy-seven marks and twenty shillings and two cows.' The second emendation implies a confusion, either in Pen. 20 or in RB, between xxvii and lxvii, and between xx and v. Emendation (1) involves the lesser change in RB. It is probable, however, that RB *trugein* is for 'sixty [pence]' (= Pen. 20 'five shillings'), and that no emendation is necessary. The only discrepancy is '27 marks' in Pen. 20 as against '37 marks' in RB.

110 15 **towards the end of summer**: so too RB; BS Ac yna, 'And then'; CW *s.a.* 1255 (= AC *s.a.* 1255, MS. C) die translacionis Sancti Benedicti, i.e. 11 July.

110 19–20 **And after his return to England**: RB ——; BS Ac Awst nessaf ar hynny, 'And in the August following that'; AC *s.a.* 1256 (MS. B) *Quo* (*sc.* Edwardo) *recedente* et facta uisitatione.

NOTES

page line

110 27-8 and by the end of the week he gained possession of it all: so too RB; BS *a goresgyn y Berveddwlad a Meirionydd yn vn wythnos,* 'and he conquered Perfeddwlad and Meirionnydd in one week.' Ctr. AC *s.a.* 1256 (MS. B) *et eam* (*sc.* Perfeddwlad) *infra unam ebdomadam preter duo castra, scilicet Deganho et Dissert uiriliter occupauit.*

110 29-34 And the land that belonged to Edward . . . and honour: RB *A'r rann a oed eidaw Edwart o Geredigyawn, ef a'e rodes y Varedud ap Ywein, a Buellt gyt a hynny, a thalu y Varedud ap Rys Gryc y gyuoeth gann wrthlad Rys y nei o'e gyuoeth a'e rodi y Varedud ap Rys, heb gynnal dim idaw ehun o'r tired goresgyn hynn eithyr clot a gobrwy,* 'And the portion of Ceredigion which belonged to Edward he gave to Maredudd ab Owain, and Builth along with that, and he restored to Maredudd ap Rhys Gryg his territory, expelling Rhys, his nephew, from his territory and giving it to Maredudd ap Rhys, without keeping any of these conquered lands for himself, but only fame and merit'; BS *a goresgyn Karedigion o law Edwart a'i rodd[i] i Vredudd ap Owain ap Gruffydd ap yr Arglwyd Rys. A goresgyn i Vredudd ap Rys Gryc i gyvoeth yntav,* 'and he conquered Ceredigion from the hands of Edward and gave it to Maredudd ab Owain, son of Gruffudd, son of the Lord Rhys. And he conquered for Maredudd ap Rhys Gryg his territory too.' That RB gives the best version here is shown by AC *s.a.* 1256 (MS. B) . . . *partem domini Edwardi de Keredigeaun Maredut filio Owini cum terra de Buelt dedit, quam tunc similiter in manu forti occupauit, restituendo predictum Maredut filium Resi cum terra sua et eiciendo prefatum Resum nepotem suum e sua parti et illa dicto Meredut conferendo iure hereditario, nichil sibi ex omnibus preter famam et meritum de predictis conquestibus retinendo.*

111 2 castle of Bodyddon: MS. 273*a*, 23 *a chastell Bodydon*; RB and BS *castell Bydydon*; AC *s.a.* 1287 (MS. B) *castellum Bodedon*. 'Bodyddon' is now Bydyfon, a township in the parish of Llanfyllin: see HW ii. 720, note 22. On the site of the castle see OP iv. 593.

111 10 . . . about two thousand and more: After this RB (but not BS) adds *Pann las y gwyr yn y Kymereu oed hynny,* 'That was when the men were slain *at Cymerau.*' This additional sentence in RB must have been originally a marginal rubric (as in MS. M), incorporated in the text of MS. P. Cf. CW *s.a.* 1257 *Hoc anno interfecti fuerunt multi Walenses apud Kemereu in uigilia Trinitatis in Stratewy.* A much fuller account is given in MS. B of AC *s.a.* 1257, which also mentions 'Kemereu.' The 'Walenses' of CW (see above) is not necessarily an error, for MS. C of AC has: *Interfecti fuerunt plures Anglici et Wallenses partem Anglorum fouentes apud Kemmereu in Estradtewy in uigilia Sanctae Trinitatis.* Lloyd, HW ii. 720, note 23, maintains that the site of the battle was probably at the confluence of the Tywi and the Cothi. See also B viii. 95-6, OP iv. 413-14, 430-31, and (criticizing Lloyd) B xiv. 179-86.

111 14 A year after that: RB and BS agree with Pen. 20 in starting a fresh annal here, but the events recorded belong to the second half of 1257. Cf. also AC MS. B, where the date 'Annus MCCLVIII' is given. Hence the date of the *Brut* is one year ahead here.

111 15-7 And after that . . . John the Baptist: not in RB and BS.

page line

111 22–3 **the castle of Llangynwyd**: MS. 274*b*, 5–6 *Llānkȳnwch*; RB *Llann Genev*, 'Llangenau'; BS *Llann Gynen*, an error for *Llann Gyneu*. Pen. 20 *Llannkynnwch* seems to be for Llangynwyd in Glamorgan, which is known to have been the seat of a castle in 1246: see HW ii. 721, note 29. No castle called 'Llangenau' is known in Glamorgan, but there is a parish so called in Brecknock, in the cantref of Crucywel, and a place of the same name in Pembroke. The last is impossible in this context and the Llangenau of Brecknock is very improbable. Phillimore's statement, OP iv. 427, that 'Llann Genev' 'is a scribal mistake for some old form of *Swansea*' is not to be accepted.

112 7–8 **[1259] ... king of France**: of the events placed by the chronicler in 1259 this is the only one which is correct. Henry III was absent in France from 14 November, 1259, to 23 April, 1260. This notice of Henry's going to France in November is the only event saved by Pen. 20, RB and BS from the annal for 1259. That the Latin original had other entries is suggested by AC's annal for 1259 and CW *s.a.* 1260 (= 1259). The inclusion of this one true entry for 1259 makes the chronicler's chronology correct in 1260 and for succeeding annals down to 1282.

112 29 **by treachery**: MS. 276*b*, 24–277*a*, 3 y doeth neb rei o'y kẏgor ehunein o Vaelenyd y'r kastell newyd *drwy dwyll* a oed eidaw‖yna Roger o Mortmyr ac y kawssant y kastell; RB y doeth rei o gygor gwyr Maelenyd y'r castell newyd a oed y Rosser Mortmer y Maelenyd. A gwedy *dyuot y mywn trwy dwyll* y lladassant y porthoryon, 'Certain [men], by counsel of the men of Maelienydd, came to the new castle which Roger Mortimer had in Maelienydd. And after *they had come in by treachery* they slew the gate-keepers'; BS Gwedy Gwyl Andras yr anillodd gwyr Melienydd y kastell newydd i ar Rocher Mortmer, 'After the feast of Andrew the men of Maelienydd won the new castle from Roger Mortimer.' It appears from RB that *drwy dwyll* has been misplaced in Pen. 20, possibly because it was in the margin in an earlier copy, and that it should come after *kawssant*: 'and they took the castle by treachery.'

112 30 **the new castle**: the reference is to the castle of Cefn-llys. Cf. AC *s.a.* 1262 (MS. B) Eodem anno in uigilia Sancti Andreae Apostoli per industriam hominum de Maelenit captum devastatum fuit *castellum de Kevenellis*. Cf. HW ii. 730, and CACW 26–7. Note the phrase 'by their own counsel' in the text, which suggests that Llywelyn ap Gruffudd was not responsible for the attack on the castle.

112 37 **within the castle walls**: cf. AC *s.a.* 1262 (MS. B) intrauerunt *ruinos muros de Kevenlis* cum magno apparatu molientes restaurare fracturas murorum. See CACW 27.

113 5–8 **And he came by night ... Cydewain**: MS. 277*b*, 26–278*a*, 5: Ac y doeth o hyt nos drwy Keri y Gedewein *y arnad*. A gwedy kynullaw diruawr anreith ohonaw ymchwelut a oruc ford Gedewein *y danad*. Ab Ithel, *Brut y Tywysogion* 350–51 understood *y danad* as *y Danad*, i.e. 'to (the river) Tanad,' but it cannot possibly be that: cf. OP iv. 609–10. In the text *y danad* is obviously meant to contrast with *y arnad*. Cf. RB y kyrchawd Jon Ystraens Ieuanc ... gyrch nos a diruawr lu gantaw ar traws Keri hyt yg Kedewein. A gwedy kynnullaw diruawr anreith

page line

ohonaw, ymhoelut a oruc dracheuen *y waer[e]t*, 'John Lestrange the Younger, ... and a mighty host with him made a night raid across Ceri to Cydewain. And after he had gathered vast spoil, he came back *down* again'; BS Ac y doeth o hyd nos drwy Geri i Gydewain a dwyn dirvawr anraith ganthvnt, 'And he came by night through Ceri to Cydewain and they brought vast spoil with them.'

113 12–3 **near the valley of the Clun**: MS. garllaw dyffryn *Kolunwy*; RB yn emyl *Colunwy*, 'close to Clun'; AC *s.a* 1263 Quinto Kalendarum Maii *apud Clunow* interfecti fuerunt ad minus centum uiri, inter quos cecidit Lewelinus filius Maredut flos iuuentutis totius Wallie. For *Colunwy > Clun*, see above on 102.38–9.

113 13–4 **Edward was moving ... Gwynedd**: RB yd oed Edward yn ymdeith *ardal Gwynedd* ac yn llosci rei o'r treuyd, 'Edward was traversing *the march of Gwynedd* and burning some of the townships'; BS A'r amser hwnnw y doeth Edwart ap Henrri vrenin a llosgi rai o'r trevi yn Gwynedd, 'And at that time Edward, son of king Henry, came and burned some of the townships in Gwynedd.' In Pen. 20 *yr ardal* is consistently used for 'the March,' but RB *ardal Gwynedd* could mean 'the region (neighbourhood) of Gwynedd,' for in RB *y Mars* is the phrase used generally for 'the March.'

113 16–7 **...Llywelyn, his brother**: after this RB adds: ac yd aeth y Loeger a rei o'e aruollwyr y gyt ac ef, 'and he went to England, and some of his confederates along with him.'

113 27 **the castle of Yr Wyddgrug**: so too RB and BS. The Welsh name for Mold is 'Yr Wyddgrug,' but the context shows that the reference here *cannot* be to Mold. The place meant here must have been somewhere in Montgomeryshire. See Lloyd, HW ii. 734, note 90. AC *s.a.* 1263 (MS. B) has castrum *de Weidgrut*. Phillimore, OP iv. 621–22 quotes from documents the forms *Wyrebruch* and *Wythegruc* and suggests that the Welsh form *Yr Wyddgrug* may be a corruption by Welsh annalists of an English name. Cf. note on 114.26.

113 29–32 **the strife that had been ... not forgotten**: the 'strife' referred to here was that of the preceding year, i.e. 1263. RB seems to have misunderstood the original Latin and understands 'the strife' as a reference to the struggle of 1264: Y ulwydyn racwyneb y bu gofadwy teruysc rwg Henri vrenhin ac Edward y vap a'e kymhorthwyr o'r neill tu a'r ieirll a'r barwneit o'r tu arall. Ac yn hynny y doeth hyt y maes Lewys brenhin Lloeger a'e deu vap a brenhin yr Almaen a'e deu uap ..., '*The following year [sc. 1264] there was memorable strife* between king Henry and Edward, his son, and their supporters, on the one side, and the earls and the barons, on the other side. And during it the king of England and his two sons and the king of Germany and his two sons came to the field of Lewes.' BS has nothing corresponding to the words in parenthesis in Pen. 20 and the first sentence in RB above. It is observable that the reference to 'the strife' of 1263 is given as a separate entry in MS. C of AC (*s.a.* 1262): Magna fuit discordia inter dominum Eadwardum filium Henrici regis Anglie primogenitum et barones Anglie. It is probable that in the original Latin the words 'the strife ... not forgotten' was a memorandum which was later incorporated in the main text,—as is shown by the fact that it is in Pen. 20 and RB.

T

page line

114   1   **released the king of Germany**: RB *y gellygawd y ieirll vrenhin Lloeger*, 'the earls released *the king of England*'; BS *Ac yn i kyngor y kowsant ollwng y brenin*, 'and in their counsel they decided *to release the king*.' Pen. 20 has mistranslated here, and RB and BS are correct. Cf. CW *s.a.* 1264 (= AC *s.a.* 1264, MS. C) Hoc anno captus fuit rex Henricus apud Lewes in bello, et *Ricardus rex Alemanie* et alii multi barones et multi Londonienses *interfecti fuerunt*.

114   5–6   **on the eighth day from Epiphany**: i.e. 13 January, 1265, by modern reckoning. Here for the chronicler the year began on 25 March, hence Llywelyn ap Rhys's death is recorded in the annal for 1264.

114   12–3   **and on the Tuesday next after August**: RB *A duw Mawrth nessaf wedy Awst*, 'And on the Tuesday next *after August*'; BS *A duw Mawrth kyntaf o vis Awst*, 'And on the first Tuesday of the month of August.' Pen. 20 and RB 'the Tuesday next after August' means the first Tuesday after the Calends of August. The date of the battle was 4 August, 1265.

114   15   **fell Simon and his sons**: RB *y dygwydawd Symwnt Mwmford a'e vap*, 'Simon Montford and his *son fell*'; BS *Ac y llas* Simwnt Mwnffordd *a'i veibion*, 'And Simon Montford and his *sons were slain*.' Actually, Simon Montford's sons were captured—not killed—in the battle: cf. *s.a.* 1266 below where reference is made to their subsequent escape from the king's prison.

114   26   **Kenilworth**: MS. 280*b*, 21–2 *Kelligwrd*, RB *Kelli Wrda*, and BS *Kelli* are corruptions of some form of Kenilworth. For older forms of the English place-name cf. CW *s.a.* 1266 (p. 15) *Kenelyngword*, (p. 17) *Kenelword*.

115   1–2   **on the feast-day of Pope Calixtus**: so too RB and BS, thus giving the date as 14 October. But the true date is known to be 29 September. Lloyd, HW ii. 739, note 114, explains the error in RB, Pen. 20, and BS (and so, probably, in the Latin original) as due to confusion between 'pridie *Id*. Oct.' and 'pridie *Kal*. Oct.'

115   2–5   **peace and concord ... Baldwin's Castle**: For the full terms of this agreement see LW 1–4.

115   5–7   **And for that peace ... sterling**: MS. 281*b*, 23–6 ef a edewis y'r brenhin dēgmil ar hugeint o vorkau o ysterlīg ... brenhin. The text has been retraced by a later hand, but certain letters after *ysterlīg* were and still are illegible. They were probably *ot* and *yr* or *y—ysterlīgot y'r* or *ysterlīgot y*. If the latter, the meaning is 'of the king's sterling,' but if the former the meaning may be either 'of the king's sterling' or 'of sterling to the king.' The words *y'r brenhin*, 'to the king' may have been repeated by confusing two types of sentences: (1) ef a edewis *y'r brenhin* dēgmil ar hugeint o vorkeu o ysterlīgot; (2) ef a edewis dēgmil ar hugeint o vorkeu o ysterlīgot *y'r brenhin*. In the translation the emendation 'o ysterlīg[ot y] brenhin' has been adopted. Cf. RB yd edewis Llywelin ... y'r brenhin deg mil ar hugeint o vorckev o ysterligot, 'Llywelyn promised ... to the king thirty thousand marks of sterling'; BS ... gan roddi o Lywelyn y'r brenin dair mil ar hvgain o vorkiav, ... 'Llywelyn giving to the king twenty-three thousand marks.'

Pen. 20 and RB agree in saying that the sum to be paid was 30,000 marks. Actually, Llywelyn was to pay 25,000 marks (see LW, p. 3) plus an additional 5,000 if the king should later grant the homage of Maredudd ap Rhys to Llywelyn. That homage was granted in August, 1270 (see LW xliii). The figure in the text is the sum total of the two payments to be made.

115 10–1 **and that there should be princes of Wales ... so named**: This is nearer to the correct meaning than RB is. The latter has obviously mistranslated: ac *eu* (sc. '*holl varwneit Kymry*') *galw yn tywyssogyon Kymry o hynny allan*, 'and that *they* (sc. "*all the barons of Wales*") *should be called* princes of Wales from that time forth.' For the terms of the Treaty of Montgomery see LW xlviii, and (for the text) ib. 1–5. For the true meaning underlying the Pen. 20 and RB versions here, cf. ib. 2 ... *ut idem Lewelinus et heredes sui principes Wallie uocentur et sint.*

115 15–7 **In that year ... Apulia**: The chronology of this entry is confused in Pen. 20 as also in RB and BS. Manfred was defeated and killed at Benevento on 26 February, 1266. After Manfred's death, Charles, duke of Anjou, took possession of Sicily and beheaded Conradin or Conrad the Younger in 1268. Where Pen. 20 has '*Konrat, nei y Frederic*,' '*Conrad, nephew* to Frederick,' RB has *Co[n]radin, wyr y Fredic*, '*Conradin, grandson* to Frederick,' and BS has '*nai ap brawd i Ymerodr Ruvain*,' 'nephew, brother's son, to the Emperor of Rome.' RB *wyr*, 'grandson,' is correct, for Conradin or Conrad the Younger (1252–68) was a son of Conrad IV (1228–54), who was a son of Emperor Frederick II.

115 18 **Babylon**: i.e. Cairo. Cf. above on 98.42.

115 21–5 **A year after that ... Strata Florida**: RB *Yn y vlwydyn racwynep y bu varw Goronw ap Ednyuet a Ioap, abat Ystrat Flur*, 'In the year following, died Goronwy ab Ednyfed and Joab, abbot of Strata Florida'; BS *Anno Domini* MCCLXVIII *noswyl Luc y bu varw Gronwy, distain y tywysoc. Ac y bu varw Jop, abad Ystrad Fflur*, '*Anno Domini* MCCLXVIIJ, *on the eve of the feast of Luke*, died Goronwy, *the prince's steward.* And Jo[a]b, abbot of Strata Florida, died.' On Goronwy ab Ednyfed see HW ii. 743.

115 27–8 **on the same day in the month of December**: MS. 283*a*, 1–2 *yn yr vn dyd y mis Racvyrr*; but BS *y vij dydd o vis Racvyrr*, 'on the *seventh* day of the month of December.' RB *y mis Racuyr*, 'in the month of December.' The 'vij' of BS is probably an error for *vn*.

115 31 **Hirfryn**: the original scribe wrote *Kedewein*, but a line was drawn through it and *Hyrvryn* added in the margin by the 'early corrector' of the text.

115 32–3 **on the day following the feast of St. Luke the Evangelist**: RB *trannoeth o duw Gwyl Luc* (MS. M, *Lucy* MS. R) *Wyry*, 'on the day following the feast-day of Luke (Lucy MS. R) the Virgin'; BS *drannoeth wedy Gwyl Luc*, 'on the day after the feast of *Luke*.' In MS. M of RB *Wyry* is probably intrusive and so led to the 'correction' *Lucy* in MS. R. If it is not intrusive the translator of RB must have read *v* (= virginis) for *ev* (= evangeliste). The festival of Luke was on 18 October, and that of Lucy on 13 December. Without further evidence one cannot decide whether Pen. 20 (and BS) or RB gives the correct date.

page line

115 38–9 **And Edward ... Jerusalem**: A marginal addition in the MS., written by the 'early corrector' of the text. This is not in RB and BS. RB, however, has an additional sentence not in Pen. 20 and BS: A'r Lowys hwnnw yssyd sant enrydedus yn y nef, 'And that Louis is an honoured saint in heaven.'

In Pen. 20 (MS. p. 283), at the foot of the page, under column *a*, a later hand has written: Blwydyn wedy hȳn y bu varw *mesdyr Hvw*(?) *Morgan*, 'A year after this, died Master Huw(?) Morgan.' This seems to have been written by a fifteenth century hand; but there is no indication that it is to be inserted anywhere in the main text. It may be a mere memorandum. Since there is a flaw in the vellum I cannot be sure that *Hvw* is the correct reading. If, however, this reading is correct and the entry has nothing to do with the main text, the 'Master Huw Morgan' may be identified with the person of the same name to whom the fifteenth century poet, Gutun Owain, addressed a *cywydd* of solicitation on behalf of Siôn Pilstwn: see E. Bachellery, *L'Œuvre Poétique de Gutun Owain*. Paris. Champion. 1950. pp. 87–9.

116 1 **[Maredudd ap] Rhys Gryg**: MS. Rys Gryc; so too BS, which here derives from Pen. 20. The emendation in the text of the translation is confirmed by RB *Maredud ap* Rys Gryc.

116 2–3 **on the sixth day from August**: RB *y hwechet tyd wedy* Awst, 'the sixth day after [the Calends of] August'; BS agrees with RB. See HW ii. 750, and note 179, where the date given in Pen. 20 (= 27 July) is accepted as correct.

116 13 **... Edward, his eldest son, reigned**: After this RB adds: A gweithredoed hwnnw yssyd yn yscriuenedic ynn *Ystoryaeu y Brenhined*, 'And his deeds are written in the *Histories of the Kings*.'

116 20 **his castle of Dolforwyn**: Cf. below *s.a.* 1277. See Lloyd, B x. 306–9, and Phillimore, OP iv. 592–3.

116 23–5 **and thirteen townships ... beyond the Dyfi**: RB a their tref ar dec o Gyfeilawc yssyd tu draw y Dyfi *yn Riw Helyc*, 'and thirteen townships of Cyfeiliog which are beyond the Dyfi *in Rhiw Helyg*'; BS ac vn kantref ar ddec *rwng Riw a Helygi* a rann o Gyveiliog, 'and eleven cantrefs between *the Rhyw and the Luggy* and a portion of Cyfeiliog.' Phillimore, OP i. 221, iv. 599–600 seems to regard RB as the more correct version, but other references to the land 'between the Rhyw and the Luggy' confirm Pen. 20. Cf. B viii, 253 de terris et tenementis *inter Ryu et Helegy*; CACW, 122 and 125, '13 *vills* between Rew and Elegy'; LW, 78, totam terram *inter Ryu et Helegi*, ib. 111 totam terram *inter Ryw et Helegy*. See also *Y Cymmrodor*, xxv. 1–20, xxvi. 252; LW liii and footnote. [But the *Brut* does not say that Llywelyn went to Dolforwyn 'about Palm Sunday.' The words are *amgylch y Pasc Bychan*, 'about Low Easter.'] In CACW, 79, '*fourteen* vills' are mentioned: cf. ib. 122, note 1.

On *Rhiw Helyg* of RB see OP i. 221, iv. 599–60; E. Bachellery, *L'Œuvre Poétique de Gutun Owain*. Paris. Champion. 1950. xxxi. 42, and note p. 183.

116 27 **Edward came ... Jerusalem, and**: MS. added in the margin by the 'early corrector' of the text. Cf. above on 115.38–9, where there is a similar addition to the text recording Edward's going to Jerusalem.

NOTES

page line

117   13–4   **on the fifteenth day from the Calends of August**: so too BS; RB *y pymthecuet dyd o Awst*, 'the fifteenth day *from* August,' i.e. before the Calends of August.

117   26–7   **That year the earth quaked ... of the day**: RB *Yn y vlwydyn honno, yr wythuet dyd o Wyl Veir y Medi, y crynawd y dayar yg Kymry amgylch awr echwyd*, 'In that year, on the eighth day from the feast of Mary in September, the earth quaked in Wales *about the hour of noon*'; BS *Yr ail dydd yn ol hynny* (*sc.* '*Gwyl Vair Ddiwaethaf*') *y krynodd y ddaiar ynGhymry oll am bryd anterth o'r dydd*, '*The second day after that* (*sc.* "*the last feast of Mary*") the earth quaked in all Wales *about the time of the third hour of the day.*' It is to be noticed that where Pen. 20 (MS. 286*b*, 10–11) has *am bryt anterth o'r dyd*, RB has *amgylch awr echwyd*. See G s.v. 'echŵyδ (–ẉyδ), where it is shown that in certain texts translated from the Latin *awr echwyd* and *pryd echwyd* correspond to *hora diei tertia*. Counting the beginning of the day from 6 a.m. the 'third hour' would begin at 9 a.m., but counting it from 9 a.m. the 'third hour' would begin at noon.

117   28   **merchants from Haverford**: so too RB and BS, but Lloyd, HW ii. 757, note 211, has shown that they were merchants from Bristol.

117   35   **Winchester**: but the marriage took place at Worcester. RB and BS too have '*yg Kaer Wynt*,' '*at Winchester*.' Below *s.a* 1278 it is correctly stated—in Pen. 20 and RB—that the marriage took place at Worcester. Since Pen. 20, RB and BS read *Kaer Wynt* it is probable that the common original had *Wintonia*. The marriage by proxy had taken place in 1276 (see HW ii, 757) at Eleanor's home, but the marriage in Worcester Cathedral did not take place until 13 October, 1278, as recorded below *s.a.* 1278.

118   3   **In that year ... of Ystrad**: This entry not in RB. In BS *Ystrad* has become *Ystrad Fflur!*

118   18   **And they took it by the end of a fortnight**: See CACW 30–31, where it is shown that this siege of Dolforwyn began on Wednesday, 31 March, and ended on Thursday, 8 April.

118   33–4   **till the first council**: RB *hyt y cwnsli nessaf*, 'till the next council'; BS *oni vai y kwnsel*, 'till the council would be.' Pen. 20 seems to have translated *primum* for *proximum*.

118   38   **about the feast of John the Baptist**: RB *yr wythuet dyd o wyl Jeuan*, 'the *eighth day from* the feast of John'; BS *yn emyl gwyl Jeuan*, '*close to* the feast of John.'

118   41–2   **That year ... Aberystwyth**: RB is fuller and more precise: *Y vlwydyn honno, wyl Iago Ebostol, y doeth Edmwnt, vrawt y brenhin, a llu gantaw hyt yn Llann Badarn. A dechreu adeilat castell Aber Ystwyth a wnaeth*, 'That year, *on the feast of James the Apostle*, Edmund, the king's brother, and a host with him, came to Llanbadarn. And he began to build the castle of Aberystwyth.' Cf. AC *s.a.* 1276 ... *aedificatum est castellum apud Llan Padarn super mare* a domino Eadmundo Henrici regis filio (MS. B), ... incepit (*sc.* Eadmundus) construere *castrum apud Lanpadarnuaur* (MS. C).

page line

119 2 **. . . with a ditch**: after this RB adds: a thrigyaw yno talym a wnaeth, 'and there he stayed a while.' Cf. AC *s.a.* 1276 ibique (*sc. Rhuddlan*) per aliquot dies moratus est.

119 3 **That year, about August**: RB Yn y vlwydyn honno, *dyw Sadwrn wedy Awst* . . ., 'In that year, *on the Saturday after [the Calends of] August* . . .'; BS Ac Awst nessaf ar hynny, 'And in August following that . . .' Pen. 20 'about August' means 'about the Calends of August.'

119 7–8 **And after that**: RB A *nos Wyl Vathev*, 'and *on the eve of the feast of Matthew*'; BS Ac *yna* . . ., 'And *then* . . .' RB fixes the date as 20 September.

119 9–10 **And after that**: RB A *thrannoeth wedy Gwyl Seint Ynys* . . ., 'And *on the day following after the feast of St Denis*'; BS *Yna*, 'Then.' RB fixes the date as 10 October.

119 24 **A year after that**: RB Y ulwydyn racwynep, *gwyl Edward vrenhin* . . ., 'In the following year, *on the feast of king Edward* . . .' RB fixes the date as 13 October. Cf. the next sentence in Pen. 20.

119 28 **their**: the *ei* of Pen. 20 (MS. 290b, 10) is a misprint for *eu*.

119 34–5 **'The form of exchange . . . round'**: For this prophecy see HRB 387 Findetur forma commercii; dimidium rotundum erit; BD 106, 2–3 Ef a holldir furyf y gyfnewit, hanner crwn a uyt (altered in margin to 'a'i hanner a vydd crwn'); RBB 146, 19 Ef a holltir furyf y gyfnewit. Haner crwn a vyd; *Brut y Brenhined, Cotton Cleopatra Version* (ed. J. J. Parry). Cambridge, Mass., 1937, p. 127, Ef a hollir furyf y gyfnewit; a'r hanner a vyd crwn. Round half-pence were coined by Edward I. For the splitting of pennies see C. Oman, *Coinage of England*. Oxford, 1931, pp. 97, 162–3, G. C. Brook, *English Coins*, London, 1932, pp. 81, 103–4. For a commentary on this prophecy of Myrddin's see J. S. P. Tatlock, *The Legendary History of Britain*. Univ. of California Press, 1950, p. 404. See also J. Loth, 'La prophétie de Merlin pour le demi penny' in RC xxxii. 299.

119 37 **. . . of Christ**: the entry added in the margin (see footnote to the text) has been misplaced: the date of Dafydd's rising is not 1280 but 1282.

120 1 **abbot**: RB *y trydyd abat ar dec o Ystrat Flur*, '*the thirteenth abbot* of Strata Florida.'

120 8 **A year after that**: Dafydd took the castle of Hawarden on 21 March ('the feast-day of St. Benedict'), 1282, according to modern reckoning. This meant 1281 for the chronicler, who here reckoned the beginning of the year from 25 March.

120 17 **Rhys [ap Rhys] ap Maelgwn**: *ap Maelgwn* has been added in the margin by the 'early corrector' of the text. Actually the corrector should have added 'ap Rys ap Maelgwn,' giving 'Rhys [Fychan] ap Rhys ap Maelgwn.'

120 19 **. . . Mefenydd**: RB does not continue beyond this point. The original text of Pen. 20, too, ended here. In the MS. a later hand has added, 'Hyd yma y cyrraedd y Llyfr Coch o Hergest,' 'As far as this does the Red Book of Hergest go.'

page line

Pen. 20 is continued down to 1332, but in the MS. on p. 292*a*, 1, there is a change of hand. This new hand seems to be that of the scribe who 'corrected' the main text of Pen. 20, and it bears a marked resemblance to that of BS and *Brut y Brenhined* in BM. Cotton MS. Cleopatra B.V. On the other hand, the Welsh version of *Dares Phrygius* in MS. Cleopatra B.V. is certainly written by the same scribe as wrote Pen. MS. 20. See *Y Bibyl Ynghymraec* (ed. Thomas Jones). Cardiff, 1940, pp. lxxxviii–xc; B viii. 19. It appears that Pen. MS. 20 and the *Dares Phrygius*, *Brut y Brenhined*, and *Brenhined y Saeson* of Cleopatra MS. B.V. (which is a composite MS.) are products of the same *scriptorium*.

120 26 **the bridge over the Menai**: BS ac a wnaethant bont ar Venai *o ysgraffav*, 'and they made a bridge across the Menai *with boats*.' Cf. Hemingburgh, ii. 10 fecitque fieri pontem ultra aquam Meneth ad ingressum de Snawdon *super naves multas ad invicem coniunctas*, compositis lignis et conjunctis tabulis super ipsas naves ita quod in fronte una transire possent LX. armati.

120 26–7 **the bridge broke under an excessive load**: BS A phan dores honno (*sc*. y bont) *gan ffrwd y llanw*, 'And when that (*sc*. the bridge) broke *with the flow of the tide*.'

120 36 **with but a few men with him**: in his elegy on the death of Llywelyn ap Gruffudd, the poet Gruffudd ab yr Ynad Coch refers to 'the killing of the eighteen,' MA 268*b* :
   ... Uched y cwynaf—och o'r cwynaw!—
   Arglwydd llwydd *cyn lladd y deunaw*!
('How loudly I bewail—alas for the bewailing!—[him who was] the lord of prosperity before the killing of the eighteen.')
These words suggest that the 'few men' with Llywelyn were either eighteen or—if Llywelyn himself was regarded by the poet as one of the eighteen—seventeen in number.

120 39–121 2 **on the day of Damasus the Pope ... Friday**: BS Ddugwyl Damaseus Bab, *yr vnved dydd ar ddec o vis Ragfyr*, duw Gwener. Ac yna i bwriwyd holl Gymry y'r llawr, 'on the feast-day of Damasus the Pope, *the eleventh day of December*, a Friday. And then all Wales was cast to the ground.'

121 5–6 **And on the fifth day ... was born**: This entry is misplaced, for Edward of Caernarvon was born on 25 April, 1284. The same entry is added below (in the margin in MS.) under the year 1284.

121 10 **and they were taken**: BS Ac *yn ol Kalan Gaiaf* y ducpwyd *ef* (*sc*. Dafydd) yn garcharor, 'And *after the Calends of Winter he* (*sc*. Dafydd) was taken as prisoner ...'

121 12 **And then ... executed**: BS Ac yno *nos Nodolic* y llas ef o angav gorthrwm, 'And there (*sc*. Shrewsbury) *on Christmas Eve* he was put to a dire death.'

121 20 **... length of time**: BS adds: a Jhon Pennardd yn kynnal Gwynedd dan y brenin, 'and John Pennardd holding Gwynedd under the king.' For John Pennardd cf. Pen. 20 *s.a.* 1289 = 1287.

122 1 **Llywelyn ap Llywelyn ab Ynyr**: usually known as Llywelyn of Bromfield.

page line

122   3   **Geoffrey Clement**: In the 'Subsidiary Roll of 1292' (B xiii. 220) he is mentioned as the steward of the 'new castle' in Emlyn and of Cardigan. See also G. T. O. Bridgeman, *History of the Princes of South Wales*. Wigan, 1876, pp. 221–23; J. E. Morris, *The Welsh Wars of Edward I*. Oxford, 1901, pp. 169, 200, 217, 240, 241.

122   4   **at 'Y Gwmfriw' in Builth**: MS. 293*b*, 21–2 *en y Gŵriw* em Buellt. 'Y Gwmfriw' in Builth is unknown to me, and the form may be corrupt: it may be for 'Y Gamriw,' a mountain S.W. of Llanwrthwl.

122   7   **Madog ap Llywelyn ap Maredudd**: See J. G. Edwards, 'Madog ap Llywelyn, the Welsh leader in 1294–5' (B xiii. 207), where it is shown that this Madog was a son of the Llywelyn ap Maredudd who was driven out of Meirionnydd in 1256 and slain in battle in 1263, and so a fifth cousin of Llywelyn ap Gruffudd.

122   9–12   **Edward, king of England ... was executed**: BS has a much fuller entry: Anno Domini MCClxxxxiiij y roddes y brenin dywysogaeth Gymry i Edwart i vab, yr hwnn a anesid ynGhaer yn Arvon. Ac am i eni yno y gelwid ef Edwart Kaer yn Arvon. Ac oblegid roddi o'r brenin y dywysogaeth y'w vab a diddymv etiveddiaeth Gymry, y kyvodes Madoc ap Llywelyn ap Mredudd ap Rys Jevangk ap Rys Mechyll a Morgant ap Mredudd ap Rys Jevangk ap Rys Mechyll, ewythr Madoc: kanis ev nain, gwraic briod Rys Jevangk ap Rys Mechyll, oedd Wladus verch Gruffydd ap Llywelyn ap Jerwerth Drwyndwn, chwaer Llywelyn ap Gruffydd, tywysoc Kymry. Ac wedy kyvodi o naddvnt yn erbyn y brenin y lladdasant Syr Rocher o Pilstwn, littenant y brenin ynGwynedd. Ac yna y doeth y brenin i Wynedd ac yr adeilodd y kestyll yno, nid amgen, Aber Konwy a'r Dew Mares a'r Gaer yn Arvon a Harddlech. Ac y gorvv y'r brenin eisiav digon o vettel arian y'r gost yno wnevthur y vwnai o'r lledr val i daroganasai Verddin o'r blaen yn y 'Broffwydoliaeth Vawr': 'Yr arian a lithrant o ewinedd yr rai a vrevant'. Ac ychydic wedy hynny y daliwyd Madoc a Morgant, ac yn Llvndain y kroged hwynt ac y chwartoried hwynt yll dav. A Chynan ap Mredudd ap Owain ap Gruffydd ap yr Arglwydd Rys a ddelid ac a golled yn Henffordd.

'Anno Domini MCClxxxxiiij the king gave the principality of Wales to Edward, his son, who had been born in Caernarvon. And because he was born there he was called Edward Caernarvon. And since the king had given the principality to his son and abrogated the inheritance of Wales, Madog ap Llywelyn ap Maredudd ap Rhys Ieuanc ap Rhys Mechyll and Morgan ap Maredudd ap Rhys Ieuanc ap Rhys Mechyll, Madog's uncle, rose up: for their grandmother, the wedded wife of Rhys Ieuanc ap Rhys Mechyll, was Gwladus, daughter of Gruffudd ap Llywelyn ap Iorwerth Drwyndwn, sister of Llywelyn ap Gruffudd, prince of Wales. And after they had arisen against the king, they slew Sir Roger de Puleston, the king's lieutenant in Gwynedd. And then the king came to Gwynedd and built the castles there, to wit, Aberconwy and Beaumaris and Caernarvon and Harlech. And the king through lack of sufficient silver metal for his expenses there had to make his money from leather, as Myrddin had prophesied before in the "Great Prophecy": "Money shall flow from the claws of those that bellow." And a little after that Morgan and Madog were captured, and in London

NOTES

both of them were hanged and quartered. And Cynan ap Maredudd ab Owain ap Gruffudd son of the Lord Rhys was captured and put to death at Hereford.'

It will have been noticed above that Gutun Owain calls Madog ap Llywelyn ap Maredudd a son of Rhys Ieuanc ap Rhys Mechyll. Robert Vaughan, the antiquary of Hengwrt, has added a note (now partly illegible) at the foot of the page: Mae'n debic na chafas ac na cheisiodd gwr o Ddeheubarth bendifigaeth trwy [. . .] a'r hen lyfre sydd yn dywedyd mae Mad. ap Ll̄n ap Mered. o Wynedd oedd ef, 'It appears that no man from Deheubarth obtained or sought chieftainship through [. . .] and the ancient books say that he was Madog ap Llywelyn ap Maredudd from Gwynedd.' See note on 122.7.

122 17 **and he was expelled from this island**: Actually, Bailliol was kept in prison till 1299. It was upon his release in that year that he went to the Continent.

122 20–1 **died Gilbert, earl of Clare . . . English**: The chronology is wrong here: Gilbert died on 7 December, 1295.

122 23–4 **And the sun . . . autumn**: BS ac y kolles yr haul i lliw ynechrav y kynhaiaf, *kanis lliw gwaedol oedd arni y dydd hwnnw*, 'and the sun lost its colour at the beginning of autumn, *for there was a bloody colour upon it that day.*'

122 26–7 **John, earl of Warenne, died**: He died on 27 September, 1304.

122 28 **The Pope of Rome**: i.e. Benedict XI.

123 12 **Anno ix**: BS adds: Ac yn y vlwyddyn racwyneb y priodes Edwart Kaer yn Arvon, brenin Lloegr, Jsabel verch Phylip Dec, brenin Ffraingk, 'And in the following year Edward Caernarvon, king of England, married Isabella, daughter of Philip le Bel, king of France.' But the actual date of Edward II's marriage was 25 January, 1308.

123 14 **Edward the Third was born**: Edward III was born on 13 November, 1312. Hence the chronicler's dating is one year in arrear.

123 15–6 **on the feast-day of Stt. Gervasius and Protasius**: i.e. 19 June: but the date of Gaveston's death is 13 June, 1312.

123 21 **the encounter in the Pools**: MS. y kyfranc en *y Polles*; BS gyfrangk yn *y Pollys*. The reference is to the battle of Bannockburn. The form *Polles* (= Pools) is found in Hemingburgh, ii. 140 in his account of the battle of Stirling, 1297: . . . confestim recesserunt ad suos qui in silvis latitabant juxta *Polles*; qui nefandae rei videntes eventum, egressi sunt obviam nostris, et multos particulariter fugientes peremerunt ibidem ad *Polles*, asportantes spolia multa et quadrigas onustas abducentes; non enim poterunt quadrigae vel summarii a fugientibus abduci de facili in lucubro et mariscis. Cf. W. M. Mackenzie, *The Battle of Bannockburn*. Glasgow, 1913. pp. 43–4: '. . . the river banks, and the banks of the Bannock as it draws to its exit, be fringed with great blobs or lagoons of water, probably flooded at high tide, and soaking round in muddy patches and channels. So marked a feature of the ground were these lagoons that it was known as

page line

"the Pools"; and it was while struggling through these that the English baggage was picked up after Stirling Bridge by the Steward and Lennox . . .' Cf. ib. p. 67.

123 25 **Dafydd**: i.e. Dafydd ap Bleddyn, who was consecrated bishop on 12 January, 1315.

123 29-31 **Anno vij . . . was seized**: These entries not in BS. The revolt of Llywelyn Bren took place after the Parliament at Lincoln, which assembled on 27 January, 1316, by modern reckoning. Counting the beginning of the year from 25 March, it would fall in 1315 for the chronicler. Llywelyn Bren was captured in July, 1316, and so the next annal is two years ahead in its dating. It is probable that 'Anno vij' also is two years ahead. See H. H. Knight, 'On the Insurrection of Llewelyn Bren' in *Archaeologia Cambrensis* ii (New Series), 179-91.

124 15 **soon after that**: Actually, Bridgenorth was burned *before* the king went to Gloucester.

124 19-22 **and the earl of Lancaster . . . same year**: BS a daly Jarll Longkastl, a thrannoeth y llas i benn yn Henffordd, 'and the earl of Lancaster was seized, and on the following day his head was struck off at Hereford.'

124 23-7 **The barons . . . were imprisoned**: BS does not give the names of the traitors taken: Anno Domini MCCCxxij yr ymladdwyd a'r barwniaid ymhob lle ac i llas rai, eraill a groged, eraill a garcharwyd, 'Anno Domini MCCCxxij the barons were fought everywhere and some were slain, others were hanged, others were imprisoned.'

For fuller lists of the traitors taken in 1322 see G. L. Haskins, 'A Chronicle of the Civil Wars of Edward II' in *Speculum*, xiv. 73-81; ib. p. 75, note 1; G. Sayles, 'The Formal Judgments on the Traitors of 1322,' *Speculum*, xvi. 57. Cf. EHR LVII. 373.

124 31-3 **The earl of Warenne . . . feast of St. Brigit**: Warenne was appointed to go to Gascony on 2 March, 1325, by modern reckoning,— which was in 1324 for the chronicler reckoning the beginning of the year from 25 March. Warenne actually sailed from Portsmouth on 25 August, 1325.

124 35-6 **as messengers . . . France**: BS . . . i wnevthur heddwch rwng y brenin a brenin Ffraingk, yr hwnn oedd yn meddiannv i gywethav ef o'r tu draw y'r mor. A thra vvant yno, y peris y brenin drwy gyngor drwc grio yn Llvndain i vab a'i wraic yn draetvriaid jddo ac y'w deyrnas, '. . . to make peace between the king and the king of France, who was in possession of his territories beyond the sea. And whilst they were there, the king by evil counsel had his son and his wife proclaimed in London as traitors to him and to his kingdom.'

124 36-7 **And that Christmas . . . Bordeaux**: it was at the end of 1326 (by modern reckoning) that Warenne returned from Gascony. This was 1325 for the chronicler reckoning the beginning of the year from 25 March.

125 4-5 **And on the feast-day of Luke . . . monastery**: i.e. Arundel was caught on 18 October. He was executed on 17 November. See EHR LVII. 372, and note 3 on this entry. BS does not state that Arundel

NOTES 221

page line

was caught in the monastery, but it adds 'Ac y ffoes y brenin a Syr Huw Hen ac y llusgwyd ef. A thrannoeth y llas Jarll Arwndel yn Henffordd Wyl Saint Edmwnt,' 'And the king fled, and Sir Hugh the Elder, and he was drawn. And on the day following the feast of St. Edmund the earl of Arundel was put to death in Hereford.' Cf. the next paragraph in Pen. 20.

125 12–6 **and Simon Reding ... crowned king**: the corresponding passage in BS is: a dwyn y brenin ymraint karcharor i gastell Kilingworth ynghylch Kalan Gaiaf. Ac wedy yr Ystwyll y gwnaethbwyd Parlment yn Llvndain ac y tynnwyd yr hen vrenin o'i vrenhiniaith ac yr vrddwyd Edwart i vab yn vrenin yn bymthec blwydd o oedran Ddugwyl Vair Sanffraid. A mis Ebrill nesaf ar hynny y ducpwyd yr hen vrenin i gastell Berkle. Ac yno i gwnaethbwyd ber main a'i vrydio yn wynnias a'i hyrddu ar i hyd oddi tano a llosgi i emysgar o'r tv mewn, 'and the king was taken as a prisoner to the castle of Kenilworth, about the Calends of Winter. And after Epiphany a parliament was held in London and the old king was removed from his kingship and Edward, his son, was ordained king when fifteen years old on the feast-day of Mary [after that of] St. Brigit. And in the month of April next to that the old king was taken to the castle of Berkeley. And there a thin lance was fashioned and heated white-hot and plunged lengthwise under him and his bowels were burnt within.'

Edward III was crowned on 29 February, 1327, by modern reckoning. The coronation is placed in 1326 by the chronicler because he reckoned the beginning of the year from 25 March.

Both Pen. 20 and BS date Edward's coronation on 'the feast-day of Mary [after that of] St. Brigit,' i.e. on February 2, instead of on 29 January.

125 17–8 **the daughter of the count of Hainaut**: BS *Philipa* verch Jarll *Prouins*, '*Philippa*, the daughter of the count of *Provence*.' Pen. 20 is correct: Philippa was the daughter of the count of Hainaut.

125 38 **In that year ... Dunstable**: not in BS.

126 14–7 **In that year Roger Mortimer ... the feast of Andrew**: BS Gwyl Luc yn ol hynny i daliwyd Rocher Mortmer yn siambr yr hen vrenhin. Ac o'r achos hwnnw ac am varvolaeth tad y brenin y llvsgwyd ef ac i chwartoried yn Llvndain ac y digowethwyd i ettiwedd, 'On the feast of Luke after that Roger Mortimer was caught in the old king's chamber. And for that reason and because of the death of the king's father he was drawn and quartered in London and his heir was dispossessed.'

126 22–3 **was never reaped**: BS adds: A'r kynhaiaf hwnnw vu'r Kynhaiaf Glas, 'And that autumn was the "Green Autumn".'

126 29–30 **a site for a fortification ... Iâl**: see *Inventory of the Ancient Monuments in the County of Denbigh*, p. 19 (No. 59). Cf. EHR LVII, 374, footnote 1.

126 30–1 **In that year ... London**: not in BS. Cf. Hemingburgh, ii. 303 *Die vero Lunae post festum Sancti Matthaei Apostoli* Londoniis inter

page line

    Crucem et Soper-lane tredecim milites hastiludia contra quoscunque venire volentes *per tres dies* tenuerunt.

126 37 **. . . at Gresford**: An effigy of Madog ap Llywelyn is still preserved in Gresford church. See *Inventory of Ancient Monuments in the County of Denbigh*, p. 62. Cf. EHR LVii, 372, footnote 2.

127 1–6 **the body of Harold . . . were buried**: for the tradition that Harold died and was buried at Chester see E. A. Freeman, *The History of the Norman Conquest of England*, iii. 758–59. This entry in Pen. 20 was unknown to Freeman when he wrote his note. Cf. EHR LVii. 373.

127 7–9 **In the same year . . . Scotland**: Not in BS. Entries in BS continue to 1461 (inclusive) but they hardly refer to Wales and are very scrappy.

APPENDIX
LIST OF SAINTS' DAYS, WITH DATES

Ambrose	4 April.
Andrew the Apostle	30 November.
Benedict	21 March.
—— translation	11 July.
Brigit	1 February.
Calixtus, Pope	14 October.
Catherine	25 November.
Cecilia	22 November.
Clement, Pope	23 November.
Damasus, Pope	11 December.
David	1 March.
Denis	9 October.
Edmund, archbishop	16 November.
Edward, king and martyr	5 January.
—— translation	13 October.
Gervasius and Protasius	19 June.
Gregory, Pope	12 March.
Hilary	13 January.
Ieuan y Coed	29 August.
James the Apostle	25 July.
John the Baptist	24 June.
—— decollation	see Ieuan y Coed.
John the Evangelist	27 December.
Kenelm, king	17 July.
Lawrence	10 August.
Lucy	13 December.
Luke	18 October.
Martin	11 November.
Mary, feast of, after that of St. Brigit	2 February.
——, ——, at the Equinox	25 March.
——, first feast of, in the autumn	15 August.
——, last ——, ——	8 September.
Matthew the Apostle	21 September.
Matthias the Apostle	24 February.
Michael	29 September.
Nicholas	6 December.
Patrick	17 March.
Paul	25 January.
Peter	1 August.
Simon and Jude	28 October.
Stephen the Martyr	26 December.
Thomas the Apostle	21 December.
Thomas the Martyr	29 December.

INDEX

[The numbers refer to pages. Under each item and sub-item the references are in textual, and therefore chronological order except where, in a few cases, alphabetical order was preferable. Names of the type 'X ap Y' are listed under 'X', and those of the type 'A fitz B' under 'fitz.' N = Note.]

A.

Aber
    Dafydd ap Llywelyn ap Iorwerth dies at, 107.

Aberafan, castle
    attacked by Maredudd and Rhys, sons of Gruffudd ap Rhys, 58.

Aberconwy, castle
    commenced, 121;

——, monastery
    Gruffudd ap Cynan ab Owain Gwynedd dies in, 80;
    Hywel ap Gruffudd ap Cynan buried in, 93;
    Llywelyn ap Maelgwn Ieuanc buried in, 101;
    Llywelyn ap Iorwerth dies and is buried in, 105;
    Dafydd ap Llywelyn ap Iorwerth buried in, 107;
    Gruffudd ap Llywelyn ap Iorwerth reburied in, 108;
    abbot of, *see* Gruffudd, abbot of Strata Florida.

Abercorram, castle
    entrusted to Bleddyn ap Cedifor, 41;
    taken by Rhys ap Gruffudd, 73;
    and town, burnt by Welsh, 111.

Aberdaron, church
    Gruffudd ap Rhys ap Tewdwr seeks refuge in, 40.

Aberdovey
    see Aberdyfi.

Aberdyfi
    ship from Ireland in, 30;
    castle built at, 59;
    apportionment of lands at, between sons of Lord Rhys and sons of Gruffudd ap Rhys, 92.

Abereinion, castle
    built by Maelgwn ap Rhys, 83.

Aberffraw
    ravaged, 8.

Abergavenny
    Seisyll ap Dyfnwal and son Ieuan seized at, 69;
    Seisyll ap Dyfnwal and son Geoffrey slain at, 71;
    castle of, taken by Reginald de Breos, 90;
    castle of, destroyed by Richard Marshal and Owain ap Gruffudd, 103.

Abergelau
    Ionathal of, dies, 4.

Abergwili
    Rhain defeated in battle at, 12.

Aber-llech
    French defeated at, 20.

Aberllwchwr, castle
    burnt by Maredudd and Rhys, sons of Gruffudd ap Rhys, 57.

Abermenai
    Cadwaladr ap Gruffudd ap Cynan lands at, 53.

Aber-miwl
    barn of, English slain in, 113;
    ——, burnt by John Lestrange, ib.

Aber-rheidol, castle
    taken by Rhys ap Gruffudd, 63.

Aberriw, 37.

Abertawe
    see Seinhenydd, Swansea.

Aberteifi
    see Cardigan.

Aberystwyth, castle
    attacked by Gruffudd ap Rhys, 42-4;
    burnt by Owain and Cadwaladr, sons of Gruffudd ap Cynan, 51;
    burnt by Hywel ab Owain, 53;
    burnt by Maelgwn ap Rhys, 83;
    rebuilt by Llywelyn ap Iorwerth, 83;
    built by Falkes de Breauté, 86;
    destroyed by Maelgwn ap Rhys and brother Rhys Fychan, 86;
    subdued by Llywelyn ap Iorwerth, 98;
    built by Edmund, brother of Edward I, 118-9;
    and town of, taken by Gruffudd ap Maredudd ab Owain and Rhys Fychan ap Rhys ap Maelgwn, 120.
    see Llanbadarn-fawr.

Abraham, bishop of Menevia
    succeeds Sulien, 17;
    dies, 17.

Abraham, bishop of St. Asaph
    dies, 102.

Achilles, 105.

Acre
    Christians escorted to, by Saracens, 99;
    Louis IX, king of France, goes to, from Damietta, 108.

Adam, bishop of St. Asaph
    dies at Oxford, 72.

[Adomnán]
    see Damnani, N.

Aedd, son of Mell
    dies, 5, N.

Aeddan ap Blegywryd
    with four sons, slain by Llywelyn ap Seisyll, 12.

Aelfhere, Saxon leader
    lands ravaged by, 8, 9.

224

INDEX

Aeron, river
    land between it and the Dyfi, given by Llywelyn ap Iorwerth to sons of Gruffudd ap Rhys, 83;
    land between it and the Dyfi, granted to the king by sons of Gruffudd ap Rhys, 86.
Æthelflæd, queen
    dies, 6.
Ajax, 77.
[Alan], bishop of Bangor
    dies, 75.
Alan, king of Brittany
    succeeds Cadwaladr ap Cadwallon as ruler of Britons, 1.
Albanactus, 78.
Aldfrid, king of the Saxons
    dies, 1.
Alexander, of Macedon, 78.
Alexander I, king of Scotland
    son of Maelcoluim, 27, 37;
    succeeds brother Edgar, 27;
    leads army against Gwynedd, 37-8.
Alexander II, king of Scotland
    dies, 108.
Alexander III, Pope
    summons Henry II to Rome, 66;
    dies, 72.
Alexander IV, Pope
    consecrates Richard de Carew, bishop of Menevia, 110.
Alfred, king of Wessex
    dies, 6.
Amlaibh, king of Dublin
    dies, 7;
    sons of, Holyhead and Llŷn ravaged by, 8;
    see Sitriuc.
Anarawd ab Einion
    slain, 80.
    see Anarawd ap Rhys (*recte* ab Einion).
Anarawd ap Gruffudd ap Rhys
    daughter of Owain ap Gruffudd ap Cynan betrothed to, 53;
    slain by followers of Cadwaladr ap Gruffudd ap Cynan, 53.
Anarawd ap Gwri
    slain, 7.
Anarawd ap Rhodri Mawr
    harries Ceredigion and Ystrad Tywi, 5;
    dies, 6.
Anarawd ap Rhys (*recte* ab Einion)
    blinds brothers Madog and Hywel, 75;
    see Anarawd ab Einion.
Angharad, daughter of Maredudd ab Owain
    wife of (1) Cynfyn ap Gwerystan, 28, 46;
    —— (2) Llywelyn ap Seisyll, 40-1.
Angharad, daughter of Owain ab Edwin
    wife of Gruffudd ap Cynan, 49;
    children of, 49;
    dies, 62.

Angharad, daughter of Uchdryd, bishop of Llandaff
    sons of, 66.
Anglesey, island
    Hywel of, victorious, 3;
    ravaged by Black Host, 4;
    Sunday battle in, 5;
    battle of Ynegydd in, 5;
    Igmund comes to, 6;
    ravaged by folk of Dublin, 6;
    subdued by Godfrey, son of Harold, 8;
    ravaged by Godfrey, son of Harold, and Black Host, 9;
    conquered by Maredudd ab Owain, 9;
    ravaged by Custennin ap Iago and Godfrey, son of Harold, 9;
    ravaged, 10;
    won by Gruffudd ap Cynan, 16;
    attacked by Hugh of Chester and Hugh of Shrewsbury, 21, 30;
    king Magnus in battle against French, off, 21;
    given to Gruffudd ap Cynan, 21;
    king Magnus comes to, 24;
    held by Gruffudd ap Cynan, 48;
    Cadwaladr ap Gruffudd ap Cynan expelled from, 58;
    attacked by Henry II's fleet, 59-60;
    Maelgwn ab Owain Gwynedd expelled from, 70;
    won by Dafydd ab Owain Gwynedd, 70;
    Dafydd ab Owain Gwynedd expelled from, 70.
    subdued by Rhodri ab Owain Gwynedd, 74;
    men and chattels of, moved into Eryri by Llywelyn ap Iorwerth, 85;
    monastery of Llan-faes in, 117;
    ravaged by Edward I's fleet, 119;
    occupied by Edward I's fleet, 120;
    see Goronwy ap Tudur.
Anjou
    warriors of, in expedition (1165) against Welsh, 63;
    Henry III fails to recover territory in, 101.
Annals
    kept at Strata Florida, 108.
Anselm, archbishop of Canterbury
    reinstated, 22.
Anselm the Fat, bishop of Menevia
    dies, 107.
Antioch, city
    taken by Sultan of Babylon, 115.
Apulia
    Manfred, son of emperor Frederick, slain in, 115.
Arberth, castle
    burnt by Gruffudd ap Rhys ap Tewdwr, 40;
    burnt by Maelgwn ap Rhys and Rhys Ieuanc ap Gruffudd, 90;
    and town of, burnt by Welsh (1257), 111;
    see Cardigan (*recte* Arberth).

archbishop
　created in Damietta, 97;
　see Asser; Canterbury; Elfoddw; York.
Ardudwy, commot
　taken from Gruffudd ap Llywelyn, 98.
Arfon, cantref
　attempted invasion of, by English from Anglesey, 120.
Armagh
　ravaged and burnt, 10.
Armenia
　ravaged by Sultan of Babylon, 115.
Arnulf, son of Roger of Montgomery
　see Montgomery.
Arthen, king of Ceredigion
　dies, 3.
Arthurus, 78.
Arundel, castle
　occupied by Robert de Bellême, 23;
　taken by Henry I, 23.
———, earls of
　[Edmund fitz Alan] seized and executed, 125;
　[Richard fitz Alan], rights given to, 126.
Arwystli, cantref
　Owain ap Cadwgan's men flee to, 29;
　Llandinam in, raided by Owain Gwynedd, 62;
　subdued by Gwenwynwyn, 79;
　taken from Gruffudd ap Llywelyn ap Iorwerth by brother Dafydd, 104;
　taken from Gruffudd ap Gwenwynwyn by Llywelyn ap Gruffudd, 116.
Asser, archbishop of Britain
　dies, 6.
Athelstan, king of the Saxons
　dies, 6.
Atropos, 97.
Audley, the
　executed, 124.
Austria, duke of
　leads Christians against Damietta, 96-7.

B.

Babylon
　Christians go to, from Damietta, 98;
　Armenia ravaged by Sultan of, 115;
　Antioch taken by Sultan of, 115.
Bachglas, follower of Maelgwn ap Rhys
　slain, 86.
Badlesmere, Sir Bartholomew of
　seized and executed, 124.
Bailliol, Edward de
　seeks to win Scotland, 127.
Bailliol, Sir John, king of Scotland
　seized, with son, 122;
　expelled, 122.
Bala, castle
　taken by Llywelyn ap Iorwerth, 82.
Baldwin, archbishop of Canterbury
　takes the Cross, 73;
　goes to Jerusalem, 74;
　dies, 74.

Baldwin's Castle
　destroyed by Llywelyn ap Iorwerth, 102;
　peace between Llywelyn ap Gruffudd and Henry III arranged at, 115;
　army sent to, against Welsh (1276), 118;
　constable of, see Lestrange, John.
Bangor
　ravaged by Gentiles, 16;
　king John sends men to burn, 85;
———, bishops of
　see [Alan], Cadwgan, Gwion, Maredudd (recte Meurig), Morlais, Rhobert, [Richard].
Banolau
　battle of, 5.
bards
　of Gwynedd, 71;
　see Gwrgant ap Rhys.
Bardsey, island
　Iarddur, monk from, 11.
Basingwerk
　Owain Gwynedd encamps at, 59;
　fortification of, destroyed by Owain Gwynedd, 64.
Beaumaris
　castle of, commenced, 121.
Beaumont, Henry de
　castle of, at Swansea, 40.
Bec, Thomas de, bishop of Menevia
　succeeds Richard de Carew, 119;
　celebrates Mass at Strata Florida, 120;
　consecrated bishop, 120.
Becket, Thomas, archbishop of Canterbury
　murder of, 65, 66;
　reburial of, 97.
Bede
　dies, 2.
Beli, son of Elffin, king of Dumbarton
　dies, 2.
Bellême, Robert de
　see Shrewsbury, earls of
[Benedict XI], Pope
　dies, 122.
Benedict, St.
　habit of, 109.
Berkleys, the
　imprisoned, 124.
Bernard, bishop of Menevia
　succeeds Geoffrey, 39;
　death and encomium of, 56
Berwyn, mountain
　Henry II encamps on (1165), 63.
Black Gentiles
　ravage York, 4;
　see Black Host; Gentiles; Norsemen; Pagans (1).
Black Host
　ravage Anglesey, 4, 9;
　Maredudd ab Owain pays tribute to, 10;
　see Black Gentiles; Gentiles; Norsemen; Pagans (1).

INDEX

Black Mountain, the
    Llywelyn ap Iorwerth crosses, 95.
Blaenllyfni
    castle of, surrendered to Giles de Breos, 90;
    ——, destroyed by Richard Marshal and Owain ap Gruffudd, 103.
Blaen-porth
    castle of, held by Gilbert fitz Richard, 42;
    ——, attacked by Gruffudd ap Rhys ap Tewdwr, 42.
Blathaon, in Scotland
    promontory of, 37.
Bleddri ap Cedifor
    see Bleddyn (recte Bleddri) ap Cedifor.
Bleddyn (recte Bleddri) ap Cedifor
    castle of Abercorram entrusted to, 41.
Bleddyn ap Cynfyn, king, 28;
    defeats Ithel (recte Idwal) and Maredudd, sons of Gruffudd ap Llywelyn, 15;
    rules after battle of Mechain, 16;
    slain through treachery, 16;
    death of, avenged, 17;
    encomium of, 17;
    ——, daughters of
    see Gwenllïan, Hunydd.
    ——, sons of
    Rhys ap Tewdwr expelled by, 18.
Bleddyn ap Gwyn
    Maredudd ap Hywel slain by sons of, 52.
Bleuddydd, bishop of Menevia
    dies, 16.
Blois, Stephen of
    see Stephen, king of England.
blood-rain
    in Britain and Ireland, 1.
Blyth, castle
    occupied by Robert de Bellême, 23;
    taken by Henry I, 23.
Bodyddon, castle
    destroyed by Llywelyn ap Gruffudd, 111.
Bonheddig, bishop of Menevia
    rules, 4, N.
Bordeaux
    Henry III and queen stay at (1242), 106;
    Henry III returns from (1243), 106;
    earl of Warenne goes to and returns from, 124.
Boroughbridge
    battle of, 124.
Boulogne, count of
    makes pact with king John, 89;
    captured at Vernon, 89.
Brabant, William
    slain by Owain ap Cadwgan's men, 34.
Breauté, Falkes de
    see Falkes, sheriff of Cardiff.
Brecon, town
    Trahaearn Fychan executed at, 79;
    castle of, surrendered to Giles de Breos, 90;
    town of, surrenders to Llywelyn ap Iorwerth, 95;
    castle of, destroyed by Llywelyn ap Iorwerth, 102;
    town of, burnt by Llywelyn ap Iorwerth, 102;
    castle of, destroyed by Llywelyn ap Iorwerth, 102.
Breos, Giles de, bishop of Hereford
    sends brother Reginald into Brycheiniog, 90;
    castles surrendered to, 90;
    makes peace with king John, 91;
    dies at Gloucester, 91.
——, John de
    weds Margaret, daughter of Llywelyn ap Iorwerth, 97;
    repairs castle of Swansea, 99;
    dies, 102.
——, Matilda de, wife of Gruffudd ap Rhys
    dies at Llanbadarn-fawr, 84;
    buried at Strata Florida, 84;
——, Reginald de
    received in Brycheiniog, 90;
    castles taken by, 90;
    succeeds brother Giles in patrimony, 91;
    weds daughter [Gwladus Ddu] of Llywelyn ap Iorwerth, 91;
    king John fails to gain support of, 93;
    makes peace with Henry III, 95;
    Rhys Ieuanc and brother Owain rise against, 95;
    surrenders to Llywelyn ap Iorwerth, 95;
    Llywelyn gives castle of Seinhenydd to, 95, N.
——, William de
    makes pact with Rhys ap Gruffudd, 76;
    executes Trahaearn Fychan, 79;
    banished to Ireland, 83;
    wife of
    see Matilda of St. Valéry.
——, William de, the Younger, son of preceding
    banished to Ireland, 83;
    with family, seized by king John, 84;
    with mother, put to death, 84.
——, William de, the Younger, son of Reginald
    captured by Welsh, 101;
    release of, 101;
    hanged by Llywelyn ap Iorwerth, 101-2.
Bretagne (recte Mortaigne), William de
    imprisoned by Henry I, 27.
Brian [Boruma], king of Ireland
    slain in battle, 11;
    sons of, see Donnchadh; Murchadh.
Bridgenorth, castle
    occupied by Robert de Bellême, 23;
    taken by Henry I, 23;
    Llywelyn ab Owain [ap Cadwgan] interned in, 50;
    burnt by barons, 124.

Bristol
    Owain ap Dafydd ap Gruffudd taken prisoner to, 121;
    Edward II comes to, from Morgannwg, 125;
    earl of, at Dinwileir, 61;
    ———, Owain ap Iorwerth slain by men of, 68.
Britain
    archbishop of, *see* Asser.
———, island of
    mortality in, 1, 57, 76;
    Otir comes to, 6;
    mortality upon cattle in, 10;
    Eilaf comes to, 12;
    king Magnus purposes to conquer, 21;
    Henry I gathers host of, 37.
Britain (i.e. Wales)
    51; *see* Wales.
Brithdir
    see Owain of.
Britons (i.e. Welsh), 15, 32, 43, 55, 74;
    lose kingship, 1;
    victorious in three battles, 2;
    in battle against Picts, 2;
    ——— ——— Saxons, 2;
    Easter changed for, 2;
    harried, 2;
    defeat Saxons at Hereford, 14;
    lands of, seized by French, 19;
    revolt of, against French, 19;
    expedition of William Rufus against, 20;
    wrongs suffered by, 24;
    imprisonment of Iorwerth ap Bleddyn lamented by, 26;
    extermination of, planned, 37;
    see Welsh.
———, kings of
    see Anarawd ap Rhodri, Gruffudd ap Llywelyn ap Seisyll, Hywel the Good, Maredudd ab Owain, Rhodri, William the Bastard.
Bromfield
    see Madog ap Llywelyn of.
Bron-yr-erw
    battle of, 16.
Brotor
    slain, 11.
Brun
    battle of, 6.
Brycheiniog
    men of, slay Ithel, king of Gwent, 4;
    ravaged by Norsemen, 5;
    ravaged by Saxons, 9;
    Rhys ap Tewdwr slain by French of, 19;
    French expedition to, 20;
    men of, slay Llywelyn ap Cadwgan, 21;
    Rhys ap Gruffudd leads host from, against Rhys Fychan, 87;
    Rhys Ieuanc goes to, 88;
    Reginald de Breos received in, 90;
    Llywelyn ap Iorwerth invades, 95;
    ——— ravages, 102;
    Llywelyn ap Gruffudd receives homage of, 112–13;
    won for earl of Hereford, 118;
    Llywelyn ap Gruffudd sends men to receive homage of, 120;
    see Trahaearn Fychan of.
———, lord of
    Seisyll ap Dyfnwal and son Geoffrey slain by, 71;
    Maelgwn ap Rhys escapes from prison of, 74.
Bryneglwys, in Iâl
    fortification at, 126.
Bryn Onnen
    battle of, 5.
Builth, cantref
    won from Reginald de Breos, 95;
    Llywelyn ap Iorwerth takes from William de Breos, son of Reginald, 101;
    Llywelyn ap Gruffudd invades, 112;
    won for Roger de Mortimer, 118;
    Llywelyn ap Gruffudd occupies, 120;
    see y Gamriw.
———, castle of
    fortified by Ingelard, sheriff of Gloucester, 84;
    surrendered to Giles de Breos, 90;
    not won from Reginald de Breos, 95;
    given to Llywelyn ap Iorwerth, 101;
    fortified by John de Monmouth, 106.
Burgh-on-Sands
    Edward I dies at, 123.
Burgundy
    Henry III sails to (1253), 109.
———, prince of
    see Theobald.
Burton-on-Trent
    barons dispersed at, 124.
Bwlchydinas
    castle of, destroyed by Richard Marshal and Owain ap Gruffudd, 103.

C.

Cadell, king of Powys
    dies, 3.
Cadell ab Arthfael
    poisoned, 7.
Cadell ap Gruffudd ap Rhys
    castles overcome by, 54;
    in attack on Wizo's Castle, 55;
    repairs Carmarthen castle, 57;
    harries Cydweli, 57;
    wins Is-Aeron, 57;
    takes Ceredigion from Hywel ab Owain Gwynedd, 57;
    at taking of Llanrhystud castle, 57;
    at repairing of Ystrad Meurig castle, 57;
    injured by men from Tenby, 57;
    goes on pilgrimage, 58;
    dies at Strata Florida, 71.
Cadell ap Rhodri
    dies, 6.

INDEX

Cadfan ap Cadwaladr
 dispossessed by Hywel ab Owain Gwynedd, 57;
 see Cadwgan (*recte* Cadfan) ap Cadwaladr.
Cadwaladr ap Cadwallon
 dies in Rome, 1.
Cadwaladr ap Gruffudd ap Cynan
 encomium of, 51;
 attacks Walter's Castle, 51;
 defeats Flemings and Normans, 51–2;
 in third attack on Ceredigion, 52;
 expelled by brother Owain, 53;
 castle of, at Aberystwyth, burnt, 53;
 lands at Abermenai from Ireland, 53;
 makes peace with brother Owain, 53;
 seized by Irish, 53;
 opposed to Hywel and Cynan, sons of Owain Gwynedd, 56;
 Cynfael castle built by, 56;
 builds castle at Llanrhystud, 57;
 gives his portion of Ceredigion to son Cadwgan (*recte* Cadfan), 57;
 expelled from Anglesey, 58;
 recovers land, 60;
 at Dinwileir, 61;
 opposes Henry II's expedition (1165), 63;
 with Owain Gwynedd and Rhys ap Gruffudd expels Owain Cyfeiliog 64;
 at taking of Rhuddlan castle, 65;
 dies, 68.
Cadwaladr ap Rhys
 slain in Dyfed, 73.
Cadwaladr ap Seisyll ap Dyfnwal
 slain by French, 71.
Cadwallon ab Owain
 dies, 8.
Cadwallon ab Owain Cyfeiliog
 slays Owain ap Madog, 73.
Cadwallon ab Owain Gwynedd
 blinded, 63.
Cadwallon ap Gruffudd ap Cynan
 invades Meirionnydd and Powys, 49;
 slays uncles, 49;
 slain by first-cousins, 50.
——, son of
 see Cunedda ap Cadwallon.
Cadwallon ap Ieuaf
 slays Ionafal ap Meurig, 9;
 slain by Maredudd ab Owain, 9.
Cadwallon ap Madog ab Idnerth of Maelienydd
 escapes from French, 62;
 opposes Henry II's expedition (1165), 63;
 at council at Gloucester, 70–1;
 slain, 72.
——, sons of
 castle of Rhaeadr-gwy, burnt by, 75;
 expelled from Maelienydd, 75.
Cadwallon ap Maelgwn of Maelienydd
 dies at Cwm-hir, 103.
Cadwallon [ap Maredudd ab Owain]
 dies, 10.

Cadweithen
 expelled, 4;
 Glywysing ravaged by, 5, N.
 dies, 5.
Cadwgan, abbot of Llandyfái
 becomes bishop of Bangor, 91;
 —— a monk at the monastery of Dore, 104.
Cadwgan [ab Elystan Glodrydd]
 sons of, Goronwy and Llywelyn, in battle of Camddwr, 16;
 —— —— —— 'Gweunytwl,' 16.
Cadwgan ab Owain
 slain by Saxons, 7.
Cadwgan ap Bleddyn, 28, 30, 33;
 with brothers Madog and Rhiryd expels Rhys ap Tewdwr, 18;
 plunders Dyfed, 19;
 defeats French in Coedysbys, 19;
 war-band of, attacks Pembroke castle, 20;
 flees to Ireland and returns, 21;
 receives portion of Powys and Ceredigion, 21;
 supports Robert de Bellême, 23, 24;
 lands given to, by brother Iorwerth, 25;
 feast prepared by, 28;
 reaction to son Owain's attack on Cenarth Bychan, 29;
 boards Irish ship at Aberdyfi, 29–30;
 obtains truce from Richard, bishop of London, 30;
 redeems Ceredigion, 31;
 prisoner at king's court, 34;
 given Powys by Henry I, 35;
 slain by Madog ap Rhiryd, 35–6;
 lands given to Uchdryd ab Edwin by, 46;
——, son of, Henry as hostage, 32;
——, sons of, 47–8, 49;
——, ——, come to terms with Henry I, 48;
  invade territory of Llywarch ap Trahaearn, 49;
  slay Cadwallon ap Gruffudd ap Cynan, 50;
——, wife of, 31.
Cadwgan (*recte* Cadfan) ap Cadwaladr ap Gruffudd
 father Cadwaladr's portion of Ceredigion given to, 57.
Cadwgan ap Madog ab Idnerth
 slain, 53.
Cadwgan ap Maredudd
 slain by Walter fitz Richard, 62.
Cadwgan Fychan of Ystrad
 dies, 118.
Caereinion, commot, 35, 37;
 taken from Maredudd [ap Bleddyn], 45;
 castle in, built by Madog ap Maredudd, 59;
 given to Owain ap Madog, 64;
 castle of, destroyed by Owain Cyfeiliog, 64;

Caereinion, commot. (*cont.*)
    taken from Gruffudd ap Llywelyn by brother Dafydd, 104;
    part of, taken from Gruffudd ap Gwenwynwyn, 110–11.
Caerffili, castle
    taken by Llywelyn ap Gruffudd, 115.
Caerleon (-on-Usk)
    taken by Iorwerth ab Owain, 60;
    taken from Iorwerth ab Owain, 66;
    destroyed by Iorwerth ab Owain and allies, 66;
    taken by Iorwerth ab Owain, 70;
    taken by French, 70;
    yielded to Iorwerth ab Owain, 71;
    monastery near, 72;
    besieged by William Marshal, 96;
    burnt by Llywelyn ap Iorwerth, 102.
Caernarvon
    castle of, commenced, 121;
——, Edward of
    see Edward II.
Caerwedros, commot
    castle of, burnt by Owain and Cadwaladr, 51.
[Cairo]
    see Babylon, N.
Camber, 78.
Cambria, 77–8.
Camddwr, river
    battle of, 16.
Canterbury
    archbishops of,
        see Anselm; Becket, Thomas; Baldwin; Hubert; Langton, Stephen; Richard.
——, church of
    archbishop Thomas Becket murdered in, 65;
    St. Thomas Becket reburied in, 97.
Canton, William, of Cemaes
    dies, 101.
Cantref Bychan
    held by Richard fitz Pons, 40;
    Hywel ap Maredudd ap Rhydderch, lord of, 52;
    taken by Rhys and Maredudd, sons of Rhys ap Gruffudd, 75;
    given, excepting Hirfryn and Myddfai, to Rhys Gryg, 92.
Cantref Gwarthaf
    given to Maelgwn ap Rhys, 92;
Cantref Mawr
    portion of, given by Henry I to Owain ap Caradog ap Gruffudd, 40;
    given to Lord Rhys, 60;
    taken by Lord Rhys, 62;
    overrun by Rhys Ieuanc, 88;
    given, excepting Mallaen, to Rhys Gryg, 92.
Caradog, king of Gwynedd
    slain by Saxons, 3.
Caradog ap Gruffudd ap Rhydderch
    slays Maredudd ab Owain [ab Edwin], 16;
    in battle of Camddwr, 16;
    slays Rhys and Hywel, sons of Owain ab Edwin, 17;
    slain in battle of Mynydd Carn, 17.
Cardiff
    Henry II goes through (1172), 68;
    Owain ap Iorwerth slain near, 68;
    castle of, taken by Richard Marshal and Owain ap Gruffudd, 103.
——, sheriff of
    see Falkes.
Cardigan
    attacked by Owain and Cadwaladr and allies, 51;
    ravaged by Hywel and Cynan, sons of Owain Gwynedd, 53–4;
    burnt by Rhys ap Gruffudd, 64;
    rebuilt by Rhys ap Gruffudd, 67;
    Rhys ap Gruffudd holds court at, 71;
    castle of, taken by Maelgwn ap Rhys, 79;
——, withheld from Gruffudd ap Rhys, 80;
——, sold to Saxons, 80–1;
——, surrendered to Llywelyn ap Iorwerth, 91;
——, given to Rhys Ieuanc and brother Owain, 92;
——, given to Llywelyn ap Iorwerth to keep, 96;
——, withheld from Rhys Ieuanc by Llywelyn ap Iorwerth, 98;
——, promised to Rhys Ieuanc by Llywelyn ap Iorwerth, 98;
——, surrendered to William Marshal, 99;
    town of, burnt by Maelgwn Ieuanc ap Maelgwn, 102;
    castle of, surrenders to Maelgwn Ieuanc ap Maelgwn, 102;
——, William Marshall sent to fortify, 105.
—— (*recte* Arberth)
    destroyed by Welsh, repaired by Flemings and again destroyed by Llywelyn ap Iorwerth, 97.
cardinals, papal
    see John; Langton, Stephen; Otto.
Carew, Master Richard de, bishop of Menevia
    consecration, 110;
    dies, 119.
Carmarthen
    Walter, chief justice of Gloucester, comes to, 29;
    castle of, Welsh chieftains appointed to keep, 41;
——, men of Ystrad Tywi flee to, 44;
——, Flemings from Rhos come to, 44;
——, burnt by Owain and Cadwaladr, 52;
——, built by Gilbert, son of earl Gilbert, 54;
——, overcome by Cadell ap Gruffudd, 54;

INDEX

Carmarthen (*cont.*)
—, repaired by Cadell ap Gruffudd, 57;
—, besieged by Lord Rhys, 61;
—, burnt by Lord Rhys, 75–6;
Rhys Fychan seized at, 88;
castle of, burnt by Llywelyn ap Iorwerth, 91;
—, given to Llywelyn ap Iorwerth to keep, 96;
—, given to Maelgwn ap Rhys, 98;
—, surrendered to William Marshal, 99;
—, repaired by William Marshal, 100;
town and castle of, besieged in vain, 103;
Nicholas de Meules sent from, to dispossess Maelgwn Ieuanc, 107;
Rhys Fychan ap Rhys Mechyll brings army to, 111;
Pain de Chaworth brings army to, 118;
—, justice of
see Meules, Nicholas de.
Carn
see Mynydd Carn.
Carno (1)
see Mynydd Carno.
Carno (2)
battle of, 7.
Carnwyllion, commot
Maredudd ap Rhys slain in, 81;
subdued by Rhys Ieuanc, 90;
given to Rhys Gryg, 92.
Carreg Cennen, castle
given to French by Matilda de Breos, 108;
obtained by Rhys Fychan ap Rhys Mechyll, 108.
Carreg Faelan, castle
destroyed by Llywelyn ap Gruffudd, 113.
Carreg Hofa, castle
taken by Owain Gwynedd and allies, 62;
Owain ap Madog slain at, 73.
Castell Coch
burnt by Llywelyn ap Iorwerth, 103.
Castell Gwallter
see Walter's Castle.
Cedifor, abbot of Strata Florida
dies, 100.
Cedifor ap Daniel, archdeacon of Ceredigion
dies, 62.
Cedifor ap Gollwyn
dies, 18;
daughter of, *see* Ellylw.
Cedifor ap Goronwy
calls Gruffudd ap Rhys ap Tewdwr into Ceredigion, 41.
Cedifor ap Gruffudd
caused to be slain, with four sons, by Maelgwn ap Rhys, 82–3;
wife of, *see* Susanna, daughter of Hywel.

Cedyll
battle of, 4.
Cefn Cynfarchan
Llywelyn ap Iorwerth at, 95.
[Cefn-llys], castle
see Mortimer, Roger II de.
Cefn Rhestr Main, mountain
Rhys ap Gruffudd encamps on, 61;
Ceiriog, river
see Dyffryn Ceiriog.
Celli Tarfawg
French slain in, 20, N.
Cemaes, cantref, in Dyfed
Hywel ap Rhys slain in, 82;
plundered by Maelgwn ap Rhys and Rhys Ieuanc, 90;
men of, subjugated by Llywelyn ap Iorwerth, 91;
given to Maelgwn ap Rhys, 92;
won by Llywelyn ap Gruffudd, 111;
see Canton, William.
Cenarth Bychan, castle
built by Gerald of Windsor, 28;
attacked and burnt by Owain ap Cadwgan, 28.
Cerbhall
dies, 5.
Cerbhall, son of Muirecan, king of Leinster
dies, 6.
Ceredigion
harried by Anarawd and Saxons, 5;
Gruffudd ab Owain slain by men of, 6;
ravaged by [Iago and Ieuaf], sons of Idwal, 7;
relics brought to, from Anglesey, 10, N;
part of Maredudd ab Owain's territory, 10;
ravaged by Edwin ab Einion and Edylfi, 10;
ravaged by French, 16;
overrun by French, 19;
castles of, captured, 19;
ravaged by Welsh, 19;
given to Cadwgan ap Bleddyn, 21;
given to Iorwerth ap Bleddyn, 24;
given to Cadwgan ap Bleddyn, 25;
recovered by Cadwgan ap Bleddyn, 31;
Owain ap Cadwgan comes to, 31;
hostility of Dyfed to, 42;
attacks on, by Owain and Cadwaladr, 51–2.;
Cadwaladr ap Gruffudd's portion of, given to Cadwgan (*recte* Cadfan) ap Cadwaladr, 57;
attacked by Cadell, Maredudd and Rhys, sons of Lord Rhys, 57;
Maredudd ap Gruffudd as lord of, 58;
Owain Gwynedd comes to, 58;
Roger, earl of Clare, comes to, 60;
castles of, burnt by Rhys ap Gruffudd, 61;
taken by Rhys ap Gruffudd, 63;
given to Rhys ap Gruffudd, 67;

Ceredigion (*cont.*)
   seized by Maelgwn ap Rhys, 79;
   Llywelyn ap Iorwerth comes to, 91;
   parts of, given to Maelgwn ap Rhys, 92;
   parts of, given to Rhys Ieuanc and brother Owain, 92;
   princes from, tender homage to Edward I, 118.
——, archdeacons of
   see Cedifor ap Daniel; fitz Gerald, David; Gruffudd ap Maredudd ap Rhys; Maredudd, son of Lord Rhys.
——, kings of
   see Arthen; Gwgan ap Meurig.
Ceri, commot
   battle in, between Henry III and Llywelyn ap Iorwerth, 101;
   taken from Gruffudd ap Llywelyn by brother Dafydd, 104;
   John Lestrange goes through, on raid to Cydewain, 113;
   won for Roger de Mortimer, 118.
Cesar, 78.
Charles, king of Sicily
   Conrad killed by, 115.
Chaworth, Pain de
   makes pact with Rhys ap Maredudd ap Rhys and Rhys Wyndod, 118;
   subjugates land above the Aeron, 118;
   leads army to Carmarthen, 118;
   returns to England from Aberystwyth, 119.
——, Patrick de
   in Emlyn, at parley with Welsh leaders, 111–12;
   slain after breaking truce, 112.
Cheap, in London
   tournament at, 126.
Chester
   king Edgar brings fleet to, 8;
   French from, 46–7;
   Henry II leads army to (1157), 59;
   Henry II's host at (1165), 64;
   king John comes to (1211), 85;
   Edward I goes to, 117;
   Edward I leads army to (1276), 118;
   body of king Harold discovered at, 127.
——, constable of
   see Reginald de Crescy.
——, earls of
   see Edward, son of Henry III, later Edward I;
   Hugh I, the Fat
      leads expedition to Gwynedd, 20;
      dies, 22.
   Hugh II (fitz Ranulf)
      accuses Gruffudd ap Cynan and Goronwy ab Owain, 37;
      repairs Cymaron castle, 53;
      subjugates Maelienydd, 53.
   John
      dies, 104.

Ranulf I
   helps Madog ap Maredudd, 57;
   defeated at Coleshill, 57;
   dies, 58.
Ranulf II
   castle of Degannwy rebuilt by, 84;
   —— Holywell built by, 84;
   land of, ravaged by Llywelyn ap Iorwerth, 84;
   Gwenwynwyn flees to, 92;
   in battle of Lincoln, 94;
   goes on Crusade, 96.
Ranulf III
   dies, 102.
Richard, son of Hugh I
   succeeds father, 22, N;
   leader of host against Gwynedd, 37–8.
Christianity
   interdicted in England and Wales, 83;
   restored to the Southerners (*sc.* of Wales), 96.
Christians
   many take Cross, 73;
   defeat Saracens in Spain, 86;
   take Damietta, 96–7;
   surrender Damietta and make truce with Saracens, 99;
   host of, goes to Jerusalem, 108;
   slaughter of, at Damietta, 108.
Christmas
   Cadwgan ap Bleddyn holds feast at, 28;
   Lord Rhys holds court at Cardigan at, 71.
Church, the
   laws of, confirmed, 83;
   ——, renewed, 91.
Cilcennin
   Maelgwn ap Rhys routed at, 84.
Cilgerran, castle
   Rhys ap Gruffudd occupies, 64;
   French and Flemings fail to take, 64;
   Gruffudd ap Rhys takes, 80;
   William Marshal takes, 82;
   surrendered to Llywelyn ap Iorwerth, 91;
   given to Maelgwn ap Rhys, 92;
   built of mortar and stone by William Marshal, 100.
Clairvaux, monastery
   abbots of, *see* Peter; Richard.
Clare, Bevys de
   dies, 121.
——, Gilbert de
   drowned in battle of Lincoln, 94.
——, earls of
   see Gloucester, earls of; Hertford, earls of; Pembroke, earls of.
Cleddyf, river, 27;
   Rhys Gryg crosses, 95.
Clement, Geoffrey, justice of Deheubarth
   slain, 122.
Clement IV, Pope
   elected, 114;

INDEX

Clement IV, Pope (*cont.*)
    peace between Henry III and Lord Llywelyn ratified by, 115.
Cletwr, river
    castle of Humfrey's son in valley of, 57.
Clifford, Roger de, lord of Hawarden castle
    imprisoned by Dafydd ap Gruffudd, 120.
——, the
    executed, 124.
——, Walter
    holds Llandovery castle, 60;
    attacks Rhys ap Gruffudd's land, 60.
Clun, river
    Welsh slain in valley of, 113.
——, town, burnt by Llywelyn ap Iorwerth, 102;
    see Colunwy.
Clwyd, river
    see Dyffryn Clwyd.
Clydog ap Cadell
    slain by brother Meurig, 6.
Clynnog
    see Cyfeiliog (*recte* Clynnog).
—— Fawr
    ravaged by Hywel ap Ieuaf, 9.
Cnut, son of Sweyn, king
    wins England, Denmark, and Great Germany, 11;
    dies, 13.
Coedysbys
    battle of, 19.
Coenwulf
    ravages Dyfed, 3.
coinage
    changed by Edward I, 119.
Coleshill
    Owain Gwynedd victorious at, 57.
Colunwy, castle
    burnt by Rhys ap Gruffudd, 76;
    see Clun.
—— (*recte* Colwyn), castle
    built a second time, 53;
    left by Giles de Breos to Gwallter Fychan ab Einion Clud, 90.
Colwyn
    see Colunwy (*recte* Colwyn).
Congalach, king of Ireland
    slain, 7.
Connaught, king of
    see Toirrdelbhach.
Conrad, nephew of emperor Frederick
    slain, 115.
Conway, river
    battle of, 5;
    Dafydd ab Owain Gwynedd driven across, 70;
    king John crosses, 85.
Conwy Hirfawr
    battle of, 7.
Cormac, son of Culennán
    slain, 6.
Cornwall
    men from, with Gilbert fitz Richard, 37.

——, earl of
    Richard, brother of Henry III, repairs castle of Radnor, 102;
    ——, realm of England entrusted to, 109.
——, king of
    Dwngarth, 4, N.
'Corruonet,' ford
    sons of Rhiryd meet Uchdryd ab Edwin at, 30.
Corwen
    Welsh forces encamp at (1165), 63.
councils, Church
    in Lateran church, 91;
    see Synods.
councils, state
    at Gloucester (1175), 70-1;
    London (1176, 1241, 1275, 1320, 1329), 71-2, 105-6, 117, 123, 125;
    Ludlow (1223), 100;
    Oxford (1217), 93;
    Salisbury (1328), 125;
    Worcester (1276), 118.
Courtemain, Robert
    castle of, at Abercorram, 41.
Crescy, Reginald de
    drowned in battle of Lincoln, 94.
Cricieth, castle
    Gruffudd ap Llywelyn ap Iorwerth and son imprisoned in, 105.
Crogen, castle
    granted to Elise ap Madog, 82.
Cross, the
    king John takes, 90;
    Henry III takes, 93;
    recovered, 99.
crowders, 71.
Crusaders, 74, 96.
Cunedda ap Cadwallon [ap Gruffudd ap Cynan]
    castrated and blinded, 58.
Custennin ap Iago [ab Idwal Foel]
    ravages Llŷn and Anglesey, 9;
    slain, 9.
Cuthbert, abbot
    dies, 2.
Cwm-hir, monastery
    monks from, go to Cymer in Meirionnydd, 79;
    Cadwallon ap Maelgwn dies at, 103.
——, abbot of
    see Meurig.
Cwmwd Perfedd
    given to Cynan ap Maredudd, 116;
    exchanged by Cynan ap Maredudd for Pennardd, 117;
    subjugated by Pain de Chaworth, 118.
Cydewain, cantref
    obtained by Owain [ap Maredudd] ap Rhobert, 108;
    raided by John Lestrange, 113;
    won for Roger de Mortimer, 118;
——, lords of
    see Maredudd ap Rhobert; Owain ap Maredudd ap Rhobert.

Cydweli, castle
  built by Rhys ap Gruffudd, 74;
  destroyed by Llywelyn ap Iorwerth, 102;
——, commot
  part of Maredudd ab Owain's territory, 10;
  ravaged by Edwin ab Einion and Edylfi, 10;
  ravaged by French, 19;
  given to Iorwerth ap Bleddyn, 24;
  given to Hywel ap Goronwy, 25;
  harried by Cadell ap Gruffudd, 57;
  subdued by Rhys Ieuanc, 90;
  given to Rhys Gryg, 92;
——, town
  burnt by Rhys Gryg, 100.
Cyfeiliog, commot
  Owain ap Cadwgan and Madog ap Rhiryd in, 33;
  given to Uchdryd ab Edwin, 46;
  taken by Gruffudd ap Maredudd [ap Bleddyn], 46;
  given to Owain and Meurig, sons of Gruffudd ap Maredudd, 57;
  ravaged by Lord Rhys, 58;
  Tafolwern castle in, 62;
  taken from Gruffudd ap Llywelyn by Dafydd, 104;
  portion of, taken from Gruffudd ap Gwenwynwyn, 116.
—— (*recte* Clynnog), archdeacon of *see* Simon.
Cymaron, castle
  repaired by Hugh fitz Ranulf, 53;
  built by Roger Mortimer, 75.
Cymer, castle, in Caereinion
  built by Madog ap Maredudd, 59.
——, castle, in Meirionnydd
  taken by Einion ap Cadwgan and Gruffudd ap Maredudd ap Bleddyn, 46.
——, monastery, in Nannau, Meirionnydd
  monks from Cwm-hir go to, 79.
Cynan (1)
  defeated by Hywel, 3;
  dies, 3.
Cynan (2), of Nanhyfer
  dies, 4.
Cynan (3), abbot of Whitland
  dies, 71.
Cynan ab Owain Gwynedd
  Cardigan ravaged by, 53-4;
  Cynfael castle taken by, 56;
  imprisoned by father, 57;
  engages Henry II's army (1157), 59;
  at Dinwileir, 61;
  Gwrgenau and Llawdden slain by, 65;
  dies, 70.
——, sons of
  see Gruffudd; Maredudd.
Cynan ap Hywel [ap Ieuaf]
  holds Gwynedd, 11;
  slain, 11.

Cynan ap Hywel [Sais]
  captured at Cilcennin, 84.
Cynan ap Maredudd ab Owain
  receives Cwmwd Perfedd, 116;
  exchanges commots, 117;
  submits to English, 118;
  returns from king's court, 119;
  with Maelgwn ap Rhys, chief over Deheubarth, 122;
  executed, 122.
Cynan ap Seisyll
  slain, 13.
Cynfael, castle
  built by Cadwaladr ap Gruffudd ap Cynan, 56;
  taken by Hywel and Cynan, sons of Owain Gwynedd, 56.
Cynfyn ap Gwerystan, 28, 41;
  daughter of, *see* Iwerydd;
  sons of, *see* Bleddyn; Rhiwallon.
Cyngen (1)
  slain by Pagans, 4.
Cyngen (2), king of Powys
  dies in Rome, 4.
Cyngen ab Elisedd
  poisoned, 7.
Cynioedd, king of the Picts (1)
  dies, 2.
——, king of the Picts (2)
  dies, 4.
Cynwrig ab Owain
  slain by followers of Madog ap Maredudd, 52.
Cynwrig ap Rhiwallon
  slain by men of Gwynedd, 16.
Cynwrig ap Rhys ap Gruffudd
  blinded, 63-4, N.
  dies, 104.
Cyprus, island
  Morgan ap Cadwgan dies in, 50.

D.

Dafydd, abbot of Strata Florida
  dies, 73.
Dafydd ab Owain Gwynedd
  engages Henry II's host (1157), 59;
  ravages Tegeingl, 63;
  slays brother Hywel, 65;
  wins Anglesey, 70;
  wins Gwynedd, 70;
  imprisons brother Maelgwn, 70;
  imprisons brother Rhodri, 70;
  marries Emma, 70;
  dispossessed, 75;
  seized by Llywelyn ap Iorwerth, 79;
  expelled from Gwynedd, 82;
  dies in England, 82.
Dafydd ap Bleddyn, bishop of St. Asaph
  elected and consecrated, 123.
Dafydd ap Gruffudd ap Llywelyn
  parleys with Maredudd ap Rhys Gryg and Patrick de Chaworth, 111-12;
  breaks with brother Llywelyn, 113;
  fugitive with Edward I, 117;
  takes Hawarden castle, 120;

INDEX

Dafydd ap Gruffudd ap Llywelyn (*cont.*)
  set to guard Gwynedd, 120;
  goes into outlawry, 121;
  seized and executed, 121.
Dafydd ap Llywelyn ap Iorwerth
  princes of Wales swear allegiance to, 104;
  territories taken from brother Gruffudd by, 104;
  imprisons brother Gruffudd and latter's son, 105;
  succeeds father and does homage to Henry III, 105;
  summoned to London by Henry III, 105-6;
  rises against enemies, 106;
  Henry III fortifies Degannwy against, 107;
  dies and is succeeded by nephews, 107.
Damietta, city
  taken by Christians, 96-7;
  Christians go from, to Babylon, 98;
  surrendered to Saracens, 99;
  taken by Louis IX of France, 108;
  retaken by Saracens, 108;
  again taken by Louis, 108.
Damnani, 1, N.
Daniel ap Sulien, archdeacon of Powys
  dies, 50;
  son of, *see* Cedifor ap Daniel.
Daugleddau, cantref
  ravaged by Llywelyn ap Iorwerth, 98.
David I, king of Scotland
  dies, 58.
David II, king of Scotland
  marries [Jeanne], daughter of Edward II, 125.
David, St.
  shrine of, despoiled, 18;
  sanctuary of, at Llanddewifrefi, 30;
  church of, at Menevia, Maredudd, archdeacon of Ceredigion, buried in, 101.
Dean, Forest of
  Henry II and Rhys ap Gruffudd meet in, 66.
Decemnouenalis, 11, 12, 15, 17.
Degannwy
  burnt by lightning, 3;
  destroyed by Saxons, 4;
  castle of, rebuilt, after destruction, 84;
  ———, king John at, 85;
  ———, destroyed by Llywelyn ap Iorwerth, 86;
  ———, taken by Llywelyn ap Iorwerth, 88;
  Henry III fortifies castle at, 107;
  ——— leads army to, 111;
  castle of, destroyed by Llywelyn ap Gruffudd, 113.
Deheubarth, 37, 40, 53, 63, 65, 66, 74, 76, 99, 105;
  territory of Maredudd ab Owain in, 10;
  held by Llywelyn (*recte* Gruffudd ap Llywelyn), 13;
  ravaged, 14;
  men of, moved into Ystrad Tywi, 60;
  Henry II's expedition (1158) to, 61;
  ——— ——— (1163) to, 62;
  Rhys ap Gruffudd justice of, 68;
  princes from, on expedition (1215) to Dyfed, 91-2;
  lands of, apportioned, 98;
  William Marshal comes to, 99;
  leaders of, at siege of Carmarthen, 103;
  princes of, sent to dispossess Maelgwn Ieuanc, 107;
  Llywelyn ap Gruffudd in (1257), 111;
  Llywelyn ap Gruffudd traverses, 112;
  Maredudd ab Owain [ap Gruffudd] as defender of, 114;
  last princes of, to submit to English, 118;
  chiefs over, in 1294, 122;
  ———, justices of
  see Clement, Geoffrey; Rhys ap Gruffudd.
Denmark, 25;
  won by Cnut, 11;
  ruled by Cnut, 13;
  ———, kings of
  see Harold.
Despenser, Sir Hugh the Elder
  barons invade territory of, 124;
  queen placed on livery by, 124;
  executed, 125.
———, Sir Hugh the Younger
  barons want to seize, 123;
  flees to Morgannwg, 125;
  drawn at Hereford, 125.
Deuddwr, commot, in Powys, 37.
Dewma, monastery
  founded, 72.
Diarmaid, son of Mael-na-mbo, king of the Irish
  death and encomium of, 16.
Diarmaid MacMurchadha, king of Leinster
  expelled, 64;
  returns, 65;
  Richard fitz Gilbert weds daughter of, 65;
  dies, 66.
Dinasnewydd
  battle of, 6.
Dinefwr
  land at, taken by Rhys ap Gruffudd, 62;
———, castle
  taken by sons of Rhys ap Gruffudd, 75;
  taken from French, 79;
  lost by Maelgwn ap Rhys, 82;
  taken by sons of Gruffudd ap Rhys, 82;
  taken by Rhys Fychan, 83;
  fortified by Rhys Fychan, 87;
  taken by Rhys Ieuanc, 87-8;
  given to Rhys Gryg, 92;
  Rhys Fychan ap Rhys Mechyll leads army against, 111;

Dinefwr (cont.)
   Rhys Ieuanc ap Rhys Mechyll dies in, 116.
  —— (recte Dinwileir), castle
   built by earl Gilbert, 54;
   overcome by Cadell ap Gruffudd, 54;
   built by sons of Gruffudd ap Rhys, 57;
   see Dinwileir.
Dineirth, castle
   burnt by Owain and Cadwaladr, 51;
   taken by Roger, earl of Clare, 60;
   built by Gruffudd ap Rhys, 80;
   attacked by Maelgwn ap Rhys, 80;
   completed by Maelgwn ap Rhys, 82;
   burnt by Maelgwn ap Rhys, 83.
Dingeraint, castle
   built by Gilbert fitz Richard, 34.
Dinneir
   battle of, 6, N.
Dinwileir, castle
   opponents of Rhys ap Gruffudd at, 61;
   see Dinefwr (recte Dinwileir).
Diserth, in Tegeingl
   Henry III fortifies castle at, 105.
Dolforwyn, castle
   Llywelyn ap Gruffudd at, 116;
   taken by earl of Lincoln and Roger de Mortimer, 118.
Donnchadh, son of Brian
   dies on way to Rome, 15.
Dore, monastery
   Cadwgan, bishop of Bangor, becomes monk at, 104.
Dover
   earl of Warenne awaits Edward III at, 125.
Dryslwyn, castle
   [Maredudd ap] Rhys Gryg dies in, 116;
   Rhys ap Maredudd, lord of, 121;
   taken by English, 121.
Dublin, 53;
   folk of, ravage Ireland and Anglesey, 6;
   ravaged by Irish, 11;
   Gentiles of, capture Gruffudd ap Llywelyn ap Seisyll, 13;
   ships from, support Henry II (1165), 64;
   taken by Richard fitz Gilbert, 65;
  ——, kings of
   see Sitriuc.
Dumbarton
   fortress of, destroyed by Pagans, 5.
Dunstable
   tournament at, 125.
Dwngarth, king of Cornwall
   drowned, 5.
Dwnwallon (1)
   slain by Gentiles, 7.
Dwnwallon (2), king of Strathclyde
   goes to Rome, 8.
Dyddgu, daughter of Owain ap Caradog
   son of, 66.
Dyfed, 10, 37;
   ravaged by Coenwulf, 3;
  —— Iago and Ieuaf, 7;
  —— men of Godfrey, son of Harold, 9;
  —— Edwin ab Einion and Edylfi, 10;
   part of Maredudd ab Owain's territory, 10;
   ravaged by Gentiles, 11, 13;
  —— Eilaf, 12;
  —— Gruffudd ap Llywelyn [ap Seisyll], 14;
  —— French, 16;
   plundered by Cadwgan ap Bleddyn, 19;
   overrun by French, 19;
   castles of, destroyed, 19;
   ravaged by Welsh, 19;
   Arnulf [Montgomery] comes to, 22;
   half of, held by [William] fitz Baldwin, 24;
  ——, —— Iorwerth ap Bleddyn, 24;
   taken from Iorwerth ap Bleddyn, 25;
   given to Saer, 25;
   Flemings come to, 27;
   Owain ap Cadwgan's men flee to, 29;
   plundered by Owain ap Cadwgan's men, 33;
   Gruffudd ap Rhys returns to, 39;
   hostile to men of Ceredigion, 42;
   diverse peoples in, 42;
   overrun by Gilbert fitz Gilbert, 54;
   held by Maredudd ap Gruffudd ap Rhys, 58;
   castles in, burnt by Rhys ap Gruffudd, 61;
   Cadwaladr ap Rhys slain in, 73;
   army from, with Falkes de Breauté, 85;
   attacked by Maelgwn ap Rhys and Rhys Ieuanc, 90;
   portion of, given to Maelgwn ap Rhys, 92;
   castles in, burnt by Welsh, 111;
  ——, kings of
   see Maredudd; Rhun (recte Rhain).
Dyffryn Ceiriog
   Henry II in (1165), 63.
Dyffryn Clwyd
   Hywel ab Ithel and confederates in, 46;
   people of Tegeingl moved into, 63.
Dyfi, river, 51;
   castle of, taken by Roger, earl of Clare, 60;
   land between it and the Aeron given to nephews of Maelgwn ap Rhys, 83;
   land between it and the Aeron granted to king John, 86;
   portion of Cyfeiliog beyond, taken from Gruffudd ap Gwenwynwyn, 116.
Dyfnwal
   Sannan, daughter of, 45.
Dyfnwal ap Tewdwr
   dies, 2.

INDEX

E.

Eadric, the Saxon
  ravages Menevia, 11.
earthquakes, 1;
  in island of Britain, 18;
  in Jerusalem, 81;
  in England, 107;
  in Wales, 117.
Easter
  changed for the Britons, 2.
eclipses
  lunar, 3, 4;
  solar, 3, 52, 73, 74, 126.
Edeirnion, commot
  Welsh army in (1165), 63.
Edgar, king of the Saxons
  brings fleet to Chester, 8;
  dies, 8.
Edgar, son of Maelcoluim, king of Scotland
  dies, 27.
Edmund [Crouchback], son of Henry III
  captured in battle of Lewes, 113;
  builds castle at Aberystwyth, 118;
  returns to England, 119;
  with Edward I, gives Eleanor de Montford as wife to Llywelyn ap Gruffudd, 119.
Edward [the Confessor], king of the Saxons
  death of, 15;
  good laws of, 89.
Edward, son of Maelcoluim III of Scotland
  slain by French, 19.
Edward I, king of England
  born, 105;
  as co-regent, 109;
  left to hold Gascony, 109;
  comes to Gwynedd, 110;
  in the Welsh March, 113;
  rising against, 113;
  captured at Lewes, 113-14;
  escapes from Hereford, 114;
  in battle of Evesham, 114;
  goes to Jerusalem, 115;
  succeeds father as king, 116;
  returns from Jerusalem, 116;
  holds council in London, 117;
  Llywelyn ap Gruffudd refuses homage to, 117;
  Dafydd ap Gruffudd and Gruffudd ap Gwenwynwyn as fugitives with, 117;
  returns to London, 117;
  at marriage of Llywelyn ap Gruffudd and Eleanor de Montford, 117, 119;
  sends three armies against Wales, 118;
  comes to Perfeddwlad, 118-19;
  makes peace with Llywelyn ap Gruffudd, 119;
  releases Owain Goch ap Gruffudd and Gruffudd ap Gwenwynwyn, 119;
  changes coinage, 119;
  invades Gwynedd, 120-21;
  breaks with Rhys ap Maredudd, 121;
  overruns Wales, 122;
  war with Scotland, 122-23;
  makes peace with Flanders, 122;
  dies, 123.
Edward II, king of England
  born, 121;
  crowned king, 123;
  flight from the Pools, 123;
  war with barons, 123-24;
  goes to Shrewsbury, 124;
  war in Gascony against, 124;
  makes for Morgannwg, 125;
  taken prisoner, 125.
Edward III, king of England
  born, 123;
  goes to Paris, 124;
  lands in England, 124-25;
  crowned king, 125;
  betrothal to count of Hainaut's daughter, 125;
  does homage to king of France, 125;
  son born to, 126.
Edwin ab Einion
  ravages Maredudd ab Owain's territory, 10;
  ravages Menevia, 10.
——, sons of (Hywel and Maredudd)
  in battle against sons of Rhydderch [ap Iestyn], 13;
  hold Deheubarth, 13;
  see Hywel ab Edwin; Maredudd ab Edwin.
Edwin ap Hywel
  dies, 7.
Edylfi, the Saxon
  lands ravaged by, 10.
Efelffre, commot
  given to Rhys ap Gruffudd, 67.
Egypt, 97, 98.
Eifionydd, commot
  won by Llywelyn ap Iorwerth, 81.
Eilaf
  comes to Britain, 12;
  flees to Germany, 13.
Einion, bishop of St. Asaph
  called 'Black Friar of Nannau,' 121;
  dies, 121.
Einion ab Anarawd ap Gruffudd
  takes Humfrey's Castle, 61;
  slain in sleep, 62.
Einion ab Einion Clud
  see Einion of Porth.
Einion ab Owain
  slays Cadwallon ap Gruffudd ap Cynan, 50.
Einion ab Owain [ap Hywel Dda]
  ravages Gower, 8, 9;
  Saxons ravage lands of, 9;
  Saxons slain by, 9;
  slain by men of Gwent, 9.
Einion ap Cadwgan ap Bleddyn
  mother of, 45;
  in attack on Cymer castle, in Meirionnydd, 45-6;

Einion ap Cadwgan ap Bleddyn (*cont.*)
    takes half of Penllyn and Meirionnydd, 46;
    leagued with Hywel ab Ithel, 46-7;
    opposes Henry I's expedition, 47-8;
    comes to terms with Henry I, 48;
    Meirionnydd taken from Uchdryd by, 49;
    portion of Powys held by, 49;
    dies, 49.
Einion ap Caradog
    slain at Cilcennin, 84.
Einion ap Cynan
    dies, 73.
Einion ap Rhys of Gwerthrynion
    at council at Gloucester, 70-1.
Einion Clud ap Madog ab Idnerth
    seizes brother Cadwallon, 62;
    opposes Henry II's expedition (1165), 63;
    at council at Gloucester, 70-1 (but see N.);
    slain, 72.
Einion Fonheddig, bishop of Menevia (N.)
    dies, 5.
Einion of Porth (i.e. Einion ab Einion Clud)
    slain by brother, 74.
Einion Sais, abbot of Strata Florida
    monastery burnt in time of, 120.
Elen, wife of Hywel Dda
    dies, 6.
Elenid
    see Elfed.
Elfael, cantref, 70, 76, 79, 102;
    subjugated to French, 53;
    left to Gwallter Fychan ab Einion Clud, 90;
    raided by Gwilym ap Gwrwared, 109;
    men of, claim pastures of Elfed (*recte* Elenid), 109;
    see Owain ap Maredudd of.
Elfed (*recte* Elenid)
    men of Elfael claim pastures of, 109.
Elfoddw, archbishop of Gwynedd
    changes Easter for Britons, 2;
    dies, 3.
Elise ap Cyngen
    brother Griffri slain through treachery of, 3.
Elise ap Madog
    refuses to join Llywelyn ap Iorwerth against Gwenwynwyn, 82;
    dispossessed, 82;
    land given to, 82.
Elisedd ap Rhodri
    slain by Saxons, 7.
Ellylw, daughter of Cedifor ap Gollwyn
    Morgan, son of, 45.
Emlyn, cantref
    new castle in, taken by Llywelyn ap Iorwerth and allies, 91;
    given to Maelgwn ap Rhys, 92;
    parley in, between Welsh leaders and Patrick de Chaworth, 111-12.

Emma, sister of Henry I
    Dafydd ab Owain Gwynedd weds, 70.
Eneurys, bishop of Menevia
    dies, 7.
England, 60, 63, 64, 66, 68, 79, 81, 104, 111, 113;
    ravaged by Norsemen, 5;
    won by Cnut, 11;
    ruled by Cnut, 13;
    ravaged by Magnus and Gruffudd ap Llywelyn, 14;
    government of, entrusted to Walter, chief justice of Gloucester, 29;
    Henry I returns to, from Powys, 48;
    south of, subdued by Stephen, 51;
    Matilda comes to, 52;
    subdued by prince Henry, 58;
    Henry II returns to (1171), 66;
    Dafydd ab Owain dies in, 82;
    Hubert, chief counsellor of, 82;
    interdiction of Christianity in, 83;
    king John returns to, from Ireland, 84;
    ——, from Gwynedd, 85;
    three leaders from Wales hanged in, 87;
    churches in, interdicted by Pope, 87;
    Church of, wronged by king John, 88;
    made tributary to Roman See, 88;
    king John returns to, from Poitou, 89;
    Louis, son of Philip II of France, invades, 93;
    Louis comes again to, 94;
    laws and customs of, restored by Henry III, 96;
    foresworn by Louis, 96;
    churches in, absolved, 96;
    Crusaders from (1218), 96;
    Stephen Langton, primate of, 97;
    William Marshal sails to, from Deheubarth, 100;
    Cardinal Otto comes to, 104;
    Cardinal Otto leaves, 105;
    Henry III returns to, from Gwynedd, 107;
    regents of, 109;
    Henry III returns to, from Gascony, 109;
    strife between foreigners in, 111;
    magnates of, rebel against Edward, son of Henry III, and foreigners, 113;
    ——, intercede for release of Eleanor de Montford, 117;
    Jews expelled from, 121;
    wars against Scotland and Flanders, 122;
    leaders of, go against Scots, 125;
    peace with Scotland, 125;
    see North, the; Northerners, the.
England, kings of
    see Cnut; Edward [the Confessor]; Edward I, II, III; John; Henry I, II, III; Richard; William I.
——, papal legate in
    see Gualo.

INDEX

English
    victorious against reinforcements for Louis, 95;
    driven out of Gower by Rhys Gryg, 96;
    send Walter Marshal to Cardigan, 105;
    slaughter of, after raid on Cydewain, 113;
    Wales has peace from, 114;
    last princes of Deheubarth submit to, 118;
    from Llanbadarn, land seized by, 119;
    see Saxons.

Enilfre
    dies, 14.

Erfyn, bishop of Menevia
    dies, 13.

Eryri, mountains
    ravaged by Saxons, 3;
    Welsh retreat to, 37, 85;
    king John makes for, 85.

Ethelbald, king of the Saxons
    dies, 2.

Ethelred, son of Edgar, king of the Saxons
    territory of, invaded by Sweyn, 11.

Ethelstan, king
    dies, 6. N.

Eurialius, 77.

Euron, daughter of Hoeddlyw ap Cadwgan ab Elystan
    Maredudd, son of, 45.

Evesham
    battle of, 114.

Ewilfre, bishop of Menevia
    dies, 17.

Ewyas
    see Piggott, de.

F.

fair
    at Moel-yr-Wyddfa, 121.

Falkes, sheriff of Cardiff
    sent against Rhys Ieuanc and Owain, sons of Gruffudd ap Rhys, 85;
    builds castle at Aberystwyth, 86;
    commanded to support Rhys Ieuanc, 87;
    joins Rhys Ieuanc, 87;
    in battle of Lincoln, 94.

Falkes (*recte* Ingelard), sheriff of Hereford
    commanded to support Rhys Ieuanc, 87.

Falkirk
    Scots massacred at, 122.

famine
    mortality because of, 10;
    in Maredudd ab Owain's territory, 10.

Ferns, city
    Diarmaid, king of Leinster, buried in, 66.

Ferrars, earl
    goes on Crusade, 96.

Ffinnant
    battle of, 4.

Ffyrnfael ab Idwal
    dies, 10.

fish
    abundance of, in estuary of Ystwyth, 83.

fitz Alan, Edmund
    see Arundel, earls of.

—— ——, Richard
    see Arundel, earls of.

—— Baldwin, Richard
    holds half of Dyfed, 24;
    repairs castle of Rhyd-y-gors, 26.

—— ——, Stephen
    slain by Llywelyn ap Madog ap Maredudd, 58.

—— ——, William
    castle of Rhyd-y-gors established by, 20;
    dies, 20.

—— Gerald, David
    archdeacon of Ceredigion, 56;
    becomes bishop of Menevia, 56;
    entertains Henry II, 67;
    brothers of, 67;
    dies, 71.

—— ——, William
    given custody of Tenby castle, 58;
    brothers of, 67.

—— Gilbert, Gilbert
    Dyfed overrun by, 54;
    builds Carmarthen castle, 54;
    —— Mabudryd castle, 54;
    dies, 56.

—— ——, Richard
    slain by Morgan ab Owain, 51.

—— Hai, William
    at siege of Llanstephan castle, 54.

—— John, Payn
    imprisons Llywelyn ab Owain, 50.

—— Martin, Robert
    defeated by Owain and Cadwaladr, 51.

—— Odo, William
    defeated by Owain and Cadwaladr, 51.

—— Pons, Richard
    holds Cantref Bychan, 40.

—— Ranulf, Hugh
    see Chester, earls of.

—— Richard, Gilbert
    receives Cadwgan ap Bleddyn's land, 34;
    comes to Ceredigion, 34;
    accuses Owain ap Cadwgan, 37;
    leader of host against Powys, 37;
    Blaen-porth in hands of, 42;
    Ralf, officer of, 42;
    castle of, at Ystrad Meurig, 42;
    dies, 46.

—— ——, Walter
    slain by Cadwgan ap Maredudd, 62.

—— Stephen, Robert
    imprisoned by Rhys ap Gruffudd, 64;
    goes to Ireland, 65;
    captured at Cardigan, 67;
    family relations of, 67.

—— Walter, Robert
    captured in battle of Lincoln, 94.

—— Wizo, Philip
    with family, captured, 75.

Flanders, 34, N., 63, 89;
  folk from, come to Dyfed, 27;
  war against England, 122;
  peace with Edward I, 122.
——, count of
  pact with king John, 88-9;
  captured at Vernon, 89;
  see Theobald.
Flemings, 61, 64;
  attacked by Gruffudd ap Rhys, 40;
  in Dyfed, 42;
  in Is-Coed, Ceredigion, 42;
  come from Rhos to Carmarthen, 44;
  Owain ap Cadwgan slain by, 45;
  defeated by Owain and Cadwaladr, 51-2;
  fail to take Llanstephan castle, 54;
  harried by Rhys ap Gruffudd, 63;
  defeated by Maelgwn ap Rhys, 73;
  attack Hywel Sais and brother Maelgwn, 75;
  make peace with Llywelyn ap Iorwerth, 95-6;
  attack Welsh, 97;
  attacked by Llywelyn ap Iorwerth, 97-8.
Flint
  fortified by Edward I, 118-19;
floods, 109.
foreigners
  in England, 111;
  English magnates and Welsh rise against, 113.
France
  Henry II goes to, 68;
  mortality in, 76;
  harassed by King John and allies, 89;
  Louis, son of Philip II, goes to, 96;
  Henry III seeks to regain lands from, 106;
  aid for Damietta sought from, 108;
  Henry III goes to, 112;
  sons of Simon de Montford sail to, 114;
  messengers from Edward I to, 124;
  Edward III goes to, 125.
——, kings of
  see Louis, son of Philip II; Louis VII, VIII, IX; Philip II, VI.
Franks
  see Pippin.
Frederick II, emperor
  excommunicated, 105;
  seizes cardinal Otto, 105.
—— ——, nephew of
  see Conrad.
—— ——, son of
  see Manfred.
French, the, 19, 25, 31, 37, 39, 43, 60, 61, 64, 95;
  slay Maredudd ab Owain, 16;
  ravage Ceredigion and Dyfed, 16;
  overrun Ceredigion and Dyfed, 19;
  ravage Gower and Cydweli and Ystrad Tywi, 19;

  attack Brycheiniog, Gwent, and Gwynllŵg, 20;
  defeated at Aber-llech, 20;
  attack Gwynedd, 20-1;
  Hywel ap Goronwy slain through treachery of, 26-7;
  harassed by Owain ap Cadwgan and Madog ap Rhiryd, 32;
  attacked by Gruffudd ap Rhys, 40;
  in Dyfed, 42;
  from Chester, support sons of Owain ab Edwin, 46-7;
  accuse Gruffudd ap Rhys, 50;
  Elfael subjugated to, 53;
  fail to take Llanstephan castle, 54;
  defeated by men of Anglesey, 60;
  Welsh unite against, 63;
  win Caerleon, 70;
  seize Gwladus, wife of Seisyll ap Dyfnwal, and slay her son, 71;
  lose castle of Dinefwr, 79;
  at Cilcennin, 84;
  in Rhys Ieuanc's host against Llandovery, 88;
  take Lincoln, 94;
  defeated in battle of Lincoln, 94;
  defeated in naval battle, 95;
  Carreg Cennen castle given to, 108;
  see Normans, the.
Friars, Barefooted
  monastery of, at Llan-faes in Anglesey, 104, 117.
Furnevaus, Gerald de
  drowned in battle of Lincoln, 94.

G.

Gamage, Pain de
  imprisoned by Dafydd ap Gruffudd, 120.
Garth Grugyn, castle
  fortified by Maelgwn Ieuanc ap Maelgwn, 106.
Gascony
  warriors from, 63;
  Henry III returns from, 109;
  war in, against Edward II, 124;
  earl of Warenne sent to, 124.
Gaveston, Piers
  rule and death of, 123.
Gawain, 74.
Genau'r Glyn, commot
  men of, flee to Gwynedd, 119.
Gentiles
  slay Dwnwallon, 7;
  ravage Tywyn, 8;
  capture Iago ap Ieuaf, 9;
  with Maredudd ab Owain, 10;
  ravage Dyfed, 11;
  capture Meurig ap Hywel, 13, N;
  defeated by Hywel ab Edwin, 13;
  capture Gruffudd ap Llywelyn ap Seisyll, 13;
  ravage Menevia and Bangor, 16;
  see Black Host; Black Gentiles; Dublin, folk of; Norsemen; Pagans (1).

INDEX

Geoffrey, bishop of Llandaff
  dies, 58.
——, bishop of Menevia (1)
  dies, 39.
——, bishop of Menevia (2)
  dies, 89.
——, son of Seisyll ap Dyfnwal
  slain, 71.
Gerald (of Windsor), the officer
  given keepership of Pembroke castle, 20, 26, 39;
  sent to Ireland, 23;
  Nest, wife of, violated, 27;
  castle of Cenarth Bychan built by, 28;
  escape from Cenarth Bychan, 28;
  supreme in Dyfed, 29;
  comes to Carmarthen, 45;
——, sons of
  defeated by Owain and Cadwaladr, 51;
  at siege of Llanstephan castle, 54.
Gerard, bishop of Hereford
  succeeds Thomas, archbishop of York, 22.
Germany
  won by Cnut, 11, 13;
  Eilaf flees to, 13;
——, emperor of
  goes to Jerusalem, 55.
——, king of
  captured at Lewes, 113;
  released, 114, N;
  see Magnus, son of Harold.
Gilbert, abbot of Gloucester
  becomes bishop of Hereford, 56.
Gilbert Strongbow
  see Pembroke, earls of.
Glamorgan
  ravaged by Maredudd ab Owain, 10;
  host of, with Falkes, sheriff of Cardiff, 85;
  invaded by Llywelyn ap Gruffudd, 111;
  see Hywel ab Owain; Hywel ap Maredudd; Morgan ap Caradog.
Glasgrug
  men of Gruffudd ap Rhys [ap Tewdwr] encamp at, 42.
Gloucester
  lands around, ravaged, 68;
  Welsh princes at council at, 70–1;
  Giles de Breos dies at, 91;
  Henry III crowned at, 93;
  Dafydd ap Llywelyn does homage to Henry III at, 105;
  barons at, 124.
——, abbot of
  see Gilbert.
——, earls of
  Gilbert
    Rhys Gryg weds daughter of, 97.
  Gilbert (d. 1295)
    makes pact with Llywelyn ap Gruffudd, 114;
    takes London and submits to Henry III, 114–5.
    dies, 122.

Gilbert the Younger
  slain by Scots, 123.
Richard
  siezes territory of Hywel ap Maredudd, 107;
  dies, 112.
——, sheriff of
  see Ingelard.
Gluniairn, son of Amlaibh
  slain, 10.
Glywysing
  ravaged, 4.
Godfrey, son of Harold
  ravages Anglesey, 8;
  ravages Llŷn and Anglesey, 9;
  ravages Dyfed, Menevia, and Llan-weithefawr, 9;
  ravages Anglesey, 9.
Godred
  son of, helps Rhodri ab Owain, 74.
Godwin, earl
  son of, see Harold, king of the Saxons.
Gorchwyl, bishop
  dies, 6.
Goronwy ab Ednyfed, steward to Llywelyn ap Gruffudd
  death and encomium of, 115.
Goronwy ab Owain
  accused by Hugh, earl of Chester, 37;
  makes agreement with Owain ap Cadwgan, 37–8;
  slain, 49.
Goronwy ap Cadwgan
  in battle of Camddwr, 16;
  —— 'Gweunytwl,' 16;
  dies, 22.
Goronwy ap Rhys
  dies, 25.
Goronwy ap Tudur of Anglesey
  dies, 126.
Gorwydd, Y
  ravaged by Owain [ap Hywel Dda], 7, N.
Gower, commot
  ravaged by Einion ab Owain, 8, 9, 10;
  part of Maredudd ab Owain's territory, 10;
  ravaged by French, 19;
  given to Iorwerth ap Bleddyn, 24;
  given to Hywel ap Goronwy, 25;
  castle in, burnt by Gruffudd ap Rhys, 41;
  attacked by sons of Gruffudd ap Rhys, 57;
  Rhys Ieuanc goes to, 90;
  Llywelyn ap Gruffudd approaches, 95.
Gregory IX, Pope
  relieves Cadwgan, bishop of Bangor, of his episcopal care, 104;
  sends Otto to England, 104;
  excommunicates emperor Frederick, 105;
  dies, 106.
—— X, Pope
  elected, 116;
  holds synod at Lyons, 116.

Gresford
  Madog ap Llywelyn buried in church of, 126;.
Griffri ap Cyngan
  slain, 3.
Griffri [ap Griffri ap Trahaearn]
  blinded, 50.
Griffri ap Trahaearn ap Caradog
  slain by Owain ap Cadwgan, 27.
Grosmont, castle
  taken by Reginald de Breos, 90.
Gruffudd, abbot of Strata Florida
  settles debt to Henry III, 108;
  with abbot of Aberconwy, obtains body of Gruffudd ap Llywelyn, 108.
——, abbot of Strata Marcella
  dies, 76.
Gruffudd ab Idnerth ap Cadwgan
  with brother Ifor defeats French, 20.
Gruffudd ab Ifor ap Meurig of Senghenydd
  at council of Gloucester, 71;
  dies, 86.
Gruffudd ab Owain, king of Gower
  slain by men of Ceredigion, 6.
Gruffudd ap Cadwgan, chief counsellor of Maelgwn ap Rhys
  captured, 84.
Gruffudd ap Cadwgan ap Bleddyn
  mother of, 45;
  dies, 74.
Gruffudd ap Cynan, king of Gwynedd
  wins Anglesey, 16;
  in battle of Bron-yr-erw, 16;
  —— Mynydd Carn, 17;
  flees to Ireland, 21;
  receives Anglesey after return, 21;
  accused by Hugh, earl of Chester, 37;
  makes agreement with Owain ap Cadwgan, 37-8;
  Henry I imposes tribute on, 38;
  betrays Gruffudd ap Rhys, 39-40;
  refuses to unite with sons of Cadwgan, 48;
  death and encomium of, 52.
——, daughter of
  see Gwenllian.
——, sons of
  see Cadwaladr; Cadwallon; Owain.
——, wife of
  see Angharad, daughter of Owain ab Edwin.
Gruffudd ap Cynan ab Owain Gwynedd
  dispossesses Dafydd ab Owain, 75;
  death and encomium of, 80.
Gruffudd ap Gwenwynwyn
  given rights in Powys, 106;
  submits to Dafydd ap Llywelyn, 106;
  Llywelyn ap Gruffudd's campaign against, 110-11;
  dispossessed by Llywelyn ap Gruffudd, 111;
  destroys castle of Yr Wyddgrug, 113;
  lands taken from, 116;
  territory of, subdued, 116-17;
  fugitive with Edward I, 117;
  gains Powys, 118;
  in fatal attack on Llywelyn ap Gruffudd, 120-1.
Gruffudd ap Gwyn
  dies, 58.
Gruffudd ap Llywelyn ap Iorwerth
  quarrels with father, 98;
  loses Meirionnydd and Ardudwy, 98;
  waylays William Marshal, 100;
  in battle near Carmarthen, 100;
  returns to Gwynedd, 100;
  released from prison, 103;
  territories taken from, by Dafydd, 104;
  with son, imprisoned by Dafydd, 105;
  imprisoned in London by Henry III, 106;
  killed in escape from prison, 106;
  body of, brought to Aberconwy, 108.
——, daughter of
  see Gwladus.
——, sons of
  see Dafydd ap Gruffudd; Llywelyn ap Gruffudd; Owain Goch.
Gruffudd ap Llywelyn ap Seisyll, 16
  defeats Hywel ab Edwin, 13, 14;
  captured by Gentiles, 13;
  treachery of sons of Rhydderch against, 14;
  members of war-band of, slain, 14;
  ravages Dyfed and Ystrad Tywi, 14;
  slays Gruffudd ap Rhydderch, 14;
  defeats Saxons, 14;
  helps Magnus, 14;
  death and encomium of, 15;
  see Llywelyn (recte Gruffudd ap Llywelyn).
——, mother of
  see Angharad, daughter of Maredudd ab Owain.
——, sons of
  see Ithel; Maredudd.
Gruffudd ap Madog ap Gruffudd Maelor (1)
  slain by brother Maredudd, 105.
Gruffudd ap Madog ap Gruffudd Maelor (2)
  submits to Dafydd ap Llywelyn, 106;
  makes peace with Llywelyn ap Gruffudd, 111;
  death and burial of, 115.
Gruffudd ap Maredudd ab Owain ab Edwin
  defeated and slain, 18.
Gruffudd ap Maredudd ab Owain ap Gruffudd
  gives Cwmwd Perfedd to brother Cynan, 116;
  tenders homage to Edward I, 118;
  at taking of Aberystwyth, 120;
  wins Mefenydd, 120.
Gruffudd ap Maredudd ap Bleddyn
  attacks Cymer castle, 45-6;
  takes Mawddwy, Cyfeiliog and half of Penllyn, 46;
  slays Ithel ap Rhiryd ap Bleddyn, 49;
  dies, 50.

INDEX

———, sons of
  see Owain ap Gruffudd ap Maredudd;
  Meurig ap Gruffudd ap Maredudd.
Gruffudd ap Maredudd ap Rhys, archdeacon of Ceredigion
  dies, 106.
Gruffudd ap Rhain
  see Gruffudd ap Rhun (*recte* Rhain).
Gruffudd ap Rhun (*recte* Rhain)
  dies, 3.
Gruffudd ap Rhydderch ap Iestyn
  in battle against sons of Edwin, 13;
  treachery of, against Gruffudd ap Llywelyn, 14;
  slain by Gruffudd ap Llywelyn, 14.
Gruffudd ap Rhys ap Gruffudd
  succeeds father, 78;
  exiled by brother Maelgwn, 78–9;
  given to Saxons by Gwenwynwyn, 79;
  released, 79;
  obtains portion of patrimony from Maelgwn, 80;
  builds castle of Dineirth, 80;
  takes castle of Llandovery, 81;
  death and encomium of, 81;
  brother Hywel buried in same grave as, 82.
———, wife of
  see Breos, Matilda de
Gruffudd ap Rhys ap Tewdwr
  returns from Ireland, 39;
  betrayed by Gruffudd ap Cynan, 39–40;
  escapes from Aberdaron, 40;
  attacks Flemings and French, 40;
  attacks Carmarthen castle, 41;
  burns castle in Gower, 41;
  called into Ceredigion, 41;
  comes to Is-Coed, 42;
  attacks Aberystwyth castle, 43–4;
  Owain ap Cadwgan and Llywarch ap Trahaearn set against, 44;
  slays Gruffudd ap Sulhaearn, 49;
  expelled by Henry I, 50;
  in attack on Cardigan, 51;
  dies, 52.
Gruffudd ap Sulhaearn
  slain by Gruffudd ap Rhys, 49.
Gruffudd Maelor, lord of Powys
  death and encomium of, 74.
Gualo, papal legate
  Henry III consecrated by authority of, 93.
Gwallter ap Llywarch
  slays Einion ab Anarawd, 62.
Gwallter Fychan ab Einion Clud
  land left to, by Giles de Breos, 90.
Gwenllïan, daughter of Bleddyn ap Cynfyn
  mother of Owain ap Caradog [ap Gruffudd], 41.
Gwenllïan, daughter of Gruffudd ap Cynan
  Madog, son of, 45.
Gwenllïan, daughter of Llywelyn ap Gruffudd
  made a nun, 117.
Gwenllïan, daughter of Maelgwn Ieuanc
  death and burial of, 109.
Gwenllïan, daughter of Rhys [ap Gruffudd]
  dies, 74.
Gwent
  ravaged by Norsemen, 5;
  Einion ab Owain slain by men of, 9;
  French expedition to, 20;
  best men of, slain, 71;
  Ranulf de Poer slain by young men from, 72;
  invaded by Llywelyn ab Iorwerth, 102.
———, kings of
  see Ithel; Meurig.
Gwent, Higher, cantref, 71.
Gwent Is-Coed, cantref
  won by Hywel ap Iorwerth, 70.
Gwenwynwyn ab Owain Cyfeiliog
  slays Owain ap Madog, 73;
  castle of, at Welshpool surrenders, 76;
  ——— retaken, 76;
  war-band of, at Aberystwyth, 79;
  subdues Arwystli, 79;
  besieges Painscastle, 79;
  hostages of Gruffudd ap Rhys escape from, 80;
  Llywelyn ap Iorwerth moves against, 81;
  ——— reconciled to, 82;
  takes Llandovery and Llangadog castles, 82;
  seized at Shrewsbury by king, 83;
  Llywelyn ap Iorwerth takes territory of, 83;
  recovers land, 84;
  opposes king John (1211), 85;
  makes pact with Llywelyn ap Iorwerth, 86;
  freed from allegiance to John, 87;
  with allies, wins Perfeddwlad from king, 87;
  with Llywelyn ap Iorwerth in Dyfed, 91;
  renounces pact with Llywelyn, 92;
  land of, subdued by Llywelyn, 92.
Gwerthrynion, commot, 70;
  castle of, taken by Welsh, 81;
  taken from Roger de Mortimer, 110;
  won for ———, 118.
'Gweunytwl'
  battle of, 16.
Gwgan ap Gwriad
  slain, 7.
Gwgan ap Meurig (1), king of Ceredigion
  drowned, 5.
Gwgan ap Meurig (2)
  betrays Hywel ap Goronwy, 26–7.
Gwili, river
  battle at mouth of, 12.
Gwilym ap Gwrwared, king's steward
  dies, 109, N.
  carries off spoil from Elfael, 109.
Gwion, bishop of Bangor
  dies, 74.

Gwlad Forgan
see Glamorgan.
Gwladus, daughter of Gruffudd ap Llywelyn ap Iorwerth
wife of Rhys Ieuanc ap Rhys Mechyll, dies, 112.
Gwladus, daughter of Gruffudd ap Rhys ap Tewdwr
wife of Seisyll ap Dyfnwal, 71;
seized by French, 71.
Gwladus, daughter of Rhiwallon ap Cynfyn
mother of Nest by Rhys ap Tewdwr, 28.
Gwladus Ddu, daughter of Llywelyn ap Iorwerth
wife of Reginald de Breos, 91;
dies at Windsor, 109.
Gwlfach
blinded, 11.
Gwrgant ap Rhys, poet
slain, 60.
Gwrgenau, abbot of Llwythlawr (? Ludlow)
slain by Cynan ab Owain, 65.
Gwrgenau ap Seisyll
slain by sons of Rhys Sais, 17.
Gwrgystu
battle at, 7.
Gwriad, son of Merfyn
slain by Saxons, 5.
Gwrmid
ravages Llŷn, 9.
Gwrtheyrn Wrthenau
Myrddin's prophecy to, 1.
Gwyn
sons of, slain, 8.
Gwyn ap Gruffudd
dies, 22.
Gwynedd, 50, 52, 76;
Norsemen come to, 5;
conquered by Maredudd ab Owain, 9;
sons of Meurig hostages in, 10;
held by Cynan ap Hywel, 11;
held by Iago ab Idwal [ap Meurig], 13;
held by Trahaearn ap Caradog, 16;
men of, slay Cynwrig ap Rhiwallon, 16;
castles in, destroyed, 19;
expedition by French to, 20-1;
revolt of, against French, 21;
Henry I's expedition to (1114), 37-8;
Henry II's expedition to (1157), 59-60;
won by Dafydd ab Owain Gwynedd, 70;
Dafydd ab Owain expelled from, 82;
king John's expedition to (1211), 85;
Llywelyn ap Iorwerth destroys castles in, 86;
Maelgwn ap Rhys and Owain ap Gruffudd flee to, 90;
princes from, on 1215 expedition to Dyfed, 91;
learned men of, 92;
Gruffudd ap Llywelyn returns to, from Deheubarth, 100;

Llywelyn ap Maelgwn Ieuanc dies in, 101;
William de Breos the Younger hanged in, 101-2;
Henry III takes hostages from, 105;
Henry III's expedition to (1245), 107;
Maelgwn Ieuanc and Hywel ap Maredudd flee to, 107;
Edward, son of Henry III, comes to, 110, 113;
Owain ap Gruffudd ap Gwenwynwyn taken to, 116;
Amaury and Eleanor de Montford sail for, 117;
Rhys Fychan ap Rhys ap Maelgwn and men of Genau'r Glyn flee to, 119;
Dafydd ap Gruffudd guards, 120;
John Pennardd leads men of, against Dryslwyn castle, 121;
subdued by Edward I, 121;
Madog ap Llywelyn ap Maredudd chief over, 122;
host of, goes to Hereford with Edward II, 124;
——, archbishop of
see Elfoddw.
——, kings of
see Caradog; Gruffudd ap Cynan; Iago ab Idwal ap Meurig; Llywelyn ap Seisyll; Trahaearn ap Caradog.
Gwynionydd, commot
given to Maelgwn ap Rhys, 92.
Gwynllŵg, cantref
ravaged by Norsemen, 5;
French expedition to, 20.
Gŵyr, commot
see Gower.

H.

Hainaut, count of
makes pact with King John, 89;
daughter of [William II], betrothed to Edward III, 125;
brother of, comes to England, 125.
Harclay, Sir Andrew of
at Boroughbridge, 124.
Harlech, castle
commenced, 121.
Harold, king of Denmark
defeated and slain, 15.
Harold, king of the Saxons
slays Harold, king of Denmark, 15;
body of, discovered, 127.
harpists, 71.
Haverford, town
Llywelyn ap Iorwerth approaches, 95;
burnt by Llywelyn ap Iorwerth, 98;
spared by Llywelyn ap Gruffudd, 111;
merchants from, (see N.) seize Amaury and Eleanor de Montford, 117.
Hawarden
wood of, Henry II's host in, 59;
castle of, taken by Dafydd ap Gruffudd, 120.

INDEX

Hay, castle
  surrendered to Giles de Breos, 90;
  destroyed by king John, 93;
  —— Llywelyn ap Iorwerth, 102.
Heilyn
  battle of, 2.
Henffordd
  battle of, 2;
  see Hereford.
Henri ab Arthen
  dies, 62.
Henry, emperor of Rome
  dies, 27.
Henry, prince of Burgundy
  surety for Henry II, 66.
Henry, son of Cadwgan
  as hostage, 32;
  mother of, 45.
Henry (recte Robert), son of Henry I
  dies, 56.
Henry I, king of England, 29, 36, 40;
  succeeds William Rufus, 22;
  marries Matilda, 22;
  treachery against, 22ff;
  takes Arundel castle, 23;
  gives lands to Iorwerth ap Bleddyn, 24;
  summons Iorwerth ap Bleddyn to Shrewsbury, 26;
  ejects Saer from Pembroke, 26;
  goes to Normandy, 27;
  sends Flemings to Dyfed, 27;
  releases Iorwerth ap Bleddyn from prison, 32;
  Cadwgan ap Bleddyn prisoner with, 34;
  restores Powys to Cadwgan ap Bleddyn and recalls Owain ap Cadwgan, 35;
  expedition of, against Gwynedd and Powys, 37–8;
  visit to Normandy, 38;
  gives land to Owain ap Caradog ap Gruffudd, 40;
  encomium of, 42;
  sets Owain ap Cadwgan and Llywarch ap Trahaearn against Gruffudd ap Rhys, 44;
  son of, at Carmarthen, 44;
  in Normandy, 46;
  sons of, drowned, 47;
  marries daughter of prince of Germany, 47;
  expedition against Powys, 47–8;
  returns from Normandy, 49;
  expels Gruffudd ap Rhys, 50;
  dies, 51;
  called 'Henry the Great,' 59;
  good laws and customs of, 89.
Henry II, king of England, 12, 59, 61;
  wins England, 58;
  expedition against Gwynedd, 59–60;
  makes peace with Owain Gwynedd, 60;
  expedition to Deheubarth (1158), 61;
  goes overseas, 61;
  expedition to Deheubarth (1163), 62;
  expedition to N. Wales (1165), 63–4;
  Thomas Becket slain at instigation of, 65;
  refuses to go to Rome, 66;
  returns to England, 66;
  expedition to Ireland, 66–8;
  parleys with Lord Rhys, 68;
  reconciled to son Henry, 70;
  holds Council at Gloucester, 70–1;
  holds council at London, 71–2;
  Patriarch of Jerusalem seeks help of, 72;
  takes the Cross, 73;
  dies, 73;
  sister of: see Emma.
——, Henry son of
  at Tours, 69;
  goes to king of France, 69;
  attacks father's territory, 70;
  dies, 72.
Henry III, king of England
  crowned, 93;
  takes the Cross, 93;
  supporters of, hold council, 93;
  supporters of, attack Louis's confederates, 94;
  peace with Louis, 96;
  Rhys Gryg does homage to, 96;
  summons Llywelyn ap Iorwerth to Shrewsbury, 98;
  fails to reconcile William Marshal and Llywelyn ap Iorwerth, 100;
  voyage to France, 101;
  expedition against Llywelyn ap Iorwerth, 101;
  builds Painscastle, 102;
  hostility to Llywelyn ap Iorwerth, 102;
  hostility to Richard Marshal, 103;
  marries, 104;
  son Edward born, 105;
  Dafydd ap Llywelyn and Welsh barons do homage to, 105;
  expedition to N. Wales, 105;
  summons Dafydd ap Llywelyn to London, 105–6;
  lands granted to Welsh princes by, 106;
  visit to Poitou, 106;
  fortifies castle at Degannwy, 107;
  dispossesses Maelgwn Ieuanc, 107;
  debt to, by Strata Florida settled, 108;
  in France, 109;
  leads army to Degannwy, 111;
  goes to France, 112;
  revolt against, 113;
  captured at Lewes, 113;
  death of, 116.
Hercules, 77.
Hereford
  burnt by Gruffudd ap Llywelyn, 14;
  lands around, ravaged, 68;
  king John flees to, 93;
  Edward, son of Henry III, escapes from, 114;
  Cynan ap Maredudd seized at, 122;

Hereford (cont.)
  Edward II, comes to, 124;
  Sir Hugh the Younger and Simon Reding drawn at, 125;
  see Henffordd.
——, bishops of
  see Breos, Giles de; Gerard; Gilbert; Robert.
——, earls of
  Henry de Bohun, captured at Lincoln, 94;
  Humfrey de Bohun (1) gains Brycheiniog, 118;
  —— (2) slain at Boroughbridge, 124;
  Miles, slain, 53;
  Roger, dies, 58;
——, sheriff of
  see Falkes (recte Ingelard).
Hermer, Sir Ralf de
  slain, 125;
Hertford, earl of
  Roger de Clare
    comes to Ystrad Meurig, 60;
    at Dinwileir, 61;
    Lord Rhys invades land of, 63.
Himbert, bishop of Menevia, 5.
Hirbarwch, Gwaith, 9.
Hirfryn, commot
  given to Maelgwn ap Rhys, 92;
  see Maredudd ap Gruffudd.
Hoeddlyw ap Cadwgan ab Elystan
  Euron, daughter of, 45.
Holyhead
  ravaged by sons of Amlaibh, 8.
Holy Land
  Louis IX of France returns from, 109.
Holywell, castle
  built by earl of Chester, 84.
Honorius III, Pope
  succeeds Innocent III, 93.
Hospital, the
  master of, leads Christians against Damietta, 96–7.
Hubert, archbishop of Canterbury
  takes castle of Welshpool, 76;
  dies, 82.
Humfrey's Castle
  burnt by Owain and Cadwaladr, 52;
  won by Roger, earl of Clare, 60;
  taken by Einion ab Anarawd, 61.
Humfrey, son of
  castle of [later 'Castell Hywel'], rebuilt by Hywel ab Owain Gwynedd, 57.
Hunydd, daughter of Bleddyn ap Cynfyn
  wife of Rhydderch ap Tewdwr, 40.
Hyfaidd ap Bleddri
  dies, 5.
Hyfaidd ap Clydog
  dies, 6.
Hywel (1)
  drives Cynan from Anglesey, 3;
  driven from Anglesey, 3;
  dies, 4.
Hywel (2)
  dies in Rome, 5.

Hywel (3)
  Susanna, daughter of, 83.
Hywel ab Ednyfed, bishop of St. Asaph
  consecrates monastery, 104;
  death and burial of, 107.
Hywel ab Edwin ab Einion
  with Maredudd, holds the South, 13;
  in battle against sons of Rhydderch, 13;
  driven from kingdom, 13;
  defeated by Gruffudd ap Llywelyn, 13;
  defeats Gentiles, 13;
  slain in battle, 14.
Hywel ab Einion
  see Hywel ap Rhys (recte Einion).
Hywel ab Idnerth
  calls Gruffudd ap Rhys into Ceredigion, 41.
Hywel ab Ithel
  goes to Ireland, 21;
  conflict with sons of Owain ab Edwin, 46;
  dies, 47.
Hywel ab Owain, king of Glamorgan
  dies, 13.
Hywel ab Owain ab Edwin
  slain by Caradog ap Gruffudd, 17.
Hywel ab Owain Gwynedd
  burns castle at Aberystwyth, 53;
  with brother Cynan, ravages Cardigan, 53–4;
  takes Wizo's Castle, 55–6;
  takes Cynfael castle, 56;
  dispossesses Cadfan ap Cadwaladr, 57;
  loses Ceredigion, 57;
  burns Llanrhystud castle, 57;
  at Dinwileir, 61; ..
  slain by brother Dafydd, 65.
——, castle of
  built, 57.
  subdued by sons of Gruffudd ap Rhys, 58;
  see Humfrey's Castle; Humfrey, son of.
Hywel ap Cadwallon ap Madog
  expelled from Maelienydd, 75;
  hanged in England, 87.
Hywel ap Goronwy
  in attack on Pembroke castle, 20;
  expelled from Ystrad Tywi and Rhyd-y-gors, 26;
  depredations of, 26;
  betrayed to the French and slain, 26–7.
Hywel ap Gruffudd ab Ednyfed
  leads Edward I's fleet against Anglesey, 120.
Hywel ap Gruffudd ap Cynan
  expels Maredudd ap Cynan from Meirionnydd, 81;
  opposes John's expedition (1211), 85;
  with Llywelyn ap Iorwerth in Dyfed, 91;
  death and burial of, 93.
Hywel ap Ieuaf ab Idwal Foel
  expels Iago, 8;
  ravages Clynnog Fawr, 9;

INDEX

Hywel ap Ieuaf ab Idwal Foel (*cont.*)
  dispossesses Iago, 9;
  slays Custennin [ap Iago], 9;
  slays Saxons, 9;
  slain, 9.
Hywel ap Ieuaf ab Owain, lord of Arwystli
  takes Tafolwern castle, 62;
  defeated by Owain Gwynedd, 62;
  dies, 73.
Hywel ap Iorwerth, of Caerleon
  lands ravaged by, 68;
  besieges Caerleon, 70;
  wins Gwent Is-Coed, 70;
  blinds and castrates Owain Pen-carn, 70;
  loses Caerleon, 70.
Hywel ap Madog ab Idnerth
  slain, 53.
Hywel ap Maredudd, of Brycheiniog
  at siege of Aberystwyth castle, 51;
  in attack on Cardigan, 51.
Hywel ap Maredudd, of Glamorgan
  flees to Gwynedd, 107.
Hywel ap Maredudd ap Bleddyn
  slain by own men, 53.
Hywel ap Maredudd ap Rhydderch
  slain by Rhys ap Hywel, 52.
Hywel ap Meurig, constable of Cefn-llys castle
  with wife and sons, captured, 112.
Hywel ap Rhys (*recte* Einion)
  blinded by brother, 75.
Hywel ap Rhys ap Tewdwr
  goes to Gruffudd ap Cynan, 39.
Hywel ap Rhys Gryg
  goes to Llywelyn ap Gruffudd, 118.
Hywel Sais ap Rhys ap Gruffudd
  restored to father by Henry II, 67;
  sent to France, 69;
  takes Wizo's Castle, 75;
  releases father, 75;
  death and burial of, 82.
Hywel the Good
  goes to Rome, 6;
  dies, 7.
——, sons of
  battles of, against sons of Idwal, 7.

I.

Iago ab Idwal [ap Meurig]
  holds Gwynedd, 13;
  slain, 13;
  Gruffudd [ap Cynan], grandson of, 16, 17.
Iago ab Idwal Foel
  ravages Dyfed, 7;
  seizes brother Ieuaf, 8;
  expelled by Hywel, 8;
  captured by Gentiles, 9;
  see Idwal Foel, sons of.
——, sons of
  see Custennin.
Iâl, commot
  Owain ap Gruffudd ap Cynan builds castle in, 57;
  castle of, burnt by Iorwerth Goch ap Maredudd, 60;
  monastery of Llynegwestl in, built, 81;
  see Bryneglwys; Llynegwestl.
Iarddur, monk
  dies, 11.
Iarddur ap Merfyn
  drowned, 7.
Idnerth ap Cadwgan
  French defeated by sons of, 20.
Idwal ap Meurig
  slain, 10.
Idwal ap Rhodri (1)
  slain by Saxons, 7.
Idwal ap Rhodri (2)
  slain, 8.
Idwal Foel, sons of
  battles of, against sons of Hywel, 7;
  Ceredigion ravaged by, 7;
  hold rule, 8, N.;
  kingdoms of, ravaged by Saxons, 8.
Idwal [Fychan ab Idwal Foel]
  slain, 9.
Idwallon
  dies, 4.
Idwallon ab Owain
  dies, 8.
Ieuaf ab Idwal Foel
  ravages Dyfed, 7;
  seized by brother Iago, 8;
  dies, 10;
  see Idwal Foel, sons of.
Ieuaf ab Owain
  slain by sons of Llywarch ap Trahaearn, 50;
  see Llywelyn (*recte* Ieuaf) ab Owain.
Ieuan ap Seisyll ap Rhiryd
  seized by king's men, 69.
Ieuan [ap Sulien], high-priest of Llanbadarn
  dies, 52.
Ifor ab Alan
  succeeds Cadwaladr, 1.
Ifor ab Idnerth ap Cadwgan
  with brother Gruffudd, defeats French, 20.
Ifor ap Meurig
  men of, betray Morgan ab Owain, 60.
Igmund
  comes to Anglesey, 6.
Imhar of Waterford
  dies, 11.
Ingelard, sheriff of Gloucester
  fortifies Builth castle, 84.
Ingelard, sheriff of Hereford
  see Falkes (*recte* Ingelard).
Innocent III, Pope
  frees Welsh princes from allegiance to king John, 87;
  interdiction of churches by, 87;
  king John submits to, 88;
  holds Lateran council, 91;
  dies, 93.
—— V, Pope
  intercedes for release of Eleanor de Montford, 117.

insects
    leaves devoured by, 69;
    see vermin.
Ionafal ap Meurig
    slain by Cadwallon ap Ieuaf, 9.
Ionathal, head of *clas* at Abergelau
    dies, 4.
Iorwerth, abbot of Talley and bishop of Menevia
    becomes bishop of Menevia, 91;
    arranges peace between Llywelyn ap Iorwerth and Flemings, 95–6;
    buries Maredudd, archdeacon of Ceredigion, 101;
    dies, 101.
Iorwerth ab Owain
    slain, 50.
Iorwerth ab Owain ap Caradog
    wins Caerleon and brother Morgan's land, 60;
    loses Caerleon, 66;
    with allies, destroys Caerleon, 66;
    lands ravaged by, 68;
    takes Caerleon, 70;
    loses Caerleon, 70;
    regains Caerleon, 71;
    at council of Gloucester, 71.
Iorwerth ap Bleddyn
    supports Robert de Bellême, 23;
    lands given to, by Henry I, 24;
    deserts Robert de Bellême, 24;
    reconciled to brothers, 25;
    seizes brother Maredudd, 25;
    Henry I's promises to, not fulfilled, 25;
    imprisoned after trial, 26;
    released by Henry I, 32;
    recovers territory, 32;
    acts against Owain ap Cadwgan and Madog ap Rhiryd, 32–3;
    at king's court, 34;
    slain through treachery of Madog ap Rhiryd and Llywarch ap Trahaearn, 35.
Iorwerth ap Llywarch [ap Trahaearn]
    slain by Llywelyn (*recte* Ieuaf) ab Owain, 50.
Iorwerth ap Nudd
    slain, 47.
Iorwerth ap Rhiryd
    hostage for Iorwerth ap Bleddyn, 32.
Iorwerth Goch ap Maredudd ap Bleddyn
    burns castle of Iâl, 60;
    opposes Henry II's expedition (1165), 63;
    expelled from Mochnant, 64.
Irathwy
    battle of, 13, N.
Ireland
    Pagans come to, 3;
    bread fails in, 6;
    ravaged by Norse of Dublin, 6;
    fleet of Gentiles from, supports Hywel ab Edwin, 14;
    fleet from, founders in South [Wales], 14;
    Rhys ap Tewdwr flees to, 18;
    Hywel ab Ithel goes to, 21;
    Cadwgan ap Bleddyn and Gruffudd ap Cynan flee to, and return from, 21;
    ship from, at Aberdyfi, 30;
    Owain ap Cadwgan flees to, 30, 34;
    ships from, with Owain ap Cadwgan, 33;
    Madog ap Rhiryd flees to, 34;
    —— returns from, 35;
    Owain ap Cadwgan recalled from, 35;
    Gruffudd ap Rhys ap Tewdwr taken to, 39;
    fleet from, with Cadwaladr ap Gruffudd, 53;
    ships from, support Henry II (1165), 64;
    Robert fitz Stephen goes to, 65;
    Henry II goes to, 66–8;
    Richard, son of Gilbert Strongbow, returns from, 67;
    Maelgwn ab Owain Gwynedd driven to, 70;
    king John's expedition to, 83–4;
    William de Breos and family banished to, 83;
    made tributary to Roman See, 88;
    William Marshal brings army from, 99;
    Richard, earl of Pembroke, goes to, 103;
    soldiers from, with Henry III in N. Wales, 107;
    see 'White Strand.'
——, kings of
    see Brian; Congalach; Cormac, son of Culennán; Maelsechlainn.
Irish, the, 5, 68;
    Dublin ravaged by, 11;
    boastfulness of, 12;
    Rhydderch ap Iestyn slain by, 13;
    support Gruffudd ap Cynan, 17;
    Arnulf seeks aid of, 23;
    ways and customs of, 35;
    defeated by Owain ap Gruffudd ap Cynan, 53;
    see Scots.
——, kings of
    see Diarmaid, son of Mael-na-mbo; Toirrdelbhach.
[Isabella], wife of Edward II
    prevented from entering Leeds castle, 124;
    placed on livery, 124;
    goes to France and returns, 124–5.
Is-Aeron
    won by sons of Gruffudd ap Rhys, 57;
    ravaged by Rhys Ieuanc and brother Owain, 86;
Ischerwlf
    son of, leads fleet from Ireland, 53.
Is-Coed, commot in Ceredigion
    Gruffudd ap Rhys ap Tewdwr comes to, 42.

Isles, the
  men of, destroy Menevia, 18.
Is-Rhaeadr (sc. Mochnant)
  comes to Owain Fychan ap Madog, 64.
Ithel, abbot of Strata Marcella
  dies, 73.
Ithel, king of Gwent
  slain by men of Brycheiniog, 4.
Ithel ap Gruffudd ap Llywelyn
  slain in battle against sons of Cynfyn, 15.
Ithel ap Rhiryd ap Bleddyn
  incited against Owain ap Cadwgan, 29;
  leagued with Uchdryd ab Edwin, 30;
  with brother Madog seizes portion of Powys, 31;
  hostage for Iorwerth ap Bleddyn, 32;
  land of, given to brother Madog, 36;
  released from prison, 49;
  slain by Gruffudd ap Maredudd ap Bleddyn, 49.
Iwerydd, half-sister of Bleddyn ap Cynfyn
  mother of Owain and Uchdryd, sons of Edwin, 45.

J.

[Jeanne], daughter of Edward II
  married to [David II] son of king [Robert I] of Scotland, 125.
Jerusalem
  Robert, son of William I, goes to, 19;
  ———, ———, returns from, 22;
  Morgan ap Cadwgan goes to, 50;
  Welsh pilgrims to, 53;
  Louis VII of France and emperor of Germany go to, 55;
  Patriarch of, seeks help for, 72;
  taken by Saracens, 73;
  Richard I returns from, 74, 75;
  aid to, discussed, 91;
  oppressed by Saracens, 91;
  Crusaders go to, 96;
  Louis IX of France goes to, 108;
  ——— returns from, 109;
  Papal legate and son of Louis IX on way to, 115;
  Edward I returns from, 116.
———, king of
  leads Christians against Damietta, 96–7.
———, Patriarch of
  comes to England, 72;
  leads Christians against Damietta, 96–7.
Jews
  Jerusalem harried by, 72;
  expelled from England, 121.
Joab, abbot of Strata Florida
  dies, 115.
Joan, natural daughter of king John and wife of Llywelyn ap Iorwerth
  sent by Llywelyn to sue for peace with John, 85;
  William de Breos the Younger caught in chamber of, 101–2;
  called 'Lady of Wales,' 104;
  dies at Aber, 104;
  Dafydd, son of, 105.
John, cardinal
  comes from Rome to England, 83.
John, king of England
  succeeds Richard I, 80;
  opposes election of archbishop of Canterbury, 83;
  banishes William de Breos, 83;
  expedition to Ireland, 83–4;
  support of Welsh princes, 84;
  expeditions to Wales, 85;
  land between the Dyfi and the Aeron granted to, 86;
  Rhys Ieuanc and brother Owain reconciled to, 86;
  Rhys Ieuanc seeks portion of patrimony from, 87;
  seeks to obtain Llandovery castle for sons of Gruffudd ap Rhys, 87;
  makes amends for wrongs done to clerics, 88;
  makes kingdom tributary to Roman See, 88;
  wages war against Philip II of France, 88–9;
  barons rebel against, 89–90, 96;
  takes the Cross, 90;
  makes peace with Giles de Breos, 91;
  Gwenwynwyn makes pact with, 92;
  retreats before Louis, son of Philip II of France, 93;
  death and burial of, 93.
———, daughter of
  see Joan.
John, St., church of, in Chester
  body of king Harold discovered in, 127.
Joseph, bishop of Menevia
  dies, 15.
Joseph, Teilo's bishop
  dies in Rome, 14.

K.

Kenilworth, castle
  fortified by sons of Simon de Montford, 114;
  surrendered to the king, 114.
Kent
  Roger Mortimer and queen await Edward III in, 94.
———, castle of
  Louis, son of Philip II, desists from siege of, 94.
———, earl of
  Woodstock, Sir Edmund de, lands in England from France, 124–5;
  ———, ———, executed, 125–6.
Kidwelly
  see Cydweli.

L.

[Lacy, Henry de]
see Lincoln, earl of
——, Hugh de
  sons of, land of, in Ireland taken by king John, 83-4.
Lampeter
  Maredudd, archdeacon of Ceredigion, dies at, 101;
  see Stephen's Castle.
Lancaster, earl of
  [Henry] execution of, proposed, 125;
  [Thomas] executed, 124.
Langton, Stephen, archbishop of Canterbury
  election of, opposed by John, 83;
  John submits to, 88;
  John defies, 90;
  a papal cardinal, 97;
  re-inters body of Thomas Becket, 97;
  fails to reconcile William Marshal and Llywelyn ap Iorwerth, 100.
Lateran church, in Rome
  Innocent III holds council in, 91.
Laugharne, castle
  parley between Henry II and Lord Rhys at, 68;
  destroyed by Llywellyn ap Iorwerth 91.
Lawhaden, castle
  taken by Lord Rhys, 74;
  destroyed by Welsh, 75.
Leeds, castle
  queen refused entrance to, 124.
legates, papal
  see Otto; Ottobon.
Leicester, 125.
Leinster, kings of
  see Cerbhall, son of Muirecan; Diarmaid; Maelmordha.
Lestrange, John, constable of Baldwin's Castle
  raids Cydewain, 113.
Lewes
  battle of (1264), 113-14.
L'Ile, Brian de
  goes on Crusade, 96.
Lincoln
  battle of, 94.
——, bishop of
  dies, 104.
——, earl of [Lacy, Henry de]
  with Roger de Mortimer at Baldwin's Castle, 118;
  at siege of Dolforwyn castle, 118.
Llanarthnau
  Rhys Gryg seized at, 101.
Llanbadarn-fawr, castle of
  built by Gilbert fitz Richard, 34;
  English at, 119;
  see Aberystwyth.
——, church of
  ravaged, 10;
  pillaged by Llywelyn (recte Gruffudd ap Llywelyn), 13;
  as sanctuary, 30;
  desecrated, 42;
  Matilda de Breos dies at, 84;
  Maredudd ab Owain [ap Gruffudd] dies at, 114;
  see Ieuan [ap Sulien]; Padarn, St.; Sulien ap Rhygyfarch.
Llancarfan
  ravaged, 10.
Llandaff, bishops of
  see Geoffrey; Nicholas ap Gwrgant; Uchdryd.
Llanddewifrefi
  sanctuary of St. David at, violated, 30.
Llandeilo-fawr
  burnt by Rhys Fychan, 87;
  Rhys Gryg dies at, 103.
Llandinam
  raided by Owain Gwynedd, 62.
Llandovery, castle
  attacked by Gruffudd ap Rhys ap Tewdwr, 40;
  held by Walter Clifford, 60;
  taken by Rhys ap Gruffudd, 61;
  taken by Rhys Ieuanc ap Gruffudd, 82;
  taken by Gwenwynwyn and Maelgwn ap Rhys, 82;
  taken from Maelgwn ap Rhys by sons of Gruffudd ap Rhys, 82;
  surrenders to Rhys Fychan, 84;
  Rhys Fychan refuses to give, to sons of Gruffudd ap Rhys, 87;
  surrendered to Rhys Ieuanc, 88;
  fortified by Rhys Fychan, 88;
  given to Maelgwn ap Rhys, 92;
  Rhys Gryg released for, by Rhys Fychan, 101;
  Maredudd ap Gruffudd, lord of Hirfryn, dies in, 115.
Llandudoch
  ravaged, 10;
  battle of, 18.
Llandyfái, abbot of
  see Cadwgan.
Llanegwad, castle
  taken by Rhys ap Gruffudd, 82.
Llan-faes, in Anglesey
  battle of, 3.
——, ——, monastery of
  Gwenllïan, daughter of Gruffudd ap Llywelyn, buried in, 117.
Llanfair, in Builth, castle and town
  Llywelyn ap Gruffudd fails to take, 112;
  destroyed by Llywelyn ap Gruffudd, 112.
Llanfihangel Gelynrhod
  Gwenllïan, daughter of Maelgwn Ieuanc, dies at, 109.
Llanfihangel [Genau'r Glyn]
  castle of Pen-gwern in, 57.
Llangadog, castle
  taken by Gwenwynwyn and Maelgwn ap Rhys, 82;
  taken by Rhys Fychan, 83;
  burnt by Rhys Fychan and brother Owain, 83.

INDEX

Llanganten
    Llywelyn ap Gruffudd at, 120.
Llan-giwg
    Llywelyn ap Iorwerth encamps at, 95.
Llan-gors
    Trahaearn Fychan comes to, 79.
Llangwm
    battle near, 10.
Llangynwyd, castle
    taken by Llywelyn ap Gruffudd, 111.
Llanidloes
    Hywel ap Ieuaf defeated at, 62.
Llanilltud
    ravaged, 10.
Llannerch Aeron
    Maelgwn ap Rhys dies at, 102.
Llanrhystud, castle
    built by Cadwaladr ap Gruffudd ap Cynan, 57;
    taken by sons of Gruffudd ap Rhys, 57;
    burnt by Hywel ab Owain Gwynedd, 57;
    taken by Roger, earl of Clare, 60.
Llanstephan, castle
    overcome by sons of Gruffudd ap Rhys, 54;
    defended by Maredudd ap Gruffudd, 54;
    taken by Rhys ap Gruffudd, 73;
    destroyed by Llywelyn ap Iorwerth, 91;
    with town, burnt by Welsh, 111.
Llantarnam
    see Nant-teyrnon.
Llantwit Major
    see Llanilltud
Llanweithefawr
    ravaged by Godfrey, son of Harold, 9, N.
Llawdden
    slain by Cynan ab Owain, 65.
Llech-y-crau
    battle of, 18.
Llwythlawr (? *recte* Llwytlaw = Ludlow), abbot of
    see Gwrgenau.
Llŷn, cantref
    ravaged by sons of Amlaibh, 8;
    ravaged by Gwrmid, 9;
    ravaged by Custennin ap Iago and Godfrey, son of Harold, 9;
    won by Llywelyn ap Iorwerth, 81;
    Gruffudd ap Llywelyn ap Iorwerth allowed to hold, 104;
    given to Owain Goch by brother Llywelyn, 119;
    tournament at Nefyn in, 121.
Llynegwestl, in Iâl, monastery
    built, 81;
    Madog ap Gruffudd Maelor, founder of, buried in, 104;
    Gruffudd ap Madog ap Gruffudd Maelor and brother Madog Fychan buried in, 115.

Llywarch ab Owain
    blinded, 9.
Llywarch ab Owain ab Edwin
    slain in battle against Hywel ab Ithel, 46–7.
Llywarch ap Hyfaidd
    dies, 6.
Llywarch ap Trahaearn
    attacks Owain ap Cadwgan's land, 29;
    leagued with Uchdryd ab Edwin, 30;
    with Madog ap Rhiryd, betrays Iorwerth ap Bleddyn, 35;
    land of, raided, 36;
    set against Gruffudd ap Rhys, 44;
    returns after attack on Ystrad Tywi, 45;
    territory of, invaded, 49;
    helps sons of Gruffudd ap Cynan, 49;
    sons of, slay Ieuaf ab Owain, 50.
Llywelyn (*recte* Gruffudd ap Llywelyn), king of Gwynedd
    rules after Iago [ab Idwal ap Meurig], 13;
    routs Pagans, 13;
    pillages Llanbadarn, 13;
    holds Deheubarth, 13;
    expels Hywel ab Edwin, 13.
Llywelyn ab Owain
    seized by Maredudd, his uncle, and imprisoned, 50;
    slays Iorwerth ap Llywarch, 50;
    castrated and blinded by Maredudd ap Bleddyn, 50.
Llywelyn (*recte* Ieuaf) ab Owain
    slays Maredudd ap Llywarch, 50.
Llywelyn ab Owain Gwynedd
    death and encomium of, 64.
Llywelyn ab Owain ap Maredudd
    submits to English, 118;
    placed in ward, 118.
Llywelyn ap Cadwallon
    blinded, 73.
Llywelyn ap Cadwgan
    in battle of Camddwr, 16;
    —— 'Gweunytwl,' 16;
    slain by men of Brycheiniog, 21.
Llywelyn ap Cedifor ap Gollwyn
    with brothers, calls in Gruffudd ap Maredudd, 18.
Llywelyn ap Gruffudd
    with brother Owain Goch, succeeds Dafydd ap Llywelyn, 107;
    Maelgwn Ieuanc flees to, 107;
    defeats brothers Owain Goch and Dafydd, 110;
    gains Perfeddwlad and Meirionnydd, 110;
    gives land in Ceredigion to Maredudd ab Owain, 110;
    gives Builth to Maredudd ap Rhys Gryg, 110;
    takes Gwerthrynion from Roger de Mortimer, 110;
    campaigns against Gruffudd ap Gwenwynwyn, 110–11;
    invades Dyfed and Deheubarth, 111;

Llywelyn ap Gruffudd (cont.)
  makes peace with Gruffudd ap Madog, 111;
  dispossesses Gruffudd ap Gwenwynwyn, 111;
  attacks Builth and Deheubarth, 112;
  Owain ap Maredudd of Elfael comes to his peace, 112;
  campaigns against Maelienydd and Brycheiniog, 112–13;
  brother Dafydd breaks with, 113;
  castles taken by in 1263 rising, 113;
  prince over all Wales, 114;
  pact with earl of Clare, 114;
  makes peace with Henry III, 115;
  takes Caerffili castle, 115;
  at Dolforwyn, 116;
  acts against Gruffudd ap Gwenwynwyn and son, 116–17;
  refuses homage to Edward I, 117;
  marriage by proxy to Eleanor de Montford, 117;
  fails to make peace with Edward I, 118;
  princes from Deheubarth flee to, 118;
  Rhys Fychan ap Rhys ap Maelgwn flees to, 119;
  makes peace with Edward I, 119;
  tenders homage to Edward I, 119;
  Owain Goch and Gruffudd ap Gwenwynwyn released from prison of, 119;
  gives Llŷn to Owain Goch, 119;
  actual marriage to Eleanor, 119;
  betrayal of, at Bangor, 120;
  breaks with Edward I, 120;
  slain in Builth, 120–1;
——, daughter of
  see Gwenllïan.
——, steward of
  see Goronwy ab Ednyfed.
Llywelyn ap Hofa
  dies, 126.
Llywelyn ap Iorwerth
  dispossesses Dafydd ab Owain Gwynedd, 75;
  seizes Dafydd ab Owain Gwynedd, 79;
  gains Llŷn and Eifionydd, 81;
  moves against Gwenwynwyn, 81;
  reconciled to Gwenwynwyn, 82;
  takes Bala castle, 82;
  expels Dafydd ab Owain from Gwynedd, 82;
  occupies Gwenwynwyn's territory, 83;
  rebuilds Aberystwyth castle and gains Penweddig, 83;
  destroys Degannwy castle, 84;
  ravages earl of Chester's land, 84;
  John's expedition (1211) against, 85;
  rises against John, 86;
  freed from allegiance to John, 87;
  gains Perfeddwlad from John, 87;
  takes Degannwy and Rhuddlan castles, 88;
  Shrewsbury surrendered to, 90;
  Maelgwn ap Rhys and Owain ap Gruffudd flee to, 90;
  castles taken by, on expedition (1215) to Dyfed, 91–2;
  princes with, on 1215 expedition, 91–2;
  action by, against Gwenwynwyn, 92;
  presides over apportioning of lands between descendants of Lord Rhys, 92;
  invades Brycheiniog and Dyfed (1217), 95–6;
  given custody of Carmarthen and Cardigan, 96;
  attacks Flemings, 97–8;
  acts against son Gruffudd, 98;
  subdues Aberystwyth castle, 98;
  relations with Rhys Ieuanc, 98;
  gives land to Maelgwn ap Rhys, 99;
  sends son Gruffudd to oppose William Marshal, 99–100;
  comes into Mabudryd, 100;
  Henry III's expedition (1228) against, 101;
  hangs William de Breos the Younger, 101–2;
  castles taken by, in hostilities against the king, 102–3;
  makes alliance with Richard Marshal, 103;
  Gilbert Marshal's fear of, 104;
  builds monastery for Barefooted Friars, 104;
  death and burial of, 105.
——, daughters of
  see Gwladus Ddu; Margaret.
Llywelyn ap Llywelyn ab Ynyr, bishop of St. Asaph
  elected, 122;
  dies, 123.
Llywelyn ap Madog ap Maredudd
  slays Stephen fitz Baldwin, 58;
  slain, 62.
Llywelyn ap Maelgwn Ieuanc
  death and burial of, 101.
Llywelyn ap Maredudd ap Cynan (1) [i.e. Llywelyn Fychan]
  with Llywelyn ap Iorwerth in Dyfed, 91;
  given rights in Meirionnydd, 106.
Llywelyn ap Maredudd ap Cynan (2), [i.e. Llywelyn Fawr]
  given territory in Meirionnydd, 106.
Llywelyn ap Rhys ap Maelgwn Fychan
  dies, 114.
Llywelyn ap Rhys Fychan ap Rhys Mechyll
  goes to Llywelyn ap Gruffudd, 118.
Llywelyn ap Seisyll, king of Gwynedd
  slays Aeddan ap Blegywryd and sons, 12;
  encomium of, 12;
  defeats the pretender Rhain, 12;
  dies, 12;
  kingdom of, held by Iago ab Idwal [ap Meurig], 13.

Llywelyn Bren
  war of, 123;
  seized, 123.
Locrinus, 78.
London, 125;
  taken by Henry I, 22;
  council at (1176), 71–2;
  Louis, son of Philip II of France, received in, 93;
  Louis besieged in, 95;
  Henry III's wedding feast at, 104;
  council at (1241), 105–6;
  Gruffudd ap Llywelyn ap Iorwerth imprisoned at, 106;
  taken by earl of Clare, 114;
  Henry III buried in, 116;
  Edward I holds council in, 117;
  Edward I goes from, to Chester, 117;
  Welsh princes tender homage to Edward I at, 118;
  council at (1320), 123;
  ——— (1329), 125;
  Roger Mortimer executed at, 126;
  see Cheap, in.
———, bishop of
  dies, 104, N.
  see Richard.
[Longespée, William de]
  see Salisbury, earl of.
Loughor, castle
  burnt by Rhys Ieuanc, 90;
  see Aberllwchwr.
Louis, son of Philip II of France
  sent to Poitou to oppose king John, 89;
  actions of, in England against supporters of Henry III, 93–6;
  makes peace with Henry III and sails for France, 96.
Louis VII, king of France
  goes to Jerusalem, 55;
  sends messengers to Henry II, 68;
——— VIII, king of France
  dies, 101.
——— IX, king of France
  goes to Jerusalem, 108;
  takes Damietta, 108;
  captured by Saracens, 108;
  victorious over Saracens, 108;
  returns from Jerusalem, 109;
  Henry III goes to parley with, 112;
  dies, 115;
  son of, on way to Jerusalem, 115.
Lucius III, Pope
  succeeds Alexander III, 72;
  dies, 73.
Ludlow
  council at, 100.
———, abbot of
  see Llwythlawr.
Luggy, river
  land between it and the Rhyw, taken from Gruffudd ap Gwenwynwyn, 116.
Lwmberth, bishop of Menevia
  dies, 7.
Lyons
  Pope Gregory X holds synod at, 116.

M.

Mabudryd, commot
  Gilbert, son of earl Gilbert, builds castle in, 54;
  Llywelyn ap Iorwerth comes into, 100;
  see Dinwileir, castle in.
Mabwynion, commot
  taken by Rhys ap Gruffudd, 63;
  given to Maelgwn ap Rhys, 92.
Maccus, monk
  dies, 14.
Maccus, son of Harold
  see Madog, son of Harold, N.
Machein, castle
  taken and then restored by Gilbert Marshal, 104.
Madog ab Einion
  see Madog ap Rhys (recte ab Einion).
Madog ab Idnerth
  at siege of Aberystwyth castle, 51;
  in attack on Ceredigion, 51;
  dies, 52.
———, sons of (Hywel and Cadwgan) slain, 53.
———, sons of (Cadwallon and Einion Clud) oppose Henry II's expedition (1165), 63.
Madog ap Bleddyn
  with brothers, expels Rhys ap Tewdwr, 18;
  slain at Llech-y-crau, 18;
  mother of, 45.
Madog ap Cadwgan ap Bleddyn
  leagued with Hywel ab Ithel, 46–7;
  opposes Henry I's expedition, 48;
  comes to terms with Henry I, 48.
Madog ap Gruffudd Maelor
  opposes John's expedition (1211), 85;
  makes pact with Llywelyn ap Iorwerth, 86;
  war-band of, with Llywelyn ap Iorwerth, 91;
  death and encomium of, 104.
Madog ap Llywarch [ap Trahaearn]
  slain by first-cousin Meurig, 50.
Madog ap Llywelyn ap Maredudd
  chief over Gwynedd, 122;
  with son, seized, 122.
Madog ap Llywelyn of Bromfield
  dies, 126.
Madog ap Maelgwn [? ap Cadwallon]
  hanged in England, 87.
Madog ap Maredudd
  followers of, slay Cynwrig ab Owain, 52;
  builds Oswestry castle, 57;
  gives Cyfeiliog to sons of Gruffudd ap Maredudd, 57;
  opposes Owain Gwynedd, 57;
  builds castle in Caereinion, 59;
  opposes Henry II's expedition (1157), 59;

Madog ap Maredudd (*cont.*)
  death and encomium of, 61;
  daughter of, 83.
——, nephew of
  see Meurig ap Gruffudd ap Maredudd.
——, sons of
  oppose Henry II's expedition (1165), 63.
Madog ap Rhiryd ap Bleddyn
  incited against Owain ap Cadwgan, 29;
  leagued with Uchdryd ab Edwin, 30;
  with brother Ithel, seizes portion of Powys, 31;
  protects Saxons from French, 31;
  leagued with Owain ap Cadwgan, 31-3;
  in Cyfeiliog, 33;
  returns to Powys, 33;
  goes to Ireland, 34;
  returns from Ireland, 35;
  betrays Iorwerth ap Bleddyn, 35;
  slays Cadwgan ap Bleddyn, 35-6;
  imprisoned by Maredudd ap Bleddyn, 36;
  blinded by Owain ap Cadwgan, 37;
  Caereinion held by, 45.
Madog ap Rhys (*recte* ab Einion)
  blinded, 75.
Madog Fychan ap Madog ap Gruffudd Maelor
  death and burial of, 115.
Madog (*recte* Maccus) son of Harold
  ravages Penmon, 8.
Maelcoluim III, son of Donnchadh, king of Picts and Scots
  slain by French, 19.
——, sons of
  see Alexander; Edgar; Edward.
Maelgwn ab Owain Gwynedd
  driven from Anglesey, 70;
  imprisoned by brother Dafydd, 70.
Maelgwn ap Cadwallon ap Madog ab Idnerth
  expelled from Maelienydd, 75;
  dies, 79;
  two sons of, with Llywelyn ap Iorwerth in Dyfed, 91-2.
Maelgwn ap Rhys
  with Cynan ap Maredudd chief over Deheubarth, 122.
Maelgwn ap Rhys ap Gruffudd
  ravages Tenby, 73;
  encomium of, 73-4;
  imprisoned, 73-4;
  escapes from prison, 74;
  takes Ystrad Meurig castle, 75;
  gives Ystrad Meurig to brother [Hywel], 75;
  captures brother Gruffudd, 79;
  takes Cardigan and Ystrad Meurig castles, 79;
  brother Gruffudd obtains portion of patrimony from, 80;
  attacks castle of Dineirth, 80;
  sells Cardigan castle to Saxons, 80-1;
  with Gwenwynwyn takes Llandovery and Llangadog castles, 82;
  completes castle of Dineirth, 82;
  men of, slay brother Hywel, 82;
  loses Dinefwr and Llandovery, 82;
  has Cedifor ap Gruffudd and sons slain, 82-3;
  builds Abereinion castle, 83;
  destroys Ystrad Meurig castle, 83;
  burns Dineirth and Aberystwyth, 83;
  makes pact with king John, 84;
  breaks with nephews Rhys and Owain, 84;
  routed at Cilcennin, 84;
  opposes king John's expedition, 85;
  sent against sons of Gruffudd ap Rhys, 85;
  land of, Is-Aeron, ravaged, 86;
  makes pact with Llywelyn ap Iorwerth, 86;
  helps to win Perfeddwlad from king, 87;
  Rhys Fychan, his brother, flees to, 88;
  with Rhys Ieuanc, attacks Dyfed, 90;
  flees to Gwynedd, 90;
  on 1215 expedition to Dyfed, 92;
  lands given to, in 1216, 92;
  Carmarthen castle given to, 98;
  receives portion of Rhys Ieuanc's patrimony, 99;
  death and burial of, 102;
  Trefilan castle built by, 103.
Maelgwn Ieuanc (Fychan) ap Maelgwn ap Rhys
  attacks on Cardigan by, 102;
  at siege of Carmarthen, 103;
  repairs Trefilan castle, 103;
  fortifies Garth Grugyn, 106;
  flees to sons of Gruffudd ap Llywelyn, 107;
  stewardship of lands formerly held by, 109;
  death and burial of, 111.
——, daughter of
  see Gwenllïan; Margaret.
——, son of
  see Rhys ap Maelgwn Ieuanc.
Maelienydd, cantref
  Owain ap Cadwgan's men flee to, 29;
  subjugated by Hugh fitz Ranulf, 53;
  sons of Cadwallon [ap Madog ab Idnerth] expelled from, 75;
  castle of, fortified by Roger de Mortimer, 106;
  men from, take Roger de Mortimer's new castle, 112;
  Llywelyn ap Gruffudd comes to, 112;
  see Cadwallon ap Madog; Cadwallon ap Maelgwn; Maelgwn ap Cadwallon.
Maelmordha, king of Leinster
  slain in attack by Brian, 11.
Mael-na-mbo
  see Diarmaid, son of.
Maelog Cam, son of Peredur
  slain, 6.

INDEX

Maelor
  see Gruffudd ap Madog ap Gruffudd Maelor (1), (2); Madog Fychan ap Madog ap Gruffudd Maelor.
Maelsechlainn
  dies, 4.
Maenclochog, castle
  burnt by Maelgwn ap Rhys and Rhys Ieuanc, 90;
  and town of, burnt by Welsh, 111.
Maeshyfaidd, vill
  ravaged by Maredudd ab Owain, 10.
Maes Rhosmeilon
  held by Igmund, 6, N.
Magnus, king of Germany
  brings fleet to Anglesey, 21;
  comes again to Anglesey, 24;
  goes to Man, 24;
  Robert de Bellême sues to, for help, 25;
  slain, 25.
——, ——, son of
  marries daughter of Muircertach, 24.
Magnus, son of Harold
  with Gruffudd ap Llywelyn, ravages England, 14;
  see Madog (*recte* Maccus), son of Harold.
Maig ap Ieuaf
  slain, 9.
Mallaen, commot
  given to Maelgwn ap Rhys, 92;
  Rhys ap Maredudd seized in, 121.
Man, island
  ravaged by Sweyn, son of Harold, 10;
  Magnus goes to, 24;
  Magnus leaves, 25.
Manfred, son of emperor Frederick II
  slain in Apulia, 115.
March, the, 81, N;
  king John flees to, 93;
  earls and barons of, summoned by Henry III, 98;
  Edward, son of Edward III, in, 113;
  see Wales, March of.
Marchers, the
  lament defeat by Rhys ap Gruffudd, 76.
Mare, Richard de la
  castle of, burnt by sons of Gruffudd ap Cynan, 51.
Maredudd, king of Dyfed
  dies, 3.
Maredudd (*recte* Meurig), bishop of Bangor
  dies, 62.
Maredudd ab Edwin ab Einion
  with brother Hywel, holds the South, 13;
  in battle against sons of Rhydderch ap Iestyn, 13;
  slain by sons of Cynan, 13.
Maredudd ab Owain ab Edwin
  holds the South, 16;
  slain, 16.

Maredudd ab Owain ap Gruffudd
  commanded to dispossess Maelgwn Ieuanc, 107;
  land of Builth given to, 110;
  with Llywelyn ap Gruffudd against Gwenwynwyn, 110–11;
  at parley in Emlyn, 111–12;
  death and burial of, 114;
  son Owain buried near grave of, 117.
——, sons of
  see Gruffudd ap Maredudd; Owain ap Maredudd.
Maredudd ab Owain ap Hywel Dda
  slays Cadwallon ap Ieuaf, 9;
  brings relics (N.) to Ceredigion and Dyfed, 9–10;
  pays tribute to Black Host, 10;
  ravages Maeshyfaidd, 10;
  territory of, ravaged, 10;
  ravages Glamorgan, 10;
  defeated by sons of Meurig, 10;
  dies, 10;
  Rhain claims to be son of, 12.
——, daughter of
  see Angharad.
Maredudd ap Bleddyn
  supports Robert de Bellême, 23-4;
  seized by brother Iorwerth, 25;
  escapes and regains land, 27;
  holds Iorwerth ap Bleddyn's land, 36;
  raid by war-band of, 36;
  seizes Madog ap Rhiryd, 36;
  makes peace with Henry I, 37;
  persuades Owain ap Cadwgan to submit to Henry I, 38;
  loses Caereinion, 45;
  leagued with Hywel ab Ithel, 46–7;
  Henry I's expedition against, 47–8;
  comes to terms with Henry I, 48;
  prevents Maredudd ap Cadwgan from taking Meirionnydd, 49;
  fails to take Meirionnydd, 49;
  invades territory of Llywarch ap Trahaearn, 49;
  Llywelyn ab Owain castrated and blinded by, 50, N.;
  dies, 50.
Maredudd ap Cadwgan
  Euron, mother of, 45;
  slain by brother Morgan, 49;
Maredudd ap Cynan ab Owain Gwynedd
  dispossesses Dafydd ab Owain, 75;
  expelled from Llŷn and Eifionydd, 81;
  expelled from Meirionnydd, 81.
——, sons of
  see Llywelyn ap Maredudd ap Cynan (1), (2).
Maredudd ap Griffri ap Trahaearn
  blinded by Maredudd ap Llywarch, 50.
Maredudd ap Gruffudd, lord of Hirfryn
  death and burial of, 115.
Maredudd ap Gruffudd ap Llywelyn
  dies, after defeat by sons of Cynfyn, 15.
Maredudd ap Gruffudd ap Rhys
  with brothers Cadell and Rhys, takes Llanstephan castle, 54;

BRUT Y TYWYSOGYON

Maredudd ap Gruffudd ap Rhys (*cont.*)
   defends Llanstephan castle, 54;
   in attack on Wizo's Castle, 55;
   wins Is-Aeron, 57;
   in conquest of Ceredigion, 57;
   in attack on Gower, 57;
   attacks Hywel's Castle, Tenby, Aberafan, Cyfeiliog, 58;
   with Rhys, given the authority of brother Cadell, 58;
   dies, 58;
   daughter of, 69.
Maredudd ap Hywel (1)
   slain by sons of Bleddyn ap Gwyn, 52.
Maredudd ap Hywel (2), lord of Edeirnion
   at taking of Carreg Hofa, 62.
Maredudd ap Hywel ap Maredudd, of Brycheiniog
   at siege of Aberystwyth castle, 51;
   in attack on Cardigan, 51.
Maredudd ap Llywarch
   slays son of Meurig ap Trahaearn, 50;
   blinds first-cousins, 50;
   blinds two brothers, 50;
   slain, 50.
Maredudd ap Llywelyn, of Meirionnydd
   dies, 109.
Maredudd ap Madog ab Idnerth
   slain by Hugh de Mortimer, 54;
Maredudd ap Madog ap Gruffudd Maelor
   slays brother Gruffudd, 105;
   Llywelyn ap Iorwerth seizes territory of, 105.
Maredudd ap Rhobert, of Cydewain
   opposes John's expedition (1211), 85;
   makes pact with Llywelyn ap Iorwerth, 86;
   on 1215 expedition to Dyfed, 91;
   dies, 106.
Maredudd ap Rhydderch ap Caradog
   receives refugees from Owain ap Cadwgan's land, 29;
   defends Llandovery castle, 40;
   holds chieftainship of Cantref Bychan, 40;
   set to keep Carmarthen castle, 40–1.
Maredudd ap Rhydderch ap Tewdwr
   set to keep Carmarthen castle, 40–1;
   in attack on Aberystwyth castle, 43.
Maredudd ap Rhys ap Gruffudd (1), archdeacon of Ceredigion
   death and burial of, 101.
Maredudd ap Rhys ap Gruffudd (2), chieftain
   with brother Rhys, takes castles of Dinefwr and Cantref Bychan, 75;
   imprisoned at Ystrad Meurig, 75;
   slain in Carnwyllion, 81;
Maredudd ap Rhys ap Gruffudd (3), Cistercian monk
   blinded, 63–4;
   death and burial of at Whitland, 105.
Maredudd ap Rhys Gryg
   commanded to dispossess Maelgwn Ieuanc, 107;
   acts with Llywelyn ap Gruffudd in winning Perfeddwlad, 110;
   given Builth, 110;
   on campaign against Gwenwynwyn, 110–11;
   reconciled to Rhys Fychan ap Rhys Mechyll, 111;
   breaks pact with Welsh, 111;
   at parley in Emlyn, 111–12;
   death and burial of, 116.
Maredudd Bengoch
   slays Meurig ab Addaf, 65.
Margaret, daughter of Llywelyn ap Iorwerth
   wedded to John de Breos, 97.
Margaret, daughter of Maelgwn Ieuanc and wife of Owain ap Maredudd
   dies, 110.
Margaret, wife of Maelcoluim III
   dies, 19.
——, ——, daughter of
   see Matilda.
Marshal
   see Pembroke, earls of.
Mary, church of, at Lampeter
   Maredudd, archdeacon of Ceredigion, dies in, 101.
——, ——, at Meifod
   built, 59.
——, ——, in Anglesey
   plundered, 59.
——, ——, in Worcester
   king John buried in, 93.
Mathrafal, castle
   built by Robert Vieuxpont, 86;
   Llywelyn ap Iorwerth beaten off from, 86;
   burnt by king John, 86.
Matilda, daughter of Maelcoluim III
   wife of Henry I, 22.
Matilda, empress
   comes to England, 52.
Matilda of St. Valéry, wife of William de Breos
   put to death at Windsor, 84.
Mawddwy, commot
   taken by Gruffudd ap Maredudd ap Bleddyn, 46;
   taken from Gruffudd ap Llywelyn by brother Dafydd, 104.
Mechain, cantref
   battle of, 15.
Mefenydd, commot
   subjugated by Pain de Chaworth, 118;
   won by Gruffudd ap Maredudd ab Owain, 120
Meifod
   church of Mary at, built, 59;
   Madog ap Maredudd buried at, 61.
Meilyr ab Owain ab Edwin
   slain by Cadwallon ap Gruffudd ap Cynan, 49.
Meilyr ap Rhiwallon
   slain in battle of Mynydd Carn, 17.
Meirchion ap Rhys ap Rhydderch
   slays Rhydderch ap Caradog, 16.

INDEX

Meirionnydd, cantref
  men of, join sons of Uchdryd, 33;
  Owain ap Cadwgan and Madog ap Rhiryd enter, 33;
  men of, routed by Owain ap Cadwgan, 33;
  with Cyfeiliog, given to Uchdryd ab Edwin, 46;
  taken by Einion ap Cadwgan, 46, 49;
  bequeathed to Maredudd ap Cadwgan, 49;
  invaded by sons of Gruffudd ap Cynan, 49;
  invaded by sons of Owain Gwynedd, 56;
  Maredudd ap Cynan expelled from, 81;
  subjugation and loss of, by Gruffudd ap Llywelyn, 98;
  won by Llywelyn ap Gruffudd, 110;
  see Maredudd ap Llywelyn of.
———, archdeacon of
  see Tudur ab Adda.
Menai, the
  bridge over, 120.
Menevia, church
  burnt, 3;
  destroyed, 6;
  ravaged by men of Godfrey, son of Harold, 9;
  ravaged three times, 10;
  ravaged by Eadric and Ubis, 11;
  destroyed, 12;
  ravaged by Gentiles, 16;
  pillaged, 17;
  William I comes on pilgrimage to, 17;
  destroyed by men of the Isles, 18;
  bounds of, ravaged by Gerald [of Windsor], 20;
  labours of Bernard for, 56;
  Henry II at, 67;
  William Marshal lands at, 99;
  Maredudd, archdeacon of Ceredigion, buried at, 101;
  Rhys Gryg dies at, 103;
———, bishops of
  see Abraham; Anselm the Fat; Bec, Thomas de; Bernard; Bleuddydd; Bonheddig; Carew, Richard de; Einion Fonheddig; Eneurys; Erfyn; Ewilfre; fitz Gerald, David; Geoffrey; Himbert; Iorwerth; Joseph; Lwmberth; Morgenau; Morgynnydd; Peter; Sadyrnfyw; Sulien; Thomas; Wallis, Thomas.
Merfyn [Frych]
  dies, 4.
Merfyn, son of (recte Merfyn ap Rhodri)
  dies, 6, N.
Merlin, prophet
  see Myrddin.
Meules, Hugh de
  castle of, at Tal-y-bont, taken by Rhys Ieuanc, 90.
———, Nicholas de, king's justice at Carmarthen
  sent to dispossess Maelgwn Ieuanc, 107.
———, Roger de
  keeper of Aberystwyth castle, 119.
Meurig, abbot of Cwm-hir
  dies, 72.
Meurig, bishop of Bangor
  see Maredudd (recte Meurig).
Meurig, king of Gwent
  slain by Saxons, 4.
Meurig ab Addaf
  slain by cousin Maredudd Bengoch, 65.
Meurig ab Arthfael
  slain, 12.
Meurig ab Idwal Foel
  blinded, 8.
———, sons of
  hostages in Gwynedd, 10, N.;
  defeat Maredudd ab Owain, 10.
Meurig ap Cadell
  slays brother Clydog, 6.
Meurig ap Cadfan
  dies, 8.
Meurig ap Clydog
  dies, 6, N.
Meurig ap Gruffudd ap Maredudd
  with brother Owain, receives Cyfeiliog, 57;
  escapes from prison, 59.
Meurig ap Hywel
  captured, 13.
Meurig ap Madog ap Rhiryd
  slain through treachery of own men, 54.
Meurig ap Meurig ap Trahaearn
  slays Madog ap Llywarch ap Trahaearn, 50;
  blinded and castrated, 50.
Meurig ap Trahaearn ap Caradog
  slain by Owain ap Cadwgan, 27;
  son of, slain by Maredudd ap Llywarch, 50, N.
Meurig Barach
  hanged in England, 87.
Michael, St., church of
  consecrated, 1.
Mochnant, commot
  shared between Owain Cyfeiliog and Owain Fychan, 64;
  taken from brother Gruffudd by Dafydd ap Llywelyn, 104.
Moel-yr-Wyddfa
  Edward I holds fair at, 121.
Mold, castle
  taken by Owain Gwynedd, 55.
Monks, White, Order of
  at Strata Florida, 99.
Monmouth, town
  burnt by Richard Marshal and Owain ap Gruffudd, 103.
———, John de
  fortifies castle of Builth, 106.
moon, the
  reddening of, 1;
  see eclipses, lunar.

Montford, Amaury de
    with sister Eleanor seized and imprisoned, 117;
    goes to court of Rome, 117–18.
——, Eleanor de
    with brother Amaury, seized and imprisoned, 117;
    marriage by proxy to Llywelyn ap Gruffudd, 117;
    actual marriage, 117, 119;
    returns to Wales, 119;
    death and burial of, 117.
    daughter of, *see* Gwenllïan.
——, Simon de
    Edward, son of Henry III, escapes from prison of, 114;
    slain at Evesham, 114;
    sons of, escape from prison, 114;
    ——, fortify Kenilworth castle, 114.
Montgomery, Arnulf, son of Roger of Montgomery
    treachery of, against Henry I, 22–5;
    occupies Pembroke castle, 23;
    obtains Muircertach's daughter for wife, 23–4;
    surrenders to Henry I, 25;
    Gerald, officer of, 26.
——, Hugh, Robert, Roger
    see Shrewsbury, earls of.
Mor ap Gwyn
    dies, 11.
Morfran, abbot of Whitland (*recte* Tywyn)
    defends Cynfael castle, 56.
Morgan ab Owain ap Caradog of Gwynllŵg
    slays Richard fitz Gilbert, 51;
    slain, 60;
    land of, taken by brother Iorwerth, 60.
Morgan ap Cadwgan
    mother of, 45;
    opposes Henry I's expedition, 48;
    slays brother Maredudd, 49;
    goes to Jerusalem and dies on return, 50.
Morgan ap Caradog ap Iestyn of Glamorgan
    at council of Gloucester, 70–1.
Morgan ap Hywel ap Iorwerth of Gwynllŵg
    castle of, at Machein, taken and then restored by Gilbert Marshal, 104;
    submits to Dafydd ap Llywelyn ap Iorwerth, 106.
Morgan ap Maredudd (1)
    slain, 72.
Morgan ap Maredudd (2)
    chief over Morgannwg, 122.
Morgan ap Rhys ap Gruffudd
    dies at Strata Florida, 109.
Morgan ap Seisyll ap Dyfnwal of Gwynllŵg
    with allies, destroys Caerleon, 66.
Morgan [Hen ab Owain ap Hywel]
    dies, 8.
Morgannwg
    castles of, taken by Rhys Ieuanc, 90–1;

Morgan ap Maredudd chief over, 122;
    overrun by barons (1321), 124;
    Edward II flees to, 125.
Morgenau, bishop of Menevia
    slain, 10.
Morgynnydd, bishop [of Menevia]
    dies, 12.
Morlais, bishop of Bangor
    dies, 7.
Mortaigne, William de
    see Bretagne (*recte* Mortaigne).
mortality
    in Britain, 1;
    in Ireland, 1, 68;
    upon animals, 3;
    upon cattle in island of Britain, 10;
    upon men because of famine, 10;
    in island of Britain, 57;
    upon men and animals, 69;
    in island of Britain and France, 76;
    in Damietta, 97;
    upon Henry III's army in France, 101.
Mortimer, Hugh de
    imprisons Rhys ap Hywel, 53;
    slays Maredudd ap Madog ab Idnerth, 54.
——, Ralf de, son of Roger I
    dies, 107.
——, Roger I de
    builds castle in Cymaron, 75;
    defeated by Rhys ap Gruffudd, 76;
    loses Gwerthrynion castle, 81;
——, Roger II de, son of Ralf II
    fortifies castle of Maelienydd, 106;
    succeeds father, 107;
    Gwerthrynion taken from, by Llywelyn ap Gruffudd, 110;
    castle of [Cefn-llys], taken by men from Maelienydd, 112;
——, burnt, 112;
——, re-entered, 112;
    loses Builth, 112;
    helps Edward, son of Henry III, to escape, 114;
    leads army to Baldwin's Castle, 118;
    lands won for in 1276, 118;
    at siege of Dolforwyn, 118;
    Rhys ap Rhys ap Maelgwn submits to, 118;
    attacks Llywelyn ap Gruffudd, 120–1.
——, Roger III
    lands in England from France, 124–5;
    holds council at Salisbury, 125;
    awaits Edward III in Kent, 125;
    executes Edmund de Woodstock, 125–6;
    executed, 126.
Mowbray, the
    executed, 124.
Muircertach, king of Ireland
    daughter of, wife of Arnulf de Montgomery, 23;
    ——, wife of king Magnus, 24;
    receives Owain ap Cadwgan, 30;
    dies, 47.

INDEX

Murcastell
    Henry I and Gilbert fitz Richard encamp at, 37.
Murchadh, son of Brian
    slain in battle, 11.
Myddfai, manor
    given to Maelgwn ap Rhys, 92.
Mygedog
    battle of, 2.
Mynydd Carn
    battle of, 17.
Mynydd Carno
    battle of, 2.
Myrddin, prophet
    prophecy of, to Gwrtheyrn, 1;
    ——, fulfilled, 119.

N.

Nanheudwy, commot
    Cadwallon ap Gruffudd ap Cynan slain in, 50.
Nanhuniog, commot
    Pain de Chaworth subjugates, 118.
Nanhyfer
    see Cynan of; Nevern.
Nannau, in Meirionnydd
    see Cymer in
    ——, Black Friar of
    see Einion, bishop of St. Asaph.
Nant-teyrnon
    monastery founded at, 72.
Nantyrarian, castle
    given to Rhys Ieuanc and brother Owain, 92.
Neath, castle
    Llywelyn ap Iorwerth destroys, 102.
    ——, river, 51.
Nefyn, in Llŷn
    Edward I holds tournament at, 121.
Nercu, bishop
    dies, 6.
Nest, daughter of Gruffudd ap Rhys
    Gruffudd ap Meurig, son of, 71.
Nest, daughter of Rhys ap Tewdwr, 39;
    violation of, by Owain ap Cadwgan, 28;
    children of, 28;
    Robert, son of, 67.
Nestor, 77.
Nevern, castle
    taken by Gruffudd ap Rhys, 74;
    taken from Maelgwn ap Rhys, 75;
    see Nanhyfer.
Newark
    king John dies at, 93.
Newcastle Emlyn
    see Emlyn, new castle in.
Newport (Mon.)
    see Usk, new town on.
Newport (Pemb.)
    see Trefdraeth.
Nicholas ap Gwrgant, bishop of Llandaff
    succeeds Uchdryd, 56.
Nile, river
    Damietta built upon, 97;
    floods against Christians, 98–9.

Normandy, 39, 63;
    Robert de Bellême goes to, 25;
    Henry I's visits to, 27, 38, 46, 49;
    Owain ap Cadwgan goes to, 38;
    Henry I dies in, 51;
    Diarmaid MacMurchadha goes to, 65;
    destruction of, 70;
    Henry III fails to regain territory in, 101.
Normans
    defeated by Owain and Cadwaladr, 51–2;
    men of Gwynedd exiled by, 52;
    see French, the.
——, prince of
    see William I.
Norsemen
    come to Gwynedd, 5;
    lands ravaged by, 5;
    see Black Gentiles; Black Host; Dublin, folk of; Gentiles; Pagans (1).
North, the (sc. of England), 37, 63.
Northerners, the (sc. of England)
    rise against king John, 89–90;
    take London, 90;
    confederacy with Louis of France, 93;
    attempted peace with supporters of Henry III fails, 93;
    with French, take Lincoln, 94;
    defeated in battle of Lincoln, 94.
Nottingham
    Roger Mortimer seized at, 126.

O.

Offa, king of Mercia
    harries the South, 2;
    dies, 3.
Osfeilon
    see Maes Rhosmeilon, N.
Osney, monastery
    Adam, bishop of St. Asaph, buried in, 72.
Osred, king of the Saxons
    dies, 1.
Oswestry
    Madog ap Maredudd builds castle of, 57;
    Henry II at (1165), 63;
    king John destroys, 93;
    Llywelyn ap Gruffudd burns, 103.
Otir
    comes to Britain, 6.
Otir, son of Otir
    leader of fleet from Ireland, 53.
Otto, cardinal and legate of Pope
    comes to England, 104;
    leaves England, 105;
    seized by emperor Frederick, 105.
Otto, emperor of Rome
    confederate of king John against Philip II of France, 89;
    defeated [at Bouvines], 89.
Ottobon, papal legate
    mediates between Henry III and Llywelyn ap Gruffudd, 115.

Owain, king of the Picts
  dies, 2, N.
Owain ab Edwin ap Goronwy
  brings French to Anglesey, 21;
  dies, 26;
  daughter of, see Angharad;
  sons of, 46, 49;
Owain ab Owain ap Caradog
  see Owain Pen-carn.
Owain ap Cadwallon
  slain, 80.
Owain ap Cadwgan
  slays sons of Trahaearn ap Caradog, 27;
  attacks Cenarth Bychan, 28;
  opposition to, in Powys, 29;
  boards ship at Aberdyfi, 30;
  sails to Ireland, 30;
  returns to Powys, 31;
  leagued with Madog ap Rhiryd, 31-3;
  routs men of Meirionnydd, 33;
  goes to Ceredigion, 33;
  men of, plunder Dyfed, 33;
  goes to Ireland, 34;
  Henry I recalls from Ireland, 35;
  returns from Ireland and obtains land from Henry I, 36;
  blinds Madog ap Rhiryd, 37;
  accused by Gilbert fitz Richard, 37;
  retreats to Eryri, 37;
  makes pact with Gruffudd ap Cynan and Goronwy ab Owain, 37-8;
  goes to Normandy with Henry I, 38;
  returns from Normandy, 38;
  set against Gruffudd ap Rhys, 44;
  slain in battle against Flemings, 45;
  names of brothers of, 45.
Owain ap Caradog ap Gruffudd
  set to keep Carmarthen castle, 41;
  slain, 41;
  daughter of, see Dyddgu.
Owain ap Caradog ap Rhydderch
  given portion of Cantref Mawr, 40;
  set to keep Carmarthen castle, 40-1.
Owain ap Dafydd ap Gruffudd
  seized and imprisoned, 121.
Owain ap Dyfnwal (1)
  slain, 10.
Owain ap Dyfnwal (2)
  slain, 11.
Owain ap Gruffudd
  dies, 15.
Owain ap Gruffudd ap Cynan
  see Owain Gwynedd.
Owain ap Gruffudd ap Gwenwynwyn
  seized by Llywelyn ap Gruffudd, 116;
  released from prison, 119.
Owain ap Gruffudd ap Llywelyn
  see Owain Goch.
Owain ap Gruffudd ap Maredudd
  see Owain Cyfeiliog.
Owain ap Gruffudd ap Rhys
  with brother Rhys Ieuanc, takes Dinefwr and Llandovery, 82-3;
  —— ——, given land between the Dyfi and the Aeron, 83;
  —— ——, burns Llangadog castle, 83;
  —— ——, routs Maelgwn ap Rhys, 84;
  —— ——, refuses peace with John, 85;
  army sent against, 85-6;
  comes to terms with Falkes, 86;
  grants land between the Dyfi and the Aeron to king, 86;
  reconciled to king, 86;
  with brother, ravages Maelgwn ap Rhys's land, 86;
  joins brother Rhys Ieuanc at Trallwng Elgan, 87;
  with Maelgwn ap Rhys, flees to Gwynedd, 90;
  with Llywelyn ap Iorwerth in Dyfed, 92;
  lands apportioned to, at Aberdyfi, 92;
  opposes Reginald de Breos, 95;
  succeeds Rhys Ieuanc in portion of patrimony, 99;
  at siege of Cardigan, 102;
  at siege of Carmarthen, 103;
  with Richard Marshal, castles taken by, 103;
  death and burial of, 103.
Owain ap Gruffudd Maelor
  dies, 79.
Owain ap Hywel ap Ieuaf
  see Owain of Brithdir.
Owain ap Hywel Dda
  ravages Y Gorwydd, 7;
  dies, 10.
Owain ap Iorwerth of Caerleon
  slain by earl of Bristol's men, 68.
Owain ap Madog ap Maredudd
  see Owain Fychan.
Owain ap Maredudd
  dies, 3.
Owain ap Maredudd, of Elfael
  comes to Llywelyn ap Gruffudd's peace, 112.
Owain ap Maredudd ab Owain
  with brother Gruffudd, gives Cwmwd Perfedd to brother Cynan, 116;
  death and burial of, 117.
Owain ap Maredudd ap Rhobert, of Cydewain
  obtains Cydewain, 108;
  dies, (104 N.), 112;
  wife of, see Margaret, daughter of Maelgwn Ieuanc.
Owain ap Rhydderch ap Tewdwr
  set to keep Carmarthen castle, 40-1;
  attacks Aberystwyth castle, 43.
Owain ap Rhys
  dies, 74.
Owain Cyfeiliog ap Gruffudd ap Maredudd
  with brother Madog, receives Cyfeiliog, 57;
  opposes Henry II's expedition, 63;
  takes Mochnant Uwch-Rhaeadr, 64;
  expelled, 64;

Owain Cyfeiliog—(cont.)
  destroys Caereinion castle, 64;
  submits to Rhys ap Gruffudd, 66;
  sons of, slay Owain ap Madog ap
    Maredudd, 73;
  dies, 79.
Owain Fychan ap Madog ap Maredudd
  at taking of Carreg Hofa, 62;
  takes Mochnant Is-Rhaeadr, 64;
  slain by Owain Cyfeiliog's sons, 73.
Owain Goch ap Gruffudd ap Llywelyn
  with brother Llywelyn, succeeds
    Dafydd ap Llywelyn ap Iorwerth,
    107;
  Maelgwn Ieuanc flees to, 107;
  defeated by brother Llywelyn, 110;
  released from prison, 119;
  receives Llŷn, 119.
Owain Gwynedd ap Gruffudd ap Cynan
  invades Meirionnydd and Powys, 49;
  encomium of, 51;
  attacks Walter's Castle, 51;
  defeats Flemings and Normans, 51-2;
  in third attack on Ceredigion, 52;
  daughter of, promised to Anarawd ap
    Gruffudd, 53;
  expels brother Cadwaladr, 53;
  makes peace with Cadwaladr, 53;
  defeats Irish, 53;
  grief of, at death of son Rhun, 55;
  takes Mold castle, 55;
  sons of, attack Cynfael castle, 56;
  builds castle in Iâl, 57;
  imprisons son Cynan, 57;
  defeats Madog ap Maredudd and earl
    of Chester, 57;
  has Cunedda ap Cadwallon mutilated,
    58;
  expels brother Cadwaladr from Anglesey, 58;
  opposed by Rhys ap Gruffudd, 58-9;
  Henry II's expedition against (1157),
    59-60;
  gives Cadwallon ap Madog ab Idnerth
    to French, 62;
  raids Llandinam, 62;
  takes Carreg Hofa, 62;
  Henry II's expedition against (1165),
    63;
  drives Owain Cyfeiliog from territory,
    64;
  takes Rhuddlan castle, 65;
  death and encomium of, 65.
Owain of Brithdir ap Hywel
  dies, 79.
Owain Pen-carn
  blinded and castrated, 70.
Oxford
  Adam, bishop of St. Asaph, dies at, 72;
  council at (1217), 93;
  Hywel ab Ednyfed, bishop of St.
    Asaph, dies at, 107.
Oystermouth, castle
  and town, burnt by Rhys Ieuanc, 90.

P.
Padarn, St.
  precincts of, unmolested, 30;
  church of, burnt, 111.
Pagans (1), i.e. Norsemen, etc.
  come to Ireland, 3;
  slay Cyngen, 4;
  destroy Dumbarton, 5;
  attacked by Llywelyn (*recte* Gruffudd
    ap Llywelyn), 13;
  see Black Gentiles; Black Host;
    Gentiles; Norsemen.
Pagans (2)
  take Jerusalem, 73;
  losses of, in battle in Spain, 86.
Painscastle
  taken by Rhys ap Gruffudd, 76;
  left to Gwallter Fychan ab Einion
    Clud, 90;
  built by Henry III, 102.
Paris, city
  messengers from Edward II, to, 124.
Paris, son of Priam, 77.
Patriarch, the
  see Jerusalem.
Paul, St., 88.
Pembroke, cantref
  French from, 64;
  Henry II at, 66;
  parley between Henry II and Rhys ap
    Gruffudd at, 67;
  Henry II at, on return from Ireland,
    68;
  hostages from, given to Llywelyn ap
    Iorwerth, 96;
  Llywelyn ap Iorwerth attacks Flemings of, 97-8.
——, castle, 28, 44;
  not taken by Welsh in 1094, 19;
  taken by Uchdryd ab Edwin and
    allies, 20;
  keepership of, given to Gerald of
    Windsor, 20;
  established by Arnulf Montgomery,
    23;
  occupied by ——, 23;
  surrendered to Henry I, 25;
  given to Saer, 25;
  transferred to Gerald of Windsor, 26;
  Gruffudd ap Rhys ap Tewdwr at, 39.
——, earls of
  Clare, Richard de, son of Gilbert
    Strongbow
      goes to Ireland, 65;
      marries daughter of Diarmaid, 65;
      takes Dublin, 65;
      returns from Ireland, 67.
  Marshal, Gilbert
    takes Machein castle and then
      surrenders it, 104.
  ——, Richard
    in alliance with Llywelyn ap
      Iorwerth, 103;
    castles taken by, 103;
    mortally wounded, 103.

Pembroke earls of—(cont.)
—, Walter
   sent to fortify Cardigan castle, 105
—, William
   takes Cilgerran castle, 82;
   sends aid to Lincoln, 94;
   besieges Caerleon, 96;
   Rhys Ieuanc goes to, 98;
   goes to Ireland, 99;
   castles taken by, on return from Ireland, 99;
   in battle against Gruffudd ap Llywelyn ap Iorwerth, 100;
   fails to be reconciled to Llywelyn ap Iorwerth, 100;
   repairs Carmarthen castle, 100;
   begins castle at Cydweli, 100;
   heirs of, receive patrimony, 106.
Pencadair
   battle of, 13;
   Henry II at, 62.
Pencelli, castle
   taken by Reginald de Breos, 90;
   taken by Richard Marshal and Owain ap Gruffudd, 103.
Pen-coed
   see Pen-cŵn.
Pen-cŵn (alias Pen-coed)
   battle of, in the South, 2, N.
Pen-gwern, in Llanfihangel [Genau'r Glyn]
   castle of, 57.
Penllyn, cantref
   half of, taken by Gruffudd ap Maredudd [ap Bleddyn], 46.
Penmon
   ravaged by Madog (recte Maccus), son of Harold, 8.
Pennant Bachwy
   Alexander, son of Maelcoluim, and Richard, earl of Chester, at, 37.
Pennardd, commot
   exchanged for Cwmwd Perfedd, 117.
—, John
   drowned, 121.
Penweddig, cantref
   Gruffudd ap Rhys ap Tewdwr invades, 42;
   sons of Gruffudd ap Rhys invade, 58;
   Llywelyn ap Iorwerth wins, 83;
   Maelgwn ap Rhys attacks, 84;
   Falkes, sheriff of Cardiff, and sons of Lord Rhys invade, 86;
   Rhys Fychan ap Rhys ap Maelgwn wins, 120.
Penwith, promontory, 37.
Perche, count of
   slain in battle of Lincoln, 94.
Peredur
   son of: see Maelog Cam.
Perfeddwlad
   men and chattels of, moved into Eryri, 85;
   granted to king by Llywelyn ap Iorwerth, 85;

   won from king, 87;
   won by Llywelyn ap Gruffudd, 110;
   Edward I comes to, 118–19.
Perugia
   cardinals confined at, 122.
Pessi, Simon de
   drowned in battle of Lincoln, 94.
pestilence, 10;
   see mortality; plague.
Peter, abbot of Clairvaux
   dies, 73.
—, bishop of Menevia
   succeeds David fitz Gerald, 71.
—, St., 88;
   church of, in Anglesey, plundered, 59.
Peuliniog, commot
   given to Maelgwn ap Rhys, 92.
Philip II, king of France
   takes the Cross, 73;
   goes to Jerusalem, 74;
   wars against king John, 89;
   son Louis, seeks counsel of, 93–4.
— VI, king of France
   Edward III does homage to, 125.
Philippa, daughter of count of Hainaut
   betrothed to Edward III, 125;
   awaits Edward III in Kent, 125.
Phylip Goch, abbot of Strata Florida
   dies, 120.
Picot of Sai
   daughter of, 31, 45.
Picts, the
   in battle against Britons, 2.
—, —, king of
   see Maelcoluim; Owain; Talargan.
Piggott, de, 100, N.
pilgrimage
   Cadell ap Gruffudd goes on, 58;
   see Jerusalem; Menevia; Rome.
pilgrims, Welsh
   drowned on way to Jerusalem, 53.
pipers, 71.
Pippin, king of the Franks
   dies, 1.
pirates
   Scots and Irish, support Rhys ap Tewdwr, 18.
plague, 8;
   see mortality; pestilence.
Poer, Ranulf de
   slain, 72.
poets
   see bards.
Poitou
   king John sails to, 88;
   war in, 89;
   Henry III fails to recover, 101;
   Henry III goes to, 106.
Pontefract, castle
   earl of Hereford executed in, 124.
Porth
   see Einion of.
Pools, the
   encounter in, 123.

INDEX

Popes
 see Alexander III, IV; Benedict XI; Clement IV; Gregory IX, X; Honorius III; Innocent III, V; Lucius III; Urban III.
Powys, 30, 50, 61, 62, 63, 85;
 won by Saxons, 4;
 Cadwgan ap Bleddyn receives portion of, 21;
 given to Iorwerth ap Bleddyn, 24;
 Cadwgan ap Bleddyn receives portion of, 25;
 portion of, seized by sons of Rhiryd, 31;
 Owain ap Cadwgan returns to, 31;
 Madog ap Rhiryd returns to, 33;
 Madog ap Rhiryd comes to, from Ireland, 35;
 given to Cadwgan ap Bleddyn, 35;
 Madog ap Rhiryd's portion of, divided, 37;
 Henry I's expedition against (1114), 37-8;
 Henry I's expedition against (1121), 47;
 Einion ap Cadwgan holds portion of, 49;
 invaded by sons of Gruffudd ap Cynan, 49;
 Iorwerth ap Llywarch slain in, 50;
 invaded by Llywelyn ap Iorwerth, 81;
 castle of Mathrafal in, 86;
 princes from, with Llywelyn ap Iorwerth in Dyfed, 91;
 subdued by Llywelyn ap Iorwerth, 92;
 rights in, given to Gruffudd ap Gwenwynwyn, 106;
 won by English for Gruffudd ap Gwenwynwyn, 118;
 occupied by Llywelyn ap Gruffudd, 120.
——, archdeacon of
 see Daniel ap Sulien.
——, kings of
 see Cadell; Cyngen; Madog ap Maredudd.
Provence, count of
 Henry III marries daughter of, 104.
proverbs, Welsh
 quoted, 12, 44.
Pwlldyfach
 battle of, 13.
Pwllgwdig
 battle of, 17.

R.

Radnor, castle
 burnt by Rhys ap Gruffudd, 76;
 Roger de Mortimer and Hugh de Sai defeated near, 76;
 surrendered to Giles de Breos, 90;
 destroyed by king John, 93;
 destroyed by Llywelyn ap Iorwerth, 102;
 repaired by Richard, earl of Cornwall, 102.

Ralf, officer to Gilbert fitz Richard
 castle of, burnt, 42.
 holds castle of Aberystwyth, 42-3.
Ralf, Saxon leader
 see Ranulf (*recte* Ralf).
Ranulf (*recte* Ralf), Saxon leader
 defeated by Gruffudd ap Llywelyn ap Seisyll, 14.
Rechra
 harried, 3.
Reding, Simon
 drawn at Hereford, 125.
Reginald, son of Henry I
 encamps at Dinwileir, 61.
Rhaeadr-gwy, castle
 Rhys ap Gruffudd builds, 72;
 burnt, 75;
 Rhys ap Gruffudd rebuilds, 75;
Rhain, Irish pretender
 claims to be son of Maredudd ab Owain, 12;
 defeated by Llywelyn ap Seisyll, 12.
Rhain, king of Dyfed
 see Rhun (*recte* Rhain).
Rhedynog Felen, in Gwynedd
 monks from Strata Florida go to, 73.
Rheims, city, 71.
Rhiryd ab Owain ab Edwin
 attacked by Hywel ab Ithel, 46-7;
 slain by Cadwallon ap Gruffudd ap Cynan, 49.
Rhiryd ap Bleddyn
 expels Rhys ap Tewdwr, 18;
 slain at Llech-y-crau, 18.
Rhiwallon ap Cynfyn
 defeats Ithel and Maredudd, 15;
 slain by Rhys ab Owain, 16;
 mother of, 28.
Rhobert, bishop of Bangor
 seized and ransomed, 85;
 dies, 86.
Rhobert ap Hywel
 slain, 80.
Rhobert ap Llywarch
 dies, 66.
Rhodri, king of the Britons
 dies, 2.
Rhodri ab Idwal
 slain, 8.
Rhodri ab Owain Gwynedd
 imprisoned by brother Dafydd, 70;
 drives Dafydd from Anglesey, 70;
 subdues Anglesey, 74;
 expelled, 74;
 dispossesses Dafydd, 75.
Rhodri ap Hywel Dda
 dies, 7.
Rhodri Mawr ap Merfyn
 slain by Saxons, 5;
 death of, avenged, 5.
Rhodri Molwynog
 succeeds Ifor ab Alan, 1.
Rhos, cantref, in Dyfed
 occupied by Flemings, 27-8;
 Flemings from, come to Carmarthen, 44;

Rhos, cantref, in Dyfed—(*cont.*)
    hostages from, to Llywelyn ap Iorwerth, 96;
    attacked by Llywelyn ap Iorwerth, 97-8;
    Rhys Ieuanc goes to, 98;
    ravaged by Llywelyn ap Iorwerth, 98;
    —— Llywelyn ap Gruffudd, 111.
Rhos, cantref, in Perfeddwlad
    held by Hywel ab Ithel, 46.
Rhuddlan
    battle of, 3;
    Henry II's army at (1157), 59;
    Henry II encamps at (1165), 63;
    castle of, burnt by Owain and Cadwaladr, 65;
    ——, spared by Llywelyn ap Iorwerth, 86;
    ——, taken by Llywelyn ap Iorwerth, 88;
    fortified by Edward I, 119;
    Llywelyn ap Gruffudd makes peace with Edward I at, 119;
    Edward I at, 120;
    Dafydd ap Gruffudd and son Owain taken prisoners to, 121.
Rhufoniog, cantref
    won by Saxons, 3;
    held by Hywel ab Ithel, 46.
Rhun (*recte* Rhain), king of Dyfed
    dies, 3.
Rhun ab Owain Gwynedd
    death and description of, 55.
Rhyd-y-gors, castle
    Welsh fail to take in 1094, 19;
    established by William fitz Baldwin, 20;
    repaired by Richard fitz Baldwin, 26;
    Hywel ap Goronwy expelled from, 26;
    Hywel ap Goronwy slain by French from, 26-7.
Rhyd-y-grog, ford on Severn
    Llywelyn (*recte* Gruffudd ap Llywelyn) defeats Pagans and Saxons at, 13, N.
Rhydderch, abbot of Whitland
    dies, 72.
Rhydderch, bishop
    dies, 8.
Rhydderch ap Caradog
    with Rhys ab Owain, holds the South, 16;
    in battle of Cwmddwr, 16;
    slain by Meirchion ap Rhys, 16.
Rhydderch ap Hyfaidd
    head of, struck off, 6.
Rhydderch ap Iestyn
    holds kingdom of South, 12;
    slain by Irish, 13.
Rhydderch ap Tewdwr
    with sons, set to guard Carmarthen castle, 40-1;
    wife of, *see* Hunydd.
Rhygyfarch ap Sulien
    death and encomium of, 21;
    son of, *see* Sulien ap Rhygyfarch.

Rhymni, river
    battle of, 16.
Rhys ab Owain ab Edwin
    slays Bleddyn ap Cynfyn, 16;
    with Rhydderch ap Caradog, holds the South, 16;
    in battle of Camddwr, 16;
    in battle of 'Gweunytwl,' 16;
    defeated at Pwllgwdig, 17;
    slain by Caradog ap Gruffudd, 17.
Rhys ab Owain Gwynedd
    blinded, 63, N.
Rhys ap Gruffudd ap Rhys (Lord Rhys), 69, 74, 79, 85, 101, 103;
    with brothers takes Llanstephan castle, 54;
    in attack on Wizo's Castle, 55;
    in attack on Ceredigion (1150), 57;
    takes Ceredigion from Hywel ab Owain (1151), 57;
    takes Llanrhystud castle, 57;
    repairs Ystrad Meurig, 57;
    attacks Gower, 57;
    attacks Hywel's Castle, Tenby, Ystrad Cyngen, Aberafan, and Cyfeiliog, 58;
    with Maredudd, given authority of Cadell, 58;
    opposes Owain Gwynedd, 58-9;
    lands given to, by Henry II (1158), 60;
    hostilities of, against Walter Clifford, 60-1;
    destroys castles in Ceredigion and Dyfed, 61;
    gives hostages to Henry II, 62;
    lands taken by (1163), 62;
    invades land of Roger, earl of Clare, 63;
    opposes Henry II's expedition (1165), 63;
    attacks Cardigan, 64;
    with allies, expels Owain Cyfeiliog, 64;
    at taking of Rhuddlan castle, 65;
    Owain Cyfeiliog submits to, 66;
    meets Henry II in Forest of Dean, 66;
    meets Henry II on way to Ireland, 66-7;
    lands given to by Henry II, 67;
    appointed justice of Deheubarth, 68;
    sends son Hywel to Henry II, 69;
    at council of Gloucester (1175), 70-1;
    holds court at Cardigan, 71;
    builds Rhaeadr-gwy castle, 72;
    opposed by sons of Cynan ab Owain, 72;
    castles taken by (1189), 73;
    builds Cydweli castle, 74;
    takes Nevern and Lawhaden, 74;
    rebuilds Rhaeadr-gwy castle, 75;
    seized by sons, 75;
    released by Hywel Sais, 75;
    imprisons sons Rhys and Maredudd, 75;
    takes Carmarthen, Colunwy, Radnor, Painscastle, 75-6;

INDEX

Rhys ap Gruffudd ap Rhys—(*cont.*)
   defeats Hugh de Mortimer and Roger de Sai, 76;
   makes pact with William de Breos, 76;
   death and encomium of, 76-7;
   Latin elegy and epitaph on, 77-9.
Rhys ap Hywel ap Maredudd of Brycheiniog
   at siege of Aberystwyth, 51;
   in attack on Cardigan, 51;
   slays Hywel ap Maredudd ap Rhydderch, 52;
   imprisoned by Hugh de Mortimer, 53.
Rhys ap Maelgwn
   hanged by Robert Vieuxpont, 86.
Rhys ap Maelgwn Ieuanc
   death and burial of, 109.
Rhys ap Maredudd ap Rhys, lord of Dryslwyn
   makes pact with Pain de Chaworth, 118;
   tenders homage to Edward I, 118;
   driven into outlawry, 121;
   seized, 121.
Rhys ap Rhydderch
   treachery of, against Gruffudd ap Llywelyn, 14.
Rhys ap Tewdwr, king of the South (*sc.* Wales)
   begins to rule, 17;
   in battle of Mynydd Carn, 17;
   expelled from kingdom to Ireland, 18;
   victorious at Llech-y-crau, 18;
   victorious near Llandudoch, 18;
   slain by French, 19;
   daughter of, *see* Nest.
Rhys Fychan ap Rhys ap Maelgwn
   exchange of commots by, with Cynan ap Maredudd ab Owain, 117;
   submits to Roger de Mortimer, 118;
   does homage to Edward I, 118;
   flees to Gwynedd, 119;
   takes Aberystwyth and wins Penweddig, 120;
Rhys Fychan (Mechyll) ap Rhys Gryg
   seizes father, 101;
   dies, 106.
Rhys Fychan (Ieuanc) ap Rhys Mechyll
   obtains Carreg Cennen castle, 108;
   attacks Carmarthen and Dinefwr, 111;
   host of, routed by Welsh, 111;
   reconciled to Maredudd ap Rhys Gryg, 111;
   at parley in Emlyn, 111-12;
   death and burial of, 116.
   wife of, *see* Gwladus.
Rhys Gryg (Fychan) ap Rhys ap Gruffudd
   with brother Maredudd takes Dinefwr and castle of Cantref Bychan, 75;
   imprisoned at Ystrad Meurig, 75;
   takes castles of Llangadog and Dinefwr, 83;
   makes peace with king John and takes Llandovery, 84;
   opposes John's expedition (1211), 85;
   sent against sons of Gruffudd ap Rhys, 85;
   with brother Maelgwn, destroys Aberystwyth castle, 86;
   asked to give Llandovery to sons of Gruffudd ap Rhys, 87;
   defeated at Trallwng Elgan, 87;
   goes to Maelgwn, his brother, 88;
   seized at Carmarthen, 88;
   released from king's prison, 91;
   with Llywelyn ap Iorwerth in Dyfed, 92;
   lands apportioned to, 92;
   given custody of Seinhenydd castle, 95;
   first to lay siege to Haverford, 95;
   destroys Seinhenydd castle, 96;
   drives English from Gower, 96;
   weds daughter of earl of Clare, 97;
   awaits William Marshal in Carnwyllion, 100;
   seized by son Rhys Fychan, 101;
   at siege of Carmarthen, 103;
   death and burial of, 103.
Rhys Ieuanc ap Gruffudd
   takes Llandovery and Llanegwad castles, 82;
   with Owain, takes Dinefwr and Llandovery, 82;
   with Owain, given land between the Dyfi and the Aeron, 83;
   with Owain, burns Llangadog castle, 83;
   with Owain, defeats Maelgwn ap Rhys, 84;
   with Owain, does not make peace with king, 85;
   Falkes de Breauté sent against, 85-6;
   reconciled to king, 86;
   with Owain, ravages Is-Aeron, 86;
   with allies, defeats Rhys Gryg, 87;
   takes Dinefwr castle, 87-8;
   takes Llandovery castle, 88;
   reconciled to Maelgwn ap Rhys, 90;
   attacks Dyfed, 90;
   castles taken by, 90-1;
   on expedition to Dyfed (1215), 92;
   lands apportioned to, 92;
   with Owain, opposes Reginald de Breos, 95;
   as mediator between burgesses of Brecon and Llywelyn ap Iorwerth, 95;
   does homage to Henry III, 96;
   breaks with Llywelyn ap Iorwerth, 98;
   goes to William Marshal, 98;
   complains to Henry III against Llywelyn ap Iorwerth, 98;
   Llywelyn ap Iorwerth promises Cardigan to, 98;
   death and encomium of, 99;
   disposal of patrimony of, 99;
   brother Owain buried near, 103.

Rhys Sais
   Gwrgenau ap Seisyll slain by sons of, 17.
Rhys Wyndod ap Rhys Fychan ap Rhys Mechyll
   expelled by Llywelyn ap Gruffudd, 110;
   makes pact with Pain de Chaworth, 118;
   tenders homage to Edward I, 118;
   returns from king's court, 119.
Rhyw, river
   thirteen townships between it and the Luggy taken from Gruffudd ap Gwenwynwyn, 116.
Richard, abbot of Clairvaux
   slain by monk, 71.
Richard, archbishop of Canterbury
   quarrels with archbishop of York, 72;
   dies, 72.
[Richard], bishop of Bangor
   consecrates new bell at Strata Florida, 91.
Richard, bishop of London
   king's officer at Shrewsbury, 28;
   incites sons of Rhiryd against Owain ap Cadwgan, 29;
   gives truce to Cadwgan ap Bleddyn, 30;
   demands fugitives of Madog ap Rhiryd, 31;
   gives land to Madog ap Rhiryd, 36.
Richard, brother of Henry III
   see Cornwall, earls of.
Richard I, king of England
   becomes king, 73;
   goes to Jerusalem, 74;
   imprisoned on way from Jerusalem, 74;
   comes back from Jerusalem, 75;
   slain, 80.
Robert, bishop of Hereford
   death and encomium of, 56.
Robert, brother of Louis IX of France
   slain at Damietta, 108.
Robert, duke of Normandy, son of William I
   goes to Jerusalem, 19;
   returns from Jerusalem, 22;
   imprisoned by Henry I, 27.
Robert Courtemain
   castle of, at Abercorram, 41.
Robert of Gloucester, son of Henry I
   see Henry (recte Robert), son of Henry I.
Roch, Hugh de
   drowned in battle of Lincoln, 94.
[Roger], archbishop of York
   quarrels with archbishop of Canterbury, 72.
Roger, son of Robert de Bellême
   wrongs done to Britons by, 24;
   acts against Henry I, 34.
Rogers, the
   imprisoned, 124.

Rome
   Cadwaladr ap Cadwallon goes to, 1;
   Cyngen, king of Powys, dies in, 4;
   Hywel dies in, 5;
   Hywel Dda goes to, 6;
   Dwnwallon goes to, 8;
   Joseph, Teilo's bishop, dies in, 14;
   Donnchadh, son of Brian, dies on way to, 15;
   cardinal John comes from, to England, 83;
   Thomas, bishop of Menevia, returns from, 109.;
   Amaury de Montford goes to, 118;
   cardinal from, 71-2;
   see Gualo.
——, Church of
   king John engages to make annual payment to, 88.
——, emperors of
   see Frederick, Otto.
Ropell, Robert de
   drowned in battle of Lincoln, 94.

S.

Sadyrnfyw, bishop of Menevia
   dies, 4.
Saer, Norman knight
   Dyfed and [Pembroke] castle given to, 25;
   ejected from Pembroke castle, 26.
Sai, Hugh de
   defeated by Rhys ap Gruffudd, 76.
——, Picot of
   see Picot.
St. Asaph, archdeacon of
   see Llywelyn ap Hofa.
——, bishops of
   see Abraham; Adam; Dafydd ap Bleddyn; Einion; Hywel ab Ednyfed; Llywelyn ap Llywelyn ab Ynyr.
St. Clears, castle
   taken by Rhys ap Gruffudd, 73;
   destroyed by Llywelyn ap Iorwerth and allies, 91.
St. David's
   see Menevia.
St. Dogmaels
   see Llandudoch.
St. Edmondsbury
   prince Edward [III] lands at, from France, 124-25.
Salisbury
   council at (1328), 125.
——, earl of [William de Longespée]
   makes pact with king John, 89;
   captured at Vernon, 89;
   William Marshal plans to go through territory of, 100.
Samson, 77.
Sannan, daughter of Dyfnwal
   mother of Einion ap Cadwgan, 45.
Saracens, 19, 72;
   take Jerusalem, 73;
   defeated in Spain, 86;

INDEX

Saracens—*cont.*
    Jerusalem oppressed by, 91;
    defeat of, at Damietta (1218), 97;
    imprison Christians, 99;
    Damietta surrendered to, 99;
    escort Christians to Acre, 99;
    leave Damietta (1249), 108;
    Louis IX of France captured by, 108;
    slaughter of, at Damietta, 108.
Saxons, the, 37, 42, 60, 61, 74;
    obtain crown of kingship in Britain, 1;
    in battle against Britons, 2;
    ravage Eryri and conquer Rhufoniog, 3;
    destroy Degannwy, 4;
    win Powys, 4;
    slay Meurig, 4;
    slay Rhodri and Gwriad, 5;
    harry Ceredigion and Ystrad Tywi, 5;
    slay sons of Rhodri, 7;
    ravage Strathclyde, 7;
    slay Cadwgan ab Owain, 7;
    ravage kingdoms of sons of Idwal, 8;
    ravage Clynnog Fawr, 9;
    ravage Brycheiniog and lands of Einion ab Owain, 9;
    Hywel ap Ieuaf slain through treachery of, 9;
    slay Caradog ap Rhydderch, 13;
    attacked by Llywelyn (*recte* Gruffudd ap Llywelyn), 13;
    defeated at Hereford, 14;
    defeated by William I, 15;
    robberies of, in lands of French, 31;
    harassed by Owain ap Cadwgan and Madog ap Rhiryd, 32;
    harried by Gruffudd ap Rhys ap Tewdwr, 42;
    Gruffudd ap Rhys ap Gruffudd given to, 79;
    —— —— —— released by, 79;
    defeat Welsh at Painscastle, 80;
    Cardigan castle sold to, 80-1;
    harassed by Llywelyn ab Iorwerth, 85;
    see English; Northerners.
——, leaders of
    see Aelfhere; Eadric; Ranulf; Ubis.
——, kings of
    see Athelstan; Edgar; Edward [the Confessor]; Ethelbald; Ethelred, son of Edgar; Harold; William I; William [Rufus].
Scotland, 37, 63, 66, N.;
    raided by Magnus, 25;
    Edward I wars against, 122-23;
    makes peace with England, 125;
    Edward de Bailliol seeks to win, 127.
——, kings of
    see Alexander II; Bailliol, Sir John; David I, II; Maelcoluim III; Robert I.
Scots, the
    Magnus slain by, 25;
    massacre of, at Falkirk, 122;
    slaughter English in the Pools, 123;
    English expedition against, 125.

Sea, Great
    Louis IX of France, crosses, 108.
Sea, Irish, 65, 68, 99.
Sea of Britain, 27.
Sea, Tyrrhene, 50.
Seinhenydd
    town of, burnt at approach of Rhys Ieuanc, 90;
    Llywelyn ap Iorwerth gives castle of, to Reginald de Breos, 95, N.;
    custody of castle of, given to Rhys Gryg, 95;
    castle of, destroyed by Rhys Gryg, 96.
    see Swansea.
Seisyll ap Dyfnwal, of Higher Gwent
    seized by king's men, 69;
    at council of Gloucester, 71;
    slain, 71.
Senghennydd
    see Gruffudd ab Ifor ap Meurig.
Severn, river, 125;
    valley of, king John flees to, 93;
    ——, portion of, left to Gruffudd ap Gwenwynwyn, 110-11;
    see Rhyd-y-grog.
Shrewsbury
    Iorwerth ap Bleddyn condemned at, 26;
    Gwenwynwyn seized at, 83;
    Rhys ap Maelgwn ap Rhys hanged at, 86;
    Llywelyn ap Iorwerth and earls and barons of March summoned to, 98;
    Dafydd ap Gruffudd and son Owain taken prisoners to, 121;
    Dafydd ap Gruffudd executed at, 121;
    Edward II goes to, 124;
    earl of Arundel seized at, 125.
——, castle
    occupied by Robert de Bellême, 23;
    with town, surrendered to Llywelyn ap Iorwerth, 90;
    Gwenwynwyn ap Gruffudd goes to, 116.
——, earls of
    Montgomery, Hugh
        leads expedition to Gwynedd, 20;
        opposes king Magnus off Anglesey, 21;
        wrongs done to Britons by, 24;
    ——, Roger
        wrongs done to Britons by, 24;
        castle at Dingeraint, built by, 34;
    Robert de Bellême
        treachery of, against Henry I, 22;
        castles occupied by, 23;
        deserted by Iorwerth ap Bleddyn, 24;
        territory of, plundered, 24;
        seeks truce of Henry I, 24;
        fails to obtain help from Magnus, 24-5;
        goes to Normandy, 25;
        imprisoned, 36;
        son of, acts against Henry I, 36.

Sicily, king of
  see Charles.
Simon, archdeacon of Cyfeiliog (*recte* Clynnog)
  dies, 58.
Sitriuc, son of Amlaibh, king of Dublin
  attacked by Brian and son Murchadh, 11.
Skenfrith, castle
  taken by Reginald de Breos, 90.
snow, great, 14.
Snowdonia
  see Eryri.
Solomon, 77.
South, the (*sc.* Wales), 81, 96;
  battle in, 2;
  Rhydderch ap Iestyn holds kingdom of, 12;
  Rhain accepted by, 12;
  ravaged by Llywelyn ap Seisyll, 12;
  sons of Edwin ab Einion hold kingdom of, 13;
  fleet from Ireland founders in, 14;
  held by Maredudd ab Owain ab Edwin, 16;
  held by Rhys ab Owain and Rhydderch ap Caradog, 16;
  host of, with Rhys ap Gruffudd, 95.
———, king of
  see Rhys ap Tewdwr.
Southerners, the
  Christianity restored to, 96.
Spain
  battle in, between Christians and Saracens, 86.
Stephen, constable of Cardigan castle
  defeated by Owain and Cadwaladr, sons of Gruffudd ap Cynan, 51.
Stephen, king of England
  succeeds Henry I, 51;
  wars against Henry (*recte* Robert), son of Henry I, 56;
  dies, 58.
Stephen's Castle
  burnt by Owain and Cadwaladr, sons of Gruffudd ap Cynan, 52.
Strata Florida, monastery
  monks come to, 64;
  Cadell ap Gruffudd dies at, 71;
  Hywel ap Ieuaf buried at, 73;
  Einion ap Cynan dies at, 73;
  monks from, go to Rhedynog Felen, 73;
  Owain ap Rhys dies at, 74;
  monks of, go to new church of, 81;
  Gruffudd ap Rhys dies and is buried at, 81;
  Hywel, son of Lord Rhys, dies and is buried at, 82;
  Matilda de Breos buried at, 84;
  Rhys Ieuanc ap Gruffudd dies at, 99;
  Maelgwn, son of Lord Rhys, buried at, 102;
  Owain ap Gruffudd ap Rhys dies and is buried at, 103;
  princes of Wales swear allegiance to Dafydd ap Llywelyn ap Iorwerth at, 104;
  Maredudd ap Rhobert [ap Llywarch] dies at, 106;
  settlement of debt owed by, 108;
  Annals of, 108;
  Morgan, son of Lord Rhys, dies at, 109;
  Gwenllïan, daughter of Maelgwn Ieuanc, buried at, 109;
  Rhys ap Maelgwn Ieuanc dies and is buried at, 109;
  great bell raised at, 110;
  Maelgwn Ieuanc buried at, 111;
  Maredudd ab Owain [ap Gruffudd] buried at, 114;
  Maredudd ap Gruffudd buried at, 115;
  Owain ap Maredudd ab Owain buried at, 117;
  Thomas [de Bec] sings Mass in, 120.
———, abbots of
  see Cedifor; Dafydd; Einion Sais; Gruffudd; Joab; Phylip Goch.
Strata Marcella, monastery
  Owain Cyfeiliog dies at, 79.
———, abbots of
  see Gruffudd; Ithel.
Strathclyde
  ravaged by Saxons, 7.
———, king of
  see Dwnwallon.
Suibhne, Irish anchorite
  dies, 5.
Sulien, bishop of Menevia
  becomes bishop, 16;
  resigns, 17;
  becomes bishop a second time, 17;
  again resigns, 17;
  death and encomium of, 18.
———, ———, sons of
  see Daniel ap Sulien; Ieuan ap Sulien; Rhygyfarch ap Sulien.
Sulien ap Rhygyfarch, teacher at Llanbadarn
  death and encomium of, 54.
Sultan
  see Babylon.
summer
  hot, 2, 7;
  very dry, 109.
sun
  reddening of, 122.
  see eclipses, solar.
Sunday
  battle on, in Anglesey, 5.
Susanna, wife of Cedifor ap Gruffudd, 83.
Swansea, castle
  attacked by Gruffudd ap Rhys ap Tewdwr, 40;
  repaired by John de Breos;
  see Seinhenydd.

INDEX

Sweyn, son of Harold
   ravages Man, 10;
   invades territory of Ethelred, son of Edgar, 11;
   dies, 11.
synods
   in England (1206), 83;
   at Lyons, 116;
   see councils.

T.

Tafolwern, castle
   taken by Hywel ap Ieuaf, 62;
   repaired by Owain Gwynedd, 62;
   given to Rhys ap Gruffudd, 64.
Talacharn
   see Laugharne.
Talargan, king of the Picts
   slain, 2.
Talley, monastery
   Rhys Ieuanc ap Rhys Mechyll buried in, 116.
——, ——, abbot of
   see Iorwerth.
Tâl Llwyn Pynna
   Owain Gwynedd encamps at, 59.
Tal-y-bont, in Gower
   castle of Hugh de Meules at, taken by Rhys Ieuanc, 90.
Talyllychau
   see Talley.
Tegeingl, cantref
   ravaged by Dafydd ab Owain Gwynedd, 63;
   Henry III fortifies castle at Diserth in, 105.
Teifi, river, 34;
   bridge over, broken by Maelgwn Ieuanc ap Maelgwn, 102.
Teilo, St.
   bishop of, *see* Joseph.
Teme, valley
   won by Llywelyn ap Iorwerth, 102.
Templars, master of
   leads Christians against Damietta, 96–7.
Tenby
   men from, injure Cadell ap Rhys, 57;
   castle, captured by Maredudd and Rhys, sons of Gruffudd ap Rhys, 58;
   town, ravaged by Maelgwn ap Rhys, 73.
Tewdwr ab Einion
   slain near Llangwm, 10.
Tewdwr ap Beli
   dies, 2.
Thames
   naval battle in estuary of, 95.
Theobald, prince of Burgundy and ruler of Flanders
   Theobald, son of, as surety for Henry II, 66;
   sons of, support prince Henry, son of Henry II, 70.

Thomas, archbishop of York
   dies, 22.
Thomas, bishop of Menevia
   returns from Rome, 109.
thunders, great, 3, 69.
Tickhill, castle
   see Blyth.
Toirrdelbhach, king of Connaught
   dies, 59.
——, king of the Irish
   dies, 18.
tournaments
   at Nefyn, in Llŷn, 121;
   at Dunstable, 125;
   at Cheap, in London, 126.
Tours, city
   prince Henry, son of Henry II, at, 69.
Tower, the White, in London
   the Rogers imprisoned in, 124.
Tracton, abbey
   see 'White Strand.'
Trahaearn ab Ithel
   calls Gruffudd ap Rhys ap Tewdwr into Ceredigion, 41.
Trahaearn ap Caradog
   rules Gwynedd, 16;
   in battle of Bron-yr-erw, 16;
   victorious at Pwllgwdig, 17;
   slain in battle of Mynydd Carn, 17;
   sons of, *see* Griffri ap Trahaearn; Meurig ap Trahaearn.
Trahaearn Fychan of Brycheiniog
   executed, 79.
Trallwng Elgan
   Rhys ap Gruffudd at, 87.
Trefdraeth, castle
   destroyed by Llywelyn ap Iorwerth and allies, 91;
   subdued by Llywelyn ap Gruffudd and allies, 111.
Trefilan, castle
   built by Maelgwn ap Rhys, 103;
   repaired by Maelgwn Fychan ap Maelgwn, 103.
Trinity, church of the, in Canterbury
   St. Thomas's body reburied in, 97.
Tudur ab Adda, archdeacon of Meirionnydd
   dies, 126.
Turcaill
   son of, leads fleet from Ireland, 53.
Tydeus, 77.
Tyeis, the
   executed, 124.
Tyrrell, Walter
   William Rufus shot by, 22.
Tysilio, St., church of, at Meifod
   Madog ap Maredudd buried in, 61.
Tywi, river
   battle at mouth of, 14;
   forest-land of, as refuge for Deheubarth, 60;
   crossed by William Marshal, near Carmarthen, 100;
   bridge on, destroyed and repaired, 103.

Tywyn
    ravaged by Gentiles, 8.

U.

Ubiad
    blinded, 11.
Ubis
    ravages Menevia, 11.
Uchdryd, bishop of Llandaff
    death and encomium of, 56.
    daughter of, see Angharad.
Uchdryd ab Edwin
    attacks Pembroke castle, 20;
    attacks Owain ap Cadwgan's land, 29;
    leagued with sons of Rhiryd and Llywarch ap Trahaearn, 30;
    castle of, at Cymer, taken from, 45–6;
    Meirionnydd and Cyfeiliog given to, 46;
    leagued with sons of Owain ab Edwin, 46–7;
    Meirionnydd taken from, 49;
—— ——, sons of
    in Cyfeiliog, 33.
Ulysses, 77.
Usk, river, 66.
——, new town on (i.e. Newport)
    Henry II goes to, 68.
Ussa ap Llawr
    dies, 7.
Urban III, Pope
    succeeds Lucius, 73.
Uwch-Rhaeadr (sc. Mochnant)
    comes to Owain Cyfeiliog, 64.

V.

Valle Crucis
    see Llynegwestl.
vermin
    like moles, 6.
Vernon
    counts of Flanders and Boulogne and earl of Salisbury captured at, 89.
Vieuxpont, Robert
    castle of Mathrafal built by, 86;
    Rhys ap Maelgwn ap Rhys hanged by, 86.

W.

Wales, 34, 51, 52, 66, 68, 73, 74, 76, 79, 86, 116, 117;
    princes of, make peace with Henry II (1158), 60;
    Cardigan castle as lock and stay of, 80–1;
    interdiction of Christianity in, 83, 87;
    three leaders from, hanged in England, 87;
    made tributary to Roman See, 88;
    princes of, make pact with barons of England against king John, 89;
    leading men of, at Aberdyfi, 92;
    king John fails to gain support of princes of, 93;
    princes and leading men of, invade Rhos and Pembroke, 97–8;
    Henry III's expedition to (1228), 101;
    princes of, swear allegiance to Dafydd ap Llywelyn, 104;
    barons of, do homage to Henry III, 105;
    castles fortified in, in 1242, 106;
    counsellors of, 106, 114;
    enjoys peace in 1264, 114;
    Llywelyn ap Gruffudd prince over all, 114;
    earthquake in, 117;
    Edward I sends three armies against, 118;
    Llywelyn ap Gruffudd and Eleanor return to, 119;
    overrun by Edward I, 122;
    death of leading men of, 126;
    see Cambria; Wallia.
——, Lady of
    see Joan.
——, March of, 81, N.;
    see March, the.
——, South, 52;
    see Deheubarth; South, the.
Wallace, William
    put to death, 122.
Wallia, 78.
Wallis, Thomas, bishop of Menevia
    dies, 110.
Walter, chief justice of Gloucester
    comes to Carmarthen, 29.
Walter's Castle
    burnt by Owain and Cadwaladr, 51.
war-bands
    of Cadwgan ap Bleddyn, 20;
    Gruffudd ap Llywelyn ap Seisyll, 14;
    Gwenwynwyn, 79;
    Iorwerth ap Bleddyn, 24;
    Madog ap Gruffudd, 91;
    Maelgwn ap Rhys, 75;
    Maredudd ap Bleddyn, 36;
    Rhys ab Owain, 17;
    Rhys ap Gruffudd, 61;
    Rhys Ieuanc and brother Owain, 84;
    sons of Uchdryd, 33.
Warenne, countess of
    goes to Paris, 124.
——, earls of
    John I
        dies, 122.
    —— II
        sent to Gascony, 124;
        returns from Bordeaux, 124;
        awaits Edward III at Dover, 125.
Warwick
    Piers Gaveston slain near, 123.
Waterford
    taken by Richard fitz Gilbert, 65;
    see Imhar of.
Welsh, the, 60, 61, 63, 64, 76, 84, 88, 90, 103;
    defects of, 49;
    unite against French (1164), 63;

INDEX

Welsh—(*cont.*)
    destroy castle of Lawhaden, 75;
    Gwenwynwyn seeks to restore rights of, 79;
    defeated at Painscastle, 80;
    take Gwerthrynion castle, 81;
    Ingelard's men slain by, 84;
    Rhys Fychan deserts, 88;
    rise against king John, 90;
    do not agree to barons' peace with Henry III, 96;
    attacked by Flemings, 97;
    Henry III's expeditions against, 101, 105, 107;
    make alliance with Richard Marshal, 103;
    pact of agreement between, 111;
    slain in valley of the Clun, 113;
    leagued with English magnates, 113;
    break with English, 122;
    see Britons; pilgrims, Welsh; Welshmen.

Welshmen
    lands given to, in Gower, 96;
    Henry III oppresses, 106.

Welshpool
    Cadwgan ap Bleddyn slain at, 35–6.
——, castle
    surrendered, 76;
    retaken by Gwenwynwyn, 76;
    not taken from Gruffudd ap Gwenwynwyn (1257), 110;
    Gruffudd ap Llywelyn's messengers imprisoned in, 116;
    burnt by Llywelyn ap Gruffudd, 116–7.

Wessex, king of
    see Alfred.

Wexford
    taken by Robert fitz Stephen and Diarmaid MacMurchadha, 65.

White Castle
    taken by Reginald de Breos, 90.

'White Strand,' the [i.e. Tracton], in Ireland
    monks from Whitland go to, 100.

Whitland, monastery
    Rhys ap Gruffudd and Henry II at, 67;
    Cadwaladr ap Rhys buried at, 73;
    monks from, go to the 'White Strand' in Ireland, 100;
    Maredudd Goeg, son of Lord Rhys, buried at, 105;
    Maredudd ap Rhys Gryg buried at, 116.
——, abbots of
    see Cynan; Rhydderch.

William of London
    leaves his castle, 41.

William I, the Bastard, king of England, 21, 51, 52, 59;
    defeats Saxons, 15;
    comes to Menevia, 17;
    dies, 18.

—— II, king of England
    succeeds father, 18;
    goes to Normandy, 19;
    expedition of, against Welsh, 19–20;
    second expedition of, against Welsh, 20;
    dies, 21–2;
    concubines used by, 22;
    oppression of Church by, 22.

Winchester, 61, N., 62, N.;
    Henry I goes to, on death of William II, 22;
    king John flees to, 93;
    king John burns town and fortifies castle of, 93;
    castle of, surrendered to Louis of France, 93;
    ——, taken by supporters of Henry III, 94.
——, bishop of [Peter des Roches] dies, 105.
——, earl of [Seher de Quincy] captured in battle of Lincoln, 94.
—— (*recte* Worcester)
    Llywelyn ap Gruffudd and Eleanor de Montford married at, 117, N.

winds, tempestuous, 104, 126.

Windsor
    William de Breos the Younger and mother put to death in castle of, 84;
    Gwladus Ddu dies at, 109.

winter, mild, 92.

Wizo's Castle
    taken by sons of Gruffudd ap Rhys and Hywel ab Owain, 55–6;
    taken by Hywel Sais, 75;
    destroyed by Llywelyn ap Iorwerth, 97.

Woodstock
    son born to Edward III at, 126.
——, Sir Edmund de
    see Kent, earl of.

Worcester
    king John buried at, 93;
    council of Edward I at, 118;
    Welsh princes tender homage to Edward I at, 118;
    marriage of Llywelyn ap Gruffudd at, 119;
    barons at (1328), 125;
    see Winchester (*recte* Worcester).
——, bishop of [William of Blois] dies, 104.

Wrexham
    belfry of, falls, 126;
    market-day of, changed, 126.

Wulfstan, St.
    king John buried near grave of, in Worcester, 93.

Y.

Y Gamriw
    see Y Gwmfriw, N.

Y Gwmfriw (*recte* Gamriw), in Builth
　　Geoffrey Clement slain at, 122 N.
Ynegydd, in Anglesey
　　battle of, 5.
York
　　ravaged by Black Gentiles, 4;
　　English go to, against Scots (1327), 125.
——, archbishops of
　　see [Roger]; Thomas.
Yr Wyddgrug, castle
　　destroyed by Gruffudd ap Gwenwynwyn, 113, N.
Ystlwyf, commot
　　given to Rhys ap Gruffudd, 67.
Ystrad
　　see Cadwgan Fychan of.
Ystrad Antarron, near Aberystwyth, 43.
Ystrad Cyngen, castle
　　ravaged by Rhys ap Gruffudd, 58.
Ystrad Fflur
　　see Strata Florida.
Ystrad Marchell
　　see Strata Marcella.
Ystrad Meurig, castle
　　built by Gilbert fitz Richard, 42;
　　burnt by Owain and Cadwaladr, 52;
　　repaired by sons of Gruffudd ap Rhys, 57;
　　provisioned by Roger, earl of Clare, 60;
　　taken by Maelgwn ap Rhys, 75;
　　given by Maelgwn ap Rhys to brother, 75;
　　Rhys and Maredudd imprisoned at, by father, Rhys ap Gruffudd, 75;
　　taken by Maelgwn ap Rhys, 79;
　　withheld from Gruffudd ap Rhys, 80;
　　destroyed by Maelgwn ap Rhys, 83.
Ystrad Peithyll, castle
　　burnt by Gruffudd ap Rhys, 42.
Ystrad Tywi
　　harried by Anarawd ap Rhodri, 5;
　　men of, slay men of Gruffudd ap Llywelyn ap Seisyll's war-band, 14;
　　ravaged by Gruffudd ap Llywelyn ap Seisyll, 14;
　　Bleddyn ap Cynfyn slain through treachery of men of, 16;
　　ravaged by French, 19;
　　given to Iorwerth ap Bleddyn, 24;
　　given to Hywel ap Goronwy, 25;
　　Hywel ap Goronwy expelled from, 26;
　　Owain ap Cadwgan's men flee to, 29;
　　Gruffudd ap Rhys escapes to, from Aberdaron, 40;
　　Gruffudd ap Rhys hides in, 44;
　　depredations of Owain ap Cadwgan in, 44;
　　held by Maredudd ap Gruffudd ap Rhys, 58;
　　given to Rhys ap Gruffudd, 67;
　　Rhys Ieuanc ap Gruffudd leads host to, 87;
　　parts of, given to Maelgwn ap Rhys, 92;
　　princes from, tender homage to Edward I, 118.
Ystwyth, river
　　castle near estuary of, 34, 43;
　　abundance of fish in estuary of, 83.